APPLICATIONS OF TRANSPUTERS 2

TRANSPUTER AND OCCAM ENGINEERING SERIES

Editors
Dr. M. Jane
Dr. J. Hulskamp
Prof. P. Welch
Prof. D. Stiles
Prof. T.L. Kunii

Previously published in this series:

L. Freeman and C. Phillips (Eds.), Applications of Transputers 1
T. Bossomaier, T. Hintz and J. Hulskamp, The Transputer in Australasia (ATOUG-3)
T.L. Kunii and D. May (Eds.), Transputer/Occam Japan 3
S.J. Turner (Ed.), Tools and Techniques for Transputer Applications (OUG-12)
J. Wexler (Ed.), Developing Transputer Applications (OUG-11)
A. Bakkers (Ed.), Applying Transputer Based Parallel Machines (OUG-10)
C. Askew (Ed.), Occam and the Transputer – Research and Applications (OUG-9)
J. Kerridge (Ed.), Developments Using Occam (OUG-8)
T. Muntéan (Ed.), Parallel Programming of Transputer Based Machines (OUG-7)
A.S. Wagner (Ed.), Transputer Research and Applications 3 (NATUG 3)
J.A. Board, Jr. (Ed.), Transputer Research and Applications 2 (NATUG 2)
G.S. Stiles (Ed.), Transputer Research and Applications 1 (NATUG 1)
H. Neishlos (Ed.), Parallel Processing: Technology and Applications

ISSN: 0925-4986

Applications of Transputers 2

edited by

D.J. Pritchard
University of Southampton

and

C.J. Scott
Transputer Technology Solutions

Proceedings of the Second International Conference
on Applications of Transputers
11–13 July 1990 – Southampton, UK

IOS Press
1990
Amsterdam • Washington • Tokyo

© 1990 Second International Conference on Applications of Transputers (Southampton, UK).

All rights reserved. No part of this book may be reproduced, stored in a retrieval system, or transmitted, in any form or by any means, without permission in writing from the publisher.

ISBN 90 5199 035 9

Publisher:
IOS
Van Diemenstraat 94
1013 CN Amsterdam
Netherlands

Distributor in the U.S.A. and Canada:
IOS
Postal Drawer 10558
Burke, VA 22009-0558
U.S.A.

Distributor in Japan:
IOS Japan Dept.
Highway Development Co. Ltd.
1st Golden Bldg, 8-2-9 Ginza
104 Tokyo - Chuoku
Japan

LEGAL NOTICE
The publisher is not responsible for the use which might be made of the following information.

PRINTED IN THE NETHERLANDS

Preface

The First International Conference on Applications of Transputers was held in August 1989 at the University of Liverpool, under the auspices of the SERC/DTI Transputer Initiative. Following the success of that event, this year's conference at the University of Southampton is much bigger; with 450 delegates and 75 submitted papers in 5 parallel streams. We also have 9 specially invited speakers (from 6 countries), and a keynote speech "The Transputer - the last 20 years and the next 20 years" given by Prof. Tony Hoare of the Oxford Programming Research Group. Application areas covered include: real time control, instrumentation, image and signal processing, molecular and particle modelling, operating systems, networking, programming environments and tools, graphics, hardware emulation, music synthesis, industrial inspection, commerce, computer aided design, and simulation.

In association with the conference there is a large exhibition of transputer related products. Also, immediately prior to the conference there are a number of pre-conference events:

- Introduction to Transputers Tutorial
- Image Processing Tutorial and Workshop
- DTI Parallel Software Evaluation Initiative Reports
- ESPRIT Parallel Computing Action Workshop

On behalf of the local organising committee we wish to acknowledge the financial and other support given to the conference by the SERC/DTI Initiative in the Engineering Applications of Transputers, the Institute of Electrical Engineers, the British Computer Society, the Institute of Physics, and Parallelogram International. The organisation of several of the parallel streams was undertaken by the Transputer Applications Community Clubs (TACCs). We would also like to thank those authors who managed to get their manuscripts to us in time to be included in these proceedings. For the information of delegates, where the full paper was not received in time the extended abstract has been included.

The next conferences in this series will be held in Glasgow (summer 1991) and Barcelona (1992). We hope to see you there.

David J. Pritchard

Department of Electronics
   and Computer Science
The University
Southampton SO9 5NH
United Kingdom

Christopher J. Scott

Transputer Technology Solutions
2, Venture Road
Chilworth Research Centre
Southampton SO1 7NP
United Kingdom

May 1990

Contents

Invited Papers

IBM Victor V256 Applications, *D. Shea*	1
Transputer Applications at Volkswagen Research I. Visual Simulation by Means of a Transputer Network for a Driving Simulator, *P. Zimmermann*	13
Transputer Applications at Volkswagen Research II. Control of an Active Suspension System by a Transputer Network, *H. Beduhn*	25
Military Applications of Transputers (Abstract), *I. Browning*	28
Image Synthesis for Television on a Volvox Transputer based Machine, *C. Tricot*	29
The Application of Transputers in High-Energy Physics, *L. Wiggers, J.C. Vermeulen*	34
Object Oriented Simulations in Mechatronics, *A. Eppinger*	40

Contributed Papers

Instrumentation

Transputer Architectures for Sensing in a Layered Controller: Formal Methods for Design, *P.J. Probert, D. Djian, H. Hu*	49
Particle Flow Instrumentation, *E. Mills, B.C. O'Neill*	56
A Transputer Based Instrument for the ESA/NASA CLUSTER Mission, *C.M. Dunford, J.A. Thompson, K.H. Yearby*	63
A Modular, Decentralized Architecture for Multi-Sensor Data Fusion, *H.F. Durrant-Whyte, S. Grime, H. Hu*	71
A Modular Sensing System for Robotic Control, *J.A. Ware, G. Roberts, R. Davies, R. Miles, J.H. Williams*	78

Real Time Control

Transputer Implementation of the Kalman-Bucy Filter, *G.W. Irwin, L.P. Maguire*	86
Implementation of a Multivariable Adaptive Controller by a Transputer Based Architecture, *L. Fortuna, G. Nunnari*	93
The Integration of Transputers into VMEbus Systems for Computationally-Bounded Real Time Control Applications, *C.D. James*	100
A Transputer-Based Fault-Tolerant Architecture for Gas Turbine Engine Control, *H.A. Thompson, P.J. Fleming*	111
The Structure of a Parallel Adaptive Controller and its Transputer Implementation, *A.K. Kordon*	119
Parallel Processing in Aerospace Control Systems, *G.S. Virk, J.M. Tahir, P.K. Kourmoulis*	124

Tools for Real Time Control

Implementation of Digital Controllers on a Transputer-Based System, *F. Garcia Nocetti, P.J. Fleming* ... 135

A Transputer Based Processor Farm for Real-Time Control Applications, *P.N.F. da Fonseca, P.M. Entwistle, D.I. Jones* ... 140

Simulation

Multiprocessor Solution of Nonlinear Equations for Chemical Process Simulation, *D. Juárez, C.C. Pantelides* ... 148

Image Processing

Implementation of the Binary Hough Transform in Pipelined Multi-Transputer Architectures, *L. da Fonta Costa, M.B. Sandler* ... 150

Implementation of the Radon Transform using a Dynamically Switched Transputer Network, *G. Hall, T.J. Terrell, L.M. Murphy* ... 156

Image Reconstruction on Transputer Networks, *E.L. Zapata, I. Benavides, J.D. Bruguera, J.M. Carazo* ... 164

CARVUPP Computer-Assisted Radiological Visualisation Using Parallel Processing, *J. Tyrrell, F. Yazdy* ... 172

3-D Parallel Visualisation, *B.J. Payne* ... 182

The Development of a Transputer-based Image Database, *D. Crookes, P.J. Morrow, G. Philip* ... 189

A Transputer Based Automatic Number-Plate Recognition System, *R.A. Lotufo, A.D. Morgan, A.S. Johnson, B.T. Thomas* ... 196

Identification of 3-D Objects from 2-D Images, *W. Lin, D.A. Fraser* ... 203

Automatic Traffic Monitoring Using Transputer-Image Processing System (Extended Abstract), *A.T. Ali, E.L. Dagless* ... 209

Real Time Image Analysis for Dynamic Displacement Measurement, *G.A. Stephen, C.A. Taylor, E.L. Dagless* ... 211

MARVIN & TINA: A Multiprocessor 3D Vision System, *M. Rygol, S. Pollard, C. Brown, J. Kay* ... 218

Two Parallel Algorithms for Matching Attributed Relational Graphs on a Transputer Network, *V. Vuohtoniemi, T. Seppänen* ... 226

A Parallel Processing Engine for n-tuple Pattern Recognition, *K.M. Curtis, A. Bouridane* ... 233

Textural Analysis by Transputer, *P. Smart, X. Leng* ... 240

Image Analyser of Carbon Fibre Orientations in Composite Materials, *A.R. Clarke, N. Davidson, G. Archenhold* ... 248

Molecular and Particle Modelling

Monte Carlo Simulations of Biomolecular Systems using Transputer Arrays, *D.M. Jones, J.M. Goodfellow* ... 256

Transputer Molecular Dynamics with Electrostatic Forces, *S. Miller, D. Fincham, R.A. Jackson, P.J. Mitchell* ... 264

Molecular Dynamics Simulation of Proteins on an Array of Transputers,
  A.R.C. Raine   272
Prediction of Protein Secondary Structure using Transputers, *R.A. Laskowski, M.B. Swindells, J.M. Thornton, D.S. Moss*   280

Operating Systems
Preemptive Process Scheduling and Meeting Hard Real-Time Constraints with TRANS-RTXc on the Transputer, *E. Verhulst, H. Thielemans*   288
Distributed Programming on Transputer Networks – An Object Oriented Interface to the Helios Operating System, *A. Tully*   296

Networking
The Metrobridge – An Application of Transputers in Transparent Bridging, *B. Robertson, M. Chopping, K. Zielinski, D. Milway*   303

Programming Environments
The Application of Transputers as a Network 'Compute' Server, *I.D. Hardy, A.P.H. Jordan*   311
An Environment for the Development of Large Applications in Parallel C, *C. Brown, M. Rygol*   319
Transputer Environment to support Heterogeneous Systems in Robotics, *M.M. Barata, J.C. Cunha, A.S. Garção*   327

Parallel Programming Tools
Numerical Algorithm Libraries for Multicomputers, *R.J. Allen*   335
ECCL A General Communications Harness and Configuration Language, *M. Surridge*   341
A Disk Accessing Library Utility for 3L Compilers, *J. Kerridge, G.H. Jones*   355

Applied Signal Processing
Radiation Tolerance Testing of the T425 Transputer in Support of the SOHO Satellite Mission, *J.P. Nichols*   361
A Transputer Radar ESM Data Processor, *R.D. Beton, J.B. Kingdom, C. Upstill*   368
DICARPS Transputer Signal Processing System (Extended Abstract), *J.M. Little, C.M.H. Klimpke, J.P. Madar*   376
A Versatile Sonar Transmitter Signal Generator, *J.W.R. Griffiths, D.B. Payne, T.A. Rafik, W.J. Wood, J. Zhang*   381

Signal Processing Enabling Technologies
Parallized 2D-Discrete Hartley Transform by Using IMS A100 Devices, *G. D'Angelo, L. Fortuna, G. Muscato, G. Nunnari*   386
Fast Digital Parallel Processing Module FDPP, *D. Crosetto*   392

Graphics
A Transputer Architecture for Parallel Processing of Polygonal Regions, *C. Montani, A. Tomasi* 400

Hardware Emulation
Product Label Inspection using Transputers, *M. Mirmedhi* 408

Music Synthesis
On the Solution of Some Classical Scheduling Problems Using Parallel C, *N. Bailey, A. Purvis, P.D. Manning, I. Bowler* 417

Industrial Inspection
Transputer Based Pin Compatible i80287 Accelerator Board, *D. Wong, Y.K. Chan* 425

Commercial Applications
High Performance Relational Database Systems on Transputers, *C.H.C. Leung, H.T. Ghogomu, K.L. Mannock* 430
The Application of Transputer Based Scalar Supercomputers in Financial Risk Management, *P. Bond* 437

CAD
VLSI Design Stations Using Transputers, *S. Christian* 447
A VLSI Routing System on Configurable Multi-transputer Hardware, *V.K. Sagar, R.E. Massara* 453

Continuous Simulation
ONDA: A River Modelling System, *H.K.F. Yeung* 461
Spectral Element Methods for Computational Fluid Dynamics on Transputer Arrays, *R. Watts* 472
Time Evaluation of a Transputer-Based Model of the Ventricle, *K.E. Tehrani, C.M. Shapcott, J. Anderson* 480
Non-Local Cluster Update Algorithms for Spin Models, *P. Coddington, C.F. Baillie* 488
The Numerical Solution of ODE IVPs in a Transputer Environment, *K. Burrage, S. Plowman* 495

Classical Algorithms
An Efficient Implementation of Search Trees on an Array of Transputers, *A. Colbrook, C. Smythe, D.H. Pitt* 506
Experimenting with Divide-and-Conquer Algorithms of a Parallel Graph Reduction Machine, *F.A. Rabhi, G.A. Manson* 514
The Solution of Radiation Engineering Problems on a Transputer Based System, *S.A. Khaddaj, H. Al-Bhadili, A.J.H. Goddard, C.R.E. de Oliveira, J. Wood* 523

An Occam Implementation of an Asynchronous Algorithm for Calculating
  Polynomial Zeros, *T.L. Freeman, M.K. Bane* 533
Machine Code Implementation of Basic Vector Subroutines for the T800,
  D.C.B. Watson, R. Wilkinson, C.J. Willis, P.G.N. Howard 541
Parallel Algorithms for Finding Optimal Paths on Digital Maps, *A.D. Hislop* 547

Discrete Simulation

DACAPO-III: Parallel Multilevel Hardware Simulation on Transputers, *P.
  Grabienski* 559
Distributing Gate-Level Digital Timing Simulation Over Arrays of Transputers, *K.R. Wood* 565
Parallel Neural Optimisation for Bearing Estimation (Extended Abstract), *S.
  Jha, G. Kelieff, T.S. Durrani* 573
An Investigation into the Parallelising of Genetic Algorithms (Extended Abstract), *G.D. McClurkin, R.A. Geary, T.S. Durrani* 581

IBM Victor V256 Applications

Dennis G. Shea, Mark E. Giampapa, Leendert Huisman, Gail R. Irwin,
Tom A. Johnson, Eva Ma, Tom T. Murakami, Pratap C. Pattnaik
Philip R. Varker, Winfried W. Wilcke, Deborra J. Zukowski

IBM Thomas J. Watson Research Center
P.O. Box 218
Yorktown Heights, New York 10598
dgshea@ibm.com

Abstract:

Victor is a family of multiprocessors that have been designed at IBM Research with the goal of providing researchers with a platform for experimentation in the area of highly parallel message passing MIMD machines with distributed memory. We describe the architecture of Victor V256 and discuss E-kernel, an embedding kernel that supports mapping of higher dimensional task graphs onto the Victor network. We present three applications presently running on V256: VLSI waveform relaxation based circuit simulation, fault simulation for combinational logic and Quantum Monte Carlo simulations for exploration of high temperature superconductors.

1. Introduction

The Victor project at IBM Research started in late 1986 with the intent of exploring message passing machines and their capabilities. The project has evolved in three phases. In the first phase, a V32 prototype was developed to provide a proof of concept and a platform to begin experimenting with applications as quickly as possible. V32 was functional in Summer '87 and the next phase begun, the development of V256, a 256 node partitionable system which is described in Section 2.1. The V256 system was completed and functional in 1989 and we are now in the *application* phase, the focus of this paper.

The objective of V256 is to provide researchers with a platform for experimentation in the area of highly parallel message passing MIMD machines with distributed memory. Goals are to better understand what classes of problems are well suited to this type of architecture, how one designs and develops these applications, and what tools are needed to support their development. In pursuit of these goals, a variety of applications have been developed on V256 [WS*89,TS*90,CS*88]. In this paper we focus on three important applications: VLSI waveform relaxation[ZJ89], fault simulation for combinational logic [HND90], and quantum monte carlo simulations for exploration of high temperature superconductors [FP*90]. Communication and processing requirements vary greatly for this selection of problems, Quantum Monte Carlo with its very computation intensive workload, to fault simulation, a communication intensive problem with irregular and frequent short messages that stress the communication structure of Victor. The applications are discussed and preliminary results presented in Section 3.

One tool that has proven very beneficial in support of application development on

V256 is the Victor monitor and it discussed in Section 2.1. It provides a non-intrusive view into the system and provides a graphical display of events such as link and processor activity. Another vehicle to aide in the development of applications on Victor is the development of E-kernel. It is an an embedding kernel that supports automatic mapping of parallel programs having higher dimensional mesh or torus task graphs onto the 2-d mesh network of Victor and is discussed in Section 2.2.

2. Victor V256

In this Section, we discuss the Victor V256 system architecture and monitoring facilities. Then we discuss E-kernel, an embedding kernel that supports automatic mapping of parallel programs having higher dimensional mesh or torus task graphs onto the 2-d mesh network of Victor. The E-kernel also supports the reconfiguration of the 2-d mesh network into a ring or a linear array.

2.1 Victor V256 Architecture Victor is a family of experimental message passing multiprocessors, the largest is V256, a partitionable system providing a gigabyte of main memory and ten gigabytes of distributed DASD. The overall system topology of V256 is shown in Figure 1. The 256 processor nodes form a 2-dimensional (16,16)-mesh. Four host processors (H1 through H4) are connected to the corners of the mesh and a fifth host processor (H0) serves as the operator's console. Sixteen disk nodes are attached, forming a 17th row, having connections to the upper and lower boundaries of the mesh and thus closing the mesh into a cylinder. Four graphics nodes are connected to the left and right sides of the mesh. The file system is a shared resource, and currently owned by the file server host (FS). The system is usually configured as such, but since all physical links are brought out to the backplane, the system could be manually reconfigured to a new topology if so desired.

V256 is a multiuser system that can support up to four concurrent users. A user owns a host; an arbitrarily shaped, but connected, piece of the processor network; a graphics node; and access to the disk subsystem. There are four regions in the system. The region to which a partition belongs is determined by the host of the partition, that is, if the host

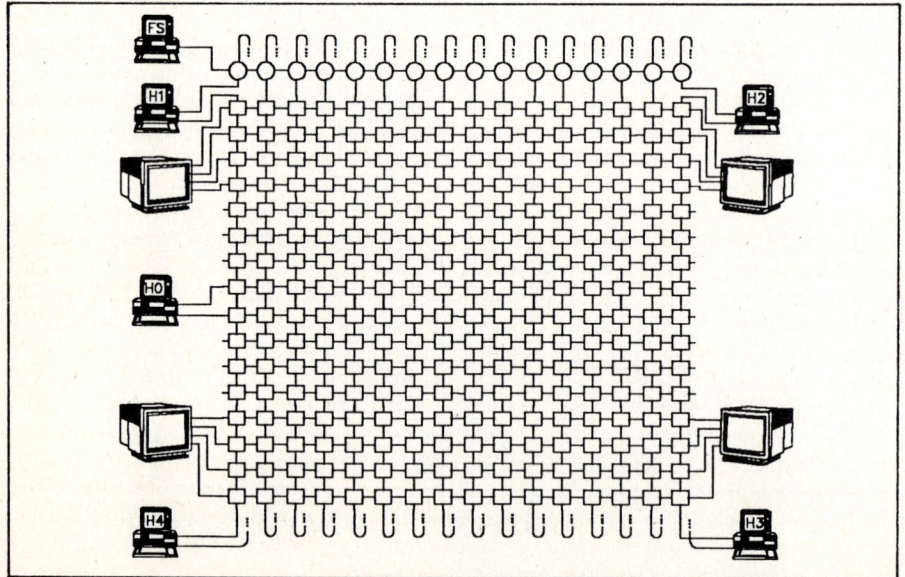

Figure 1: V256 System Topology

is H1, then the partition belongs to Region 1. Partitioning logic is provided at each node to insure that once a partition is formed, its processors only listen to its host's system service requests.

There are four distinct types of nodes in the system, *host, processor, disk,* and *graphics*. Each node contains an Inmos T800 transputer [Inm89a]. A transputer is a single VLSI chip integrating processor, memory, and communication hardware. Each T800 contains a 20Mhz processor, a 64-bit IEEE floating-point unit capable of delivering over a Megaflop, four serial links with a communication rate of 1.6 Megabytes/second, 4Kb of fast on chip RAM, and a 32 bit wide memory interface. Each link is autonomous, and has an output and an input signal, both of which are used to carry data and protocol bits. Each link can support two Occam channels.

A *host* node provides a connection path between the processor nodes in a partition and its user, providing a program load path, screen I/O, and an environment for program compilation. Currently in Victor, hosts can be IBM PS/2's, PC AT's, and RT PC's. The Victor *processor* node provides the transputer with four megabytes of ECC protected memory, partitioning logic support, and non-intrusive monitoring logic, which will be discussed below. With 256 processor nodes the total system memory is one gigabyte.

The Victor *disk* node provides the transputer a SCSI interface into 600 Megabyte drives. With 16 disk nodes currently in V256, the total DASD is 10 Gigabytes. The Victor File System is a UNIX-like hierarchical file system. Once the file system has been loaded, communication may be from any network link connected to it. The *graphics* node transputer is augmented with video ram, providing 1024x1024 screen resolution on an IBM Megapel display. A detailed description of V256 is given in [WS*89].

Since an objective of Victor was to explore the behavior and performance characteristics of the programs during their execution, the Victor monitor was designed to support such analyses. The monitor displays, in real-time on a workstation screen, a graphical representation of system activities, which include both memory activities and communication activities at each node. The monitoring is achieved with a separate hardware status bus, which is completely independent of the regular transputer links and is controlled by a dedicated PS/2 for real-time collection and display of the data. Information fed back from a node include: link activity, host id (to which partition the node belongs), memory activity, and state of user programmable LEDs.

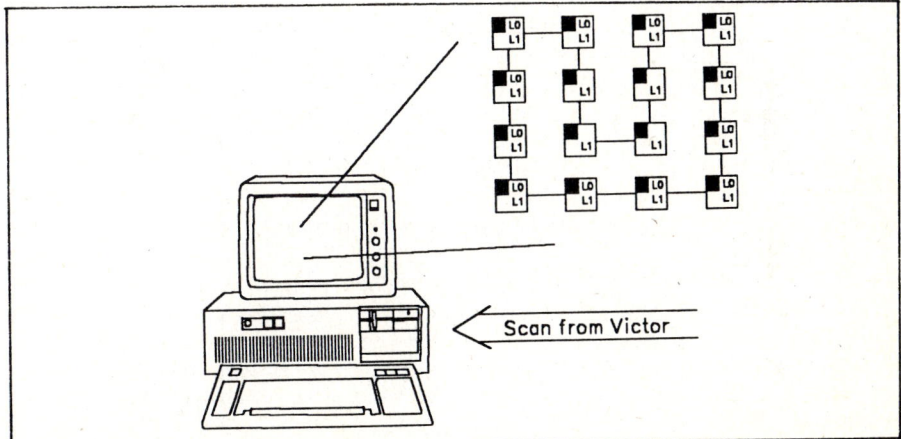

Figure 2: Example of ring embedding captured on Victor monitor

Figure 2 shows a sample instance of the monitor screen, which is an example of neighboring communication when a (4,4)-partition is reconfigured into a ring. Currently, the monitor software supports system configurations from as small as one node up to the entire V256 system. The design is extendable, only being limited by screen resolution and sampling speed of the data. The monitor is non-intrusive. As a result, there is no modification necessary to the system or application software in using the monitor. The aid of the monitor in understanding the system behavior has proven very useful in bringing up the implementation of E-kernel.

2.2 E-kernel

The processor interconnection network for V256 is a 2-d (16,16)-mesh. In order to enlarge the set of communication structures of which the system can provide efficient support, we designed and implemented an embedding kernel, called E-kernel, on Victor. E-kernel supports two levels of embeddings: in the first level, the mapping of a parallel program onto the system network; and in the second level, the mapping of a network topology onto the 2-d mesh. The first level of embeddings corresponds to the support of automatic program mapping, and the second level the support of network reconfiguration. The support of program mapping applies to both the 2-d mesh network as well as the reconfigured network.

The communication structures that we enlarge are drawn from the families of meshes and toruses of various dimensions and shapes, which include hypercube and higher dimensional square meshes and square toruses. These graphs represent many communication structures of applications in scientific computations. Further, since currently there are many existing application programs designed and optimized for systems having networks of these graph topologies, the embedding support of these communication structures allow us to port such programs to Victor with a minimum amount of re-optimization effort.

E-kernel assumes that the task graph of an application program is always chosen by the user in such a way that its has the same number of nodes as the number of processors in its requested partition. Further, in program mapping, the objective of E-kernel is to place the communicating processes as close as possible in the partition so as to minimize the maximum communicating distance. (In the terminologies of graph embedding, the mappings of the nodes in a task graph to the processors of a partition are all one-to-one onto, and the objective of the mapping is to minimize the dilation costs.) E-kernel does not address the problem of task graph contraction nor the optimization of message routing after the mapping.

For network reconfiguration, E-kernel supports the reconfiguration of the 2-d mesh into an even size ring, which can either be unidirectional or bidirectional, and a linear array. These two topologies are also members in the families of toruses and meshes. The main objective of providing this reconfigurability into Victor is to give users the ability to conduct their experiments on different networks on the same system. Further, using this reconfigurability, we are able to demonstrate the benefits of providing the support of automatic program mapping in a parallel system. We show that through the support of E-kernel, without any alteration of the code, the same program runs on Victor regardless of whether the network is configured as a 2-d mesh, a ring, or a linear array, while the support for the required communications are being optimized automatically in each case.

In addition to the objective of enlarging the communication support of Victor, an equally important objective of our work on E-kernel is to experiment with the actual implementation of an automatic program mapping software system. Using Victor as an experimental vehicle, we study the difficulties in bringing up such a software system and the ease of its use.

The embedding functions that we implement in E-kernel are based on those derived in [MT88]. The following are some example embeddings on Victor: a $(4,4,4)$-mesh (torus) on a $(8,8)$-mesh; a $(8,8,4)$-mesh (torus) on a $(16,16)$-mesh; a $(4,4,4,4)$-mesh (torus) on a $(16,16)$-mesh; and an eight dimensional hypercube on a $(16,16)$-mesh. A detailed description of E-kernel is given in [MS90].

Following the goal of Victor being a platform for experimentation, there are a variety of environments and tools available. We have just described one, E-kernel, which has been developed in Occam and allows the user application program to be written in Occam, C, Fortran and Pascal using the Inmos Toolset facilities running under DOS on a PC or PS/2 [Inm89a]. The Quantum Monte Carlo codes discussed in section 3.3 are written in 3L Fortran and use the routing functions of the E-kernel for communication support. Another environment we are currently working with is Trollius, originally developed at Cornell's Theory Center. Trollius is a distributed operating system that runs on V256 and provides a Unix front-end, currently MACH running on an IBM RT PC. We are now investigating porting it to AIX on the IBM RISC System/6000. E-kernel and Trollius are just two examples of the various kernels being tried on Victor. We continue to explore other programming environments, as we better understand the needs of the applications.

3. V256 Applications

There is a wide variety of interesting applications being developed and or ported onto Victor. In this section we focus on three applications: VLSI waveform relaxation, fault simulation, and Quantum Monte Carlo simulations for exploration of high temperature superconductors.

3.1 WR_V256: VLSI Waveform Relaxation

Circuit simulation is one example of an application that is quickly outgrowing available computational resources. Currently circuit designers may verify their designs for O[10,000] transistors, at best. However, the designs themselves are exceeding several hundred thousand transistors and in some cases surpassing one million. The gap between the number of transistors that can be simulated versus the number per design inhibits proper analysis prior to manufacturing. Incomplete analysis often overlooks design flaws that force re-design resulting in increased design costs and longer release times. This gap is expected to widen for the foreseeable future. Waveform Relaxation based circuit simulation on Victor V256 (WR_V256) project is aimed at laying the groundwork to use highly parallel production systems to help close the simulation/design gap [ZJ89].

Since the bulk of the computation done in circuit simulators is done in the analysis phase, i.e. the building and solving of a set of non-linear differential equations, the WR_V256 project is focused mainly on this phase. Waveform relaxation offers a simple way to parallelize via a divide-and-conquer approach that is well suited for digital MOS circuits. The WR_V256 project is one of many such parallelization efforts [DN84,WS*85,SW*87,ST88,OCD89], though it differs in that it is focused on very large circuits, up to 100,000 transistors. Previous efforts have provided some elegant solutions to enhance parallelism, based on much smaller circuits (from 20 to 4,000 transistors).

A serial circuit simulation program served as the base of the WR_V256 project. The program was divided into a preprocessing phase, an analysis phase, and an output phase. **Preprocessing phase:** The preprocessing phase first breaks a large circuit into smaller "subcircuits" that can be analyzed independently. This phase was augmented for V256 by adding a static work allocation mechanism that chained subcircuits based on communication requirements and grouped several chains together for each Victor node. The emphasis for static allocation is to minimize cross node communication with a first pass chaining mechanism and to balance the load and to hide communication by allocating many subcircuits to each node. The preprocessing phase is currently run on an IBM 3090 mainframe and generates a file for V256 initialization.
Analysis phase: To successfully port this serial code to multiple Victor nodes, many things had to be done. First, since Victor is a distributed memory machine, circuit voltages are distributed across all Victor nodes. These voltages are assigned to the nodes that contain the subcircuits that solve them and, when solved, are sent to other nodes that

eventually access them as input signals. Second, the entire subcircuit scheduling strategy was redesigned. In the serial program, a Gauss-Seidel relaxation method was enforced by using a single ordering among all subcircuits. Once each Victor node contained its own list of subcircuits, a cross-node "synchronization" was needed to maintain the Gauss-Seidel nature of the relaxation. Iteration tags were added to the circuit voltages, and a scheduler was added that builds a queue of subcircuits that are ready to run. As more signals arrive, either from off node or on node, the newly ready subcircuits are added to the queue. A third change to the serial code involved the addition of synchronization points. When all of the subcircuits have been analyzed on every Victor node, the nodes synchronize to determine if global convergence has been reached. This synchronization forces the parallel version to maintain the same behavior as the serial version, which is necessary for verification purposes.

Output phase: When an analysis is complete, the converged voltage waveforms are distributed across all of the Victor nodes. The output phase consists of two pieces. First, all of the voltage waveforms are collected from each Victor node and stored into a file. The file is sent back to a 3090 for a small amount of additional processing. This processing is required because of byte rotations between the 370 and transputer architectures and because of differing floating point formats. A new file is created that can then be read by a CAD program on a 3090 class machine to display the voltage waveforms. These waveforms are useful to verify that the signals behave as expected by the circuit designer.

Currently, a 256-way simulator is completely functional and has been tested with a suite of ALU circuits that range from a 4-bit ALU (282 transistors) to a 1K-bit ALU (72,192 transistors). This suite retains many of the circuit characteristics that experts expect to see in very large circuits. Average processor utilizations of 70% have been achieved with a Gauss-Seidel relaxation, as long as each Victor node is loaded as heavily as possible, i.e. with about 300 transistors. Currently, the largest simulation takes about 1/10 the time of a state-of-the-art mainframe, running similar software, as shown in Figure 3. In the figure, predicted relative preformance is shown by the dashed line. Actual relative performance for the ALU suite of circuits is shown by the solid. Victor specific preprocessing has increased the time over that needed for a serial version in the preprocessing phase by under 2%.

The future directions of this project focus on increasing the robustness of parallel execution across a wider range of large circuit characteristics. This includes more general load balancing and relaxing the Gauss-Seidel requirement. To test this work, a wider range of circuit suites will be used.

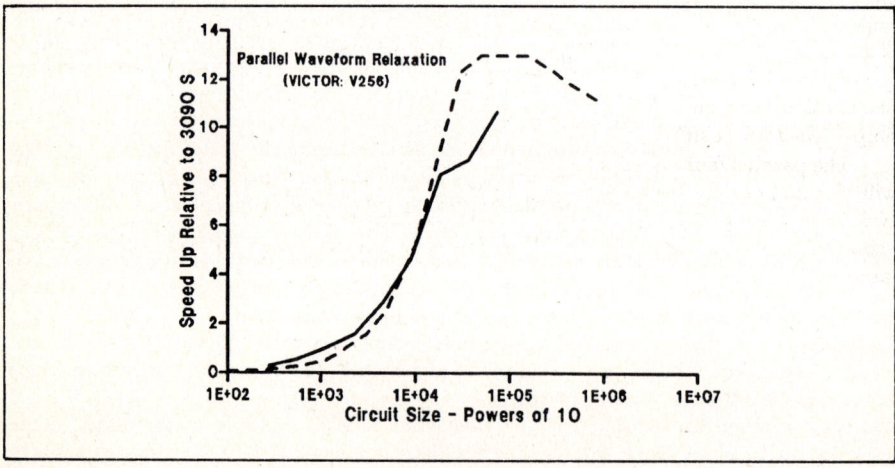

Figure 3: WR_V256 preliminary results

3.2 Fault Simulation

Fault simulation [Mic86a] means the simulation of a logic design that has been modified to reflect the presence of a fault. Simulating such faulty designs is done, among other things, to assess the ability of a proposed set of test patterns to expose faults in the real design. Typical faults that are simulated are any input pin or output pin of any gate stuck at 1 or stuck at 0. In principle, each such fault gives rise to a modified design that has to be simulated. Many such faults are equivalent however, in the sense that the corresponding modified designs behave identically. Typically there are on the order of 3 or 4 non-equivalent faults per gate in a logic design. Simulating all these modified designs is therefore very costly.

The fault simulation algorithm that we will consider in this article is (a slightly modified version of) Concurrent Fault Simulation [Mic86b]. The calculation at each gate determines which faults produce fault-effects on the output of that gate for the pattern being simulated. Implicitly, we do a loop over all faults in the fault-list, as indicated in the program fragment, but explicitly we only consider faults that have fault-effects on the inputs of the gate or that are located on the input or output pins of the gate. The overall structure of this algorithm is shown below:

```
DO all patterns;
    DO all gates in topological order;
        DO all faults;
            code;
        END;
    END;
END;
```

The innermost DO loop, the one over the faults, is treated as an unbreakable, atomic unit. It is the job unit out of which the parallel fault simulation will be built up. The output of the job is a fault table, consisting of all the faults that produce fault-effects on the output of the gate. Their sizes range from one to several thousand in the designs that we considered.

Each gate needs fault tables from its preceding gates and the corresponding job can therefore not be executed before all jobs corresponding to preceding gates have been executed. Gates will be called independent when they are not in each other's downcone. If two gates are independent, neither has to wait for the other and both can be executed in parallel. It is this parallelism that we want to exploit in our parallel fault simulation. A rough measure of the number of gates that can be treated in parallel is given by the width of the design, i.e. the ratio of the total number of gates in the design and the average number of gates between a controllable input, like a latch or a PI, and an observable output, like another latch or a PO.

Experimental results

The parallel fault simulation program has been exercised on various logic designs. We will discuss here the results for the two largest ones. The circuit characteristics for these two designs are given in Table 1. C7522 is the largest design in the ISCAS suite of test generation benchmarks [BPH85]. DESIGNA is an internal design and is almost four times larger than C7522.

	C7522	DESIGNA
Number of clusters	1155	5454
Average cluster size	3.8	2.7
Number of faults	7550	26299

Table 1: DO loop structure of Concurrent Fault Simulation

	C7522	DESIGNA
Total simulation time (secs.) :	0.7	2.0
Average job time (msecs.) :	9.50	7.65
Total number of idle per. :	271.2	404
Average idle period (msec.) :	21.57	18.35
Maximum idle period (msec.) :	194.50	202.94

Table 2: Performance statistics per pattern(32 nodes)

Overall performance

Table 2 shows the simulation time per pattern, measured by simulating five random input patterns and taking their average simulation time. The simulation time is measured from the moment an input pattern is sent to V256 to the moment the result message is returned. When doing fault simulation on mainframes, several optimizations are employed that have not been employed here. When those mainframe simulations are run without the optimizations, they run at roughly the same speed as the VICTOR based simulation.

Clearly, the single pattern simulation time for DESIGNA is not four times as much as it is for C7522. To understand this improved performance, more detailed statistics have to be taken. Two different times were measured. First of all, the time to complete a single job, i.e. the simulation of one cluster including the requesting and receiving of required input fault tables. Secondly, we want to know how much time is spent idling, i.e. waiting for another job to become ready. Such idling occurs when a processor still has some clusters to process but all of them need input tables that have not been computed yet.

Results for both designs are shown in Table 2. Clearly, the main difference between the two designs is in the average job times and the number of idle periods. The difference in average job time results from the smaller average size of the clusters in DESIGNA: the average time per gate is roughly the same in both designs. More importantly, DESIGNA has relatively fewer idle periods than C7522. This is to be expected, because a large number of idle periods indicates a lack of parallelism, which in larger designs is less likely than in smaller ones. In fact, in C7522 the idle periods account for about 25% of the total lapse time, while in DESIGNA they account for only 12%.

Performance analysis

The total time T taken by the fault simulation depends on the number of processors P, the number of clusters C, the average fault table size S and the allocation of the clusters to the processors. In practice, C is roughly one third of the number of gates in the design. The time needed for the simulation of one cluster is roughly the sum of the time needed to obtain the fault tables from other nodes and the time needed for processing these fault tables. When P becomes large, the first term will dominate and we will focus on its effects. With the random assignment of gates to processors employed here, request times are proportional to $d(P)$, the average distance in a mesh of P nodes. We therefore find:

$$T \propto \frac{d(P)}{P} CS$$

where we assumed that there is perfect load balance. The total time taken on one processor is also proportional to C and S, and the resulting speedup is therefore proportional to $P/d(P)$. With the random allocation on a rectangular mesh, $d(P)$ is roughly equal to $2\sqrt{P}/3$, and the speedup is proportional to $\sqrt{P}$.

The most interesting application of parallel processors to fault simulation occurs when we let P grow linearly with C. This a very natural thing to do, because, when C increases, the amount of memory required to hold the design description has to increase as well.

This is true even for uni-processors. In a parallel processor, a node typically has a fixed amount of memory and the easiest way to increase the total memory is therefore to increase the number of nodes P. When P is proportional to C, the total time taken for the fault simulation grows only as $SC^{0.5}$ rather than as SC when done on a uni-processor. Note also that on topologies with $d(P) \simeq lnP$ the total simulation grows only as $S\ ln\ C$.

Speedup

Figure 4 shows the speedup as function of the number of processors. The speedup is calculated as follows. First, the total simulation time as seen from the host is obtained. The speedup is then measured by dividing the total simulation time at some fixed number of processors by the simulation time at the actual number of processors. Because these designs are too large to run on a single processor, the speedup with respect to the single node parallel processor could not be measured. Instead, the speedup is calculated relative to 32 nodes and the speedup at 32 nodes is set to 8. This arbitrary speedup was obtained

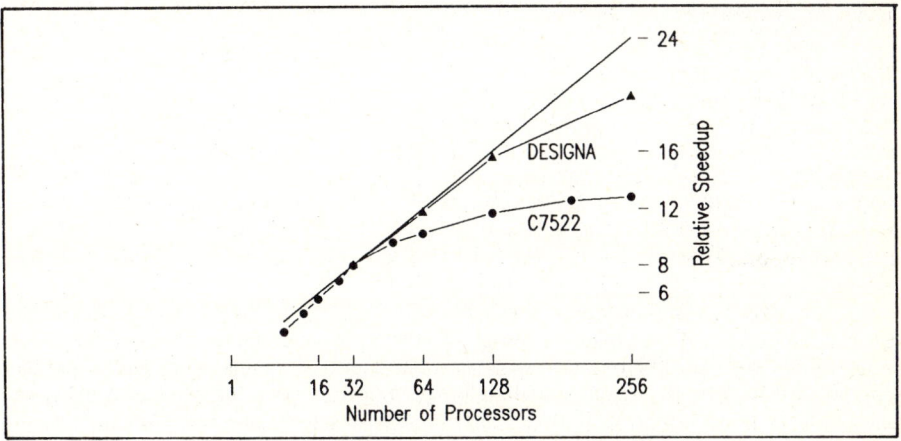

Figure 4: Fault simulation relative performance

by calculating $P/d(P)$ (see the section on the performance analysis) and using for $d(P)$ the value for random allocation on a rectangular mesh (= 4).

Speedup data are plotted in Figure 4 as a function of $P/d(P)$. The figure shows that for a range of P values, the speedup behaves roughly as $P/d(P)$, as was found in the previous analysis. For small P, the speedup is not proportional to $P/d(P)$ because the analysis was only correct for large P. For very large P, perfect load balancing cannot be maintained, because of the finite degree of parallelism in the design. However, as shown by the figure, larger designs keep their parallelism longer than smaller ones.

3.3 Quantum Monte Carlo

The study of the electronic properties of highly correlated systems has been a subject of considerable interest in Physics. High temperature superconductors, heavy fermion and mixed valence systems are examples of highly correlated systems. The main difficulty in understanding the physics of these systems arises primarily from the four operator interaction term. Since the discovery of high temperature oxide superconductor, it is commonly accepted that the Cu-Oxygen units in these systems are primarily responsible for their superconductivity. From the low carrier densities in these systems one expects the on site Columb repulsion, U i.e. the four operator interaction, of the copper d-orbital to play an important role in determining the electronic structures.

A number of models have been proposed to capture the essential properties of these oxides. The commonly used ones are the one band Hubbard model, the t-J model, the three band Hubbard model, the Anderson lattice model and the oxygen 2 level system model. Since all these models involve a large copper U, their ground state properties can not be determined from conventional band structure. A number of theoretical methods have been tried to study the ground state properties of these Hamiltonians yielding an array of results. But all these approaches involve making a priori assumptions based on ones expectation of the nature of the ground state.

We have examined the superconductivity in the three band Hubbard model using Quantum Monte Carlo simulation running on Victor V256. Unlike the analytical approaches, this method does not make any a priori assumption about the nature or the symmetry of the ground state. Over the last few years this method has been significantly developed and used by a number of groups to study the one band Hubbard model. These studies show the ground state of the one band Hubbard model is non-superconducting in the s-wave channel. Hence we examined the ground state of the three band Hubbard model for the presence of s-wave supperconductivity [WP*90].

A large number of Monte Carlo steps was used to assure proper convergence for various correlation functions. This was possible due to the development of an importance sampling algorithm, that has almost linear speed up with the number of processor. These simulations were performed using this parallel projector quantum Monte Carlo algorithm. Thus along with developing a highly parallel QMC algorithm, the availability of Victor V256 made the analysis of the three band Hubbard model feasible.

4. Conclusions

From the initial results presented in Section 3, the future of highly parallel distributed memory MIMD machines looks promising. The waveform relaxation based circuit simulation effort (Section 3.1) is aimed at laying the groundwork for using highly parallel systems to help close the simulation/design gap. As can be seen from Figure 3, the measured relative performance for the ALU circuit quite closely follows the predicted relative performance. It is clear that WR_V256 has demonstrated the potential of highly parallel distributed memory machines in the solution of very large circuits beyond the capabilities of current uni-processor machines.

The work on fault simulation for combinational logic (Section 3.2) is a good test of the fast message startup times and context switching times of V256 that are provided by the use of the transputer. The communication traffic in fault simulation is irregular and contains many short messages. It is encouraging to see from this work that the parallel implementation can be scaled in performance with the size of the application. As shown in Figure 4, larger designs keep their parallelism longer.

There is a large class of computation intensive Monte Carlo codes that will do very well on machines of this structure. The work on Quantum Monte Carlo simulations for the study of electronic properties of high temperature superconductors is an example (Section 3.3). Given today's tools and technology one can quickly put the resources of V256 to work in the solution of such problems. Of course, problems like these demonstrate the ever increasing demand for MIPS and memory for future machine designs.

A long range goal of the Victor effort is to better understand what capabilities highly parallel distributed memory MIMD machines provide. There is a growing set of applications that cannot be solved on any of today's most advanced supercomputers. We believe that this approach to machine design, as demonstrated with V256, is one viable path to the development of machines that will deliver the necessary MIPS, Gigabytes, and TeraFLOPS [Hey90]. This essentially redefines what will be considered *supercomputer class* performance. Coupling these machines with the new tools necessary to support application development will open up a set of applications not able to be solved on today's computers.

Bibliography

[BPH85] Franc Brglez, Philip Pownall, and Robert Hum. "Accelerated ATPG and Fault Grading via Testability Analysis" Proceedings of ISCAS, pp.695-698, IEEE, 1985.

[CS*88] G. Cerf, D. G. Shea, W. W Wilcke and D. J. Zukowski. "Parallelizing Back Propagation on IBM's Victor V32 Multiprocessor". *IBM Research Report RC#13788*, April 1988.

[DN84] J.T. Deutsch and A.R. Newton, "A multiprocessor implementation of relaxation-based electrical circuit simulation". *21st Design Automation Conference*, 1984, pp. 350-357.

[FJL88] G. Fox, M. Johnson, G. Lyzenga, S. Otto, J. Salmon, and D. Walker. *Solving problems on concurrent processors. Vol 1. General techniques and regular problems.* Prentice Hall, 1988.

[FP*90] M.Frick, P.C.Pattnaik, I.Morgenstern, D.M.Newns, W.von der Linden. "Monte Carlo Study of Superconductivity in the 3 Band Emery Model". *Submitted Physical Review Letter*, April, 1990.

[Hey90] Anthony J. G. Hey. "Supercomputing with Transputers – Past, Present and Future". *will appear in Proceedings of the 1990 ACM International Conference on Supercomputing*, Amsterdam, June 1990.

[Hoa78] C. A. R. Hoare. "Communicating Sequential Processes". *Communications of the ACM*, 21(8):666-677, August 1978.

[Hoa85] C. A. R. Hoare. *Communicating Sequential Processes. Prentice Hall International*, 1985.

[HND90] Leendert Huisman, Indira Nair, and Raja Daoud. "Fault Simulation on Message Passing Parallel Processes", to appear in *Proceedings of DMCC5*, Charleston 1990.

[Inm89a] Inmos. *The Transputer Databook.* Inmos, 72 TRN 203-01, 1989.

[Inm89b] Inmos. *The Transputer Development and iq Systems Databook.* Inmos, 72 TDN 219-00, 1989.

[MS90] Eva Ma and Dennis G. Shea. "The embedding kernel on the IBM Victor Multiprocessor for program mapping and network reconfiguration". *Submitted to Second IEEE Symposium on Parallel and Distributed Processing,* 1990.

[MT88] Eva Ma and Lixin Tao. "Embeddings among toruses and meshes". *Submitted to Journal of the ACM; also as technical report MS-CIS-88-63, University of Pennsylvania*, 1-60, August 1988.

[MT84] David May and R. Taylor. "OCCAM – An Overview". *Microprocessors and Microsystems*, 8(2), March 1984, 73–79.

[May83] David May. "OCCAM". *Sigplan Notices*, 18(4), April, 1983.

[Mic86a] Alexander Miczo. *Digital Logic Testing and Simulation.* Chapter 4.8, Harper and Row, 1986

[Mic86b] Alexander Miczo. *Digital Logic Testing and Simulation.* Chapter 4.8.3, Harper and Row, 1986

[OCD89] P. Odent, L. Claesen, and H. DeMan. "Feedback loops and large circuits in the multiprocessor implementation of a relaxation based circuit simulator". *26st Design Automation Conference*, 1989, pp. 25-30.

[SW*87] R.A. Saleh, D. Webber, E. Xia, and A. Sangiovanni-Vincentelli, "Parallel waveform Newton algorithms for circuit simulation". *Internation Conference on Computer Design: VLSI in Computers and Processors*, Rye Brook, NY, Oct. 1987, pp. 660-663.

[ST88] D.W. Smart and T.N. Trick. "Waveform relaxation on parallel processors". *Int. Journ. of circuit theory and applications*, V 16, 1988, pp. 447-456.

[TS*90] A.K. Thakore, S.Y.W. Su, H.Lam and D.G. Shea. "Asynchronous parallel processing of object bases using multiple wavefronts". *to appear in The 16th Annual International Symposium on Computer Architecture*, August 1990.

[Tro90] Cornell Theory Center and Ohio State University. "Trollius User's Reference

Manual", March 1990.

[WS*85] J. White, R. Saleh, A. Sangiovanni-Vincentelli, and A.R. Newton. "Accelerating relaxation algorithms for circuit simulation using waveform Newton, iterative step size refinement, and parallel techniques". *Int. Conf. of Computer-Aided Design*, Santa Clara, CA., Nov. 1985, pp. 5-7.

[WS*89] W. W. Wilcke, D. G. Shea, R. C. Booth, D. H. Brown, M. E. Giampapa, L. Huisman, G. R. Irwin, E. Ma, T. T. Murakami, F. T. Tong, P. R. Varker and D. J. Zukowski. "The IBM Victor Multiprocessor Project". *Proceedings of the 4th International Conference on Hypercubes*, Vol. 1, April 1989, 201–207.

[Wu85] Angela Y. Wu. "Embedding of tree networks into hypercube". *Journal of Parallel and Distributed Computing*, 2:238-249, 1985.

[ZJ89] D.J. Zukowski and T.A. Johnson. "Waveform Relaxation Based Circuit Simulation on the Victor Parallel Processor". IBM internal report, 1989.

Transputer Applications at Volkswagen Research I
Visual Simulation by Means of a Transputer Network for a Driving Simulator

Peter Zimmermann

VOLKSWAGEN AG, Research
Dept. 17760
3180 Wolfsburg
Germany

Abstract

Visual simulation is one of the most important parts of a driving simulator. Unfortunately it is in general the most expensive part too. CGI-manufacturers tend to develope more complex systems due to the demands of the military market. The common systems are strongly hardware-oriented.
On the basis of a new type of microprocessor, the transputer, a more software-oriented approach is introduced. Transputer in connection with the new high level language OCCAM are well suited for pipelining and parallelisation due to their communication concept. The advantages of this approach are reduced costs and development time, also the ability of fast and cheap changes in algorithms. The achievable performance meets the requirements for a driving simulator very well.

1. INTRODUCTION

In 1971 the VOLKSWAGEN driving simulator became operational. At that time it was the first dynamic simulator in the automotive industry. The simulator consists of three main parts, the cabin with the cockpit and all necessary elements of a real vehicle, the computer (formerly a three-console analog computer) and control hardware racks. The cabin has three rotational degrees of freedom. Accelerations are simulated by additional angles, e.g. the lateral acceleration is simulated by an additional roll angle, yaw and pitch likewise.
In 1983 a digital computer (Concurrent 3260 MPS) was introduced for controlling the simulator tasks. This computer with its six processors is able to run all the necessary tasks of the mathematical model in realtime with a steptime of 10 ms, including all ADC/ DAC -conversions to and from the cabin.

The current visual system is a hardware solution which was developed at the Technical University of Wuppertal. The concept of this system is no longer state of the art and shall be replaced within the next two years.

2. VISUAL SIMULATION

The need for a visual system in a driving simulator is obvious. The visual sensation is the most important stimulator for a driver. Unfortunately it is the most difficult and expensive part of a realtime dynamic simulation. Full flexibility in this environment is only achieved by a computer generated imagery (CGI), because the visual system must be responsive to driver actions. This cannot be achieved by a movie or a storage system.

A difficult problem even for the most advanced of today's systems is the level of realism on which driver acceptance depends. Realism depends not only on the generation of a scene but also on how the image is delivered to the driver (lens, projector, mirrow/ beamsplitter, helmet mounted display). For military flight simulators a wide angle in both vertical and horizontal directions is a stringent requirement.

A CT6-system from Evans & Sutherland with six channels output (180°) and a projection system costs about $ 6 Mio. The tendency of suppliers is to develope more powerful systems for the same price and not to decrease prices for the same performance. The characteristic of higher end systems is the dominance of specialized and expensive hardware (VLSI, ECL, parallelism).

2.1 Requirements on a Visual System for a Driving Simulator

The suggested requirements for this kind of application are not at the top end of todays technical possibilities, but seem to be a good compromise in the sense of cost and benefit. Requirements can be categorized as follows :

Performance
- o Task dependent rate of 20 to 35 frames/s
- o Delay time not greater than 80 ms
- o Resolution per channel of 512 x 512 minimum
- o Color with 4096 levels (12 bitplanes)
- o Soft and hard shading
- o Texturing, shadows (simple)
- o Different weather conditions

Control
- o Ability to independently control other model vehicles
- o Collision detection

Data
- o Landscape and roads with traffic signs
- o Landscape of 20 x 20 km real
- o Virtually unlimited
- o Powerful geometric data base and editor
- o Easy generation and modification

Reliability and maintenance
- o Software
- o Hardware

As pointed out earlier, many of the today`s systems are hardware oriented, which is a widely used practice to increase the speed of a system. However, time and costs to develop the hardware may be high. A software solution has a disadvantage in speed, but a great advantage in the other criteria, namely in costs (custom hardware), development time, flexibility of algorithm changes, debugging and risk minimization. Perhaps it is a good idea to change from software to hardware for certain time consuming parts after a careful research of the best algorithms.

2.2 Transputer, a New Approach to Parallelism

Transputer are a new type of 32-bit microprocessors. The IMS-T800 with floating point unit (64-bit) on the chip is a very powerful tool. The difference to an ordinary processor are its four high speed serial communication links. The unidirectional transfer rate of one link is about 1.6 Mbyte/s, and even with all links working at full speed the CPU is running at about 80%. This new approach is well suited to overcome the bottleneck of a common bus system, because with each new processor there is a proportional increase in communication power. Some other interesting features and performance data of the IMS-T800 are listed below :

o 4 Gigabyte address space
o Up to 1.5 Mflops
o Most common instructions in 1 cycle
o Interrupt delay not more than 3 μs
o Hardware scheduler
o On chip RAM of 4 kbyte

A transputer can be programmed in a variety of high level languages, e.g. PASCAL, C, FORTRAN. The language best suited to this new processor however is OCCAM [1], which is designed specifically to run transputer networks. One important command is the PAR construct, which is used to run processes in parallel on different processors. Three very effective block move commands are implemented in OCCAM too, which are hardware supported :

o block_move_1d   to move vectors within the memory,
o block_move_2d   to move two-dimensional arrays,
o block_draw   to move only bytes .ne. zero,
o block_clip   to move only bytes .eq. zero.

3. THE TRANSPUTER APPROACH FOR A VISUAL SYSTEM

From the requirements of a visual system for a driving simulator we have the "hard points" for the timing.
As one cannot exspect to do this job with only one processor, algorithms have probably to run in parallel. In the case at hand a pipeline of many processors seemed to be the best solution for the whole problem. An optimal dataflow within a pipeline can only be achieved if all processors start and terminate their tasks at

the same time, so the balance between the processes and processors is very important. Slight differences in the timing can be fitted by buffers.

3.1 Hidden Surface Removal

For the generation of a realistic perspective picture one has to consider that picture elements can hide each other. In the literature this is well known as the "hidden-surface-problem". In [2] ten different algorithms for the solution of this problem are described. Most of them are using sorting to find out the viewable parts of the object polygons. The amount of sorting depends on the number of polygons in the whole scene. The disadvantage of these algorithms is not only to sort n polygons but the fact that all polygons of the given scene have to be collected **before** starting the pipeline for the next frame. Sorting can be avoided by a method known as the "painters algorithm" /3/, where the faces are painted from back to front. Nevertheless one has to determine the order in which the faces have to be displayed. In our case we have to obey the following conditions, which are different from the problems with a CAD application, where one object can obscure another :

o No changes in landscape or objects during simulation must occur

o Penetration into an object or part of landscape causes a crash, simulation will stop

These restrictions are very useful, because it is now possible to determine the order of the polygons within all objects before the simulation starts. An algorithm which is well suited to deal with the painters algorithm with respect to the pipeline is the "binary space partitioning tree" (BSP-tree), which was suggested by FUCHS et al. [4],[5] and formerly used in a more restrictive way by SCHUMACKER.
The basic idea is that the planar polygons, which build an object in 3D-space, divide the space into positive and negative parts, depending on the viewpoint of the observer :

        PlaneF :   ax+by+cz+d = 0
        PlaneF (x,y,z) $\geq$ 0   positive halfspace of F
        PlaneF (x,y,z) < 0   negative halfspace of F

If the viewpoint is $(x_v, y_v, z_v)^T$ and PlaneF $(x_v, y_v, z_v) \geq 0$
then display
 1. polygons of negative halfspace of F
 2. Plane F itself
 3. polygons of positive halfspace of F

Each polygon is described by a node in the binary tree. The subtrees in the positive halfspace FRONT(F) and the nodes in the negative halfspace BACK(F) have the following properties :

All polygons in subtree FRONT : PlaneF $(x,y,z) \geq 0$
All polygons in subtree BACK : PlaneF $(x,y,z) < 0$

The following recursive procedure will produce the correct priority sequence with respect to the viewing position $(x_v, y_v, z_v)^T$:

```
IF
   PlaneF (x_v, y_v, z_v) ≥ 0
     THEN
       DisplaySubtree (BACK (F));
       DisplayFace (F);
       DisplaySubtree (FRONT (F));
     ELSE
       DisplaySubtree (FRONT (F));
       DisplayFace (F));
       DisplaySubtree (BACK (F));
FI
```

Each polygon treated by the procedure DisplayFace (F) is now ready for further actions in the pipeline while in the same time the remaining subtree will be passed. The generation of a BSP-tree is not time critical and is performed after editing of the objects.

3.2 Transformation and Clipping

Transformation and clipping are performed by the well established procedures. Transformation is necessary for changing the coordinate systems.

Landscape, roads and objects are described in different coordinate systems. The world-coordinate-system (WCOS) forms the basic system, all landscape and road data are described here, because they remain unchanged for the duration of simulation. Objects, which can be static (houses, trees, traffic signs etc.) or dynamic (other vehicles), are described in the object-coordinate-system (OCOS). After transformation by an orientation matrix coupled with a linear transformation-vector the WCOS-representation is obtained. Static objects are described by a simple pointer in the landscape description, because they are invariant during the simulation. Dynamic objects have to be checked against the landscape patches to determine their position. Data will then be tranformed from WCOS to the observer-position with its origin in the drivers eye (ECOS), this is associated with a change from a right to a left hand system, where y_{WCOS} becomes z_{ECOS} (Figure 1).

After all visible polygons of the entire scene have been transformed into the ECOS, z-clipping will be performed in the view volume. Polygons lying in front of yon will be discarded completely. Perspective projection of polygons is then obtained by projecting the vertex coordinates onto the projection plane, which is limited by height s_H and width s_W of the screen :

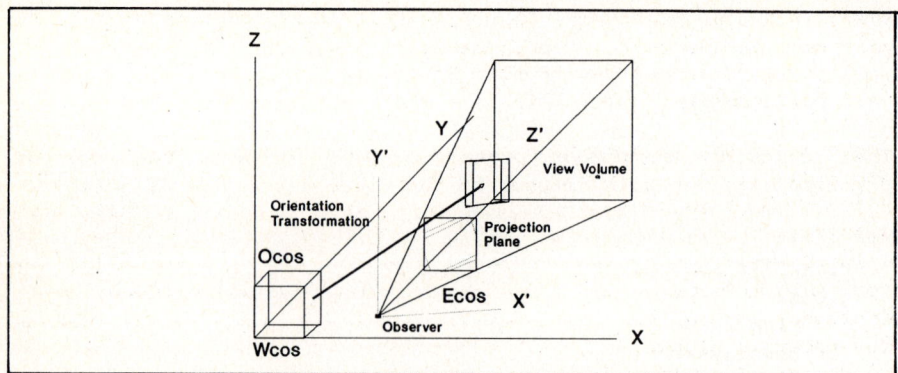

Figure 1: Interdependence of coordinate-systems

$$(x,y,z)^T \rightarrow \{\ [xD/(z+D)]+s_W/2\ ;\ [yD/(z+D)]+s_H/2\ \}_{DCOS},$$

where D means the eye distance to the projection plane. After this final transformation the vertices are transformed into the display-coordinate-system (DCOS), the depth information is not longer available. Color intensity has therefore to be computed before transformation.

3.3 Scanline Conversion

After transformation and clipping of the polygons, which are still in the correct order for hidden surface elimination, the vector description of the polygons has to be substituted by a rasterization of the polygon edges.
Let vertices (x_0,y_0) and (x_1,y_1) be the endpoints of an edge, then

$$dx := (x_1-x_0)/(y_1-y_0)$$

will be the slope in the scanline direction. Rasterization can be performed by

```
x:=x0
y:=y0
  WHILE y ≤ y1 DO
    BEGIN
       Store (Round(x),y)
       x:=x+dx
       y:=y+1
    END
```

Computing x(y) by floating-point arithmetic has two disadvantages. First, there is no guarantee to meet the endpoint (x_1,y_1) because of limited accuracy. Second, computation time is longer than with fixed-point arithmetic (which is by the way not true in the transputer case !). Several algorithms have been developed in the past to rasterize straight and curved lines (BRESENHAM [6]).

The method implemented in our application uses 32-bit integer, is very fast and meets the requirements of pipelining :

$$x := a*2^{16}+b$$

where a is the integer part of value x in the high order 16 bit and b is the binary fraction. The MSB of b has therefore the value $2^{-1}=1/2$ and so forth. With $\delta x := x_1 - x_0$ and $\delta y := y_1 - y_0$ we have $dx := \delta x * 2^{16} / \delta y$ and $x_{\delta y} := x_0 * 2^{16}$.

This algorithm requires one integer divide (dx) and one shift (x) for initialisation and only integer increment $x := x + dx$ plus an increment $y := y + 1$ for the loop, it works for positive as well as for negative slopes.

To decide if an edge is a left or a right border of the polygon is easy. As the nodes of all polygons are clockwise arranged, a left edge is characterized by $\delta y > 0$, a right edge by $\delta y < 0$. If $\delta y = 0$, the edge is horizontal and hence can be disregarded.

3.4 Shading

Shading is the next stage of the pipeline, where the scanlines of polygons are filled between the rasterized edges.

If a polygon has to be filled by constant shading, the block_move-operation of the transputer is quite useful. Let x_{left} and x_{right} of scanline y be the borders of the segment to be filled with color c, then

[Line FROM x_{left} FOR $(x_{right} - x_{left}) + 1$] :=

[ColorLine (c) FROM 0 FOR $(x_{right} - x_{left}) + 1$]

is the appropiate command of the transputer. The array ColorLine contains a complete color line for each of the entire colors of the simulation. This hardware-supported operation is much more efficient than an explicit setting and adressing of each pixel.

Soft shading of a polygon [7] is much more complicate than hard shading. Linear interpolation between the left and right border of each scanline is necessary to determine the color value of the pixels.

Let $\delta x := x_{left} - x_{right}$ and $\delta c := c(x_{left}) - c(x_{right})$, then each pixel has to be set individually when $|\delta c| \geq \delta x$. If $|\delta c| < \delta x$, there are segments of pixels with the same color and hence can be treated the same way as with hard shading.

At the present time texturing is not available in the system. As texturing is a very time consuming task for the overall scenery, it may be a possible solution to texture only certain parts of the scene like polygon-intensive traffic signs, wheels, beams etc. Beside this it may be a good idea to wait for the next transputer generation or to use special chips like vector processors.

3.5 The Topology of Processors

In the previous chapters the basic algorithms of the visual simulation were introduced. These algorithms in the form of OCCAM-procedures have to be joined together to form a functional process/ processor -network.
The balance of the overall task distribution for the network forms the basis for the design of the pipeline topology. Time measurements of the implemented algorithms are more useful than theoretical considerations in this case. Memory access time of a transputer depends on the location of code and data in the memory. Memory is divided into two sections, one is the "onchip-RAM" with 4 kbytes and access time of 50 ns (for 20 MHz), the other the external RAM with locations above, which has a longer access time with typically 100 ns. Measurements have shown that with the equipment at hand internal code is about 3.5 times faster than code and data completely in external memory.
Normally the programmer cannot influence the location of arrays and variables, because the compiler is responsible for memory organisation. Compiler starts with memory location in the onchip-RAM depending on the length of variables, arrays and program code.
Time consumptions of the tasks in the pipeline are different. Link speed and the amount of data to be transferred between the various processors are influencing the balance too. The following table shows the first four stages of the pipeline and the timing of a typical test scene with 466 four-sided polygons :

Process	Time [ms]
BSP-process	11
Transformation	9
Front clipping, projection	12
X/ Y - clipping	10

Table 1 : Timing of processes

Scanline conversion has to be the next stage of the pipeline. There are some possibilities to distribute this task over several processors. Using the assumption of equally distributed polygons in the scene, a static task distribution would be a good approach. Static means, that each processor is responsible for a fixed segment of the display. This assumption has to be valid not only for the quantity but also for the size of the displayed polygons. One can imagine that in the case of a driving simulation this is not true. In worst case, if all objects are contained in only one display segment, only one processor would be in action and cause serious overload to the whole system.
A distribution of the dynamic load to a "processor pool" may be another alternative to the static segmentation. This method may work quite well, if there are enough polygons in the scene, but it has a serious disadvantage too. As it cannot be assumed that all

polygons have equal size and direction, a smaller polygon of high priority may leave the processor pool earlier than a bigger one with low priority. The consequence of this would be an inconsistency in the order of polygons leaving the pool, the painters algorithm would no longer be applicable without resorting the entire polygon stream.

A modification to the prediscribed method is sharing one polygon to several processors. The implemented scanline-algorithm uses modulo arithmetic for the distribution of a polygon to n processors. The i-th processor works on those scanlines for which number y is

$$y \bmod n = i$$

Attachment of scanlines to the n processors can be fixed before starting simulation because this distribution is static.

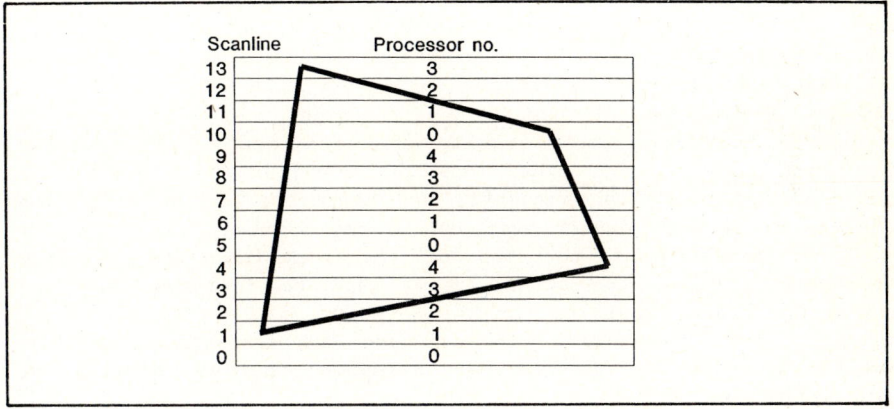

Figure 2: Modulo distribution of a polygon for n=5 processors

This method leads to a much better distribution of scanlines over the processors. Neither the location of objects in the scene nor the size of any polygon has an influence on the efficiency of the processor pipeline.

As described earlier, each transputer has 4 independent links. In case of scanlining, two of them are used for receiving data from the clipper stage and transmitting the results to the painter processors. With the remaining two links a tree-like structur can be organized for the scanline processors. Data paths between root and leafs of a binary-tree are proportional to the logarithm of the sum of nodes. As data distribution via the links of a transputer runs in parallel, there is nearly no additional load on the CPU. Measurements show that with a tree of 16 processors and running at a rate of 25 frames/s, 600 polygons (2400 edges) can be scan-converted and displayed [8]. In this case it was a typical simulation scene with both constant and soft shading.

Another important factor for the realtime visual simulation is the time delay of the whole system. For a vehicle simulator 80 ms

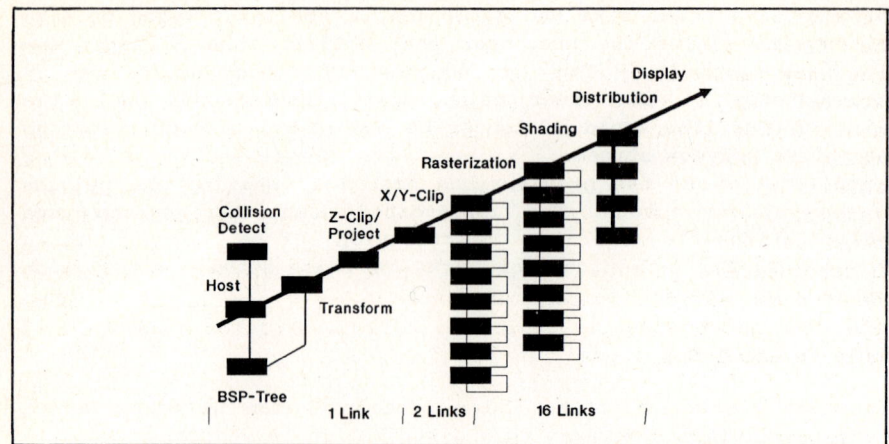

Figure 3: Topology of processors

should be the upper limit. The proposed transputer-pipeline yields a delay time < 60 ms at a frame rate of 25/s with 600 polygons.
The frame rate of the system depends highly on the amount of displayed polygons, which itself is a function of the modeled landscape, objects and other vehicles. Obviously the number of scene-polygons changes frequently and therefore has an effect on the frame rate. To detect overload of the system, data frequency will be measured at the top of the pipeline. If frequency decreases rapidly, the actual frame will be finished, but the following frame will be omitted, which leads to a slight oscillation in frame rate. In our case the differences are too small to have a considerable influence on the quality of simulation.

3.6 Increasing the Performance of the System

The analysis of the proposed visual system shows that because of the restrictions by the transformation- and clipping part of the pipeline it makes not much sense to increase the partitioning of the scanline- and shading-processors. With a second pipeline in parallel problems would occur with the order for the painters algorithm, so it would be necessary to resort the polygons after clipping.
The proposed system can be understood as somewhat like a visual channel. Normally one channel displays about 30° to 40° depending on the generation type (mirror, projection etc.). This corresponds to a static distribution, which was discussed earlier in this chapter. To increase the viewing angle means that the whole pipeline has to be replicated, for example 6 times to achieve an angle of 180°. An additional increase of performance could be achieved, if the channel in front of the driver would be statically segmented into 4 subchannels (somewhat like "area of interest").

The transputer used for the described prototype system is one of the first T800-types available. The current supplied clock frequency is 20 MHz, 25 MHz are available now (together with 70 ns external RAM), 30 MHz are announced. With todays available hardware the potential speed-up of the system would be in the amount of 30%. A further increase of system throughput can be achieved by software. The number of polygons which have a certain distance from the observer can be reduced without loss of accuracy.

In conclusion a potential system with 6 channels of 30° each with one channel divided into 4 subchannels could run at 25 Hz frame rate with about 6000 polygons. The today's price of such a system would be about $ 800.000.

4. GEOMETRY DATA BASE AND EDITOR

The geometry data base consists of two parts. One part contains data for the landscape and roads, the second part data for the objects including vehicles. The editor, which is still under development, has the same structure. Data base and editor are residing on a PC. The reason for this arrangement is the availability and flexibility of the MS/DOS-world.

Visual simulation data will be downloaded in the initialisation phase. Apart from this the transputer-network has to be connected with the simulation computer, because a small amount of data concerning the location of the vehicles has to be send each simulation cycle. On the other hand, crash information from the visual system has to be reported to the host computer in order to inform the mathematical vehicle model.

For the mathematical description of landscape, objects and roads BEZIER-polynoms of third degree were chosen. Working with curves and surfaces of this or similar type has several advantages [3]. The most interesting are easy handling of the so called control points, the parametric type of curve and surface and the convex hull property.

A slight disadvantage may be computation time, but as we do not act with the coefficients during realtime simulation, this is not important.

5. ACKNOWLEDGEMENT

I wish to thank T. Umland for his excellent diploma work during his time at VOLKSWAGEN Research. T. Umland worked out many of the algorithms and programmed procedures and networks.

REFERENCES

[1] Pountain, D.; A tutorial introduction to OCCAM programming.
     INMOS Ltd., 1987

[2] Sutherland, I.E., Sproull, R.F., Schumacker, R.A.; A characterization of ten hidden-surface algorithms. Computing Survey, 6(1974), 1-55
[3] Foley, J.D., Van Dam, A.; Fundamentals of Interactive Computer Graphics. Addison-Wesley, 1983
[4] Fuchs, H., Kedem, Z.M., Naylor, B.F.; On visible surface generation by a priori tree structures. Computer Graphics, 14(1980), 124-133
[5] Fuchs, H., Abram, G.D., Grant, E.D.; Near real-time shaded display of rigid objects. Computer Graphics, 17(1983), 65-72
[6] Bresenham, J.E.; Algorithm for computer control of digital plotter. IBM Syst.J., 4(1) (1965), 25-30
[7] Gouraud, H.; Continous shading of curved surfaces. IEEE Transactions on computers. 20(1971), 623-629
[8] Umland, T.; Zur Parallelisierung von Algorithmen für einen Realzeit-Sichtsimulator auf der Basis von Transputern.

Transputer Applications at Volkswagen Research II
Control of an Active Suspension System by a Transputer Network

Harald Beduhn

VOLKSWAGEN AG, Research
Dept. 17760
3180 Wolfsburg
Germany

Automotive experts know that there exists a conflict in building vehicles which are comfortable in ride and safe in driving stability too. Ride comfort generally requires reduced damping and spring forces, whereas good handling and stability properties are achieved with increased damping and spring rate.
The aim of the active suspension control system is to adapt the forces acting between vehicle body and wheels to the different driving situations.
This will be achieved by a closed loop system, where up to 32 sensors supply their information about the driving conditions to a transputer network shown in Fig.1. The network is responsible for digital filtering of input signals, calculating the actuator forces and controlling the hydraulic devices. This realtime loop will be performed within 1 ms.

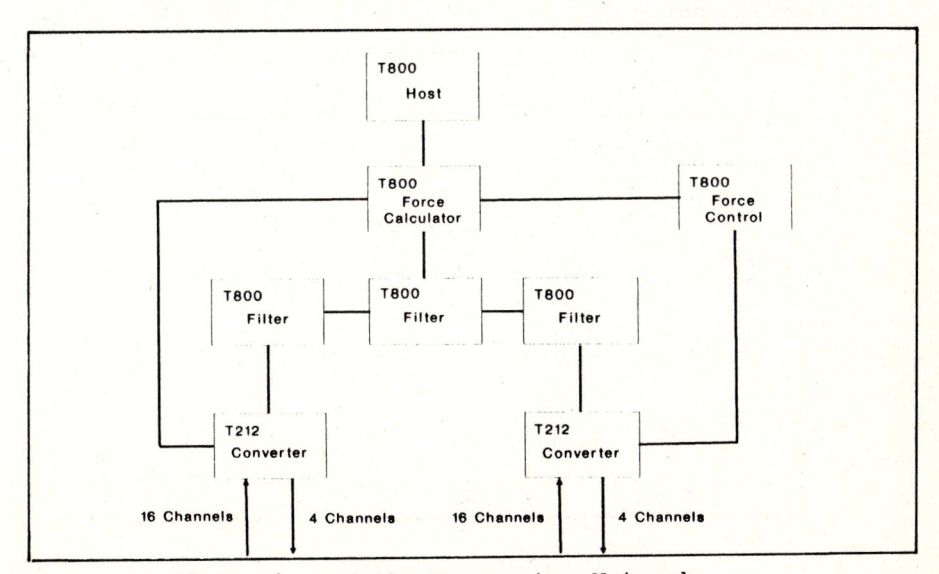

Fig.1   Configuration of the Transputer Network

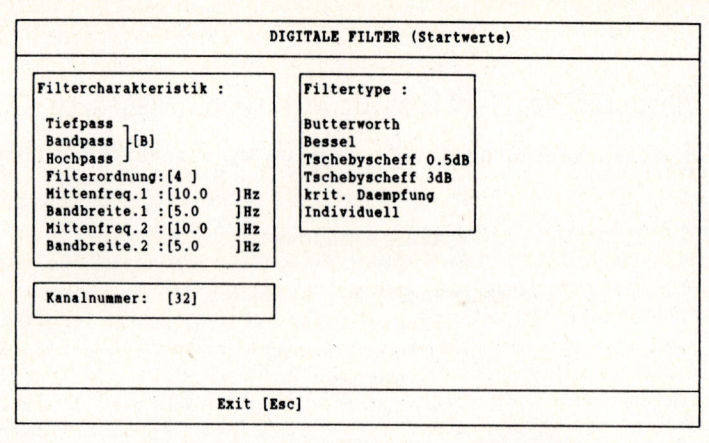

```
┌─────────────────────────────────────────────────────────────┐
│                   DIGITALE FILTER (Startwerte)              │
│  ┌─────────────────────────────┐ ┌─────────────────────────┐│
│  │ Filtercharakteristik :      │ │ Filtertype :            ││
│  │                             │ │                         ││
│  │   Tiefpass    ┐             │ │   Butterworth           ││
│  │   Bandpass    ├[B]          │ │   Bessel                ││
│  │   Hochpass    ┘             │ │   Tschebyscheff 0.5dB   ││
│  │   Filterordnung:[4 ]        │ │   Tschebyscheff 3dB     ││
│  │   Mittenfreq.1 :[10.0  ]Hz  │ │   krit. Daempfung       ││
│  │   Bandbreite.1 :[5.0   ]Hz  │ │   Individuell           ││
│  │   Mittenfreq.2 :[10.0  ]Hz  │ │                         ││
│  │   Bandbreite.2 :[5.0   ]Hz  │ └─────────────────────────┘│
│  └─────────────────────────────┘                            │
│  ┌─────────────────────────────┐                            │
│  │ Kanalnummer:   [32]         │                            │
│  └─────────────────────────────┘                            │
│                                                             │
│                        Exit [Esc]                           │
└─────────────────────────────────────────────────────────────┘
```

Fig.2   Menu for controlling the digital filters

```
                        F A H R Z E U G R E G L E R
 ┌───────────────────────────────────────────────────────────────────────┐
 │ Parameter :        vr      vl      hr      hl    Regelstrategien      │
 │                                                                       │
 │ cw: [F1] <       14700   14700   14700   14700  < [F2]  [O] full active│
 │ d1: [F3] <         150     150     150     150  < [F4]  [R] semi active│
 │ d2: [F5] <         150     150     150     150  < [F6]  [Q] conventional│
 │ w : [F7] <          50      50      50      50  < [F8]  [U] pitch and roll│
 │ n : [F9] <          50      50      50      50  <([F10]) [ ]          │
 │                                                         [ ]           │
 │                                                         [ ]           │
 │                                                         [ ]           │
 │ [Cw] [d1] [d2] [N] [W]  einzeln ändern :                [ ]           │
 │           wvl  [N] :  50.0                              [ ]           │
 │           wvr  [N] :  50.0                              [ ]           │
 │           whl  [N] :  50.0                                            │
 │           whr  [N] :  50.0                                            │
 │                                                                       │
 │ [D] Digitale Filter                                                   │
 │ [K] Kraftregler                      [S] Werte auf Diskette speichern │
 │                                      [B] Betriebssystem (MS-DOS)      │
 │ [M] ONLINE-Modus                     [P] Pufferbetrieb                │
 └───────────────────────────────────────────────────────────────────────┘
  START = 3 x <ENTER>                                  3 x ESC = STOP
```

Fig.3   Menu for set and vary vehicle control stragegy

```
              ══< KRAFTREGLER (Online.modus) >══
 ┌───────────────────────────────────────────────────────────────────────┐
 │         │  Vordere Aktuatoren      │  Hintere Aktuatoren              │
 │         │   rechts  │   links      │   rechts  │   links              │
 │         │ einf.│ausf.│einf.│ausf.  │ einf.│ausf.│einf.│ausf.          │
 │   PV  : │  1.0   1.0   1.0   1.0  │  1.0   1.0   1.0   1.0            │
 │   TI  : │  0.35  0.35  0.35  0.35 │  0.0   0.0   0.0   0.0            │
 │   TV  : │  0.2   0.2   0.2   0.2  │  0.0   0.0   0.0   0.0            │
 │   AB  : │  0.0   0.0   0.0   0.0  │  0.0   0.0   0.0   0.0            │
 │   AR  : │  0.0   0.0   0.0   0.0  │  0.0   0.0   0.0   0.0            │
 │   AG  : │  0.6   0.0   0.0   0.0  │  0.0   0.0   0.0   0.0            │
 │   RB  : │  0.78  0.78  0.78  0.78 │  0.0   0.0   0.0   0.0            │
 │   RG  : │  0.0   0.0   0.0   0.0  │  0.0   0.0   0.0   0.0            │
 │   RW  : │  0.0   0.0   0.0   0.0  │  0.0   0.0   0.0   0.0            │
 │   DD  : │  0.0   0.0   0.0   0.0  │  0.0   0.0   0.0   0.0            │
 │   DT  : │  0.0   0.0   0.0   0.0  │  0.0   0.0   0.0   0.0            │
 │                                                                       │
 │   VR-Regelguete  VL-Regelguete  HR-Regelguete  HL-Regelguete          │
 │       0.3994         1.0014          0.0            0.0               │
 │                                                                       │
 │                           Exit [Esc]                                  │
 └───────────────────────────────────────────────────────────────────────┘
```

Fig.4   Menu for set and vary force controller

Several softkey driven menus are available for observation and control of the tasks, special keys are available to change parameters on the fly during process is running.
Fig 2 shows the menu for controlling the digital filters. Filtering is necessary to separate vibrations of engine and metal sheet from the input signals. The program includes various filtertypes like Butterworth, Bessel and Chebyshev of the order up to 10 and low-, high- and bandpass characteristics.
A comfortable way to find the optimal parameters to a given vehicle control strategy is using the menu shown in Fig.3, which makes it possible to change e.g. the vehicle roll angle during curve driving thus determining the best compromise for drivers feeling.
Another menu -shown in Fig.4- is used for control the actuator units, where proportional, differential and integral components can be set and varied, feedback of current state is possible too.

Military Applications of Transputers

Ian Browning
RSRE, Malvern, UK

Abstract

The Ministry of Defence (MOD) realised the importance of parallel computing machines at an early stage of the development of the transputer. Some eight years, on its research establishments have a wide ranging programme of transputer based research and development covering a broad range of application areas. These areas of work will be examined and compared with the original application areas envisaged for the transputer. The attractions of transputer based systems for military systems will be examined along with some comments on the present state of hardware and software platforms. The special requirements and timescales for the development of military systems will be examined and compared with the state of transputer system development. This paper will use a number of selected applications with differing requirements to illustrate the wide applicability of transputer systems, these will include the ARMADA speech recognition system developed by the Speech Research Unit (SRU) at RSRE which performs real-time continuous speech recognition of spoken airborne reconnaissance reports. The ROVA Unmanned Land Vehicle project at RARDE which is being used as a testbed for the development and assessment of control methods and algorithms and the Battlefield Sensor Simulator (BSS) a multi-user high resolution transputer based simulator for the assessment of future generation sensor systems, currently being developed for RSRE.

Image Synthesis For Television on a Volvox Transputer based machine

Christian TRICOT - Jean-Marie FEST

Archipel S.A.
P.A.E. du Levray
4, Route de Nanfray
Cran-Gevrier
74000 ANNECY
FRANCE

Tel : (+33) 50.69.20.58   Fax : (+33) 50.69.20.65

Abstract:

This application deals with image synthesis to produce movies for TV, adverts, video clips.... The parallelism is introduced at pixel computation and on facet presentation. The architecture is based upon an N-ring of two transputers per node. This application is used in industry to produce movies, image per image. Some of these movies have been produced for French TV (Canal+, La 5).

This application proves the Archipel approach in terms of 'direct parallel programming' to produce embedded systems with optimum performances, at modular costs.

INTRODUCTION

ARCHIPEL is a French manufacturer specialised in transputer-based products. The systems, named VOLVOX, are connected to an host using one of the communication boards. Currently, hosts like PCs, Apollos, SUNs, CETIA and general implementation of VME Bus based work-stations are supported. A communication board, hosted typically in a work-station, controls a Volvox-transputer-system, built using Archipel's network boards. These systems can be accessed by multiple hosts, either by a transputer interface or by Ethernet. Associated to this hardware, software tools allow an easy and fast integration of existing software written in C, Fortran and Pascal. Being a manufacturer, Archipel provides training, support and assistance. In this context, the following applications have been developed using Volvox systems.

This application treats image synthesis for the industrial video world. This application has been used for french TV (Canal+, La 5) and developed by the french company BSCA, located in Paris. Their product, named 'RenderWoman', is used in-house for image-production.

I. The 'RenderWoman' machine

BSCA is a company specialised in 3D image synthesis production for video, cartoons, adverts, etc... It is well known that image synthesis is a computer intensive application, and that the goal of any company is to decrease the production prices of images. In a first stage, BSCA produced images on IRIS 3130 from Silicon Graphics, with an in-house developed software. In a second stage, considering that they had not enough performances for image production, they chose to adapt their software on an Archipel machine.

This is typically the type of application where an user wants to develop rapidly, making profit of easy-to-use and performant software tools, in order to provide an embedded system that he will exploit on a commercial basis.

II. The system architecture

Today, they produce images on a transputer based machine hosted by a PC-AT under Xenix, and then transfer them to the Iris machine for final assembly. Image modelling is done on the PC, image rendering on the transputer network, assembly and storage on the Iris.

The system architecture is the following :

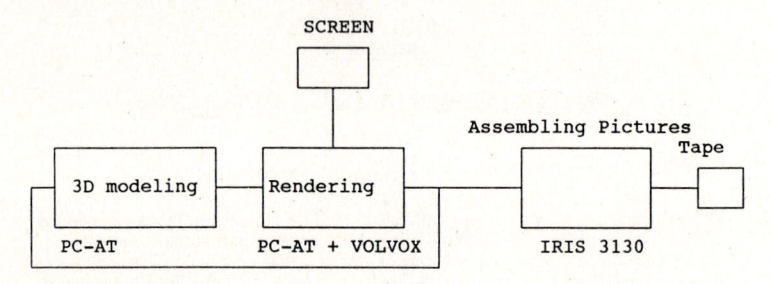

```
                        SCREEN
                          |
                                        Assembling Pictures
                                                         Tape
        ┌─────────────┐  ┌───────────┐  ┌─────────────────┐ ┌──┐
        │ 3D modeling │──│ Rendering │  │                 │─│  │
        └─────────────┘  └───────────┘  └─────────────────┘ └──┘
           PC-AT          PC-AT + VOLVOX       IRIS 3130
```

III. The Scenario of a movie

The movie which illustrates this application deals with part of the life of an spidder, named René, and its friends (bugs...). They live in a non-reliable computer (whose manufacturer is unknown!). Called 'ComputerHome', this movie been broadcasted by the French Canal+ TV channel and projected in cinemas.

IV. Creating the movie

Once the scenario has been defined, the main actor René and its friends are modellised (structure and expressions). The main parameters are the dimensions, the squeleton and the moving possibilities. The scenes (the environnement) are modellised. All the modelisation is done using the 'facet technics'.

The paths of the different actors are then defined. These trajectories are given using main points, the trajectory between these points being interpolated. At any stage, the creator may check the motions of its actors using wire representation.

Once the trajectories are defined, the colors are added to the scene. Different possibilities can be used at this stage, like zoom effects and shading.

Finally, the 'virtual' camera is introduced using a travelling technic. A graphic tool is used to define the motion speed, the trajectory, the angle and the focal.

This produces a contiguous set of image to render. This set is sent to the 'RenderWoman' machine.

V. Architecture and algorithm of the 'RenderWoman' machine

The image is described with a 3D facet model. The software is based on a classical scan-line (Watkins) algorithm, associated to a Phong shading.

V.1 The architecture

The rendering machine has the following organisation :

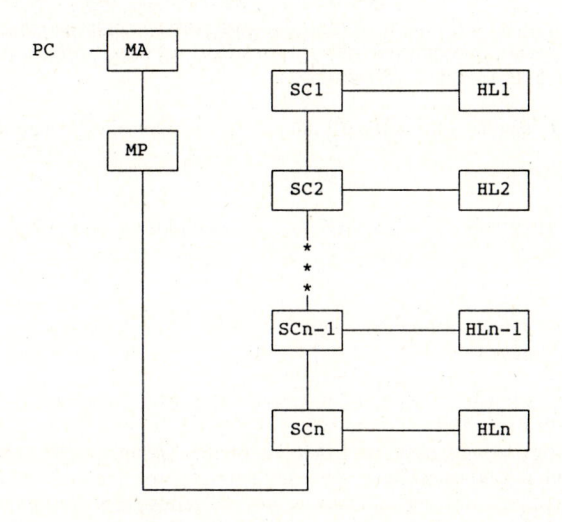

```
PC ---- MA ----+----- SC1 ----- HL1
               |
        MP     |----- SC2 ----- HL2
               |        *
               |        *
               |        *
               |----- SCn-1 --- HLn-1
               |
               +----- SCn ----- HLn
```

MA : Master task, needs 8 Mbytes

SC : Scanning and Phong Shading task, needs 2 Mbytes

HL : Holder task, needs 4 to 8 Mbytes

MP : Mapper (optional), needs 4 to 8 Mbytes

V.2 The algorithm

The algorithm mapping used is of a geometric type.

Each line of the image to compute is distributed over the network of transputers, one line per couple of transputers.

An image is produced line by line, in two phases. Each couple SCi and HLi computes a number of lines depending on the number of couples in the network. During the first phase, all the modelised objects are sent on the primary ring, to all the SC tasks, each of these exploiting the object to build the lines it has to compute. Image rendering is done in phase 2, data being sent back in the ring to the master.

Phase 1 :

The Master sends each facet on the primary ring of transputers.

For each object, the Scanner (SC) intersects the object with the plans corresponding to the lines it has to compute, to determine the intersected segments. Thus, the SC is building its image data base, which is sent as and when required to the Holder (HL).

Line by line, the HL sorts out the segments and keeps the foreground one (elimination of the hidden segments).

Then, the Master (MA) defines virtual objects, which are shade cones : zones in which the hidden light sources are eliminated. This is a preliminary for the later shading computation.

These virtual objects are also sent into the primary ring at the destination of the SCs, which apply the same scanning algorithm and send the resulting segments to the HL. These associate the informations (for instance, useful light sources) to the corresponding foreground segments.

Phase one is completed when all the real and virtual objects have been exploited.

Phase 2 :

During this phase, the HLs send all the segments of one line to the SCs, which now compute the Phong shading. Once a line is computed, the SC sends it to the Master.

The lines being computed asynchronously, the MA has to re-organise the complete image.

Finally, this image is displayed or stored in a file.

This methodology allows easy modification of the lightning parameters (source light intensity, object colors) : one can refine the parameters of images without going back to the first step, thereby offering time saving whilst 'debugging'. This functionnality is, of course, integrated in the 'RenderWoman' software. For this, the render tool keeps the image database in the transputer network, therefore avoiding the first phase computing. The creator can modify the parameters interactively. The new resulting image will be produced with the existing database and the new parameters by just going through phase two.

This methodology, together with the power of transputers, increases global productivity.

VI. Performances/price Ratio

The 'RenderWoman' machine used for image production integrates 9 T800 transputers, of which 4 are SC-HL couples. Tests have shown that performances scale up, up to 8 SC-HL couples.

Before the Volvox machine BSCA used a specific image synthesis oriented machine. The two machines having about the same price, there is an acceleration ratio greater than 30 for a 4 couples machine.

One should note that this is the computing acceleration ratio, the increase of productivity due to the methodology being added to this figure.

With the Volvox-System, BSCA produces today in 1 to 2 weeks what needed before 3 to 4 months, and this with a higher degree of quality.

VII. Conclusions

This application is used in the real industrial world. This application is caracterised by the need of high computation power and a large amount of data. For this application, only a multi-processors architecture could provide an adequate solution, associated to a distributed data base. Further, there is no need for a reconfigurable network of transputers. A fixed topology network of transputers provides an affordable solution with the best performances to build powerful dedicated systems.

REFERENCES:

.Parallelism in Rendering Algorithms (CROW, 1989, communication ACM SIGGRAPH)

.The Design of Image Space Graphic Display Algorithms for MIMD Architectures (WHITMAN & GUENTER, 1989, communication ACM SIGGRAPH).

.Illumination for Computer generated Pictures (PHOG-BUI-TUONG, 1975, communication ACM SIGGRAPH).

.Models of light reflection for computer synthesized Pictures (BLINN, 1977, communication ACM SIGGRAPH).

.A reflectance Model for computer graphics (COOK & TORRANCE, 1981, communication ACM SIGGRAPH).

.A characterization of 10 hidden surfaces Algorithms (SUTHERLAND, SPROUL & SCHUMACKER, 1974, Computing Surveys).

.Shadow algorithms for computer Graphic (CROW 1977, communication ACM SIGGRAPH).

.Computer Home, une histoire de puce savante (TECHIMAGES N°8, SEGURA, October 89).

.Two Examples of Transputer Industrial Applications (BIRA89, 1989, TRICOT & FEST).

The application of transputers in High-Energy Physics

L.W. Wiggers and J.C. Vermeulen
ZEUS Collaboration
NIKHEF-H
P.O. Box 41882, NL-1009 DB Amsterdam

May 11, 1990

Abstract

Transputers are applied in several High-Energy Physics experiments. They serve as processing and transport engines for data-acquisition and compression, event-selection and data-monitoring. In this paper examples will be presented of their use in the largest-scale High-Energy Physics application at the moment: the on-line system of the ZEUS experiment.

1 Introduction

High-Energy Physics experiments aim for the identification of elementary particles, the determination of their properties and the study of their interactions. The main experimental technique consists of measuring the direction, energy and momentum of the particles produced in interactions of colliding high-energy particles at accelerator centers like CERN in Geneva and DESY in Hamburg. Large scale experiments with typical costs of about 30 M£ require a long construction time (typically of the order of 7 years). A few hundred physicist, backed by even more technicians, from many institutes in the world participate in the design, construction and operation of the experiment and later in the analysis of the data. The experiment is operating continuously for half a year periods during 5-10 years after startup.

The numbers of electronic channels to be read out in a typical experiment is a few hundred thousand. The rate of the reactions makes it necessary to "trigger" on relevant "events" and to reject "background" and uninteresting events, *i.e.* to select on-line. The trigger has to reduce the initial event rate to a few events per second with -after data-compression- an eventlength of 100-200 KByte. This rate is dictated by storage capabilities and analysis requirements. In this sample the interesting events just form a small fraction; they are selected later off-line by sophisticated analysis programs.

To use the ZEUS experiment as an example: in Spring 1991 the HERA electron-proton collider at DESY is scheduled to start its operation. ZEUS is one of the two detectors at that collider. Every 96 nsec beam-bunches cross at the interaction point in the detector. The rate of hard electron-proton interactions is about 1-10 Hz, while the background rate of interactions of beam particles and residual gas molecules along the beam-line is about 400 KHz. The "first-level" trigger has the task to set a trigger rate of 1 KHz by eliminating most of the beam-gas background. The data of all crossings is kept in buffers until a decision is taken. Programmable logic is applied for the trigger at this level. At the "second-level" commercially available microprocessors -here mainly transputers- will analyze the digitized data of the subdetectors. Combining the results of those processors should result in a further reduction of the trigger rate to 100 Hz. After a positive decision the data of all subdetectors is gathered and sent to a "third-level" processor farm. RISC Processors (MIPS R3000) will reduce the rate to 3-10 Hz by an analysis of the whole event.

Transputers are applied in the second-level trigger, the read-out of the subdetectors after a second-level trigger and the building of the events out of the data of the subdetectors [5].

2 Why Transputers?

The choice for the Transputer microprocessor of INMOS for application in High-Energy Physics experiments is based on :

1. the dma-driven data transport over 4 links, providing simple communication between different parts of a detector

2. the multi-tasking with task-switching times of just a few microsec

3. the powerful cpu

4. the support in the OCCAM language for parallel processing and for interprocess communication and synchronization, eliminating the need for an operating system

The parallelism is geometric and event based: each transputer reads and processes a small part of the subdetector data while several events are simultaneously present in the system and treated in parallel.

The real-time aspect of the systems demands that they must be able to transport and process the mean rate of events. Statistical fluctuations are flattened out by extensive buffering. Each step in the system should take less time than the average time between events.

3 Transputers for read-out of front-end electronics

3.1 Strategy

After a positive first level trigger decision the data of a subdetector are stored in buffers in read-out modules. There are a few possibilities:

1. equip every module with a transputer and connect the modules via transputer links

2. read many modules by a transputer over the extended transputer bus

3. read many modules by a transputer over a standard bus, like VME

An experiment at CERN aims for applying strategy 1 [7], in ZEUS both strategy 2 [1, 2] and 3 [5] are applied. For solution (1) more transputers are needed, for (2) the interfacing to the bus is simple, for (3) the potential is more general.

3.2 The NIKHEF 2TP-module

Following strategy 3 a read-out controller has been developed at NIKHEFH with 2 transputers interfaced to the VME bus. In fig 1 the layout is sketched for the 2TP-module, applied in the read-out and triggering of several subdetectors in ZEUS, the Event Builder and the Global Second-Level Triggering [3, 4].

In the read-out system of the "calorimeter" subdetector a 2TP-module handles the data of all front-end cards in a VME crate. After a first-level trigger a part of the digitized data in the cards is read over the VME bus by transputer Y into the TPM. Transputer X will analyze those data, *i.e.* to search for clusters of energy. After a positive second-level trigger all data in the front-end cards is read and transported via the links of transputer Y to the Event Builder.

Both transputers have access to the VME bus and can issue VME instructions. The TPM is also accessible by another master on the VME bus. The transfer speed for the

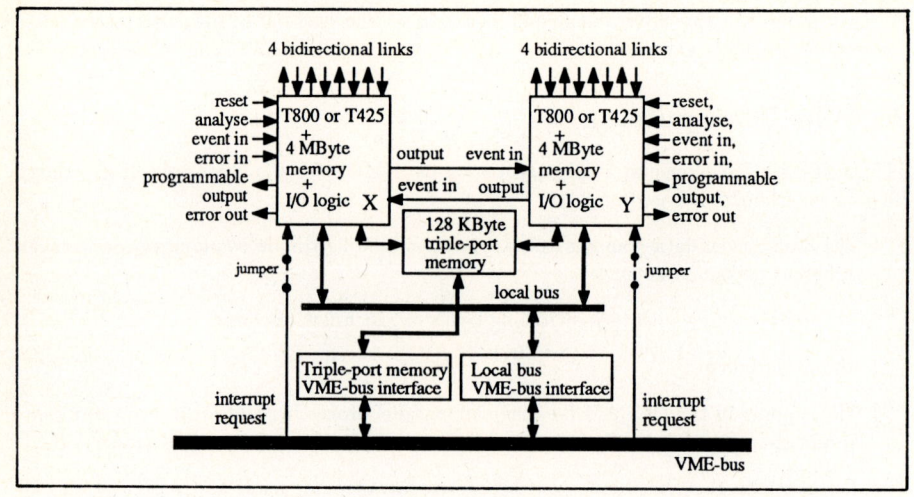

Figure 1: Read-out controller (2TP-module) in development at NIKHEF.

present prototypes is 7 MByte/s for reading by transputer Y and 10 MByte/s for direct write into the TPM of the 2TP-module from outside.

In Spring 1990 a production of 234 modules has started.

4 Transputers in ZEUS

4.1 Transport to the Sub-System Crate

After a second-level trigger the data stored in the front-end cards in ZEUS have to be transported further to the third-level trigger system. at an expected frequency of 100 Hz. First the data of each subdetector are assembled in a 2TP-module in the Sub-System Crate (SSC) of each subdetector. When the general readout system is down, every subdetector can redirect its output from there to its local controlling MicroVax.

The transputer networks of the subdetectors will have different configurations. Here the configuration for the calorimeter subdetector applying a crossbar switch, will be discussed. The use of a mesh network has been considered but was rejected because of the more complicated routing software and the less predictable behaviour of such a network.

The data of the 36 read-out crates are sent from the collecting 2TP-modules over a multiplexer to 3 2TP-modules in the SSC's of the calorimeter. This multiplexer, Control and Switch Box (CSB), is built around the INMOS crossbar C004 Link Switch (fig 2). At maximum 16 crates are connected via each switch to the receiving transputer of the 2TP-module in the SSC. A transputer sends a request for a connection to the 2TP-module in the SSC over a link to a controlling T222. This request is latched in an C012 (serial to parallel converter) connected to the external bus of the T222 transputer. After the transport over the C004 the connection is released. The CSB also has a simple uni-directional broadcast circuit to fan-out trigger decisions over many links [6].

The transport from a read-out crate to the SSC crate over in total 7.5 m plus linkswitch proceeds with a transfer speed of about 1 MByte/s per link.

4.2 Event Building

Instead of building an event out of the data of all subdetectors at a central place (see [8]) and transporting it from there to the third-level trigger and thereby perhaps creating a bottleneck, in ZEUS a solution is adopted where the event is built in each individual third-level trigger

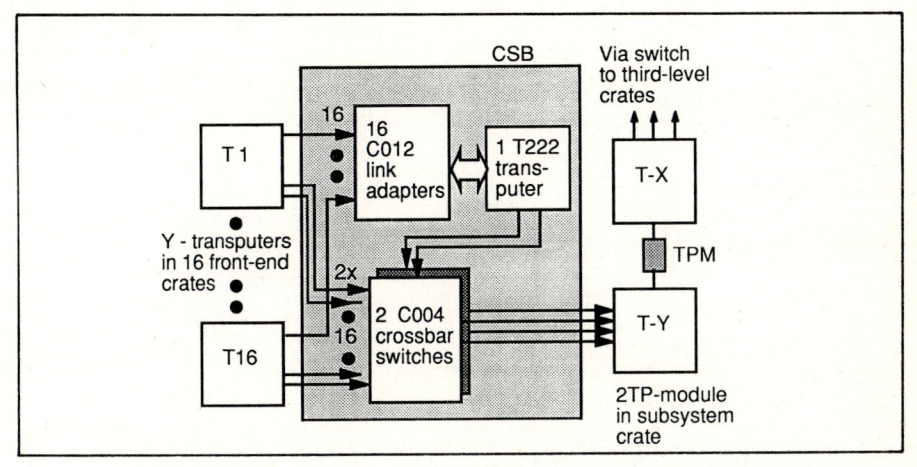

Figure 2: Layout of the read-out network of the calorimeter with a Control and Switch Box (CSB) multiplexing the data of the read-out crates (T1 to T16) to a transputer in the Sub-System Crate (T-SSC).

crate directly. The data is transported from a 2TP-module in the SSC over a switch to the 2TP-modules in the 6 third-level crates (fig 3). Like for the calorimeter read-out a request for connection is sent to a controlling T222. This transputer makes a connection to an 2TP-module in a third-level trigger crate. Over 4 links in parallel an event is assembled in the 2TP-module. For each subdetector 3 links are used for transport, at most 12 events are built simultaneously in the third-level crates.

In total 16 subdetectors are connected to the Event Builder, over 48 links data are flowing into the third-level crates. The transfer speed over the links and link switch is about 0.9 MByte/s per link. So the maximum throughput of the system is about 40 MByte/s.

4.3 Second-Level Local Processing

Five of the ten second-level triggering systems in ZEUS will use transputers. In this section one subdetector trigger, *i.e* the calorimeter system, will be discussed in more detail.

The X transputer of fig 1 processes part of the front-end data after a first-level trigger, searching for clusters of energy, signaling the presence of leptons or hadron jets. The results of the local processing of the 36 trigger transputers are combined to get an overview over the calorimeter. A tree structure (fig 4) is chosen, since it minimizes the latency in the network compared to mesh structures. Data of 7 trigger transputers are assembled in a 2TP-module. One transputer receives data over 4 links, the other over 3. After combining the results the data are transferred to the next layer where finally one transputer sends the results to the global second-level trigger. The total latency is about 2.7 ms.

4.4 Global Second-Level Triggering

In the global trigger (fig 5) the results of the local processors are combined. A final decision is taken, determining whether an event has to be assembled or has to be skipped from the buffers in the read-out crates. About 10 subdetectors are participating in the local second-level processing. In the global trigger different algorithms run in parallel on 8 trigger transputers in 4 2TP-modules. From every subdetector the data is broadcasted to those processors. The results of the processing are sent from the trigger transputers over the VME bus to a master processor, that takes the final decision. The decision is broadcasted to the subdetectors via the Event Builder.

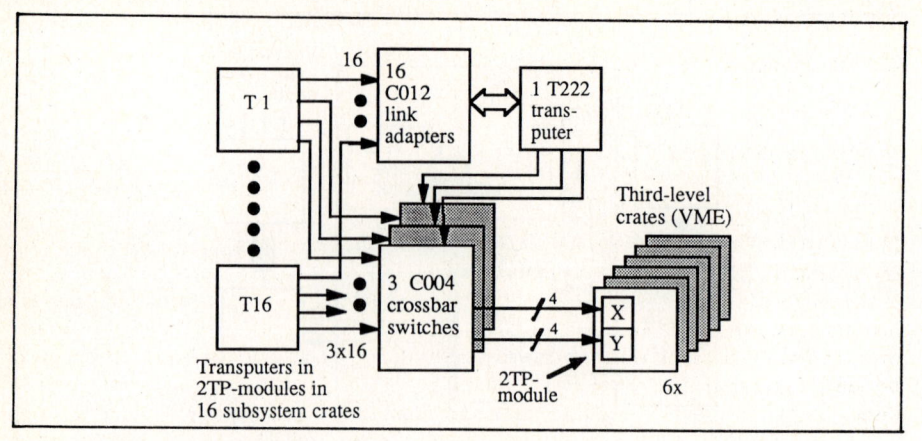

Figure 3: Layout of the Event Builder. Data from 16 subdetectors are sent via 3 C004 Link Switches to 6 2TP-modules in the Third-Level Crates.

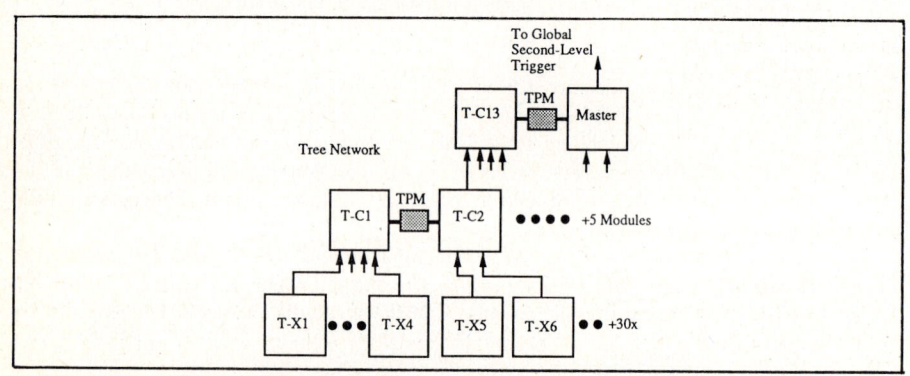

Figure 4: Structure of the network of trigger transputers (T-X1 to T-X36) and the combining transputers (T-C1 to T-C13 plus the Master) in 7 2TP-modules.

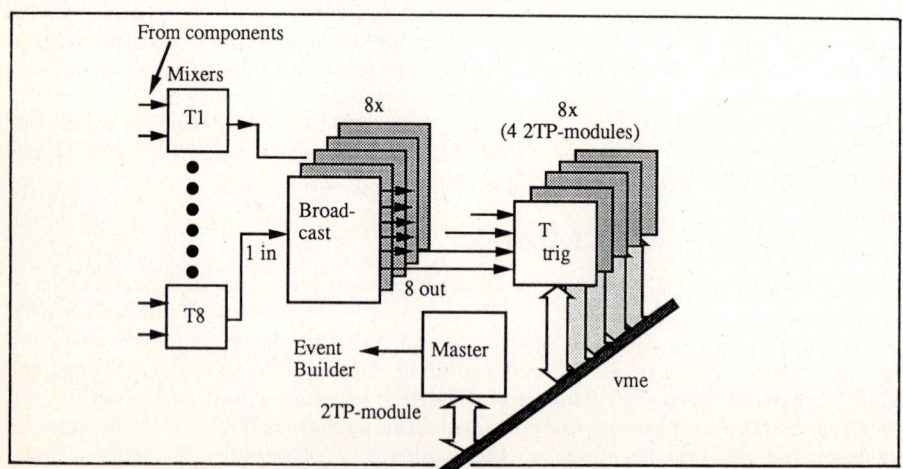

Figure 5: Structure of the Global Second-Level Trigger, combining the results of the local second-level processors and providing a yes/no decision for all subdetectors.

4.5 Monitoring

The transputers in the various systems should monitor:

1. the correct functioning of the front-end channels
2. the results of the analysis
3. the behaviour of the network

In the calorimeter transputer system a low-priority monitoring process will be scheduled when the processing tasks are not busy. Histograms of the outputs of the front-end channels and of the results of the analysis will be stored locally. Regularly they will be sent to a dedicated monitor transputer. The behaviour of the network will be analysed by measuring the traffic over the links and the idleness of the transputers. The number of words of a message will be added to a variable and read by the monitoring process, the idleness will be measured by measuring the frequency of the scheduling of a dummy process (analogue to [9]).

4.6 Interface to host systems

A general solution has been adopted in ZEUS. The MicroVaxes controlling the subdetectors, are equipped with an Q-Bus to Transputer link interface of CAPLIN Cybernetics Corporation. Via such an interface four users can simultaneously connect to four transputers. Programs are developed at the MicroVax and stored on disk. Monitor data are sent from the Transputer systems to the MicroVaxes, displayed there and messages sent to the main data-acquisition Vax for control and monitoring. Every transputer systems will be reset and booted separately.

5 Concluding remarks

Parallel triggering and read-out in High-Energy Physics experiments can be handled naturally with transputers. The ZEUS collaboration, where the use of transputers is now widely accepted, is at present the largest scale application (more than 500 transputers used) in this field.

References

[1] R. Belusevic and G. Nixon, Nucl. Instr. and Meth. A277(1989)513.

[2] S. Quinton et al., "Data Acquisition for the ZEUS Central Tracking Detector", Proceedings of the 1989 IEEE Nuclear Science Symposium, to be published.

[3] H. Boterenbrood et al., Proc. Int. Conf. on the Impact of Digital Microelectronics and Microprocessors on Particle Physics, ed. M. Budinich et al. (World Scientific Publishing Co., Singapore, 1988) p. 217.

[4] H. Boterenbrood et al., Proc. of VMEbus in Research, ed. C. Eck and C. Parkman (North-Holland, Amsterdam, 1988) p. 109.

[5] L.W. Wiggers and J.C. Vermeulen., Comp. Phys. Comm. 57 (1989) 316.

[6] H. Boterenbrood et al., Proc. 10th occam User Group Technical Meeting, ed. A. Bakkers (IOS, Amsterdam, 1989) p. 289.

[7] D. Crosetto, "Fast Digital Parallel Processing module FDPP", Workshop on On-line Applications of Transputers in Nuclear and High-Energy Physics, CERN 1990.

[8] A. Bogaerts, "The Jetset event builder", Workshop on On-line Applications of Transputers in Nuclear and High-Energy Physics, CERN 1990.

[9] G. Barret, OCCAM Newsletter No. 12 (1990) p. 57.

OBJECT ORIENTED SIMULATIONS IN MECHATRONICS

A.Eppinger
Robert Bosch GmbH, Abteilung ZWI
Postfach 106050
D-7000 Stuttgart 10

ABSTRACT: The artificial word "Mechatronics" represents the symbiosis of 'classical' mechanical systems and 'modern' electronics that has opened up a wide range of new possibilities. A typical application is an Anti-Lock-Bracking-Systems (ABS), a very complex combination of sensors, microprocessor based controllers, electromagnetic actuators and mechanical as well as hydraulic components.

Increasing complexity and their mostly nonlinear behaviour are the major challenges in designing, implementing and testing of these systems. A very promising design methodology is based on the idea of integrating real hardware via interfaces into a system simulation ('Hardware-in-the-Loop'). Development may start with a completely simulated model. With hardware being designed and becoming available, it is step by step incorporated into the system. This methodology significantly reduces development time since there is an early feedback on the design approaches and the final solution is proved under real operating conditions.

Obviously the realtime simulation of fast mechatronical systems requires tremendous computing power. Supposed one finds a way to express the simulation problem in a parallel form, a Multi-Transputer-System could provide the necessary computing power for a relatively small price.

One solution is a modelling approach that decomposes the systems hierarchically into components with a strong relationship to the physical world. Each component is described by a set of equations operating on the component's own local state. The communication of physical interface data is modelled by sending messages via connections between the components.

This approach may be attributed as 'object oriented' since computer science defines objects as independent elements maintaining their own internal state and communicating via message-passing mechanisms.

Taking a close look at a Transputer, it reveales a very 'object' like architecture: Local memory to maintain its own local state and links designed to pass messages between transputers.

Therefore Transputers are the ideal vehicle to realize fast realtime simulation by following the principle of object orientation starting at system modelling all the way down to simulation.

2 Introduction

No other technological step had nearly as much impact on modern system design as the microelectronic revolution. It makes new solutions feasible many of them to be found in the car industry: Electronic motor control, Anti-Lock Bracking Systems (ABS), active suspension /10,11/ etc. They may be characterized as follows:

* Complex, mixed electrical, mechanical, hydraulic, pneumatic and thermal systems with both continuous and discrete elements
* Rapidly changing environment conditions and high noise levels
* Strong nonlinear behavior
* Time constants covering a wide range:
  - Mechanical time constants: 1 ms .. 1 s
  - Position control: 100 us .. 10 ms
  - Underlying current control: 10 us .. 1 ms

Designing, producing and testing these complex, nonlinear mechatronical systems requires a new generation of tools. Fortunately microelectronics also provides the appropriate technology in the form of powerful computers. Up to now CASD

(Computer Aided System Design) is in most cases done in an offline fashion with simulation, analysis and graphical output performed on a mainframe. With computing power becoming available for a very small price, it is possible to provide this power to the engineer in the lab or test site. Some examples should give a basic understanding of the value of an interactive 'computer integrated' system development:

Modelling and Identification

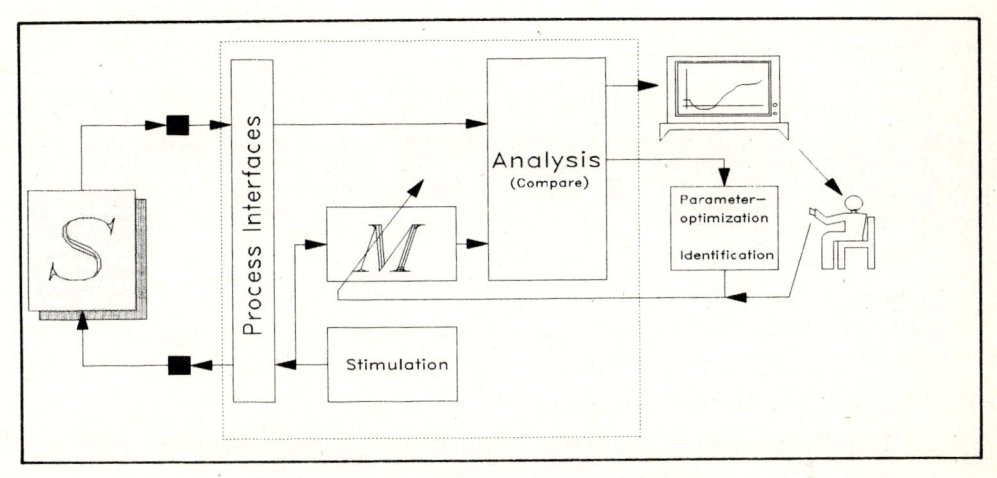

Fig. 1: Modelling and Identification

Fig. 1 shows the elements needed to find a model of a given mechatronical system S. Stimulating S we measure its response and compare it to the response of the simulated model M. The results of this analysis are displayed and may be used to manually change the model's structure and/or tune parameters. The engineer may be supported by identification algorithms or by a parameter optimization strategie.

Controller design

Controller design for a nonlinear system is a interactive task which heavily depends on simulation with some special demands:
* Flexibility in changing structures during the design phase
* Realistic simulation with integer arithmetic of selectable resolution
* Availability of typical control engineering elements like characteristic tables and switching nonlinear elements

Quality Control in Production

The same technique already known from modelling may be useful for quality control procedures. The system S is now supplied by the production line. The model M serves as a reference system. The result of the analysis methods in this case may be a simple 'ok' or 'error' indication.

Summarizing the examples given above results in a list of demands:
* process interfaces
* realtime simulation
* integrated analysis methods
* online changes of model structure, parameters and characteristic tables
* immediate display of results
* online parameter optimization

To make these demands become reality we should begin with the system representation (chapter 3), consider an appropriate simulation technique (chapter 4) and finally discuss ASCET, a tool currently being developed at Robert Bosch GmbH central research laboratories (chapter 5).

3 Object Oriented System Representation

3.1 Managing Complexity

There are two basic techniques to manage the complexity of typical mechatronical systems, **hierarchical decomposition** and **modularity**.

Large systems are built physically from subsystems which may in turn contain subsystems or basic components. Expressed in more general words, we may decompose a system hierarchically into entities (physical components) and their relations (physical interfaces). Obviously there are several advantages in preserving this 'natural' decomposition through the design and implementation phases.

* The data base will contain entries with a one to one relation to physical components.
* Structural changes in a complex model only have local effects
* HW-in-the-Loop is made possible by inserting process interfaces

3.2 Block Diagrams and Objects

Control engineers prefer to represent their systems as block diagrams /9/ with blocks representing anything from physical components to controller algorithms. Due to their high level of abstraction they are useful when dealing with mixed systems. The other basic elements in block diagrams are the connections between blocks. They show the energy flow, data flow etc.

Comparing the block diagram representation of technical systems with the object oriented programming techniques one finds a very interesting relationship:

Computer science defines objects as independent units with private variables representing their internal structure and state and a set of methods defining their behavior /12/. The only way objects interact is via communication ('message passing') using the interface provided by the object's methods [15].

Assigning a block to each physical component and a connection to each physical interface follows the idea of object orientation considering that each block has its own internal structure (equations) and state (state variables) and that blocks communicate through exactly defined interfaces (block in- and outputs) and channels (connections).

Physical components work in parallel. Therefore its obvious that an adequate simulation technique may be based on modern parallel computing techniques.

4 Objektoriented Simulation

OCCAM /7/ is a programming language which provides basic mechanisms for parallel processing and synchronization. It is based on a process and channel model. 'Processes' and 'Channels' may be used to implement an object oriented approach by assigning objects to processes and communicating data via channels.

One of the most advanced concepts in parallel computing is the INMOS transputer family /6/. OCCAM is especially suited for programming Transputers since the Transputer directly implements a process- and channel concept /5/. A closer look into its internal structure reveals the Transputer as a hardware element that realizes the idea of an object (Fig. 2): It has private memory holding the Transputer's internal state and 4 'Links' which serve as communication channels.

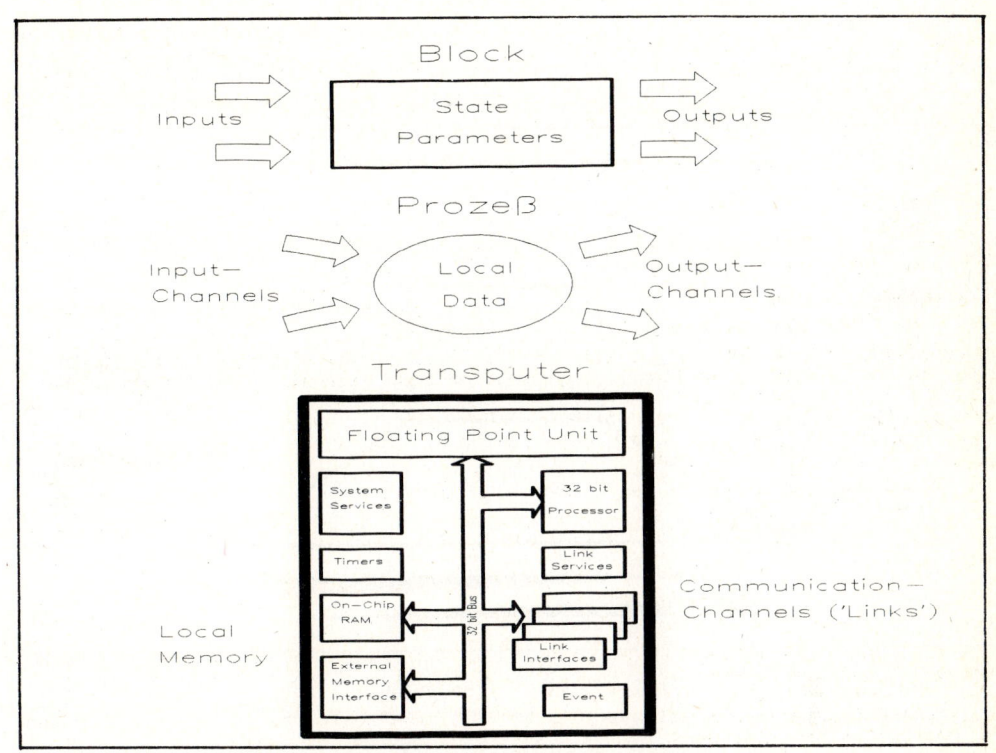

Fig. 2: Block -> Process -> Transputer

Fig. 3 gives a simulation example which involves 6 Transputers and demonstrates the direct correspondence between model structure and Transputer network structure.

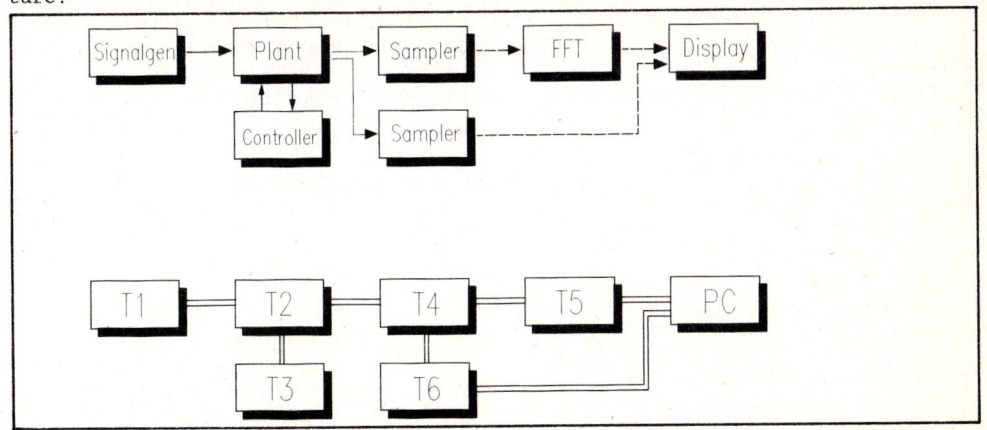

Fig. 3: Object-Oriented Simulation on a Multi-Transputer-Network

The major advantage of a Multi-Transputer-System is the lack of central resources (shared memory or a bus) which easily become the bottleneck in other parallel processing architectures. Another nice feature is the capability of adapting the link structure to the problem requirements via 'Linkswitches'.

5 ASCET System

5.1 System Overview

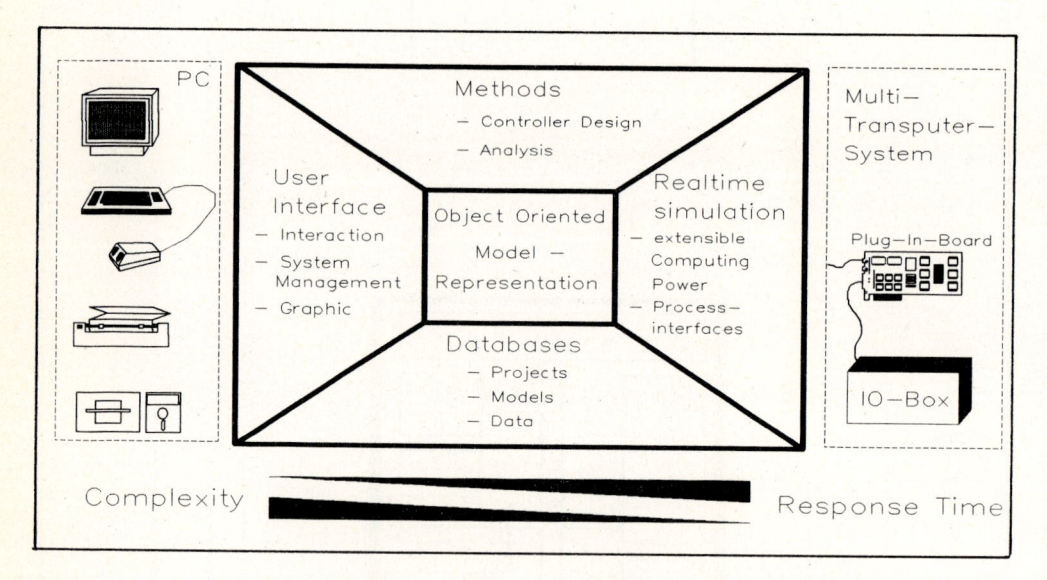

Fig. 4:   ASCET - Overview

ASCET is an integrated, interactive design tool based on the ideas outlined in the previous chapters (Fig. 4). The user of ASCET is able to change the model structure, parameters and characteristic table values 'online' without interrupting the simulation or violating realtime conditions.

The ASCET system structure emerged from two conflicting demands:

* Realtime simulation requiring simple data structures in order to be fast and a
* comfortable, interactive user interface requiring complex data structures.

In order to solve this conflict we split the ASCET system into two parts:

* Highly interactive methods, system management and data bases are implemented on a workstation. The software is written in SMALLTALK, an object-oriented language /1,2,3,4/.
* Computing power and communication bandwidth as well as process interfaces are provided by a Multi-Transputer-System.

5.2 Hardware

The workstation is currently a PC with a 80386-CPU, 4 MB of RAM, 80 MB harddisk and VGA-graphic. A plug-in board holds up to eight Transputer modules each consisting of a T-800 /7/ and 1MB of RAM. One dedicated Transputer communicates with the PC software via an 8-bit parallel port /8/.

External 'IO-Boxes' may be connected to the PC-internal Transputers via normal link connections. Each IO-Box provides 8 slots holding either a card with Transputer modules (B008 or B012) or an interface-card. The interface-cards are developed at Bosch and contain one T-800, RAM and peripherie circuits like D/A coverters, A/D converters, Timers, digital IO etc.

5.3 Hierarchical Blockdiagrams in ASCET

Blocks are the basic elements a control engineer builts his model structures from. Blocks communicate with each other via connections between in- and outputs of the blocks. To manage large systems requires hierarchical decomposition. This concept is implemented in ASCET by two types of blocks, 'Baseblocks' and 'Structureblocks'.

Structureblocks serve as structuring elements. They contain other blocks and the connections between them (Fig. 5).

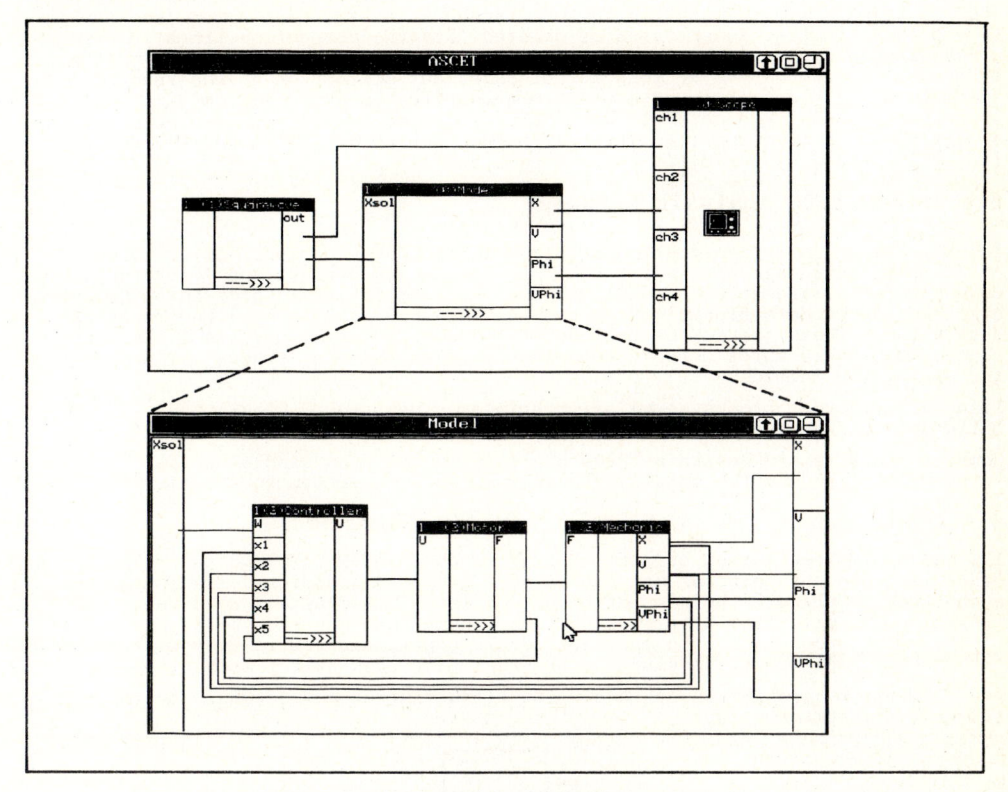

Fig. 5: Hierarchical Blockdiagram

At the lowest hierarchy level ASCET uses nonlinear differential and algebraic equations contained in ***Baseblocks***. The multi-window editor shown in Fig. 6 lets the user define inputs, outputs, parameters and characteristic tables of a Baseblock as well as its differential equations.

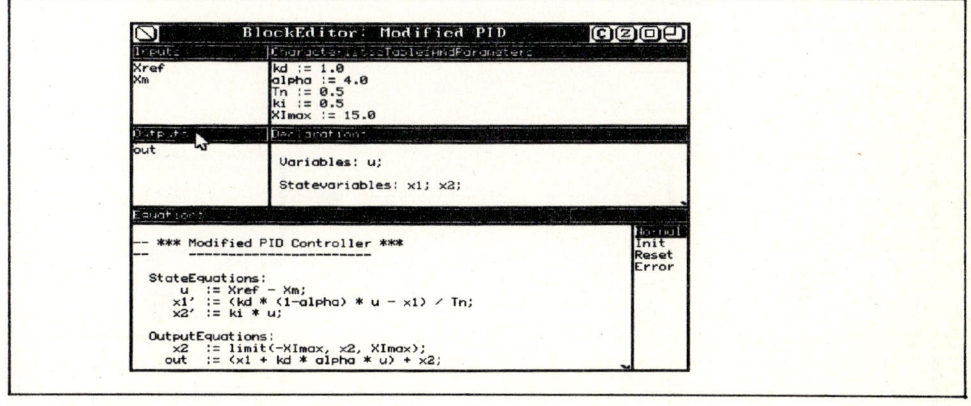

Fig. 6: Baseblock-Editor

The textual information is then compiled to code executable on a Transputer /5/. The compiled block may be stored at or retrieved from a data base. As soon as a block is added to the model on the graphical user interface level the block's code is immediately transferred to the Transputer system. Each block may separately been activated, deactivated or deleted. Drawing connection lines in the block diagram causes communication processes to be created dynamically on the Transputer system. These actions do not cause any disruption of the running simulation and there is never a need to recompile the whole system since an operating system takes care of the modular addition or removal of blocks and the synchronisation of operation. This gives the user an analog computer like fealing appreciated by engineers for a long time.

5.4 Integrating Analysis Methods

The block diagram representation provides a high level of abstraction which ASCET takes advantage of. By introducing 'Packetdata-Blocks' and 'Packetdata-Connections' we are able to integrate analysis and design methods into the block diagram. 'Packetdata-Blocks' operate on packages of data rather than on single data values. These operations include FFT, detection of properties (like overshoot), mean sqare error between two data packages and many others, even parameter optimizing methods.

Transient recorder blocks serve as interfaces: They record simulation data, build data packages and communicate them via 'Packetdata-Connections'.

Complex analysis and design methods are constructed from simple operations hierarchically like complex models are constructed from simple subsystems.

5.5 Execution on the Multi-Transputer-System

The actual implementation of a block diagram onto the Multi-Transputer-System takes into account that one may not be able to spend a dedicted Transputer for each block. Therefore the simulation of complex block diagrams requires a small operating system that multiplexes several blocks onto one Transputer and multiplexes many connections onto one link. Still the Transputer is very well suited for such an implementation since it provides fast task switch mechanisms (1us).

Fig. 7 gives an example on how a complex block diagram may actually be implemented on a Transputer network.

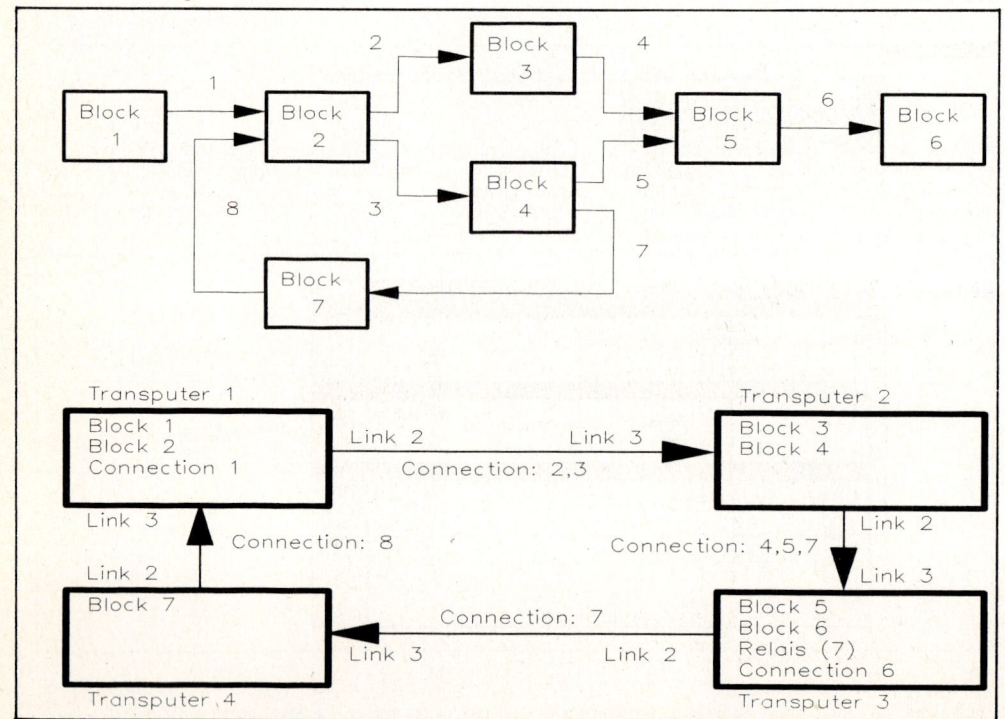

Fig. 7:   Transputer Operating System

5.6 Elements of Interactive Simulation

ASCET implements several elements supporting interactive simulation. The following list gives some examples:

Data Monitor

A data monitor displays the current value on a connection line and may be plugged to any block output.

Scope

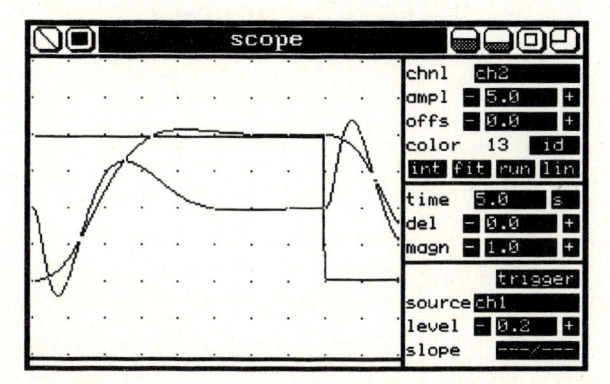

The scope implements the functionality of a digital storage oszilloscope. It provides a graphical user interface that displays data on multiple channels simultaniously.

Potentiometer

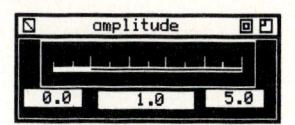

Potentiometers are useful to change parameter values during simulation. The user may also set minimum and maximum values for a parameter.

Characteristic Table Editor

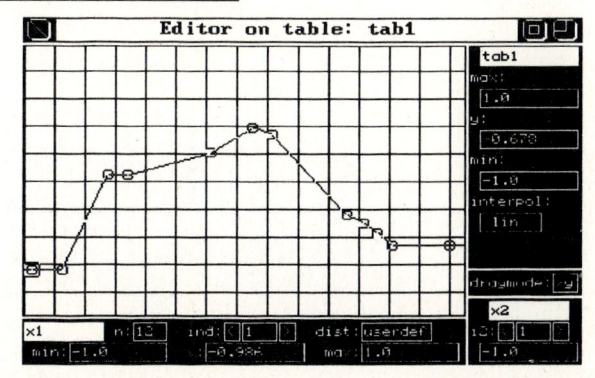

The characteristic table editor allows the user to define characteristic tables with one or two independent variables. He may choose between several interpolation methods. This editor also works in an online mode so that the user may change a table during simulation.

6 References

/1/ Adele Goldberg, David Robson:
SMALLTALK-80 - The Language and its Implementation
Addison-Wesley Publishing Company, 1983
ISBN 0-201-11371-6

/2/ Adele Goldberg:
SMALLTALK-80 - The Interactive Programming Environment
Addison-Wesley Publishing Company, 1984
ISBN 0-201-11372-4

/3/ Glenn Krasner:
SMALLTALK-80 - Bits of Historie, Words of Advice
Addison-Wesley Publishing Company, 1984
ISBN 0-201-11669-3

/4/ SMALLTALK V/286
Digitalk Inc., May 1988

/5/ The transputer instruction set - a compiler writers' guide
INMOS Limited, 1986
72 TRN 119 03

/6/ IMS T800 transputer. Engineering Data
INMOS Limited, April 1987
42 1082 01

/7/ Dick Pountain: A tutorial introduction to OCCAM programming
INMOS BSP professional books, Oxford 1988

/8/ IMS C011 link adaptor. Engineering Data.
INMOS Limited, 1987.
42 1412 00

/9/ Otto Föllinger: Regelungstechnik
AEG-Telefunken Aktiengesellschaft, 1980
ISBN 3-87087-116-4

/10/ H. Braess, B. Thomson:
The motor vehicle - a good example of the wide range of modern control engineering
IFAC 10th World Congress, 1987

/11/ J.Lückel, R.Kasper, K.-P.Jäker:
A practical control concept for the active suspension of road vehicles
IFAC 10th World Congress, 1987

/12/ Object-Oriented Programming
Byte, August 1986, pp. 137-233

Transputer Architectures for Sensing in a Layered Controller: Formal Methods for Design *

P.J. Probert, D. Djian, Huosheng Hu
Department of Engineering Science, Oxford University

1 Introduction

We describe a sensing architecture which we are developing for our autonomous vehicle programme [4]. Each sensor uses a transputer as its local processor and is designed either as a standalone sensor or as one in a network of similar or complementary devices. Such sensors exploit several features of the transputer: its bandwidth for data acquisition, its facilities for handling input/output and the ease with which networks of transputers can be built up. The latter is of particular importance in the context of sensor integration and an expanding system.

An advantage of transputer architectures is that the language Occam is amenable to formal specification techniques. Predictable performance is especially important in real time systems in which any unexpected events, however occasional or unlikely, may cause disaster. We have used formal methods of specification in the design, especially the *Communicating Sequential Protocols* language [3], which has a close relationship to transputers and Occam.

To improve reliability further our architecture allows us to combine the information from several sensors. Graceful degradation, rather than catastrophic failure, should result from a sensor's malfunction.

1.1 Integration of sensory information

In the context of large real-time systems, key requirements for sensing are for reliability and high bandwidth. In mobile robotics typical needs are to assess range and geometric properties of the environment so that the robot can path plan in a changing environment. Since information from a single sensor is noisy and incomplete combining the data available from several is an important requirement.

Traditionally sensor integration has been done through the maintenance of a central world representation using a blackboard architecture [5]. However the blackboard architecture has several problems particularly related to bandwidth and the control of system complexity. We have chosen a more structured architecture, in which integration is either through *action* or *communication*.

The overall architecture is shown in Figure 1 (autonomous vehicles are a demanding testbed for sensor architectures owing to the tight perception-action loop at several response levels). The vehicle is given a number of behavioural competences in the layered controller, following some of the ideas originally proposed by Brooks [1]. The

---
*This work is funded by SERC

principle of the architecture is that all layers operate concurrently with access to the actuators, but that the lower layers can subsume the operation of the higher ones as necessary; only one layer at any time actually controls the vehicle. Thus the vehicle may be controlled by the path planning layer which plans actions through sophisticated sensing, but if the obstacle avoidance layer sees an obstacle it takes control to guide the vehicle around that obstacle before allowing the higher layers to take control again.

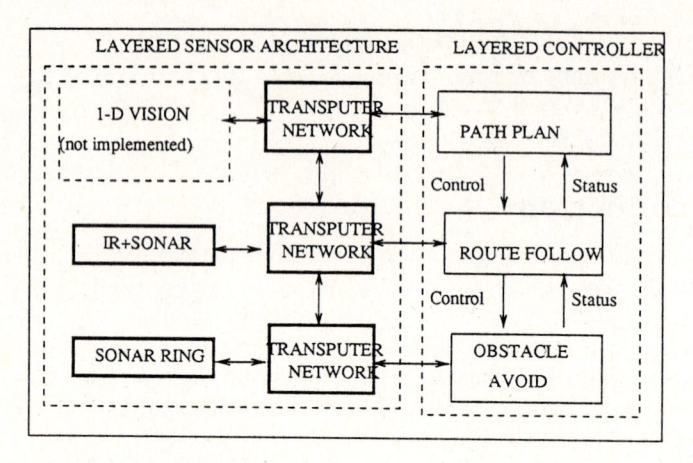

Figure 1: Layered Architecture for control and Sensing

Currently only the lowest level is operating under sensor control (a sonar ring), although outlines of higher levels are implemented.

1.2 Integration through action

This architecture is designed for minimal interaction between layers. Sensor outputs may be available to more than one layer, but the sensory information in each layer is treated independently. The only interaction is through the subsumption mechanism at the vehicle actuators, leading to integration of sensory information through the *action* of the vehicle. Minimising the communication in this way simplifies overall design. Graceful degradation is inherent in the architecture since if one level fails lower layers will take over; however even so malfunction of the lowest level can lead to catastrophic failure.

Each layer of sensing is controlled by a transputer network which communicates to a transputer in the layered controller. Messages are sent between layers using transputer links. The advantage of using transputers is the easy expandability of the system.

1.3 Integration through communication

Within each layer there may be interaction between several sensors which communicate to establish a unified environmental model: integration through *communication*. This introduces the usual concept of sensor integration, in which incomplete or partial information is combined. Without careful design such integration may be a cause of bottlenecks or inconsistency.

The sensors in each layer are to be implemented as nodes of a communicating, distributed network. Distribution gives us the following advantages:

- A high bandwidth in gathering and processing information
- Easy expansion of the system when new sensors become available
- Robustness if an individual sensor should fail

The remainder of this paper discusses the design of a sensor to fulfil these requirements.

2 Communicating Sensors

An immediate target of this work is a sensor which integrates sonar and infra-red transducers to assess range, for use in the second level of our architecture. An embedded transputer provides local control and intelligence [2]. Sonar and infra-red complement each other in their use, sonar providing good range information and infra-red good angular resolution.

The sonar and the infra-red part of the sensor are implemented as separate intercommunicating nodes. In system terms, the sensors differ most importantly in timing. Readings from the sonar sensor are limited by the speed of sound and are expected to take several tens of milliseconds whereas the infra-red sensor should respond in hundreds of nanoseconds (limited by the electronics).

2.1 Overall Specification

Sensors vary in their physical characteristics (such as in the transducers employed, in the time to gather and process data and in their error models). To be a member of an integrated, adaptable network each sensor must present a common interface.

Each sensor in the network is expected to do the following:

- Communicate with others asynchronously
- Send messages to an external party (in this case control information to the autonomous vehicle) based on its own and other sensors' observations
- Include a facility to assess its own condition (for example to disassociate itself from the network if it believes itself to be faulty) - developed in outline but not included at this stage
- Include the possibility of being implemented on several processors - for example to allow special purpose processors or hardware

2.2 Specification of processes and communication

In this section we describe a sensor architecture in terms of concurrent processes and their intercommunication. At this stage there is no attempt to include algorithmic detail, although the sensor has been designed with algorithms such as the distributed Kalman filter [6] in mind.

Consider the simple sensor model shown in Figure 2: The sensor is shown as three separate logical entities.

The *HARDWARE-CONTROL* represents the hardware interface to the transducer and any low level data processing.

The *DATA-PROCESSING* takes in slightly processed data *data.stream* from the hardware control and, in conjunction with global data, processes it through a suitable algorithm. It also co-ordinates with the hardware through a control signal: *get.data*. (In implementation, we have allowed the algorithmic processing to take place at the same time as a process controlling the data acquisition through *get.data* by using concurrent synchronising processes). Processed data *l.assertion* is sent on in local co-ordinates. Since the data processing module works in local co-ordinates it does not need any global knowledge.

The *SENSOR-INTEGRATION* process communicates with the outside world. It converts local data to global data for send to the other sensor *g.assertion*. In addition it contains a local internal model, based on the consensus of its own data and that from the other sensor. Whenever an assertion is sent from either sensor, *SENSOR-INTEGRATION* updates its own global model from the assertion just received. It works in global co-ordinates, accessible through its path to the outside world. As often as new data is available, it sends global updating signals to the mobile robot.

The two sensors under immediate consideration, the sonar and infra-red, may be controlled by a single transputer or have a transputer built into each. Figure 2 shows the links configuration for a sensor with a dedicated transputer. Three links are in use. One goes to the transducer through the hardware control, one to the other sensor and one to the outside world, the mobile robot. The fourth link is left free so that more sensors can be added. However it may be desirable to introduce more transputers: for example for a vision sensor a small network of transputers may even be needed for the data processing. The structure has been developed to support a flexible implementation.

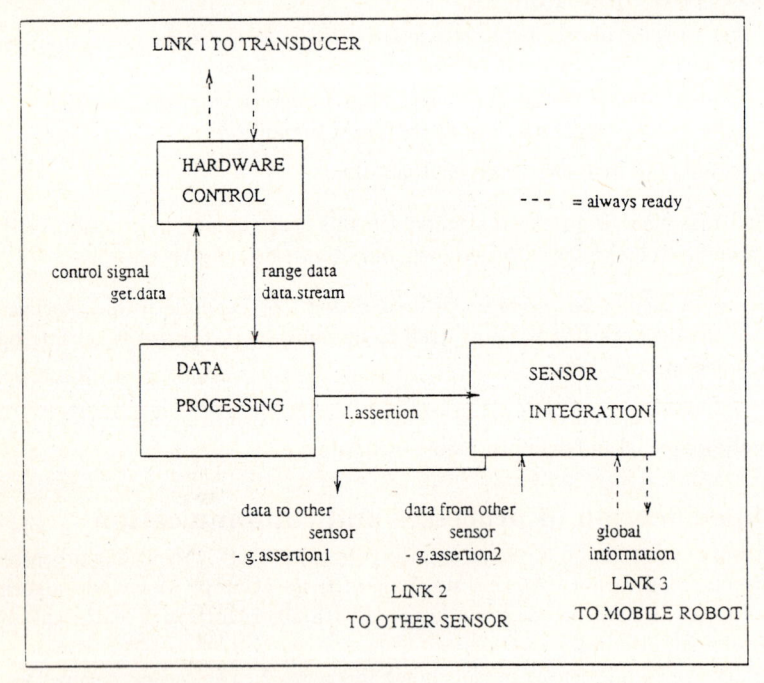

Figure 2: Process components of individual sensor

2.2.1 CSP specification

Difficulties in designing asynchronous concurrent systems are manifold. Intercommunicating by messages rather than shared memory imposes an explicit burden on the early specification to avoid difficulties such as deadlock and livelock (the same problems arise in a shared memory system but tend to be more transparent, encouraging less rigorous specification with consequent later problems). We have found the use of the *Communicating Sequential Processes* language very helpful in design.

The simplest concepts in *CSP* are the *event, process* and *alphabet*. A *Process*, which is defined as in Occam consists of a number of events, constituting its *alphabet*. Processes with common events in their alphabets must synchronise on those events when run together.

Various operators are possible to combine processes. The ones relevant here are the *choice* operator | and the *parallel* operator ||. The *choice* operator allows one of several processes to run depending on which initial event arises first (ie it selects the process whose guard is satisfied first). It is coded in Occam by **ALT**. The *parallel* operator is for processes running concurrently with some synchronising events - ie some common events in their *alphabets* - **PAR** in Occam. The parallel operator is the one which may lead to deadlock.

The sensor may be described 'in the large' by putting in parallel the three processes: $DATA-PROCESSING \parallel HARDWARE-CONTROL \parallel SENSOR-INTEGRATION$. The || operator shows that the processes run concurrently with common synchronisation events. Each of the main processes may then be broken down into their constituent processes and described in terms of the events they handle.

In subsequent sections, we use the numbers 1 and 2 to distinguish between the two sensors.

2.2.2 Sensor Integration

Omitting the global signals, the sensor-integration process is described formally as follows (for sensor 1):

$$SENSOR - INTEGRATION1 =$$
$$l.assertion1? \to g.assertion1! \to SENSOR - INTEGRATION1$$
$$\mid g.assertion2? \to SENSOR - INTEGRATION1$$

This reads as follows: *SENSOR-INTEGRATION1* either takes in a signal *l.assertion1* and sends *g.assertion1* and then recurses (updating from local data), or it reads in *g.assertion2* and then recurses (updating from data from the other sensor).

The ? and ! signs have the same meaning of input and output as they do in Occam. Note that our specification in *CSP* is not concerned with algorithms but only with intercommunicating events and processes. The algorithm inside *SENSOR-INTEGRATION*, whereby it updates its global representation, may be omitted (although could be included in a timed implementation by a time delay).

2.3 Analysis of deadlock

Following the specification of individual processes in *CSP* we can use formal rules to examine their interaction. In particular we can prove the absence of deadlock.

2.3.1 In a single sensor

First each sensor was analaysed for deadlock. Only signals which are common to more than one process need be included in the analysis. This simplifies matters considerably.

In addition the analysis is simplified by including some signals as *always ready* so there is no need for synchronisation on these signals. The *always ready* condition can be achieved through the use of buffers. The need for buffers here is because of the inclusion of asynchronous events in an essentially synchronous protocol.

Events which are *always ready* may be omitted in examining deadlock and livelock.

In examining deadlock, the transducer response must be included. We have assumed that it always returns a signal, either through a genuine reading or through a timeout. Hence its signals may be considered *always ready*.

The single sensor was shown to be deadlock free.

2.3.2 Two sensors in parallel

Examination of the expression for *SENSOR-INTEGRATION1* above shows that it operates off alternative events $g.assertion1$ and $g.assertion2$. The other sensor, *SENSOR-INTEGRATION2*, has an identical specification, interchanging the two assertion events. The overall sensor definitions include similar expressions. The two sensors may be put in parallel using the $\|$ operator.

Deadlock may occur from this. This may be seen from inspection or from using the *CSP* proof rules. Deadlock occurs if both sensors simultaneously enter the symmetrical upper guards (ie receiving signals $l.assertion1$ and $l.assertion2$). Each will wait for synchronisation from the other on the outputs $g.assertion$ before recursing.

This problem results from allowing the sensors to operate asynchronously; for synchronous operation it could be avoided by providing a suitable synchronisation signal. We have removed the deadlock by including an additional process to schedule the two sensors using a synchronising signal. This allows genuine event driven operation of each sensor and avoids the need for a buffer.

2.4 From CSP to Implementation

The use of *CSP* was of great benefit in enforcing a specification discipline. It offered a simple brief method whereby we could expose and interpret the important aspects of a process and was invaluable in helping us to formulate synchronisation events. In addition the proof rules allowed us to check the absence of deadlock in a simple mechanistic way. The use of such a language clearly affected our design and a different approach may well have resulted in alternative definitions.

The *CSP* specification makes no assumptions on the mapping of process to processor. This allows us to write general and versatile specifications. In implementation we may want to use different mapping for different sensors, depending on their complexity: in particular sensors with computationally intensive data processing may use a transputer (or even a network) dedicated to the processing algorithm.

In a real implementation some processes will probably run on a single transputer - in pseudo-concurrence controlled by the microcoded scheduler in the transputer. The deadlock freedom proved in the *CSP* holds for all scheduling algorithms. However *CSP* has no notion of fairness; that is a function of the scheduler.

The main difficulties we found in the translation from *CSP* to Occam arose from the Occam implementation of the *choice* structure. In Occam the | operator is implemented as a deterministic choice, normally as a `PRI ALT`. This may lead to problems as the first guard will always be entered, to the exclusion of all others, if it is always ready. A solution to this is to ensure that the guards are not always in the same order by using more than one `PRI ALT` structure. The inability to implement a genuine *choice* can lead to other problems too, especially where there is asynchronism.

3 Conclusion

We have demonstrated an architecture for sensor integration, using *action* between layers in a subsumption-type architecture and *intercommunication* within a layer. An architecture for a robust, intelligent sensor been developed and proved to be deadlock free using *CSP* rules for two such asynchronous intercommunicating sensors. The immediate further area of work lies in extending the analysis to a greater number of sensors and to a multiple transputer implementation.

4 References

[1] R.A. Brooks. A layered intelligent system for a mobile robot. In *Third Intl. Symp. Robotics Research*, 1985.

[2] S.Grime H.F.Durrant-Whyte and H.Hu¡. A modular, decentralised architecture for multi-sensor data fusion. In *Transputer Applications Conference*, 1990.

[3] C. Hoare. *Communicating Sequential Processes*. Prentice Hall, 1985.

[4] Huosheng Hu M.D.Adams and P.J. Probert. Towards a real time architecture for obstacle avoidance and path planning in mobile robotics. In *To be presented at IEEE Conference on Robotics and Automation*, 1990.

[5] H.P. Nii. Blackboard systems: the blackboard model of problem solving and the evolution of blackboard architectures. *A.I.Magazine*, 1986.

[6] B.S.Y. Rao and H. Durrant-Whyte. A fully decentralized algorithm for multi-sensor kalman filtering. 1989.

PARTICLE FLOW INSTRUMENTATION

Dr. E.Mills & Dr. B.C.O'Neill
Dept. of Electrical & Electronic Eng.
Nottingham Polytechnic
Burton Street
Nottingham NG1 4BU, UK

Abstract. This paper describes the development of a real-time particle flow meter for pneumatic conveyance systems. The subject is approached by a brief overview of the pneumatic transportation process and method of particle detection, moving to the decisions taken on the choice of host processor system, the design of the final system and the results obtained to date.

The application of this work is not only confined to commercial pneumatically conveyed products such as epoxy powder paint for electrostatic paint spraying, but the measurement system itself is of interest to the CEGB for determining the efficiency of their electrostatic precipitators and exhaust gas driven turbine protection.

1. Introduction

This project is concerned with instrumentation to measure the flow rates and velocities of particles in ducts and pipes. The main applications for such an instrument is to monitor the particle concentration of effluent gases in industrial processes and to control the flow from spray guns in the electrostatic powder coating process.

At present there is no method of continuously measuring powder flow rates while spraying and therefore any instrument which did this would offer considerable benefits to the industry. Some car manufacturers consider powder coating to be technically superior to liquid coating but are reluctant to implement it at plant level because of the lack of good control of the coating process. For flue gases the method of measurement used in this project would offer a more detailed and reliable method of measuring particle density compared with optical techniques which offer only an average reading across the entire cross-section of the duct.

Measurement of mass-flow is achieved by a pulse charging technique [1]. A pulse of charge is injected into the powder/air stream via a corona needle located along the axis of the detector. Sensors downstream measure the amount of charge conveyed.

The powder density is related to the ratio of injected charge to conveyed charge, and the velocity is obtained by "time of flight" measurements between two sensors.

This technique has the advantage of injecting a measurable quantity of charge into the flow and then comparing this with the downstream sensors while other techniques such as optical [2], capacitance [3,4] and microwave are dependent on the transmission of a signal through the walls of a pipe. This transmission can therefore be affected by deposition of powder on the walls of the sensor. For the pulse charging technique to be successful the processing of the signals must cope with two major points. The first is that the sensor signals are non linear and can depend on the velocity of the powder flow. The second point is that the fluctuations in transducer signals are significant from one injection to the next. It is therefore necessary to carry out a large amount of signal processing to convert the sensors reading into a mass flow rate.

The aims of this project were:

(a) to produce an instrument to continuously measure the mass flow rates in pipes

(b) to study low density flow conditions which are more typical of the particles flows found in flue gas ducts

2. Experimental Apparatus

Figure 1 shows the block diagram of the main components of the experimental equipment. This consists of a commercial pneumatic transport unit where the powder is stored in a fluid air bed container and is sucked into the pipe by a venturi system. The powder sucked into the pipe passes through the experimental injection and

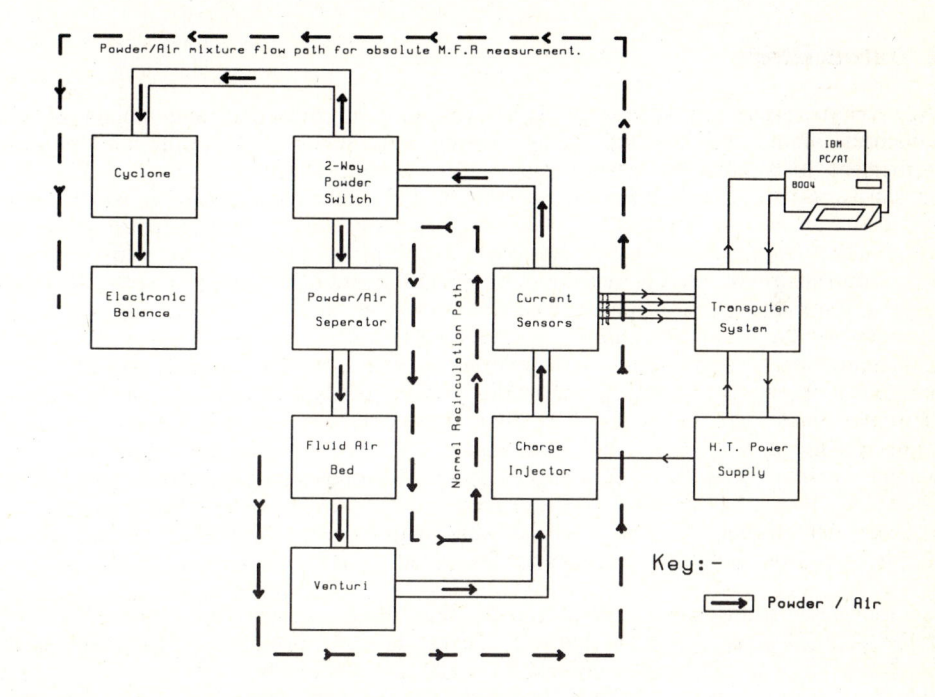

Figure 1 Experimental Apparatus.

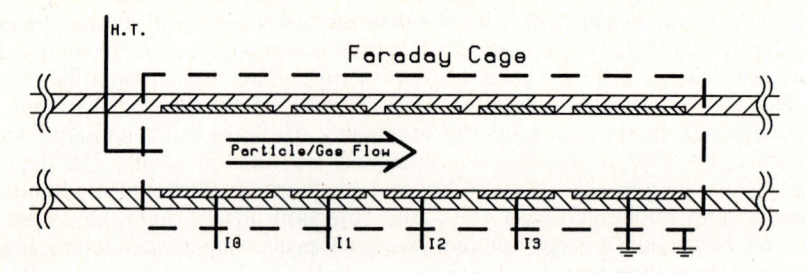

Figure 2 Sensor Unit.

sensor unit and is either returned to the hopper or directed to the a balance for accurate flow rate measurements.

The transducer system is shown in figure 2. This consists of a needle electrode and ground plain followed by three down stream electrodes which can detect the charge carried by the powder. The transported charge is detected by current sensors and these signals are processed to produce a mass flow measurement. There are two main parameters of interest for the analysis. One is the total charge reaching each sensor which can be obtained by integrating the current over a set time period and the other parameter is the peak current of each sensor. The velocity was obtained by measuring the time difference of the waveform of two sensors and this was used in the analysis of mass flow. Also the velocity measurement can be used to determine some degree of quality of the flow because pulsation of the flow, which is unacceptable for many applications, is directly related to low powder velocities.

3. System Design

The various processes of charge measurement, peak detection and timing of the waveforms could be realised using analogue circuits. This approach requires duplication of circuits for each channel. An alternative approach is to digitize the waveforms and then use a microprocessor to carry out the analysis. It was clear if this technique was to succeed then two or more processors would be required due to the complex nature of the signals involved. Two types of processor were investigated, the Motorola 68000 using dual-ported RAM for inter-processor communications and the INMOS T414 transputer. The 68000 system is not a 'standalone' processor and requires the addition of RAM and ROM to build a minimum system. The T414 in its minimum configuration offers program download to on board RAM a parallel processing operating kernel and automatic transfer of data to one of four fast inter-transputer links. The T414 will also allow expansion to external RAM or ROM and memory mapped I/O. The major disadvantage of the T414 was the initial price but assurances were obtained from INMOS that this would be substantially reduced in the future. Recently there has been a dramatic drop in the price of the transputer to such an extent that the new T400 32-bit processor is cheaper than most other 32-bit processors and is very economically priced.

The transputer solution was chosen and the final design showing the interconnections of the processors is shown in figure 3. There are six transputers in this octahedral structure, with a transputer controlled data acquisition unit at the top of the diagram. The data from this unit is distributed to one of four transputers, one for each sensor, for processing. The transputers in the array then pass the results of their calculations to the bottom transputer for further processing. This transputer is also used for the master control of the system. Only this control processor has an additional 1 Mbyte of RAM, the four array processors are completely stand alone, while the acquisition unit board has the hardware to support A to D operations.

The data acquisition board consists of a transputer with links as described above plus interfaces to a fast A to D converter, a gain control unit and multiplexer to select one of eight channels. The gain of each channel can be controlled for each sample and the number and order of the channels can be selected by software. The best mode of operation is a cycle of 4000 samples per channel with the gain of each channel unaltered throughout the cycle. The conversion system produces a 16 bit value with a resolution of only 8 bits. It was found that, in this mode of operation, a maximum conversion rate of 435 KHz/(number of channels) could be obtained from the transputer system.

The system was designed and then implemented on printed circuit boards. The circuit layouts were achieved using CAD packages which were new to the department. Some time was spent mastering these packages, nevertheless it was considered to be the only practical solution when using embedded microprocessors which require such a large number of interconnections.

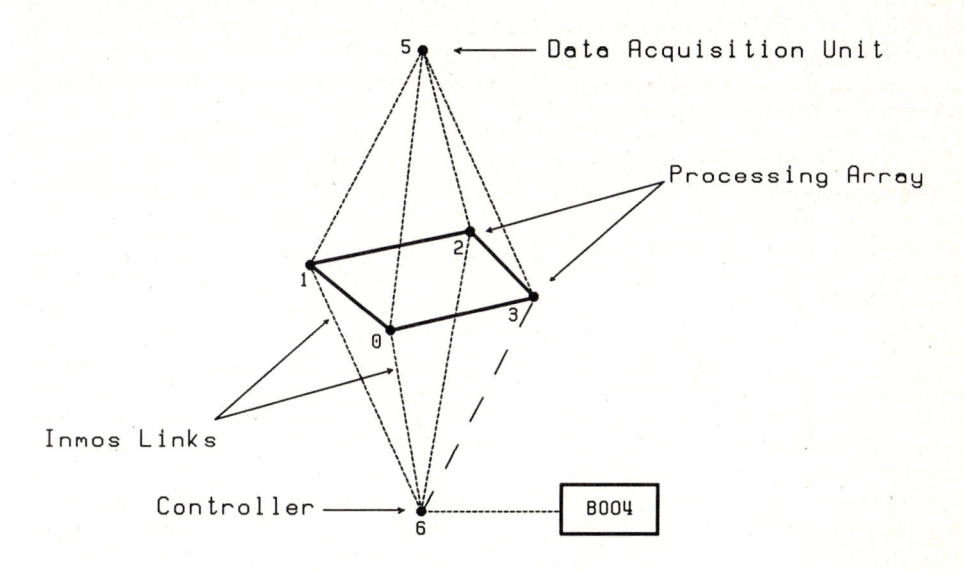

Figure 3 System Configuration.

The initial development of the transputer software was carried out using an INMOS TDS system on a VAX mainframe. This proved to be inadequate for downloading software to the target system and so was replaced by a IBM AT development system provided by a SERC/DTI loan and later a similar system was provided by the department. This TDS system with the folding editor provided a good environment for software development and the tools enabled successful debugging of the system.

Since one of the main design criteria of the system design was to operate the upper system processors, nodes 0 to 3 and node 5, without any external memory, to minimise the overall hardware complexity, it is important that the code generated by the compiler be as compact as possible. Our experience of the Occam 2 compiler is that the code generation produces very compact solutions which with optimised programming techniques allowed the speed of system operation to be increased.

4. Results

The system has two main modes of operation. The first is a waveform capture and store mode and the other is as its main design function as a real-time parallel signal processing unit. In the waveform capture mode it was possible to make detailed comparisons of transducer signals obtained over a wide variety of powder flow conditions and also to vary the processing algorithms without the need to repeat the experiment.

For each setting of the powder flow rate an absolute value of mass flow was obtained from the balance reading along with a variety of readings from the four transducers for 2000 attempted charge injections. Each injection is processed in real-time, firstly to detect if injection occurred and, if successful, to obtain the integral of the transducer currents, the negative and positive peak heights and time of each peak. These results were then passed to the control processor for further analysis. Data was collected from 198 flow settings in the range of 0.2 to 6.0 g/sec with a velocity range from 3.5 to 14.0 m/sec. Some readings were automatically rejected because of low velocities which caused unacceptable pulsation of the flow. The remaining readings were automatically sorted by analysis in several regions and a mass flow prediction was obtained. These results are shown in figures 4, 5 & 6 and show that it is possible to obtain the mass flow rate from the transducer readings to an accuracy of 15% of each scale. Once the method of analysis was verified it was then possible to obtain real-time mass flow readings by including the appropriate code in the control processor.

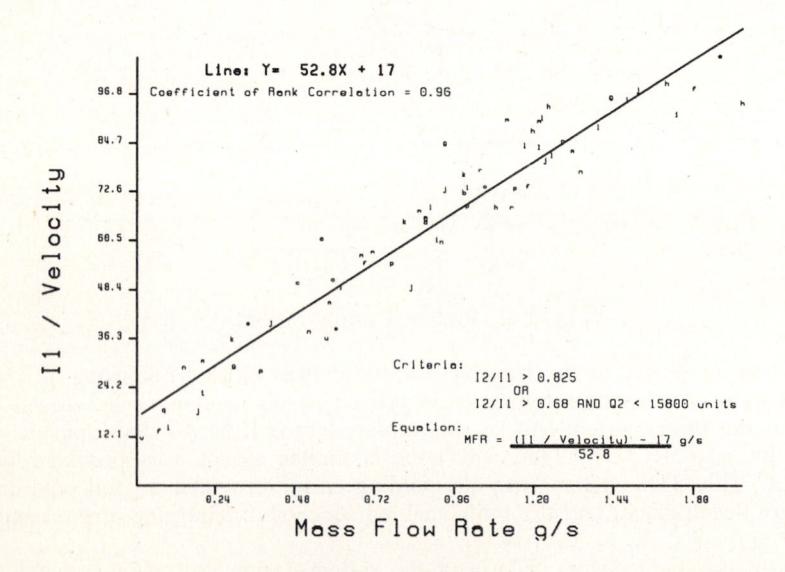

Figure 4   Region 1.

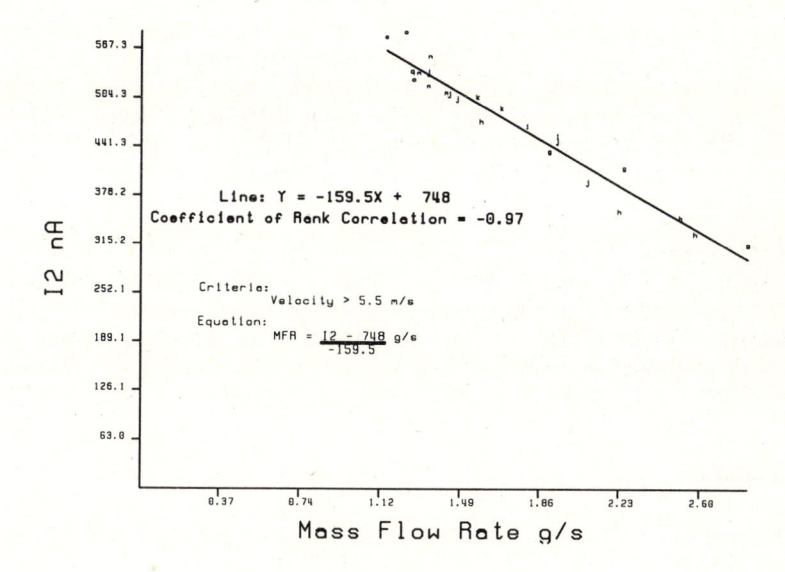

Figure 5 Region 2a.

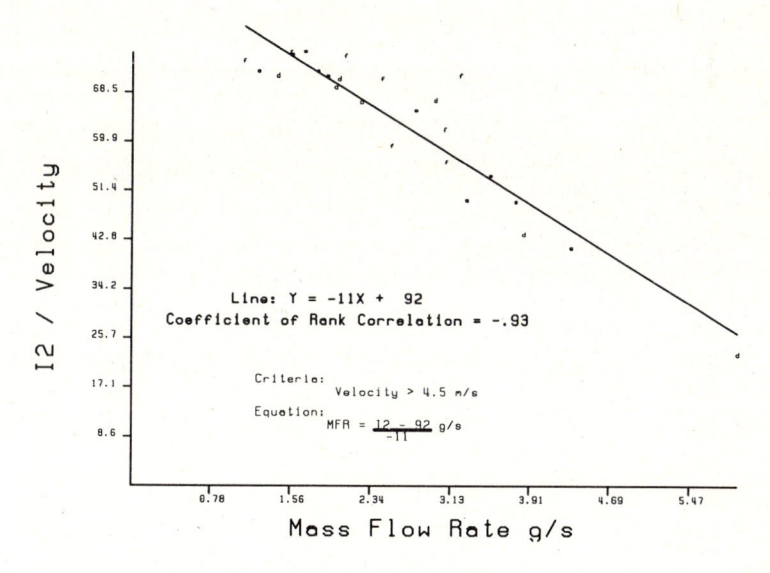

Figure 6 Region 2b.

5. Conclusions & Future Work

The system was successful in measuring powder flow rates and the time taken to process the transducer signals was less than the interval between injection pulses. The transputer has proved to be a processor which offers great flexibility in design. The main flexibility is the ability to use the processor in a stand alone mode and ease of interconnection to similar processors. This solution is a cost effective one for this application.

Future work will concentrate on two aspects of the work. One is the low density measurements for flue gas ducts. In this environment the technique would be use a moveable probe so that quick and reliable information could be obtained from many points on the cross-section of the duct. The transducer design will require modification for this application. Discussions are taking place with CERL who are interested in this application with the view to implementing this in their test facilities.

The other application is in powder spray systems. To be successful it is necessary to use this measurement to control the flow in several spray guns by one system. To control the flow further work is required to study the fluctuations in a standard commercial spay system before a reliable control method can be implemented. This research will continue at the Polytechnic and it is anticipated there will be considerable industrial interest in this final stage of the project.

6. Acknowledgments

This work has been supported by the Science and Engineering Research Council and Nottingham Polytechnic.

7. References

[1] B.C.O'Neill and C.A.Willis. *Corona Charging of Pneumatically Conveyed Powders*. Journal of Electrostatics June 1985.

[2] F.R.G.Mitchell, J.M.Proctor and E.Turnbull. *An Optical Method of Measuring Particle Mass Flow Rates*. J. Physics E:Sci. Instrum., Vol. 17, pages 183–184, 1984.

[3] M.S.Beck, J.H.Hobson and P.J.Mendies. *A Mass Flowmeter for Airborne Solids*. Proceedings of Powtech 71; International Powder Technology and Bulk Granular Solids Conference, pages 63–65.

[4] R.G.Green, S.H.Foo and R.Thorn. *Microcomputer−Based Mass Flow Rate Measurement of Solids in a Pneumatic Conveying System*. The Arabian Journal for Science and Engineering, Vol. 7. N°. 4, pages 411–418.

A Transputer based instrument for the ESA/NASA CLUSTER mission

C.M.Dunford[*], J.A.Thompson[*], K.H.Yearby[+]

[*]Computer Science Department
[+]Control Engineering Department
University of Sheffield
Sheffield S10 2TN

Abstract. This paper describes the evolution and implementation of a multiple transputer based instrument, the Digital Wave Processor (DWP), for the ESA Cluster mission. The DWP is a fault-tolerant instrument responsible for the control of five wave processing experiments, and the data processing and compression of their output. Novel features include low power modes of the DWP where some transputers are powered off and others may run at a reduced clock speed.

1. Introduction

A team from the departments of Physics, Control Engineering and Computer Science at Sheffield University has an expanding involvement in space instrumentation. A wave instrument [1] was provided for the AMPTE mission (launched in 1984). A wave correlator for the Russian INTERBAL programme to be launched in 1992 is almost complete and the design of an instrument for the Russian Mars94 mission is about to commence.
   The Cluster mission [2] is intended to study the wave and plasma environment of the Earth's magnetosphere. It involves four identical spacecraft in an orbit with an apogee of ~20 earth radii and a perigee of ~3 earth radii with a lifetime of at least two years. The use of four spacecraft will allow a three dimensional view of the environment for a number of wave and particle detectors.
   The plasma wave instruments on Cluster are grouped into a consortium, the 'Wave Experiment Consortium' (WEC), to allow the sharing of resources in an optimum manner. Five instruments are all under the control of a central data collection and processing instrument, the Digital Wave Processor [3], the subject of this paper.

2. Requirements

The functions that the Digital Wave Processor (DWP) must perform, in as reliable and fault tolerant manner as possible, are:
   - Data collection from other WEC instruments.
   - Control and sequencing of other WEC instruments.
   - Data processing and compression.
   - Packaging and transmission of telemetry to the spacecraft.

- Reception and decoding of telecommands.
- Wave-particle correlations.

To fulfil these processing requirements, along with the need to provide some redundancy and fault tolerance, a multi-processor architecture has been adopted.

Telemetry is passed to the spacecraft at rates up to 38 kbps. Data rates from the WEC instruments may be up to twice this. This gives a peak data rate of around 114 kbps, a bandwidth that can be easily accommodated by a bus architecture.

The mass allocated to the DWP is ~2 kg. This figure includes the box, fixings, boards, connectors, any internal wiring, electronic components, etc.

In its normal mode of operation, DWP is allowed 1.5W of electrical power. More power is consumed during initialisation and in some special modes.

The orbit of the Cluster spacecraft takes them through some of the more hazardous regions of the magnetosphere. Over the two year life, current estimates predict a radiation dose of around 20 kRads(Si) behind 4 mm of aluminium. This means that radiation tolerant components have to be selected.

3. Instrument Evolution

The design of the Cluster DWP evolved through two distinct stages. A design based around three radiation hardened, CMOS, 8086 microprocessors was originally proposed. Subsequently, the microprocessors were changed to Inmos T222 transputers, with a consequent simplification of some of the circuitry, as outlined below.

3.1 Design As Originally Proposed

The original design study for this project produced an instrument based around three processor modules communicating with each other and with interfaces to the client instruments over an internal bus. A pair of redundant busses was considered but eliminated for mass and power reasons. Each processor module was to consist of a Harris HS80C86RH microprocessor with ROM and RAM. The HS80C86RH was chosen because it was a well known device with an established radiation hardness pedigree.

There were a number of problems with this original concept. One was the requirement for inter-processor communications. Two solutions were investigated, one involved a block of RAM connected to the bus that could be accessed by all three processors, the other allowed a part of each processor module's RAM to be accessed by the other two processors over the bus. This latter solution was preferred because of the inherent greater redundancy. Both solutions involved use of the bus, thus vastly increasing the bus bandwidth requirement.

A second problem was the processing power of the 8086. The capabilities of all three processors were expected to be barely enough to fulfil the peak processing requirements. If a processor failure occurred, drastically reduced functionality would ensue.

Thirdly, merely programming the three processors to cooperate flat out in a reliable manner was expected to be difficult. Added to that the requirement that some operation was still to occur with the failure of any one or even two processor modules, and the programmers could expect problems.

Another problem was the unambiguous communication of initial health check results between processors, preferably without using the bus. The proposal included a small state machine in each processor module that accepted a short two bit, multi-word, protocol from the microprocessor. Only the correct sequence of two bit words would cause the machine to end in the state that caused its output signal to be active. This signal was then broadcast to the other two processor modules. In this way, each processor could inspect the results of the other two processors' health checks without the worry that a processor running wild was likely to produce an erroneous OK result.

There was one aspect of the design that proved to be easy. This was the implementation of the power saving modes. Since the HS80C86RH was a purely static CMOS device, merely stopping the processors main clock would reduce its power consumption to virtually zero. No complex power switching arrangements would be required to turn off individual processor modules.

3.2 Enter the Transputer

Members of the team had been working with transputers for some years, but the transputer had not been considered as a candidate processor because of its unknown radiation tolerance. The ESA Space Technology Centre (ESTEC) then published the results of some radiation tests that had been carried out on the T414 transputer [4]. This indicated that the T414 was capable of withstanding the radiation dose expected for the Cluster DWP.

Selecting the transputer directly addressed all the problems foreseen with the original concept. Inter-processor communication using the links reduced the bus bandwidth requirement and increased redundancy. Significantly more processing power was available, and occam, the transputer's associated language is specifically aimed at multi-processor and multi-process systems. Lastly, the communication of health checks could be done over the links with no hardware overhead.

Implementing low power modes was not so easy however. Power consumption could not be reduced by stopping the clock because of the internal phase-lock loop which would free-run in the absence of a clock. So power switching circuitry had to be included.

A 16 bit transputer is the microprocessor of choice rather than a 32 bit device. The main reasons for this are that fewer RAM and ROM chips are accessed in one cycle, thus reducing power consumption and most instruments use a 16 bit data length.

A programme of test irradiation of the T222 transputer was carried out using the facilities at ESTEC. [5] The results established the viability of the T222 for the Cluster mission.

4. Hardware Implementation

The basic architecture of the DWP is shown in figure 1. Each of the WEC instruments is provided with a dedicated interface to the common instrument bus. An interface to the spacecraft On Board Data Handling (OBDH) system is also included. Three processor modules are provided, interconnected by links to provide inter-process communications and interfaced to the instrument bus to provide for instrument and spacecraft communication.

4.1 The Processor Module

A T222 transputer with 32 Kbytes of external RAM (the internal memory is disabled to provide increased radiation tolerance) and 16 Kbytes of PROM forms the core of each module. In addition each has a HS82C37A DMA controller, event multiplexor and instrument bus interface.

Power down circuitry enables the PROM or an entire processor module to be switched off to conserve power. Series resistors or tri-state buffers are employed to ensure that the inputs of powered down circuits are not driven. The PROM is powered down on command from the transputer after the initial boot up procedure has copied its contents into RAM. Whole processor modules are only powered down by a hardware command from the OBDH interface.

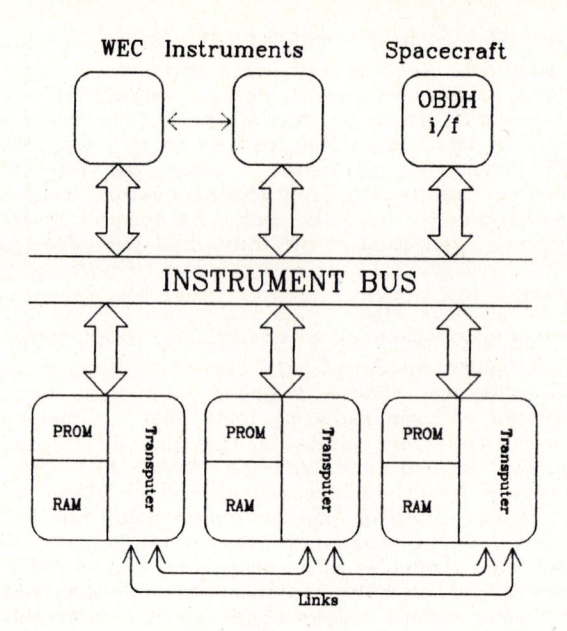

Figure 1 - DWP Architecture

The design of the DWP allows the transputers to be operated at input clock frequencies of 2.5 or 5 MHz, the lower rate requiring less power. The clock frequency select signal is applied to the transputer link speed input (as well as to the clock divider) in such a way that the links always operate at the standard speed of 10 Mbits/s. This allows processor modules operating at different speeds to communicate. Speed selection is made by hardware command from the OBDH interface.

4.2 The Instrument Bus and Interfaces

The instrument bus allows 16 bit parallel communication between the processor modules and the instrument interfaces. Events and DMA transfers are also requested over this bus. Only one transputer (chosen at boot time) is allowed access to the instrument bus. This removes the requirement for any complex instrument bus arbitration logic. However, simple logic is provided to prevent damage to DWP if, due to some fault, more than one processor does try to drive the instrument bus simultaneously.

A variety of interfaces are used to control and obtain data from the instruments of the wave consortium. Interfaces with a relatively low data rate employ registers allocated one of the 16 instrument bus addresses and in some cases an event request line. High data rate interfaces use the DMA channels.

4.3 The Spacecraft OBDH Interface

The OBDH interface contains telemetry, telecommand, and timing circuitry, duplicated for telemetry and telecommand to provide redundancy in case of failure.

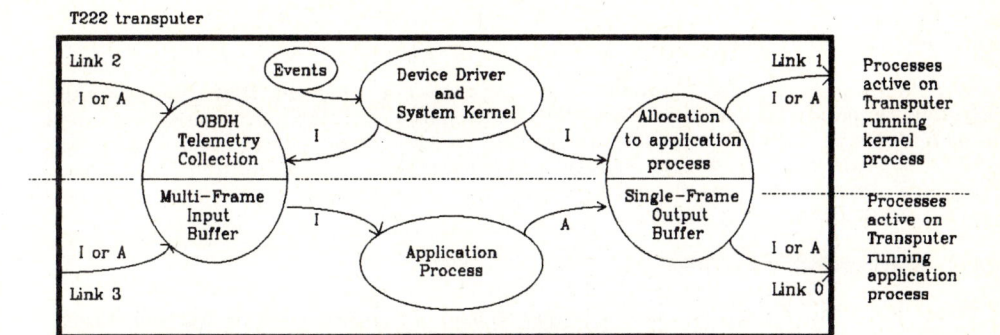

```
T222 transputer
```

```
                                                                    Processes
Link 2                                              Link 1           active on
 I or A    ┌──────┐   Events  ┌────────────┐       ┌──────┐  I or A  Transputer
           │ OBDH │────────→  │Device Driver│      │Allocation│       running
           │Telem.│           │    and      │      │to appl. │       kernel
           │Collec│           │System Kernel│      │ process │       process
           └──────┘                                └──────┘
           Multi-Frame          I            I     Single-Frame
            Input                                   Output        Processes
            Buffer                                  Buffer        active on
 I or A                      Application            I or A       Transputer
Link 3                        Process                Link 0       running
                                                                  application
                                                                  process
```

KEY:
I Instrument data from WEC instrument
A Output from application process

Figure 2 – occam process running on a DWP transputer

The telemetry interface is the route for all data leaving the DWP. A DMA channel is used to provide high data throughput. Data may be output on either of the redundant interfaces as requested by the spacecraft OBDH.

The telecommand interface enables the DWP software to receive commands from the spacecraft OBDH. Separate command registers and interrupt request lines are assigned to the two redundant parts of this interface. An extension of this interface (hardware commands) allows the OBDH to directly command parts of the DWP hardware without software intervention (processor speed and power on/off).

The OBDH provides a high frequency clock and a reset pulse (occurring at the start of every major telemetry frame) to allow time tagging of received data. The timing interface consists of a prescaler and a 16 bit counter. The reset pulse resets the counter and generates an event request. A processor module can read the counter over the instrument bus and thus tag data received from instruments with the spacecraft time.

5. Software Implementation

The software can be partitioned into three levels of functionality. These are System Kernel, Data Compression and Added Science. For DWP to function at a minimum level, one and only one transputer must run the System Kernel. Any other active processors may run the Data Compression or Added Science modules. The software architecture is shown in figure 2.

5.1 System Kernel

The system kernel contains routines that control all the hardware interfaces and perform the basic data collection and transmission functions. The code runs at two priority levels. At the high level of priority, events are noted and buffered for further processing by the main, low priority, driver. Because of some tight timing constraints and possible low clock speed of the transputer running the kernel, some events have to be handled at high priority. This requires careful design of the code to ensure that timing requirements for all instruments are met.

5.2 Data Compression

DWP is responsible for filtering and compressing data so that the available telemetry bandwidth is not exceeded. Extensive research into this topic has been done at the Universities of Sheffield and Sussex, and tested on data from the AMPTE, GEOS and Viking missions [6,7]. An intelligent controlling process then selects and combines packets of compressed data into a single fixed length telemetry frame.

5.3 Added Science Modules

Some scientific functions are also performed by DWP. These include wave-particle correlations and resonance sounder tracking.

Wave-particle correlations are detected by a software module that performs the cross-correlation function between particle counts and electric field data. Electric field data are already available to the DWP from one of the WEC instruments, but an extra hardware interface to a particle instrument is required.

The resonance sounder (WHISPER) is an instrument that transmits pulses of electromagnetic radiation into the space plasma and then listens for resonances. This device can be operated in a mode in which the DWP analyses its data on-board to identify significant resonances. DWP then controls the frequency of transmission to track them.

5.4 Process Partitioning and Communication

DWP must be able to function with three, two, or only one processor module active. All essential tasks are grouped together into a single process, the System Kernel, which will execute on a single transputer (determined at boot time). Data Compression and Added Science modules will then be farmed out to other transputers. These latter functions will be progressively sacrificed if other processor modules are not available.

5.5 Booting

Upon application of power to the DWP, each transputer boots up from PROM. Selection of the transputer to run the system kernel is based upon the outcome of self-test routines, and a pre-determined priority amongst the working transputer modules. Other working processor modules are allocated data compression and added science tasks, depending on the desired mode. After the successful booting of a transputer from PROM, the required code is copied from the PROM into local static memory. The PROM is then paged out of the memory map of the transputer, and switched off to save power.

During the boot sequence, the self test routine has to access the instrument bus. To avoid two processors accessing the bus simultaneously, each waits a unique length of time after the power on reset, before commencing its tests. These delays are achieved using the transputer's internal timer. However, because there are two possible speeds each processor can run at, these delays must be carefully selected, as shown in figure 3.

The next major phase in the bootstrap, is the establishment of communication with the other processors, if possible, and the allocation of processing functions. All transputers attempt, in parallel, to output and input on all their links. The Inmos routines *output.or.fail* and *input.or.fail* are used to prevent the test process hanging in the event of a failure. Using the results of this test, kernel and application processes are allocated to processors as shown in figure 4. The basic criteria is that processor 0 has the highest priority for executing the kernel, unless another transputer has greater connectivity. In the worst case, if processors 1 and 2 cannot

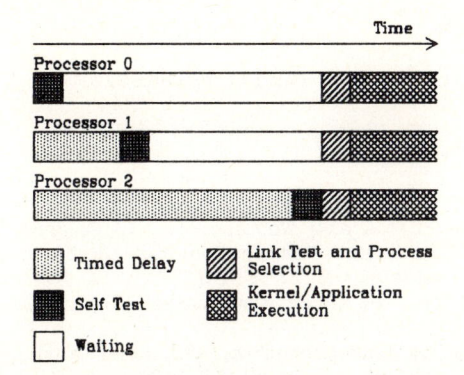

Figure 3 - Timed delays before executing self-test for each processor

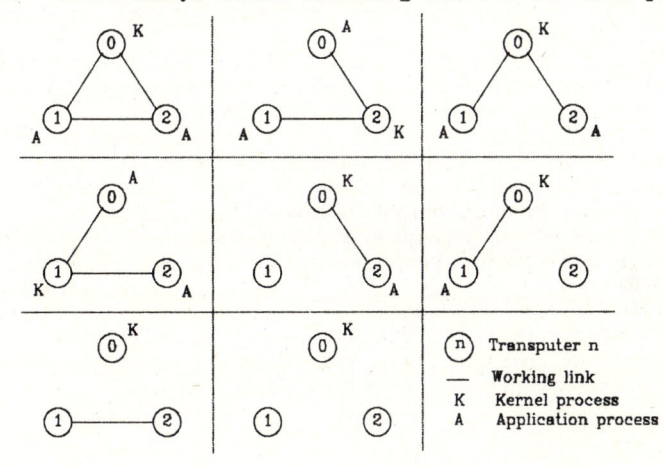

Figure 4 - Allocation of Kernel and Application tasks after link failure

communicate with processor 0, then they will stop. This simple scheme prevents more than one processor from running the kernel, and driving the bus. This allocation mechanism can be over-ridden by the use of hardware commands.

6. Conclusion

A fault tolerant, multi-transputer instrument has been designed for the ESA/NASA Cluster mission. A single transputer prototype has been built and successfully tested with early prototypes of the other WEC instruments. The engineering model design has just been completed and boards are in the process of being laid out.

Using the transputer rather than the 8086 simplified much of the design. It solved the problems of:
 - inter-processor communication
 - shortage of processing power
 - difficulty of programming multi-processor systems

It is even cheaper!

7. Acknowledgements

The Cluster DWP programme is funded by BNSC/SERC.

8. References

[1] Darbyshire A G, Gershuny E J, Jones S R, Norris A J, Thompson J A, Whitehurst G A, Wilson G A and Woolliscroft L J C; 'The UKS wave experiment' IEEE trans on Geoscience and Remote Sensing, GE-23, 3, pp 311-314, (1985).
[2] Schmidt R and Goldstein M L; 'CLUSTER - A fleet of four spacecraft to study plasma structures in three dimensions' ESA document SP-1103, pp 7-13, (1988).
[3] Woolliscroft L J C, Thompson J A, (19 other authors); 'The Digital Wave Processing Experiment' ESA document SP-1103, pp 49-54, (1988).
[4] Thomlinson J, Adams L and Harboe-Sorensen R, 'The SEU and Total Dose Response of the Inmos Transputer', IEEE Transactions on Nuclear Science, Vol. NS-34, No. 6 (1987)
[5] Thompson J A and Hancock B K; 'Report on the suitability of the Inmos T222 and C011 for use in the Cluster mission radiation environment', University of Sheffield departmental report (1990).
[6] Sumner A E, Battersby A D, Thompson J A, Woolliscroft L J C, Gough M P A and Powell T J; 'The use of data compression for wave experiments', presented at 4th Symposium on spacecraft instrument engineering, Frunze USSR, and accepted for publication in proceedings (1989).
[7] Gough M P, Germon R, Thompson J A and Woolliscroft L J C; 'Simulation of data compression of satellite geophysical data', Int J Remote Sen, 8, no. 8, pp 1219-1227 (1987).

A Modular, Decentralized Architecture for Multi-Sensor Data Fusion[*]

H. F. Durrant-Whyte, S. Grime, and H. Hu
Department of Engineering Science
University of Oxford
Oxford OX1 3PJ

May 9, 1990

1 Introduction

Systems that employ a variety of different sensors to obtain information are becoming increasingly common in a range of different application domains; from process plant systems to military command and control, from robotics to surveillance. The main advantages of using many different types of sensors to obtain information are that the good points of one sensor can be used to overcome the weakness in another, and that by providing redundancy overall system robustness can be increased [2].

The main problem with multi-sensor systems is how the information obtained from all these sensing devices can be integrated into a robust and consistent description of the state of the environment; this is the multi-sensor data fusion problem. The fusion process is clearly not only a function of the complexity of the sensing device, but also depends on the geometric complexity of the state description, and the geographical dispersion of the sensors themselves. The underlying fusion mechanism may range from a simple least-squares fitting algorithm, in the case of some simple, homogeneous and co-located sensors, to quite complex statistical inference methods employing large models of system function and the observation process.

The complexity of the multi-sensor data fusion problem has given rise to a considerable interest in the development of suitable architectures for multi-sensor systems. Most architectures currently used in such systems rely on having a central processor where global fusion takes place (hierarchical systems for example [5]), or in having a central communications medium through which all messages between sensors must pass (blackboard systems for example [4, 7]). Such centralized architectures give rise to problems with communication and computational bottle-necks, and are not able to deal with sensor failure in a graceful manner.

This paper describes a fully decentralized, Transputer-based architecture for data fusion problems. This architecture takes the form of a network of sensor nodes, each with it's own processing facility, which together do not require any central processor or any central communication facility. In this architecture, computation is performed locally and communication occurs between any two nodes. Such an architecture has many desirable properties including modularity of sensor devices, robustness to sensor failure, and flexibility to the addition or loss of one or more sensors. The Transputer is an ideal machine for implementing such a decentralized architecture; it can be easily packaged with a sensor and it's associated electronics in a modular form, it is easily extendible, and it takes care of the considerable communication problem in a flexible, transparent manner.

In this paper, we will concentrate on describing the hardware architecture rather than the details of the data fusion algorithm itself. A detailed description of the algorithm can be found in [3]. We first outline the decentralized data fusion algorithm, describing the flow

---

[*]This work is supported in part by ESPRIT 1560 (SKIDS)

of information through the sensor network and the quantities that need to be computed at each node or communicated between sensors. We then show how this algorithm can be mapped into hardware, and briefly describe three different implementations; the first on a physically centralized Transputer-based multi-camera vision system, the second on a modular, Transputer-based, surveillance network (based on sonar and infra-red sensing) that we have constructed, and finally on a pilot process plant, using this same modular sensing architecture, that we are currently constructing.

2 The Algorithm

The starting point for the decentralized sensing architecture is an algorithm which permits the complete decentralization of the Extended Kalman Filter (EKF) equations. We call this algorithm the Decentralized Kalman Filter (DKF). The DKF is an implementation of a multi-sensor EKF which has been divided up into modules, one associated with each sensor. In the EKF, a joint prediction is made about what each sensor is expected to observe and when these observations are made, they are centrally combined into a single composite description of the environment. In a DKF, each individual node makes its own predictions about what will be observed, and initially only integrates its own observation to obtain a local, partial estimate of the environment. An additional stage is then evoked in which these partial estimates are broadcast to other nodes where they are assimilated to provide the full environment estimate.

The DKF algorithm has a number of features which make it more than just a mathematical curiosity:

- The estimates arrived at by each node are guaranteed to be *exactly* the same estimates as those obtained by a fully centralized EKF (Our algorithm differs from the sub-optimal decomposition described in [1]). Thus, although processing is now distributed, there is no degradation in performance.

- Each sensor node deals with its own pre-processing and estimation problems; the failure of any one of the nodes will not result in a whole system failure. Thus, the decentralized sensing architecture is highly survivable and robust, being able to degrade gracefully in the face of sensor or processor failure.

- The amount of additional computation required is quite small and is certainly outweighed by the advantages of distributing computation.

- The communication overhead is also low, indeed it is actually *less* than is required for similar hierarchical organizations [5].

- The fact that all signal processing and estimation algorithms can be implemented locally with each sensor allows the packaging of sensors and processing in to modular units.

These advantages have led us to pursue the DKF as an algorithmic foundation for developing a fully decentralized data-fusion architecture.

We do not think that this conference is an appropriate place to describe the theoretical details of the DKF algorithm which can be found elsewhere [3]. We shall, instead, outline what functions each node performs and what information needs to be communicated between different nodes. The DKF is based on the *information filter* form of the extended Kalman filter. It encorporates a full description of state dynamics, process and observation models. The DKF can be applied to any problem which can also be solved using a standard Kalman filter, including non-linear models of process and observation, or multi-target problems, for example.

The basic building block for the DKF algorithm is shown in Figure 1. The observations made by the ith nodes sensor at time-step k are described as an information vector $\mathbf{I}_i(k)$. The information matrix is defined as the inverse covariance matrix, and the information vector as the transpose of the observation matrix times the information matrix times the observation

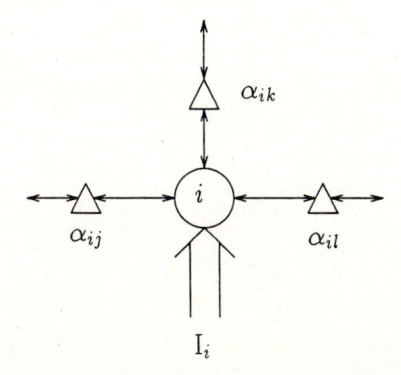

Figure 1: The basic building block for the DKF algorithm: Each node i obtains information I_i from it's associated sensor. It then integrates this information into a local estimate of state and communicates the result to it's nearest neighbours. The information communicated to each sensor is recorded by the associated channel α_{ij} and used to determine how new information form adjacent sensors should be assimilated with the sensor's own local estimate.

vector itself. The information filter for each independent node can be written as:

$$\tilde{\mathbf{y}}_i(k+1) = \hat{\mathbf{y}}_i(k) + \mathbf{I}_i(k+1) \tag{1}$$

Simplistically, this just states that each node's new partial estimate $\tilde{\mathbf{y}}_i(k+1)$ at time $k+1$ is composed of the previous global estimate $\hat{\mathbf{y}}_i(k)$ plus the new local information $\mathbf{I}_i(k+1)$. To produce a new global estimate $\mathbf{y}_i(k+1)$ at each node, information from adjacent sensors needs to be incorporated into this local estimate. This is achieved through an assimilation stage,

$$\begin{aligned} \hat{\mathbf{y}}_i(k+1) &= \sum_{j \in N_i} [\mathbf{I}_j(k+1) + \hat{\mathbf{y}}_j(k) - \alpha_{ij}(k)] \\ &= \sum_{j \in N_i} [\tilde{\mathbf{y}}_j(k+1) - \alpha_{ij}(k)] \end{aligned} \tag{2}$$

where the summation is taken over all nodes in the ith neighbourhood N_i (which includes i), and each channel filter $\alpha_{ij}(k)$ is defined as

$$\alpha_{ij}(k) = \mathbf{I}_i(k) + \mathbf{I}_j(k) + \alpha_{ij}(k-1), \tag{3}$$

with $\alpha_{ii}(k) = 0$ The interpretation of Equations 2 and 3 is as follows: Each node assimilates each adjacent nodes new partial estimate $\tilde{\mathbf{y}}_j(k+1)$ only after subtracting what it knows they have in common; that is, the information previously communicated down their common channel. Thus, the global estimate obtained at node i is composed of; (i) node i's new information, (ii) each adjacent nodes' new information, and (iii) the information at each adjacent node which has not previously been communicated to node i (information obtained from nodes which are not in direct communication with node i).

It can formally be shown that a network of these nodes, in an *arbitrary topology*, is identically equivalent to a fully centralized Kalman filter, with the proviso that the information communicated from one node to another will be delayed by a time proportional to the minimum path length between them.

3 The Hardware

The Transputer is an ideal machine for implementing this decentralized architecture. This is because it can easily be embedded locally with a sensor and networked with other, spatially distributed, sensor nodes by passing the links through an RS422 communication network.

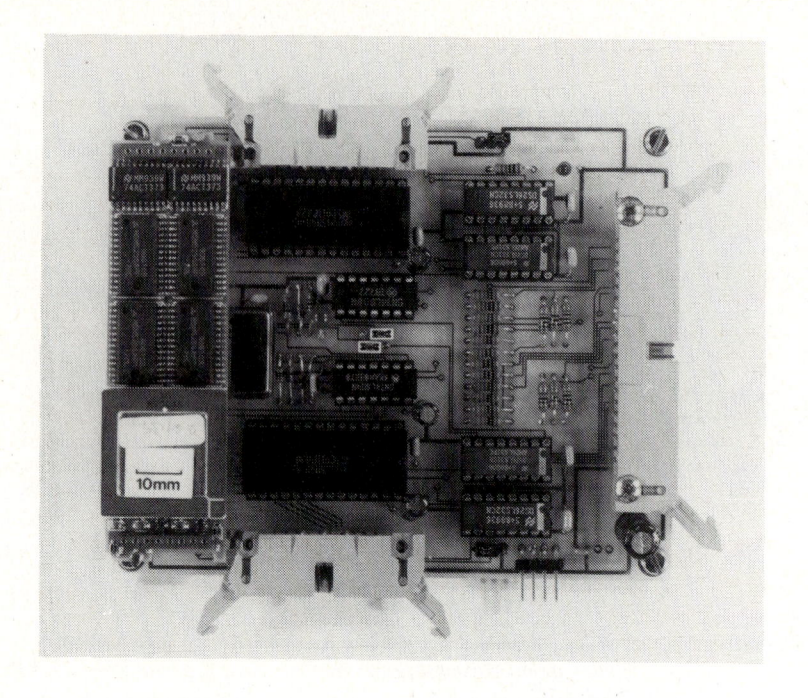

Figure 2: A LISA module based on a TRAM2/T800

In addition, the links provide a simple standard interface between the processor and sensor driver boards.

We have designed and built a number of different types of sensor node. Each sensor node is based around a standard "LISA"[1] board (Figure 2). Each board contains a TRAM2/T800 with 128Kb of local memory, two C011 link to parallel interface chips, three link to RS422 communication channels, a local clock, and various diagnostic and interface logic. One link is always dedicated to drive a sensor, two links are always dedicated to communicating with other sensor nodes, the remaining link can be configured to drive a second sensor or to provide an additional communication channel or to provide a boot from EPROM. This is the second version of the LISA board we have built. Future versions are planned which will aim to allow modules to be stacked for either increased computational power or increased communication fan-out.

We have built three other basic boards which interface to LISA and which drive different sensors and motors. These boards can be packaged in various combinations to provide different types of sensor node (Figure 3). The first drives an active infra-red ranging sensor, the second drives a standard ultra-sonic ranging sensor, and the third is able to drive four small DC servo motors. All of these boards are the same size, the power supply and interface to each board can be daisy-chained so that they can be stacked together in any combination. Photographs of a completed node are shown in Figures 4 and 5.

A number of other basic boards are under development: We are now designing a linear-CCD driver to augment the infra-red and ultra-sonic sensors for a surveillance application. We are also designing AD/DA boards to support different types of process plant sensors for an IED project[2].

---
[1] Locally Intelligent Sensor Agent
[2] IED4/1/1199 "Distributed Sensing and Sensor Fusion in Complex Man-Machine Systems", in Collaboration with British Aerospace PLC and Marcol Computer Systems Limited.

Figure 3: Sonar, Infra-red and Motor-driver Boards

4 Implementations

Our first implementation of the DKF algorithm involved the use of four widely spaced cameras to track, in real-time, objects and people moving through a room[3] [6]. The sensing system used consists of four CCD cameras mounted at the top corners of a room (10m×10m in size), and pointing at the approximate center of the floor. Special purpose hardware (Data-Cube) was used to capture and preprocess images at frame-rates. In addition to this, the cameras each have three T800 Transputers associated with them. Two of these processors are used to extract targets from the processed image, the third is employed to run the local node's DKF. Each DKF algorithm employs a third-order multi-target model of motion dynamics. The target detection process is able to cycle at about 2Hz, limited by the time it takes to extract events from the preprocessed images.

The intended application of the LISA system described in the previous section is in surveillance problems where people and vehicles need to be tracked and identified. Each LISA node is self-contained and can be placed at any suitable location in the application domain. Each sensor node implements the DKF algorithm by creating local tracks based on local observations and by assimilating track information from other neighbouring sensor sites. Four nodes (two infra-red and two ultra-sonic) are employed to track moving events in two dimensions. The infra-red sensors are used to acquire fast reflectance scans of the environment. Changes between successive scans are used to obtain target bearings. The sonar is then directed to acquire range information data at the indicated bearings. The DKF is used to integrate this range information with the bearing information. A third-order model of motion dynamics is employed by each local filter For each target, the cycle rate for the DKF is about 40ms. The intention of this implementation is to physically demonstrate the

---

[3]This work was conducted in collaboration with British Aerospace Sowerby Research Center.

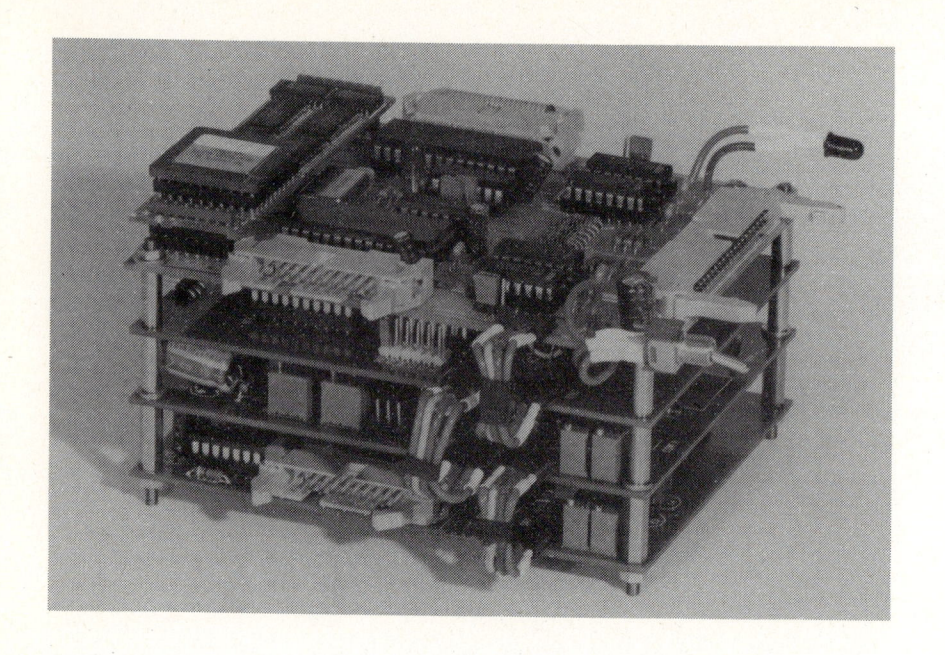

Figure 4: A completed node showing the different modules stacked together

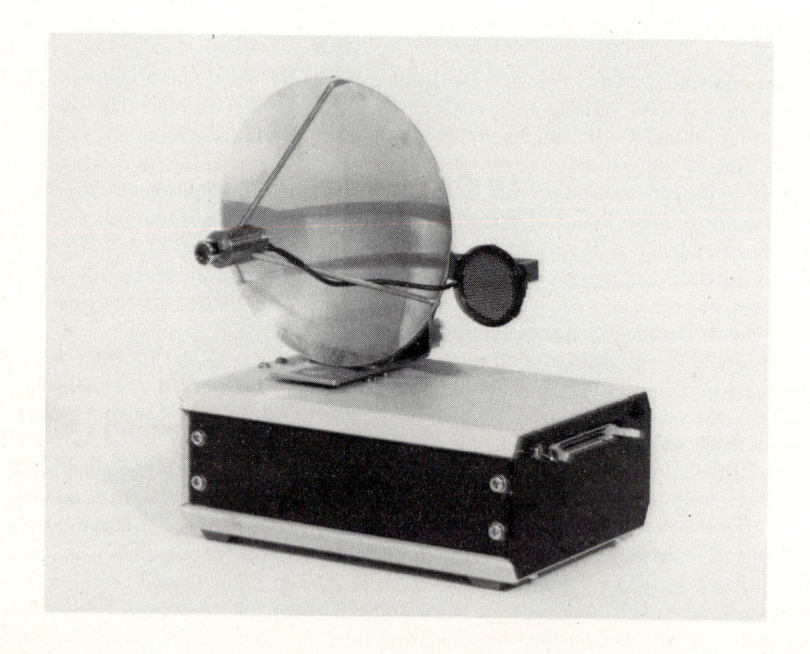

Figure 5: A completed node

robustness, modularity and flexibility of the architecture by allowing new sensors to be added, "failed" sensors to be removed, and the sensor network to be reconfigured on-line. A further ten nodes are currently being added to this demonstrator.

We are currently working toward applying this architecture to data fusion problems in process plant. This application is characterized by a huge amount of simple data, by complex models of plant behaviour, and by stringent reliability requirements. We will be using twenty identical LISA boards, with either a 32-channel AD sensor board (for thermocouples and flow meters), or a 4-channel DA valve controller board.

References

[1] C. Chong, K. Chang, and Y. Bar-Shalom. Joint probabilistic data association in distributed sensor networks. *IEEE Trans. Automatic Control*, 31(10):889–897, 1986.

[2] H.F. Durrant-Whyte. *Integration, Coordination, and Control of Multi-Sensor Robot Systems*. Kluwer Academic Press, Boston, MA., 1987.

[3] H.F. Durrant-Whyte, B.Y. Rao, and H. Hu. Toward a fully decentralized architecture for multi-sensor data-fusion. In *Proc. IEEE Int. Conf. Robotics and Automation*, 1990.

[4] S.Y. Harmon. Sensor data fusion through a blackboard. In *Proc. IEEE Int. Conf. Robotics and Automation*, page 1449, 1986.

[5] H.R. Hashemipour, S. Roy, and A.J. Laub. Decentralized structures for parallel kalman filtering. *IEEE Trans. Automatic Control*, 33(1):88–93, 1988.

[6] B.S.Y. Rao and H.F. Durrant-Whyte. *A Fully Decentralized Algorithm for Multi-Sensor Kalman Filtering*. Technical Report 1787/89, Oxford U. Robotics Research Group, 1989.

[7] S.S. Shafer and C.E. Thorpe. An architecture for sensor fusion in a mobile robot. In *Proc. IEEE Int. Conf. Robotics and Automation*, page 2002, 1986.

A Modular Sensing System For Robotic Control

J.A.Ware and G.Roberts,
Dept Of Mathematics and Computing,
The Polytechnic Of Wales, Pontypridd,
Mid Glamorgan, CF37 1DL.

R.A.Davies,
Dept Of Computer Studies,
The Polytechnic Of Wales.

R. Miles
The Transputer Centre,
Bristol Polytechnic,
Bristol, BF16 1QY.

J.H.Williams,
School Of Electrical Electronic and Systems Engineering,
University Of Wales, Cardiff, CF1 3YH.

Abstract. One of the main factors that inhibits the widespread use of robotic systems is the complexity of adding sensors to the robot's workspace. The majority of sensing systems that are currently available are inflexible in that the addition of extra sensors requires, at the very least, substantial changes to both hardware and software. This paper describes a transputer based system that contains the facility to add additional sensors without requiring major changes to hardware and software.

The process of extracting the information from the sensors is separated from the processes that use the information. This separation of information provider from information user enables the software that controls the sensors (and even the sensors themselves) to be upgraded with no corresponding changes to the information user software. Additional sensors can easily be added to the system while obsolete sensors and those with poor imaging characteristics can simply be removed.

1. Introduction

The manipulation of objects by a robot within its workspace requires knowledge about each object's location and orientation. A 3-D representation of the robot's workspace is thus required. This 3-D representation can be built up from information obtained from various sensors within the workspace.

At the outset of the research it was envisaged that before a 3-D model of workspace could be constructed the following would have to be addressed:-

(1) The information extracted from different sensors will generally be at different resolutions.

(2) The representation of 3-D space will require large amounts of computer memory.

(3) The production of the 3-D model, particularly when a large number of sensors are involved will probably require a substantial amount of processor time.

It was also proposed that (1) and (2) may be solved by using a hierarchical data structure while (3) might be addressed by identifying parallel aspects of the processing and implementing them using a network of processors. The development and description of this data structure is detailed elsewhere [1]. The present paper describes the process by which the information to build the structure is obtained from multiple sensors in parallel with the process of identifying objects.

2. Modelling System Developed

The information extracted from multiple sensors is used to provide "upper bounds" on the locations of the objects within the robot's workspace. The accuracy of this "upper bound" in locating the object depends on the number and nature of the sensors used, but always encloses the object. The software is responsible for taking into account the reliability of information provided by different sensors.

To construct this 3-D model, the projection of each 2-D sensor image through the workspace is calculated [2, 3]. The dimensions of this projection will depend on the orientation and angle of view of the sensor. The composite 3-D model of the robot's workspace is then constructed by taking the intersections of each of the projections. Where an intersection occurs, the values contained in the intersecting voxels are added to the values already stored, the values being weighted according to the sensor's reliability. Thus, each voxel in the composite model will contain a value representing the 'certainty factor' (not, strictly speaking the probability) of the voxel being part of an object.

Once the workspace has been modelled, the next step is to use that model to locate the objects within it. The location of an object refers to its coordinates in space. Since an object occupies a finite volume of space, its coordinates would typically be defined relative to a specific point on the object. A correct physical interpretation of location of object would require the determination of its centre of gravity. However, in the system implemented the model is used to produce three two-dimensional views of the workspace (plan, side elevation and front elevation). The centroid (i.e., centre of gravity for the two-dimensional image) of each view is then calculated and used to give an estimate of the location of that object.

The system developed allows the following functions to be carried out:-
    1) Update the model,
    2) Display view of model,
    3) Modify workspace characteristics,
    4) Modify sensor characteristics.

2.1. Update the model

The update of the model may be broken down under the following headings:-

(a) Obtain a view of workspace via sensor.
(b) Calculate projection of view through workspace.
(c) Add projection information to workspace model.

This process may be executed concurrently on any number of transputers; each transputer being connected to a different sensor.

2.2. Display views of workspace model

This process produces the three two-dimensional views of the workspace used to give an estimate of the location of objects within the workspace.

2.3. Modify Workspace Characteristics

It is envisaged that the sensing system being developed will be suitable for employment in a large number of different applications. As the application changes, so the characteristics of the robot's workspace will vary. In one application the robot's workspace might be a room while in a second application the robot's workspace might be a workbench. It was therefore necessary to build into the system a means by which changes in the dimensions of the workspace could be reflected in the workspace model. The resolution of the workspace model is constrained by the memory available on the transputers holding the model.

2.4. Modify Sensor Characteristics

Each time a new sensor is added to the system or a characteristic of an existing sensor is changed the sensor has to be calibrated. After sensor calibration the information obtained is stored for future reference.

3. Identification Of Objects Using Feature Extraction

All objects can be described in terms of their features. For some objects several features may be required to correctly identify them. These features may be anything from the volume and mass to the average curvature of an object.

For cases in which several object features must be measured to identify an object, a simple factor weighting method may be used to consider the relative contribution of each feature to the analysis. For example, to identify a valve stem from among a group of stems of several sizes, the image area may not be sufficient by itself to ensure positive identification. The measurement of height may add some additional information, as may the determination of the centroid of the object. Each feature would be compared with a standard for the goodness-of-fit measurement. Features that are known to be the most likely indicators of a match would be more heavily weighted than others. A weighted total goodness-of-fit score could then be determined to indicate the likelihood that the object has been correctly identified.

In the system developed, this feature extraction process is carried out in parallel with other modules in the system. To facilitate recognition of the object, a set of describing features is first produced for all objects within the object set. These features include:-

(1) Ratio of the length of two lines which intersect at right angles at the centre of gravity of the object; one line being the axis of least moment of inertia of the object.
(2) Ratio of perimeter length to object area.
(3) Euler Number.

As the features are extracted they are added to a table of features. (Each entry in the table consists of a feature type together with a feature value.) If only a limited amount of computer power is available for object recognition then it is better to utilise it in extracting those features that uniquely identify an object from within a set. However, if there is sufficient processor power to extract the whole set of features for each object in view then a more reliable classification of objects may be obtained.

Using a Transputer network (where processor power can be expanded to meet demand) a feature table may be produced for the object set. Each object in the table will have a set of features associated with it together with a set of values for those features. The feature values are calculated using model data.

As objects within the object set change so will the usefulness of the various features extracted. For example, if the object set contains various shaped assembly pieces then the average degree of roundness of their edges may give a good indication as to their identity. However, in another case, such as a set of various sized disks, then knowing the average degree of roundness of edges does not help in object identification.

To allow for this change in feature usefulness, each feature value will have a weighting factor associated with it that will be recalculated each time the object set is changed. Thus for each set of objects, those features best suited to uniquely identifying objects will have the greatest weighting.

When an object is to be classified, an attempt is made to extract from it all the features listed in the table. The extracted features are then compared with the table values. Thus, the degree of correlation between each table entry and the object to be classified can be calculated.

When the system has completed the process of analysing object features, some conclusions must be made about the findings, such as the verification that an object is, or is not part of the recognisable object set. Based upon these conclusions, certain decisions can be made about the object or the production process.

On the one hand, the decision might be that the identified object should be manipulated in a given fashion. On the other hand, the decision arrived at might be to halt production until some unrecognised object is removed.

4. Configuration Of Transputer Network

The model of the prototype workspace was held on eight transputers, each storing the model for one eighth of the workspace. From figure 1 it can be seen that a more detailed description of the cell is held for the Y axis than for the X and Z axis. The level to which each axis is represented can be varied by the user depending on application.

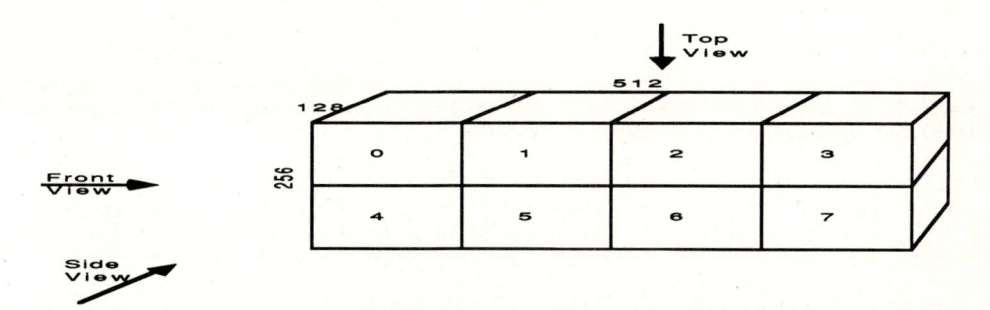

Figure 1 - Prototype workspace. The workspace which was 465 by 250 by 650 millimetres in size being held on eight transputers. Each section is broken down into 128 by 128 by 128 voxels.

Initially, multiple 2-D camera images were obtained using a CCD camera mounted on a SCARA robot arm. The robot arm gave great flexibility in positioning the camera in relation to the workspace. The CCD camera was connected to a 'Harlequin* frame grabber and image processing' board that in addition to processing the multiple views from the camera was used to display the three orthogonal views of the workspace model.

The transputer configuration for the prototype system is illustrated in figure 2. The transputers that held the data structure were arranged so that they formed an extendible bidirectional loop.

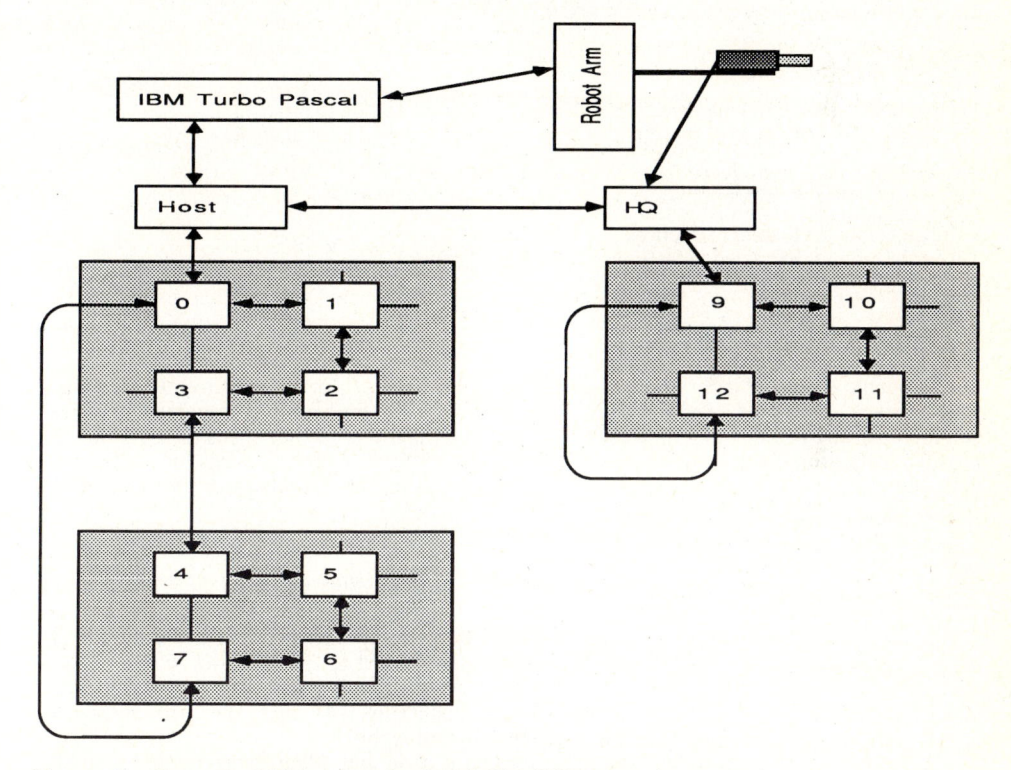

Figure 2 - Shows the initial system developed. The CCD camera is connected directly to the Harlequin frame grabber / graphics board. Transputers 0-7 hold the workspace model while transputers 9-12 are responsible for feature extraction.

---

*Manufactured By Quintek Of Bristol.

Data to be sent from one processor to another is packaged into a one-dimensional array (that is a list of numbers). The first element in the array indicates the destination address of data, the second the source address of data and the third the quantity of data being sent. The sending processor uses the first two pieces of information to determine the best route to the required destination. This communication packet is depicted in figure 3.

To	From	Amount Of Data	No Of Sets(n)	Prob	Op-Code	X (1)	Y (1)	Z.Start (1)	Z.End (1)	- - - - -	X (n)	Y (n)	Z.Start (n)	Z.End (n)

Figure 3 - Format For Passing Data From Sensor To Model.

Harlequin

1) Obtain image from CCD camera.
2) Threshold image and remove noise.
3) Project image through workspace.
4) Build view of workspace model from partial views provided by network transputers and analyse.

Host

1) Provide interface between user and system.
2) Provide interface between Harlequin and network.

Transputers in network (0 - 7)

1) Update data structure with data received from Harlequin relating to projection.
2) Create a view of the workspace and send it to the the Harlequin for analysis.

Transputers in network (9 - 12)

1) Responsible for feature extraction.
2) Use the features extracted to facilitate object identification.

5. Implementation Principles

To enable the processes, which were coded in OCCAM, to run concurrently on several processors a means of sending data from processor to processor is required. To keep communication overhead to a minimum it is important that this facility sends data via the best possible route around the network and that the number of times a process needs to communicate with other processors is optimised. It is also important to ensure that processor power is used as effectively and efficiently as possible.

To help meet these criteria the following rules were developed:-

1) Start the processors doing useful work as soon as possible and keep them doing useful work for as long as possible.
2) Data transfer between processors should be via the best possible route around the network. The best route is not necessarily the shortest as "traffic jams" might develop along certain paths. Obviously, it would be quicker if these were bypassed, but if there is no possibility of deadlock occurring [4] and the probability of "traffic jams" developing is low then they are best ignored.
3) Data transfer should be keep at an optimum level and when transfer is required it should be given priority over other tasks (this enables the receiving transputers to make use of the transferred information as soon as possible).

The optimum level of information transfer depends on two factors. First, it may be quicker to duplicate processes on more than one processor than to send information from processor to processor. Second, if one processor is generating information to be shared by other processors in the network then the information can be passed at one of three stages. These three stages being:-

(i) after all the information has been generated,
(ii) after a given amount of information has been generated,
(iii) as and when the information is generated.

While the choice of option will depend on the system being implemented the correct decision is crucial to the efficient execution of parallel processes. When making a decision the system designer should bear in mind rule 1. In the system being described, option (ii) proved to be the best choice.

Each transputer in the network therefore has the following processes executing concurrently:-

(1) a 'get info' process to receive data from both nearest clockwise and anti-clockwise transputers.
(2) a multiplexer to send data to the nearest clockwise transputer. This data may have been processed by the sending transputer, or the sending transputer may be acting as a link in the chain. (The multiplexer is required to collect data from the 'get info' and 'process request' routines and pass it on via a single connection.)
(3) a multiplexer to send data to the nearest anti-clockwise transputer. Again this data may have been processed by the sending transputer, or the sending transputer may be acting as a link in the chain.

In addition to the above, the first transputer in the network has the facility to communicate with the host transputer. Figure 4 shows the processes that run concurrently on the first transputer, while the other transputers in the network have all but the multi-word process running concurrently on them.

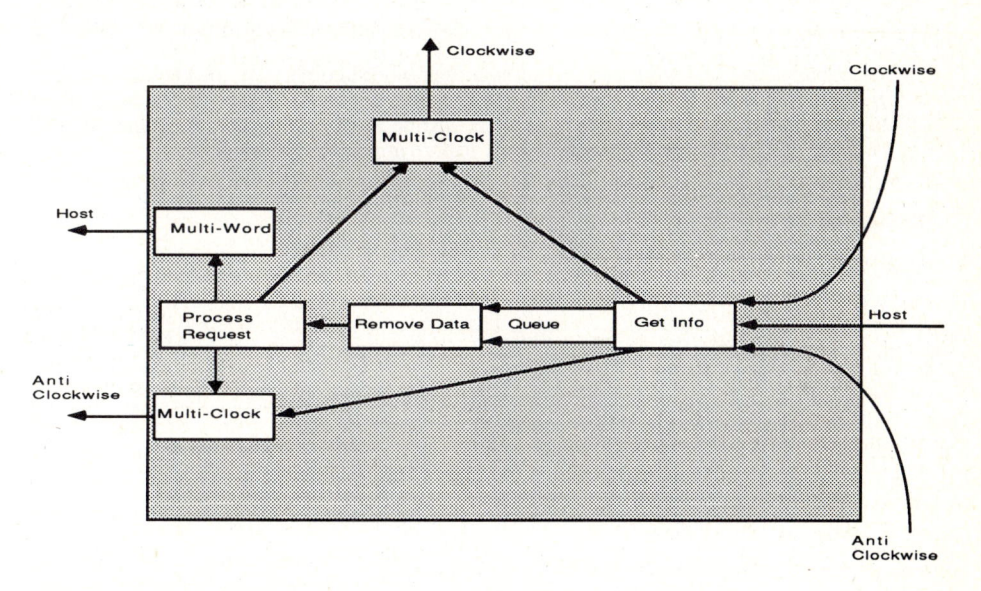

Figure 4 - A diagrammatical view of the processes running concurrently on the first processor in the network.

6. Testing The System

After the system outlined had been implemented, the next stage was to test its ability to locate and recognise objects, from a predefined object set, within a prototype workspace. To enable testing, the processes running on the network were extracted. Extraction puts all the code necessary for the loading, communication and execution of processes into a file that is 'bootable' by a program running on host PC [5].

A Turbo Pascal program was written to interface the robot arm with the transputer network (the Pascal program running on the host PC). The Pascal program was responsible for driving the robot arm so that the camera repeatedly scanned the workspace until an object was detected. Once an object was detected the scanning was stopped and the orientation of the camera adjusted so that the object became located in the centre of the camera's field of view.

The 2-D image was then processed to remove noise and its projection through the workspace calculated. The information associated with projection was then packaged before being sent to the transputers that held the associated parts of the model.

The camera was then raised to a position vertically above the object's location. The robot then moved the camera so that it scanned through an arc between the horizontal and vertical plane until the object was relocated. As with the first view the camera was adjusted automatically so that the object became located in the centre of the camera's field of view. This 2-D image was then processed as before.

In parallel with the object location process a second procedure attempts to identify the objects. The identification process matches features extracted from each object with a database of predefined object features. A statistical analysis is then used to determine the identity of each located object.

The next stage was to use the workspace model produced to determine the intersection of the two projections. This intersection was then used to determine the three two-dimensional views of the object within the workspace. The centroid of each view was then calculated and used to give the location of the object.

The system testing revealed that while on the whole the system worked well there are several areas of design which need refining. If objects within the workspace are occluded then in certain cases the intersecting views obtained from the different sensors will produce incorrect results. This can be overcome by better selection and placement of sensors, but a more satisfactory solution will be the inclusion of A.I. techniques to overcome any anomalies.

An additional problem is that the workload of the transputers is not as balanced as it might be. This leads to valuable processor power being wasted. A more dynamic processor allocation strategy will therefore be developed.

The object identification module also requires further work in order that a wider set of objects can be identified. At present only objects that come from sets with a fair degree of dissimilarity can be recognised. This increase in recognition ability will be achieved by increasing the range of features extracted and by improvements to the way feature importance is calculated.

7. Discussion

The availability of an easily adaptable sensing system would help to motivate an expansion in the use of robots in manufacturing industries. One factor that limits the adaptability of current systems is their lack of modularity. What is required is a system where by manufacturing industries can acquire different modules to meet their changing requirements without having to purchase a complete new system.

The nature of the task under consideration suggests that an extendible parallel architecture would be better suited to providing the processing requirements of such a system, than a traditional Von Neumann architecture. In general, one of the difficulties in using parallel architectures is that it is difficult to recognise inherent parallelism in problems. However, in the present task the parallel operation of modules is self evident.

The design of the transputer makes it a cost effective processor to meet the computational requirements of such a system. The transputer allows processor power to be expanded and applied, when and where needed. For example, if it were required to double the size of the prototype work cell without loss in resolution this could easily be achieved by doubling the number of network transputers from 8 to 16. Similarly, if an extra camera were to be added to the system (as in figure 5) then that would simply require the addition of an extra Harlequin board.

One disadvantage of using a transputer system however, is the lack of shared memory. In the object identification module, for example, it would have been simpler and more efficient to have a single copy of the image being shared by several processors.

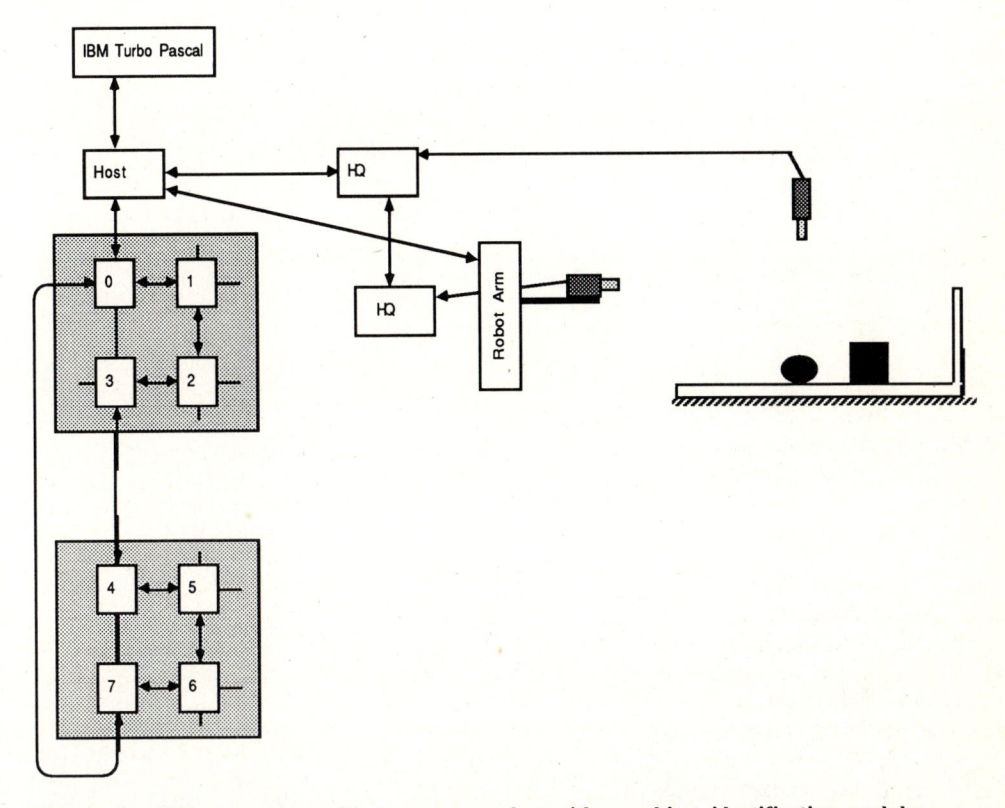

Figure 5 - Shows a system with two cameras but with no object identification modules.

8. Conclusions

This paper has outlined a prototype of a transputer based modular sensing system. The authors believe that such a system could form the basis for an adaptable system that could be configured to meet the requirements of a wide variety of applications in automated manufacturing.

9. References

[1] Ware,J.A., Davies,R.A., Roberts,G., Williams, J.H.,"A method for storing a 3-D workspace", Draft version available from Dept Of Mathematics and Computing, The Polytechnic Of Wales, Pontypridd, Mid Glamorgan, CF37 1DL.

[2] Chien,C.H., and Aggarwal,J.K., "Model Construction and Shape recognition from occluding Contours", IEEE Transactions on pattern analysis and machine intelligence, Vol 11, No. 4, April 1989, pp 372-389.

[3] Martin,W.N., and Aggarwal,J.K., 1983, "Volumetric descriptions of objects from multiple views", IEEE transactions on pattern recognition and machine intelligence, VOL PAMI-5 No 2.

[4] Ditel,H.M., 1984, "An introduction to operating systems", Addison-Wesley Publishing Company, London.

[5] Inmos, 1987, "Transputer development system", Prentice Hall International (UK) LTD.

Transputer Implementation of the Kalman-Bucy Filter

Prof. G.W. Irwin and L.P. Maguire
Department of Electrical and Electronic Engineering
The Queens University
Belfast BT9 5AH

Abstract

This paper considers the problem of realising the continuous-time, state-space Kalman filter on a fixed-dimension transputer array. This involves using the highly parallel analogue flow diagram representation of the filter for mapping purposes. The transputer implementation is bench-marked against ACSL simulation results for a test system of varying state dimension.

1. Introduction

The trade-offs between the complexity of the control algorithm and the processing speed needed for real-time applications has limited the full exploitation of much of modern, matrix-based control theory. In particular, the Kalman filter, which uses a state space model of a dynamical system to generate recursive optimal state estimates from noisy measurements, requires $O(n^3)$ arithmetic operations for each state update, where n is the state dimension. This has prompted considerable interest in concurrent architectures, such as systolic arrays and transputers, for real-time implementation [1-4]. These have been proposed for the discrete-time form of the Kalman filter with comparatively little attention to the continuous-time domain.

The aim of this paper is to report on the realisation of a continuous-time Kalman filter on an array of transputers. The mapping strategy utilises the analogue flow diagram representation of the filter. Historically this has been used for continuous-time simulation of control systems but it can also provide a highly parallel description due the inherently concurrent operation of the functional blocks [5]. The estimation was bench-marked against ACSL simulation results for a test system of varying state dimensions.

2. Preliminaries

The Kalman-Bucy filter is based on the linear, continuous-time system model defined below :

$$\underline{\dot{x}}(t) = A(t).\underline{x}(t) + B(t).\underline{u}(t) + \underline{w}(t) \qquad \ldots (1)$$

$$\underline{z}(t) = C(t).\underline{x}(t) + \underline{v}(t) \qquad \ldots (2)$$

where $\underline{x}(t)$ is the nth order state vector, $\underline{z}(t)$ is the mth order measurement vector and $\underline{u}(t)$ is the rth order input vector. A(t) is the system matrix, B(t) the input matrix and C(t) the measurement matrix. The vectors $\underline{v}(t)$ and $\underline{w}(t)$ are independent, zero- mean, Gaussian, white noise processes representing the measurement and system noises respectively. These noise sources are uncorrelated and their statistics are described by the respective covariance matrices :

$$E\{ \underline{v}(t).\underline{v}^T(\tau) \} = V(t).\delta(t-\tau)$$
$$E\{ \underline{w}(t).\underline{w}^T(\tau) \} = W(t).\delta(t-\tau)$$
$$E\{ \underline{v}(t).\underline{w}^T(\tau) \} = 0$$

where $\delta(t-\tau)$ is the Dirac delta function.

The Kalman-Bucy filter, which produces the minimum mean-square estimate of the state vector from noisy measurements, is defined by the following equations [6] :

$$\dot{\hat{\underline{x}}}(t) = A(t).\hat{\underline{x}}(t) + B(t).\underline{u}(t) \qquad (3)$$

Here $\hat{\underline{x}}(t)$ is the estimated state vector and the filter gain matrix is given by :

$$K(t) = P(t).C^T(t).V^{-1}(t) \qquad \ldots (4)$$

where P(t) is the estimation error covariance matrix and is obtained by solving the differential Riccati equation :

$$\dot{P}(t) = A(t).P(t) + P(t).A^T(t) - P(t).C^T(t).V^{-1}(t)C^T(t).P(t) + W(t)$$
$$\ldots (5)$$

The test application employed was the state-feedback control of a 4th order, linear missile model moving in the vertical plane against a stationary target [7]. Here the control requirement was to track a ramp trajectory and the estimation problem was to determine the missile states from a single, noisy measurement of height error.

The analogue flow diagram representation of the Kalman-Bucy filter, for this application, is shown in Figs. 1 and 2. Fig. 1 represents the 4 differential equations of the state update corresponding to equation (3) and Fig. 2 represents the 16 differential equations of the Riccati equation (5). These two

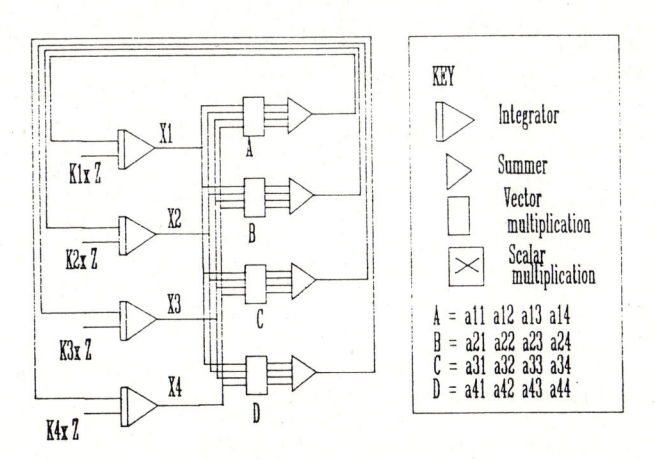

Fig. 1 : Analogue flow diagram for state update

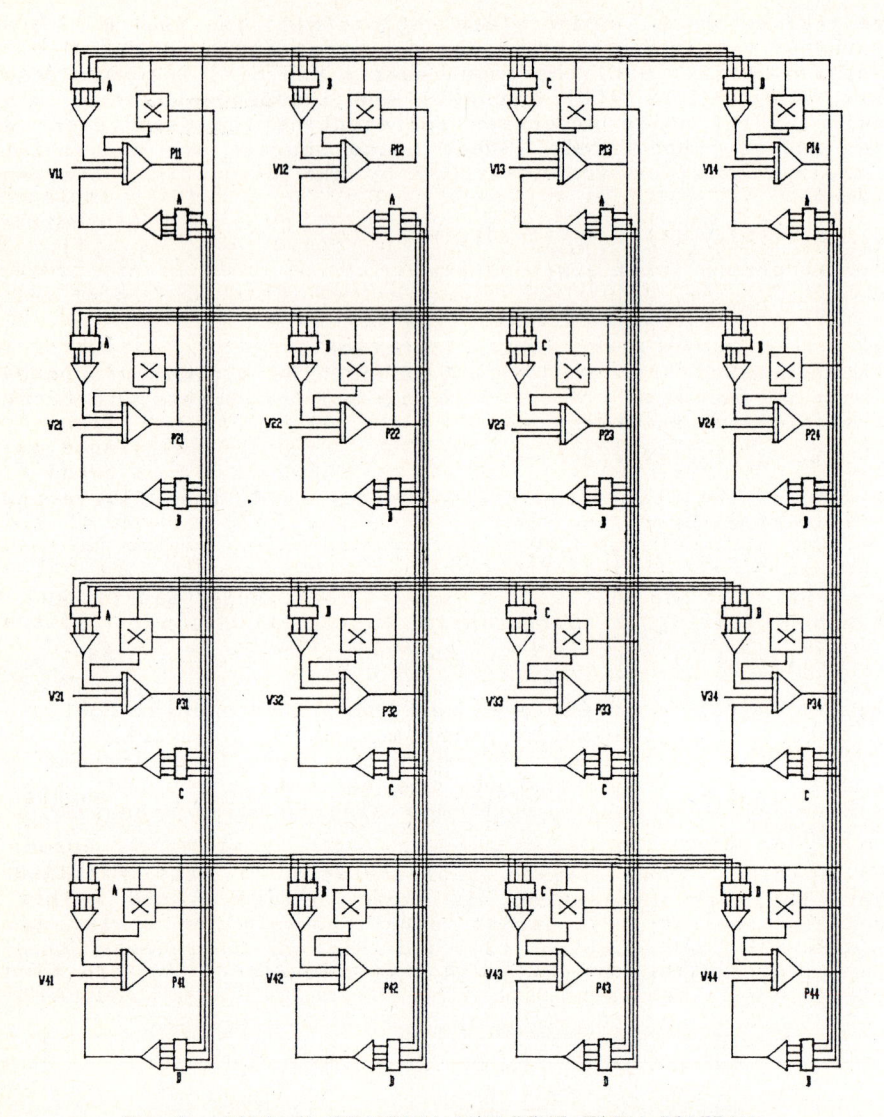

Fig. 2 : RICCATI EQUATION ANALOGUE FLOW DIAGRAM

parts are linked by the filter gain matrix. Higher order estimation problems were produced by multiplying up the test system to achieve a 8th order system with 2 measurements, a 12th order system with 3 measurements etc.

3. Transputer Implementations

Any implementation of a continuous-time system on a digital computer requires the selection of a suitable numerical integration routine for solving the differential equations [8,9]. This choice must consider the trade-offs between the computational burden and the numerical accuracy of the integration procedure.

The Runge-Kutta 4th order integration algorithm, with a step-size of 5 msec, was found to be satisfactory from simulation studies of the filter using a powerful continuous-time simulation package, ACSL, which is hosted on a VAX mainframe computer.

3.1 Single Transputer Implementation

Analogue flow diagram representations can be readily implemented on a transputer by considering each functional block (integrators, summers and gain blocks) as an occam process [5]. This correspondence, with the occam model of concurrent processes communicating via channels, illustrates the high degree of natural parallelism in the flow diagram description.

However such a fine-grained description leads to an inefficient implementation because of the excessive number of parallel processes. To improve efficiency, yet retaining a high degree of parallelism, functional blocks are coalesced into first-order sections. Furthermore, the symmetry of the error covariance matrix means that only the upper-triangular section in Fig. 2 needs to be implemented, so reducing the computational requirements. Applying these techniques to the analogue computer flow diagram of Fig. 2 produces the schematic shown in Fig. 3. This can now be readily implemented on a single transputer. The results, on T414-G20 transputers, in terms of the average time required to produce one state estimate, for varying orders of the system, are illustrated graphically in Fig. 5. Note the rapid reduction in speed of a state update for increasing state dimension.

3.2 Multiple Transputer Implementations

The analogue flow diagrams (Figs. 1 and 2) suggest a multiprocessor implementation involving the state update on one transputer and the Riccati equation partitioned across a transputer network. This partitioning strategy implies a subdivision of the filter equations into a small number of computationally equal processes in order to utilise the target hardware effectively.

The "coarsening" of the analogue representation of the Riccati equation, as described in the last section, reduces the

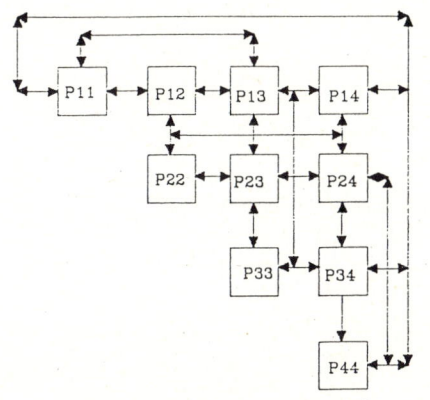

Fig. 3 : Coarse description of Riccati equation analogue computer flow diagram

description to a collection of first-order processes each of which provides the update for one element of the error covariance matrix and which communicates with all other such processes in its row or column. The processes within a row can be further coalesced into a single row-process. This strategy projects the computational structure into a linear set of row processes connected together in a Hamiltonian graph since each row process communicates with every other one.

This projected structure can now be readily realised on a transputer network by assigning row-processes to transputers. However, this assignment must be done with care due to the computational imbalance of the row-processes resulting from the upper triangular section. This is evident with the 4th order Riccati equation which needed to be partitioned across 3 transputers to obtain the best possible computational balance. The resulting transputer network is shown in Fig. 4.

With higher order problems, the interconnectivity of the row-processes facilitated the mapping of non-neighbouring rows onto the same transputer to give a more balanced distribution of computation. The variation in the average state update times with increasing order on T414-G20 transputers is illustrated graphically in Fig. 5.

4. Discussion

The transputer implementations need to be compared to the ACSL simulation bench-mark to determine the accuracy of the results. This showed that the percentage error in the transputer implementations was less than 0.5%, illustrating the effectiveness of using the transputer and the occam programming language for such an application.

The results in Fig. 5 indicate, as expected, that the average time required to produce one state update on a single processor increases exponentially with the order of the problem. Furthermore, the multi-transputer implementations considerably reduced this time.

Speed-up, defined as :

$$\frac{\text{time for implementation on 1 transputers}}{\text{time for implementation on a transputer array}}$$

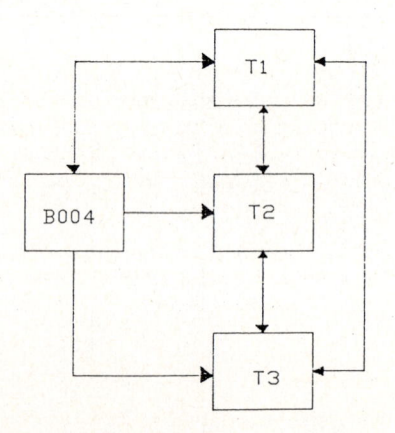

Fig. 4 : Transputer network for 4th order problem

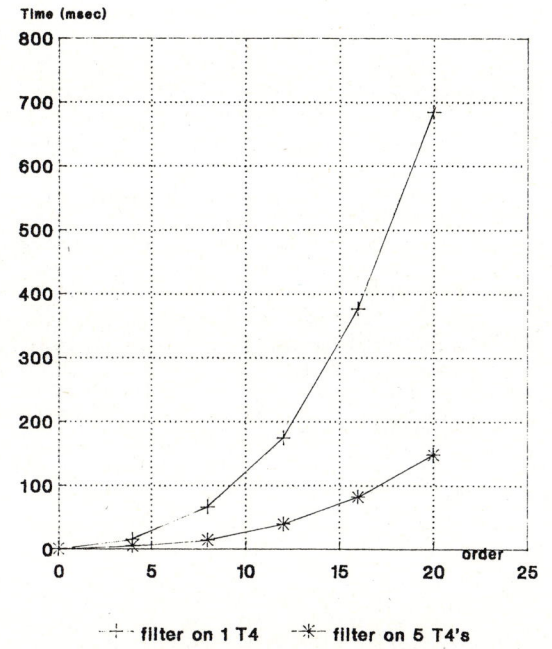

Fig. 5 : Transputer Implementation Results

provides a measure of the effectiveness of the parallel processing approach [10]. Analysing the results showed that the speed-ups ranged from 4.5 to 4.9 with five transputers. The latter figure was obtained with the 8th order problem when the Riccati equation was partitioned equally across four transputers. Similarly, the 4th order multi-transputer implementation provided a speed-up of 3.6 using only four transputers. These, almost linear, speed-up results are attributed to the high interconnectivity of the coarser analogue flow diagram description of the filter and its similar architectural relationship with the target hardware.

5. Conclusion

The analogue flow diagram provided a useful parallel description of the Kalman-Bucy filter which matched the occam model of concurrent processes communicating via channels. Almost linear speed-up figures were obtained for the average state update time on an array of five transputers using a test system of varying state order. More generally, the analogue flow diagram provides a powerful framework for the realisation of continuous-time control systems onto transputer networks and it has the added advantage that it is a familiar representation to control engineers.

References

1. Jover, J.M.; Kailath, T. : "A parallel architecture for Kalman filter measurement update and parameter estimation", Automatica Vol. 22, no. 1, pp 43-57, 1986.
2. Yeh, H.G. : "Systolic implementation on Kalman filters", IEEE

Trans. on Acoustics Speech and Signal Processing, Vol. 36, no. 9, pp 1514-1517, 1988.
3. Gaston, F.M.F; Irwin, G.W : "Systolic approach to square-root information Kalman filtering", Int. J. of Control, Vol.50, no. 1, pp 225-248, 1989.
4. Maguire, L.P; Irwin, G.W : "Transputer implementation of Kalman filters", to be presented at American Control Conference, San Diego, May 1990.
5. Hamblen, J.O : "Parallel continuous system simulation using the transputer", Simulation, pp 249-253, Dec. 1987.
6. Brammer, K; Siffling, G : "Kalman-Bucy Filters", Artech House Inc., 1989.
7. Roddy, D.J.; Irwin, G.W.; Wilson, H. : "Approaches to roll-loop design for BTT CLOS guidance", IEE Proc. Pt. D, Vol. 132, no. 6 pp 268-276, 1985.
8. Davis, P.J; Rabinowitz, P.P. : "Methods of numerical integration", 2nd Edition, Academic Press, 1984.
9. Krosel, S.M; Milner, E.J : "Application of integration algorithms in a parallel processing environment for the simulation of Jet engines ", Annual Simulation Symposium, pp 121-143, 1982.
10. Modi, J.J : "Parallel algorithms and matrix computations", Oxford Applied Maths and Computing Series, 1988.

Acknowledgements

Liam Maguire would like to acknowledge the financial support of the Department of Education for Northern Ireland and the Institute of Advanced Microelectronics.

IMPLEMENTATION OF A MULTIVARIABLE ADAPTIVE CONTROLLER BY A TRANSPUTER BASED ARCHITECTURE

L. FORTUNA, G. NUNNARI
Istituto di Elettrotecnica ed Elettronica
Universita' di Catania
Viale A. Doria, 6
95125 Catania (Italy)

Abstract The aim of this paper is to show the peculiarities of a transputer based parallel architecture for the implementation of multivariable adaptive control algorithms, which can be very useful in controlling MIMO systems with fast dynamical behavior such as in robotics or in tracking applications. In particular aclassical multivariable control algorithm, as proposed by Koivo, is considered. The parallelization strategy is outlined and the implementation, using a transputer array composed by four T800 transputer is illustrated. The experimental results are reported and discussed referring to the typical algorithm parameters. Finally the suitability of the implementation is shown with an example.
The criteria which have been described to obtain the parallelization of the described algorithm can be easily applied to other parallel control strategies.

1. Introduction

Several multivariable adaptive control schemes have been proposed in the literature in the last few years and many papers have been published where the analysis of robustness properties has been widely investigated. However, usually the computation problems underlying such control strategies are not emphasized enough, even if in some cases they can lead to algorithms unimplementable by low cost single microprocessor based systems, despite the increased capability of present day VLSI technology. Recently the use of systolic-like arrays to implement high-speed RLS estimators has been proposed [1] . However, it seems that this kind of VLSI structures, which has been introduced to speed-up simple operations, such as the matrix by matrix product, are not oriented to parallelize complex control strategies where several different tasks have to be implemented. In fact it is well known that the drawback of the systolic architectures is that their fixed function allied to their neighbor connectivity, and hence long throughput delay, intrinsically restricts their application area [2]. Indeed, for control applications the MIMD (Multiple Instruction, Multiple Data) parallel architectures are more suitable. Such a kind of processor arrays allows that different algorithms can be performed simultaneously and also each processor element can be a powerful one capable of executing a complex task. In a previous paper [3] the Authors described the use of a Transputer based parallel architecture for the implementation of self-tuning control algorithms for SISO systems. The aim of this paper is to illustrate the peculiarities of such a kind of parallel architectures for the realization of multivariable adaptive control algorithms which can represent a solution for controlling MIMO systems with fast dynamical behavior.

2. Hardware and Software Framework

The particular transputer array used to implement the parallelization of adaptive control algorithms made-up by a INMOS B009 card and four T800 transputers is shown in Fig. 1.
In the same figure two cards, an IDM 534/1 Transputer Multi-channel ADC and an IDB 534/2 transputer Multi-channel DAC, which assure the interfaces between the external world and the controller, are also represented. All the software routines required to implement the controller described in this paper have been coded by using the OCCAM 2 concurrent programming language.

3. An Outline of the Control Algorithm

In this paper we consider a typical multivariable controller as

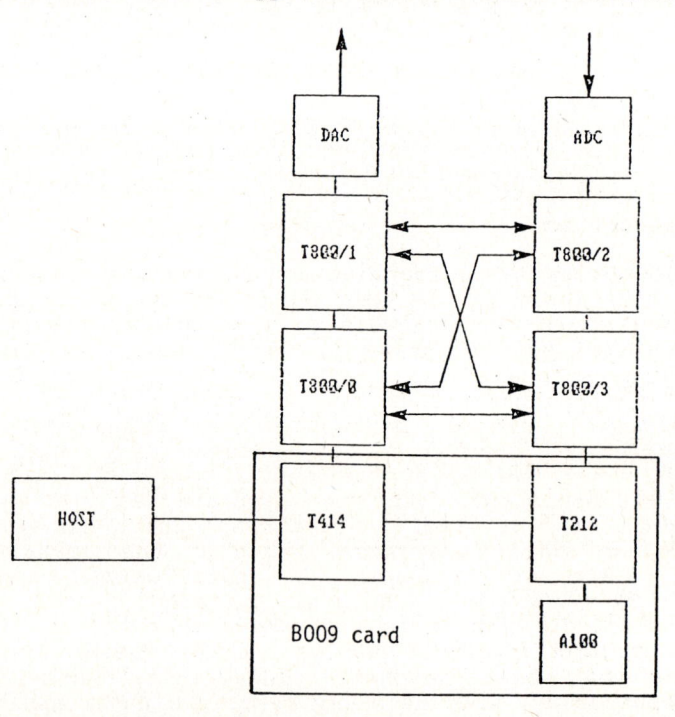

Fig. 1 - Hardware framework for executing the Transputer development system and for implementing the multivariable controller

proposed by Koivo [4] for MIMO systems represented in ARMAX form:

$$A(q^{-1}) \, y(t) = B(q^{-1}) \, u(t-k) + d + C(q^{-1}) \, \xi(t)$$

It has been proved, that the optimal control law, which minimizes an appropriate index, is given by:

$$G_0 u(t) = - \left[\sum_{i \geq 0} F_i y(t-i) + \sum_{i \geq 1} G_i u(t-i) + \sum_{i \geq 0} H_i w(t-i) + \gamma \right]$$

where $w(t) \in R^m$ is the known reference signal vector, $y(t) \in R^m$ the output signal vector; and $F_0, F_1, \ldots G_0, G_1, \ldots H_0, H_1, \ldots \gamma$ unknown matrices. Defining the matrix

$$\Theta = \left[\vartheta_1, \ldots \vartheta_i \ldots \vartheta_m \right] := \left[F_0, F_1, \ldots G_0, G_1, \ldots H_0, H_1, \ldots \gamma \right]^T$$

the unknown parameters ϑ_i can be recursively estimated as follows:

$$\hat{\vartheta}_i(t+1) = \hat{\vartheta}_i(t) + K(t) \left[\phi_i(t) - x(t-k) \, \hat{\vartheta}_i(t) \right] \quad (i = 1, \ldots m) \quad (1)$$

$$K(t) = P(t) \, x^T(t-k) \left[1 + x(t-k) \, P(t) \, x^T(t-k) \right]^{-1} \quad (2)$$

$$P(t+1) = \left[P(t) - K(t) \left[1 + x(t-k) \, P(t) \, x^T(t-k) \right] K^T(t) \right] / \beta \quad (3)$$

where $x(t)$ is the data vector defined and $\phi_i(t)$ are the elements of the vector

$$\phi(t) = y(t) - R \, w(t-k) + \lambda \, u(t-k).$$

In the expressions above P and R are polynomial matrices.

4. Parallelization Strategy

The guide line of our approach in parallelizing the control algorithm can be summarized as follows:

1) The whole control procedure is partitioned, i.e. a number of segments well defined from the functional point of view are recognized. This is a condition for minimizing the data flow between transputers. In fact even when links between processors make the data exchange fast, these exchanges are slow compared with the internal computation speed of the T800 processors. Data dependencies between tasks are accurately pointed out.

2) The execution times of each code segment are determined by accurate measurements and, whenever possible, analytically, in order to find the dependencies of the execution time on the control algorithms parameters. This information is useful for making correct decisions in balancing the computational load between the processors.

3) A set S of possible parallel solutions is hypothesized and represented by graphs, referring to a parallel architecture

based on n processors. Let t_{cp} be the time required to execute the critical path, which is considered as the shortest possible execution time. The best parallelization solution is the one which minimizes t_{cp}, over the set S.
Let

$$\hat{t}_{cp} = \min_{S} t_{cp}$$

The speed-up ratio is then computed as:

$$S = \frac{t_{sp}}{\hat{t}_{cp}}$$

where t_{sp} is the required time for a single-processor based architecture to execute the whole algorithm.

The following assertions are true for the Koivo's multivariable control algorithm:

a) the effort in computing K(t) and P(t+1) is greater than the total effort required to perform the remaining steps in the control algorithm. In fact the complexity in computing any of this two arrays is $O(\rho^2)$, where ρ is the dimension of the vector x(t), while for the remaining steps is $O(\rho \cdot m)$, or $O(\rho)$. It is to observe that $m \ll \rho$.

b) the computation of K(t) must be completed before to start the computation of P(t+1). This is the main bottleneck in parallelizing this particular control algorithm which leads to a significant limitation of the attainable speed-up.

Based on these considerations and looking at expressions (1÷3), to improve the execution time of the parallel implementation, we find that the best solution consists in distributing the computation of the product $P(t) \cdot x^T(t-k)$ over n-1 transputer as schematically shown in Fig. 2, where n=4 is assumed.
The corresponding synchronization graph is reported in Fig. 3.

5. Results

The experimental results are shown in Table I for typical values of ρ and m.
The time values (in milliseconds) indicated in this table for the algorithm sequential version refer to the execution on a T800 processor, while for the parallel version refer to a four T800

TABLE I

m	ρ	time (msec) seq. vers	time (msec) par. vers.	speed-up factor
2	11	2.60	1.30	2.00
2	13	3.30	1.69	1.95
2	15	4.12	2.20	1.87
2	17	5.00	2.77	1.80
3	19	6.78	3.54	1.91
4	25	11.93	6.05	1.97

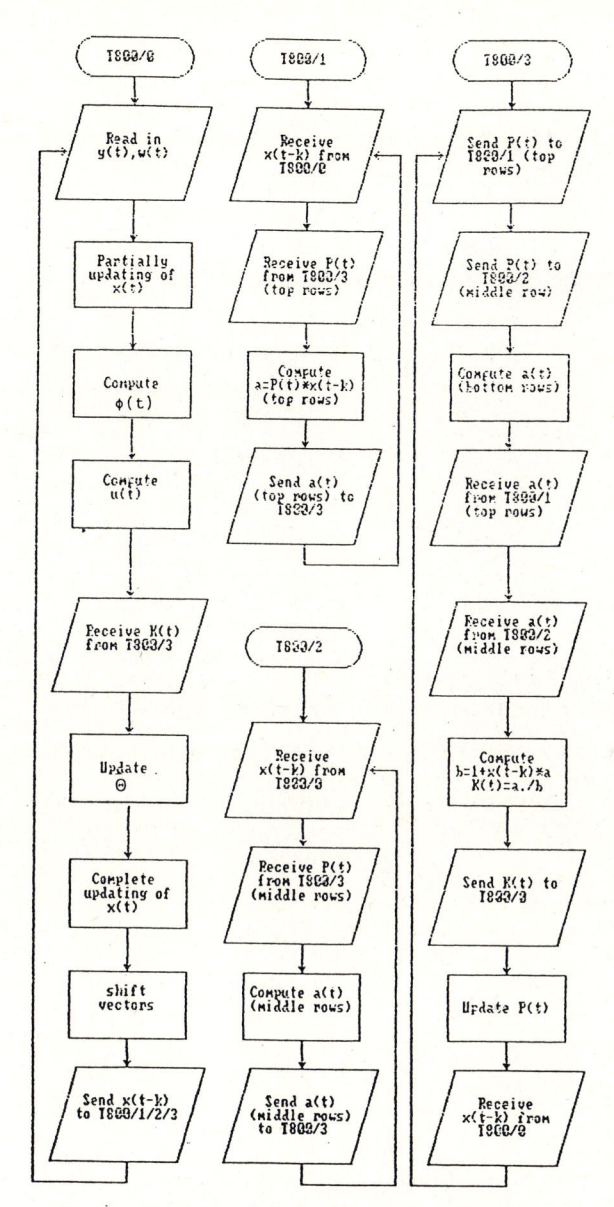

Fig. 2 - Flow-chart representing the sub processes executed by each individual transputer of the array shown in Fig. 1.

transputer array.
We have found that for a given value of m, better results in terms of speed-up are obtained for low values of ρ. However for a set of m values, the speed up is quite independent from this parameter.

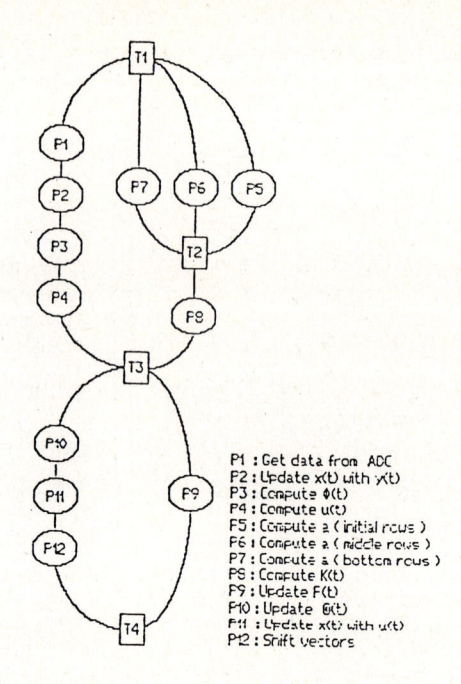

Fig. 3 - Synchronization graph of the parallel control algorithm

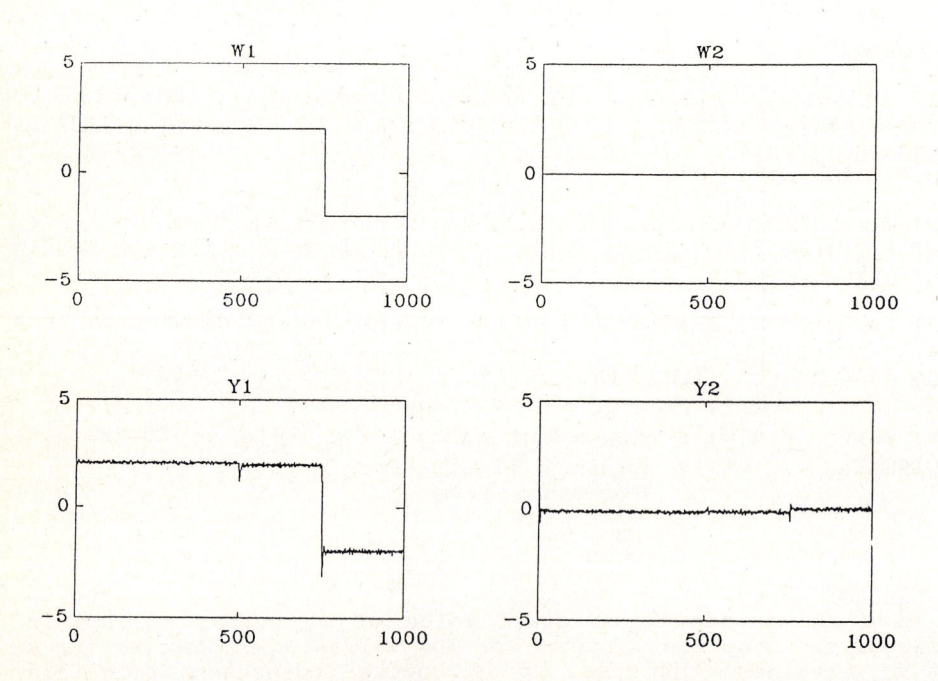

P1 : Get data from ADC
P2 : Update x(t) with y(t)
P3 : Compute φ(t)
P4 : Compute u(t)
P5 : Compute a (initial rows)
P6 : Compute a (middle rows)
P7 : Compute a (bottom rows)
P8 : Compute K(t)
P9 : Update F(t)
P10 : Update θ(t)
P11 : Update x(t) with u(t)
P12 : Shift vectors

Fig. 4 - Reference and output signal for the described example.

The goodness of the implementation is shown by an example where a nonminumum-phase system with an uncertain parameter is controlled:

$$y(t) = A_1 y(t-1) + B_0 u(t-1) + B_1 u(t-2) + \xi(t)$$

where:

$$A_1 = \begin{bmatrix} 0.9 & -0.5 \\ -0.5 & 0.2 \end{bmatrix}; \quad B_0 = \begin{bmatrix} 0.2 & 1 \\ 0.25 & 0.2 \end{bmatrix}; \quad B_1 = \begin{bmatrix} 1 & 0 \\ 0 & 1 \end{bmatrix};$$

$$E\{ \xi(t) \xi^T(t) \} = \text{diag} \{ 0.1, 0.1 \}.$$

A variation in $A_1(1,1)$ from 0.9 to 0.5 has been supposed in correspondence of t=500. In Fig. 4 the simulation results are reported showing a satisfactorily performance of the controller.

6. Conclusions

A parallel scheme, based on a transputer hardware architecture, to implement multivariable adaptive controllers has been proposed. This approach appears promising to implement high performances controllers for systems with fast dynamics such as in robotics or in tracking applications.
The criteria which have been described to obtain the parallelization of the described algorithm can be easily applied to other parallel control strategies.

Reference

[1] Chisci L. (1988). High-speed RLS parameter estimation by systolic-like arrays ", Proc. Application of Advanced Computing Concepts and Techniques in Control Engineering, pp.471-485,Spring-Verlag,Berlin.

[2] Jones S.(1988). Parallel Processing Computer Architectures, IEE Workshop on Parallel Processing and Control - The Transputer and other architectures, Digest N.1988/95, London, 1/1 - 1/10.

[3] Fortuna L., Gallo A., Nunnari G., (1989).Implementation of a Self-Tuning Regulator by Using a Transputer Network, Proc. of the IFAC Second Symposium on LowCost Automation, Milan.

[4] Koivo, H.N., (1980). A Multivariable Self-Tuning Controller, Automatica, vol.16, pp. 351-366.

The Integration of Transputers into VMEbus Systems for Computationally-Bounded Real Time Control Applications

by C D James

The author is currently with British Aerospace plc,
Space Systems, Filton, Bristol, BS12 7QW

Abstract. This paper reports on the work conducted by AEA Technology, Culham Laboratory, (ACAP Department) to assess the Transputer's ability to accommodate requirement changes and performance upgrades for existing VMEbus, 680x0, OS9 control systems. In particular, such an upgrade for a robotic teleoperation facility developed for the European Space Agency to investigate earth based operator performance in satellite servicing type tasks is discussed. The similar input/output topologies of CSP design theory and control engineering block diagram design methodology, illustrated in Figure 0, combined with the control engineering background of ACAP staff has resulted in a process farm orientated design architecture.

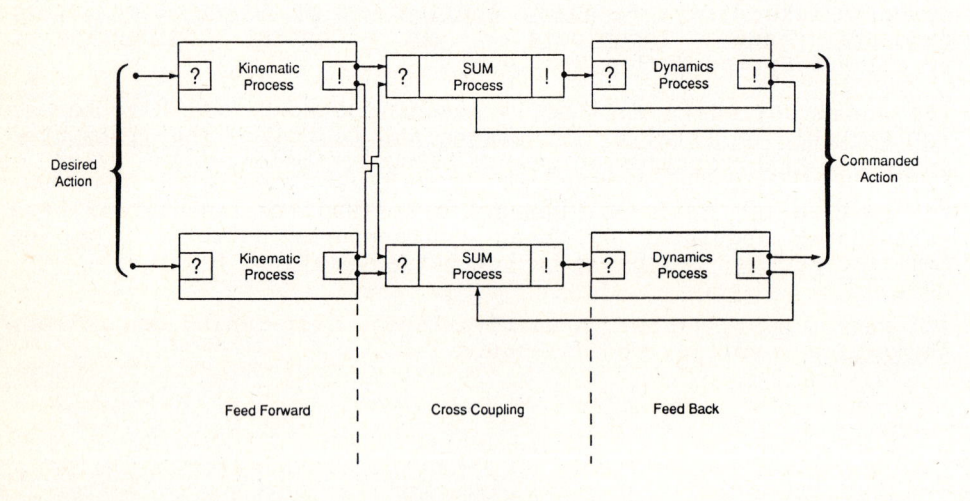

(Occam/Control Engineering)
Block Diagram

Figure 0

1. Introduction

The ACAP Group was established in 1985 to undertake Advanced Control and Power projects for high tech industry. Work reported here is closely connected to one such contract undertaken for the European Space Agency on Telerobotic Spacecraft Servicing. In 1986 ACAP standardised on the VMEbus combined with the OS9 operating system. The wide range of digital and analogue I/O VME boards complemented the real time capabilities of OS9 and, what was then, high performance of the 68020 microprocessor. The teleoperation and control study number 2 (TELCO2) undertaken for ESA in 1986 used this technology for a joystick driven robotic testbed. This is capable of simulating the delayed robot response aspects of low earth orbit servicing operations using an industrial robot and closed circuit TV.

As with all engineering projects, but more expectedly with this prototype project, the system requirements changed. Unlike most projects, where the changes occur just before or just after delivery to the customer, our change in requirements came about in the form of a follow-on contract teleoperation and control study number 3 (TELCO3). It was immediately obvious that TELCO3 required duplication of certain existing algorithms, which would defeat the processing capabilities of the existing single 68020 system. We chose to avoid the known problems of using multiple 68020 OS9 systems and not risk just scraping through with a 68030. Instead a transputer solution was proposed both for the TELCO3 project and to enable evaluation for future ACAP projects.

This paper reports on prototype work conducted to prove that the transputer could indeed be used for the TELCO3 contract. It has highlighted the simple, and immensely powerful, adaptability of transputer software/hardware systems to requirement changes thereby providing an attack on the heart of the engineering problem through the simplicity of the CSP theory and its OCCAM translation.

2. TELCO2 Testbed

2.1 Requirements Resume

2.1.1 Upgrade Capability

The new testbed had to be flexible in its design such that future extensions and developments can be carried out effectively by ESTEC. This flexibility should permit development of the testbed to such a level that it can be used ultimately as a development or training simulator, and possibly even as a back-up system to an operational ground based RTS workstation.

2.1.2 Number of Controllable Degrees of Freedom at any One Time

It is important for the purposes of the investigation that all six degrees of freedom can be controlled simultaneously. The robot end effector will be required to be translated and rotated in the X, Y and Z axes. This 'resolved motion rate control' will require the integration of simultaneous movements from all degrees of freedom if the end effector is to make accurate translational and rotational movements.

2.1.3 Time Delays

Three time delays are identified for use during the series of investigations. These are:
a) Human Perceptual Threshold Time Delay (around 60ms)
b) Human Control Disruption Threshold (around 200ms)
c) Maximum Delay likely to be experienced in a Space Teleoperation System (around 1.01 secs)

2.2 Testbed implementation

These requirements resulted in the testbed shown in figure 1. The standard ASEA IRB6 controller proved unsuitable in three respects.

a) The source code is not available to permit modification to the controller functioning.
b) It required an ancillary switch to respond to a six degree of freedom joystick (or a 2 x 3 joystick configuration). It is therefore unable to respond in six degrees of freedom simultaneously.
c) It has an inherent 200ms time delay between commanded action and robot response.

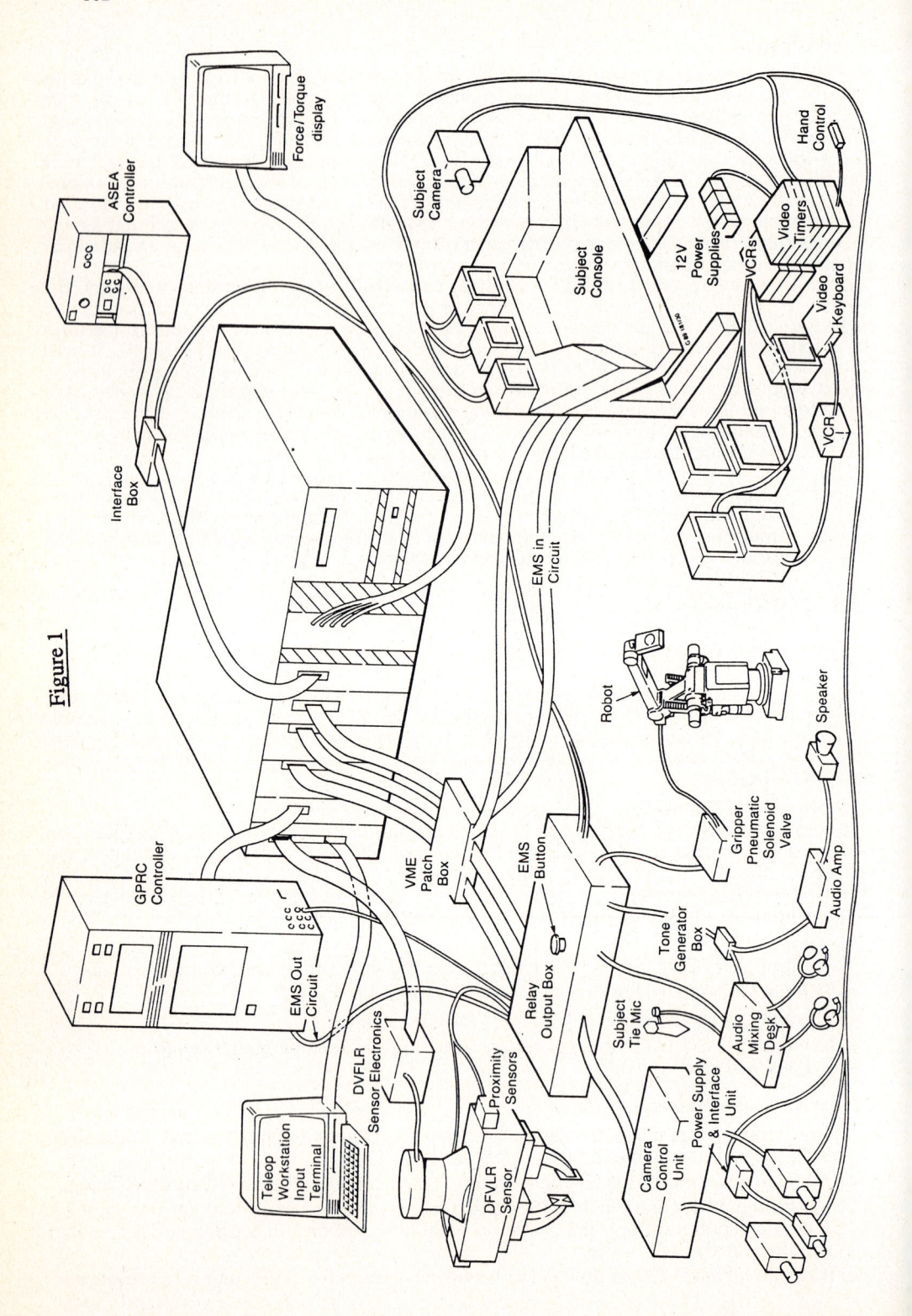

Figure 1

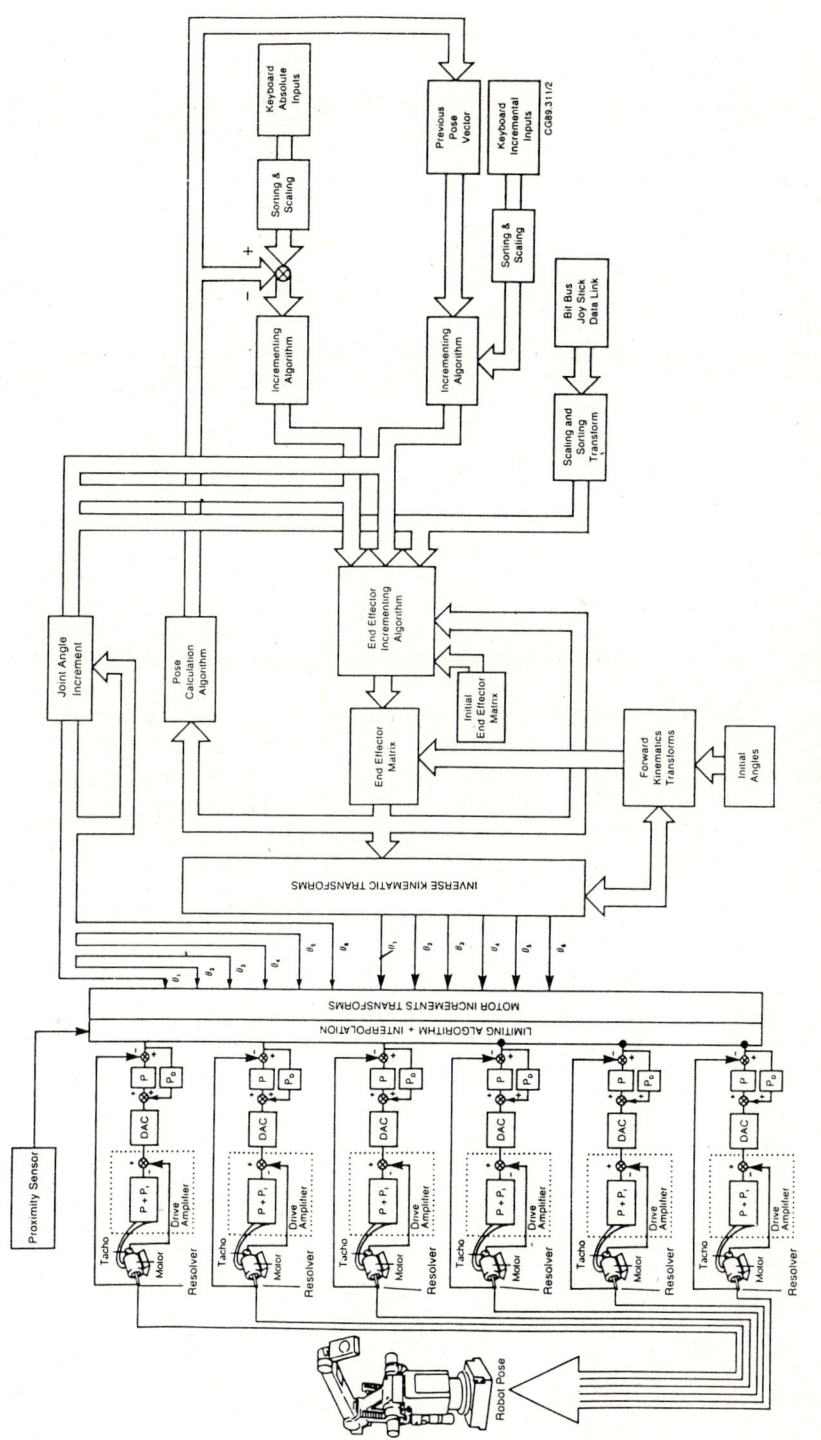

Figure 2 GPRC Control System Schematic

Culham developed and supplied to ESA a General Purpose Robot Controller (GPRC) for their IRB60 robot to overcome these shortcomings. This controller was based on VMEbus 68020 and OS9 technology, connected to the workstation VMEbus 68020 via a bitbus serial link for robot commanding. The essential operations performed by the controller are shown in figure 2 for the prototype system software. The software was known to take 7ms out of the 10ms OS9 time slice.

3. TELCO3 TESTBED

3.1 Requirement summary

3.1.1 The teleoperator workstation will be modified to enable local impedance control in the vicinity of the primitive task elements.

3.1.2 The teleoperator workstation will be modified to enable discrete switching from low earth orbit type time delays (1 sec) to data relay satellite (5 sec) type time delays, and back a number of times, during the execution of a primitive task.

3.1.3 The teleoperator workstation will be modified to provide the operator with a graphical display of the robot's position and orientation, with regard to primitive task elements, of the robot end effector in two instances simultaneously.

Instance 1: The graphical robot being driven directly from the joysticks with no time delay. Known as the robot predicted pose.

Instance 2: The graphical robot being driven by the joysticks after the joystick data has been delayed by the simulated time delay. The graphical robot motion will correspond with actual robot motion. It is therefore known as the robot actual pose.

In *Instance 1*, only the final two links and the gripper of the robot will be depicted to ease clutter and simplify processing.

3.1.4 The teleoperator workstation will facilitate the use of a commercially available direct voice input (DVI) system for:

a) Camera control

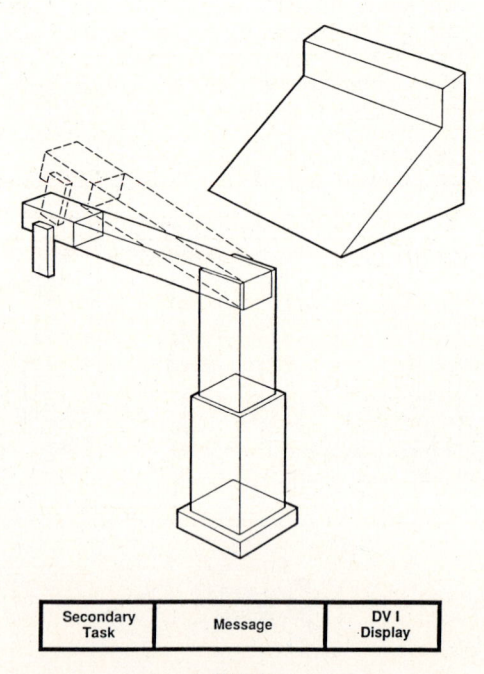

Figure 3

b) Graphic switching
c) Gripper switching
d) Secondary task identification acknowledgement by the operator
e) Predictive graphic control

3.2 Implications on TELCO3 Implementation

The local impedance control, time delay change over and DVI requirements are easily achievable using existing TELCO2 68020 system. Provision of the predictive graphic does not imply that robot joint angles have to be available at the teleoperator workstation (TWS) computer in order to orientate the oblongs of figure 3 for drawing.

Here the solid lines represent the actual robot and the dotted line the predicted robot. It would be possible to implement the following algorithms of figure 2 solely on the TWS system and operate GPRC in a joint coordinated frame.

a) Tool/World Coordinate End Effector Matrix update
b) Inverse Kinematics
c) Motor Increments Transforms
d) Joint Limiting
e) Forward Kinematics·

This would lead to a more complicated TWS TELCO3 software and modified GPRC software. Instead, the GPRC robot angles are returned and used with undelayed joystick data in duplicate routines. This achieves parallel computation of the predicted and actual robot angles on the TWS and GPRC machines respectively, thereby achieving a more balanced loading of the available resources.

The hardware implications were simple as seen by comparison of figure 1 with figure 4, suffice to say that the Parsytec RS422 link conversion allowed our standard 10 metres between equipment at 20 Mbits/sec.

3.3 Architectural Layout

The similar input/output topologies of CSP design theory and control engineering block diagram design methodology, illustrated in figure 0, combined with the control engineering background of ACAP staff resulted in a process oriented farm, rather than a data oriented farm, architecture illustrated in figure 5. The existing 68020 processor was allocated the man machine interface (MMI) task, the link to the robot controller and communication with the transputer network via an OS9 version of the afserver task. The afserver was developed a part of this work.

The Parsytec BBK-V2 VMEbus bridgehead card was logically allocated the analogue and digital I/O, whilst the 2 T8 transputers on the Parsytec MTM2 card were used to simulate the time delay and perform any pre-processing of data required for the graphics calculation process. One also performed the graphics calculations. The Parsytec GDS card was simply to provide the graphics monitor display. It was anticipated that all processes other than the communications servers would be written in C.

4. TELCO3 Proof of Concept

The eventual architecture that emerged to prove the proposed solution was feasible is shown in figure 6. The differences occurred courtesy of the simplicity of programming in OCCAM and the usable software supplied by Parsytec. The alien filer/afserver provided the C I/O when connected to our C "equivalent OCCAM processes " correctly, and the comms servers provided useful timing capabilities. Adaptation of our existing C routines proved to be simpler than anticipated and resulted in the following processes.

bridgehead server C
  Accessing the digital and analogue VME cards, passing the joystick data to the OS9 process afserver and to the joy.to.angles process. The afserver forms the link to the GPRC bitbus serial link.

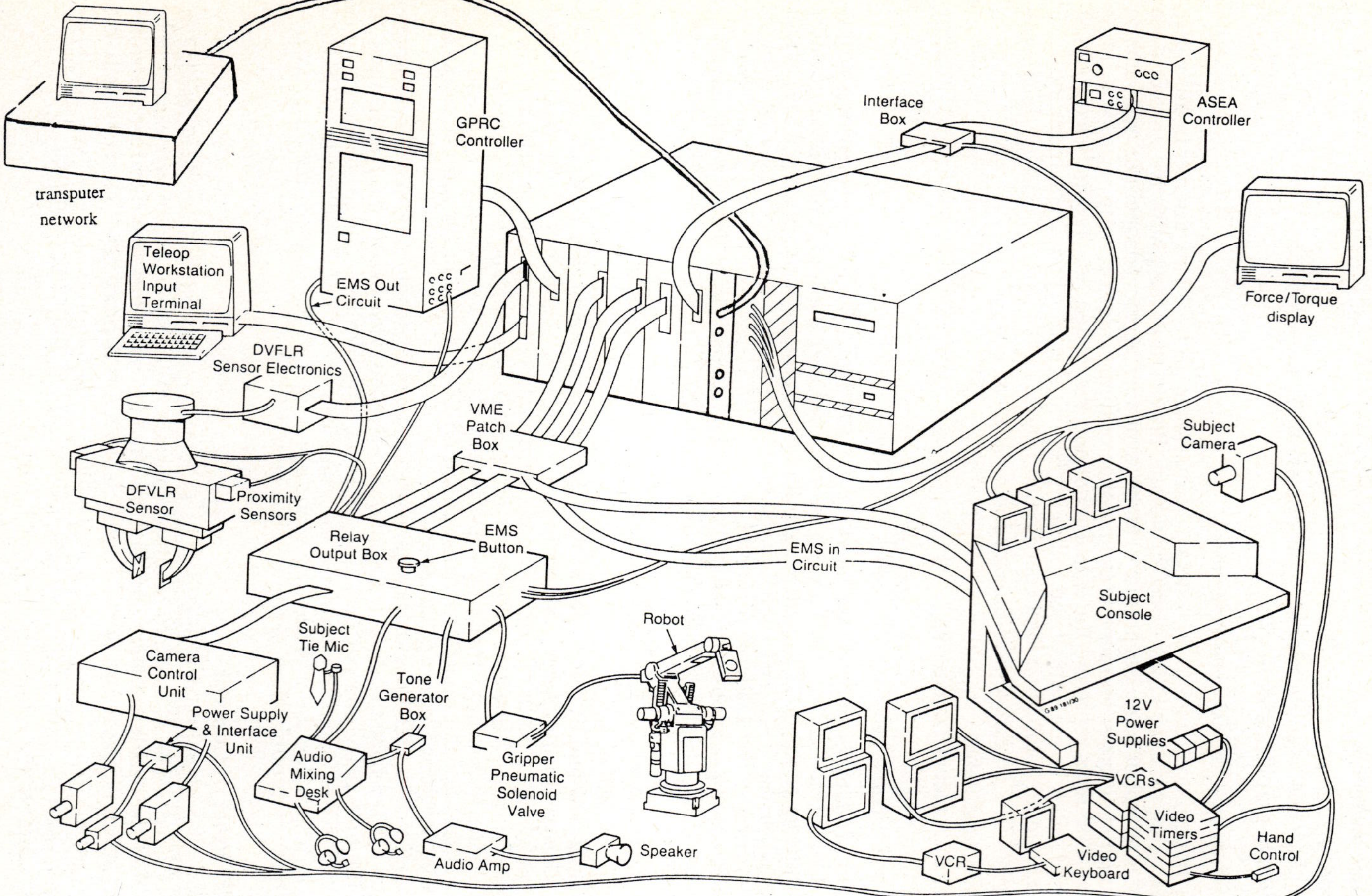
transputer network
GPRC Controller
Interface Box
ASEA Controller
Teleop Workstation Input Terminal
EMS Out Circuit
Force/Torque display
DVFLR Sensor Electronics
VME Patch Box
DFVLR Sensor
Proximity Sensors
Subject Camera
Relay Output Box
EMS Button
EMS in Circuit
Subject Console
Robot
Subject Tie Mic
Camera Control Unit
Tone Generator Box
Power Supply & Interface Unit
12V Power Supplies
Audio Mixing Desk
Gripper Pneumatic Solenoid Valve
VCRs
Video Timers
Speaker
Audio Amp
VCR
Video Keyboard
Hand Control

Figure 4

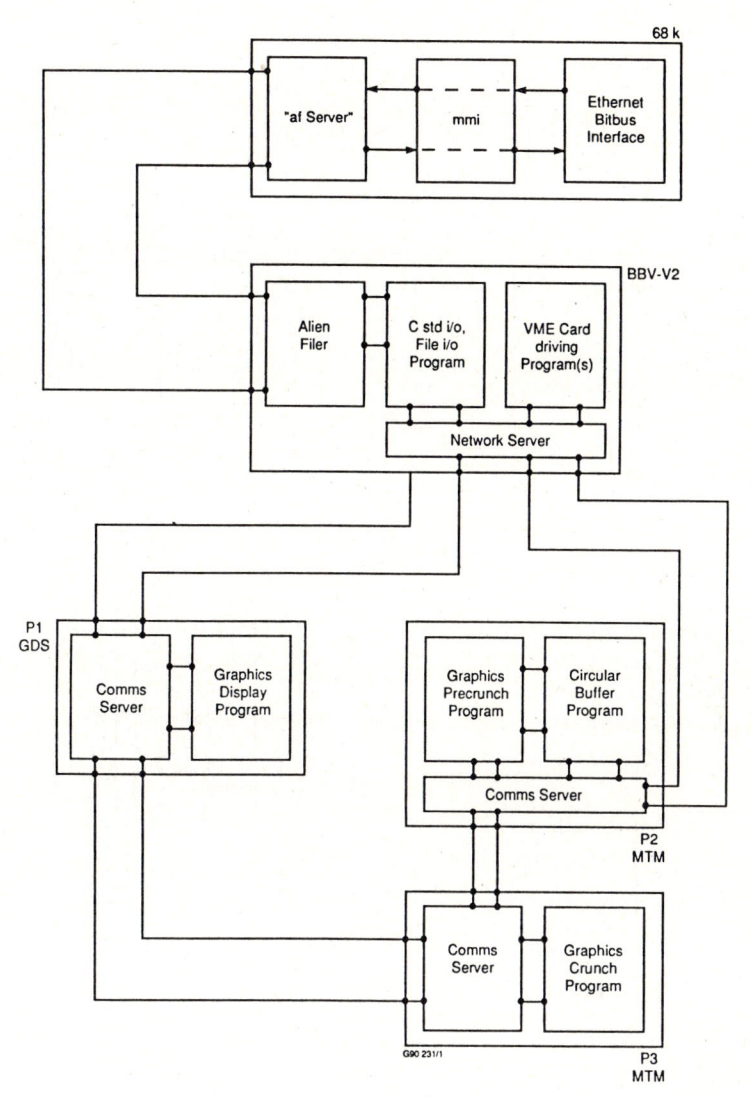

Figure 5

joy.to.angles C
  Takes the joystick values and stores them in a circular buffer for time delay simulation. Time delayed joystick data is converted to angular demands on the graphical robot, via a kinetic algorithm, before transmission to the angles.to.lines process.

angles.to.lines OCCAM
  Takes in the relative angular rotations of each robot link and the viewing angle, before computing the required beginning and end screen coordinates for each line. It passes these values to the robotdraw process in a block format.

robotdraw OCCAM
  Takes the screen coordinates buffer and plots straight lines between beginning and end points.

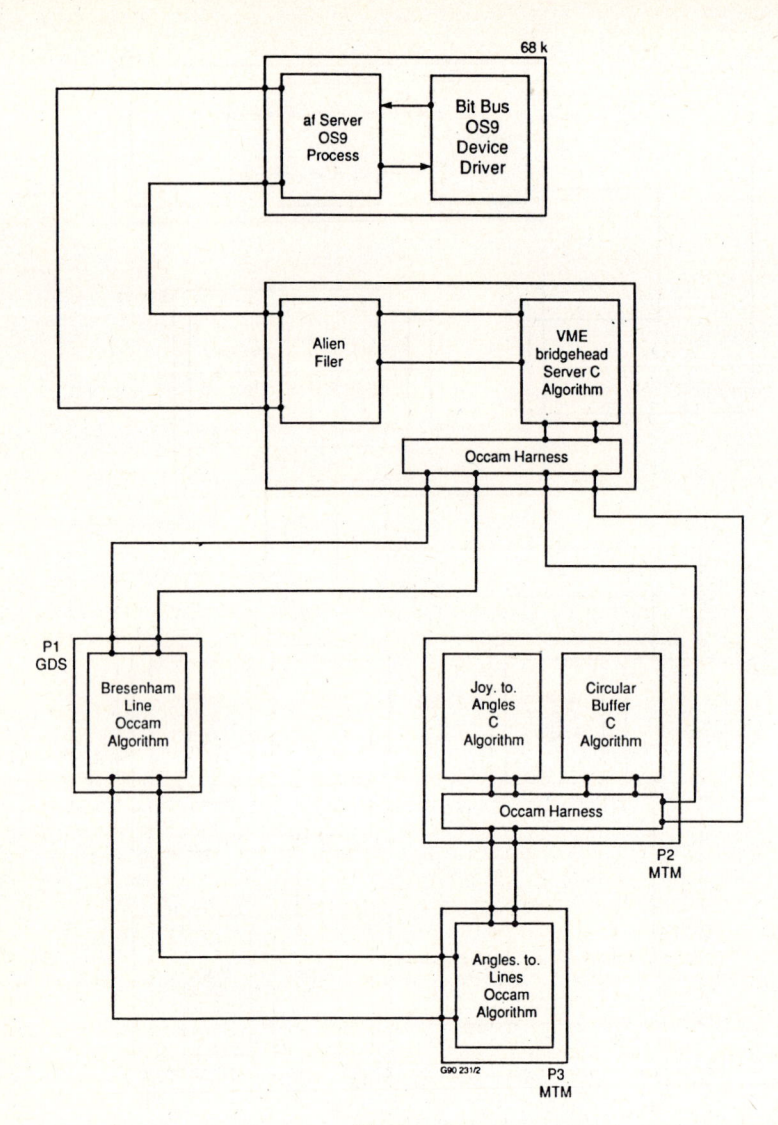

Figure 6

The drawing of the robots proved to take approximately 70ms whilst the robot controller required and provided data every 10ms. This meant that the joy.to.angle kinematics algorithm condensed the input data before outputing, and the robot draw process operated on a complete buffer of data. The essential features of these processes was derived with the following structure in mind.

PAR

... Worker Process

... Buffer Process

... Gluing Process

... Delay Process

The process... Gluing Process requires the architectural structure:

ALT

(from .previous. transputer ? data)
... Send data to buffer

(from .worker. process ? request)
... Ask buffer process to unload to worker

(from .delay. process ? EMS)
... Default actions

If the worker process on the previous transputer naturally ran faster than the worker process, the buffer process had to operate a condensing (averaging) algorithm. If the worker process on the previous transputer naturally ran slower than the worker process, the buffer process had to operate an interpolating algorithm.

5. CONCLUSIONS

The raison d'etre of the transputer is to implement the OCCAM2 language programme model (ref1). The raison d'etre of the OCCAM2 language is to implement parallel computing by means of the theory of Communicating Sequential Processors (ref 2).

This elegant theory is based on sound engineering principles and has resulted in both hardware and software elements that are designed for building parallel computing machinery. It is this designed-in expandability that can be invaluable in an engineering environment, since most systems throughout their full life cycle have to be adjusted to meet new requirements.

It is therefore anticipated than the transputer and primarily OCCAM2 based systems will be considerably cheaper to maintain, whether the requirement changes occur in the design phase or operational phase.

The OCCAM2 language itself is particularly simple with few control construct and data types. This is in marked contrast to the other CSP based multitasking language Ada; it is felt that a precursory design in OCCAM2 as a pseudo code language would aid immensely the parallel processing aspects of an Ada designers solution.

The folding editor supplied with the Transputer Development System (TDS) tends to encourage the production of top down self documenting designs, that are consistent with the software engineering ideals of

a) Understandability
b) Modifiability
c) Abstraction
d) Information Hiding
e) Modularity
f) Localisation
g) Uniformity
h) Completeness

Unlike Ada, the designer is not forced to adhere to these ideals. Used correctly, the folding editor can greatly increase the productivity of software design and implementation.

OCCAM2 provides easy access to hardware address locations and simple implementation of multitasking, whilst the transputer provides two levels of priority, 64us and 1us time slicing for low and high priority respectively. These elements support the software engineering ideal of efficiency, whilst the mathematical provability of CSP designs supports reliability and confirmability. Research on a 3 transputer system (Smiths Associates Ltd) has shown that a genuine No Single Point Failure System can be constructed.

The network analyser supplied with the TDS can be used to examine the point (on any processor) in the source code where a process halted, and also inspect variables placed at chosen locations. This allows effective debugging of transputer networks by use of break points, but does involve recompilation.

The VME based system described in this report has been shown to be suitable for implementation of the Teleoperation and Control Study 3 requirements. The system has been configured in a similar manner to that of TELCO3 and has been used for

a) Control of Camera Pan/Tilt Servos
b) Indicative lamp displays
c) Joystick analogue data acquisition
d) Digital data acquisition
e) Drive of predicted/actual calibrated graphical robots

The integration with the conventional OS9 systems has taken approximately six man months of effort and has integrated, with relative ease, existing conventional C algorithms with the main body OCCAM2 code.

References

1. OCCAM2 Reference Manual
ISBN 0-13-629312-3
INMOS Ltd

2. Communicating Sequential Processes
ISBN 0-13-153289-8

Acknowledgements

This work was conducted by AEA Technology on a duplicate of the ESA robotic testbed, at Culham Laboratory. It has been in support of the ESA teleoperation and control program.

Marketbroad Communications and Parsytec's UK distributor, Dean Microsystems, have encouraged and assisted in the writing and production of this paper.

A TRANSPUTER-BASED FAULT-TOLERANT ARCHITECTURE FOR GAS TURBINE ENGINE CONTROL

H.A. Thompson and P.J. Fleming
University of Wales, Bangor
Gwynedd LL57 1UT

Abstract. This paper describes the implementation of operational fault tolerance using transputer arrays for gas turbine engine control. Two such High Integrity Controllers are described which highlight the current architectural constraints of transputer hardware.

1. Introduction

With the ever increasing performance requirements being demanded from aircraft systems the need for parallel processing to accomplish real-time system goals has now been found to be highly desirable. In addition to this, the need for increased monitoring and safety checking also introduces a major software burden upon the control computers. In order to meet current performance demands aircraft which are inherently unstable are being designed which rely on highly complex digital fly-by-wire control systems for successful operation. The loss of a controller in such systems (even for a short period of time) can be catastrophic. Thus there is much interest in producing fault tolerant systems for these safety-critical applications.

In this paper a collaborative project, with Rolls-Royce Military Aero-Engines (Bristol), investigating the use of transputers to provide the necessary processing power to meet future demands for more complex engine control strategies and increased health monitoring while at the same time exploiting the inherent redundancy in a parallel system for fault tolerance, is described. Three main areas of investigation have been performed:-

- Mapping of Engine/Controller Simulations onto transputers
- Integration of reheat control into the main engine control
- Implementation of a transputer based High Integrity Controller

This paper concentrates on aspects of introducing operational fault tolerance into gas turbine engine controllers using transputer arrays to produce a High Integrity Controller. This is the primary concern when considering safety-critical applications. During the course of the project advantages of the Occam language and restrictions imposed by the current transputer hardware have been highlighted and these are discussed in this paper.

2. Design Constraints

In aircraft systems triple modular redundancy (TMR) is the norm due to the fault masking properties it provides, preventing propagation of failures throughout the system [1,2]. Powerplants, although vital to the aircraft's operation, in general, only use a dual redundant system. The are a number of reasons for this. Being hydraulically actuated, weight and size constraints prohibit the use of redundant hydraulic lanes.

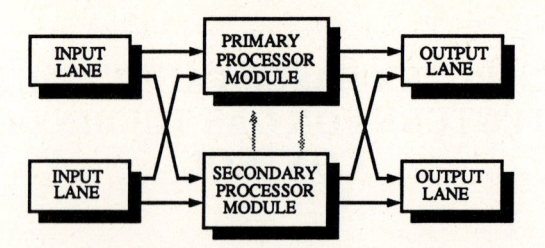

Fig. 1 Dual-Lane Controller Architecture

Even if this were possible switching between the lanes reliably would produce problems as the switching element would be a single point of failure. Thus, to provide the necessary fault tolerance to meet reliability levels, dual wound actuators are used. For engine parameter sensing only two lanes of sensors are provided, this is again due to weight and cost considerations. The sensors are extremely expensive, having to survive in a hostile environment. Therefore conventional TMR is not possible and the designer is left with the problem of trying to introduce the benefits of a TMR system into an inherently dual-lane architecture with two lanes of inputs and two lanes of outputs as shown in Fig. 1.

3. Design Criterion

The design criterion was that the system should survive any single failure and as many multiple failures as possible, failing safe in the event of a total loss of control. Also each processor within the multiprocessor array must be monitored since the use of self-checking in processors had been found from experience to be unreliable [3]. A complete failure modes and effects analysis of a processor was deemed impossible.

Three fault-tolerant strategies have been implemented on transputers. The first of these utilising two controller modules consisting of five transputers was based around the existing controller (see Fig. 1) and used a mixture of TMR and Backward Error Recovery to survive permanent and transient faults. It was felt, however, that the number of transputers being used was in itself a reliability concern and so a minimum processor implementation was sought. The restriction of four transputer links was found to be a major restriction on the topologies which could be employed. Although six-link transputer nodes can be formed, as in Fig. 2, initially work was confined to consideration of 4 links per transputer.

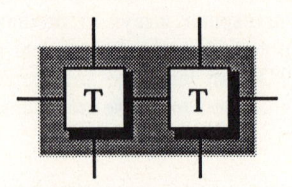

Fig. 2 6-link transputer node

signal is sent to both of the output transputers from both monitors. These are compared and, if they agree, sent to a processor shutdown circuit. Thus, processor deselection is a voted response from the system,. Transient data errors due to a malfunctioning processor or memory are logged in the monitor transputers using a fault integrator scheme. Persistent errors will therefore eventually result in the shutdown of a processor. At the beginning of each sample validated data is sent to each member of the triads. Thus, any corruption of data within a processor experiencing a transient fault will not result in a permanent failure.

4.4 Output Selection

The outputs connected to the actuators are selected by a changeover relay. This is preferred as a failure modes and effects analysis of this element is simple. The relay will fail in one of two ways, both of which will both leave it connected to a valid set of outputs.

4.5 Communication Failure Handling

The problem of handling link failures between processors introduces interesting problems. If watchdog timers are introduced on communications in the asynchronous transputer array all synchronisation is lost. Thus a system synchronisation strategy has to be developed. Since the design criterion dictates that there should be no single point of failure in the system the use of a common clock connected to the transputer event pins is ruled out. In the Overlapping Triad configuration a compromise solution had to be found giving the possibility of a complete system "lock-up". To cope with this, two separate external watchdog timers are used, one for each triad to produce a reset signal if "lock-up" occurs. A second problem is that a processor experiencing a watchdog timer will itself be "skewed" with respect to the rest of the system. If other communications are attempted with the "skewed" processor these will also fail and so a failure can propagate throughout the system. In order to mask the effect of the original failure time redundancy was incorporated by allocating tasks and communications to time frames. However, using this technique it was found that the system could no longer meet its real-time requirements and so a modified topology had to be adopted. The use of task overlapping also had to be abandoned in order to reduce interprocessor communication. Thus the system was modified to that of Fig. 4 which allows direct communication between the two monitor transputers and each processor now performs a complete set of control tasks.

As can be seen from Fig. 4 if a monitor processor now fails the integrity of the system is reduced. The input data from T4 has to pass through T1 and so the integrity of this data is dependent upon this processor, however, it is retained to allow access to the two lanes of sensors.

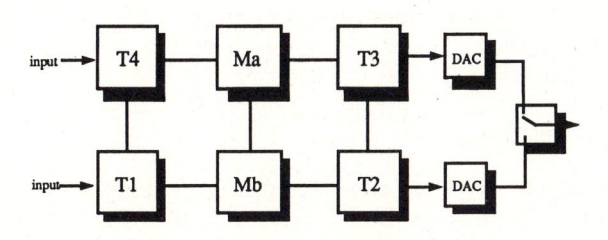

Fig. 4 Modified Topology

4.1 Evolution of Processor Topology

The topology evolved as follows. Fig. 3a shows a basic three-lane voter with two monitors which both have access to three processors. The inputs are exchanged between transputers and compared. Since four-link transputers are being used there is no direct connection between the monitors and it is assumed that there is some sort of comparison of outputs. If a single transputer fails the system reverts to a dual-lane comparison. If T1 or T3 fails, then a set of inputs is lost. If a monitor fails, then a set of outputs is lost. By adding another transputer (Fig. 3b), both monitor transputers have access to three processors. The inputs are exchanged between T1 and T4 and compared in each. As before, there is no direct communication between the monitors and a single processor failure will have the same consequences as for the previous case.

If T2 and T3 are used as the output transputers, as for Fig. 3c, then there is a link spare from each of the monitor transputers which allows each monitor to be connected to four processors. Therefore, if a single link fails a three-lane vote is still possible, but either a set of inputs or a set of outputs would be lost. However, not all of the links have been used in the system so it is possible to add further redundancy.

If T2 and T3 are used as the output transputers, as for Fig. 3c, then there is a link spare from each of the monitor transputers which allows each monitor to be connected to four processors. Therefore, if a single link fails a three-lane vote is still possible, but either a set of inputs or a set of outputs would be lost. However, not all of the links have been used in the system so it is possible to add further redundancy.

Fig. 3d redraws Fig. 3c to clearly present the balanced topology. This shows that a major advantage of this system is that if a monitor transputer fails, the remaining monitor transputer still has access to two sets of inputs and outputs. (It should be noted that there is no direct path for communication between the two monitor processors due to the restriction of four links.)

4.2 Overview of system operation

The system consists of processors in an "overlapping triad" configuration. Each triad comprises an input, monitor and output processor. Each triad, e.g. T1-Ma-T2 (Fig. 3d) performs a complete set of control tasks. Data is read from the analog-to-digital converters (ADC's) in both lanes of input transputers. This data is exchanged between the two input transputers and rate, range and drift checks are performed. Since it is impossible to distinguish a slowly drifting sensor in a dual-lane system, a drift failure is indicated to the pilot who can perform manual reversion between lanes. If a sensor fails, the appropriate secondary sensor value is used. The sensor flags are exchanged between the two input transputers and compared. If they disagree then an input transputer failure is flagged to the two monitors. However, it is possible for a monitor transputer to receive conflicting messages from two input transputers, i.e. a Byzantine fault. If this is the case, the monitor orders the two input transputers to pass their data to them and the data is retested in the two monitors. Thus, a third lane is introduced indicating which one of the input transputers has failed.

4.3 Controller Task Calculation

The controller code was organised into three parallel tasks. Each member of the two overlapping triads performs two of the three control tasks. The results from these are compared in both of the monitor transputers, Ma and Mb, using exact voting. If an error is found, the results from the members of the opposing triad are accessed, thus allowing a three-lane vote to be performed. Once the offending processor is identified, a shutdown

The result of this was the evolution of the topology shown in Fig. 3 showing the Overlapping Triads topology. This will be discussed in more detail in the following sections. Finally, the restriction of 4 links per processors was removed and a "Hot Sparing" system was developed using a transputer and C004 programmable link switch to provide an 8-link transputer.

4. Method of Overlapping Triads

The design objective is to produce a fault tolerant system with as few transputers as possible which would be able to access two lanes of inputs and two lanes of outputs. One solution uses a Dual Triple Modular Redundant (DTMR) system.

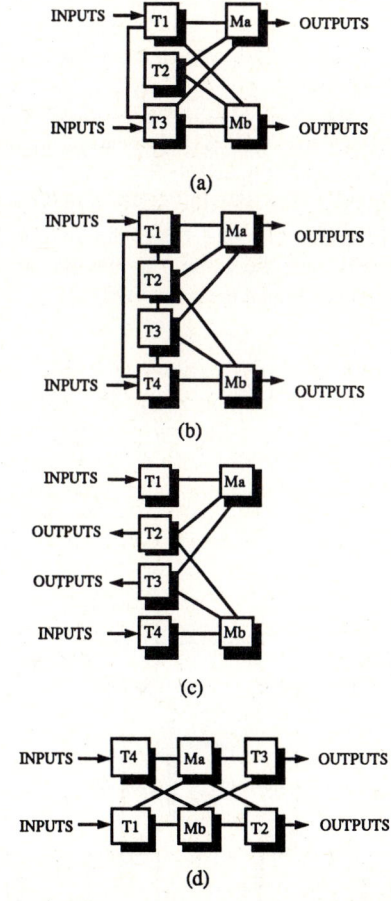

Fig. 3 Evolution of Overlapping Triads Topology

Main Fuel
Actuator
(Normal Operation)

Main Fuel
Actuator
(Failed System)

Time at which
System
Reconfigured

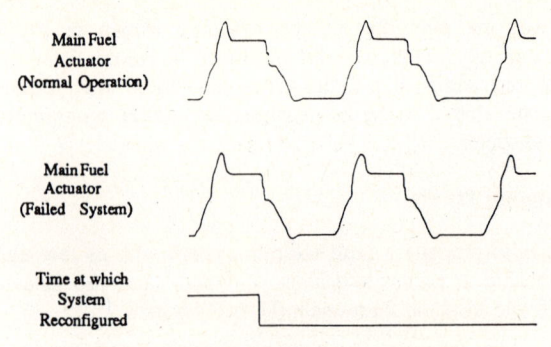

Fig.5   Response of System to Link Failure

The output is switched to T2 as the output data will only be as reliable as the data from T2. However, if an output actuator were to fail in the secondary lane the output can be switched back to the first lane

4.5 System Testing

The system was tested by introducing software faults to corrupt data. Sensor values were corrupted to produce rate, range and drift failures and the data within transputers was corrupted to simulate the effects of memory failures and transmission corruption. The fault integrator was exercised with transient and intermittent faults. Communication failures were also injected by removal of links.

Since two triads of transputers are available, each performing a full set of controller tasks, if a processor failure occurs in one triad, the output from the other triad of transputers is used immediately and the failure is masked from the output so that no reconfiguration delay is experienced which is shown in Fig. 5.

5. Hot Sparing Technique

The "Hot Sparing" technique was devised based on the assumption that an 8-link transputer will become available in the future. In the system (Fig. 6) a spare transputer is able to take over the tasks of any of the outer four transputers. To accomplish this an 8-link transputer is necessary to allow connection to all inputs and outputs.

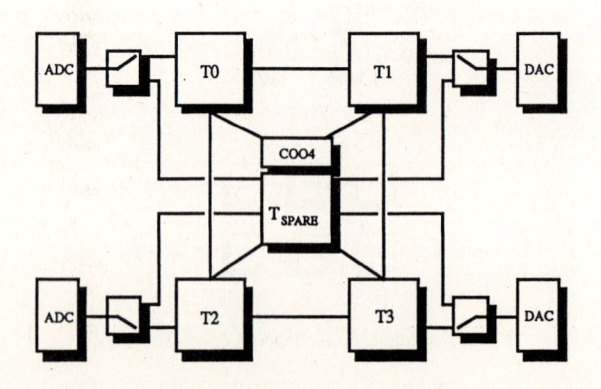

Fig. 6 "Hot Sparing" Transputer System

5.1 Overview of System Operation

The input sensor data validation is the same as for the overlapping triad configuration. The validated data is then distributed to the output transputers T1 and T3 and also to the spare transputer to check for Byzantine disagreement.

5.2 Controller Task Calculation

To exploit the parallelism available, the controller tasks would have to be split into four tasks and then a modified form of the overlapping task method used previously could be used. However, the Overlapping Triads study had already shown that the amount of communication would prevent this method being feasible within the demanded sample time on present transputer hardware. Therefore a "total control task" was allocated to each of the processors.

The controller results are exchanged, firstly, between the two input transputers and the two output transputers in pairs, and then finally between the input and output transputers. This ensures that each member of the outer quadrant has three values of the controller outputs to compare. The output from the spare transputer is also sent to the two output transputers. Here it is compared against the voted valid output of the triad comparison to test for failure of the spare. Flags are sent to the spare transputer by the main transputers whose values are dependent on the result of the three-way vote. In this way a failure in any one of the main transputers will be reported to the spare by its two neighbours. Reconfiguration of the 4 relays was performed by a link adaptor connected to the spare transputer. This introduces a single point of failure and in a final system this would need to be a voted response from the four main transputers. A pin settable from software on each transputer to provide this facility would be helpful.

5.3 Data Output Selection

Finally the voted controller results are sent to the output DAC's. The DAC output sent to the actuator is selected via a separate relay controlled by a link adaptor connected to the spare transputer. Thus, if the failure of one of the output lanes is detected, the spare switches control to the secondary output DAC lane. Failure of a spare will result in the relay being connected to one or other of the healthy output lanes. It is possible that the spare may fail in an indeterminate manner which will cause it to continuously switch between the output lanes. The outer transputers would, however, detect the failure of the spare and could be used to disconnect it.

5.4 System Testing

The system was again tested with a variety of software induced failures. Link failures were also introduced by removal of links. The implementation of the "8-link transputer" by using a programmable crossbar switch highlighted a serious omission from the switch's hardware. The programmable link switch has no arbitration logic similar to that found on dual-port RAMs. Thus, if an attempt is made to read from it or write to it while it is reconfiguring, either incorrect data is read or the link deadlocks. The status of the switch can be accessed via the control link, but this information is not available to the other transputers in the system unless it is passed via some indirect route from the control transputer increasing communication. It is thus up to the programmer to carefully synchronise communication with the switch to prevent this situation.

6. Concluding Remarks

Strategies for the management of fault tolerance in gas turbine engine controllers have been investigated. This paper describes two approaches which has been implemented based on the parallel processing device, the Inmos transputer. The successful harnessing of parallel processing capability is an important objective; advantages and shortcomings of current versions of this hardware have been revealed in this study. Hardware constraints have been found to largely dictate the final structure. Constraints of software validation for flight control using formal methods have been found to dictate the complexity of the software. At present, the main problem is that the parallelism available cannot be exploited because of the current link communication overheads. Thus there is a need for increased communication rates as well as more links. The implementations have also highlighted the need for a software-settable semaphore pin on the transputer and the need for arbitration logic to be added to the C004 programmable link switch. Fuller descriptions and subsequent developments are reported in [4].

7. Acknowledgements

The authors wish to thank Chris Legge and Sam Shutler of Rolls-Royce, Bristol for their co-operation and help throughout this project and gratefully acknowledge the financial support of SERC and Rolls-Royce, Bristol.

8. References

[1] Dennis, R.W. and Hills, A.D. :" A fault tolerant fly by wire system for maintenance free applications" AGARD Guidance and Control Panel 49th Symposium , Toulouse, France, October 1989.

[2] Urnes, J.M., Stewart, J. and Eslinger, R. :"Flight demonstration of a self repairing flight control system in a NASA F-15 fighter aircraft" AGARD Guidance and Control Panel 49th Symposium, Toulouse, France, October 1989.

[3] "Digital Flight control system - general purpose digital controller", RR Report BEAS 236, Part 2, Rolls-Royce (Bristol), 1976.

[4] Thompson, H.A. :"Parallel Processing Applications for Gas Turbine Engine Control", PhD. Thesis, UCNW, Bangor, 1990.

The Structure of a Parallel Adaptive Controller and its Transputer Implementation

Arthur Karl Kordon[1]

May 15, 1990

1. Introduction

Adaptive controllers have wide application in different branches of industry - chemistry, pulp and paper industry, industrial robots, etc [4]. The increasing complexity of modern technological processes demands the design of highly reliable, multivariable, adaptive controllers working under a wide range of operating conditions. At the same time the existing adaptive controllers do not guarantee the convergence of adjustment processes in practice, the quality of control is assured only for certain operating points, and the adaptation algorithms are sensitive to a priori information. To overcome some of these problems a supervisor module is introduced; it performs a set of actions which improve the quality of the adaptive system [9,15].

The recent developements [7] in parallel programming languages, computer architectures, and the availability of relativily cheap, general purpose, parallel processors, of which the transputer [8] is one of the best examples, make the implementation of control systems on parallel hardware very attractive. Some of the problems of employing transputers and Occam in the implementation of control systems are considered in [6], together with examples of PWM inverter control and flight control. Reference [16] gives an overview of the issues in the industrial application of transputers, with an emphasis on real-time control and robotics, and [3] presents the experimental results of using various analogue I/O strategies for transputers - host based systems, external bus systemsand wholy transputer based systems. Anderson [1] proposes the use of transputers in complex manufacturing systems with distributed hierarchical control using ideas developed by in the Supernode project [7]. He believes that such an integrated plant control system will be designed using a varaety of languages - Occam, C, Lisp or Prolog.

The aim of this paper is to present the evolution of the ideas introduced in [17],to define the structure of a parallel adaptive controller, to formulate the functionality of its components, and to discuss its implementation on transputers networks.

2. Requirements for a Universal Adaptive Controller

The principal requirements for a universal adaptive controller are as follows:

fault - tolerance, allowing functional integrity of the plant and the control system in all operating modes;

stability under conditions of undefined initial structure and parameters of the model;

high quality control over the whole range of operating points and during transition between points;

self- learning functions.

These maximalistic requirements can not be satisfied by the available adaptive controllers. The most popular among them - the Self-Tuning Regulators (STRs), are a combination of an identification algorithm and a control algorithm, the former being the RLS and the latter being one of Minimum Variance (MV), General Minimum Variance (GMV), Dead - Beat (DB), General Predictive Control (GPC), and others. They all are synthesized with their own performance criteria and are suitable for certain operating modes and control goals. The plant models also differ - eg., ARMAX and ARIMAX. As long as RLS gives a shifted estimation in case of corelated noise, it is necessary to use other identification algorithms - RELS, RML [9]. The existing adaptive controllers only achieve quality control when the structure of the model is known a priori. The approach taken by Isermann [9] of combining several algorithms for control with identification algorithms exhibits higher flexibility, but it also needs some prior exploration of the plant in order to choose the proper combination.

It is our belief that satisfying most of the aforementioned requirements can be achieved by a parallel adaptive control system.

---

[1]PAROS Laboratory, Center of Informatics and Computer Technology, Bulgarian Academy of Sciences, Varna Drava Soboltch str. 7a, Bulgaria

3. Structure of a Parallel Adaptive Controller

The studies of Lainiotis [10] show that STRs have no inner concurrency, therefore parallelism in the structure of the Parallel Adaptive Controller (PAC) is achieved at a higher level, by the concurrent action of a number of adaptive controllers. The structure of the PAC is shown in figure 1.

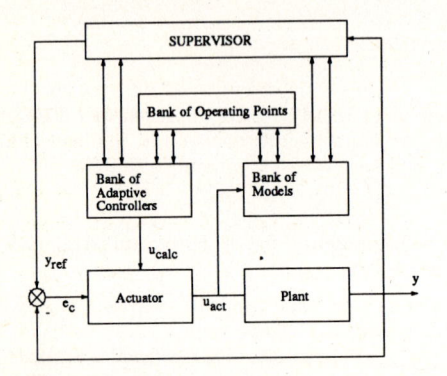

Figure 1: Structure of a Parallel Adaptive Controller.

The plant is of a MIMO (Multiple Input - Multiple Output) type with p-inputs and l-outputs. The actuator block consists of different types of actuator for different inputs (eg. valves, drives, heaters, etc.). The actual control input to the plant u_{act} reflects the limitations of the actuators and differs from the theoretical control input u_{act}.

The main components of the proposed structure have the following functions:
• Unit "bank of models" - computes concurrently the reaction of certain number of models for control signal from the plant. The number of the models is determined by the number of operating points, the stage of evolution (initial experimentation or operating exploitation), and the type of the plant.

• Unit "bank of adaptive controllers" - contains a certain number of combinations of identification and control algorithms. The following adaptive controllers are concurrently activated :
(i)adaptive controller with current control goal for the current operating point on a model with minimal error;
(ii) the later for the 2 adjacent possible operating points;
(iii) back-up control.

• Unit "bank of operating points" - contains all operating points and the related to each one of them multitude of models and controllers. The unit ensures the continuity of actions in any of them and includes the emergency situations handlers.

Without doubt, the "supervisor" unit is the most complicated and crucial unit. It has to provide the following functionality:
(i)choice of model that suites best the chosen operating point;
(ii)performance evaluation of the performance of the adaptive controllers chosen in (i);
(iii)evaluation of the future operating point by forecasting the systems behaviour;
(iv)choice of the control signal to be applied to the actuator;
(v)user-friendly dialogue with the operator inteneded to acquire and use some of the operator's knowledge about the process;
(vi)procedures for initial experimentation to obtain the necessary structural information for the different models, the exact bank of operating points, adaptive algorithms and models;
(vii)supervising of the adaptation process and taking actions in case of deteriorating quality of control;
(viii)self-learning;

While (i) - (v) predominantly compute and evaluate different quantitative measures, (vi) - (viii) have to resort to using expert control methods.

At sample instant k the output vector of the plant $y(k)$ is read and compared with the reference $y_{ref}(k)$. In the same time the control signal u_{act} is entered into the bank of models for the appropriate operating point and their outputs are sent to the supervisor unit. After the choice of the best model has been made, the bank of adaptive controllers is activated and a vector of possible control signals u_{calc} is calculated. The supervisor predicts the response for every controller action and chooses the control signal with minimal error.

4. Implementation of a PAC on Transputers

The INMOS transputer [8] is probably the most successful microprocessor to date to help the implementation of parallel process control systems. Among the advantages of using Occam and the transputer for designing and implementing complex control systems are the explicit description of the structure of a parallel system, the connectivity and communication protocol among its components, availability of timers, and explicit resource allocation. In the same time, there are some limitations and shortages - for example, lack of dynamic structures, difficult error handling, and insufficient on-chip memory.

Implementing all the PAC functions in Occam is very difficult and hard to justify. On one hand, the description of the set of system models, adaptive controllers, and the functions (i) - (v) of the supervisor as independent concurrent Occam processes seems to reflect well our intuitions about the overall system structure and behaviour. On the other hand, the rest of the supervisor functions which incorporate the expert control aspects of the system are best expressed in C and PROLOG.

We are investigating the implementation of a PAC in two versions - on one and on four transputers. The latter is used during the set-up adjustment phase, when the information available about the plant is scant and the range of possible operating points, models, and adaptive control algorithms is quite wide.

5. An Example of a PAC Implementation on Four Transputers

Some experiments in implementing a PAC on a network of four transputers under the control of an IBM AT/PC host have been made. The plant simulated was a 2 input - 2 output plant with 2 operating points and the parameters of the models (the A and B matrices in an ARMA model) are as follows.

- Operating point 1.

$$A_1 = \begin{bmatrix} -0.585 & 0.076 \\ 0.019 & -0.075 \end{bmatrix}$$

$$A_2 = \begin{bmatrix} -0.255 & -0.008 \\ -0.067 & 0.05 \end{bmatrix}$$

$$B_1 = \begin{bmatrix} 0.073 & -0.009 \\ -0.001 & 0.024 \end{bmatrix}$$

$$B_2 = \begin{bmatrix} 0.017 & 0.01 \\ 0.017 & 0.008 \end{bmatrix}$$

- Operating point 2.

$$A_1 = \begin{bmatrix} -0.652 & -0.124 \\ -0.028 & -0.62 \end{bmatrix}$$

$$A_2 = \begin{bmatrix} -0.135 & 0.109 \\ -0.03 & -0.195 \end{bmatrix}$$

$$B_1 = \begin{bmatrix} 0.244 & 0.022 \\ 0.025 & 0.43 \end{bmatrix}$$

$$B_2 = \begin{bmatrix} 0.067 & -0.076 \\ -0.064 & 0.112 \end{bmatrix}$$

Three candidate models are activated for every operating point. The identification algorithm is a Recursive Least Squares (RLS) algorithm with U-D factorisation of the covariance matrix [11]. The control algorithms used are General Minimum Variance (GMV), General Predictive Control (GPC), and Multivariable (MV) PID as a back-up.

The computational complexities of the control algorithms are given by the following expressions.

$$GMV = (degA + max(degB, 1) + 3)m^3 + m + 2inv(m)$$

$$GPC = mN_n(N_r + N_nN_r + N_n^2\sqrt{N_n} + 1)$$
$$PID = m^3 + 6m^2inv(m)$$

where,

m is the number of loops,
$degA, degB$ degrees of the polynomial matrices A and B in the ARMA models,
N_n is the control horizon, and
N_r is the prediction horizon.

The supervisor module consists of an algorithm for initial experimentation of the type described in [15], procedures for choosing the appropriate model, predicting the future behaviour of the system, and choosing the control signal.

The computational graph of this particular structure of PAC on four transputers is shown in figure 2. The mapping of this graph onto the network

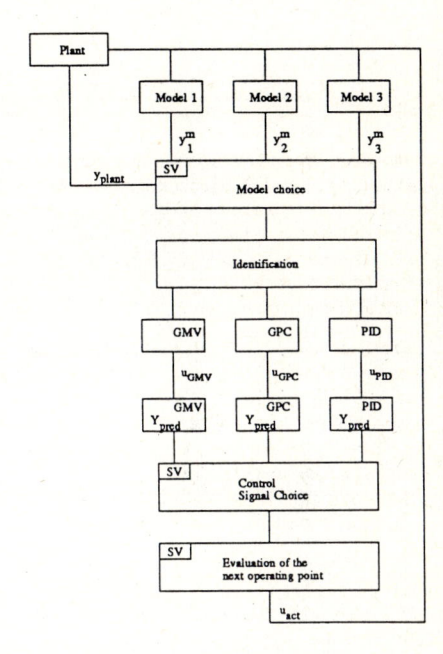

Figure 2: The Computational Graph of PAC.

resources is as follows. The computational complexity of the identification algorithm is approximately the same as the complexity of the model calculation, the controller, and the prediction block, and is mapped onto a single transputer. On that same transputer is mapped the supervisor unit and a model, a controller, and a prediction blocks are mapped on every one of the remaining three transputers. The traffic between different transputers is about 200 bytes per conveyor cycle and is nearest-neighbour only. The effect on performance is negligible since computation proceeds concurrently with intertransputer communication and computation costs outweigh the communication costs.

The reactions of both loops of the simulated system over a period of 500 samples are shown in figure 3 and figure 4. In this case the chosen adaptive control algorithm was a GPC with $N_n = 1, N_r = 5$. When the initial adjustment phase (the first 10-12 samples) is completed, the control in both loops is of a good quality.

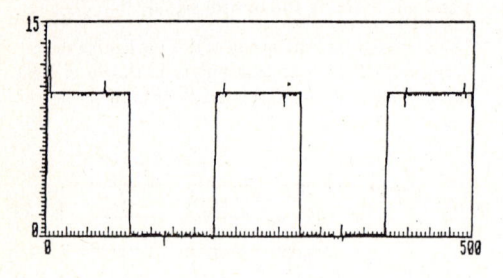

Figure 3: Output and Reference Signals - Loop 1.

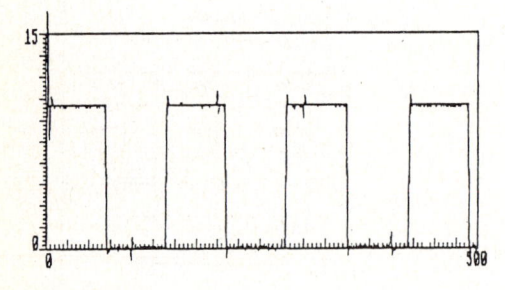

Figure 4: Output and Reference Signals - Loop 2.

The experience obtained during this initial experimentation stage makes clear the difficulties in implementing more complex supervisor structures using the Transputer Development System. Such structures will be implemented when a distributed operating environment (DIOGEN) [13], currently being developed by PAROS, is available later this year. It will allow the transparrent mapping of processes and communication on arbitrary networks of transputers. In the mean time the work is concentrated on performance evaluation and optimisation of the first-cut PAC implementation.

6. Summary

The paper discussed some of the shortcommings of the existing adaptive controllers and formulated a set of requirements for a universal adaptive system. From that position it described in more detail the structure of a Parallel Adaptive Controller (PAC), which combines banks of operating points with the corresponding models and controllers, operating concurrently. The implementation of a PAC on four transputers was described in some depth and a possible mapping of processes onto network resources was suggested. The inter-transputer traffic was found to be about 200 bytes per one conveyor cycle and these communication costs were outweighed by the computation costs.

The simulation results obtained showed that after a short initial adjustment phase (about 10-12 samples), the control in both loops was of a good quality.

References

[1] Anderson A., van Renterghem P., The Use of the Transputer and Occam in the Design of Distributed Control Systems, Journal A, 30, 4, 1989, pp 55-61.

[2] Astrom K., Anton J., Artzen K., Expert Control, Automatica, 22, 3, 1986, pp 277-286.

[3] Barlow M., Konnanov P., Burge S., Analogue I/O Strategies for Transputers, Microprocessors and Microsystems, 13, 6, 1989, pp 387-395.

[4] Chalam V., Adaptive Control Systems, Marcel Dekker, 1987

[5] Elizabeth M., Aliabadi A., Real-Time System Implementation - the Transputer and Occam Alternative, Microproc. and Microprogramming, 26, 1, 1989, pp 77-84.

[6] Fleming P. (ed.), Parallel Processing in Control, Peter Peregrinus Ltd, 1988

[7] Hockney R., Jesshope C., Parallel Computers 2, Adam Hilger Ltd, 1988

[8] Isermann R., Digital control systems, Springer Verlag, 1981

[9] INMOS, Transputer Reference Manual, Prentice Hall, 1988

[10] Lainiotis D., et al, Adaptive Ccontrol Algorithms: a Comparative Computational Analysis - Parallelism, Control and Computers, Vol.

16, 1, 1988, pp 22-27.

[11] Ljung L., Soderstrom T, Theory and Practice of Recursive Identification, MIT Press, Cambridge, Mass., 1983.

[12] Middleten R, et al, Design Issues in Adaptive Control, IEEE Trans Automat. Control, AC-33, 1, 1988, pp 50-57.

[13] Nedelchev I, Parashkevov A., Distributed Operating Environment - DIOGEN, WP&DP, Sofia, May, 1990, (to appear in LNCS).

[14] Ornedo R., et al, Design and Experimental Evaluation of an Automatically Reconfigurable Controller for Process Plants, American Control Conference'87, 1987, pp 1662-1668.

[15] van Renterghem P., Transputers for Industrial Applications, Concurrency: Practice and Experience, 1, 2, 1989, pp 135-169.

[16] Tomov I., Kordon A., Application of a Hierarchical Multivariable Self-Tunning Regulator for Adaptive Control of Chemical Processes, Proc. of IFAC Symposium ADCHEM'88, 1988, pp 88-93.

[17] Warwick K., Parallel Controller Structure for On-Line Performance Assesment, American Control Conference'89, 1989, pp 2822-2823.

[18] 3L, Parallel C User Guide, 3L Ltd, UK, 1988.

Parallel Processing in Aerospace Control Systems

G S Virk, J M Tahir and P K Kourmoulis
Department of Control Engineering, University of Sheffield,
Mappin Street, Sheffield S1 3JD

Abstract

The paper deals with two computationally intensive control problems in the area of aerospace systems. The first of these considers automatic flight control for aircraft, and the second is related to vibration suppression in flexible structures such as aircraft wings. It is shown that, by functionally decomposing the computational tasks and using a suitably configured transputer system, it is possible to achieve real-time performance in both cases.

1 Introduction

There are several problems in the control of aerospace systems that are of a complex and computationally demanding nature, and which require significant processing capabilities for on-line computer implementation. The paper deals with research being conducted in collaboration with British Aerospace (Military Aircraft) Ltd, Brough and considers two important areas, which are flight control and vibration suppression. In both of these cases simulations are conducted using optimal control laws designed for linear models and implemented in real-time to achieve desired performance levels. The paper splits naturally into two halves as we discuss the two applications areas in turn.

2 Real-time Optimal Autopilot

An aircraft in flight is a nonlinear time varying system, see Babister [5], and Blakelock [6], which can be difficult to control adequately over its entire flight regime. In principle, nonlinear optimal control techniques can provide the ability to design suitable strategies but are rarely implemented due to the large computational requirements for solving such problems in real-time. A new real-time longitudinal autopilot has been determined for an aircraft whose engineering data was supplied by British Aerospace, Brough [4] using multi-transputer processors, see [1], [2]. Here we extend the results to include the lateral dynamics and hence determine an optimal autopilot for the complete aircraft. The cross-coupling terms are handled in a novel way, where they are assumed to be constant over short intervals over which linearisations of the aircraft equations are performed for calculating the optimal control laws. In this way the known constant cross-coupling effects can be handled. The precise control engineering details will be presented in a later paper, but here we concentrate on the computational aspects and due to the lack of space, we have to be brief. First we present the mathematical model of an aircraft.

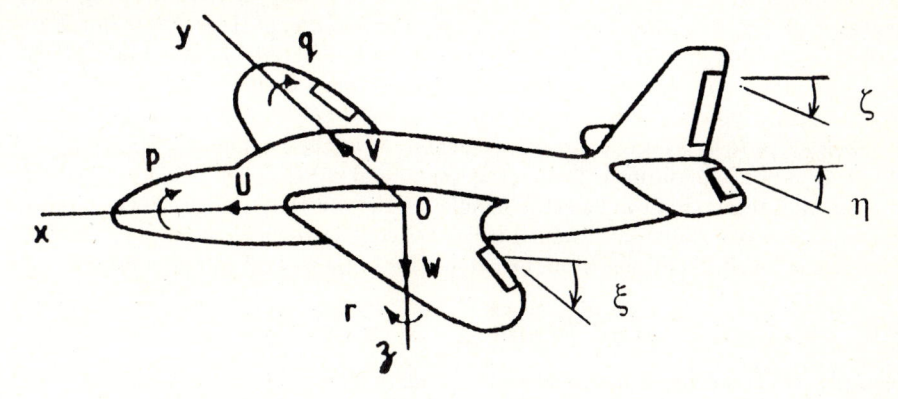

Figure 1: Aircraft in flight with notation and axes

When considered as a rigid body (see Figure 1) the motion of the aircraft is defined by a set of nonlinear equations, see [5], [6]

$$\dot{x}(t) = f(x(t), u(t)) \tag{1}$$

where the state vector $x = \begin{bmatrix} x_1 \\ x_2 \end{bmatrix}$ is made up of variables related with the longitudinal motion, $\left(x_1 = [U, W, Q, \theta, H, E_s]^T\right)$ and those connected with the lateral motion $\left(x_2 = [V, P, R, \Phi, \Psi]^T\right)$, and the control input vector $u = [\eta, \gamma, \xi, \zeta]^T$. Standard notation is used, see for example Babister [5], Blakelock[6], Virk and Tahir [1], [2], [3]. These equations can be written in a linearised form to highlight the cross-coupling terms between the longitudinal and lateral motions as

$$\begin{bmatrix} \dot{x}_1(t) \\ \dot{x}_2(t) \end{bmatrix} = \begin{bmatrix} A_{11} & A_{12} \\ A_{21} & A_{22} \end{bmatrix} \begin{bmatrix} x_1(t) \\ x_2(t) \end{bmatrix} + \begin{bmatrix} B_1 & 0 \\ 0 & B_2 \end{bmatrix} u(t) \tag{2}$$

where A_{11}, A_{12}, A_{21} and A_{22}, are the partial derivations of the nonlinear functions f in equation (1) with respect to the states and B_1 and B_2 are the derivatives with respect to the controls, see Virk and Tahir [3]. Hence A_{12} and A_{21} represents the cross-coupling terms, and if these are absent the longitudinal and lateral motiuons can be easily decoupled and handled independently of each other.

It is well known that the cross-coupling terms can be removed by assuming:

(i) the aircraft is in straight and unaccelerated flight and then disturbed by deflections of the control surfaces.

(ii) the elevator deflection causes only a pitching moment about the OY axis and causes no rolling or yawing moments.

(iii) the aileron and rudder deflections causes rotations only about the OX and OZ axes respectively.

These assumptions are not strictly valid in many modern aircraft and the situation is worsening with more weight being concentrated in the fuselage and the aircraft wings becoming thinner and shorter (and lighter). This weight shift is causing the cross-coupling effects to be increased considerably hence necessitating the consideration of these effects in the controller design. Such allowances have been made in our work, described in detail in Virk and Tahir [3], by assuming that the cross-coupling effects, although clearly present, are constant over short linearing intervals. For example when considering the longitudinal motion, the lateral variables (V, P, R, Φ, Ψ) are assumed to be constant at their values $(V_0, P_0, R_0, \Phi_0, \Psi_0)$ when the linearisation is performed. In this way the lateral variables are found to appear as separate constant terms that can be easily handled in the controller design. In the lateral motion equations, the (constant) longitudinal terms are combined with the (varying) lateral terms. Even so the longitudinal effects can be catered for in the lateral autopilot design.

2.1 Optimal Control Problem

The approach taken here is to formulate an optimal control problem for the complete linearised aircraft, separate the motions into the longitudinal and lateral dynamics, taking into account the cross-coupling effects, and solve the two subproblems using a multi-transputer network in real-time.

The nonlinear aircraft system, equation (1) can be linearised about an operating point (X_0, U_0) and the equations written as

$$\dot{e} = Ae(t) + B\Delta u(t) \tag{3}$$

where the A and B matrices are of the form shown in equation (2), e is the error in the system states and Δu is the control deviation from the operating point U_0. The elements of the A and B matrices were obtained using the aircraft engineering data supplied by British Aerospace, Brough, [4]. Equation (3) is assumed to be time invariant for a short interval T_l over which optimisation is performed, cross-coupling effects assumed to be constant as discussed above, and the resulting control actions applied to a simulation of the nonlinear time-varying aircraft. The receding horizon technique is used so that real-time, on-line optimal control of the aircraft is possible. Starting at time t_0 a linear quadratic performance index having the form

$$\begin{aligned} J(u, t_0) = &\ 1/2 \int_{t_0}^{t_0+T} \left[e^T(t) Qe(t) + \Delta u^T(t) R\Delta u(t) \right] dt \\ &+ 1/2 \left[e^T(t_0+T) Fe(t_0+T) \right] \end{aligned} \tag{4}$$

is considered and minimised, where Q and F are 6×6 positive semi-definite matrices for the longitudinal mode and 5×5 positive semi-definite matrices for the lateral mode, and R is a 2×2 positive definite matrix for each mode.

It is well known that the receding horizon optimal control law, see Kwon and Bruckstein [7], is given for our problem by

$$\Delta u^*(t) = -R^{-1}B^T P(t_0, t_0+T) e(t) \tag{5}$$
$$u^*(t) = U_0 + \Delta u^*(t) \tag{6}$$

where $P(\cdot)$ is computed by solving the following Riccati equation backwards

$$\dot{P}(t) = -P(t)A - A^T P(t) - Q + P(t)BR^{-1}B^T P(t) \tag{7}$$
$$P(t_0+T, t_0+T) = F \tag{8}$$

Once the time t has reached $t_0 + T_l$, a new linearising interval of length T_l can be started by setting $t_0 = t_0 + T_l$ and repeating the cycle indefinitely.

2.2 Parallel Implementation

The above optimisation and control procedure can be stated in the following algorithm form:

Step 0: Initialise parameters and variables.

Step 1: Linearise aircraft equations about the current point.

Step 2: Integrate Riccati equations over the receding horizon of duration T seconds and store the initial gains $P(t_0, t_0 + T)$.

Step 3: Calculate the control $u^*(t)$ necessary to be applied.

Step 4: Calculate the states for the nonlinear aircraft.

Step 5: If the end of the linearisation interval (T_l) has been reached, update the variables and goto step 1, else goto step 3.

Clearly for real-time performance all these computations have to be performed iteratively within the time scales of the aircraft. A sampling rate of approximately $200Hz$ is usually required to achieve satisfactory control. Hence the above algorithm should be processed to provide control updates every $5msec$. It has been shown in Tahir and Virk [1], that the aircraft can be adequately controlled using a time invariant linearised model for a specified time interval of T_l seconds, which can be made equal to the execution time for Steps 1 and 2 of the above procedure.

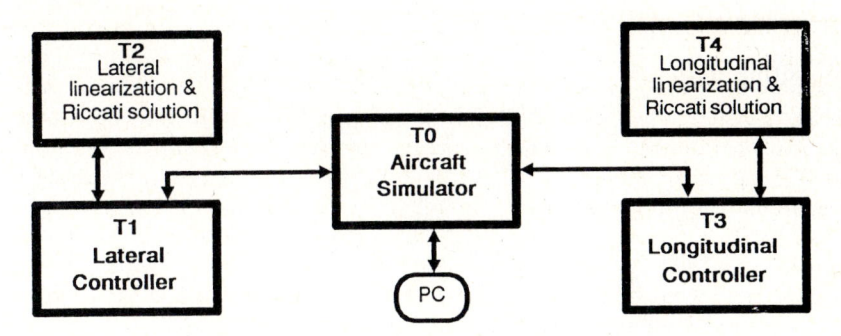

Figure 2: Transputer array for aircraft autopilot

A transputer network system as shown in Figure 2 is used to provide real-time control as follows:

Transputer T0 is the aircraft simulator.

Transputers T1 and T2 handle the lateral motion, (i.e. provide aileron (ξ) and rudder (ζ) control actions in real-time).

Transputers T3 and T4 control the longitudinal motion of the aircraft (i.e. provide the elevator (η) and engine throttle (γ) controls in real-time).

Both the lateral and longitudinal autopilots read the complete state from the simulator to allow for the cross-coupling effects as discussed earlier. In practice an observer is necessary to estimate the states which are not directly measured for use in such a control design.

For a receding horizon $T = 0.5$ sec, and if the integration step used in Step 2 is 10 $msec$ then it is found that the lateral Riccati equations can be updated every 40 $msec$ ($= T_{l,lat}$) and the longitudinal ones every 50 $msec$ ($= T_{l,long}$) (see Tahir and Virk [1] for the computational complexity and detailed timings).

2.3 Autopilot Results

The real-time algorithm was coded on a T800 transputer network of Figure 2 using Parallel C. Using the state vector $x = [U, W, Q, \theta, H, E_s, V, P, R, \Phi, \Psi]^T$, an initial state

$$x_{ic} = [\,150,\ 5,\ 0,\ 0.033,\ 5000,\ 6615,\ 0,\ 0,\ 0,\ 0,\ 0.2\,]^T$$

and a desired state of

$$x_d = [\,150,\ 5,\ 0,\ 0.033,\ 5000,\ 6615,\ 0,\ 0,\ 0,\ 0,\ 0\,]^T$$

is assumed, that is the aircraft is required to change its direction by 11.5°.
The following weighting matrices were used.

Longitudinal motion autopilot

$$\begin{aligned} Q_{long} &= diag\left[\,5,\ 0,\ 500,\ 1000,\ 0.6,\ 5 \times 10^{-5}\,\right], \\ R_{long} &= diag[\,5,\ 1\,], \\ F_{long} &= 0 \end{aligned}$$

Lateral motion autopilot

$$\begin{aligned} Q_{lat} &= diag[\,0.1,\ 10,\ 1000,\ 15,\ 1500\,], \\ R_{lat} &= diag[\,1,\ 50\,], \\ F_{lat} &= 0 \end{aligned}$$

The optimal controlled trajectories are shown in Figure 3 where we can see that the real-time performances are adequate. Hence the linear time-invariant aircraft and the cross-coupling assumptions are valid and useful when considering problems of this kind.

3 Vibration Suppression

The vibration control of flexible structures is, in a sense, even more challenging than the real-time flight control problem discussed in the last section because the structures possess an infinite number of modes, although some are very important and others less important. Several different vibrational problems arise in aerospace systems, including,

(i) oscillation of fixed wing aircraft (wing flapping) and causing large stresses and lift variations

(ii) vibrations of aircraft fuselages causing uncomfortable ride and failures in avionic systems.

(iii) oscillations of satellite solar panels which cause errors in pointing angles.

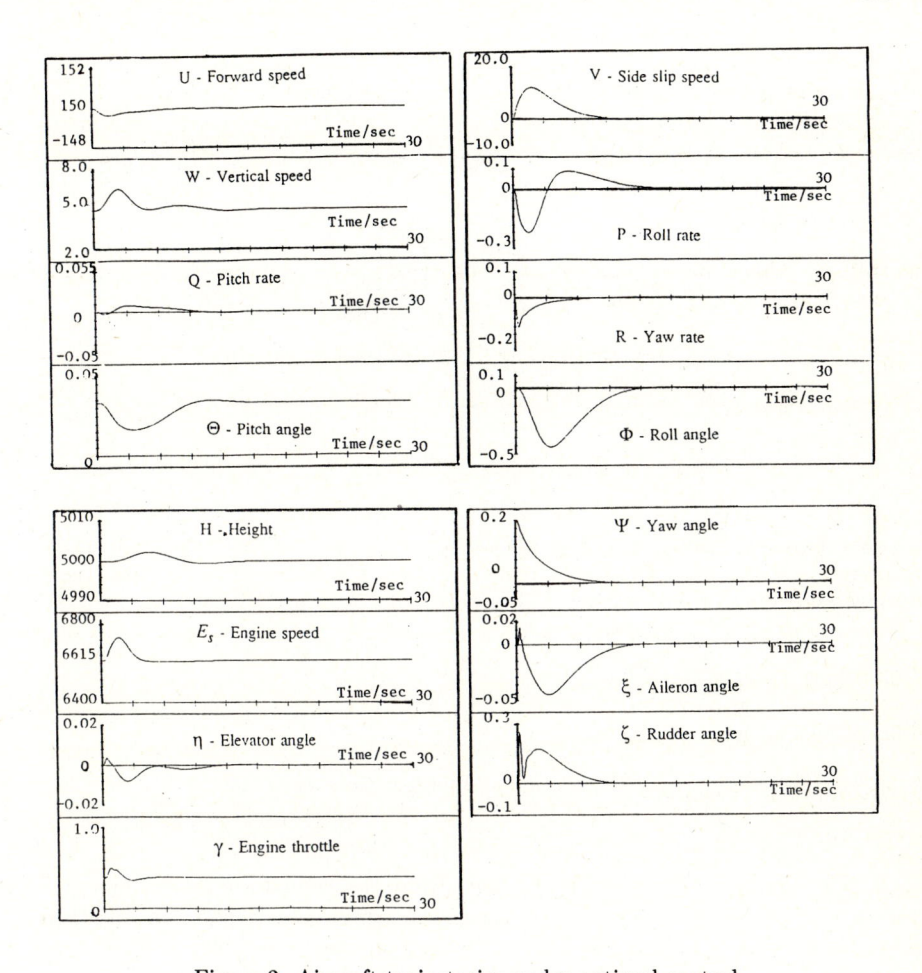

Figure 3: Aircraft trajectories under optimal control

(iv) vibrations in helicopter roters causing poor ride, and large stresses in the fuselage structure.

In addition such vibrations cause problems of excessive noise and fatigue in the aircraft structures.

A first attempt at consideration of some of these applications can be made by looking at vibration of a simple flexible beam structure. In this section a cantilever system in transverse oscillation (see Figure 4) is considered and an active controller is designed which damps out the unwanted vibrations. The motion of the cantilever is described by the fourth order partial differential equation

$$\mu \frac{\partial^4 y(x,t)}{\partial x^4} + \rho A \frac{\partial^2 y(x,t)}{\partial t^2} = f(x,t) \qquad (9)$$

where $y(x,t)$ is the deflection at a distance x from the fixed end at time t, μ, ρ, and A are beam constants and $f(x,t)$ is a force causing the beam to deform. Various applications can be considered by changing the boundary conditions. For example free-free beams can be considered for aircraft fuselage vibrations and hinged-free beams for satellite solar panels vibrations.

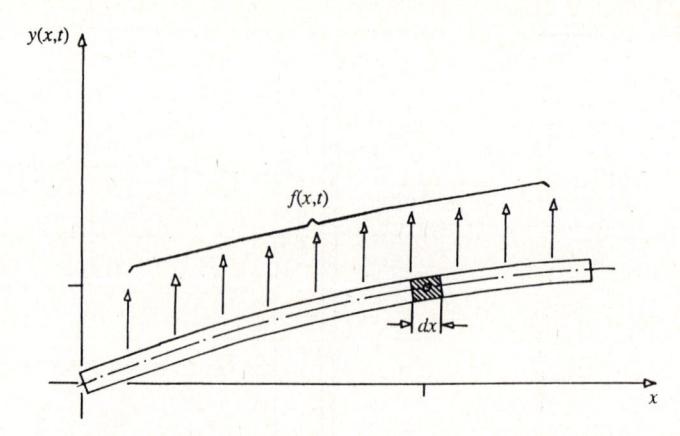

Figure 4: Cantilever system in transverse vibration

The cantilever system has been simulated using finite difference methods see Virk and Kourmoulis [8], [10] and forms the basis of vibration control considerations. Since the complete computational task is enormous it is advisable to divide it in to smaller portions. In general control engineering terms these include the formation of the following four main sub-tasks:

(i) System simulation.

(ii) Modelling (reduced-order).

(iii) Controller design, implementation and performance assessment.

(iv) User interface.

Since each of these sub-tasks can in principle require vast computational resources it is important to have the flexibility to be able to design the appropriate computer architecture so that the execution time is not excessive and real-time performance possible. A design is presented using the above functional decomposition approach for the control of flexible structure beam systems in Virk and Kourmoulis [10]. Here each of the above sub-tasks is solved, in real-time, on a suitably configured transputer network system using the network topology shown in Figure 5. Each block shown in the configuration is in fact a smaller network of processors onto which the above sub-tasks are mapped.

Due to the structure of the two main algorithms, namely the system and model simulations, modified tree networks are used. This is due to the fact that the software needs to be split algorithmically and not in a data-distributed fashion. The configuration adopted in this work is a highly parallel configuration for generating the real-time performance required. The distributed system is a set of separate sites where each site is a system of separate processors, each processor has its own memory (typically 256KBytes) and thus each system has independent local memory. The three major blocks introduced in this work are interconnected by transputer links/channels and are driven by a master processor, able to store up to 8MBytes of software code and data. The three blocks, namely the system simulator, the model simulator, and the controller, need to be synchronised so that each site proceeds in distinct steps with each step producing a numerical result. The result, as well as being local to the site, is also transmitted to the rest of the network and is available for global use.

A short description of the main blocks is now presented.

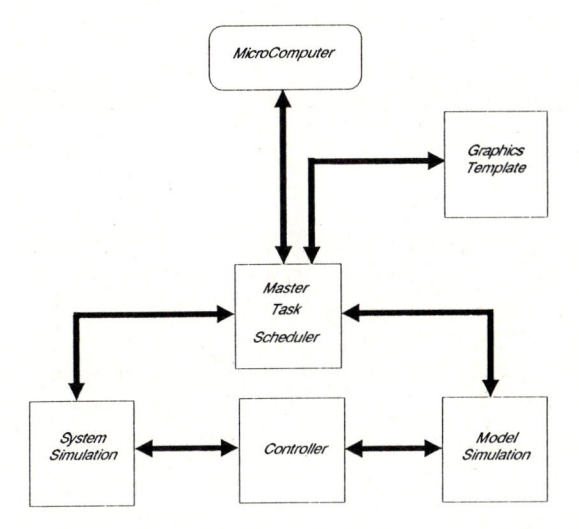

Figure 5: Functional decomposition of the control problem

3.1 System Simulation

Since the cantilever system did not exist in practice for testing of the modelling and controller design results, it was necessary to simulate the beam system equation (9). The finite difference (FD) scheme available to do this numerical simulation require extensive computational effort and sequential computing methods usually yield long execution times. The technique is however ideally suited for parallelism and it has been shown that parallel FD methods can yield dramatic speed improvements, see Virk and Kourmoulis [8].

The solution of the PDE exists in a space-time grid where it is possible to use either first central finite difference (FCFD) approximations in both the time and space dimensions or use FCFD in t and second central finite difference (SCFD) in x. The numerical solution then follows by using the difference equation together with known initial conditions to give $y(x, t)$ at the chosen number of node points in a row-by-row progression satisfying the boundary conditions at each iteration. The beam was partitioned into 20 sections or stations and these were split over four processors to achieve real-time simulation. Table 1 shows the simulation timing on various computing hardware systems.

3.2 Modelling

Since the infinite system modes are difficult to handle, a reduced-order model is derived. Assuming that 5 modes are present, a 10th order state-space representation can be obtained with each mode being decoupled from the other modes considered. This allows easy implementation on a parallel processing system since communication overheads are low, and the different modes can be solved on different processors for the speed-up.

The resulting state-space equations were distributed onto five transputers and then integrated using the fourth order Runge-Kutta method. This yielded a performance well within real-time bounds as shown in Table 1 where other configuration timings are also given.

The model thus obtained can provide estimates of the dominant states which can therefore be used in controller implementation, such as in for example, state feedback compensation.

Table 1: System and Modelling simulation timings

System simulation		Model simulation	
Network	Processing time (sec)	Network	Processing time (sec)
$SUN\ 3$	519.42	$SUN\ 3$	44.29
$1 \times T414$	1352.75	$1 \times T414$	155.82
$1 \times T800$	131.08	$1 \times T800$	13.81
$4 \times T800$	40.46	$5 \times T800$	4.26

Actual real-time over which simulations are performed = 60 seconds

With such a model the need for the construction of a state observers in controlling situations of this kind is removed.

3.3 Controller Design

Various design methodologies can be considered for obtaining a suitable control law. The approach taken was to design an optimal control law that minimised a linear quadratic performance index for the reduced order state-space model. We concentrate on the problem of optimising the transverse vibrations of the cantilever by using a number of control actuators placed along the beam. The solution to the resulting minimisation problem is given by the well known linear feedback control law which requires the solution of the corresponding matrix Riccati equation already discussed in Section 2. The Riccati equations can be solved off-line and the gains stored for on-line use or the complete processing can be performed on-line.

The resulting optimal control law is applied to both the model and system simulation block on-line for various disturbance signals and Figure 5 shows the result of typical responses. Due to possible variations in the system and model behaviour, differences between the two outputs can occur, these errors can however be eliminated by feedback techniques to fine tune the individual blocks. Table 2 shows the overall transputer system timing performance, as well as timings for other hardware implementations.

Table 2: Timings of vibration control transputer system

Actual time of simulation (sec)	Network Processing Time (sec)			
	$SUN\ 3$	$1 \times T414$	$1 \times T800$	$17 \times T800$ $2 \times T414$
1.0	26.44	81.96	7.55	0.68
30.0	793.29	2538.53	214.4	18.97
60.0	1586.57	5235.68	453.31	40.82

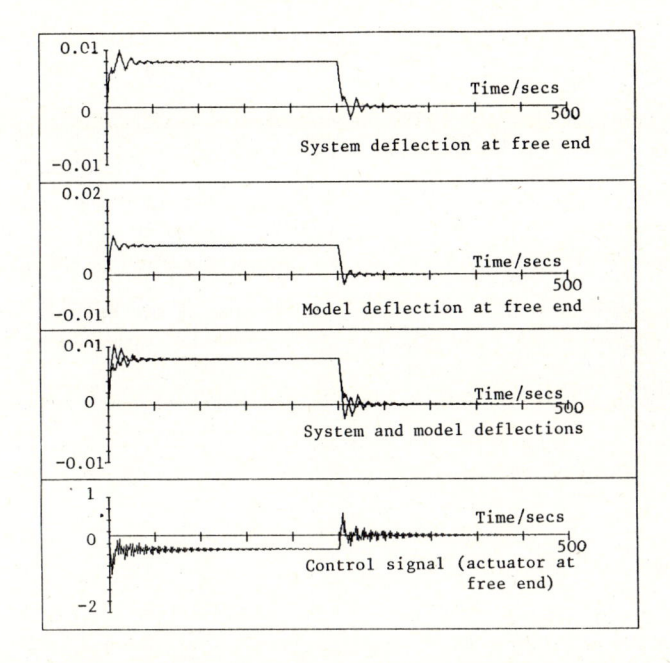

Figure 6: Optimal control results of cantilever system

4 Conclusion

The use of parallel processing techniques in obtaining real-time performances in two important areas of aerospace control systems have been clearly demonstrated. It has been found that the computational tasks can be split functionally into smaller sub-tasks which can be processed on different devices configured in suitable architectures for optimising the communciation aspects. It is imperative that such flexibility be available to the control engineer if he is to succeed in using parallel methods to a wide variety of applications.

References

[1] Tahir J,M and Virk G S, A real-time distributed algorithm for an aircraft longitidinal optimal autopilot to appear Concurrancy: Practice & Experience, 1990.

[2] Virk G S and Tahir J M, Parallel optimal control algorithms for Aircraft, IEE Colloquium on Navigation, Guidance and Control in Aerospace. Digest No.1989/142, 3/1 - 3/5, November 1989.

[3] Virk G S and Tahir J M, A real-time distributed optimal autopilot, in preparation.

[4] British Aerospace aircraft engineering data,(private correspondence).

[5] Babister A W, Aircraft dynamic stability and response, Pergamon Press 1980.

[6] Blakelock J H, Automatic control of aircraft and missiles, John Wiley & Sons 1965.

[7] Kwon W H, Bruckstein A M and Kailath T, Stabilising state feedback design via the moving horizon method, Int J Control, Vol.37, No.3, pp 631-643, 1983.

[8] Virk G S and Kourmoulis P K, On the simulation of flexible structure, IEE Conference Control 88, Oxford, pp 318-321, 1988.

[9] Kourmoulis P K and Virk G S, Parallel processing in the simulation of flexible structures, IEE Colloquium on Recent advances in parallel processing for control, Digest No 1988/94, 1988.

[10] Virk G S and Kourmoulis P K, Distributed simulation and optimal control of flexible beam structure systems, to be submitted to IEE Proc D Control Theory & Applications.

IMPLEMENTATION OF DIGITAL CONTROLLERS ON A TRANSPUTER-BASED SYSTEM

F Garcia Nocetti and PJ Fleming
School of Electronic Engineering Science
University of Wales, Bangor
Gwynedd LL57 1UT, UK

1. INTRODUCTION

Application goals of parallel processing in real-time digital control might be reduction in control law execution, the management of more complex algorithms or a fault-tolerant system architecture. Such applications make special demands of the parallel processing implementation since they invariably require that computations are carried out within relatively short sample intervals. When contemplating the implementation of control laws and associated software on these systems, we need to organise the control law to realise the maximum benefits of parallelism. To support the application of parallelism in this way we have developed tools to automate this process and to assist the control engineer to determine the likely speedup, the number of processors to be used, and experiment with alternative system topologies.

Here we describe how we have integrated the control system design package, MATLAB, with TDS (Transputer Development System) in a PC environment and developed new tools for automating the implementation of control algorithms onto transputer-based systems. The tools are used to map control laws onto transputer systems of different sizes and topologies, and to evaluate strategies, by displaying, on-line, task allocation, processor activity and performance data. Both static and dynamic task allocation strategies are studied.

2. CONTROLLER DEVELOPMENT WORKSTATION

The controller development workstation is a PC environment integrating MATLAB with TDS plus tools to automate the implementation of control algorithms on transputer systems. The need for such an environment arose out of our previous work on mapping strategies for implementing controllers onto transputer networks [1]. The effort involved in this task stimulated this research into the development of software tools to automate the process. The tools within the controller development workstation (see Fig.1) are grouped in two sets: *MATLAB Tools* for parallel partitioning, and *OCCAM Tools* for task allocation.

3. MATLAB TOOLS FOR PARALLEL PARTITIONING

MATLAB [2] is a collection of software tools for use in linear algebra, matrix manipulation and computation, and numerical analysis. MATLAB capabilities are extended by providing the user with a set of low-level commands and the prospect of defining new higher level functions with specific objectives through use of *m-files*. A number of Toolboxes are now available through this provision:- these include tools for Control Systems, Signal Processing, Identification and Multivariable Frequency Domain design.

The tools developed for parallel partitioning, based on MATLAB, generate a parallel representation of the original control algorithm as a number of independent tasks. A continuous controller description in block diagram form may be input. The software

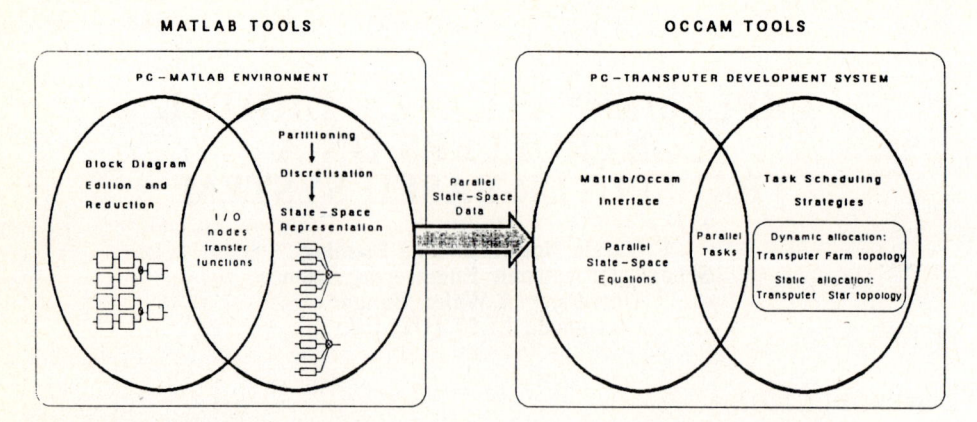

Fig.1 Software tools for mapping controllers on a transputer-based system

performs the partitioning, discretisation and parallel representation of the system as a number of state-space equations.

3.1 Block Diagram Data Entry

A MATLAB tool called *blkedit.m* has been developed to facilitate input of controller information. This tool automates the entry of transfer function blocks and interconnection data of a control algorithm, starting from a block diagram description. Nonlinear elements such as highest-wins, lowest-wins and relays cascaded to the outputs, can also be driven.

3.2 Generation of Parallel Tasks Representation

First, a MATLAB program, *blkpart.m,* transforms the control law into a number of independent tasks. It obtains the relationship between each input and output variable, and reduces each of these input-output transform relationships to a set of independent path transfer functions.

In order to avoid errors due to quantisation of coefficients and obtain a representation of the system as a number of parallel tasks, the high-order path transfer functions generated during the partitioning process are expanded into partial fractions. The resulting functions are discretised and finally represented in state-space form. The whole process is automated using a specially developed function called *paradata.m*. This tool produces an output database, which includes the state-space equations data and their relationships to form the controller outputs. The output database is ported to the Transputer Development System, where OCCAM-based Tools have been written, to evaluate a number of task allocation strategies on a parallel processing transputer-based system.

The software enables the user to perform automatic partitioning of control algorithms into a number of independent tasks. This is achieved by using the tools in the following sequence:

$$blkedit.m \rightarrow blkpart.m \rightarrow paradata.m$$

The technique is illustrated using a specific control law in Fig.2.

4. OCCAM TOOLS FOR TASK SCHEDULING

The Occam tools, developed in the TDS, automate the mapping of the controller tasks (as a collection of state-space equations) onto a number of transputer-based topologies, using either static or dynamic task allocation strategies. The tools also permit the simulation and evaluation of both strategies, by monitoring and displaying processor activity and performance. The important point to note here is that the different strategies are tested on the *actual* hardware, thus avoiding simulation inaccuracies associated with imperfect knowledge of system behaviour (e.g. task switching, communications).

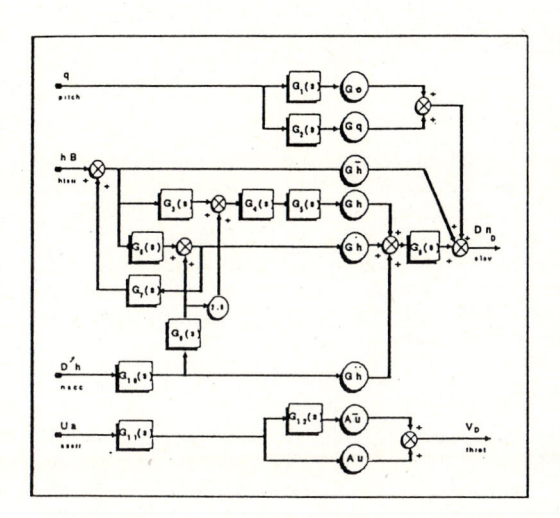

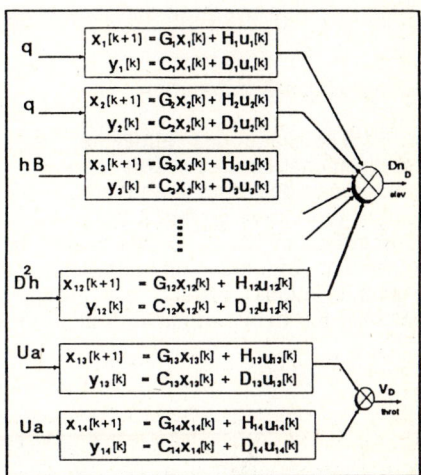

(a) (b)

Fig.2 (a) VAP flight control law; (b) Parallel state-space representation

```
Command (A)        PROCESSOR FARM ACTIVITY        EXE.TIME:  2.612 ms

                 ------    ------    ------    ------    ------    ------
  ! MASTER !===!  W 1 !===!  W 2 !===!  W 3 !===!  W 4 !===!  W 5 !===!  W 6 !
                 ------    ------    ------    ------    ------    ------
    No.Tasks    Tsk Ord   Tsk Ord   Tsk Ord   Tsk Ord   Tsk Ord   Tsk Ord
     [14]        1   1     2   1    . 3   1    4   1     5   2     6   1
                 7   1     8   1     9   1    10   1    12   1    14   1
 t:  3.5   s    11   2    13   1
```

Fig.3 Processor activity -farm topology

4.1 Dynamic Task Allocation

The dynamic task allocation tools are a number of OCCAM programs based on a processor farm computational model. This model uses a single processor for scheduling tasks, as they are required, to a number of worker processors connected in a linear array, see Fig 3. The application code, in our case, the evaluation of a state-space equation, is run in each of the worker processors and routers are used to perform data and results routing pass through the network. Tasks are passed to processors for execution as they are required in order to utilise the full processing potential of the system, thus providing an automatic mechanism for dynamic load balancing. Results are collected from the master as they are produced from the network. Finally, these results are used to compute the system controlled outputs.

We have investigated schemes for scheduling the data to the processors in the farm which keep the overhead of communicating data to the minimun. Also, the original farm model has been further extended by configuring the system as a triple linear topology. The extended model has the same conceptual architecture as the basic model - a single controller processor with a number of workers - but in this extended case the workers are grouped on three lanes. This required a more sophisticated tasks allocation mechanism, which means a greater scheduling overhead. However, there is a shortest path between the controller and any worker. This extended version, then, has the aim of reducing communication overhead and increasing the effective bandwidth of the system.

4.2 Static Task Allocation

The static task allocation tools are based on a processor star topology as the computational structure. This topology, illustrated in Fig.4, employs a master processor for controlling input and output and distributing a package of fixed tasks to a number of worker processors arranged around the central node. The tasks are allocated to the worker processors and bound to that processor for its lifetime. The master also allocates to itself a number of tasks and processes them in a similar way to the other workers. Communications between task groups only takes place during the initial distribution of data and the final computation to form the output values.

```
Command {A}    PROCESSOR   ACTIVITY    Exe.Time:   0.921 ms
=========================================================
         ============================================
  "      ----"---     --------       "      --------       "      --------
 "=| Master |========|    W1   |    "==|   W2   |    "==|   W3   |   No.Tasks
  ---------            --------       --------       --------        [14]
     Tsk Ord          Tsk Ord       Tsk Ord        Tsk Ord
      1   1            4   1         7   1          10  1
      2   1            5   2         8   1          11  2
      3   1            6   1         9   1          12  1
     13   1
     14   1
```

Fig.4 Processor activity -star topology

4.3 Occam Tools Performance

In its current realisation the processor farm approach (dynamic task allocation) displays an inferior performance when compared with the static approach, see Fig.5. Following [3], this result was expected and is well understood; implementing the scheduler in software presents a formidable overhead in real-time control systems, where individual tasks are relatively short. Communications overhead is another significant component and is exacerbated when the linear array is long. For example, no further speedup can be obtained for more than 5 workers in the test case presented in Fig.5.

The extended version, using the triple linear topology, offers an improvement in performance, reducing the executing time significantly. In this case the master is able to allocate tasks to each line in parallel.

The static allocation approach exhibits the best performance. This strategy has the virtue of minimising communication between task groups since this only takes place during the initial distribution of data and the final computation to form the output values.

Work at Bangor, by the authors of Ref 2, to produce a hardware version of the processor farm scheduler is expected to make this approach more attractive. Besides computational speedup issues, topology choice may also be influenced by other issues such as fault tolerance and hardware uniformity.

5 CONCLUDING REMARKS

A number of tools have been developed for automating the partitioning of control

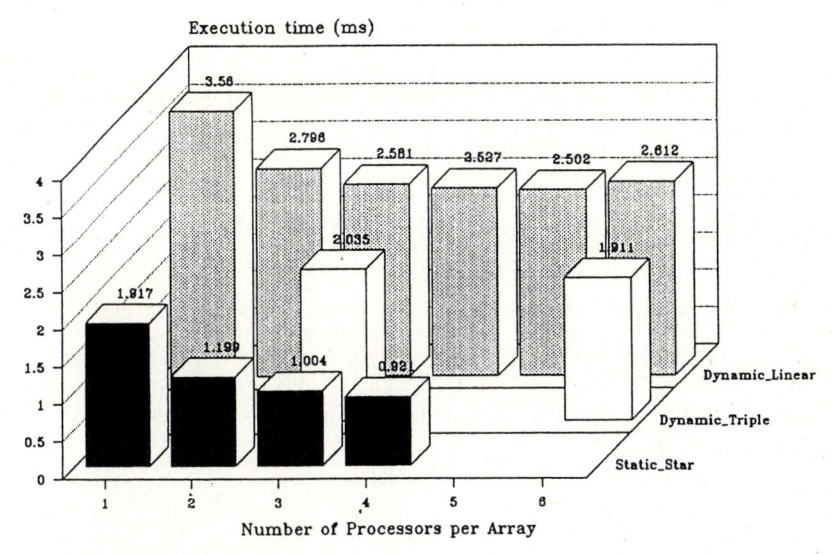

Fig.5 Performance analysis: dynamic v static task allocation

algorithms as a number of parallel tasks and for the scheduling of these on a transputer-based system. Strategies of dynamic and static task allocation have been implemented and their features described. The tools permit simulation and evaluation of strategies, by displaying processor activity and performance.

A number of tools have been developed for automating the partitioning of control algorithms as a number of parallel tasks and for the allocation of these tasks on a transputer-based system. A MATLAB-based Toolbox provides a number of tools for automating the parallel partitioning of controllers into modules or tasks. Strategies of dynamic and static task allocation have been implemented through an OCCAM-based Toolbox and their features described. The tools permit evaluation of the various strategies on-line, by displaying processor activity and performance.

ACKNOWLEDGEMENTS

F Garcia Nocetti wishes to acknowledge the support of CONACYT and National University of Mexico (UNAM) for the support of his research work at University of Wales, Bangor.

REFERENCES

1. Fleming, PJ, Garcia Nocetti, DF and Thompson, HA: "Implementation of a transputer-based flight controller", Proc. IEE Control '88 Conference, Oxford, April, 1988, pp.719-724.

2. Moler C, Little J, Bangert S and Kleinman S: PC-MATLAB User's Guide, The MathWorks, Inc., Sherbon, MA 01770, USA, 1985.

3. Jones DI and Entwistle PM: "Parallel computation of an algorithm in robotic control" Proc *IEE Control 88 Conference,* Oxford, April 1988, pp 438-443.

A transputer based processor farm for real-time control applications.

P.N.F. da Fonseca, P.M. Entwistle, D.I. Jones

School of Electronic Engineering Science,
University College of North Wales,
Dean Street, Bangor, Gwynedd LL57 1UT.

Abstract: This paper describes how a transputer network organised as a processor farm was applied to the implementation of a real-time control algorithm, specifically the computation of the Newton Euler (NE) inverse dynamics equations for robot control. A simulation of the processor farm which includes a detailed model of the transputer was written in Simscript II. This presents information on processor activity, task timing and communication overhead during execution of the computation. Its role in determining the critical factors affecting the execution of the NE algorithm is described. The design of a task scheduler implemented as specialised hardware is presented and its performance evaluated by simulation and direct measurement.

1. Introduction.

One of the attractions of parallel processing for control engineers is the prospect of implementing complex real-time control algorithms at a high computational rate [1]. The transputer appears to offer a straightforward and relatively low-cost means of implementing parallel processing. It has a number of features which have made it popular for parallel processing implementation over a wide range of application areas, including control engineering [2].

A well-known method of organising a network of transputers is the *processor farm*, where a Master scheduler is responsible for allocating the tasks which compose the algorithm to a number of Slave processors. The dynamic scheduling which is characteristic of the processor farm has a number of advantages [1,3]. The prospect of circumventing the explicit coding of parallelism or the determination of a static task schedule is particularly appealing. For these reasons we were motivated to investigate the applicability of this approach to real-time control problems.

2. Robot inverse dynamics.

The application chosen for the investigation was the calculation of the inverse dynamics for a robot manipulator [4]. This was a good problem to consider for several reasons:

o   A good body of literature on applying parallel processing to this algorithm already existed [5]; indeed it has become something of a benchmark algorithm for parallel computation in robotics. Previous work concentrates on static task allocation and often assumes a specific robot type (which reduces the problem size). In contrast, the work described here uses dynamic task allocation and preserves the full generality of the NE equations;

o   The standard NE algorithm [6] has a mix of parallel and sequential sections (though recently a version that is more amenable to parallel partitioning has been reported [7]);

○ The computation must typically be completely computed within a few milliseconds (i.e. it is a *hard* real-time problem since it is within a feedback loop and any latency will have a destabilising effect on the dynamic response).

It should be noted that the scale of the computation is quite small (about 1500 flops) but the short sampling time of the real-time controller requires a high computational rate - say 1 Mflop for a 1.5ms sampling interval.

The general NE inverse dynamics computation consists of a set of ten equations to be evaluated for each of the robot's joints (typically 6). Quantities such as the velocities, accelerations and torques are computed for each robot link; essentially this involves a large number of 3x3 matrix additions and multiplications. Each equation was considered to be a *task* and the task graph for the case of a 3 link robot is shown in Fig.1.

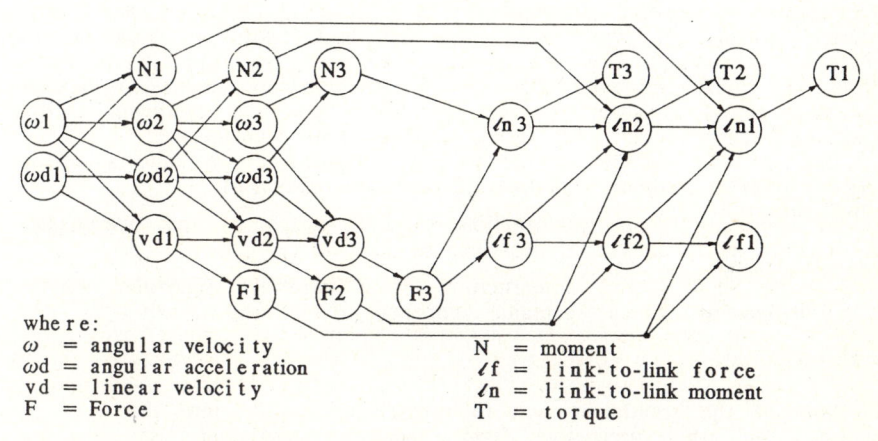

where:
ω = angular velocity
ωd = angular acceleration
vd = linear velocity
F = Force

N = moment
ℓf = link-to-link force
ℓn = link-to-link moment
T = torque

Fig.1 Task graph for modified 3 link NE inverse dynamics.

It is possible to obtain more parallelism from the algorithm by considering individual terms within equations as tasks [5]. However we chose not to do this as the finer granularity would have adversely affected the Run-time / Communicate-time (R/C) ratio and increased the size of the task set to be scheduled.

3. The processor farm.

The processor farm architecture is shown in Fig.2. There are three chains of Worker processors arranged in a star configuration about a central scheduler. The code for each task is held in each one of the Worker processors. When supplied by the scheduler with a data packet (consisting of a processor identifier, task identifier and input data), execution on that Worker may proceed. It was also found beneficial to incorporate a task buffer within each Worker process. Each Worker processor may therefore be allocated a second task which is ready to proceed immediately the current task is complete. Communication of data up the Worker chain and results back to the scheduler is by means of data-router processes which are run at the higher of the transputer's two priority levels.

The central scheduler consists of a separate transputer on which the scheduling software is run. The fourth link is connected to the TDS as an external interface. The scheduling software continually searches a table for a task which can run, by virtue of all its input data being available, and assigns it to a free processor as soon as possible.

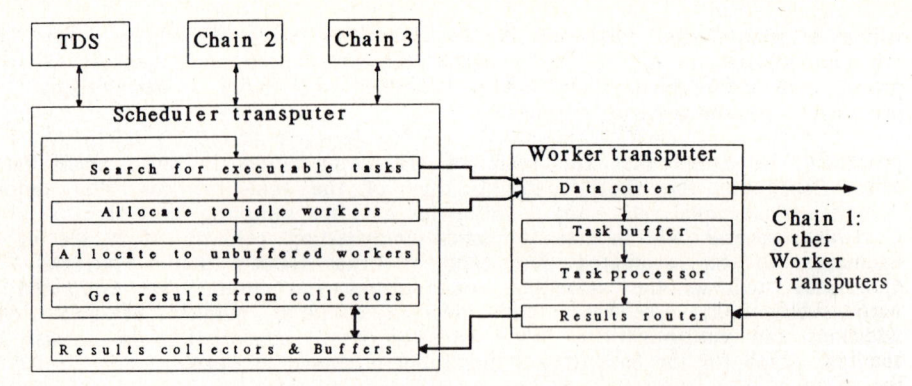

Fig.2 Structure of the transputer based processor farm.

The results of initial experiments with a T414-15 processor farm, were reported in [4]. It was found that the best execution time on multiple processors was about 25% *greater* than the execution time on one processor! While this figure improved with new compiler releases and some re-coding it was nevertheless apparent that *on this time scale* the overheads incurred in maintaining the processor farm fatally prejudiced its performance.

Rather than abandoning the potential benefits of dynamic scheduling for other methods of implementing this algorithm we opted for:

o A more thorough investigation of the causes of the overheads, leading to the simulation described in the next section;

o Design, and partial construction, of a hardware scheduler which considerably reduces the major component of overhead.

4. The Simulation.

The goal of the simulation was to provide an insight into the very complex behaviour of the processor farm and, in particular, to identify any 'bottlenecks' responsible for restricting the computational performance. A computational model of the transputer was devised [8] and embedded within the structure of a processor farm. A *static* description of the computational model is given in Fig.3.

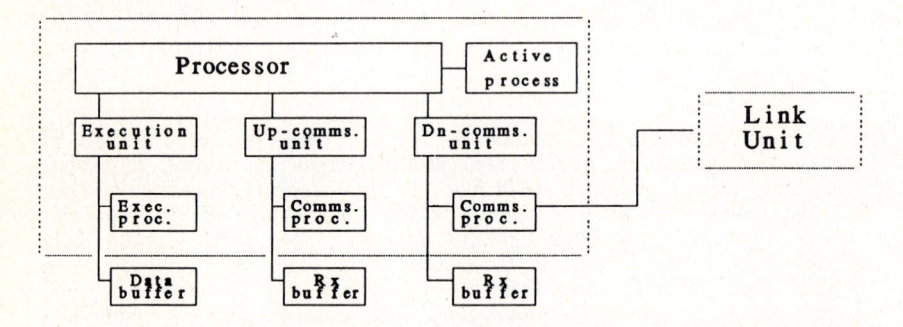

Fig. 3 Computational model of transputer used in the simulation.

The transputer is viewed as being composed of three Units - one for execution and two for communications - and an active process register which points to which of the Units' processes is currently active. Each Unit is responsible for one (or more) of the actions occurring within the transputer. A 'Link' process, external to the transputer model, acts as a medium for inter-processor communication.

Dynamically, each transputer's action is modelled in terms of three processes - Communication, Execution and Transmission - each of which is strictly defined:

Communication Process : The Communication process is assigned to the Communication Unit and is responsible for identifying the destination of a data packet and either sending it to the appropriate neighbour or lodging it with that processor. This process is parameterized by the *interrupt time* which is the time interval between receiving an incoming data packet and sending it to its next destination and the *context switching time* which is the time interval between sending a data packet and releasing the transputer for other processes.

Execution process : The Execution process is assigned to the Execution Unit and is responsible for the (notional) execution of a task. The time spent in the Execution process is the computational length of the task plus overheads associated with searching for the appropriate section of code and the overhead associated with preparing a results packet for return to the scheduler. The task length and overheads are defined by 3 parameters: *pre-processing overhead, processing speed and post-processing overhead.*

The scheduler itself is a special case of an Execution process and is defined by a single parameter, the *scheduling time*, which is the time required for one pass of the scheduling algorithm. Variants of the basic scheduling policy may be specified, to allow for task prioritisation.

Transmission process : The transmission process is assigned to a Link Unit and is responsible for collecting a data packet from a sending processor, transmitting it (notionally) along a link and storing it in the receiving processor. The process is parameterized by the *trasnmission time* which depends on the volume of data within the packet to be transmitted and an additional overhead.

Each process may exist in one of six states and the activation, or de-activation, of processes is determined by an operating system kernel. This implements a set of rules to define the transition of each process from one state to another. The operating system continually searches the processes for conditions which cause a state transition. Each transition is recorded as a discrete event and the simulated time at which it occurred is calculated from the timing parameters. Hence a complete account of the progress of the computation can be obtained.

The user supplies the simulation package with information about the algorithm (task times, precedence relationships, amount of input/output data), the architecture (interconnection paths between the processors), and the environment (scheduling policy and timing parameters for the transputer model).

The simulation output consists of a text file containing a trace history of the computation and which may be analyzed in detail by the user. There is also a facility for visualizing the results by means of a colour graphic display which provides global, qualitative information about the simulation run. There are several display types. For instance, the *Gantt Chart*, as shown in Fig.4, gives a time history of the state of each processor with a colour code to denote whether a processor is idle, communicating, executing or suspended. The *Activity Map*, as shown in Fig.5, shows the architectural layout with a colour coded representation of the average activity of the processors and links. There are also *Activity Charts* which yield information about the effectiveness of the scheduling procedure and histograms for the queue lengths of ready tasks and free processors.

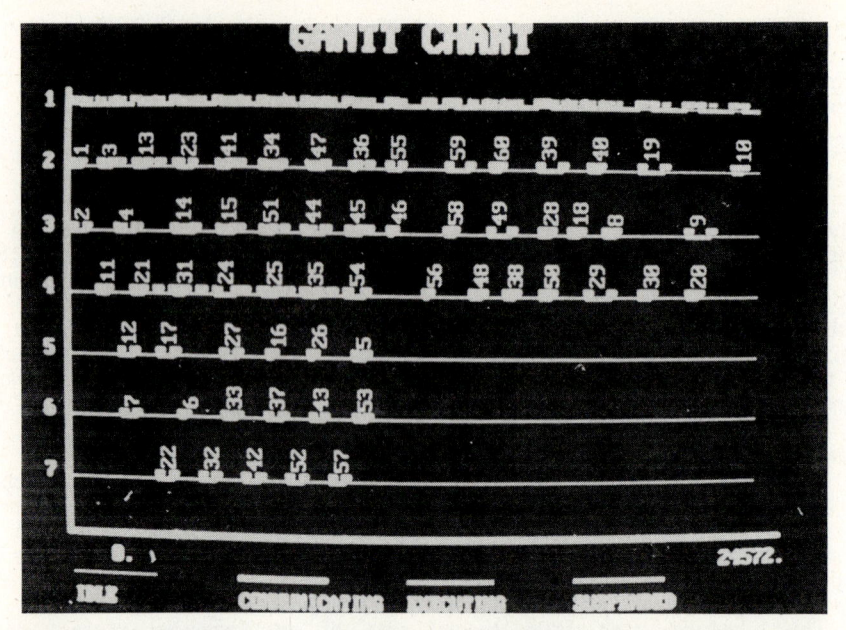

Fig. 4 Typical Gantt chart showing time history of processor farm state.

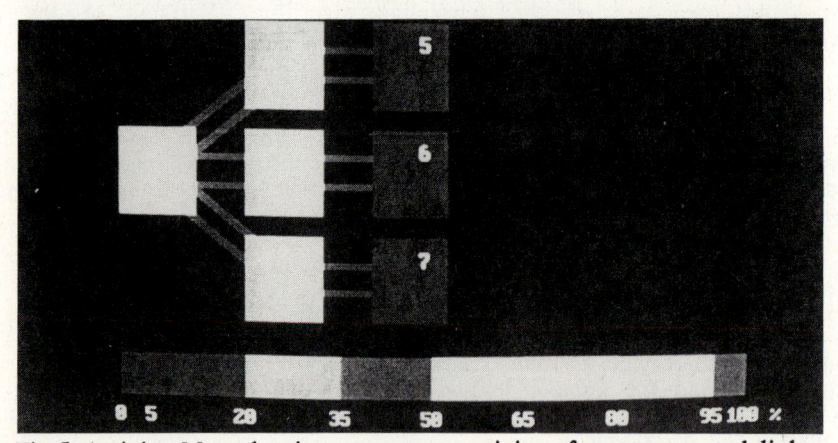

Fig.5 Activity Map showing percentage activity of processors and links.

5. Applying the simulation to the processor farm.

Data for the simulation was obtained by measuring the time taken to execute the code for each task by means of the transputer's high priority timer. Further measurements allowed values of the timing parameters to be estimated [9]. The simulation was used to predict the execution time of the NE equations for a robot with 6 links. The top two curves show that the predicted values and the values measured from the processor farm itself agree quite closely. Scrutiny of the simulation results showed that the dominant overhead was due to the scheduler [8] because each pass of the scheduler takes about $560\mu s$, which is longer than the average task time of about $350\mu s$.

The simulated execution rate of the scheduler was increased by a factor of 16 which yielded a substantial improvement as shown in the lower curve in Fig.6. Further, the simulation strongly indicated that very little improvement was obtainable by a further increase in scheduling rate; the limiting factor was now the algorithm itself. The *lower bound* on execution time, given the parallelism available with these task definitions, is estimated to be about 55% of its measured value on the processor farm.

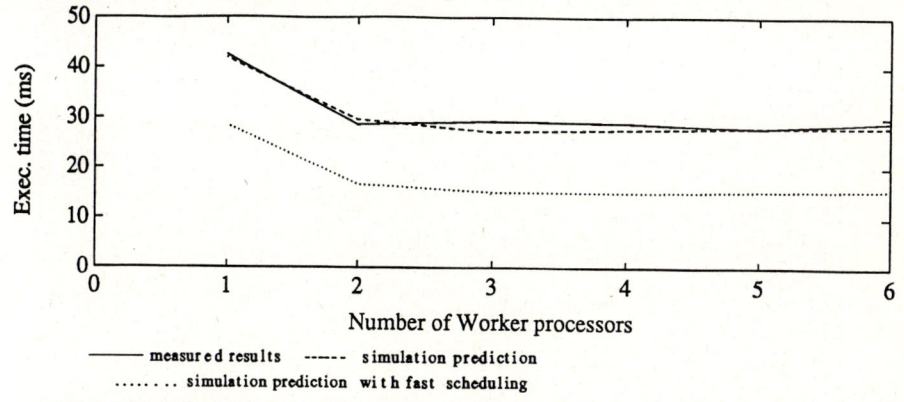

Fig.6 Simulation results predicting execution time of processor farm.

6. A hardware scheduler.

Further measurements of the execution time of the scheduler code showed that almost 70% of the total was spent searching a table for tasks that were ready for execution. In view of the simulation results, it was decided that this section of the scheduler should be realised as separate hardware. It was estimated that this would reduce the search time by two orders of magnitude, the remaining scheduler time amounting to about 30% of its previous value. In turn, the simulation predicted that this would reduce the total execution time to about 70% of its previous value (noting that 55% is the best improvement possible).

Fig. 7 is a block diagram of the hardware scheduler which performs the search for executable tasks. The condition matrix is realised as a bipolar static RAM memory which stores the precedence relationships between the tasks. The FINEXEC register sets a bit for each task that has been completed by the processor farm. A counter is used to extract successive entries from the matrix which are compared with the contents of the FINEXEC register to identify executable tasks. The task identifier is then passed to the support processor interface where it is associated with a free processor number and the correct numerical data to form a packet; this is passed to the Worker chain for processing.

The prototype hardware [9] was constructed to handle a maximum of 32 tasks and was therefore limited to handling the NE equations for a 3 link robot. The hardware was interfaced to the transputer network by means of two link adaptors and the root processor's code modified to take account of the new hardware.

The results are shown in Fig.8. The bottom curve shows the lower bound on execution time with negligible scheduling overhead, as predicted by the simulation. The top curve shows the measured execution time using software scheduling. The middle curve shows that the hardware scheduler has yielded a distinct improvement in the execution time.

7. Conclusions and Reflections.

We have shown that it is possible to obtain improved execution times over 1 processor even when using dynamic scheduling on these very small time scales. The reduction from 9.7ms on a single processor to 8.8ms on 3 processors is small, but significant. It is to be expected that the hardware scheduler when

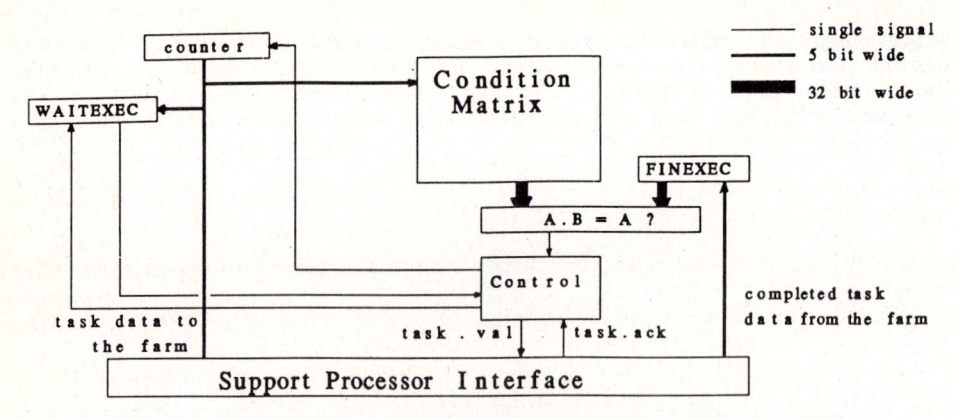

Fig.7 A block diagram of the 'executable task search' part of the hardware scheduler.

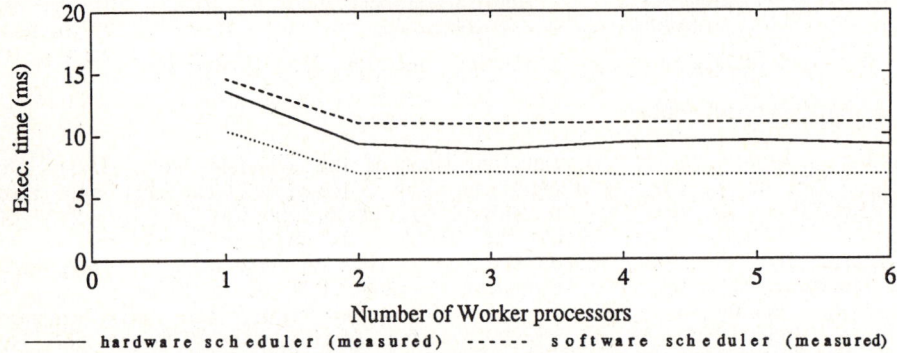

Fig.8 Performance of the processor farm with a hardware scheduler.

applied to the 6-link robot case would yield more substantial savings. The simulation shows that a further reduction is possible by exporting *all* the scheduling to hardware.

Undoubtedly, a lower execution time could have been achieved by specifying a particular robot type, partitioning for a finer grain parallelism by sub-dividing the NE equations into smaller tasks and static allocation of clusters to fixed processors. However this would have meant foregoing the potential benefits of the processor farm and would have been contrary to the aims of the investigation. In any case, it has been shown that an adequate computational rate for the NE equation set can be achieved using digital signal processors - Kabuka & Escoto [10] have recently demonstrated a 3KHz sampling rate.

In fact, it is reasonable to suppose that a single T800 transputer is capable of accomplishing the computation. The floating point operation on the T414-15, used throughout this investigation, is about $14\mu s$ whereas the T800-20 is quoted at about 500ns [11] - a factor of 28 times greater. One T414-15 took 21.5ms to compute the NE equations, so it is likely that the T800 would achieve of the order of 1ms. Though an interesting case to study, it appears that the computation of the NE equations no longer requires parallel processing. Nevertheless, the idea of the processor farm and dynamic scheduling is applicable to the larger computational tasks which the future will inevitably bring.

It is interesting to note that, when this study was started (in 1986), there was no single microprocessor on the market capable of executing the whole algorithm within the required sampling time. A typical performance capability at this time is that quoted by Kasahara & Narita [5] who used multiple 8086/8087 processors on a common bus with shared memory. They computed the NE equations specifically for the Stanford Manipulator thus reducing the computation to 30-50% of the general case. They reported an execution time of 29.7ms on a single processor, falling to 6.73ms for 5 processors. Yet, within 2 or 3 years, the technology had caught up. In a recent article, Aspinall [12] remarks that:

"The performance (*of parallel processors*) is often disappointing when compared to a monoprocessor structure. Apart from some extreme examples the degree of parallelism is quite modest. Thus the speed advantage is modest, soon to be eliminated by technology improvements which the monoprocessor can readily exploit. If the degree of parallelism offers only an order of magnitude improvement in performance it may be worth waiting for the technology to improve and then to implement a simple serial structure".

This implies that software and hardware development for a parallel processor must take no longer than required for a sequential processor. We therefore see an urgent need for software tools [13], and an underlying architecture, to expedite this approach. Our further work is aimed at extending the simulation software and scheduler hardware to meet this goal [9].

Acknowledgements.

This work was partly funded by grant GR/E 1664.9 awarded by the Science & Engineering Research Council. Mr. Entwistle was supported by a S.E.R.C. studentship and Mr. da Fonseca by a European Social Fund studentship.

References.

[1] Jones, D.I., *Parallel architectures for real-time control*, Electronics & Communications Engineering Journal, 1 (5), 217-223, 1989.
[2] Fleming, P.J. (ed), *Parallel Processing in Control*, Peter Pergrinus, London, 1988.
[3] Entwistle, P.M., da Fonseca, P.N.F. & Jones, D.I., *Task scheduling for a transputer based multiprocessor with applications in control engineering*, Proceedings of International Workshop on Algorithms and Parallel VLSI Architectures, Pont-à-Mousson, France, June 1990.
[4] Jones, D.I., Entwistle, P.M., *Parallel computation of an algorithm in robotic control*, Proceedings I.E.E. International Conference CONTROL'88, University of Oxford, April 1988, pp.438-443.
[5] Kasahara, H. & Narita, S., *Parallel processing of robot arm control computation on a multi-microprocessor system*, IEEE Journal of Robotics & Automation, RA-1 (2), 1985, pp.104-113.
[6] Craig, J.J., *Introduction to Robotics : Mechanics and Control*, Addison Wesley, 1986.
[7] Hemami, H., *A state space model for interconnected rigid bodies*, IEEE Trans. Automatic Control, AC-27 (2), 1982, pp.376-382.
[8] da Fonseca, P.N.F., *A tool for the designer of multiprocessor systems*, MSc Thesis, University of Wales, Bangor, 1989.
[9] Entwistle, P.M., *Parallel processing for real-time control*, PhD thesis, University of Wales, Bangor, 1990.
[10] Kabuka, M. & Escoto, R., *Real-time implementation of the Newton-Euler equations of motion on the NEC uPD77230 DSP*, IEEE Micro, February 1989, pp.66-76.
[11] INMOS, *Transputer Technical Notes*, Prentice Hall, 1989, p.208
[12] Aspinall, D., *Structures for parallel processing*, Computing & Control Engineering Journal, 1 (1), 1990, pp.15-22.
[13] Garcia-Nocetti, F. et al, *Implementation of a transputer based flight controller*, Proc. IEE (D), 137 (3), 1990, 130-136.

MULTIPROCESSOR SOLUTION OF NONLINEAR EQUATIONS FOR CHEMICAL PROCESS SIMULATION

D. Juárez   C.C. Pantelides

Centre for Process System Engineering
Imperial College of Sci Tech & Med
Prince Consort Road
London SW7 2BY
U. K.

ABSTRACT

In the steady-state simulation of continuous processes, the underlying numerical problem is the solution of large sparse systems of nonlinear algebraic equations. The work presented here concentrates on exploiting parallelism in evaluating equation residuals and their Jacobian matrices; often these calculations consume a large percentage of the total computational effort, especially when rigorous thermodynamic property calculations are involved.

A Newton-type iterative process was parallelised by employing two types of concurrent processes, the coordinator and the executive. The former controls the overall convergence, while each of the executives evaluates, upon request, a part of the residual vector, or the related section of the Jacobian matrix.

The application of the above algorithm to the simulation of three typical chemical processes is presented.

The necessary software was developed using the 3L parallel C compiler running on a network of 4 T800 transputers hosted by a PC.

SUMMARY

Chemical processes consist of networks of interconnected processing units performing different types of operations, such as reaction, separation and heat exchange. Output streams from one unit (generally consisting of mixtures of several components) enter other units for further processing. Unreacted feedstocks are recycled so as to improve the overall efficiency of the process. Thus most processes involve strong interactions among their constituent elements, the analysis of which necessitates a high degree of detailed mathematical modelling.

The behaviour of chemical processes under steady-state conditions is normally described by large sets of nonlinear algebraic equations, which are often solved by a member of the Newton family of methods. The most computationally expensive parts of this type of method are the linear algebra calculations (mainly the solution of a large, sparse unsymmetric linear system at each iteration), and the evaluations of the equation residuals and their partial derivatives (the Jacobian matrix).

Significant attention has already been devoted in the literature to the parallelisation of linear algebra calculations. However, in many chemical process simulations by far the dominant cost (in excess 80%) is that of residual evaluations. This is especially so when rigorous physical property calculations are required. The situation is further exacerbated by the fact that exact analytical expressions are often not available for the partial derivatives required by Newton's method; finite difference perturbations can be used to approximate them, but these require additional residual evaluations.

The work described in this paper represents an attempt to parallelise the calculation of equation residuals and Jacobian approximations. This was achieved by splitting the computational load between a main coordinator process, and multiple copies of worker processes. Each worker process is given responsibility for the calculation of part of the residual vector, with the loads being roughly balanced among different slaves.

The above algorithm was implemented in C using the 3L parallel C compiler running on a network of 4 T800 transputers hosted by a PC. The resulting code was tested using several process engineering problems. Performance comparisons with a purely sequential code are presented for some of these problems.

Acknowledgements

This work was supported by SERC grant ref. GR/F 32721.

Implementation of the Binary Hough Transform in Pipelined Multi-Transputer Architectures

Luciano da Fontoura Costa[*][†] and Mark B. Sandler[*]

[*] Dept. of Electronic and Electrical Eng., King's College London, University of London, Strand, London, WC2R 2LS

[†] Instituto de Fisica e Quimica de Sao Carlos, Universidade de Sao Paulo, Caixa Postal 369, Sao Carlos, SP, 13560 Brazil

> **Abstract.** This paper discusses the implementation of the binary Hough transform in pipelined multi-transputer architectures and presents actual execution times.

1. Introduction

The binary Hough transform (BHT) [1],[2] is a simple and efficient technique for detection of lines and line segments in digital images. It is based on a modification of the Hough transform with slope/intercept parameterization which, for image and accumulator arrays with appropriate dimensions, gives the following advantages over the standard Hough transform with normal parameterization and other previous HT variations:

a. only additions and binary shifts are needed during its calculation;
b. it provides exact representation of the sampled parameter (slope);
c. the calculated parameter (intercept) can be determined with full precision;
d. optimal efficiency of memory utilization for representation of the parameter space can be achieved with little additional effort [3];
e. at least for 128x128 images, it allows better accuracy and effectivity than the standard Hough transform with normal parameterization [3].

These advantages have motivated the proposal of three systolic architectures for the BHT [1],[2]; the VLSI design of a basic BHT module [4]; the proposal of a complete and efficient system for real time detection of line-segments [5] and the implementation of the BHT as a sequential algorithm [2] which was later improved and used to evaluate the accuracy and effectivity of BHT [3]. This paper is intended to discuss the implementation of the BHT in pipelined multi-transputer architectures and determine actual times for its execution over 128x128 images. For comparison purposes, the standard Hough transform with normal parameterization (SHT) [6] is also implemented in T414 and T800 single-transputers which represent two broad classes of processors: with slow and fast multiplication. As the SHT was found to be considerably slower than the BHT it has not been considered for implementation in multi-transputer architectures.

Although the presented BHT algorithm implementation can be used in multi-transputer systems for general application in pattern recognition, the authors have been specially interested in the speed allowed by transputers for extension of the evalution of accuracy and effectivity of the BHT and its comparison with other HT variations [3].

The paper starts with a brief review of the BHT and follows by presenting an efficient sequential BHT algorithm, adapting it to pipelined operation in multiple transputers and presenting and discussing the obtained execution times in a multi-transputer pipelined T800 architecture. More details about the Hough transform and the BHT can be found respectively in [7] and [1]-[5].

2. The Binary Hough Transform

For images with dimension NxN, $N=2^i$ and accumulator arrays (AA_1, AA_2, AA_3 and AA_4) with dimension $N_M \times (N_C+1)$, $N_M=2^j$ and $N_C=2^k$; $i,j,k \in \{1,2,3,...\}$, the BHT consists of the calculation of expressions (1)-(4) and subsequent update of the accumulator arrays for a series of m_v's, $v=1,2,3$ and 4, for every edge element (x,y) in the image.

$$c_1(m_1) := \text{Round}\{(y - m_1 2^{-j} x + N)/2^{i-k+1}\} \qquad (1)$$

$$c_2(m_2) := \text{Round}\{(y + m_2 2^{-j} x)/2^{i-k+1}\} \qquad (2)$$

$$c_3(m_3) := \text{Round}\{(x - m_3 2^{-j} y + N)/2^{i-k+1}\} \qquad (3)$$

$$c_4(m_4) := \text{Round}\{(x + m_4 2^{-j} y)/2^{i-k+1}\} \qquad (4)$$

The respective resolution for calculation of parameters slope and intercept are $\Delta M = 2^{-j}$ and $\Delta C = 2^{i-k+1}$. Each peak in the accumulator arrays describes a possible line with parameters slope and intercept which can be determined from mv and cv as described in [1] [2]. A connectivity analysis [8] can be applied in order to confirm the line candidates and to determine the extremities of line segments.

3. A Sequential Algorithm for the BHT

An efficient and quite simple sequential BHT algorithm, presented in [3], is based on the use of successive additions and subtractions and is composed of four main parts respective to expressions (1)-(4) which differ from one another by the initial value (ai_1, ai_2, ai_3, ai_4) and by the use of additions or subtractions. For ai_1=(INT y)+N; ai_2=(INT y); ai_3=(INT x)+N; ai_4=(INT x); op_1, op_3 = "-"; op_2,op_4 = "+"; b_1,b_2 = x and b_3,b_4 = y; the basic OCCAM BHT procedure to be applied over each edge element (x,y), x and y are of type BYTE, is presented in the following:

$$
\begin{aligned}
&m:=0 \\
&s:=k-i+j+1 \\
&b:=1<<(s-1) \\
&av:=ai_v<<j \\
&\text{WHILE } m<=nm \\
&\quad \text{SEQ} \\
&\quad\quad \text{IF} \\
&\quad\quad\quad av/\backslash b=0 \\
&\quad\quad\quad\quad cv:=av>>s \\
&\quad\quad\quad \text{TRUE} \\
&\quad\quad\quad\quad cv:=(av>>s)+1 \\
&\quad\quad add:=(m<<nm)+(\text{INT } cv) \\
&\quad\quad aav[add]:=aav[add]+1 \\
&\quad\quad av:=av\ op_v\ b_v \\
&\quad\quad m:=m+1
\end{aligned}
$$

It should be observed that limits are imposed by the finite word length in integer arithmetic to ΔC and the image size. We assume henceforth N_M = 16 and N = 128, which do not violate those limits.

4. BHT in Pipelined Multi-Transputers Architectures

HT techniques are especially suitable for parallel implementations [7]. Most of HT techniques, BHT and SHT included, are characterized by basic operations whose inputs are the edge elements coordinates only. Although other parallelization strategies can be used, the afore mentioned characteristic can be effectively exploited by making each processing element (hence PE) responsible for the determination of the calculated parameter (intercept in the BHT and normal distance in the SHT) for a series of sampled parameters (slope in the BHT and angle in the SHT). This task assignment implies that each pixel has to be processed by every PE in the architecture and the ideal way to do this is by broadcasting each edge element to every PE. However, this is not straightforward with transputers and alternative configurations have to be considered. We have found the use of pipelining especially suitable due to its inherent simplicity and straightforward implementation on transputers.

A natural implementation of the BHT is as four pipelines, each one responsible for the calculation of one of the four main BHT parts (v=1, 2, 3 and 4), as depicted in figure 1. As there are N_M sampled values of the intercept parameters to be calculated in each of the four branches in the BHT, each of the p PEs is assigned to a range of N_M/p of such values (for the sake of simplicity we have assumed that N_M is an integer multiple of p). The previous algorithm can be directly executed by each PE for ai_1=((INT y)-(Kx))+N; ai_2=(INT y)-(Kx); ai_3=((INT x)+(Ky))+N and ai_4=(INT x)+(Ky) and K=Nm/p.

Figure 2 shows the assumed operation of the pipeline where Tt and Tr are respectively the time to transmit and

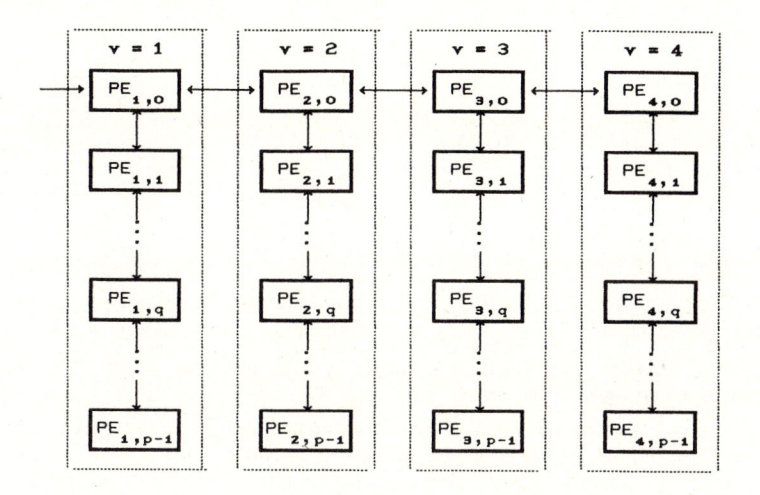

Figure 1 - Pipelined multiprocessor architecture for the BHT

receive the coordinates of all N_e edge elements (i.e. $2N_e$ bytes have to be transmited, one for x and one for y) and Tp is the time to determine the respective range of calculated parameters and subsequent updating of the accumulator array for all Ne edge elements to be processed by the BHT.
Although the distribution by broadcasting presents an upper limit of $4N_M$ to the total amount of PEs, in the pipelined configuration no more than p_{max} PEs, given by (5), should be used for each of the four main branches in order to avoid idle operation.

$$p_{max} = Tp/Tt + 2 \tag{5}$$

5. Results

The system used was composed of one Sension QUAD board (four T800 with 20MHz, link speed of 20Mbit/s and memory of 100 ns/5 cycles). The software was developed under the Transputer Development System (TDS) on a PC-AT compatible machine.

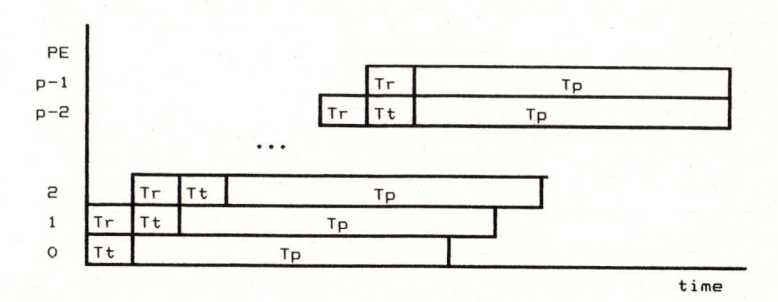

Figure 2 - Timing diagram for pipelined execution of the BHT.

Table 1

	BHT	SHT
T414	1.602	23.110
T800	1.602	2.635

Table 2

N_e	Execution time
500	50.82
1000	101.50
2000	203.01
4000	406.85

5.1. Single Transputer Implementation

We have implemented the BHT and SHT (with table look-ups for SIN and COS, $N_\theta=64$ and $N_R=128$ [2]-[3]) on a single T800 and T414. The total execution times in seconds for N=128 and $N_e=4000$ are given in table 1.
Although the SHT is faster on the T800 (faster multiplication) than on the T414, the BHT is faster than the SHT for both processors. So, the SHT will not be considered for multi-transputer implementations in this paper.

5.2. Multi-Transputer Implementation

From table 1 and Tt = 11 Tck N_e we determine $p_{max} \cong 16 \ N_M/p$. For the case considered in this paper, i.e. $N_M=16$ and p=4, p_{max} is approximately 64. However, due to the parallelism during the link transfers, a smaller Tt can be obtained which implies larger p_{max}. The execution times (in ms) for the BHT, executed on the described 4-PE pipelined T800 multi-transputer architecture, are given in table 2.

6. Concluding Remarks

We have described briefly the BHT, presented a simple and efficient algorithm for its execution, extended it for execution on a pipelined multi-transputer architecture and presented actual execution times for 128x128 images. The use of transputers T800 and T414 have allowed the following advantages and disadvantages:
Advantages: Both T414 and T800 present fast binary shifts and integer addition/subtraction, the main operations in the BHT. The T414 and T800 can be used to represent two broad classes of processors (with and withouth fast product) for evaluation purposes.
Disadvantages: Broadcast of the edge elements is not directly provided.
    The proposed architecture is quite simple and specially efficient for small amount of PEs, the case addressed by the authors. In the present case only four of the eight links are used in most PEs. More ellaborated architectures, which use more serial links, should be used for larger amounts of PEs.

7. Acknowledgements

Luciano da Fontoura Costa is grateful to Fundacao de Amparo a Pesquisa do Estado de Sao Paulo - FAPESP, Brazil, for the support.

8. References

[1] COSTA, L. D. F. and SANDLER, M. B.: "A binary Hough transform and its efficient implementation in a systolic array architecture", *Pattern Recognition Letters*, vol. 10, no. 5, pp. 329-334, Nov. 1989.

[2] COSTA, L. D. F. and SANDLER, M. B.: "The binary Hough transform and its implementation", *1990 SPIE/SPSE Symposium on Electronic Imaging Science and Technology*, paper no. 1251-21, Santa Clara, USA, Feb. 1990.

[3] COSTA, L. D. F. and SANDLER, M. B.: "Performance improvements and performance evaluation of the binary Hough transform", *V European Signal Processing Conference*, Barcelona, Spain, Sep. 1990.

[4] COSTA, L. D. F.; TZIONAS, P. and SANDLER, M. B.: "On the VLSI implementation of the binary Hough transform", *IEE Colloquium on "VLSI signal processing architectures"*, Savoy Place, London, May 1990.

[5] COSTA, L. D. F. and SANDLER, M. B.: "A complete and efficient real time system for line segment detection based on the binary Hough transform", *Euromicro Workshop on Real Time Systems*, Horsholm, Denmark, Jun. 1990.

[6] DUDA, R. O. and HART, P. E.: "Use of Hough transformation to detect lines and curves in pictures", *Comm. of ACM*, vol. 15, pp.11-15, 1972.

[7] ILLINGWORTH, J. and KITTLER, J.: "A survey of the Hough transform", *Computer Vision, Graphics and Image Processing*, vol. 44, pp. 87-116, 1988.

[8] COSTA, L. D. F.; BEN-TZVI, D. and SANDLER, M. B.: "Performance Improvements to the Hough Transform", *UK IT 90 Conference*, Southampton, Mar. 1989.

Implementation of the Radon Transform using a Dynamically Switched Transputer Network

G. Hall, B.Sc(Hons), M.Phil., Ph.D., C.Eng., MIEE.

T. J. Terrell, Dip.EE., M.Sc., Ph.D., C.Eng., FIEE.

School of Electrical and Electronic Engineering,
Lancashire Polytechnic,
Preston, PR1 2TQ, England.

L. M. Murphy, B.Sc.(Hons), M.Sc.

Space Department,
Royal Aerospace Establishment,
Farnborough, GU14 6TD, England.

Abstract. Previously reported work resulted in a transputer tree network using thirty T800 transputers to perform the Radon Transform. The Radon Transform was used to enhance linear features in noisy Synthetic Aperture Radar images.
The work presented here describes modification of the transputer network by the addition of INMOS B004 link switches, and controlling T222 transputer. The tree configuration is replaced such that link switches now dynamically switch between the image data source transputer (farmer) and the transputers which perform the calculations (workers). It is shown that this arrangement is more efficient since the worker transputers are all relieved of their data routing role. The paper includes a comparison of the previous tree network, and the new switched network, and presents results for both techniques.

1. Introduction.

This paper briefly describes the Radon transform and its application to the enhancement of linear features in noisy images. Previous work carried out to perform the Radon transform on a network of thirty T800 transputers is briefly described, together with results which illustrate some of the shortcomings of the system. The main emphasis of this paper is on a modified version of the transputer system which uses link switches to implement a more effective allocation of work through the transputer network.

2. The Radon Transform.

The Radon transform of an image intensity function f(x,y) defined on two-dimensional Euclidean space is given by:

$$R(p, \theta) = \int_{-\infty}^{\infty} \int_{-\infty}^{\infty} f(x,y) \, \delta(p - x\cos\theta - y\sin\theta) \, dx \, dy$$

where $\delta(\rho)$ is the Dirac delta function.

The term $\delta(p - x\cos\theta - y\sin\theta)$ forces the integration of f(x,y) along the line $p - x\cos\theta - y\sin\theta = 0$, and consequently the value $R(p,\theta)$ for any line (p,θ) is the sum of the values of f(x,y) along this line. Each line integral in image space f(x,y) produces a point function in feature space (p,θ).

The integration process causes noise contributions along lines in an image to tend to cancel, (leaving an average (d.c.) image intensity contribution,) whereas contributions derived from a linear feature tend to be accentuated. The signal-to-noise ratio of the point in Radon feature space is therefore higher than that of the linear feature in image space which produced that point. The Radon feature space representation can be used directly to detect the positions of linear features in image space, or a computer simulation can display corresponding synthesized feature space line diagram. Alternatively, non-linear enhancement may be applied in Radon feature space, and an inverse Radon transform applied, to give an enhanced image space representation. Both alternatives have been used to advantage for synthetic aperture radar (SAR) images which are inherently prone to speckle noise [1],[2]. Figure 1 shows a typical noisy 256x256 pixel SAR image containing a linear feature. Figure 2 shows the Radon transform of this image, and Figure 3 shows the Radon transform after square law contrast enhancement. The improvement in signal-to-noise ratio of the point in Radon space, compared to the linear feature in image space is obvious by inspection of these Figures. Figure 4 shows a synthesized image space representation produced by back-projecting the data shown in Figure 3 [1]. Figure 5 shows an image space representation obtained by applying an inverse (modified) Radon transform to the data shown in Figure 3 [2].

A method of implementing the Radon transform via the frequency domain is now briefly described. The steps involved are summarised below:
(i) Compute the two-dimensional fast Fourier transform (FFT) of the image (f(x,y)) with the origin at the centre to give F(u,v)
(ii) Take slices through the centre of F(u,v) at various angles θ. Compute the inverse one dimensional FFT of these slices to give the projections at various values of θ. The Radon transform is then a plot of these projections against their corresponding angles.

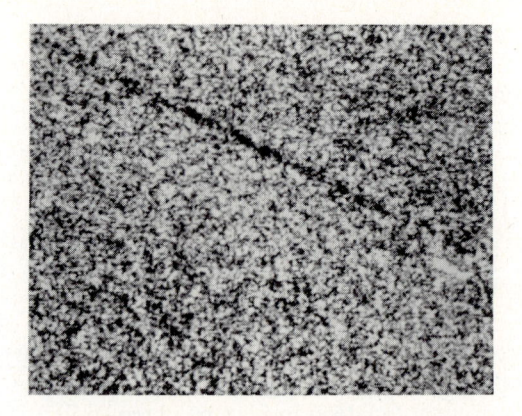

Figure 1 Typical SAR Image

Figure 2 Radon Transform of Figure 1

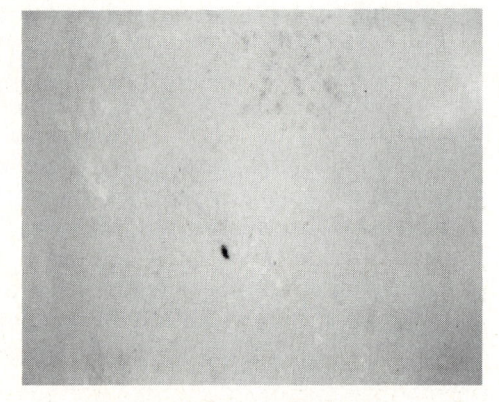

Figure 3 Effect of Contrast Enhancement of Figure 2

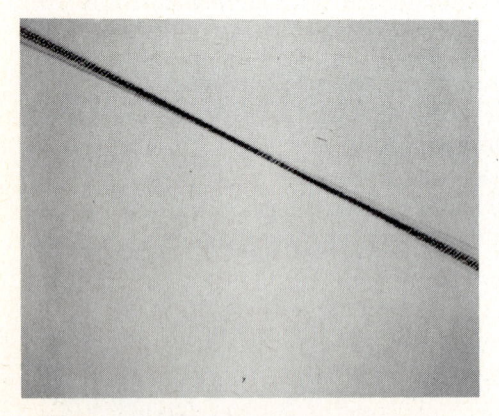

Figure 4 Synthesized Image Space representation of Figure 3

Figure 5 Inverse Radon Transform of Figure 3

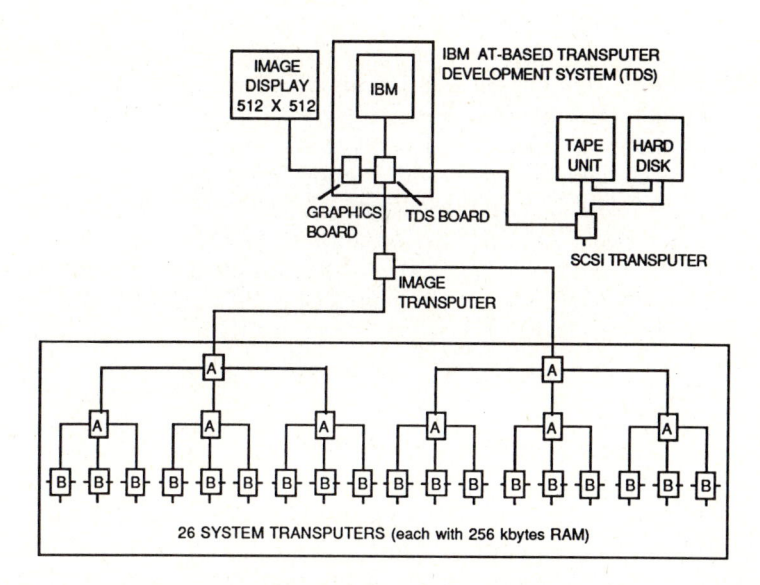

Figure 6 Transputer Tree Network

3. Transputer Tree Network.

A network of thirty T800-20 transputers programmed in OCCAM has been built to perform the Radon transform within a few seconds [1], [2], [3]. The network is shown in Figure 6.

The "Image Transputer" at the top of the tree holds the image whose Radon transform is required, and has 4 Megabytes of Dynamic RAM. The "System Transputers" perform forward or inverse one-dimensional FFTs on sections of image data allocated to them on a farming basis and on boards designed in-house containing 256 k bytes static RAM. The Radon transform is implemented by the "Image Transputer" farming out to the tree network, sections of its stored data corresponding to rows, columns, and angular slices. It has been found that the majority of the computation is performed by the transputers labelled "B" in Figure 6. The transputers labelled "A" run parallel computation and farming processes, and the ratio of time spent on computation to time spent farming is lowest for transputers located furthest up the tree. In fact the system performance was found to be improved if all but the "B" transputers were relieved of computation, and were allowed to spend all their time allocating work to the transputers lower in the tree, and sending results up the tree. Therefore in this network comprising 26 "System Transputers" (workers), only 18 were actually performing calculations. The limiting factor affecting the performance of the network was found to be the speed at which the "Image Transputer" could fetch data from its two-dimensional arrays. The row data was fetched using OCCAM *segments* , and this method did in fact provide an adequately fast data access to make full use of the available "System Transputers". Unfortunately, the use of OCCAM segments is limited to data which is contiguous in the X dimension of a multi-dimensional array, so could only be used for row data access. The column data access was implemented using the T800 Block Move instruction, the data having first been retyped to bytes. The fetching of data along slices of the two-dimensional array could only be achieved by using a WHILE loop, the calculation of X and Y coordinates being calculated for each element using SINE and COSINE functions. It was found that the time taken to compute the SINE and COSINE was negligible compared to the time taken to fetch the data from the arrays. In detail, the performance of the tree network for a Radon transform on 256x256 image data (using 256x256 FFT and 256 angular slices) was as follows:

Row FFTs	0.368 seconds
Column FFTs	0.545 seconds
Angular Slice FFTs	1.067 seconds

It should be noted that the link communications speed was 20 Mega bits per second on the critical links out of the "Image Transputer". It should also be noted that all data arrays stored by the "Image Transputer" were in 32-bit floating point format, and that two arrays were used, corresponding to real and imaginary data.

4. Dynamic Work Allocation Using Link Switches.

It was obvious from the practical results obtained from the tree network that some T800 transputers were not being used effectively. Eight of the 26 T800 "System Transputers" were being used for simple data routing. The system has been modified to utilize INMOS C004 link switches to perform dynamic allocation of work from the "Image Transputer" to the "System Transputers". All 26 "System Transputers" are now able to be employed wholly for computation, the switching being achieved by two C004 link switches controlled by a T222 transputer. Figure 7 shows a block diagram of the new arrangement using link switches. Two INMOS C004 link switches are used to connect two links of the "Image Transputer" to two "System Transputers" for allocation of FFT data and return of FFT results. The third available link of the "Image Transputer" is used to control the T222 transputer to change connection to the next two "System Transputers" once data transfer is complete. The software executes as follows:
(i) The controlling T222 transputer first connects all the transputers in a pipeline, and then the Radon transform transputer code is downloaded from the development system into the transputers.
(ii) The "Image Transputer" then repeats the following steps. Communication to the T222 controlling transputer requests connection of two links to two "System Transputers". Handshake communication is received to confirm that the links have been successfully set up. Line-identifying words are sent to the two "System Transputers". Two lines of data are fetched from two-dimensional arrays and sent to the two "System Transputers" in parallel with the return of results and line identifier from the last lines transmitted. This process is repeated, cycling through the "System Transputers" two at a time.

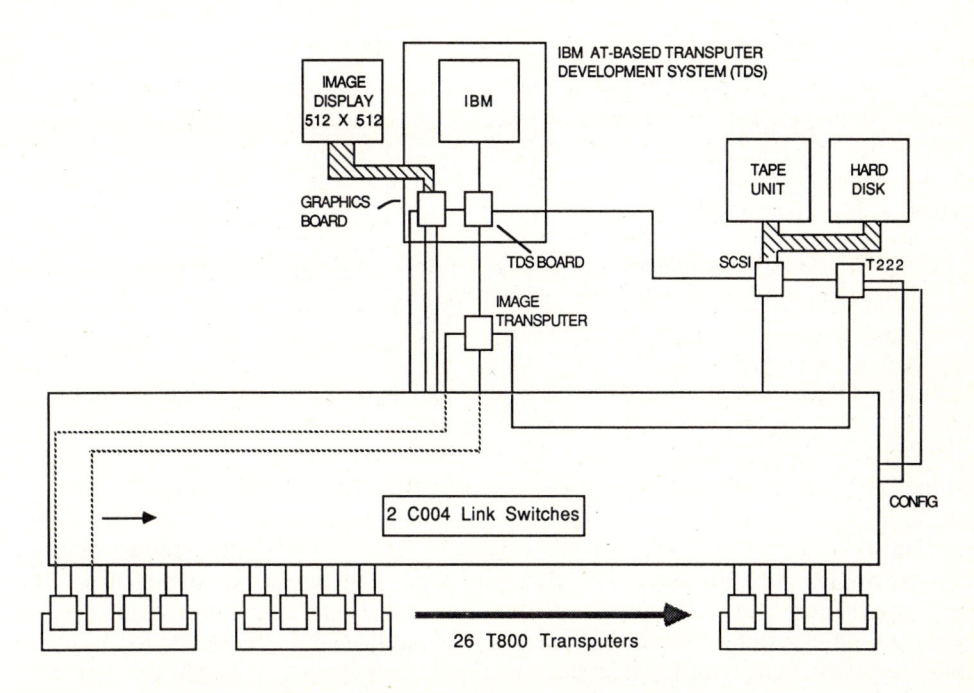

Figure 7 Dynamic Work Allocation Using Link Switches

The results for the performance of this system for a Radon Transform on 256x256 image data, using a 256x256 FFT, and employing 256 angular slices showed a slight deterioration in performance compared to the tree network used previously. This can be explained by two factors:
(i) The COO4 link switch introduces an average 1.75 bit time delay on link transmission.
(ii) There is a software overhead in link switch control. The "Image Transputer" has to generate control messages to the T222 transputer to indicate when the link switches need to connect to the next two "System Transputers", and to receive messages back from the T222 to confirm that connection is complete. It has been found that the time to set up a link via the link switches is 58 micro seconds.

The use of this arrangement means that the number of transputers used as workers (i.e. the "System Transputers") can be changed by minor software changes. Table 1 shows that the Radon transform can be implemented using twelve worker transputers with the same speed as with 26 worker transputers. In practice, the addition of a further "Image Transputer" (with 4 Mega bytes of RAM) would enable the system to work at optimum speed performing two Radon transforms concurrently.

5. Concluding Remarks

The work has shown that for applications where data is stored at one point

Workers	26	22	12	10	8	6
Row FFTs	0.44	0.44	0.44	0.52	0.65	0.86
Column FFTs	0.62	0.62	0.62	0.62	0.67	0.88
Angular Slice FFTs	1.05	1.05	1.05	1.19	1.45	1.89

Table 1   Performance in seconds for various numbers of workers (note: Link communication speed 20 M bits/sec)

and has to be communicated to worker transputers for processing, then the use of link switches to dynamically switch between transputers forms an effective solution. Many image processing applications fall into this category, since the image data often is produced at one source. In the example described in this paper, the system performance was limited by the speed at which the farmer could access data. It has been shown that in this example, the advantage of dynamic link switching, as opposed to the previous static tree network, resulted in fewer farmer transputers being required. In systems where the worker computation time is the factor limiting overall performance rather than farmer data access time, it would be expected that the use of link switching would improve overall performance.

A decision has to be made as to how large to make the sections of data to be processed. The smaller the sections the more switching (and therefore the more switching time), but the less memory each worker transputer requires. In practice the switching time of 50-60 micro seconds is short enough to enable small data packets to be used in many applications. The use of small data packets means that the worker transputers only need a relatively small amount of RAM, and this can then be fast static RAM.

It is interesting to consider applications where the calculation time is not constant such as in ray tracing. Information is required by the transputer controlling the switching to enable it to direct work to those workers which have completed their task. This would enable a switched processor farm to be implemented. The most straightforward method of implementing this would probably be to connect the workers in a pipeline using their third and fourth links, and to transmit messages down the pipeline to the controller transputer from each worker as it completed it's calculation.

In the production of the Radon transform, it will be noted that the worker transputers all perform FFT calculations. A more cost effective solution would have resulted from the use of FFT hardware (special purpose silicon), but the transputer solution was chosen to make the system "general purpose", and thus enable it to be programmed for other applications. Future work may well use a hybrid system, perhaps comprising transputers and vector processor chips.

6. Acknowledgements

This work has been carried out with the support of the Procurement Executive, Ministry of Defence; in particular the authors wish to thank the Space Department at the Royal Aerospace Establishment, Farnborough, for their support.

7. References

[1] **Hall**, G. and **Terrell**, T.J., **Murphy**, L.M., and **Senior**, J.M.: *'Transputer Implementation of The Radon Transform for Image Enhancement'* , Proc IEEE International Conference on Acoustics, Speech, and Signal Processing, Vol 3, pp1548-1551, Glasgow ,UK, May 1989.

[2] **Hall**, G. and **Terrell**, T.J., **Murphy**, L.M., and **Senior**, J.M.: *'A New Fast Discrete Radon Transform for Enhancing Linear Features in Noisy Images'*, Proc IEE Third International Conference on Image Processing and Its Applications, pp187-191, Warwick, UK, July 1989.

[3] **Hall**, G. and **Terrell**, T.J., **Murphy**, L.M., and **Senior**, J.M.: *'A Modified Radon Transform for Linear Feature Enhancement in SAR Data'* , Proc IEEE International Conference on Image Processing, Vol 2, pp676-680, Singapore, September 1989.

Copyright (C) Controller HMSO London 1990

IMAGE RECONSTRUCTION ON TRANSPUTER NETWORKS*

E.L. Zapata, I. Benavides, J.D. Bruguera and J.M. Carazo
Dept. Electronics. University of Santiago de Compostela. Spain

Filtered backprojection is a popular algorithm for the reconstruction of n-dimensional signals from their (n-1)-dimensional projections (in the sense of line integrals). In this work we analyze the implementation of the filtered back projection method in a transputer based hypercube computer. The flexibility of the algorithm is rooted in the metodology developped for embedding algorithms into hypercubes. Finally, the algorithmic complexity is analyzed, and we present some results of runtime for the 3D reconstruction of the Chaperonina Gro EL obtained from Escherichia coli.

1. Problem

The problem of the 3D reconstruction of an object from its 2D projection images (in the sense of line integrals) is a very common situation is such diverse fields as astronomy, medical imaging and electron microscopy, among many others [1-2]. A simple approximation to the reconstruction of an object from its projections is by using the direct back projection [1]. However, the so obtained volume cannot be an exact reconstruction. The unaccuracies introduced by the use of the direct back projection can also be modelled as the convolution of the exact 3D reconstruction with a 3D point spread function (PSF), which, in general, is space-variant. In principle, a correction by this PSF can be implemented in Fourier space by multiplying (filtering) the Fourier transform of each of the projection images with the inverse of the Fourier transform of the PSF. The general filter function so derived is the inverse of a summation of sinc functions along the direction perpendicular to each one of the images that are used to generate the filter [3].

Let PW be the projection image that we want to filter and PG the projection image generating the sinc functions. Let RW_w be a vector in the coordinate system associated to PW (that is, any system with the x and y axis in the plane PW), and RW_g the same vector in the coordinate system associated to PG.

Let R be a vector in a fixed coordenate plane, and [DW] the matrix of rotations from R to RW (RW=[DW]*R). In the same way, let [DG] be the matrix of rotations from R to RG (RG=[DG]*R). Then, the argument of the sinc function is proportional to Z_g, the z coordinate in the coordinate system associated with PG.

$$RW_g = [D]*RW_w = [DG]*[DW]^{-1}*RW_w \tag{1}$$

where

$$[DG] = \begin{bmatrix} \cos(\theta_g) & 0 & -\sin(\theta_g) \\ 0 & 1 & 0 \\ \sin(\theta_g) & 0 & \cos(\theta_g) \end{bmatrix} * \begin{bmatrix} \cos(\phi_g) & \sin(\phi_g) & 0 \\ -\sin(\phi_g) & \cos(\phi_g) & 0 \\ 0 & 0 & 1 \end{bmatrix} \tag{2}$$

$$[DW]^{-1} = \begin{bmatrix} \cos(\phi_w) & -\sin(\phi_w) & 0 \\ \sin(\phi_w) & \cos(\phi_w) & 0 \\ 0 & 0 & 1 \end{bmatrix} * \begin{bmatrix} \cos(\theta_w) & 0 & \sin(\theta_w) \\ 0 & 1 & 0 \\ -\sin(\theta_w) & 0 & \cos(\theta_w) \end{bmatrix} \tag{3}$$

---

*This work was supported by Ministry of Education and Science (CICYT) of Spain under contracts TIC88-0094, MIC88-0549, the Xunta de Galicia XUGA80406488, and the Spanish institution Fundación Ramón Areces (Transputer Applications'90).

being φ and θ the azimuthal and tilt angles of each projection, respectively (here, and in the following, we have arbitrarily placed the tilt axis parallel to the y axis both in PW and PG). A very interesting and useful simplification happens in those cases in which the set of projection images to be filtered is the same set than the one of images generating the filters. In this case the matrix $[DW]^{-1}$ is the transpose of $[DG]$.

The value of the filter function corresponding to the point (x^i, y^i) in the i-th image will be:

$$\text{weight}(y^i, x^i) = (\sum_{g=1}^{M} d \cdot \text{sinc}(\arg(y^i, x^i)_g))^{-1} \tag{4}$$

where $\quad \arg(y^i, x^i)_g = \frac{\pi d}{N} [y^i, x^i, 0][D^{2\,0}_g, D^{2\,1}_g, D^{2\,2}_g]^T \tag{5}$

Being M the number of generating projections, d the diameter of the 3D volume to reconstruct, N the dimensions of the image that we want to filter ($0 < y^i, x^i \leq N$) and $D^{j\,k}_g$ is the element (j,k) of the g-th matrix of transformation D ($[\ ]^T$ is the transpose). Without lose of generality, in the following we will consider the images of square dimensions (N^2 pixels) and the final volume to be a cube of dimensions NxNxN (N^3 voxels). In order to take into account the periodicities of the FFT's, the former formulas have to be corrected in the following way:

$$\text{if } x^i \text{ (or } y^i) \geq N/2 \text{ (or } N/2) \text{ then } x^i \text{ (or } y^i) = x^i - N \text{ (or } y^i - N) \tag{6}$$

As the last step in the definition of the filtering function we introduce a threshold value α on the values calculated from (4) (if $\text{weight}(y^i, x^i) < 1/\alpha$ then $\text{weight}(y^i, x^i) = 1/\alpha$) as a way to prevent the boosting of those frequencies which were less determined (sampled) from the geometrical arrangement of the input projection images. In our applications to 3D reconstruction from electron microscopy projection images a value of α = 0.6 has been found to be adequate [4-5].

After calculating the filter function, the next step in the process of 3D reconstruction is the direct back projection. At this step the input projection images (which have already been filtered) are uniformly back projected in the reconstruction volumen.

The geometrical relationship between the coordinates of the object (z^o, y^o, x^o) and the corresponding ones in each one of the projections (y^i, x^i) are described by the rotation matrix $[A]$ through the following equation

$$[y^i, x^i] = [A][z^o, y^o, x^o]^T \tag{7}$$

being (z^o, y^o, x^o) the coordinates relatives to the geometrical center of the object and

$$[A] = \begin{bmatrix} -\sin(\theta) & \cos(\theta)\sin(\phi) & \cos(\theta)\cos(\phi) \\ 0 & \cos(\phi) & -\sin(\phi) \end{bmatrix} \tag{8}$$

In this way, the direct back projection can be implemented by applying the matrix $[A]$ to each one of the voxels of the object, equation (7), in order to obtain the coordinates corresponding to the projections that we are analyzing and, then, perform a summation over all the contributions to each voxel.

As the result of equation (7) we have two different situations. The first one happens when the generated coordinates (y^i, x^i) are outside the image ($0 \geq y^i, x^i > N$) and, therefore, the i-th projection do not contribute to the (z^o, y^o, x^o) voxel of the object. The second situation happens when the generated coordinates (y^i, x^i) are within the image ($0 < y^i, x^i \leq N$). In general, y^i and x^i will be real numbers, hence the intensity value at those coordinates has to be calculated by means of some interpolation algorithm. A bilineal interpolation scheme has been used here.

$$a + (b-a)\delta_x + (c-a)\delta_y + \{(d-c)-(b-a)\}\delta_x\delta_y \qquad (9)$$

where a, b, c, d are the intensities of the image at pixels (y^j,x^i), (y^j,x^i+1), (y^j+1,x^i) and (y^j+1,x^i+1), respectively, and δ_x and δ_y are the fractional parts resulting from equation (7).

The final step in the process of 3D reconstruction of an object is the attenuation of the non-significant high frequencies that are present in the calculated volume. This process has to performed after the volume has been reconstructed since the actual interval of meaningful frequencies is only known "a posteriori" by statistically comparing different 3D reconstructions [4]. Obviously, in those applications in which the meaningful range of frequencies can be stimated "a priori", this low-pass filtration should be performed at the time each projection is weighted before back projection. In this application a very simple low-pass filter has been used, namely a radially symmetric step with a cosine attenuation (although more sophisticated filters have been discussed [13] and could be easily implemented).

$$\text{filter}[r] = \begin{bmatrix} 1 & 0 < r \leq p \\ \cos(\pi(r-p)/(2(q-p))) & p < r < q \\ 0 & q \leq r \end{bmatrix} \qquad (10)$$

where r is the radius of the 3D filter, q and p are the limits of the step function and the width of the cosine attenuation, respectively. As in the case of the image filtering (weighting), we will also take into account the symmetry of the 3D FFT (see conditions (6) for the bidimensional case).

In short, the filtered back projection reconstruction method, expressed in pseudocode, comprises the following functions:

Algorithm Filtered back projection
{
  Compute matrix [DG] for each projection: equation (2);
  for(w=1;w≤M;w++) {
    Read image(w);
    Compute 2D-FFT(image(w));
    Weight/Filter the transformed image(w): equations (4) and (5) with condition (6);
    Compute inverse 2D-FFT(image(w));
    Back projection(image(w)): equations (7) and (9);
  }
  Compute 3D-FFT(object);
  Weight/Filter the transformed object: equation (10) with condition (6);
  Compute inverse 3D-FFT(object);}

2. Hypercube Architecture

A q-dimensional hypercube computer is a machine with $Q=2^q$ processing elements interconnected like the vertices of a binary q-dimensional cube are interconnected by its edges. In this way, each PE(r) (r=0,1,..Q-1) has q bidirectional and non-shared links with the others q $PE(r^{(b)})$ (b=0,1,..,q-1), where $r^{(b)}$ is the number whose binary representation differs of the one of r only in bit b. References [6] show various examples of commercial hypercube concurrent computers.

Recently, Zapata et al. [7] analyzed how to partition a sequential algorithm in order to be processed in parallel by a hypercube computer. Their design procedure was as follows: (1) Identification of the maximum nesting level of the independent loops of the sequential algorithm (this will define the number of dimensions of the algorithmic space), (2) partitioning the dimensions of the hypercube into subset associated with the independent loops of the sequential algorithm, (3) distribution of the data arrays that are to be used in the algorithm among the PE's according to the indexing scheme of the PE's and the data distribution mode that have been chosen, (4) make the parallel algorithm, (5) performance optimization by optimazing the partition in step (2). This procedure has been succesfully applied to the "parallelization" of numerous sequential algorithms [8-12].

3. Parallel Algorithm

The sequential algorithm can be divided into three parts, filtering of the projections (2D-FFT, calculation of the weight function according to equations 4 and 5 and inverse 2D-FFT), backprojection of each of the projections and filtering of the three-dimensional object (3D-FFT, calculation of the weight function according to equation 10, and inverse 3D-FFT).

The parallelization of the FFT-2D transform (direct and inverse) has been analyzed by Zapata et al. [10], and they have obtained a performance which is close to the optimum with a 2-partition of the dimensions of the hypercube. The calculation of the weight function associated to each projection is carried out by means of equations (4) and (5). From the analysis of these equations we can deduce that there are three main nested loops (rows and columns of the projection and the number of projections). The three loops are independent and therefore can be parallelized.

In order to minimize interprocessor communications we have chosen a 2-partition for all the functions included in the filtering of the projections. This solution reduces the potential parallelism of equations (4) and (5), as we could use a 3-partition; nevertheless, this reduction is more apparent than real due to the fact that a 2-partition permits the use of up to N^2 PEs, which is quite enough.

The partition of the dimensions of the hypercube into two subsets, q_1 and q_0 where $q = q_1 + q_0$ permits the representation of the index r of each PE by means of a vector (r_1, r_0), where $r = r_0 + r_1 2^{q_0}$, and where r_i is associated to the subset q_i.

The second part of the algorithm is the backprojection of each one of the projections on the volume (equations 7 and 9). In this process there are three independent nested loops associated to the dimensions of the three-dimensional object. We, therefore, perform a partition of the dimensions of the hypercube into three subsets, q_2, q_1, q_0, where $q = q_2 + q_1 + q_0$, which are associated to the dimensions of the object; this partition permits the representation of the index r of each PE by means of a vector (r_2, r_1, r_0) where $r = r_0 + r_1 2^{q_0} + r_2 2^{q_0 + q_1}$.

The third part of the algorithm is the filtering of the three-dimensional object. In this case there are also three independent nested loops. Because of this, we keep the 3-partition of the dimensions of the hypercube [10].

The sequential algorithm presents a high level of locality in the operations that it is necessary to perform. Because of this, the most convenient is to perform a distribution of the variables that take part in the algorithm according to a consecutive scheme and to adopt a purely binary indexing for the processing elements of the hypercube.

According to the partition chosen and the consecutive distribution scheme, the distribution of the projection, with a dimension (N*N) and the matrix of the object, with a dimension (N*N*N) is the following:

a) The element of the row i and column j of the projection will be stored in the position (i mod w_1, j mod w_0) of the local submatrix LIMAG(r_1, r_0) in all the PEs for which index r_1 and r_0 are $r_1 = \lfloor i/w_1 \rfloor$ and $r_0 = \lfloor j/w_0 \rfloor$, being $w_1 = \lceil N/2^{q_1} \rceil$ and $w_0 = \lceil N/2^{q_0} \rceil$.

b) The element in the position (i,j,k) of the object will be stored in the position (i mod v_2, j mod v_1, k mod v_0) of the local submatrix LOBJ (r_2, r_1, r_0) in all the PEs for which index r_2, r_1 and r_0 are

$r_2 = \lfloor i/v_2 \rfloor$, $r_1 = \lfloor j/v_1 \rfloor$ and $r_0 = \lfloor k/v_0 \rfloor$, being $v_2 = \lfloor N/2^{q_2} \rfloor$, $v_1 = \lceil N/2^{q_1} \rceil$ and $v_0 = \lceil N/2^{q_0} \rceil$.

Thus, each PE stores two local submatrices, LIMAG with dimensions $(w_1 {*} w_0)$ and LOBJ with dimensions $(v_2 {*} v_1 {*} v_0)$.

The program, in pseudocode, for filtering the image (equations 4 and 5) is the following

```
void weight(k)
{
1   for(x=0; x<w1; x++)
2       for(y=0; y<w0; y++){
3           p:=0;
4           ag':=r1*w1+x;                  /* global coordenates */
5           bg':=r0*w0+y;
6           ag':=N-ag      {bg>N/2 && ag!=0};     bg':=N-bg    {bg>N/2};
7           for (j=0; j<M; j++){
8               z:=d21[j]*(N-ag)   {ag≥N/2};     z:=d21[j]*ag   {ag<N/2};
9               z:=z+d20[j]*bg;
10              dx:=PI*z/N;
11              arg:=d*dx;
12              p:=p+sin(arg)/arg  {dx!=0};       p:=p+1        {dx==0}; }
13          pint:=1/p          {p>α};              pint:=1/α     {p≤α};
14          p:=pint;
15          LIMAG[i1][j1]:=p*LIMAG[i1][j1];}}
}
```

where d is the diameter of the three-dimensional volume that has to be reconstructed. We have supposed that matrix D has been previously calculated and that it has been distributed among the local memories of the PEs. The calculation of equation (4) implies the nesting of three loops (sentences 1, 2 and 7). The loops of sentences 1 and 2 go through all the points of the image and obtain their global coordinates from their local coordinates (sentences 3-6). In the innermost loop, sentences 7-15, the value of the weight function is obtained for each one of the points of the image. The filtering operation is carried out in sentences 13-15 where each of the points of the image is multiplied by its weight function.

The program for the backprojection of the images is the following

```
void backpr()
{
1   for (z=0; z<=v2; z++)
2       for (y=0; y<=v1; y++)
3           for (x=0; x<=v0; x++){
4               zg':=r2*v2+z;
5               yg':=r1*v1+y;
6               xg':=r0*v0+x;
7               rx':=(xg-ctr0)*A00+(yg-ctr1)*A01+(zg-ctr2)*A02+ctr3;
8               ry':=(xg-ctr0)*A10+(yg-ctr1)*A11+(zg-ctr2)*A12+ctr3;
9               (ix,iy):=(floor(rx), floor(ry));
10              MASK:=((ix≥0)&&(iy≥0)&&(ix<N)&&(iy<N));
11              (xd,yd):=(rx-ix, ry-iy)             {MASK};     /* interpolation */
12              ph00:=LIMAG[ix][iy]                 {MASK};
13              (ph01,ph11):=(0,0)                  {MASK && (ix==N-1)};
```

14	$ph^{01} := LIMAG[i_y][i_x+1]$	{MASK && !($i_x==$N-1)};
15	$y_d := 0$	{MASK && ($i_y==$N-1)};
16	$(ph^{10}, ph^{11}) := (0,0)$	{MASK && ($i_y==$N-1)};
17	$ph^{10} := LIMAG[i_y+1][i_x]$	{MASK && !($i_y==$N-1)};
18	$ph^{11} := LIMAG[i_y+1][i_x]$	{MASK && (($i_x<$N-1) && ($i_y<$N-1))};
19	$dt_0 := ph^{00} + (ph^{01}-ph^{00})*x_d$	{MASK};
20	$dt_1 := ph^{10} + (ph^{11}-ph^{10})*x_d$	{MASK};
21	$LOBJ[z_1][y_1][x_1] := LOBJ[z_1][y_1][x_1] + dt_0 + (dt_1-dt_0)*y_d$	{MASK};

```
        }
}
```

where ctr_i represents the center of the 3D object. This process implies three parallelized nested loops (lines 1, 2 and 3) which go through all the voxels of the object. In sentences 4-10 we obtain the general coordinates of each voxel and determine if they are or not in the image, multiplying these coordinates by matrix [A]. When they are in the image, the bilineal interpolation expressed in equation (9) is carried out, sentences 10-21, to accumulate in the voxel the intensity associated to the point within the corresponding image.

When the filtering of each projection is finished, each PE has a part of the projection in a local submatrix $LIMAG(r_1, r_0)$ in its local memory. To perform the backprojection it is necessary for each PE to store the whole projection, therefore we must perform a stage for exchanging data between PEs. The parallel program for this data routing is the following:

```
void routing()
{
1   u1:=r1*w1;      u0:=r0*w0;
2   IMAG[u1:u1+w1-1][u0:u0+w0-1] := LIMAG[0:w1-1][0:w0-1];
3   c:=w0;   f:=w1;
4   for(t=0, t<q0; t++) {
5       IMAG[u1:u1+f-1][u0:u0+c-1](neigh[t]) <-- IMAG[u1:u1+f-1][u0:u0+c-1];
6       BUFF(neigh[t]) <-- u0;
7       c:=c*2; }
8   for(t=q0, t<q; t++) {
9       IMAG[u1:u1+f-1][u0:u0+c-1](neigh[t]) <-- IMAG[u1:u1+f-1][u0:u0+c-1];
10      BUFF(neigh[t]) <-- u1;
11      f:=f*2; }
}
```

The routing stage starts storing the projection local submatrix of each PE, in the appropiate position into a matrix (IMAG) with the same dimensions that the global projection matrix (sentences 1-2). In sentences 4-7, routing of matrices IMAG in relation to hypercube dimensions associated with columns of the matrix is performed. In sentences 8-11 we perform the routing in the hypercube dimensions associated with the row of the matrix IMAG.

The process of filtering the three-dimensional object is similar to the filtering of the image and, therefore, its program could be obtained by modifying the program *weight*.

4. Evaluation

The complexity of the parallel algorithm for filtered backprojection is a function of the number and the size of the projections, of the size of the object to be reconstructed and of the partition of the dimensions of the hypercube:

$$O[1 + M * (2B_0 + B_1 + R + B_2) + (2C_0 + C_1)]$$

where M is the number of projections; B_0 and B_1 are the algorithmic complexities of the basic projection filtering processes: 2D-FFT [10] and calculation of the weight functions ($B_1 = O[1+w_1*w_0*M]$), respectively. R is the complexity of the routing stage corresponding to the change from 2-partition to 3-partition ($R = O[1+q*w_1*w_0]$) and B_2 is the complexity of the backprojection ($B_2 = O[1+v_2*v_1*v_0]$). Finally, C_0 and C_1 are the complexities of the processes for filtering the three-dimensional object: 3D-FFT [10] and calculation of the weighting function ($C_1 = O[1+v_2*v_1*v_0]$), respectively.

Table I. Algorithmic Complexity of the Parallel Filtered backprojection

q_2	q_1	q_0	n.PEs	2D weight	backproj.	3D weight
0	0	0	1	N^2M	N^3	N^3
0	0	n	N	NM	N^2	N^2
0	n	0	N	NM	N^2	N^2
0	n	n	N^2	M	N	N
n	n	n	N^3	M	1	1

Table II. Runtime and Speed up of the 3D Reconstruction.

q	n.PEs	T (Backproj.)	S^{-1} (Backp.)	T (3D filter)	S^{-1} (3D filter)
3	8	8801.2	0.142	390.3	0.168
2	4	16711.2	0.270	706.2	0.305
1	2	31584.5	0.511	1265	0.547
0	1	61796.6	1	2311.9	1

a)

q	n.PEs	T (Backproj.)	S^{-1} (Backp.)	T (3D filter)	S^{-1} (3D filter)
3	8	40834.2	0.141	3582.3	0.158
2	4	78400	0.270	6622.7	0.292
1	2	146673	0.507	12149.1	0.536
0	1	288814	1	22638.5	1

b)

In table I we show the complexities of these stages for different dimensions of the hypercube and different sizes of the problem with $n = \log_2 N$. The partitions we have chosen permit the reduction of the interprocessor communication times, obtaining thus, a behavior which is close to the optimum.

5. Simulation

We have executed the 3D reconstruction on hypercubes made up of T800 Transputer with 2 Kbytes on-chip memory. Table II shows the runtime, in miliseconds, and speed up obtained in the reconstruction of objects with size (16^3), part a), and size (32^3), part b), from 64 images. The speed up is improved if we increase the size of the object. We have chosen as maximum size (32^3) because this puts us in the limit of the memory capacity of the Transputer.

The runtime obtained in the 3D reconstruction of the Escherichia coli show that Transputer based hypercube computers are adequate tools for applications which require a intense interchange of information among PEs, due to its good calculation time-communication time rate. When the hypercube dimension increases the runtime decreases by a factor which is close to 2; nevertheless the maximum hypercube dimension which can be obtained with Transputers is 4. This limits the maximum speed up that can be reached. Therefore, it will be desirable to have Transputer processors with a larger number of communication links.

References

[1] G.T. Herman, Image Reconstruction from Projections: The Fundamentals of Computerized Tomography (Academic Press, New York, 1980).

[2] R.H. Bates and M.J. McDonnell, Image Restoration and Reconstruction (Oxford University Press, London, 1986).

[3] M. Radermacher, T. Wagenknecht, A. Verschoor and J. Frank, , A New Reconstruction Scheme Applied to the 50S Ribosomal Subunit of E.coli, J. Microscopy 141 (1986) RP1-P2.

[4] M. Radermacher, T. Wagenknecht, A. Verschoor and J. Frank, Three-dimensional Reconstruction from a Single-exposure, Random Conical Tilt Series Applied to the 50S Ribosomal Subunit of Escherichia coli, J. Microscopy 146 (1987) 113-136.

[5] J.M. Carazo, T. Wagenknecht, M. Radermacher, V. Mandiyan, M. Boublik and J. Frank, Three-dimensional Structure of 50S Escherichia coli Ribosomal Subunits Depleted of Proteins L7/L12, J. Molecular Biology 201 (1988) 393-404.

[6] W.C. Athas and C.L. Seitz, Multicomputers: Message-Passing Concurrent Computers. IEEE Computer, 21 (8), (1988). 9-24.

[7] E.L. Zapata, F.F. Rivera and O.G. Plata, On the partition of algorithms into hypercubes. In Advances on Parallel Computing (D.J. Evans, Ed.). JAI Press (to be published).

[8] E.L. Zapata, F.F. Rivera, O.G. Plata and M.A. Ismail, Parallel Fuzzy Clustering on Fixed Size Hypercube SIMD Computers, J. Parallel Comput. 13 (3), (1989). 291-303.

[9] E.L. Zapata, J.D. Bruguera, O.G. Plata and F.F. Rivera, A Parallel Markovian Model Reliability Algorithm for Hypercube Computers, J. Microprocessing and Microprogramming, 27, (1989). 501-508.

[10] E.L. Zapata, F.F. Rivera, J.I. Benavides, J.M. Carazo and R. Peskin, Multidimensional Fast Fourier Transform into Fixed Size Hypercubes, J. IEE Proceedings Part E: Computers and Digital Techniques (to be published).

[11] F.F. Rivera, M.A. Ismail and E.L. Zapata, Parallel Squared Error Clustering on Hypercube Arrays, J. Parallel and Distr. Comput. 8, (1990). 292.

[12] F.F. Rivera, R. Doallo, J.D. Bruguera, E.L. Zapata and R. Peskins, Gaussian Elimination with Pivoting into Hypercubes, J. Parallel Comput. (to be published).

[13] O.G. Plata, ACLAN , Un Lenguaje Paralelo para Sistemas Multiprocesador, Ph.D. Univ. Santiago de Compostela (Spain). Feb. 1989.

CARVUPP

Computer-Assisted Radiological Visualisation Using Parallel Processing

Jon Tyrrell, Farzad Yazdy,
Mark Riley, and Norman Winterbottom

IBM UK Scientific Centre
Athelstan House, St. Clements Street
Winchester, SO23 9DR, United Kingdom

Abstract

CARVUPP (Computer-Assisted Radiological Visualisation, Using Parallel Processing) is an experimental project to develop a system to help visualise a set of 2D images of slices through a 3D object, such as those from a hospital body-scanner.

The system will generate rendered, pseudo-3D views from a set of parallel 2D-slice images.

The power of Parallel Processing will be used to enable very fast display generation and interactive display manipulation.

The system can also be used to help visualise not only medical images, but also other volumetric data produced in fields such as Oceanography, Meteorology, Geology, etc.

1 Introduction

CARVUPP is an experimental project to investigate and demonstrate the value of, and problems with:

- Volume Rendering
- Interactive Graphics
- Parallel Processing

As a vehicle to investigate the above topics, we chose to develop a transputer-based system which could generate rendered views (i.e. shaded to look like 3D) from a set of parallel 2D-slice images. The user can specify the density value ranges or thresholds of the data to be viewed (e.g. skin or bone) and also the angles from which the data is to be viewed.

We also chose to concentrate on medical (body-scanner) images, not only because they were readily available from the many contacts that we have in the medical profession, but also because of the inherent interest and usefulness of body-scanner image visualisation. Of course, the system can be used to visualise volumetric data from other fields.

2 Background

2.1 X-Rays

X-rays, discovered in 1895 by Wilhelm Roentgen, are the same phenomenon as ordinary visible light i.e. electromagnetic radiation, but they can travel through material, such as skin, that would be opaque to ordinary light.

X-rays penetrate softer tissues such as skin and fat without much attenuation but denser material such as bone or teeth are much more opaque to X-rays. Thus, denser materials cast darker shadows on a photographic plate and produce a picture of the internal composition of the body.

Although X-ray pictures are an extremely helpful aid to medicine, they do have some problems. They are, in effect, only "shadow-pictures": 2D pictures of a 3D space with all the data in the 3rd dimension squashed into 2 dimensions. This leads to a lot of detail being obscured when two or more structures in the body cast their shadows onto the same spot on the plate. For instance, a tumour may be half obscured by a bone or other structure. Also, it is very difficult to get any impression of the true 3D shape of objects from a single X-ray picture. For this reason, two or more X-rays from different positions are usually taken in order to get a more detailed view of the internal structures.

2.2 Body-Scanners

A more modern breakthrough in the Medical Imaging area was the invention of the body-scanner by Godfrey Hounsfield in the 1970's.

The body-scanner fires a very thin beam of X-rays through the body from many positions around it. The amount of X-ray radiation falling on detectors on the opposite side of the body from the X-ray source is collected and a computer is used to calculate what the internal composition of the body must be in order to produce the detected amounts.

This type of body-scanner is called a CT-scanner, CT standing for Computed Tomography or computed pictures of slices. These slices give much more detail than ordinary X-rays because they are not just shadow-pictures, but pictures of sections through the body - it is as if the body has been sliced up into very thin sections like a sliced sausage. An example CT scanner image is shown in Figure 1.

CT-scanners are now in use in many medical centres and hospitals throughout the world and their use is growing all the time.

There are also other types of body-scanners which use different techniques to produce the slice images of sections through the body. MR (Magnetic Resonance) scanners use radio waves beamed at the body whilst in a very powerful magnetic field. Different atoms in the body absorb and re-emit the radio waves at different frequencies and these differences are collected, analysed and used to form cross-sectional slices.

Another technique, called PET (Positron Emission Tomography) relies on measuring the particles of antimatter that are emitted when certain compounds are injected into the body. These measurements are again used to produce cross-sections through the body.

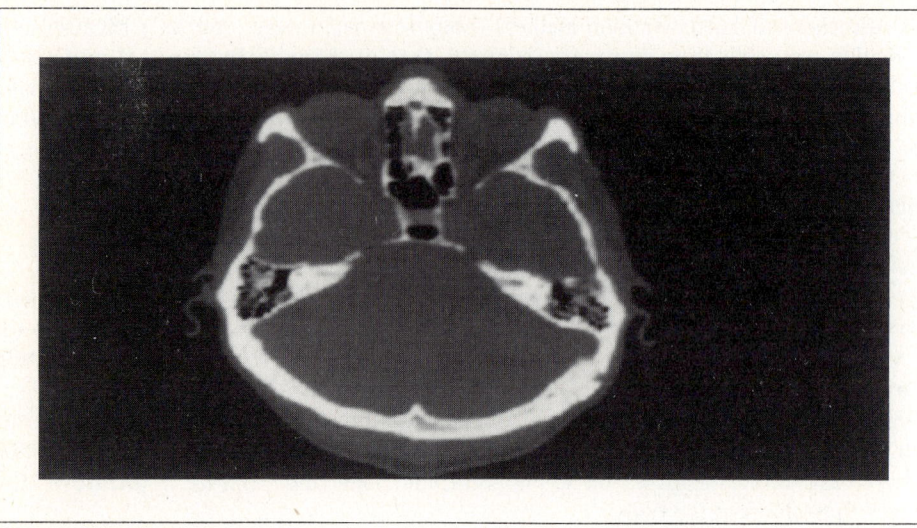

Figure 1. Example CT-scanner image

Thus, body-scanner images improve upon ordinary X-ray pictures by giving a clearer, more detailed, unobscured view of the interior of the body.

2.3 Data Visualisation

One problem with body-scanner images is that one must mentally blend together a set of cross-sectional pictures in order to get any idea of the three-dimensional shape of structures in the body. This is analogous to looking at cross-sectional plans of a ship in order to visualise the shape of the hull, or looking at contours on a map in order to visualise the topographical appearance of the land. With medical images, although each slice shows a great deal of useful information, it takes special training to be able to interpret the images, and so hospitals employ diagnostic radiologists to do this.

The next breakthrough in this area is the use of a computer to generate pictures showing a three-dimensional reconstruction of the body from the set of cross-sectional slices.

This can be done by storing a stack of slices as a cube of data in computer memory and then generating a view of the cube of data from a particular angle, by simulating what a person would see if the cube was held in front of the eyes (e.g. by calculating the paths of light rays impinging on the cube of data and reflecting back to the viewers eye). Techniques to perform this simulation have been developed by several researchers, and are usually termed "Volume Rendering" techniques. The individual elements of the cubic volume of data are called "voxels", a contraction of volume elements (as pixels is a contraction of picture elements). Further details of these techniques may be found in [1, 2, 3, 4]

In addition to Medical Imaging, there are many other fields in which visualisation of a three-dimensional block of data would be of great benefit. The volumetric data involved range from the largest (cosmological data, colliding galaxies, stellar evolution etc.) through many intermediate ranges (geographical data, oil reservoir, architecture, etc) down to the smallest (molecular models, atomic forces etc).

A great deal of research is currently underway to find the best ways of visualising this type of data. All attempts so far have shown one thing: a huge amount of processing power is needed to get the best visualisation. This processing power is needed to generate accurate and detailed views from the usually very large amount of data to be visualised and/or to generate the views as quickly as possible in order to use the effect of motion as a visualisation aid.

2.4 Parallel Processing

Parallel Processing is a recent development in computing technology. Computer processor chip speeds have been increasing dramatically and consistently since the earliest days of the computer. There is, however, a physical limit to the speed which a single processor can reach, due to technological (materials) and physical (speed of light) limits.

It was seen by many that an alternative way of getting processing done faster was by having more than one processor performing the work. It also turned out, in many cases, that the price/performance ratio when using parallel processors could be lower than that for single processors.

This line of research led to many solutions, one of which is commercially available today in a fairly economical, simple way in the Inmos Transputer chip together with its associated hardware and software support.

3 CARVUPP Volume Rendering Algorithm

In CARVUPP, we use a variation on the 'Front-to-Back' ray-casting algorithm when generating views. The stack of 2D slice images is read into memory to form a 3D volumetric array of voxels. Interpolation between adjacent slices may be used to 'fill-in' data from missing slices.

The object or objects of interest are chosen via user-specified voxel value ranges (i.e. via thresholding). A viewing orientation is chosen via user-specified angles of rotation about the axes of the object's frame of reference (x,y,z) to give an (x',y',z') viewer's frame of reference (see Figure 2). The $z'=0$ plane is the viewing plane on which the rendered view will be painted.

The paths of rays of light from the object of interest to the viewing plane are then calculated. The algorithm steps through every point (x',y') in the viewing plane, and at each point, casts a ray into the rotated volume of data, looking for a voxel value which is within the user-specified range of values.

The volume of data is not physically rotated in CARVUPP: instead, we set up an inverse transformation matrix which can be used to transform a voxel's position in the viewer's frame of reference (x',y',z') into the object's frame of reference (x,y,z).

Thus, as the algorithm casts a ray from a particular (x',y') position in the viewing plane along the z' direction, we find the corresponding voxel in the object's (x,y,z) frame of reference, and examine it to see if it lies within the user-specified thresholds.

If it does not, then we move one step in the z' direction and repeat the above operation.

If it does, then we note the z' depth in a z-buffer (i.e. depth table), and calculate the local surface normal (surface orientation) from values in neighbouring voxels. This value is used to calculate the amount of light reflected from this point onto the viewing plane (i.e. to render the view). Ray-casting for this particular ray is then stopped and we move on to the next position in the (x',y') viewplane. Thus, for each ray, we only ray-

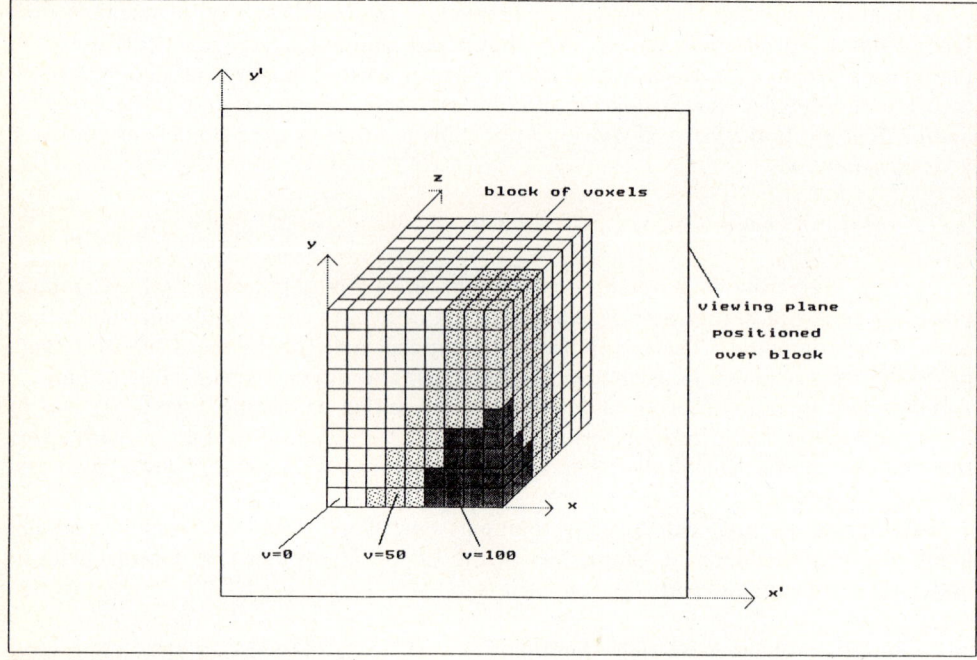

Figure 2. View generation

cast up to the first voxel whose value lies within the user-specified threshold and so do not examine every voxel: only those in front of the object, in the line of sight.

4 Parallelisation

There are many ways of parallelising sequential algorithms (e.g. pipelined operations, subdivision of object or image). We decided to take the simple approach of subdividing the volume of data among multiple processors, and having each processor calculate a local view from its part of the data, and then merging all the local views into one global view which can then be displayed.

5 Implementation

The first version of CARVUPP was completed in September 1989. Before this, we had experimented with a prototype system which used WINSOM [5, 6, 7], a solid modelling program developed at the UK Scientific Centre, to perform similar view generation from CT scans.

Subsequent versions have improved the rendering, speed, user-interface, and capabilities of the system.

5.1 System Overview

The first version of CARVUPP was created using the basic system hardware and software as shown in Figure 3. Subsequent versions have employed more worker nodes and

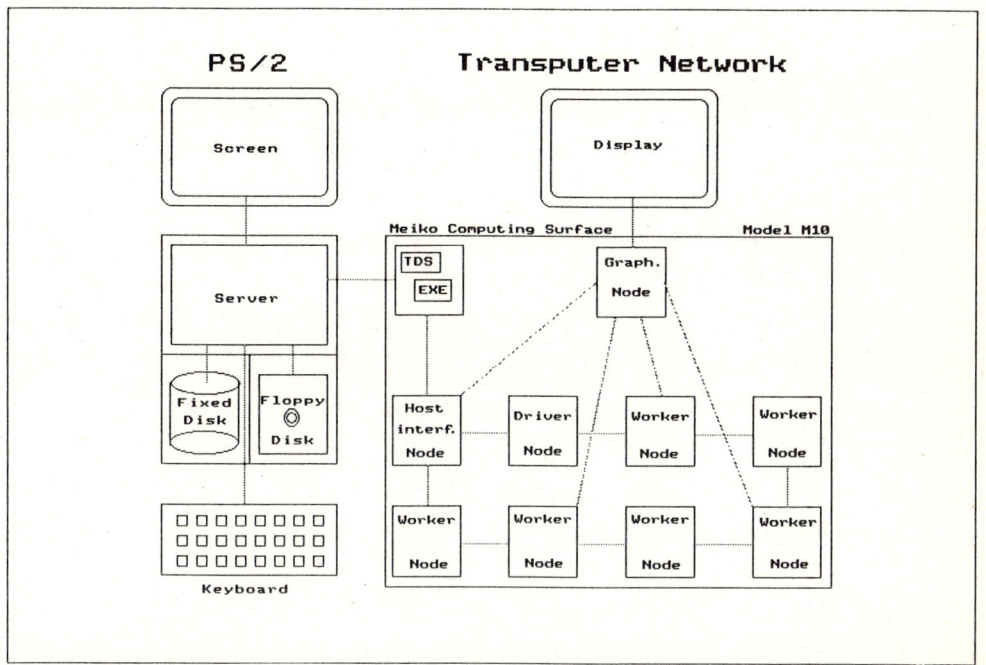

Figure 3. System overview

an additional node with extra memory, called a mass store node, to contain all the data before distribution amongst the worker nodes, and also to act as the driver node.

An IBM PS/2 supplies the control (e.g. keyboard and screen) and file I/O components of the system while the transputer network supplies the processing and graphics display components.

The PS/2 runs a program called the server, which provides the communication between the PS/2 and the transputer network.

The server communicates with the first node (i.e. transputer) in the network via an interface card in the PS/2 (not shown in the diagram).

A Meiko Computing Surface, model M10, provides the transputer network. The network consists of several printed circuit boards in a cabinet, each board containing transputers, memory, and associated hardware.

Each transputer with its associated memory and hardware acts as a node of the network. The nodes are connected together via the four two-way links that each transputer has. The user can change the topology of the network by changing the link connections via a patch panel at the back of the cabinet.

This first node runs the TDS (Transputer Development System) and a TDS-format executable program (EXE) which acts as a monitoring program, listening out for messages from the network and passing them on to the server in the PS/2, (and vice-versa: passing input from the PS/2 on to the network).

This first node is connected into the main ring of nodes in the network via the Host Interface Node. The main ring consists of several Worker Nodes and a Driver Node, and the Host Interface Node.

The Host Interface Node contains routines to transform output messages from other nodes into a format that can be passed on via the monitoring EXE to the server and thus be put on to the PS/2 screen or onto floppy or fixed disk files. The routines also handle messages travelling in the other direction such as keyboard input and file data.

The Driver Node contains the controlling or driving part of the network code. It contains the main-line logic of the system: communicating with the user and controlling the worker nodes.

Worker Nodes act as slaves to the Driver Node: the Driver passes them messages commanding them to perform specific processing.

5.2 GNW

The system uses the functions provided by GNW (Generalised NetWorking) for message passing around the network. GNW is a package of Occam routines, written at the IBM UK Scientific Centre, which simplifies the programming of networks of nodes by providing easily-used functions for routing messages around the network.

The functions allow the programmer:

- to send/receive messages from/to any node in the network
- to route messages to the nearest available node which is capable of processing the message
- to open/close communication channels from/to any node

A copy of the GNW program resides as a high priority parallel process on each node and works as follows:

- each piece of application code (residing as a low priority parallel process on each node) first of all passes a message to its copy of GNW, stating which functions it is capable of doing
- GNW passes this information around the network so that eventually each node knows which direction to send messages for processing on other nodes.
- any application process can then pass a message to its copy of GNW, requesting that GNW pass the message on to the nearest node capable of processing the message
- any application process can also request its copy of GNW to send/receive a message to/from any other node
- any application process can dynamically change its capabilities by simply telling its copy of GNW its new capabilities. GNW will propagate this information around the network to all the other nodes in order for them to update their information on capabilities and routing directions
- several extra functions allow any application process to open/close communication channels with other application processes, to easily extract data from messages, etc

Programming a network of nodes thus becomes simply a matter of deciding what processes should reside on what node, and using procedure calls to:

- inform GNW of each node's capabilities
- request GNW to send a message to the nearest node capable of processing the data in the message
- send messages containing data to be processed to other nodes

- receive messages containing data to be processed
- open communication channels on which to send/receive data

For further details about GNW see [8]

5.3 Driver node

The Driver Node allows the user to control the system. The system uses facilities provided by GNW (Generalised NetWorking), for message-passing functions (see section on GNW above).

The driver first of all opens communication channels (via GNW functions) with all the workers, it then reads in the set of CT slices, and distributes the data (again via GNW) to the worker nodes.

The driver then asks the user for viewing parameters such as rotation angles about the x, y, and z axes, and voxel density thresholds. It broadcasts these parameters to the workers, and each worker then generates a local view of its data.

The local views are then sent back to the driver which merges them into a global view which is then displayed on the graphics display screen.

5.4 Worker node

Each worker node first of all notifies its copy of GNW that it is "open-for-business". This is done by a simple call to GNW. GNW then routes this information around the network. The driver node can thus open communication links to all workers.

Each worker node is then sent a part of the global data which it stores in its local memory.

The worker then receives the viewpoint angles and threshold values from the driver and proceeds to calculate its local view. As each view is generated, it is sent back to the driver node, along with calculated values such as the global position of this local view, and the driver merges all the local views together into a global view which is then displayed on the screen.

6 Results

Examples of generated views from a set of 44 CT scans, (such as the example image shown in Figure 1) are shown in Figure 4 and Figure 5.

Slice resolution was 128 by 128 pixels, 8 bits per pixel, and, because the original slices had physical gaps between them, the number of slices was doubled by interpolating between every slice.

The approximate times to compute and display these example views were 7 seconds using 4 processors, 6 seconds using 8 processors, and 5 seconds using 16 processors.

7 Conclusions

CARVUPP is a successful project which has shown the value of Volume Rendering and Parallel Processing.

We have demonstrated the CARVUPP system to several of our contacts in the medical profession, and all have been very enthusiastic about the possibilities of such a system.

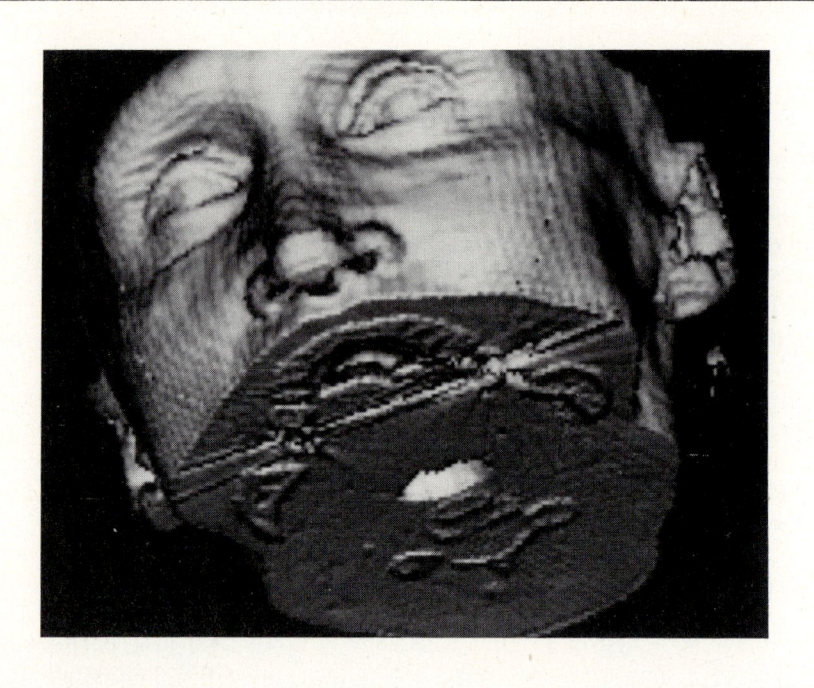

Figure 4. Example generated view - skin

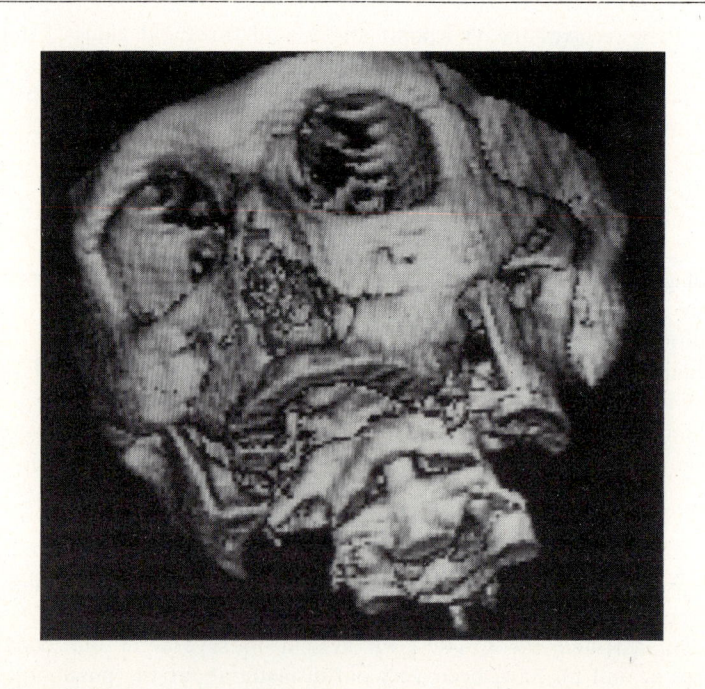

Figure 5. Example generated view - bone

Our initial results prove clearly that parallel processing can be used to speed up compute-intensive algorithms dramatically. These times are very much shorter than the 10-15 minutes that our mainframe prototype system took to produce similar views.

We have also gained much experience in Volume Rendering and Parallel Processing techniques.

8 Future Directions

We aim to enhance the CARVUPP system with additional facilities such as the ability to specify cutting planes through the data, different rendering techniques such as transparency, a measurement facility, a better user-interface, as well as enhancing the algorithms for better performance and better parallelisation and scalability.

References

1. K H Höhne et al, "3D Visualization of tomographic volume data using the generalized voxel model", *The Visual Computer*, **6**, 1, 1990.

2. R A Reynolds, D Gordon, and L Chen, "A Dynamic Screen Technique for Shaded Graphics Display of Slice-Represented Objects", *Computer Vision, Graphics and Image Processing*, **38**, 1987.

3. S M Goldwasser and R A Reynolds, "Real-Time Display and Manipulation of 3-D Medical Objects: The Voxel Processor Architecture", *Computer Vision, Graphics, and Image Processing*, **39**, 1987.

4. G Russell and R B Miles, "Display and perception of 3-D space-filling data", *Applied Optics*, **26**, 6, 1987.

5. J M Burridge et al, "The WINSOM solid modeller and its application to data visualisation", *IBM Systems Journal*, **28**, 4, 1984.

6. P Quarendon, "WINSOM User's Guide", *IBM UKSC Report*, **123**, 1984.

7. P Quarendon, "A system for displaying three-dimensional fields", *IBM UKSC Report*, **171**, 1987.

8. N Winterbottom, "General Network (GNW)", IBM UKSC Internal Report, (in preparation), 1990.

3-D PARALLEL VISUALISATION

Dr B J Payne, Transputer Technology Solutions, 2 Venture Road
Chilworth Research Centre, Southampton SO1 7NP. E-mail bjp@uk.ac.soton.tts

Abstract

This paper describes the implementation of a 3-D graphics visualisation system on an array of transputers. The work is being undertaken as part of a contract for British Aerospace (Commercial Aircraft) Ltd. The author would like to thank BAe for their kind permission to report on the work here.

1. Introduction

The aim of this project is to produce a parallel graphics package which will implement the graphics pipeline shown in figure 1 on the hardware system shown in figure 2.

The M40 Computing Surface is used to run a proprietary flow-simulation code. Data files from each simulation are transferred to the M10 box for display using the graphics package which is the subject of this report.

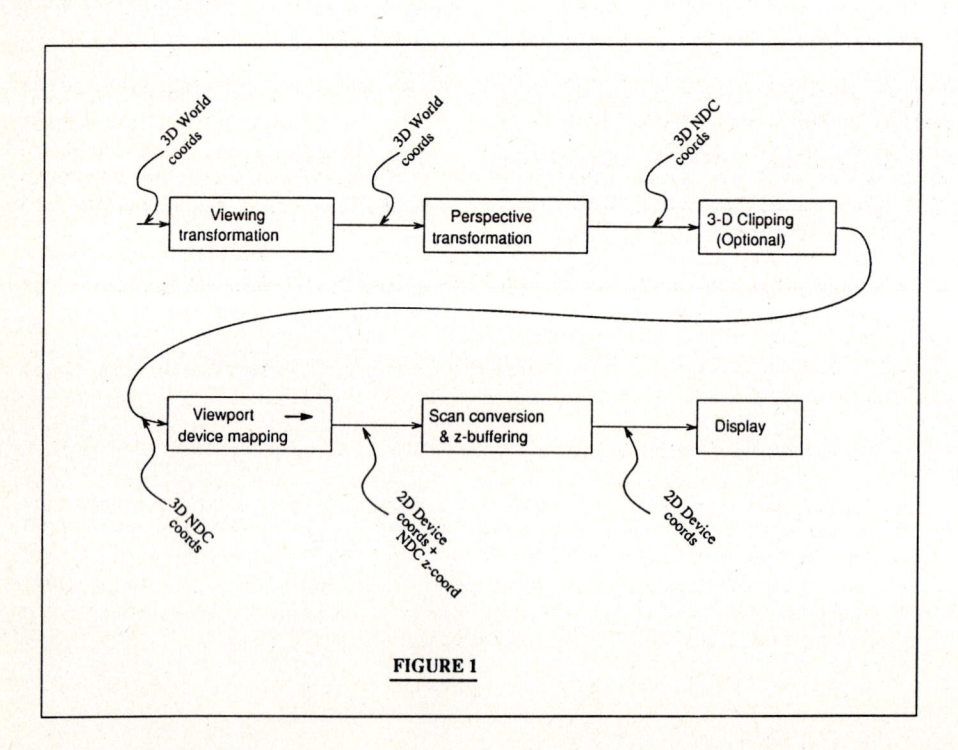

FIGURE 1

The flow code produces estimates of physical parameters such as air pressure, Mach number, etc. around a model aircraft frame. It is anticipated that the visualisation system will be used by BAe's designers and engineers as an interactive aid to the interpretation of data from simulation runs.

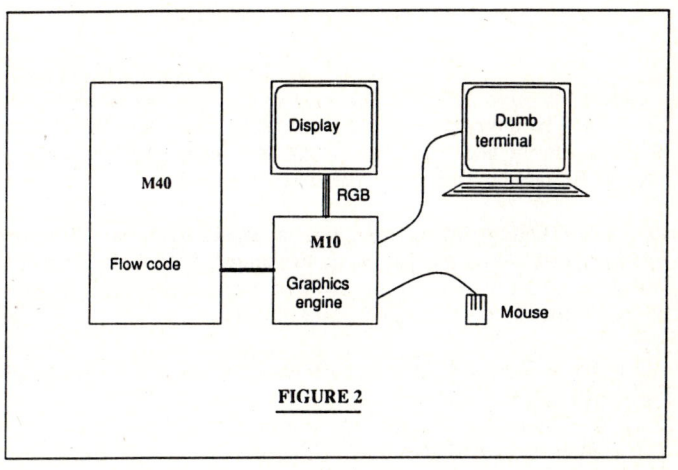

FIGURE 2

In the following sections I will report on progress towards the design goals, my experiences with the development environment, parallel distribution strategies and optimisation techniques.

2. Design Criteria

BAe's h/w setup is shown in figure 2. The "Graphics Engine" consists of a Meiko M10 populated with 16 T800s each with 4 Mb of DRAM plus a single MK015 display board. User interaction is via keyboard and mouse. Several constraints have directly affected the development of the visualisation system:

The major part of the graphics code is written in Fortran 77.

The Fortran implementation was specified by BAe. Interprocess communication is handled by small occam harnesses in the usual way. Using Fortran presents a potential performance degradation due to the inefficiency of existing transputer Fortran compilers as compared with the occam compiler. However, against this are the important advantages that Fortran will allow easy maintainability of code and the potential for functional enhancement by BAe's own engineers.

The package must make use of 3-D solid rendering techniques (including flat polygon shading and hidden surface removal) for visual realism.

Currently BAe use a VAX-based visualisation package which produces only wire-frame displays, due to the limited processing power of the VAX CPU.

The system must be fast to allow interactive use.

Essentially the idea is that the engineer/designer should be able to "walk around" the model in near real-time. An 8-bit colour display of 768 x 576 pixels requires 0.44 Mb of data. Given that each link on a 20 Mhz T800 can operate at a maximum of 1.7 Mb s^{-1}, all four links give a throughput of 6.8 Mb s^{-1}. In theory therefore, the MK015 board should be able to attain an animation rate of 15 frames s^{-1}. In practice it is expected that 5 - 10 frames s^{-1} will be achievable.

3. Comments on the Development Environment

The project is being carried out at TTS using local facilities. The main difference between the h/w development system and the target h/w system is that the worker T800s in the development M10 box have only $1/4$ Mb local DRAM. In practice this rather small memory resource is not too restrictive: it just means that smaller datasets have to be used during development of the code.

The s/w development environment is Meiko's Occam Programming System (OPS) — which is more or less equivalent to Inmos' TDS environment — plus Meiko's Fortran utility. Use of this environment was dictated by circumstance rather than choice: the Fortran utility is not available stand-alone.

There are a few negative aspects to using the OPS to develop what is essentially a Fortran program:

Necessity of writing host format files.

The Meiko Fortran utility requires input files in host format: thus after every edit to the code the user is required to explicitly write the changed file to disk. This is very inconvenient.

Lack of program integrity.

This is really a consequence of the first point mentioned. A feature of OPS when used for occam program development is that every time a file is altered the change is flagged so that the program has to be recompiled. With the current Fortran compiler, if one of the stages of writing a host file, compiling and linking is inadvertently overlooked after editing the source file, the wrong version of the Fortran library file will be linked in to the occam harness.

"Fragile" OPS File Handler functions

A major disadvantage of the current OPS implementation is that several of the File Handler functions can have unfortunate consequences when reading/writing to the host filing system. In particular, if the READ HOST function is called to read a file from the host's filing system into a fold within OPS, and the fold name is the same as the host file name, the operation will fail and the contents of the file will be wiped clean! Though it might not seem a sensible idea to attempt such an operation, when reading and writing to the host filing many times (as is necessary when developing a Fortran program), such a situation can easily arise.

Within the Fortran utility itself, there are no high-level debugging facilities (eg such as a symbolic debugger), so that finding mistakes can be a time-consuming chore.

On the plus side, the folding editor is not bad (though an equivalent editor called Origami is available standalone). It is also possible to use dynamic code loading (in which the Fortran library files are loaded dynamically into the occam harness at run-time, as opposed to statically at compile/link time) to speed up recompilation time. This works because most of the editing is done on the Fortran source rather than on the occam harness; dynamic loading avoids the need to recompile the occam harness each time.

4. Program Details — Current Status

The main steps in the 3-D graphics pipeline are shown in figure 1.

Data files from the flow-code simulation consist of (x,y,z)-coordinates of points on the airframe, plus associated attribute values (airspeed, pressure, etc). These are read in to the visualisation package where the coordinates are transformed and (optionally) clipped according to the user-specified viewing parameters, before being mapped to the device display coordinates.

The next stage is to manipulate the data from vertex format to polygon format, prior to scan-conversion and z-buffering. The latter are standard techniques for polygon filling and hidden-surface removal respectively, and are well described in the literature [1,2]. Scan conversion and z-buffering are most easily performed in one combined operation, collectively referred to as *rendering*, and represent one of the most computationally intensive steps of any 3-D graphics program. This makes it a prime candidate for distributed processing: this aspect is discussed in the next section.

The model airframe is displayed in flat shaded polygon format with polygon edges demarcated in a different colour. The vertex attributes calculated by the flow simulation code (which are the quantities of primary interest to the engineer/designer) are then overlaid in colour-shaded polygon format, where colour graduations are linearly mapped to attribute value.

Various parameters affecting the appearance of the display are under user control, including viewpoint, zoom factor, colour mapping, and so on. User interaction is via both keyboard and mouse: the latter is attached to the M10 host board, via one of the UART ports. Some examples of pictures produced by the system will be presented at the conference.

5. Distribution Strategies

The actual implementation of the graphics pipeline falls into two main steps:

> *Development and debugging of the sequential Fortran code to perform the major steps shown in figure 1.*
>
> *Determining the most efficient scheme for code distribution and data communications across the transputer array.*

To date most effort has been put into achieving the first of these objectives, since the imperative is to produce a robust working system. However, some of the aspects central to distributing the code effectively are discussed below.

The most important consideration is the communications/computation ratio. This translates to achieving a balance between the distribution of the algorithm over the physical array, and the size of the data packets used for communication via the physical links between the array elements.

It is tempting to mirror the graphics pipeline in hardware, with the algorithm split into many small sub-units corresponding to each pipeline step, and with single data points flowing through. However, the nature of the occam communications protocol augers against such a simple-minded approach. External communications are handled by autonomous link DMA engines which transfer data independently of, and concurrently with, the CPU. To initiate a data transfer, the transmitting and receiving processes must be scheduled by the CPU, which represents a fixed start-up cost. This means that the CPU load imposed depends critically on the *number* of communications, more than the amount of data transmitted: it is better to send a small number of long messages than vice-versa. Thus the distribution scheme should be sufficiently large-grained to ensure that the transputers are compute-bound, not communications bound. It is also sensible to build in communication buffering processes running at high priority to decouple compute/link activity by exploiting the DMA hardware/CPU independence (as discussed in [3]).

5.1 Code Distribution

In any distribution scheme the graphics algorithm must be split between the transformation & clipping stage and the rendering stage. This is because the ordering of polygons on scan lines is not known until after the transformation stage. This property of the algorithm constrains the number of sensible schemes, and in fact two main approaches are known to the author. In the first of these [4] an algorithmic

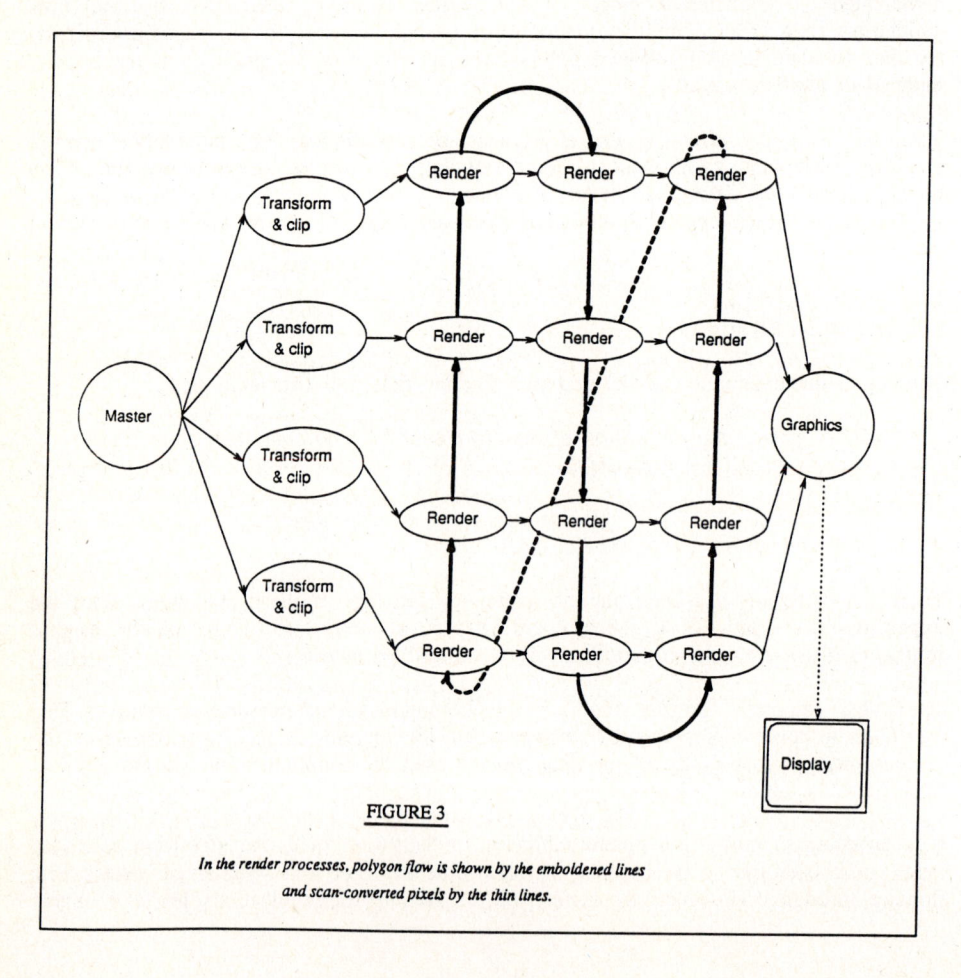

FIGURE 3

In the render processes, polygon flow is shown by the emboldened lines and scan-converted pixels by the thin lines.

pipeline is used for the transformation and clipping stages, followed by a "selective" processor farm scheme for the scan-conversion and z-buffering stage. (Selective in the sense that the workers pick off only those polygons corresponding to their subsection of the display). The second approach [3] utilises a processor farm for the transformation stage followed by a selective processor farm (as in [4]) for the rendering stage.

The distribution scheme proposed here is closest to that described in [3], and is illustrated in figure 3. Due to both the size of the flow simulation data files and the interactive nature of the package, the data has to be distributed over several transputers. It therefore makes sense to duplicate the transformation, clipping, and polygon generation code locally on these "database" transputers.

The rendering stage should also be distributed, employing rather more transputers than in the transformation step to take account of the increased computational requirement. Each of the n processors will take care of every n^{th} horizontal strip of the display. This method of distribution ensures reasonable load-balancing compared to, say, simple block division of the display area, where one display block might contain a large number of small polygons. Distributing whole scan lines also allows the property of "scan line coherence" to be exploited effectively.

5.2 Data Packet Size

Now that the strategy for the physical distribution of the algorithm is clear, there remains the question of choosing the optimum sizes for the data packets used to send polygons between the transformation and rendering transputers, and the packets used to send scan-converted pixels from the rendering transputers to the display transputer. The performance of the graphics package using various packet sizes is still under evaluation, and the latest results will be presented at the conference.

6. Optimisation Tricks

There are several simple means by which program execution time can be reduced:

Compile in reduced mode

Once a program has been fully developed and debugged, it may be compiled in reduced mode, which will remove the run-time overhead of error checking ([5], page 46).

Ensure that time-critical sections are coded optimally

For instance, the routine which forms the product of a coordinate vector with the transformation matrix is repeated many thousands of times, so efficient coding is crucial. The best way to do this is to unfold the DO-loop as described in [4], section 12.4.

Incorporate modifications to the standard graphics algorithms to take advantage of the T800's architecture.

One example of this is to utilise the on-chip FPU to draw polygon edges, by using the long arithmetic instructions (LONGADD & LONGSUM) in place of the usual digital differential analyzer or Bressenham line drawing algorithms. Sections of occam code can be linked with Fortran code by using the Meiko EXTRACTF utility [6].

Place crucial buffers in internal RAM

Normally a program whose workspace and code requirements exceed the transputer's on-chip cache size (4 Kb on a T800) is compiled so that arrays are placed in off-chip memory — ie if the compiler parameter "separate vector space" is in its default TRUE state. In the graphics pipeline, the transformation matrix is accessed very frequently and so it is important to hold it in local memory, if possible. This is done by overriding the default allocation with code which (in occam) looks something like this:

```
[4][4]INT transformation.matrix:
PLACE transformation.matrix IN WORKSPACE:
```

See [5], page 47, for more details.

7. Conclusions

This report has described the successful implementation of a 3-D parallel graphics visualisation system programmed primarily in Fortran. Final performance figures are in preparation and will be presented at the conference. Some of the techniques which were found to be useful for program optimisation are also presented for general interest; these are not just restricted to graphics applications.

8. References

1. Foley, J D & Van Dam, A "Fundamentals of Interactive Computer Graphics", pub. Addison-Wesley ISBN 0-201-14468-9.

2. Hearn, D & Baker, M P "Computer Graphics", pub Prentice-Hall ISBN 0-13-165598-1.

3. Barton, E "Data Concurrency & the Computing Surface", Meiko Guidance Note.

4. "High Performance Graphics with the IMS T800", Inmos Technical Note 37.

5. Inmos Ltd. "Transputer Development System", page 46, pub. Prentice-Hall ISBN 0-13-928995-X.

6. Meiko Ltd. "Computing Surface Fortran Reference Manual", D0400-0301.00, page 4.3.

The Development of a Transputer-based Image Database

D Crookes & P J Morrow, Department of Computer Science
G Philip, Department of Information Studies
The Queen's University of Belfast
Belfast BT7 1NN. Northern Ireland

Abstract

An image database is described which contains a selection of old photographs of historic interest. The project is investigating the application of image processing techniques, in two areas in particular: image enhancement, during the image capture phase; and image compression/decompression. Decompression operates during image retrieval. Because of the large processing requirements, we have used a transputer network as the image processing engine. The project is still in progress; but initial findings suggest that transputers are successful in providing the raw processing power; on the other hand, lack of software tools and software portability considerations have proved to be something of a drawback.

1 Introduction

An image database is being constructed to hold a selection of historical photographs which are currently held in a local museum in Northern Ireland. These photographic collections, many dating from as early as the 1870's, are valuable items and are of great interest to students of local history. Unfortunately, the demand for access to these photographs cannot be met, partly because of the large number of photographs available (some 100,000 in one collection alone), and also because of security considerations (many of the photographs are on glass plates). Users typically need to browse through the collections, or search for particular points of interest. To improve access to this valuable resource, we are developing a pilot image database which will hold around one or two thousand items in the first instance. The photographs are chosen from the Welch collection; this collection is held in the Ulster Museum, and covers the development of Belfast and Northern Ireland from around 1870 into the early twentieth century. Rather than merely using straight image capture, storage and retrieval, the project is investigating the application of image processing techniques in the development of the database. To provide the necessary processing power, we are using transputers as the image processing engine.

2 Use of Image Processing

Image processing techniques are being applied in the construction and access of the database, in two main areas of the project: image enhancement, and image compression.

2.1 Image enhancement

Although many of the old photographs are of superb quality, some are rather indistinct; some pictures, although containing very valuable information, are of poor quality. Some suffer from poor contrast, perhaps through incorrect exposure; others are blurred; others have a large amount of grain noise, and some are damaged. Image enhancement techniques can sometimes be used to improve the quality of the images, and to increase the amount of information absorbed quickly by a user who is browsing through the collection.

Another reason for requiring image enhancement is the loss of resolution during image capture. To capture as much as possible of the very fine detail in the photographs, a camera with at least 1K by 1K resolution would be desirable. Unfortunately, cost constraints have ruled out this type of equipment in our case, and we use a camera and frame grabber resolution of approximately 700 by 512. In practice, the quality of captured images is less than the optimum, and fine detail often appears rather blurred. Simple edge sharpening algorithms have been effective in restoring some of the the lost resolution.

One other advantage of image processing techniques is that images can be input in negative form. By projecting the glass plate negative using a light box, the captured (negative) image can be made positive by simple processing. This can eliminate the inconvenient intermediate stage of producing prints chemically.

2.2 Image compression

The potentially large number of items for inclusion in the database means that image compression techniques must be considered. Each uncompressed image in our system occupies around one third of a megabyte. On the other hand, since interactive retrieval and display of a set of stored (compressed) image requires processing power to do the decompression, a balance has to be struck between storage requirements and processor requirements. Also, when choosing a compression algorithm, it is important to preserve as much detail as possible, since it is often the fine detail in a picture which contains the most significant information (such as the style of dress of people in the picture, or the wording on advertisements in the background, and so on).

We are investigating a multi-algorithm approach, combining both information preserving and non-information preserving techniques: those parts of the image identified as containing significant detail are encoded using an information-preserving method.

3 Application of Transputers

Because of the significant amount of image processing which can be required for both image enhancement and image compression/decompression, we have opted for a transputer network as the processing engine for the image database. An application of this nature has a definite requirement for significant processing power, during the two different phases of the database's life cycle:

(i) *Data Input*
   We have found that input of images to the database, including image enhancement and cataloguing information, is extremely time consuming, and requires a lot of user intervention. During image input, the 'user' may have to experiment with different image enhancement techniques (edge sharpening, histogram equalisation, etc). Particularly when working with high resolution images, this takes a lot of computation time. And given the large number of items involved, the time for a single item has to be minimised. Thus data input has two specific requirements: an interactive experimentation environment for image enhancement, and very fast execution time for image enhancement operations. For the latter, we are using a network of transputers, together with a MicroEye TC II transputer-based framegrabber. To meet the first need, we are making use of a transputer-based experimentation environment—an image processing Programmer's Workbench—which has been developed as a separate project. The use of this workbench will be described below in more detail in section 3.1.

(ii) *Image Compression and Decompression*
   The reason for using transputers in the context of image compression has mainly to do with the need for fast *decompression* during image retrieval, rather than fast compression (which needs to be done only once per image, and has no real time requirement). A promising approach would be to use the INMOS A121 chip which has specific application to image compression and decompression: but resource considerations have led us to rely instead on the transputer network used for data input (above). In browsing mode, the system's response to a query may be to present batches of pictures to the user in miniature format, with up to twelve pictures on the screen. It is acceptable to the user if it takes something of the order of a second to decompress and display each miniature picture. Subsequently, the user may select individual pictures, and have them displayed full size. We can take advantage of the fact that miniature pictures need not convey the full detail of a photograph, and therefore the decompression process can afford to be approximate (and thus faster) when displaying miniature formats. The ability to vary the degree of restoration is a factor which influences the range of compression algorithms to be considered.

3.1 Using the QUB Image Processing Programmer's Workbench

The process of image enhancement needs a highly interactive environment, with facilities for experimenting with different algorithms and techniques. One drawback of using transputers has been the lack of suitable software tools which provide this sort of environment. Some time ago we recognised the need for a tool which enables users to exploit the parallelism of transputers, while hiding the details of the parallelism from the user. As a result, we are in the process of developing a programmer's workbench for developing and using image processing software systems on a transputer network [1]. A prototype version of this workbench provides the following features:

- A program is made up of a sequence of standard library components.
- The program is represented graphically (as a simple linear flowchart), and is drawn and edited using a mouse.
- Parameters can be specified interactively for each component, where appropriate. A simple case would be the setting of a suitable threshold value (which often needs some experimentation to determine the best value). A more powerful facility is the ability to select a specific algorithm from a menu of possible algorithms which all carry out the same basic operation (for instance, we could have an edge sharpening operation which provides a range of alternative algorithms, such as Laplace, high pass filters, and so on).
- Images can be viewed at various stages of the process by attaching *probes* to the diagram—rather like connecting a logic analyser.
- The user can interactively change the image size and the number of transputers, without the need for recompilation. Thus the only exposure of the transputer implementation to the user is that the user must say how many transputers are to be used.

Using this workbench, a typical enhancement program can be drawn as shown in figure 1. This shows two main enhancement stages: firstly, edge sharpening, followed by contrast enhancement (perhaps implemented by histogram equalisation). The figure is a snapshot of the programmer's screen at a point when the user is experimenting with different edge enhancement algorithms.

4 The image database system

The system comprises a database (of images and associated text) which is accessed in two different modes. In the first (data input) mode, images and descriptive textual information for each image can be added to the database. It is in this mode that image enhancement is carried out, and the image is compressed before being added to the database. In the second (user) mode, images and textual information are retrieved in response to user queries. The main user interface for the database is menu-driven, and runs on the *host* to the transputer network rather than on the transputers themselves. Images are displayed on a separate graphics monitor connected to the framestore. Figure 2 shows the use of the system.

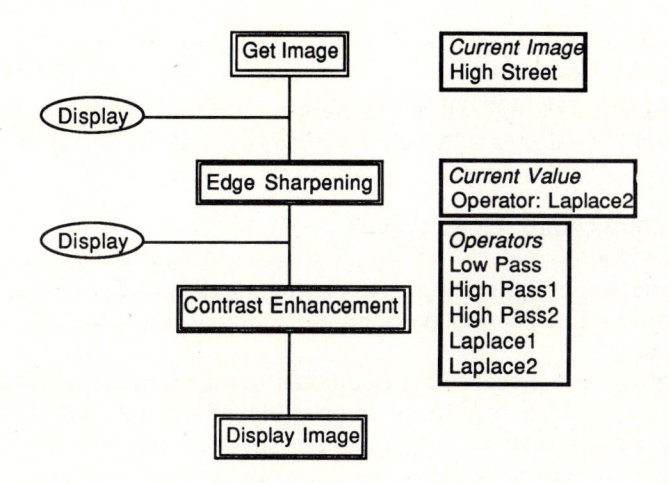

Figure 1 *An enhancement program as developed on the Programmer's Workbench*

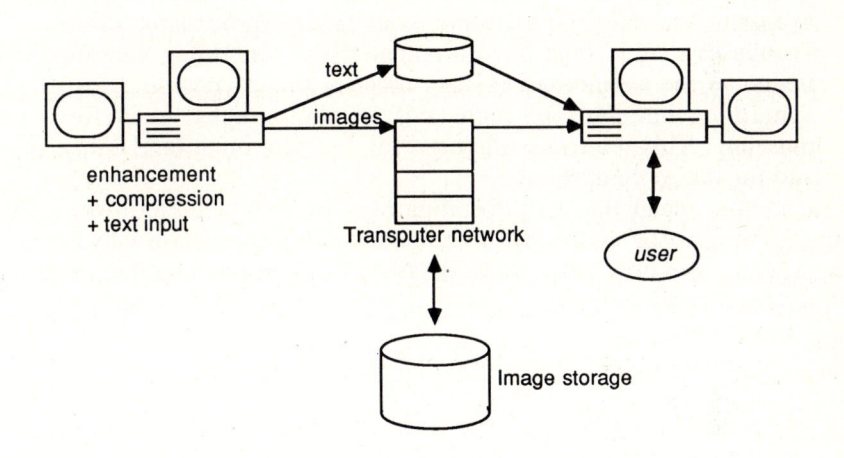

Figure 2 *Use of transputer-based image database*

The transputer system is hosted by a PC front end, which provides the menu-driven interface. Searching the database is achieved primarily using a keyword approach. A browsing facility is being incorporated, whereby the system may display a set of photographs in 'stub' format, allowing the user to zoom into a selected picture if required. The images are held on a hard disk, interfaced directly to the transputer network by a SCSI TRAM. At present, the textual information is held on the PC's hard disk; this is partly because PC-based database development tools are readily available, and the speed of operation of the system is not slowed down significantly by holding the text on the PC.

5 Experience and Conclusions

An image database application such as this one has some intrinsic properties which have a major bearing on the computational requirements for servicing the database:
- To capture and preserve the fine detail in the photographs, it is necessary to go for as high resolution as possible. This has two implications: it firstly means that any image processing will require correspondingly greater computing power; it secondly makes the need for image compression more pressing.
- There will always be loss of quality in the image capture process. Together with the existing scope for enhancement because of poor quality originals, there is a clear need for interactive experimentation with different image enhancement techniques. To be effective, this needs to be as fast as possible, and therefore requires large processing power.
- Databases of this type have a potential for containing vast numbers of items. If the technology existed, there is already potential for databases containing hundreds of thousands of photographs, even for a single museum. This reinforces the need for fast data input (and enhancement), and for image compression.

These factors mean that major computing power is a prerequisite, and the main question to be addressed is the nature of the hardware which provides this power. We now give some details of our initial experience of using transputers for this purpose.

5.1 Experience with a Transputer Solution

To date, some of our practical experience and conclusions of using transputers as the image processing engine could be summarised as follows:

Advantages
- Using a network of transputers (up to 16 in our case) has successfully delivered the computing power to provide a highly interactive image enhancement capability. We are still in the process of developing the image compression and decompression facilities, and results for this are not yet available.
- The parallelism of transputers is scalable (given a proper approach to software construction in the first instance), so that further speedup can merely be bought, with no ensuing changes in the software being necessary.
- With higher resolution graphics TRAMS now becoming available (and cheaper), the cost for a standalone *user* version of the database is more

reasonable than initially appeared. A frame grabber (by far the most expensive item in the system) is of course not necessary for image retrieval.

Disadvantages
- The initial difficulty experienced was the lack of a good image processing software development environment for transputers. This is of course the common difficulty experienced in any development of transputer-based applications. Fortunately, our separate image processing Programmer's Workbench project has reached the prototype stage, and is proving a very effective tool for applications of this nature.
- One of the problems we now face is the lack of portability which results from the fact that a transputer system needs a *host front end*, and there is a whole range of different host computers available. This means that there is yet another dimension to the hardware platform. It isn't enough to develop a transputer-based system; it must be transputers plus IBM PC, or transputers plus Sun, or whatever. There were several reasons why we didn't decide to program the entire system, including the mouse-driven user interface, on transputers: at the start of the project, software tools for generating mouse-driven menu systems on transputers were not available; also a standard size graphics screen is not big enough to support properly the display of a set of images as well as the database query interface. The moral of the story is that transputer software developers need to be constantly aware that host-dependent user interface software is not portable, and should be avoided. This increases the need, however, for landscape-sized megapixel colour graphics displays.

Acknowledgements

The image database aspects of this work are being supported by a grant from the British Library. The Programmer's Workbench project is being supported by SERC, grant number GR/F 01611.

References

1   D Crookes, P J Morrow, B Sharif and I McClatchey, 'An environment for developing concurrent software for transputer-based image processing'. Microprocessors and Microprogramming, vol.27, 1989. pp. 417–422.

A Transputer Based Automatic Number-Plate Recognition System

R. A. Lotufo   A. D. Morgan   A. S. Johnson   B. T. Thomas

Faculty of Engineering, University of Bristol, Bristol, UK.

Abstract. This paper describes recent research into the application of image processing techniques to the automatic decoding of vehicle licence plates. A fast, scalable transputer based framestore system has been designed and built at the University of Bristol to support the various image processing operations. Recent results and conclusions are presented explaining the range of applications.

1. Introduction

Traffic engineers and the police often wish to be able to uniquely identify road vehicles at different points in a road network for a number of reasons[1], such as:

- automatic toll-collection, road pricing schemes, and operation of car parks for revenue collection;

- fleet control for monitoring and optimising the movements of particular types of vehicles (e.g. heavy goods vehicles);

- speed- and weight-limit enforcement purposes;

- crime detection/prevention; and

- traffic data collection (e.g. vehicle journey times, origin/destination and entry/exit flow patterns, etc.) for traffic operation and planning.

Until quite recently, vehicle identification has largely been a labour intensive manual activity, aided where possible by electromechanical actuators. With the continuing increase in volume of road traffic, such manual techniques have proved impractical. Improvements in electronic sensor technology has allowed for the development of automatic vehicle identification (AVI) equipment.

Conventional AVI systems employ R.F., microwave and inductive loop technologies[2]. In such systems, a unique code identifying each vehicle is stored on a vehicle mounted transponder. As the vehicle passes specific points in the roadway, a roadside reader unit detects vehicle presence and reads the coded information on the vehicle mounted transponder unit. Most AVI installations additionally use a video/CCTV subsystem for photo/videologging vehicles that are unequipped with transponders. These video recordings are often manually reviewed, off-line, for extracting the registration number plates of each defaulting vehicle.

Although conventional AVI installations are becoming widespread, the practical implementation of such systems on a large scale requires mounting transponders on a very large number of vehicles. They also have the need to ensure the reliable operation and maintenance of these transponders. The latter requires some means of performing automatic checks to detect any malfunction in the vehicle mounted transponder. The alternative, involving the manual interpretation of vehicle registration number plates from video recordings of traffic is tedious and expensive, especially for heavily used AVI installations.

1.1. AVI Using Computer Vision

Recent advances in computer vision technology and the falling prices of related devices has extended the use of video/CCTV by making it practical to automatically identify vehicles visually either on-line or off-line.

The objective of our research is to develop a Computer-Vision based AVI system to achieve vehicle identification using optical character recognition (OCR) techniques. Our work involves investigations into real-time automatic Number-Plate Recognition (NPR) and its extension to other aspects of road traffic monitoring and control.

Automatic Number-Plate Recognition avoids the need to equip vehicles with a special transponder, since all vehicles already have a unique registration number plate. Furthermore, most of the conventional AVI systems currently in operation already incorporate some form of video/CCTV subsystem. This means that the only additional cost to existing installations will be that of the automatic image analysis subsystem.

2. The Number-Plate Recognition System

2.1. Design Requirements

The basic requirement for any Number Plate Recognition system, for practical implementation, is real-time performance with a high recognition accuracy. Thus, the following basic performance requirements can be identified:

1. High recognition speed (approx. a second per vehicle);

2. High recognition accuracy (typically more than 95%);

3. High level of consistency

The specification for a number plate image consists of a clean picture with the number plate occupying at least 25% of the width of the image and with a minimum contrast factor of 4 between the characters and background.

2.2. Configuration

A typical application consists of a configuration where a camera is mounted so as to capture an image of the front number plate of a vehicle entering a car park. When a vehicle arrives at the barrier, an inductive loop detector triggers the number plate recognition system. The number plate is extracted from the image and decoded, which can then be compared to a data base, or stored for later analysis. In most applications, the requirement of real-time operation is fundamental: the number plate must be decoded within couple of seconds from the capture time. This imposes a large demand on the speed of image processing operations.

2.3. System Architecture

The number plate recognition system can be divided in two main parts: image acquisition and image analysis. The image acquisition part consists of the vehicle sensor, the camera and the video digitiser. The image analysis is divided in three further sections: the location of the number plate in the captured image, character feature extraction and character classification.

The successful operation of the number plate reader depends on both parts. The image acquisition must deliver a clean picture of the number plate with good illumination, minimum blur and reasonable resolution. The image analysis must identify the number plate and correctly decode it within seconds.

2.4. Hardware Architecture

The system consists of four basic components: vehicle sensor input, video interface input, video interface output and transputer frame-store. The functions of each component are as follows.

- vehicle sensor input: a digital input port, addressable by the processor to detect the right time to acquire a picture.

- video interface input: analog video input is digitised to 8 bits, passed to a lookup table and output to buffer memory. The interface can be synchronised externally with the video synchronism extractor and frequency lock circuit. This uses a gated oscillator with good start-up characteristics rather than the common phase-locked loop solution which can often require a time-base corrector with VCR signals. This enables the grabbing of pictures both from a Video Cassette Recorder and TV camera.

- video interface output: converts digitised video data from the video bus to RGB analog TV signals suitable for displaying in a colour monitor. The colour map function is implemented using three 6 bit by 256 lookup tables.

- transputer frame-store: the digitised video data is stored in a dual memory static RAM addressable by the transputer. The video memory is organised as a double buffer allowing video data to be grabbed in one buffer concurrently with the processing of the previously captured frame. The transputer frame-store has also a digitised video output port to transmit video data to the video interface output. The processor is based on the 20MHz T800 32 bit transputer with 512 Kbyte of fast static RAM. Four INMOS serial links are provided together with the standard network signals Error, Reset and Analyse. This interface enables the expansion of the CPU power capability by an indefinite number of transputers.

- host: a PC IBM compatible fitted with a transputer card or an Inmos link interface adapter.

A prototype system based on three different board types has been designed, involving:

- a video interface card providing A/D and D/A conversion of video signals for image capture and display, and vehicle sensor interface,

- a processor card, based on the T800 32 bits floating point transputer,

- a framestore card consisting of a dual 256x256x8 double buffer or a single 512x512x8 buffer memory accessed independently from the video interface card and from the processor card.

The processor card and the framestore card make the transputer framestore component of the system. Each of the cards uses a double Eurocard form factor so they may be racked together with a variety of commercially available boards.

2.5. Image Analysis

The Number Plate Reading algorithm is divided into three main tasks: number plate location, character detection and character classification:

- The number plate location task scans the image looking for the area of the number plate and outputs the coordinates of the number plate.

- The character detection task operates on the number plate region, identifying each individual character and extracting its relevant features.

- The character classification task gathers the features extracted for each character and classifies them using a pre-stored data base.

For number plates with a known structure, such as British number plates, where there are rules for the position of letters and numbers, a further step can be used: a syntax checker and corrector which uses the alphanumeric rules and probabilities from the character classification task to confirm or correct the selected characters.

2.6. The algorithm

The images acquired are often visually noisy and invariably the scene is unevenly illuminated. A significant feature of the system is its ability to operate under typical lighting conditions. For this reason, the system first executes an adaptive thresholding algorithm on the entire scene. This thresholded image is shown in figure 1. This aids in properly segmenting the vehicle number plate and its constituent characters from the rest of the scene.

A boundary following algorithm is then applied to the resulting binary image to locate the number plate. This is achieved by a spatial scanning procedure which searches for closed contours that have an appropriate size and aspect. If a number of these closed contours are found in a localised region, then it is assumed that their position is in the area of the number plate.

Once the location of the number plate has been found, a second threshold is computed and applied to the number plate area to properly segment the characters from the rest of the plate background. A similar boundary tracking technique is then performed, within the plate area, to extract the character features. Fig 1 shows this scanning process. Typical features include number of holes, corners, boundary chain codes, bounding box, etc.

Figure 1: Original image and threshold image showing the boundary tracking in the region of the number plate.

In extreme lighting conditions such as reflections off the plate and when the plate has marks on it from dirt or fixing bolts, the segmentation/boundary tracking approach can fail to detect the presence of a character. The position and size of each character is checked against each other looking for possible missing or connected characters. The algorithm converts abnormally wide gaps into characters, splits wide characters and checks for the presence of missing end characters.

After the characters have been detected and have had their features extracted, a character classification process is performed that is based on Firschein and Fischler's method [3]. The characters are divided into classes and subclasses, with subclasses expressing the variations within a class, e.g. the possible different fonts of the character *4* form subclasses of the class *4*. The method uses a training set to iteratively split and merge subclasses until an stable condition is met. The classes and subclasses are stored in a database of reference features. Likelihood/confidence measures are computed from the Euclidean distance from the candidate character to each subclass in the database. The classes having the highest confidences are selected as potential candidates for the final classification.

Following this, the format of the extracted characters is checked against the standard number plate format to validate whether in fact this string of characters constitutes a valid vehicle number plate. This is achieved using a syntax checking/forcing algorithm. This examines the type and positional validity of each character for each syntax type (only the four most prolific syntax types have been examined so far) and performs syntax forcing if an incorrect type is detected. This is achieved by replacing the incorrect character with the appropriate type from the other potential candidates recorded earlier in order of likelihood.

3. System Performance and Evaluation

There are two basic figures relevant to number plate reading: the response time and the confidence of the extracted number plate. These figures are related and a trade-off is required to achieve the desired confidence and response time. The hardware architecture enables the expansion to parallel processing in order to speed-up the intermediate tasks simply by adding standard off-the-shelf transputer products. Most of the tasks allow natural parallel decomposition and could benefit from this parallel processing capability using both task and data parallelism:

- number-plate location: different thresholds can be applied in parallel, or different horizontal scan lines can be assigned to each processor.
- feature extraction: each character can be processed in parallel using, for instance, a processor farm approach.
- character matching: each character can be matched in parallel with the same decomposition used for feature extraction.

3.1. Evaluation

An important aspect of the project is the method used to evaluate the system. An appropriate measurement of the confidence and response time parameters of the systems requires the application of a very large number of typical images to the number plate reader. The evaluation procedure must be repeated to assess the results of a modification to the recognition algorithm.

To continuously assess the system during development, an automatic evaluation procedure was designed:

After recording scenes of real situations onto a video cassette recorder, a sound burst signal was dubbed onto the audio channel to simulate the vehicle sensor input. A reference file is created with the correct number plate sequence recorded in the tape. The number plate reader can autonomously process the video tape digitising the image at each sound trigger, reporting the processing results into a "log" file. At the end, an evaluation program, reading the "log" file and the reference file computes the performance figures of the system.

4. Results and Conclusions

The results of running the evaluation system on more than one thousand cars, considering only those number plate which are within the specification are 84% of correctly decoded number-plates. This figure was computed considering the character pairs D and O as a single class. This assumption is valid for car park or traffic data collection applications where the probability of having two number-plates which differ only by the D and O is negligible.

The prototype number-plate reader will be evaluated by field tests over the next few months. The main advantage of the transputer based architecture consists of enabling a future system upgrade to achieve improvements on both response time and the decoding of out-of-specification number-plates. The upgrade can use off the shelves transputer modules and benefit from the continuing development of more complex image analysis algorithms.

5. Acknowledgements

This research is funded by Golden River Limited, (Remote Data Collection Systems) Oxford, UK. The authors would like to acknowledge the advice and encouragement given by Professor E.L.Dagless, and Dr D.J.Milford and the assistance of Dr.R.Danbury and Mr

P.Clarke. R.A.Lotufo is supported in part by CNPq, Brazil under grant n.200172/86-EE and Universidade de Campinas, Brazil. A.S.Johnson would like to thank the British Council for their financial support.

6. References

[1] Salter, D. R. "The Potential of Automatic Vehicle Identification", IEE Conf. on Road Traffic Data Collection, 242, pp 79-82, (1984).

[2] Ayland, N. and Davies, P. "Automatic Vehicle Identification for Heavy Vehicle Monitoring", IEE 2nd Int. Conf. on Road Traffic Monitoring, 299, pp 152-155, (1989).

[3] Ullmann, J.R. "Pattern Recognition Techniques", London Butterworths, (1973).

IDENTIFICATION OF 3-D OBJECTS FROM 2-D IMAGES

W Lin and D A Fraser

Department of Electronic and Electrical Engineering
Kings College, Strand, London.   071 836 5454

Abstract.   An algorithm is presented for recognizing objects arriving under a TV camera on a conveyor belt.   A stored description of a 3-D object is rotated and translated, and its projected image is matched to the observed image.
Implementations in parallel C on 1,2,4,or 8 T414 transputers show full speed-up.

1. Introduction

This work has a dual interest: to explore the extent to which an apparently regular task can be speeded up by distributing it over a network of processors, and to develop an image recognition system suitable for a common industrial application.

A further aspect of interest was to confirm the suitability of a high-level language as a parallel programming instrument.

2. The Task

Object recognition is very difficult [1],[2] when an object has to be recognized anywhere, against any background, in any lighting, and in any orientation.

We study a simpler problem, which nevertheless has a clear industrial application. We consider objects arriving on a conveyor belt, passing into the field of view of a fixed TV camera (fig 1).

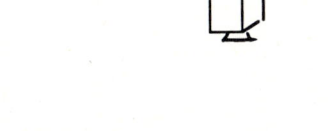

Figure 1.   The model task.

There will be only a few distinct objects that could get onto the conveyor belt (legitimately). The distance of the object from the camera is known, and the object will be in one of a small number of stable positions, in each of which it may be regarded as a distinct object.. There remain three degrees of freedom : the object when viewed may be anywhere on the surface of the conveyor belt, and may be rotated at an arbitrary angle round a vertical axis.

The computational task is to identify an image as representing one of a number of known objects, and to report the position and orientation of the source object on the conveyor belt. The transformation of an object can be found using the data from a vertex and an edge directional vector[3].

The problem has been attacked with T414 transputer networks and 3L parallel C programs.

3. Image Transforms and Matching

We are trying to match 2-D information from an image to 3-D information from a stored model of an object. The strategy is to extract a 2-D projection from the 3-D model, and then to match the two sets of 2-D data. What is needed is a set of identifiable features on the object. We have used the vertices of wire-frame solids, but the only properties of the objects that have been used are the coordinates of vertices, and any other property that could be located would do as well.

An initial attempt at solution tried to repeatedly reduce the difference between a trial projection of an object, and the image. Convergence was only satisfactory when the initial guess was very good[4].

A closed solution[3],[5],[6] is available which can determine the three possible unknown values (shift along two axes of the plane and rotation) to align the vertices from the model with vertices of the image. Expressed functionally,

$$Proj\ (Rot\ (Shift(\ Object))) = Image$$

where *Proj. Rot.* and *Shift.* are matrix operators acting on the coordinates of the object vertices. Only four observational values are needed, and these may be taken from either two , three or four distinct vertices. If the choice of vertices is not correct, then there may be no solution.

In the coordinate system shown in Fig.2, object vertices V1,V2 are related to their image points V_1', V_2' by

$$R V_1 + D = \alpha_1 V_1' \qquad (1)$$
$$R V_2 + D = \alpha_2 V_2' \qquad (2)$$

where R and D are rotation and translation matrix operators, respectively, and α_1, α_2 are coefficients related to the depth of these two object vertices.

Define $V_1 - V_2 = [\ e_1\ e_2\ e_3\ ]^T \qquad (3)$

$\alpha_1\ V_1' - \alpha_2\ V_2' = [\ g_1\ g_2\ g_3\ ]^T \qquad (4)$

Lens Center O(0,0,0)

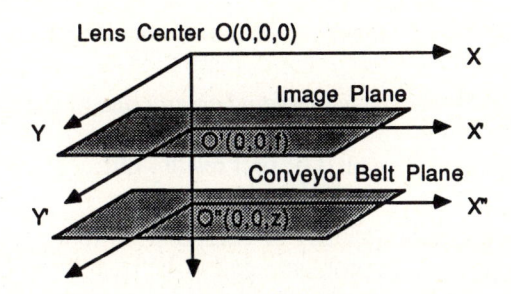

Figure 2 The coordinate system.

The solution of the transformation parameters can be expressed as:
$$\theta = \arcsin[(e_2 g_1 - e_1 g_2)/(e_1^2 + e_2^2)] \quad (5)$$
$$D = \alpha_1 V_1' - R V_1 \quad (6)$$

A major factor in the size of the computation is the large number of possible trial matches. In the worst case, if the object has M vertices and the image has N vertices, there are
$$M \times N \times (M-1) \times (N-1) /2$$
cases to try, if two vertices provide the data.   The present computation makes the full number of trials, as there has been interest in the way the computation maps onto transputer networks. There are ways of shortening the number of trials : picking a probable set of vertices for the first trial, and avoiding repetition of calculations. These are discussed in section 5.

The results of applying the algorithm to two test objects are shown in fig 3. Noise has been added to the image vertex coordinates to simulate errors introduced in image capture and data reduction.   The figures show the image, and a refined overall fit where the errors in the previous case are minimized on a least squares basis.

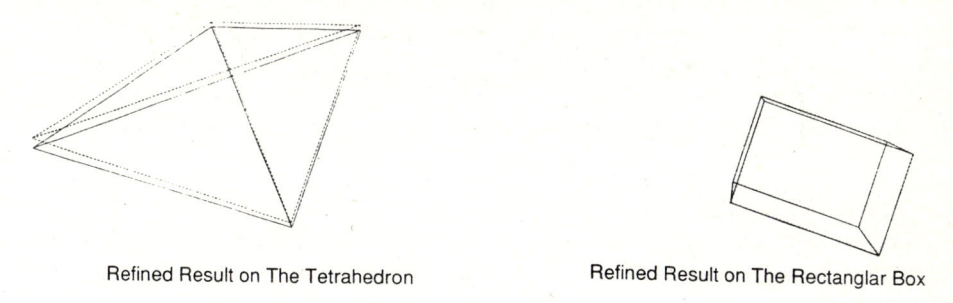

Refined Result on The Tetrahedron   Refined Result on The Rectanglar Box

Figure 3.   Image Matching results.

4.Task Structure.

A distinction can be made between problems where a solution is found when all the parts of the task are complete,

$$\text{Full result} = \text{part result}_1 \text{ AND part result}_2 \text{ AND , , , ,}$$

and problems where a solution is available when any one of the parts of the problem is solved

$$\text{Full result} = \text{part result}_1 \text{ OR part result}_2 \text{ OR , , , ,}$$

For AND problems, the total quantity of computation to a solution will be roughly the same for all examples of the problem, and if the part of the problem can be given to different processors, then the whole job will be done more quickly. With OR problems, the time to find a solution could depend on how lucky you were in guessing which sub-task to try first, or leave to last. In this case, distributing the whole task among many processors would not change the minimum time in which a solution is ever found, but the maximum time would be reduced when more processors were used. Of course, if the sub-task can itself be broken up, the argument has to be applied again at the finer scale.

The image recognition task considered here fits the OR classification, but initially no account was taken of the success of any matching in ending the computation, so every problem ran for the same , maximum , time.

5. Transputer Implementation

The task has been implemented on transputer networks with 1, 2, 4, and 8 transputers (Fig.4). A tree structure was used, which could be extended with the minimum of alteration to the program.

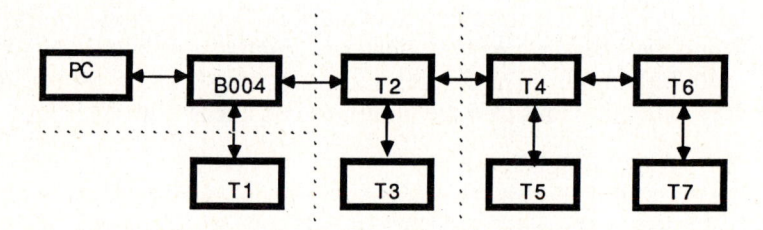

Fig.4   Configurations of the Transputer Networks.

Fig 5 shows the running times for two matching tasks on networks of 1,2,4 and 8 transputers. One task matched an object with 8 vertices and the the second, one with 16 vertices. It is apparent that there is close to full speed up in the execution of the task. Two contributary reasons are the regularity of the task , and the high ratio of computing to communication.

It is also clear that the time for recognizing an object is too long to be practically useful. Two ways of reducing the computing time have been adopted: when a successful match is found, the news is broadcast, and work is stopped; also an educated guess is used for which vertices to try matching first.

The result of introducing these ideas is to reduce the calculation time for matching a 16 -vertex object and image from 317 sec to about 1 sec. This points up an old moral : a good algorithm is the beginning and end of program design.

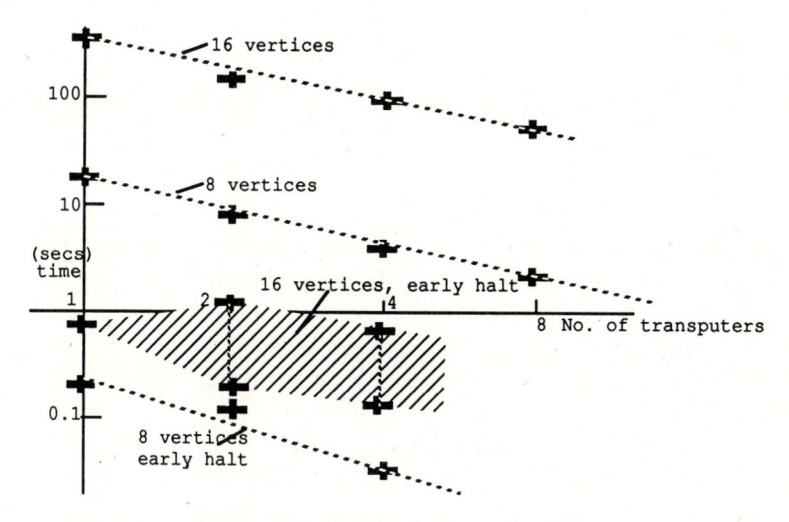

Figure 5. Run times for different numbers of transputers.

As already noted, a major factor in the size of computation is the large number of possible trial matches. An heuristic argument that suggests good choices for vertices to be matched goes like this: Two vertices in the object that are close together cannot produce image vertices that are far apart. Two vertices in the image that are widely separated must have been widely separated in the object. So we start by matching the most widely separated vertices in object and image. Run times are then reduced by a large factor.

The parallel C language [7] provides a number of facilities of multi-processor use. The task was equally split three times when being distributed over eight transputers. The chan-out and chan-in constructs in C were used to transfer data, with 'strands' being created to receive data. The semaphore function was used to control access for data flow towards the root of the processor tree.

Fig. 5 shows relative speeds for each configuration. When the program runs to the bitter end, there is full speed-up as expected, and the run time is reproducable. When a halt was called as soon as a match was found, there are three points to be noted. The run times are reduced by a factor of about a hundred. The run times also show significant variation when the details of the task are changed, and the minimum time no longer shows a full speed-up. This is all consistent with the expectations of an OR-task.

6. Future Work

This system will be interfaced to vertex generation system currently under development, so that real rather than synthetic objects will be analysed. It is possible to see already how to apply this technique to images of objects where some of the vertices are obscured, or to more than one object at a time. The T800 floating-point transputer will allow the matrix transformations to be speeded up.

REFERENCES

[1] P.J.Best and R.C.Jain, "Three-Dimensional Object Recognition", Computing Surveys, Vol 17, 1985, pp 75-145.

[2] T.O.Binford, " Survey of Model-Based Image Analysis Systems",The International Journal of Robotics Reaearch, Vol 1, 1982 pp 18-64.

3] T.M.Silburburg, et al. :"Object Recognition Using Oriented Model Points", Computer Vision, Graphics, and Image Processing, 35(1),July 1986, pp. 47-71.

[4] .D.Worrall et al," Model Based Perspective Inversion"' Image and Vision Computing , vol7, Feb. 1989 , pp 17-23.

[5] R.Nevatia,,Machine Perception, Prentice-Hall,1982

[6] L.G.Roberts,Machine Perception of Three-Dimensional Objects, Garland Publishing Inc., 1980

[[7] 3L Ltd , Parallel C User Guide, 1988.

[8] D.Holder and H.Buxton, "Polyhedral Object Recognition with Sparse Data in SIMD Processing Mode", Proc 4th.Alvey Vision Conference, Manchester , 1988

[9] D.W.Murray, "Strategies in Object Recognition", GEC Journal of Research, Vol 6,1988, pp80-95.

AUTOMATIC TRAFFIC MONITORING USING TRANSPUTER-IMAGE PROCESSING SYSTEM

A.T. Ali   E.L. Dagless

Faculty of Engineering, University of Bristol, Bristol, UK.

SYNOPSIS

An important application of transputers is in the the field of image processing due to the high processing power made available by parallel operation of a large number of transputers. The flexible topology of transputer networks makes them suitable in several different configurations, for the task of handling the huge amount of image data which needs to be processed in real-time application.
Transputers have been successfully applied to many image processing tasks. Traffic scene analysis is an area of much interest to many researchers [1,2,3,4,5,6,7].
This paper addresses the application of a transputer based image processing system(TIPS) to monitor road traffic in real time. A number of detection and tracking algorithms that have been coded in OCCAM and run on a network of transputers are reported.

Transputer-Image Processing System(TIPS)

A real-time transputer-controlled frame grabber forms the heart of a home built transputer-image processing system(TIPS) shown in fig.1. The frame grabber can capture video images via a video camera or a video recorder at a standard TV rate of 50 frame/sec in a non-interlaced mode, digitize it into $256*256(8$ bit) pixels and store it a framestore. The framestore is a double buffered and is mapped directly into the address space of a transputer. The framebuffer works in an overlapping manner so that while one frame store is involved in frame grabbing or displaying, the other can be accessed by the transputer for read/write operations.
The network transputers are linked to a B004-transputer hosted in an IPM compatable PC which runs concurrently with the operation of the other transputers to perform the extraction of the required traffic data. The host transputer is also used for program development and loading of the network transputers.

Traffic Scene Analysis

Once a video frame is digitized and stored in one of the transputer's framestores, The network transputers perform all the processing steps that form the 'detection process'comprising of frame differencing, thresholding, image size manipulation and object centeriod and dimensions extraction. The extracted center and size of each moving object in the open world traffic scene is used by the 'tracking algorithm' to predict the position of moving objects frame by frame until they leave the monitored area.
The paper will describe the results achieved in evaluating these detection tasks. The performance characteristics of these tasks will be shown.

Traffic Data Collection

While the tracking algorithm is handling and maintaining a record of the instantanuous position of each moving object in each frame, that position, as a function of time is sent via a transputer link to the host transputer and fed to the 'calibrating algorithm'. The calibrating algorithm uses the 'geometrical transformation parameters' to transfer the image coordinates of a moving object to its corresponding real-time coordinates in a traffic scene. The distance moved by a vehicle or pedestrian in each frame is used to calculate a number of traffic parameters like traffic volume, speed, headway, etc. in an on-line process.

A video film will be shown of real-time operation of the reported algorithms on a number of transputers.

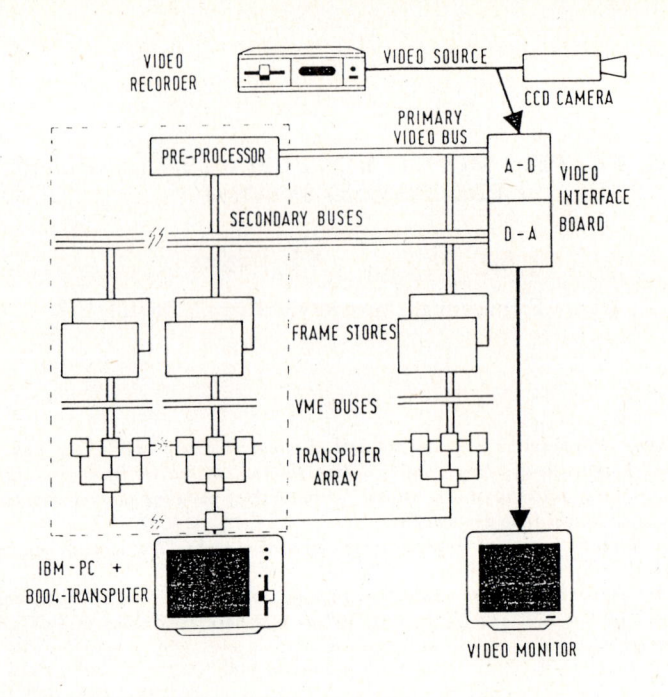

Fig.1 Transputer-Image Processing System(TIPS)

REFERENCES

1. **Radford. C. J.** *"Vehicle detection in open-world scenes using a hough transform technique."* Proceeding IEE 3rd international conference on 'image processing and its applications.', Univ. of Warwick, UK. 18-20 July. 1989, pp.78-82.

2. **Vicencio. M. A. & Hartley. M. G.** *"Algorithms and architectures for the analysis of ROAD-TRAFFIC MOVEMENTS."* Proceeding IEE 3rd international conference on 'Image processing and its applications.', Univ. of Warwick, UK. 18-20 July. 1989, pp.182-186.

3. **Dickinson. K. W. & Waterfall. R. C.** *"Image processing applied to traffic."* Traffic Engineering and control, 25(1), 6-13.& 25(2), 60-67. *1984*.

4. **Hoose. N.** *"Queue detection using computer image processing."* IEE 2nd conference on Road traffic monitoring. London, Feb. *1989*.

5. **Houghton. A. D., Hobson. G., Seed. N. & Tozer. R.** *"Automatic vehicle recognition."* IEE 2nd conference on Road traffic monitoring. London, Feb. *1989*.

6. **Ali. A. T. & Dagless. E. L.** *"Vehicle and Pedestrian Detection and Tracking."* IEE Colloquium on 'Image analysis for transport applications.' IEE, Savoy Place, London. Feb., 1990.

7. **Ali. A. T. & Dagless. E. L.** *"Computer Vision for Security Surveillance and Movement Control."* to appear at IEE Colloquium on 'Electronic images and image processing in security and forensic science.' IEE, Savoy Place, London. May, 1990.

Real Time Image Analysis for Dynamic Displacement Measurement

G. A. Stephen, C. A. Taylor
Department of Civil Engineering

E. L. Dagless
Department of Electrical Engineering

Bristol University, Queen's Building, University Walk, Bristol BS8 1TR, UK.

Abstract. A transputer based system has been developed for determining dynamic displacements in real time by visually tracking an object. Input is from a CCIR video source such as a monochrome video camera or a video tape recorder. Various predictive tracking algorithms have been assessed and implemented on the transputer network. The system is primarily intended for applications such as the monitoring or testing of large physical structures where actual displacements may not easily be otherwise determined. Results from the monitoring of the behaviour of the Humber Bridge at the centre of its span are presented.

1. Introduction

Image processing techniques are being used for monitoring the motion of objects where conventional instrumentation methods fail. Monitoring of Civil Engineering structures can provide valuable information for the validation of mathematical models. For example, determining the response of the Humber Bridge over a range of ambient conditions allows its behaviour in abnormal wind loading to be predicted. However, the physical size of the bridge and the lack of suitable stable locations to use as datum points preclude the use of conventional displacement transducers. Integration of accelerometer signals to determine displacement is also ruled out due to the very low frequency components involved in the motion. Visual analysis is therefore an ideal means of measuring dynamic displacements in this application. The availability of transputer based image processing equipment now makes real time motion detection a viable proposition. This paper describes a visual system used to determine both vertical and lateral (horizontal) displacement time histories of the Humber Bridge deck using a scheme employing an image correlation technique guided by a predictive search algorithm.

2. Real Time Tracking

The motion of large Civil Engineering structures can contain very low frequency components and long term measurements must be conducted to characterise them. Although video recording techniques can permit the capture of 2-3 hours of motion, shorter tapes have to be used for high quality recording. In order to avoid the need to digitise and store these long experimental data sets on disk, real time processing of the image sequence is essential.

The transputer provides a good arrangement for conducting experiments in real time processing. A single processor is capable of performing complex image processing tasks in real time provided that the processed image area is small. Keeping the processing area to a minimum requires clever development of the basic techniques used. However, important benefits accrue from using robust predictive techniques to determine the location of the area to be processed in the next frame. Again the transputer architecture aids this approach by allowing easy expansion of the processing power by allocating the prediction procedures to additional processors. Furthermore, by careful development of the algorithms, the system can be organised so that a minimum of data is passed between extraction and prediction processes.

The following sections describe the hardware used, and the method adopted for both a non-predictive and a predictive system.

2.1. Hardware Configuration

The non predictive system comprised a PC compatible with two expansion cards, namely a B004 (T414) development board and a Quintek Harlequin (T800) board. The Harlequin is a B007 compatible transputer controlled graphics board with dual 512x512x8 frame stores. It is also capable of digitising images from an external monochrome video source. The video timing is controlled by a 6545 CRTC, allowing various scan rates to be programmed. The internal 8 bit pixel (256 grey shades) values are scanned as a raster and mapped to the board's Red, Green and Blue output channels via a programmable look up table. This allows the RGB output, which is displayed on a separate multisync monitor, to use up to 256 colour combinations from a total of 256k.

Software to drive the system was written in Occam in the TDS environment, with the B004 acting as TDS host. The B004 process provided an interface to the user console (PC keyboard, screen and filestore) and also supervised the operation of the Harlequin by sending it commands and parameters and receiving back results.

2.2. Object Tracking

The object tracking procedure uses a copy, or template, of a distinctive feature of the target object to locate the new position in successive frames. This position is deemed to be the point where the correlation between image and template is at a maximum. This tracking scheme is described in detail below.

During the tracking process, images are grabbed into one of the Harlequin's two frame stores, while the other contains a copy which is processed and displayed. Each field of the video input is digitised as a 256x256 pixel image. One field, of constant parity (i.e. always even or always odd), per frame is (potentially) used for analysis. The procedure is initiated by the B004 process sending a command to the Harlequin together with the screen coordinates of a user selected object feature. The processes which subsequently execute are shown in figure 1.

The process *sync.detect* synchronises the process *track* to the video input frame sync using channels *comms1* and *comms2*. It also supervises the timely termination of both Harlequin processes if it should receive a shutdown signal via *to.HQ*. As the start of each new frame is detected a sequential number is assigned to it and if *track* is ready and waiting to proceed, *sync.detect* sends it this number allowing it to continue. Process *track* takes a copy of the image just acquired and then uses this as input to the tracking procedure. The number of the frame and the time taken to process it, together with the new object position, are then sent to *rttrack*, which stores the values and issues the command to shutdown if it has detected any key press on the PC keyboard. A transformation from logical to physical coordinates is then made based on parameters determined from an a priori knowledge of the scene being viewed. The sequence of object positions and corresponding frame numbers may then be saved to a file for subsequent analysis.

The tracking procedure finds the position of a feature from one image in the sequence to the next. Several approaches to solving this "correspondence problem" [1] have been proposed. An overview of which may be found in [2]. The technique employed here is that of template matching. A 12x12 pixel template of the user selected feature is extracted from the initial frame in the sequence. The position of this feature in subsequent images is then determined by evaluating a least square error (LSE) similarity measure over a 32x32 pixel sub image, or search window, centred on the previous known position. The detected object position is indicated by superimposing a red cross hair marker on the output image being displayed. For the template and window dimensions given, the procedure updates every 3 frames i.e. at 8.3 Hz, and can follow objects moving at speeds of up to 83 pixels/s with a spatial resolution of 0.4 % of the field of view.

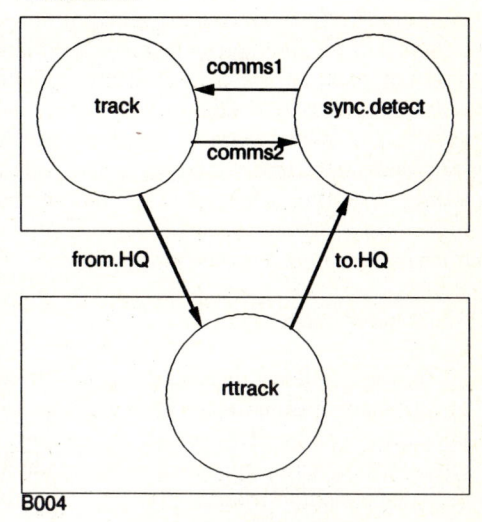

Figure 1: Tracking processes

3. Predictive Tracking

In the tracking procedure described in the previous section, the search for the object was centred on its last known position. The maximum permissible object velocity can, however, be increased if the search is centred on a reliable prediction of the object's position. If the prediction is good, then the size of the search region can be reduced. The processed frame rate can thus be increased, thereby reducing the object's inter frame displacement. There would therefore appear to be significant benefits to be gained from applying many processors to achieve rapid prediction and rapid template matching. However, if the target object is lost this system cannot recover and a more global target location algorithm has to be invoked. A predictive tracking scheme was implemented and is described below.

The work detailed in this section was carried out using the Harlequin together with a Quintek Fast9 PC compatible expansion card. The Fast9 was fitted with 4 T800 transputers - the Master, with 4 MBytes of RAM, and 3 Slaves each with 1 MByte RAM. The Slave processors are hardwired in a pipeline configuration, with their unused links connected to a C004 link exchange. The Master transputer was used as the TDS host.

3.1. Predictive Tracking Processes

The process arrangement is similar to that previously described, with the addition of another processor running the prediction procedure. This is depicted in figure 2. Process *rttrack* again supervises the other processors. Having received the results from one frame from *track* via *from.HQ* it sends the current position to *predict* via *to.slave* and relays the predicted position back to *track*. A separate channel, *stop.HQ* is used to issue the shutdown command to the Harlequin on termination. Process *predict* terminates on receipt of the appropriate code on *to.slave*. The timing is such that the prediction procedure executes concurrently with process *track* performing a screen copy operation.

3.2. Prediction Algorithms

The target object's trajectory is resolved into two orthogonal components i.e. it is a sequence of points given by their screen coordinates. A one step prediction can therefore be made for each component independently.

By assuming that the component trajectory can be approximated by a given function, such as a polynomial, over a certain number of time steps, an extrapolation of the function can be used to predict the next point. Using a linear function implicitly assumes the object to have constant velocity over the period in question. The more general assumption of constant acceleration is made when a quadratic extrapolating function is used. The minimum number of points required for this has been used [3], where the predicted value, $x_p(n)$, of $x(n)$ can be expressed as

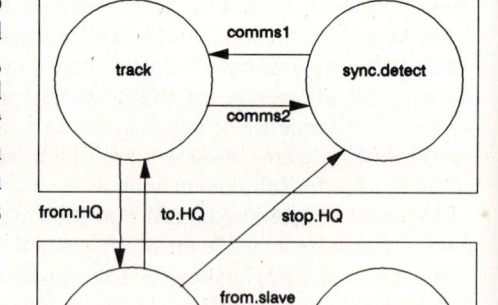

$$x_p(n) = 3x(n-1) - 3x(n-2) + x(n-3)$$

Figure 2 : Predictive tracking processes

This can, however, lead to consequential errors if the position sequence is subject to noise; for example in the case of small amplitude object vibration where quantisation noise becomes significant or when position detection accuracy is compromised by a noisy video input. Higher order polynomials may afford more generality to the form of the trajectory but become increasingly prone to the effects of noise as their potential maximum curvature increases with their degree.

In order to reduce the effects of noise a least mean square (LMS) procedure has been implemented as part of the prediction process. An LMS parabolic approximation is made to the trajectory using the previous six points. This is evaluated using the following expression

$$x_p(n) = 1.5x(n-1) + 0.3x(n-2) - 0.4x(n-3) - 0.6x(n-4) - 0.3x(n-5) + 0.5x(n-6)$$

This was found to work well with the experimental data presented later. The simplicity of the calculation leads to a fast computation time (less than 64 μs for *predict* to execute).

More accurate results were, however, achieved by employing optimum linear prediction techniques when more demanding synthetic test signals were used as input. Theoretical maximum permissible speeds in excess of 400 pixels/s have been achieved with synthesised chirp signal inputs. By making an autoregressive model of the position sequence, which is equivalent to making an all pole approximation to the signal in the z domain, a new set of non recursive prediction weights can be calculated at each step to provide the optimum prediction, in the sense of minimum mean square error. The calculation of the predictor weights involves solving a Toeplitz matrix form of the Wiener-Hopf equation [4]. An algorithm [5] originated by Burg to do this without explicitly evaluating autocorrelation functions has been modified and implemented. A 5 pole signal model calculated using the previous 15 points has been found to work well and executes in 1.6 ms.

4. Application of the Measurement System: Humber Bridge Monitoring

The measurement system has been used in a study of the behaviour of the Humber Bridge at mid span under ambient aerodynamic loading [6]. With a main span of 1410 m, the bridge has the longest single span of any bridge in the world. Data obtained from such studies are important for verifying the original design and models and are also valuable as input for future designs. The wind input to the bridge excites a number of vibration modes and also causes a low frequency sway of the bridge deck. Visual analysis is particularly suited to this application as the displacements arising from the very low frequency swaying motion cannot be reliably determined from accelerometer measurements and the deployment of physical displacement transducers is not practicable in this instance.

A monitoring station was located at the pier level of one of the bridge towers, from which the movement of a target affixed to the bridge was video taped. The station to target distance was approximately 710 m. A Pulnix monochrome CCD video camera, fitted to a 1200 mm focal length lens was used and its output was recorded using a Sony U Matic video recorder. On digitisation, the resulting image had a square field of view of approximately 2.7 m. A typical digitised target image is shown in figure 3. The camera used has an adjustable γ characteristic, allowing a linear output signal to be obtained. It can also employ a 1/1000 s electronic shutter, reducing motion blur by a factor of 20 compared to the standard CCIR TV field integration time.

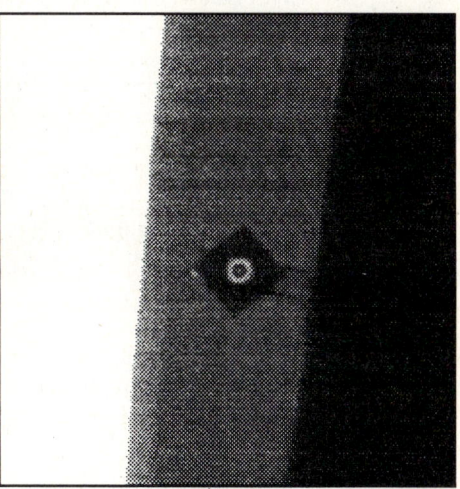

Figure 3 : Typical digitised target image

4.1. Results

Using the vision system, the bridge motion tapes were subsequently processed in real time to provide horizontal and vertical component displacement records to a spatial resolution of approximately 10 mm, sampled at 4.2 Hz. The correlation between these time histories and other parameters, which were measured concurrently, such as wind speed and direction and bridge deck accelerations has been studied [7].

Examples of the displacement records obtained are given in figures 4 and 5. These show motion over periods of 5 and 45 minutes respectively. The ordinate scales give an indication of relative motion in metres, as the absolute position values are with reference to an arbitrary datum. Frequencies of the first few vibration modes obtained from spectral analysis of the acquired displacements are in close agreement with those obtained from a thorough study of the bridge's acceleration response to ambient loading [8].

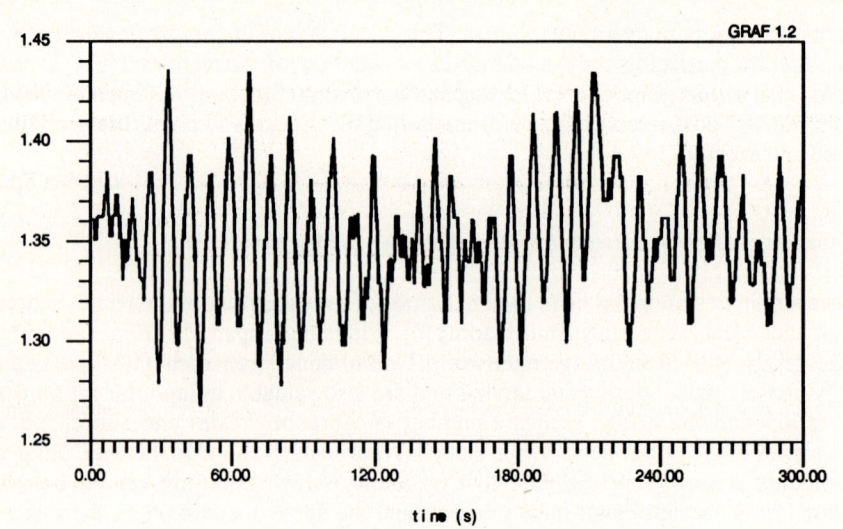

Figure 4 : Humber Bridge mid span vertical displacement (m)

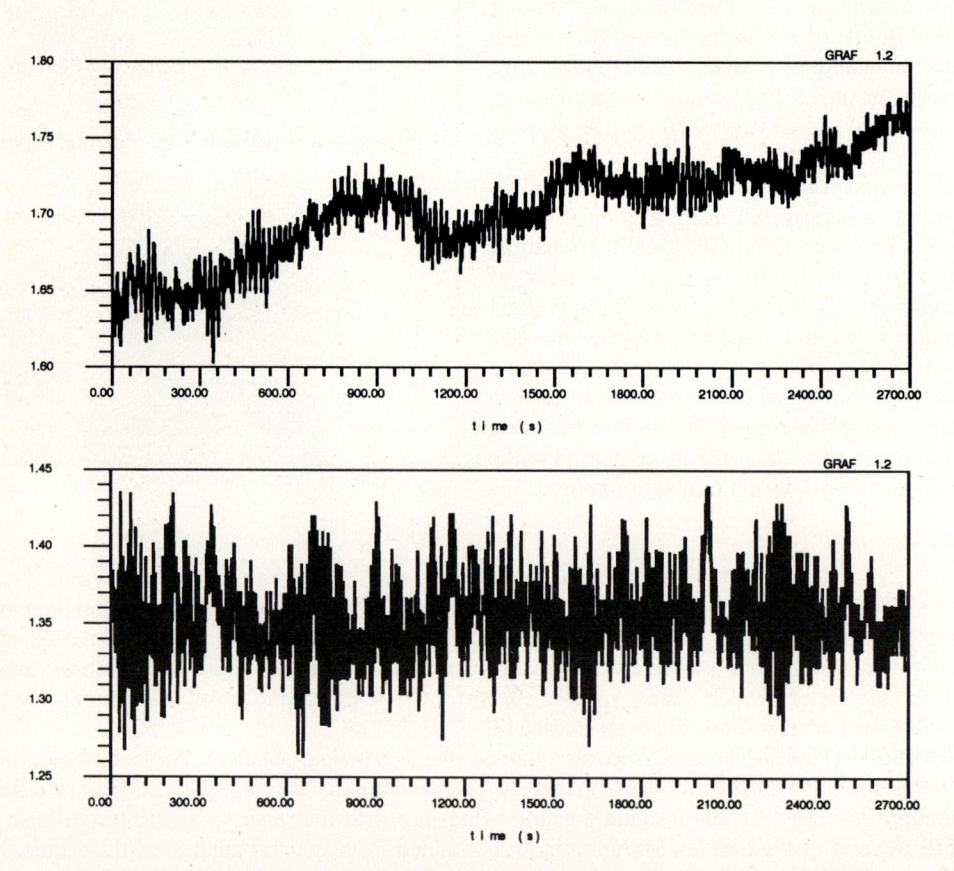

Figure 5 : Humber Bridge mid span lateral (upper) and vertical (lower) displacements (m).

5. Acknowledgments

The research described herein was funded by an SERC postgraduate studentship and part of the work was carried out using equipment supplied by the SERC/DTI Transputer Initiative loan pool (Reference TR/100).

The Humber Bridge monitoring programme was supported by Stretto di Messina SpA, and the cooperation of the Humber Bridge Board is also gratefully acknowledged.

6. References

[1] R.O. Duda, P.E. Hart, *Pattern classification and scene analysis*, John Wiley and Sons, 1973.

[2] W.B. Thompson, S.T. Barnard, *Lower-level estimation and interpretation of visual motion*, Computer August 1981 vol. 14 p.20-8.

[3] J. Wiklund, G. Granlund, *Tracking of multiple moving objects* in V. Cappellini (Ed.) *Time varying image processing and moving object recognition*, Elsevier Science Publishers 1987 p. 241-50.

[4] N. Wiener, *Extrapolation, interpolation, and smoothing of stationary time series with engineering applications*, MIT Press 1949.

[5] W.H. Press, B.P. Flannery, S.A. Teukolsky, W.T. Vetterling, *Numerical Recipes*, Cambridge University Press 1986, p. 430-5.

[6] G.A. Stephen, *Visual determination of ambient wind induced deflections of the Humber Bridge at mid span*, Bristol University report number UBCE-EE-90-07, December 1989.

[7] J.M.W. Brownjohn, *Humber Bridge monitoring*, Bristol University report number UBCE-EE-90-08. December 1989.

[8] J.M.W. Brownjohn, A.A. Dumanoglu, R.T. Severn, C.A. Taylor, *Ambient vibration measurements of the Humber Suspension Bridge and comparison with calculated characteristics*, Proceedings of the Institution of Civil Engineers Part 2 September 1987, vol. 83 p. 561-600.

MARVIN & TINA : A Multiprocessor 3D Vision System

Michael Rygol, Stephen Pollard, Chris Brown and Jennifer Kay,
Artificial Intelligence Vision research Unit,
University of Sheffield,
Sheffield S10 2TN
Tel: +44 742 768555 Xtn 6551
email: mike@aivru.sheffield.ac.uk

Abstract. We describe a multi-transputer vision system which is able to recover 3D geometry from binocular image pairs of scenes. The system incorporates a parallel model matching algorithm which is able to accurately locate modelled objects within these scenes and subsequently control a robot arm to "pick and place" these objects.

1. Introduction and Overview

We describe the implementation of AIVRU's machine vision system, called TINA, (early (sequential) versions of which are described in [1] & [2]) on a locally developed transputer-based hybrid parallel processing engine hosted by a Sun workstation, named MARVIN (Multiprocessor ARchitecture for VIsioN) [3]. TINA delivers 3D geometry from binocular image pairs of natural (though carpentered) scenes and incorporates a model matching algorithm that is able to accurately locate known objects within them. The computational complexity of these algorithms is such that their use in industrial environments is limited when executing on conventional sequential computer architectures, prompting the design of a parallelised version of this system to run on our parallel machine. The competence of this transputer based implementation of the vision system is demonstrated by visually guiding a robot arm to pick up various objects in a cluttered scene with a total processing time of approximately 10 seconds.

2. The Hardware Architecture/Software Environment

MARVIN's processor array has 3 rows and 8 columns and is further described in [3]. The processors (T800s) are firm-wired as a regular fully-connected mesh, with an anomalous extension for the root processor. Two links from the root transputer are connected to the host machine. Link 0 provides the usual boot path and I/O interface whereas link 1 provides a dedicated communications path to *tditool* (a multi-window tool, running in Sunview) allowing multi-processor console I/O [4].

One of the rows of the mesh consists of locally developed transputer cards (named TMAX) provided with 4 frame-rate byte-wide bidirectional video busses (the industry standard MAXbus, by Datacube Inc) and circuitry to control the operation of these busses, including selection of a region of interest from the video stream to be read into the 1MByte of video RAM also located on the board (in addition to 2-4MBytes of DRAM). These busses may also be ganged to allow the transfer of wider data streams, i.e. 16, 24 or 32 bits. All other processors are standard T800 + 2Mbyte TRAMs (Transputer Modules).

The stereo images (which are 512 pixels square) are simultaneously grabbed from a pair of ccd cameras via two Datacube Digimax framegrabbers into Datacube framestores. The framestores share a number of MAXbus ports with the row of TMAX cards through which synchronised image acquisition can be achieved by the TMAX cards (utilising a shared interrupt

---

This research was supported by SERC project grant no. GR/E 64497 awarded to Prof. J.P. Frisby and Dr. J.E.W. Mayhew under the ACME programme in collaboration with GEC Hirst Research Centre, Wembley

signal). It is our intention to exploit further the MAXbus facility by adding compatible cards to perform frame rate image processing operations (eg. convolution, warping, edge detection, etc).

The entire system is programmed in Parallel C and runs within a locally developed run-time environment [4]. The root processor performs no vision processing but holds the highest levels of the control architecture and runs various servers to provide host facilities to the rest of the network. A front-end has been added to the system via tditool which allows the user to interactively change system operations at runtime.

System operations are based upon the *client-server* model. A process requesting services present elsewhere in the network uses a *remote procedure call (RPC)* mechanism to obtain access to these services. The underlying message protocol necessary to implement the operation is hidden within a function call. The system has been designed to be both general purpose and easy to use. Vision processing is broken down into a number of tasks each of which may itself be multi-threaded.

3. Recovery of 3D Scene Geometry

This is achieved using the latest versions of the TINA system which employs edge based stereo triangulation as a basis for three dimensional description. Edges are obtained, *to subpixel acuity,* from grey-level images by a single scale high frequency application of the Canny edge operator [5]. The effect of the operator is essentially to identify contours corresponding to above-threshold maxima of image intensity gradients. Noise suppression and scale selection are achieved by a pre-smoothing stage involving convolution with a gaussian mask. The high frequency operator used here employs a gaussian mask of sigma 1.0 (diameter of 9 pixels when thresholded at 0.001 of the peak value). Convolution is computationally expensive but fortunately the two dimensional gaussian smoothing can be achieved through two 1 dimensional convolutions (eg. first along the rows and then the columns).

Further improvements in efficiency are possible through the use of recursive filtering techniques [6], however it is our preferred intention, in the longer term, to use specialised convolution boards directly on the MAXBus video stream. Whilst Canny is fairly computationally expensive, it has the advantage that it is relatively insensitive to noise and is able to deliver edge strength, position and orientation information. Following detection, edge strings are formed by linking edge pixels (edgels) into chains of connected components.

Stereo matching is the process of identifying which edgels from the right image correspond to edgels obtained from the left image. Achieving robust stereo matching is non-trivial as the process is very prone to ambiguities, resulting in incorrect matches. We use a locally developed algorithm, PMF, for stereo matching. In PMF, matches between edges from the left and right images are preferred if they mutually support each other through a disparity gradient constraint and if they satisfy a number of higher level grouping constraints, most notably uniqueness, ordering (along epipolars) and figural continuity. Using information about the geometry of the cameras obtained from a calibration stage allows the matching problem to be reduced to a *one dimensional* search along corresponding epipolars. Furthermore if the edge maps are transformed to an alternative parallel camera geometry that is equivalent to the original, the epipolar constraint becomes a *same-raster* constraint, with obvious benefit in reducing the complexity of the stereo matching algorithm.

As well as being matched, edge strings are processed to recover descriptions of the two dimensional geometrical elements they may represent. This process is limited to straight line descriptions though in previous implementations we have also recovered circular descriptions, and are currently developing methods to identify ellipses. The algorithm uses a recursive *fit and segment* strategy. Segmentation points are included when the underlying edge string deviates from the current line fit. Robustness of the system (and its speed) relies upon the fact that a heuristic search strategy is used to identify those regions of strings/segmented sub-strings that are most amenable to straight line fit. The actual fit is computed by orthogonal regression. We have found this scheme to be more reliable at identifying true straight line segments consistently than traditional polygonal approximations but less able to deal with data that does not arise from a linear feature.

Given descriptions of the two dimensional geometry (in a single view) and the results of the application of the stereo algorithm to the underlying edge strings, it is possible to recover three dimensional geometrical descriptions. Disparity values can be obtained along the 2D geometrical descriptors for each matched edge point. A second stage of 2D fitting (in arc length against disparity) computes the fit in disparity space. An iterative least squares fit and segmentation scheme, similar to that for 2D description, is employed. Finally disparity data is projected into the world using transformations based upon the camera calibration.

4. Model Matching

The model matcher is able to give accurately the position and rotation of modelled objects (defined in terms of their 3D geometrical primitives) from the geometry recovered by TINA.

The adopted strategy [7] is to base initial matching hypotheses on congruencies identified between 3D scene descriptions and a chosen subset of features from the model. Following hypotheses, potential matches are ranked on the basis of the extent to which further support exists for the three dimensional transformation they implicitly represent (between model and scene).

The algorithm exploits ideas from several sources: the use of a partial pairwise geometrical relationships table to represent object model and scene description from Grimson and Lozano-Perez [8], the least squares computation of transformations by exploiting the quaternion representation for rotations from Faugeraus et al [9], and the use of focus features from Bolles et al [10].

Whilst exhaustive search for maximal cliques of consistent scene and model descriptions is avoided, the algorithm still requires a considerable amount of searching to be performed. Furthermore the computational expense of the algorithm (which increases roughly linearly with the scene complexity and much faster with the number of features in the model) is replicated for each modelled object.

5. Parallelising TINA

A large vision system such as TINA offers much potential for improvement through the use of parallel processing, however, realising that potential is not entirely straightforward. The processing in TINA is not homogeneous, with different tasks having different data requirements. The low level tasks such as Canny (and to a lesser extent PMF) are spatially localised and a large degree of spatial parallelism may be exploited. The process of obtaining 2D and 3D scene description can be extended across arbitrary large regions of the image but is independent for each edge string. The model matching task has no geometric parallelism (the 3D data could be partitioned) but potential does exist for model instance and model sub-feature parallelism. Furthermore the compute time of many processes is not fixed *a priori;* often the spatial distribution of the data, rather than simply the quantity, has a significant effect upon the computational effort required. However, it is important that at key points in the processing cycle, the processing across the image is synchronised.

One important consideration in the parallel implementation of TINA is that the computation of descriptions higher in the processing chain is dependent upon large amounts of previously computed data. For example the 3D data structure is dependent upon both 2D polygonal approximations and the matched edges. Accordingly, the use of the traditional processor farm is inappropriate as the amount of data flow required would make it unusable.

Resident on each TMAX is a server providing network-wide facilities. Any task on any processor may request operations from these servers. Such operations include region-of-interest acquisition, data plotting and low level control operations. Access to these operations is via the RPC mechanism.

Copies of the collection of vision tasks which comprise TINA are distributed across the network. Each task has a predefined control message (implemented as a C structure). This structure contains all of the necessary runtime parameters for that task, including such commands as whether or not (and where) to display the output data, amongst others. This technique allows dynamic changes of operation in the system.

5.1. Recovering the 3D Geometry

Initially each image is divided into into eight horizontal slices approximately 64 rasters wide. A small overlap (2 rasters) between adjacent slices is incorporated to avoid boundary effects and simplify the processes of combination that occur later. There is a limit to how thin the image slices can be without adversely effecting the reliability of the stereo matching procedure. However potential does exist for further subdivision of images in the horizontal direction with a small increase in the complexity of the stereo matching algorithm.

Each image slice pair is acquired simultaneously into an allotted TMAX, controlled remotely by the control task on the root processor. A typical (left) image of a number of objects ("widgets") is shown in figure 1. The pair of transputers vertically adjacent to the TMAX are used to process the left and right image slices in parallel. The size of the right image slice is adjusted to take into account the warping effect of the rectification of edge locations into the parallel camera geometry. This is determined from a copy of the calibration data resident upon each processor (this may be updated dynamically to allow for updated calibration estimates to be incorporated).

Each Canny process obtains the raw image slice via the RPC mechanism from the local TMAX server. The Canny task processing the left image slice packs the resultant edgemap into a data packet and sends it to a collection thread running within the right Canny task. Upon completion, the right Canny task and the collection thread rendezvous and send a reply to the control task running on the root.

The PMF task runs on the processor that now holds both edgemaps (the one that held the right image slice). The edge structures are organised so as to make both spatial location and connectivity explicit. To avoid major data transfer and recomputation the PMF control packet (from the root) simply contains a pointer to the edge structures in the memory shared by the threads. The 2&3D descriptors are computed on completion of PMF for each slice of the image.

The sequence of operations taking place on each pair of processors is shown in figure 3.

At this point in the processing, there exists over a number of processors, a spatial distribution of the three dimensional geometry of the current scene. This data needs to be integrated into one data set as if it came from a single processor. A Joiner task (figure 4) communicates with all of the local 3D geometry tasks, receiving both 2D and 3D information. These descriptions are optimally combined where valid 2D connectivity is identified between image slices. Upon completion the Joiner returns the integrated geometry to the main control task resident on the root processor. The controller then forwards this information to a number (defined at runtime) of model matcher tasks distributed throughout the network.

Figure 2 shows an example of the 3D geometry recovered from a scene projected over a ground plane.

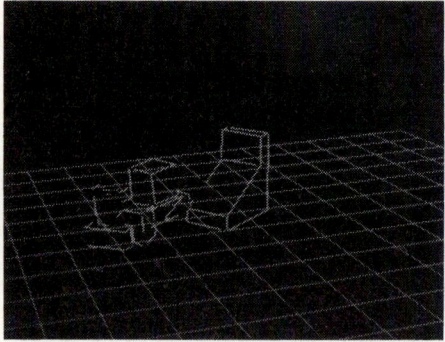

Figure 1. Raw image

Figure 2. 3D Geometry with ground plane

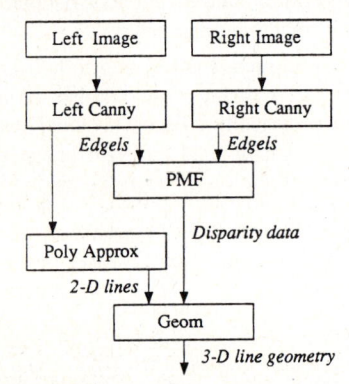

Figure 3. Data flow for recovery of scene geometry for each image pair slice

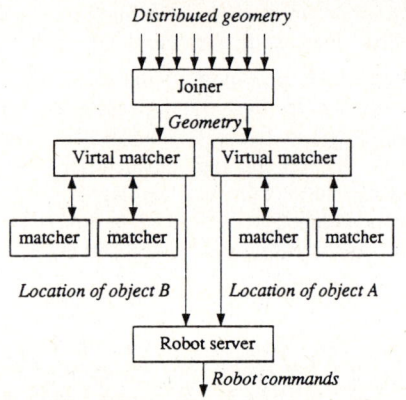

Figure 4. Geometry joining and object location for two objects (A & B) each with two subordinate matchers

5.2. Parallelising the Model Matcher

The most obvious way to exploit the architecture of MARVIN in the model matching phase is to run multiple instances of the model matcher on different processors, thereby searching the same data for different models. This limits the parallelism to the number of models being searched for and is still too computationally time-consuming. A further degree of parallelism can be obtained by employing a multi-level control architecture within the matching process itself. The model matching algorithm decomposes into separable searches for *characteristic views* of the object. This, in effect, allows the distribution of the search tree over a number of processors.

To realise this in a consistent manner, a *virtual matcher* is used. The virtual matcher simply receives a control message describing the name of the model to become its responsibility and a list of processors available for use (allocated at runtime, typically 6) which have a resident matching task which will search for a particular characteristic view of the object. The virtual matcher obtains all relevant information about the model (from files on the host machine) and the current geometry (from the Joiner) and distributes this information to its subordinates. Each subordinate matcher attempts to locate a *subset* of the model features.

Upon completion the virtual matcher chooses the best match obtained from all of its subordinates and feeds this result up to the next higher level in the control hierarchy. This technique allows a search to be made for multiple objects (with no extra time penalty) in a consistent, flexible and highly efficient manner (figure 4). Figure 5 shows the reprojection of three matched models onto the original image along with their grasp positions.

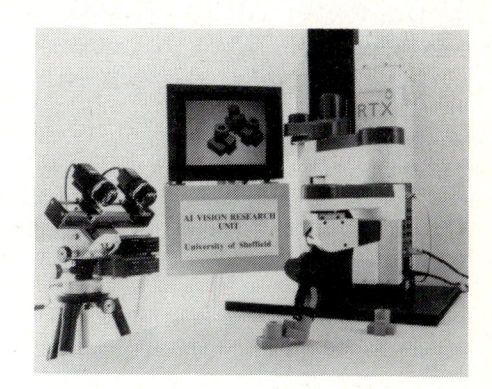

Figure 5. Matched models

Figure 6. Robot picking up a widget

6. Controlling the Robot Arm

A UMI robot (of educational rather than industrial specifications) controlled by an IBM PC is used to perform the pick and place. The IBM PC is in turn connected to a SUN 3 workstation over a serial line. MARVIN may talk to any SUN in our network by means of the UNIX socket mechanism. Locally developed additions to the *afserver* protocol and our runtime environment allow any task on any transputer to open and communicate with sockets to the outside world[4].

Each virtual model matcher returns a rotation and position of the relevant object. This information is used to transform a precomputed grasp position from the model coordinate frame to the world coordinate frame.

This information is sent over a socket to a server controlling the robot (figure 4) on a remote machine according to an agreed protocol, specifying the name of the model, where to pick it up and what to do with it. MARVIN need have no concern with solving the inverse kinematics, camera to robot transformations and path planning in order to pick the objects from the workspace, these issues are computed in different areas of the *computer* network.

An example of the robot picking up a widget is shown in figure 6.

The *hand-eye* calibration (the transformation between camera space and robot space) is obtained by using TINA to locate a flag held in the gripper of the robot arm. This is repeated numerous times in various positions of the robot workspace. A least-squares method is used to obtain the best transformation.

7. Control Architecture

The system control is mostly resident on the root processor. A control thread is created for each group of processors, allowing asynchronous control, if necessary. These threads synchronise with a central thread, the highest level in the hierarchy. Each process has no built-in knowledge of where its data comes from or where it is going. The action of the machine is completely fluid, all dataflow being determined by the control architecture at runtime.

Each vision task communicates with its control thread upon completion with a small reply packet. The controller then uses this information to instruct the next task. In this way, the various tasks are kept independent of each other as much as possible.

Some of the tasks require asynchronous control operations. In this case, control information is received by a separate thread running within the task, allowing control information to be asynchronously decoupled from data flow.

The MARVIN Software Infrastructure [4] allows us to ignore the physical communication paths between tasks and the physical interconnections between processors, allowing any logical topology to be chosen and changed dynamically.

8. Conclusions and Results

A multiprocessor transputer-based 3D vision system has been described. We have employed two different techniques to utilise the parallel hardware. The recovery of the scene geometry employs *geometric* parallelism by decomposing the image pairs into horizontal image slices. This is a natural approach as depth data is obtained by matching elements between left and right images. After recovering the scene geometry the algorithms to locate instances of modelled objects are parallelised on a *featural* basis, using a hierarchical control strategy.

Our runtime environment greatly simplifies the programming (at a coarse grain of parallelism) of a transputer-based machine such as MARVIN. It allows the easy integration (and development) of communicating sequential processes in the network, providing various services to a task anywhere in the network via sets of library functions.

Using MARVIN we have a system that in a former incarnation took well over one hour to to locate *one* object, now runs in around 10 seconds, locating *numerous* objects, making it far more practicable to perform interactive "what-if" experiments.

A more detailed breakdown of processing timings for a typical scene is shown in table 1. The two vision processes which have benefited most from being parallelised are the Canny and model matching stages, the two most costly tasks on a sequential machine.

Work is in hand to implement a parallel feature tracker on MARVIN which will follow (at near real-time) features identified as being those from a modelled object. This beacon tracking is to provide some of the information required to enable our in-house vehicle to navigate through an unknown environment.

Vision Process	Time (ms)
Canny	5500
PMF	1000
2D Geometry	100
3D Geometry	200
Geometry joining	100
Model Matching	1600
System Overheads	1000
Total	~10000

Table 1. Processing times

9. References

1. Porrill J, Pollard S B, Pridmore T P, Bowen J, Mayhew J E W, and Frisby J P (1987) TINA: The Sheffield AIVRU vision system, IJCAI 9, Milan 1138-1144.

2. Pollard S B, Pridmore T P, Porrill J, Mayhew J E W, and Frisby J P (1989) Geometrical modelling from multiple stereo views, International Journal of Robotics Research, vol 8, No 4, 3-32.

3. Brown C. and Rygol M. (1989), Marvin : Multiprocessor Architecture for Vision, *Proceedings of the 10th Occam User Group Technical Meeting*

4 Brown C. and Rygol M. (1990), An Environment for the Development of Large Applications in Parallel C *Transputer Applications '90*

5 Canny J (1986), *A computational approach to edge detection,* Trans. Patt. Anal. & Mach. Intell, 679-698, PAMI-8.

6 Pollard S B (1990), *Obtaining reliable geometrical description from stereo vision.* In preparation.

7 Pollard S B, Porrill J, Mayhew J E W and Frisby J P (1986) Matching geometrical descriptions in three space, Image and Vision Computing, Vol 2, No 5 (1987) 73-78.

8 Grimson W.E.L. and T. Lozano-Perez (1984), Model based recognition from sparse range or tactile data, *Int. J. Robotics Res.* 3(3): 3-35.

9 Faugeras O.D. and M. Hebert (1985), The representation, recognition and positioning of 3D shapes from range data, *Int. J. Robotics Res*

10 Bolles R.C., P. Horaud and M.J. Hannah (1983), 3DPO: A three dimensional part orientation system, *Proc. IJCAI 8,* Karlshrue, West Germany, 116-120.

Two Parallel Algorithms for Matching Attributed Relational Graphs on a Transputer Network

Vesa Vuohtoniemi and Tapio Seppänen

Computer Laboratory
Department of Electrical Engineering
University of Oulu
SF-90570 Oulu, Finland

Abstract. Two parallel graph matching algorithms and their implementations on a transputer network are described. The first generates state space in a breadth-first manner and the second in a depth-first manner. The results indicate that the second algorithm is preferable because it can be used for matching larger graphs and allows high speed-up values to be achieved when a lot of processors are in use.

1. Introduction

Attributed relational graphs are suitable representational data structures for many AI applications. The components of the graphs (nodes interconnected by links) are usually named and have attributes describing the properties and relations of the primitives they represent. Graphs are used for describing structural properties of objects and their interrelationships in computer vision, for example. Object recognition with these graphs proceeds by comparing model graphs with the scene description. Unfortunately, the comparison of two graphs is inherently an NP-complete problem, which means that the matching of two k-node graphs may require the construction and evaluation k!*k! solution candidates in the worst case [1]. Graphs have been employed at the University of Oulu for a number of automatic visual inspection purposes, e.g. the inspection of printed wiring boards, turbine blades and flat surfaces [2, 3, 4]. Defect candidates are analyzed by matching the graphs describing them with context-dependent defect models in the data base. An enhanced version of the matching algorithm of Eshera and Fu was developed for this purpose by our vision group in which the number of paths to be constructed is only the factorial of the number of the nodes in graph [2].

The matching of graphs with more than a few nodes often takes too long in practical applications using conventional uniprocessor computers, and one potential way of reducing the execution time would be to parallelize the algorithm and run it in a multiprocessor environment. We therefore decided to explore the possibilities of transputer-based multiprocessor systems for speeding up our application software.

2. The Hathi-2 Transputer Network

Experiments were carried out using a Hathi-2 parallel computer containing 100 T800 transputers, each of which has 1.25 Mbytes of memory. Hathi-2 consists of 25 module boards, each of which has four T800 transputers, one T212 transputer and a C004 crossbar switch for configuration

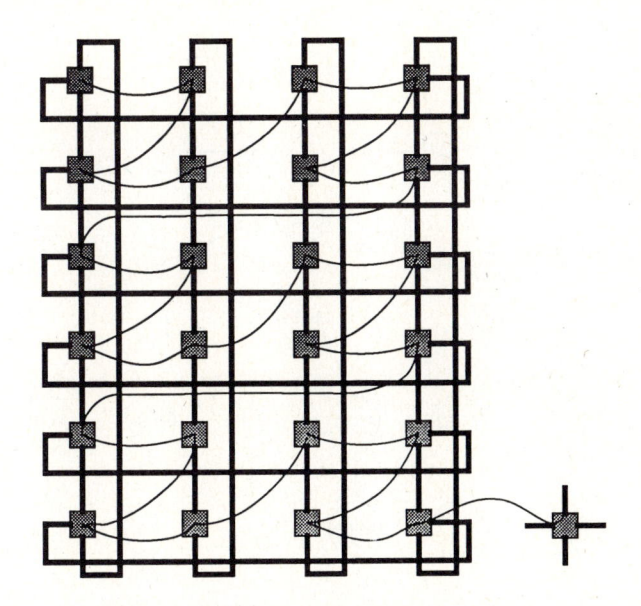

Figure 1. The topology of Hathi-2 multiprocessor.

of the system (Fig. 1). A Sun 3/160 workstation with Niche's NT1000 board and an IBM AT can be used as a host computer. There is also a hardware monitoring system based on the T212 transputers, which are connected in a ring topology and are controlled by a separate host computer [5].

The Hathi-2 can be divided into separate partitions, allowing several users to use their own multiprocessor systems. Each user can reconfigure his own partition to form the desired topology using configuration software. In addition to TDS and Occam, it is possible to use the Trollius operating system and C-language for programming the Hathi-2.

3. Sequential Algorithm for Graph Matching

The matching algorithm generates a state space tree and evaluates the paths by computing edit distances for them [2]. Each path of the tree from the root node to the leaves corresponds to a different matching alternative. For an example of the state space tree, see Fig. 2 (nodes and links usually have attributes, which are not shown in the figure). The edit operations allowed are addition and deletion of an attribute, link or node. The path with the smallest edit distance then represents the best match. The shorter the distance, the more similar the graphs are to each other.

The algorithm employs a look-up table technique for storing edit distances associated with the states in each path of the state space tree [6]. The look-up table is accessed each time a new state is to be evaluated. If the state has already been evaluated, the precomputed value is read from the table.

4. Parallel Implementations

We describe two parallelization approaches that were applied to the sequential algorithm. The

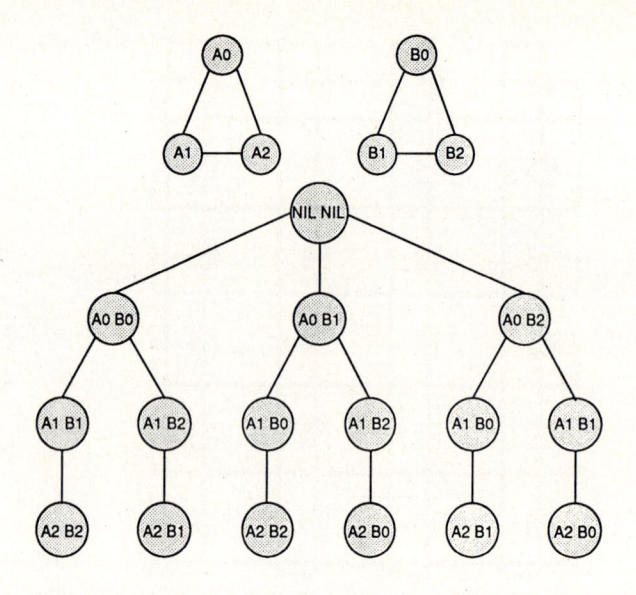

Figure 2. An example of the graphs and corresponding state space.

first algorithm, BF, generates a state space in a breadth-first manner, and the second, DF, in a depth-first manner. Evaluation proceeds in a path by path manner in both algorithms.

4.1 Experiments with the BF Algorithm

This version first generates the whole state space in a breadth-first fashion and then evaluates it in a path by path fashion. The algorithm is parallelized by assigning a processor for generating and evaluating each main branch of the state space [6, 7].

The network topology is a linear array. One of the processors acts as a network controller and communicates with the host computer, configures the array to match the problem size in hand, feeds the graph properties to the slave processors, and finally merges the partial results generated by the system. The size of the state space increases quickly (with the factorial of the graph size), and thus graphs larger than 8 nodes cannot be analyzed with this program version because of memory overflow.

The control transputer initializes the state space generation by broadcasting a parameter describing the problem size. Each processor immediately starts generating the subtree assigned to it once it has received the parameter. Meanwhile the control transputer (which does not participate in the generating step) broadcasts the data structures describing detailed properties of the graphs. The properties include information on the adjacency of the nodes and the attributes of each node and link.

After the generation step, each processor evaluates all the paths in its portion of the state space. When the evaluation is completed the processors in the network search for the local minimum paths and send them through the network to the control transputer, which finally selects the global minimum.

Experiments were performed with graph sizes from 4 to 8 nodes (Table 1.), the corresponding

Table 1. Timing measurements with the BF algorithm.

Graph size (number of nodes)	Processing time sequential / ms	Processing time parallel / ms	Speed-up
4	22	14	1.6
5	60	23	2.6
6	276	64	4.3
7	1994	385	5.2
8	17130	2830	6.1

Note: The number of processors executing parallel graph matching equals to the number of nodes in graphs which equals to the number of main branches in state space tree.

numbers of paths in the state space ranging from 24 to 40320 (the factorial of the number of nodes).

The results reveal that an almost linear speed-up is achieved when the graphs are comparatively large and complex, but the speed-up is poor with smaller graphs. The dominating factor for sublinearity in our implementation is the communication overhead caused by the broadcasting of the graph properties in the network. The processors start evaluating their subtrees immediately after their construction, provided that the graph information has been received. Otherwise they have to wait for the message, which increases the execution time. With small graphs (4...6 nodes) the state space is generated so rapidly that the graph properties are still being broadcast when the evaluation step should start, whereas with larger graphs the transfer has already been completed by that time. This results from the fact that the duration of the generation step increases combinatorially with increasing graph size, whereas the sizes of the data structures to be transmitted increase only linearly. Thus the broadcasting can be fully overlapped with the computation.

4.2 Experiments with the DF Algorithm

This version works on the state space in a depth-first fashion, by first generating a path and immediately evaluating it [8]. Two different implementations were explored, a conventional single-farm structure and a multiple-farm structure.

In the single-farm structure, a task generator processor generates paths and a variable number of worker processors evaluate them. More processors are used for evaluation than for generation because its execution time is a few times (4...6) longer. The network topology is a linear array.

In the multiple-farm structure, a control processor manages a number of processor farms, each consisting of a task generator and a variable number of workers. Each main branch of the state space is assigned to its own farm. The network topology is a cluster of linear arrays, the heads of which are connected together.

The control processor sends the input data to the task generators, which send the data needed for the evaluation step to their worker processors. After completing the work, the task generators send the subresults or paths with minimum edit distances to the control processor for selection of the global solution.

Path delivery in the network works as follows. A pool server process in the task generator processor receives paths from a path generator process through pipelined buffer processes and sends them to workers for evaluation. As soon as a path is delivered from the pool server to the evaluator network, the paths in the buffer pipeline advance one stage. A new path is fed into the pipeline as soon as it becomes ready and the first stage is empty. As the pool server process receives a path

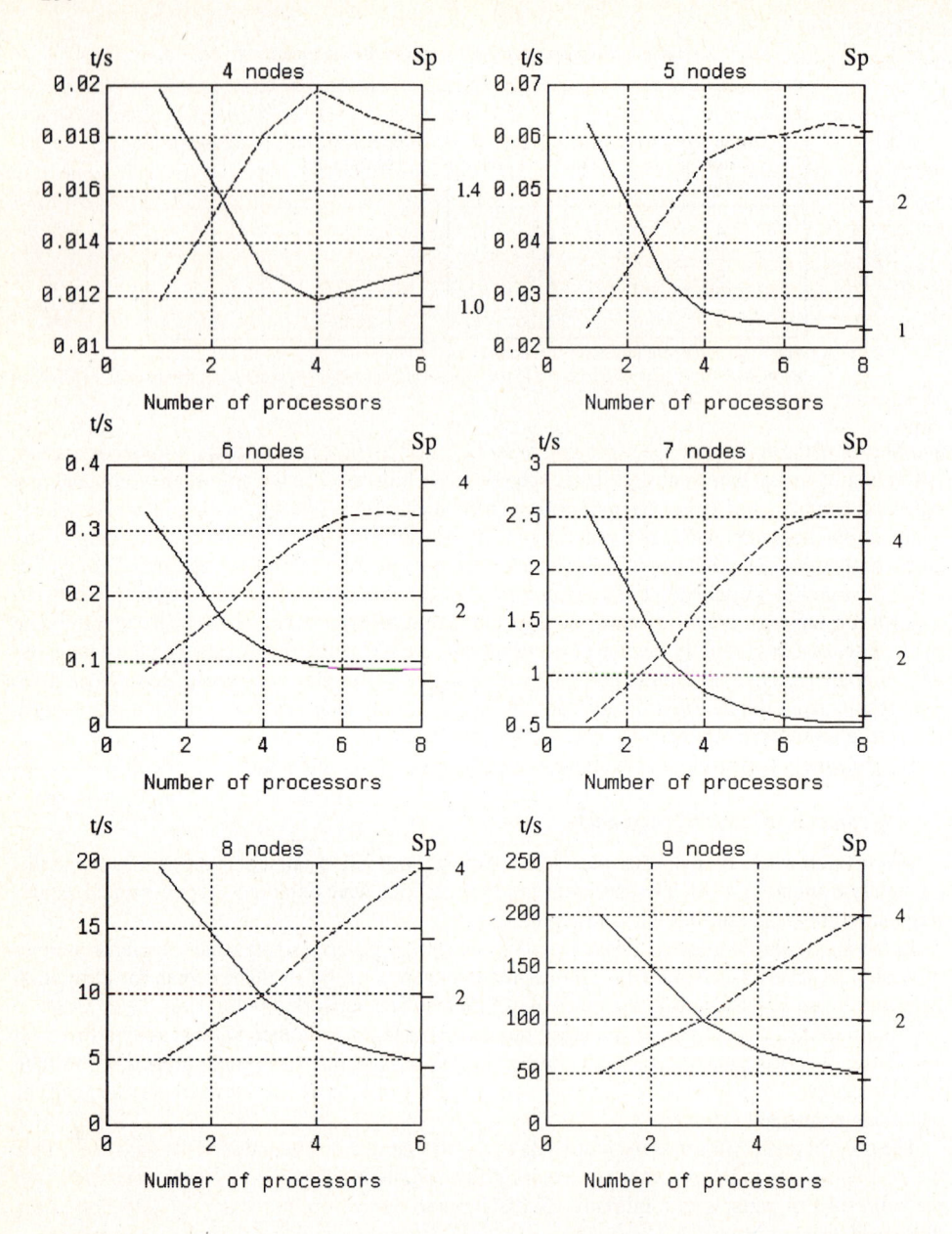

Figure 3. Execution times and speed-up curves for experiments on a single-farm structure.

request from the network, it sends a new path to the farm without assigning any address to the message. Therefore any evaluator transputer which is out of work can pick up the path message when it passes through the router process in the processor. The evaluators at the end of the farm receive less paths than the foremost ones.

The graph sizes in our experiments varied from 4 to 9 nodes and the number of paths in the state space ranged from 24 to 362880, respectively. The maximum number of processors is 54, i.e. a cluster of 9 processor farms each containing one generator and 5 evaluator processors. The execution times and speed-up curves are shown in Figures 3 and 4.

The speed-up increases with the number of evaluator processors in each farm, up to the point at which a balance is reached between the speeds of path generation and evaluation. The ratio of the number of the evaluator processors to the number of generator processors is about 5 in the case with the best balance. The number of paths evaluated in each processor decreases as one goes farther away from the generator processor in a transputer farm, the decrease is not large until the threshold value in the number of processors is achieved, after which a sharp decrease occurs. This is due to the path delivery technique described above. When the worker processors at the heads of the farms take nearly all the paths that are delivered, the processors at the tails receive only a few paths.

The speed-up is bad with small graph sizes, since evaluation time for one path is of about the same order as the time required to deliver the paths to the workers, causing the frontmost workers in the farm to consume most of the paths and resulting in bad processor utilization in the farm and a poor speed-up. This effect is amplified by the look-up table technique used in our program, which speeds up the evaluation more in the frontmost processors, as these receive more paths to fill up the look-up table. This process accelerates constantly during the evaluation.

5. Comparison of the Algorithms

If the graphs are small (less than 7 nodes), the single-farm DF algorithm is slightly faster than

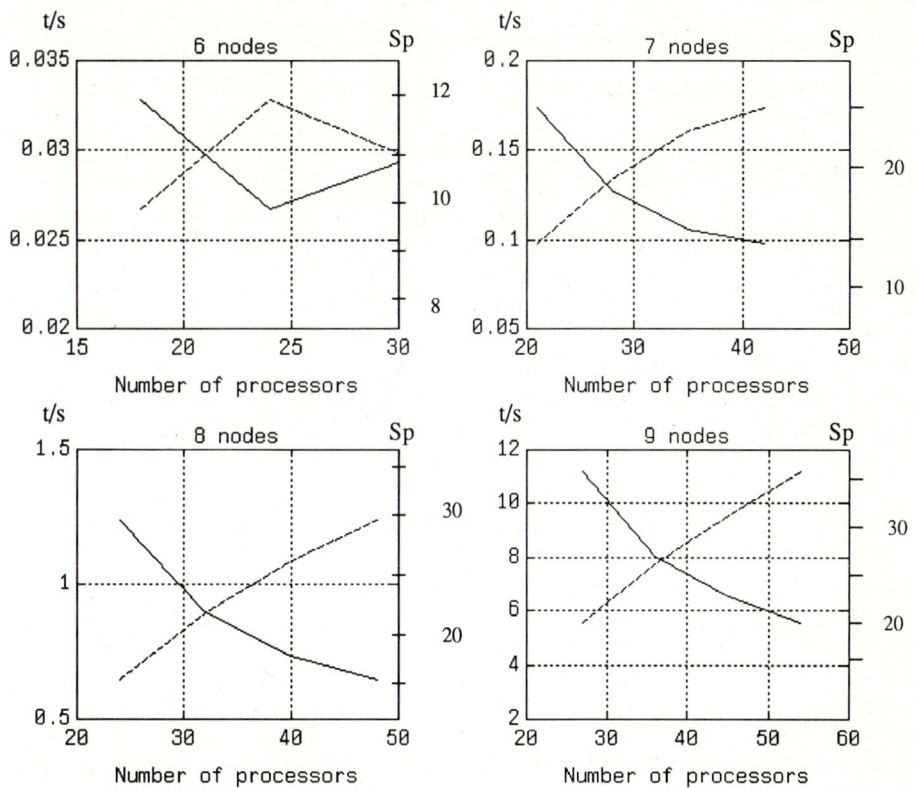

Figure 4. Execution times and speed-up curves for experiments on a multiple-farm structure.

the BF version, but when graph sizes increases beyond this points, the BF algorithm is faster. The main reason for this is the overlapping computation and communication functions in the path generation phase, but it is also influenced by the large amount of communication needed in the case of the DF algorithm because every path must be sent from path the generator processor to the evaluator. When large speed-up values are desired, the multiple-farm DF method is suitable.

There is a major difference in the amount of memory needed to implement these algorithms. This is due to a combinatorially growing state space, which must be kept in the memory in the case of the BF algorithm. Thus the memory of 1.25 Mbytes contained in our transputers is insufficient for storing the state space for graphs larger than 8 nodes, as the amount of memory needed in the case of 9-node graphs would be 9 times more, and so on. DF implementation needs only few tens of Kilobytes of memory practically independently of the size of the graphs.

6. Conclusions

These experiments with two parallel graph matching algorithms implemented on a transputer network reveal differences in speed-up behavior and the amount of memory needed which indicate that the DF algorithm in single-farm implementation is preferable to the BF-algorithm because it can be used for larger graphs, although in some cases the speed-up is slightly smaller. If considerably larger speed-ups are required, the DF algorithm in multi-farm implementation should be used.

Acknowledgments

This research was supported financially by the Technology Development Center of Finland.

References

[1] Eshera, M., Fu, K-S., "A Graph Distance Measure for Image Analysis", IEEE Transactions on Systems, Man, and Cybernetics, Vol. SMC-14, No. 3, May/June 1984, pp. 398-408.

[2] Silven, O., Westman, T., Huotari, S., Hakalahti, H., "A Defect Analysis Method for Visual Inspection", Proceedings of the 8th International Conf. on Pattern Recognition, Paris, France, 1986, pp. 868-870.

[3] Piironen, T., Silven, O., Laitinen, T., Strömmer, E., Pietikäinen, M., "An Automated System for Metal Strip Inspection", Proc. IAPR Workshop on Computer Vision -Special Hardware and Industrial Applications, Tokyo, Japan, 1988, pp. 397-400.

[4] Maliniemi, H., Ailisto, H., Hakalahti, H., "Vision System for Turbine Inspection", Proc. 9th International Conf. on Pattern Recognition, Rome, Italy, 1988, pp. 1202-1206.

[5] Aspnäs, M., Malen, T-E., "Hathi-2 Users Guide, Version 1.0", Reports On Computer Science & Mathematics, Ser. B, No 6, Åbo Akademi, Turku, Finland, 1989.

[6] Seppänen, T., Westman, T., Pietikäinen, M., "Parallel Matching of Attributed Relational Graphs". Technical Report, Center for Automation Research, University of Maryland, Md., 1988, p. 32.

[7] Vuohtoniemi, V., Seppänen, T., Virtanen, I., "Matching Semantic Nets on a Transputer-based Multiprocessor System", Proc. Finnish Artificial Intelligence Symposium (STeP-88), Helsinki, Finland, 1988.

[8] Seppänen, T., Vuohtoniemi, V., Pietikäinen, M., "A Benchmark of Two Parallel Computers: Experiments with Three Machine Vision Problems", Proc. SPIE Advances in Intelligent Robotic Systems and Visual Communications and Image Processing Symposium, Philadelphia, PA, 5.-10.11.1989.

A Parallel Processing Engine for n-tuple Pattern Recognition

By K M Curtis and A Bouridane
Department of Electrical and Electronic Engineering
UNIVERSITY OF NOTTINGHAM

Abstract. Quality control has always been an important part of the manufacturing process, with visual inspection playing an ever increasing role in this process. The automation of production lines calls for rapid automatic visual inspection techniques. This paper describes such a technique, the n-tuple technique, which offers an attractive solution to the inspection of 2-D images for the detection of unacceptable flaws. The technique is statistically based and uses unconnected attributes for the detection process. This unconnectivity renders the technique ideally suited to being implemented on a network of Transputers. Results are presented for the application for tuples using 3 x 3 and 5 x 5 matrices, implemented on an IBM/AT compatible, one Transputer and finally a network of five Transputers. Conclusions are drawn as to the suitability and efficiency of the application in each case for binary images.

1. Introduction

The rapid automisation of production lines necessitates a fast, cost-effective inspection system so as to maintain quality. In the case of the inspection of printed 2-D images the n-tuple technique offers an excellent statistical method for the detection of unacceptable flaws [1].

The n-tuple method relies upon the generation of abstract shapes called attributes. The frequency distribution of these attributes can then be used as signatures for various images. A straight comparison of the frequency occurrence of individual attributes can be used as a measure of correlation between different images or different classes. This technique attempts to address the problem of the introduction of generality in pattern recognition unlike most visual pattern recognition systems that use specific features in the recognition process [2]. It does this by introducing an element of generality, thus making the choice of features independent of the task at hand. The n-tuple technique requires black and white binary images. Using these binary images pictorial attributes can be formed from selected combinations of black and white pixels in groups of n-pixels. These groups form a window which can be used to scan the image and analyse the data through considering the joint occurrence among pixels which define the features and shapes of objects in the image. Using this type of analysis two types of approach predominate.

The first of these is the original idea proposed by Bledsoe and Browning and is of an analytic nature. Using this approach a certain number of n-tuple attributes are arbitrarily chosen. Then by recording the frequency of occurrence of each n-tuple attribute signatures are generated which may be used to distinguish between images [3]. During a training session, the signatures are used to define classes of patterns. Several techniques can then be used to recognise and subsequently classify unknown patterns. One such technique is the nearest neighbour technique [4]. Another technique utilises Bayes' Law [4] which relies on the estimation of the conditional probability of occurrence of each possible state of each of the n-tuples. For a certain state this probability assumes a maximum value which determines the classification of the unknown patterns. The main problem with the analytical approach is the large computation time required.

The second approach is a logical approach based on boolean algebra. With this approach logical functions which give the desired reaction to patterns of a particular class are generated during the training session [5]. These logic functions

In the case of the system configuration being corrupted or incorrectly setup, please use the SETAT16.COM to restore the AT-16 configuration, see the READ.ME file for more details.

Fig.1. Reference image

In the case of the system configuration being corrupted or incorrectly setup, please use the SETAT16.COM to restore the AT-16 configuration, see the READ.ME file f more deatails.

Fig.2. Corrupted image('or' missing)

In the case of the system configuration being corrupted or incorrectly setup, please use the SETAT16.COM to restore the AT-16 configuration, se the READ.ME file for more details.

Fig.3. Corrupted image('e' missing)

In the case of the system configuration being corrupted or incorrectly setup, please use the SETAT16.COM to restore the AT-16 configuration, see the READ.ME file for more details.

Fig.4. Corrupted image('c' and 't' incomplete)

are then used to distinguish between inputs from different classes by providing cumulative information about members of each class. In this way discriminators can be formed for each pattern of interest where each pixel is related by a logical function. These discriminators are then used to categorise the image using a scanning process [6]. This type of approach is ideally suited to parallel application. Thus this type of application is ideally suited to be implemented on a multi-transputer system.

2. N-Tuple Implementation

To gauge the effectiveness of the parallel implementation of the n-tuple technique it was implemented on an IBM/PC compatible computer, a single transputer and a five transputer network. The image chosen for the investigation was a piece of printed text (see Fig 1). This text was then corrupted in three ways (see Figs 2, 3 and 4). Fig 2 represents a large amount of corruption, Fig 4 a small amount and Fig 3 an amount between the two. The images were captured with a resolution of 512 x 512 pixels using a Matrox PIP1024 frame stored board.

2.1 Choice of Attribute

An important aspect to both the success of the n-tuple recognition and its parallel implementation is the choice of attributes. This choice of the most appropriate parameters revolves around the size of the window and the number of attributes to be used. Any size of window or number of attributes could be used. It has been shown that apart from totally black or totally white tuple categories, the number of occurrences of each n-tuple category is usually limited to less than 10% of the total number of window positions on the image field [7]. It has also been shown that the n-tuple number and size should be simple and small in number [8]. Another important feature for the attributes is that they are capable of rejecting noise. The attributes should not contain redundant information. Thus a matrix form for the n-tuples was seen to be best suited. Two sizes were adopted for the study, namely a 3 x 3 matrix and a 5 x 5 matrix to investigate the effect on various amounts of corruption. In the case of the 3 x 3 matrix a combination of 512 possible n-tuples exist. Nine of these were selected (see Fig 5) as the others either represent noise, are the complements of the remaining nine or contain redundant information. In the case of the nine attributes, they can be considered to be made up of a central pixel surrounded in the four cardinal positions by other pixels. The decision for each attribute to sit on a central pixel which belongs to the foreground was taken as shapes of objects are wider than one pixel. The compact combination of several pixels of the same luminance determines the shape of an object or pattern in a binary image. Each of the cardinal pixel positions are allocated a different value. Thus for each attribute there exists a unique value if the values of the attributes constituent pixels are added together. In the case of the 5 x 5 matrix, the attributes are the same as in the 3 x 3 matrix case except that the cardinal pixels are extended to the edge of the matrix.

2.2 Hardware Implementation

In the case of implementing the technique on the PC, the image was written directly into a 512 by 512 array from the frame store and the attribute analysis was then carried out upon this array. The program to carry out the analysis was written in Turbo Pascal.

When one Transputer was used for the analysis, the image was first passed to the PC from the frame store using a communications program written in Turbo Pascal. It was then passed to a B008 Transputer board, again using the Turbo Pascal communications program. The attribute analysis was then carried out by a 20MHz T414 programmed in Occam. The results are then passed back to the Turbo Pascal program for display.

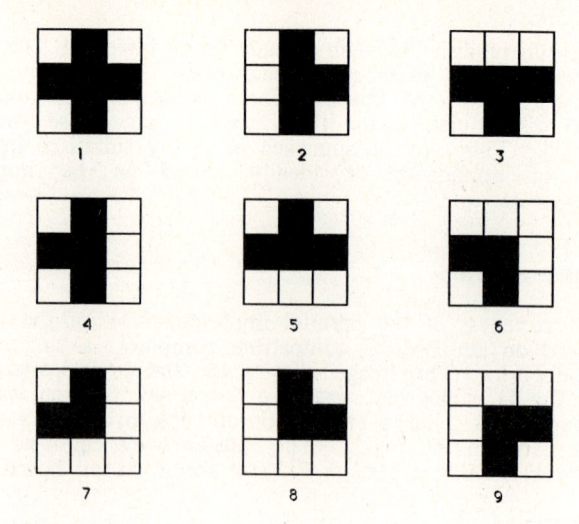

Fig.5. N-tuple Patterns used in the Analysis for a 3x3 matrix

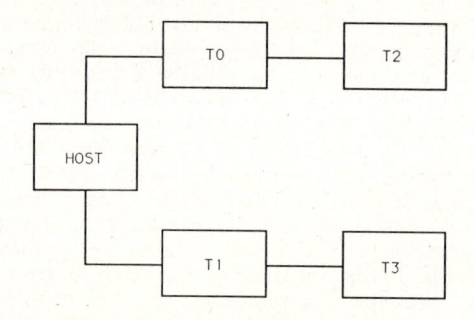

Fig.6. Multi-Transputer System

In the case of using a multi-Transputer network for the analysis then many factors have to be taken into account when deciding upon the system structure. These range from the accessing of the image down to the amount of parallelism introduced into the recognition on a pixel basis. It has been shown that when applying low-level image processing algorithms on a transputer network that "image parallelism" provides superior performance over "task parallelism" [9]. It has also been shown that careful consideration must be paid to the inter-transputer communications overhead [10] when implementing algorithms on multi-transputer systems. Thus the system constructed comprised five T414 transputers as shown in Fig 6. One of these acted as a host for the TDS system and the other 4 acted as the workers. The host transputer has 2 MBytes of RAM so as to be able to run the D700D software whilst the other four transputers each have 1 MByte of RAM. Each of the four worker transputers acted on $\frac{1}{4}$ of the image in parallel thus carrying out "image parallelism" thus minimising the inter-transputer communication times. The host transputer splits the image up into half and transfers one half to transputer T0 and the other half to T1. These then split the two halves into quarters and pass a quarter to T2 and a quarter to T3 whilst retaining a quarter each. These four transputers then perform the n-tuple recognition process on their respective image data. The image data is passed to the network in the same way as for the single transputer system.

2.3 Attribute Analysis

During the scanning process the original image and test image are exclusive ORed so as to produce a difference image. The difference image is then scanned and the occurrence of each attribute is recorded. This attribute measure of occurrence can then be used during a statistical analysis to ascertain the degree of corruption. This allows for a measure of the quality of the image under inspection to be ascertained.

To determine the occurrence of the attributes, each pixel in the image is scanned and depending on the state of the pixel, various actions undertaken. If the pixel is black then the cardinal pixels are scanned, the attribute is identified and its occurrence value is updated. If the pixel is white then this is regarded as either background or noise and thus checking for the attributes is not required.

The carrying out of the analysis is effectively the same for each of the different hardware configurations and consists of two distinct phases.

The first phase is the learning phase which comprises of three processes. First the reference image is taken and stored in a buffer. Then guideline positions are computed to distinguish the beginning of the image from the background. Finally the image is scanned, the number of tuples calculated, and a histogram produced that can be used to select the threshold values.

The second phase of the analysis is the processing phase and this also comprises of three processes. First the test image is aligned with the reference image using the guideline positions. In the case of the Transputer analysis, both the images and also the threshold vlaues are sent to the Transputer hardware, where the difference image is calculated. The attribute measure of occurrence for the difference image is then calculated and the results passed back to produce a difference histogram. Figures 2.1, 2.2, 3.1, 3.2, 4.1 and 4.2 show the attributes frequency of occurrence for the 3 x3 and 5 x 5 matrix applications on the difference images produced for Figs 2, 3 and 4 respectively.

3. Results

The occurrence of a large amount of attributes (especially in the case of attribute 1) in the difference image indicates corruption in the image under test. From Fig 2.2 we can see that the 5 x 5 matrix application has been successful in detecting the large amount of corruption as has the 3 x 3 matrix as shown by Fig 2.1. In the case of the least amount of corruption then the 3 x 3 matrix has been successful in the detection as shown by Fig 4.1 whilst the 5 x 5 matrix has not as shown in Fig 4.2, by the small amount of attributes detected. In the case of the image having an amount of corruption between the other two then Fig 3.1 shows that the 3 x 3 matrix has been successful in the detection whilst Fig 3.2 shows that the success of the detection for the 5 x 5 matrix is marginal.

For an IBM/AT clone having a 286 processor running at 10MHz, then the application of the n–tuple technique took 29s for the 3 x 3 matrix, for a 512 by 512 image with the program written in Turbo Pascal.

For the system comprising a single T414 transputer running at 20MHz then the application of the technique took 6.11s when applying the 3 x 3 pixel matrix and 6.13s when applying the 5 x 5 pixel matrix.

For the network of five transputers comprising of T414's running at 20MHz utilising "image parallelism" in the application of the n–tuple technique, then the analysis took 1.38s when applying the 3 x 3 pixel matrix and 1.41s when applying the 5 x 5 pixel matrix. The timing for the running of the algorithm on the PC alone was over the period from when the image had been loaded into the Pascal array upto the production of the results. In the case of the transputer systems, the timings are taken from when the image data has been loaded into the transputer in

Fig.2.1

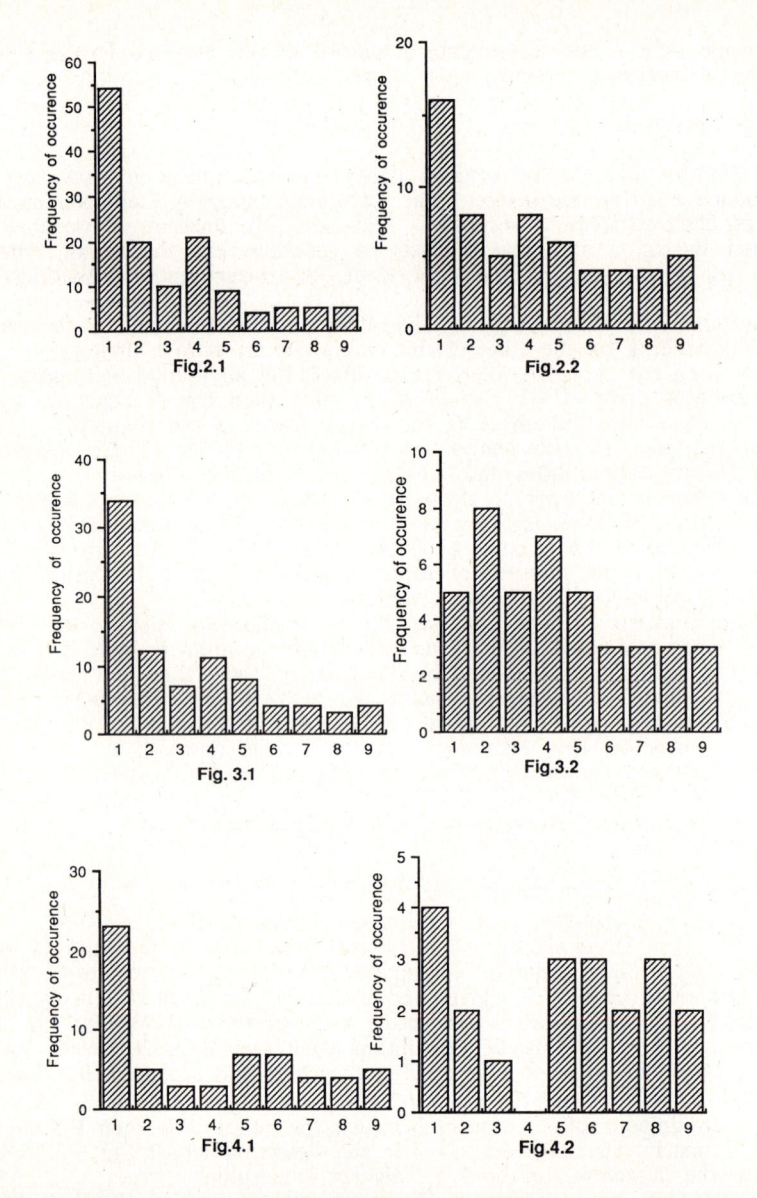

Fig.2.2

Fig. 3.1

Fig.3.2

Fig.4.1

Fig.4.2

the single transputer case and into the host transputer in the case of the five transputer network, upto the production of the results.

Thus the application of the technique on a single transputer is 4.6 times faster than on an IBM/AT as expected due to the higher processing power of the transputer. For a network of five transputers then an increase in speed of 4.43 times is obtained over a single transputer. Thus each transputer is running at 88% efficiency.

4. Conclusions

Analysis has been carried out, utilising the n-tuple technique, on test images containing known amounts of corruption and has proved to be successful without having to apply filtering prior to the analysis. This has been undertaken for both 3 x 3 and 5 x 5 masks. It has also been shown that the n-tuple technique is ideally suited for the detection of unacceptable flaws and that a network of transputers is an ideal medium for its execution with a five transputer system exhibiting an efficiency of 89% when using a 3 x 3 pixel mask and 87% when using a 5 x 5 pixel mask. Thus careful selection of the attributes and their size is required for optimisation of the analysis system. The multi-transputer system is ideally suited to carrying out n-tuple analysis due to the unconnected nature of the attributes and the high "image parallelism" possible for the technique. We have shown that the n-tuple technique can be used to generate simple and quick algorithms for the recognition of image faults whilst providing a substantial reduction in the amount of storage required by the recognition system. Work is currently underway in using the n-tuple technique for the analysing of multi grey-level images. A series of images at different threshold levels are generated. This has the effect of slicing the image into several parallel binary planes representing adjacent grey levels. These images will then be analysed in parallel by a multi-transputer system.

References

[1] Bledsoe, W W and Browning, I, "Pattern Recognition and Reading by Machines", Proc Eastern Comp Conf, 1959, p225
[2] Fu, K S, "Pattern Recognition for Automatic Visual Inspection", SPIE Vol 336: Robot Vision, 1982
[3] Stonham, T J and Aleksonder, I, "Advanced digital information systems:, Prentice Hall Inc, USA, 1985, pp 251-271
[4] Cover, T, "Recent Books on Pattern Recognition", IEEE Trans Information Theory, Vol IT-19, Nov 1973
[5] Bledsoe, W W and Bisson, C C, "Improved memory matrices for the n-tuple pattern recognition method", IRE Trans Electronic Comput EC-11, June 1962, p414
[6] Stonham, T J and Aleksonder, I, "Advanced digital information systems", Prentice Hall Inc, USA, 1985, pp 251-271
[7] Aleksander, I, "Artificial vision for robots", The Camelot Press Ltd, Southampton, UK, 1982
[8] Chan, Y C, "Automatic Visual Inspection", BEng Thesis, Nottingham University, UK, 1988
[9] Morrow, P J and Perrot, R H, "An investigation of Low-Level Image Processing Algorithms on a Transputer Network", Parallel Architectures and Computer Vision Workshop, Oxford, March 1987,
[10] Curtis, K M, Race, P and Aziz, A A, "Parallelism and the Transputer in the Automatic Translation of Text to Speech", ICASSP 89, pp 809-811

TEXTURAL ANALYSIS BY TRANSPUTER

P. Smart and X. Leng

Civil Engineering Department,
Glasgow University, Glasgow G12 8QQ.

9th May 1990

Introduction

Novel methods of recognising features in images on the basis of their textural characteristics are being developed. The first of these methods is capable of mapping features on the basis of local preferred orientation or local random orientation of the fine-scale structure within these features, and it is being applied to study the structural changes resulting from the deformation of clay as seen in electron micrographs. For this method of analysis, an efficient algorithm for uniform large filters was designed. This algorithm extends at once: to non-circular filters; to alternative methods; and to automatic methods of classification using inter- and intra-feature measurements. The method also extends to coloured images.

Table 1 Time (minutes) for mapping and display, approx.

Method	Analysis	Display	Remarks
Hand mapping	960	-	A4 prints
PC	200	3	simple code
mainframe	20	-	no display
T414	2	3	display via host
6 x T800	0.6	0	display in parallel

These methods are numerically intensive, approximate timings are given in Table 1. The first practical implementation was made using a single transputer; this is now being replaced by a 6-transputer machine, the design of which has been planned for expansion to 18-transputers; transputers which run the system are discounted here.

Method of analysis

For over 20 years, it had been necessary to use hand mapping to analyse the structure of clayey soils as seen by electron-microscopy. The soils are made of clay particles, which are platelike. They tend to come together face-to-face in sub-parallel fashion to form elongated straight or curved groups of various sizes called domains; the perfection of packing within domains is variable, and the intra-domain void ratio (ratio of voids to solids by volume) varies also. The clay plates also come together edge-to-face to form random clusters. Isolated clay plates are possible but rare. Mixed amongst these features are larger granular particles (i.e. silt); small fossils; etc. Between these features, there may be relatively large inter-feature voids. Although much valuable information had been obtained by hand mapping, it was too slow and expensive for modern conditions, and almost all of the intra-feature information was inaccessible to it. Plates 1 and 2 show results from the new system.

The micrographs concerned here are cross-sections. Most of the clay plates are seen as thin lines where they intersect this section. In order to bring as many features as possible into the field of view, the magnification is reduced, so each micrograph contains a very large number (up to 10000) of very small particles. In dense soils, the particles merge together and cannot be separated; at the other extreme, the voids may take up more than half of the area of the micrograph and the concept of a discrete void becomes inapplicable.   Obtaining such micrographs is extremely expensive; so it will be necessary to re-examine several existing archives of micrographs, and this will involve making allowance for various artefacts which were unavoidable when these micrographs were obtained.   The method of analysis is designed to cater for all these factors.

The original method (Smart et al. 1988) concentrated on local preferred orientation (or lack of it) of the clay plates.   The almost circular 20,14-formula (Smart + Tovey 1988) was used to calculate the intensity gradient:

$$\underline{U} = -\text{grad } I$$
$$U = \text{mod } \underline{U}$$
$$\theta = \text{arg } \underline{U}$$

where I is intensity.   When $\theta = := \text{atan } (0/0)$, θ was labelled as undecided. θ was then coded to a small number of directions, the number depending on the image.   A large circular filter was used to decide whether preferred orientation existed, and if so in which direction, thus mapping the image into random and directed areas.   Typically, a radius of 20 pixels is required for this filter for micrographs specially taken with controlled contrast and magnification.   Larger radii have been required in other cases.   Originally, the operator set: the definition of an undecided direction; the definition of randomness; and the scale of discrimination (through the radius of the filter).   We have now developed satisfactory approximate logical algorithms for the first two choices. Table 2 shows the result of a modified chi-square test, suggesting 24 pixels radius to be the best; this test is still under evaluation.

Table 2   Choice of radius.

RAD, pixels	$\sum \text{error}^2$
16	5865000
20	1070000
24	682000
28	755000
32	1137000

Images with long thin anisotropic features may require large inclined elliptical or rectangular filters, and the code has been designed to use these.

The code has also been designed to use alternative mapping algorithms.   In particular, work is in hand to map curved domains (which are subdivided arbitrarily by the original method) and to discriminate between areas of high and low contrast.

For multi-spectral coloured images, Smart (1988) showed that there exists a vector gradient, which could be used in the same way as the intensity gradient for monochromatic images, although other possibilities also exist.

Implementation

The course of development has been: main-frame Fortran 77;   PC Fortran 77; T414 Occam 2;   6 x T800 Occam 2.   Our experiences so far are as follows.

<u>Language</u>:   Occam 2 was chosen because it looked easy and promised fast execution. Both these hopes were realised; but our home-made Fortran development environments were more efficient and produced programs which were ready to be called by an operating system director program.   However, most commercial image processing packages transputers now use C, because of its wide availability on other processors.

```
         HOST              MASTER          4 x WORKERS        HARLEQUIN

         SEND DATA--->---GET DATA          INITIALS           INITIALS
                         SEND ICON--->---GET ICON    --->---GET ICON
                         SEND DATA--->---GET DATA    --->---DISPLAY D
         SHOW H.D ---<---FIND H.D          FIND U     --->---DISPLAY U
         SEND CONT--->---GET CONT
         SHOW H.U ---<---ADD H.U  ---<---SEND H.U
         SEND CONT--->---SEND ICON--->---GET ICON
                                          FIND A,C  --->---DISPLAY A
         SHOW H.A ---<---ADD H.A  ---<---SEND H.A
         SEND CONT--->---PASS CONT--->---GET CONT
                                          SEND C    --->---DISPLAY C
                                          FIND T    --->---DISPLAY T
         SHOW H.T ---<---ADD H.T  ---<---SEND H.T
         SEND CONT--->---PASS CONT--->---GET CONT
                                          FIND B    --->---DISPLAY B
                                          FIND F
         SHOW F   ---<---ADD F    ---<---SEND F
```

Fig. 1. Simplified flow chart for interactive use. D (= data), U, A, C, T, and B, are images; F is a vector (field data); H = histogram; ICON is a vector of control numbers; CONT is a command from the keyboard to continue. For fast use, some displays and histograms are omitted, and most CONTs originate from the master, these being used to ensure that a complete set of partial histograms are obtained and added together before the next set start to arrive.

<u>Basic Data structure</u>: Images are normally scanned left–to–right top–to–bottom; so we use left–handed coordinates (i,j) origin top left. Mathematical and surveying coordinate systems normally use right–handed coordinates origin centre of field or bottom left or beyond bottom left. Procedures x(i), y(j) are being considered to simplify programme development:

$$x(i) = +i - i_0,$$
$$y(j) = -j + j_0.$$

Table 3 Program structure vs. hardware.

Level	Language	Processors
Director	SCL/DOS	80386
Executive	F77, etc.	T800
Worker	F77, etc.	4 x T800
Service	F77, etc.	Harlequin

<u>Program structure</u>: Conventionally, we use mixed–language programs four levels deep, Table 3. This structure maps onto transputer hardware as indicated. Using Occam, which has no labels, it is simple to replace the Fortran service subroutines by in–line code, thus freeing a large slice of memory. The Harlequin board can do some post–processing of images; but, as an aid to program development, it is primarily set up to display images as they are processed. Histograms are calculated on the fly.

<u>Operation</u>: The Occam programs are required to run either automatically as sub–programs within the mixed–language environment of Table 2 or manually from the development environment. In addition, it will be necessary to replace the code on the workers whilst leaving the data on these transputers in place. It would also be desirable

to be able to reboot these four transputers from the master transputer without rebooting the Harlequin. Alternative ways of linking the boards and transputer for achieving these objectives are being evaluated.

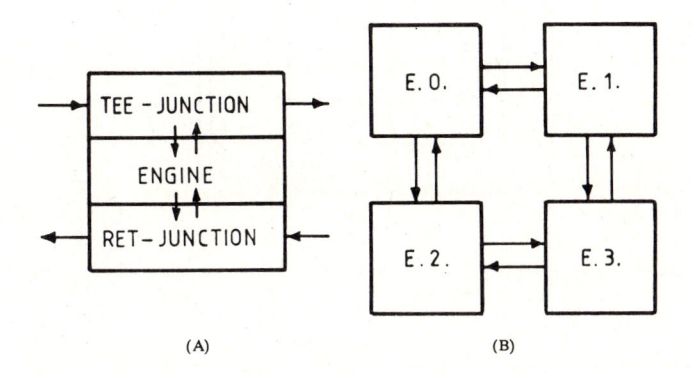

Fig. 2. (A) All six transputers are linked in two unidirectional pipes, M, 0, 1, 2, 3, H, and H, 3, 2, 1, 0, M, using four links per transputer. (B) The engines of the four workers are directly linked in a matrix using the remaining four links.

Parallel processing: Image analysis is a matter of producing an answer A by applying an operation O to some data D:

$$A = O.D$$

This equation may or may not decompose conveniently in various ways. If:

$$A = O_n.O_{n-1}...O_2.O_1 D$$

then a pipeline of transputers may be appropriate. This arrangement is more appropriate for small scale operation than for the large filters needed here. If:

$$A = A_1 + A_2 + ... + A_n = O_1.D + O_2.D + ... + O_n.D$$

then a tree structure may be best. For example, it had originally been intended to perform three operations in parallel: mapping clay; finding silt; finding large voids. However, these operations would each take different times. If:

$$A = A_1 + A_2 + ... + A_n = O.D_1 + O.D_2 + ... + O.D_n$$

then a matrix structure or farm is required, depending on whether the data is partitioned evenly or unevenly. For the earlier of the operations used here, the data is partitioned evenly, so a matrix structure was used. Partition into both strips and tiles was considered. These entail swapping large borders from transputer to transputer; tiles require more complicated code but about 30% less swapping, so tiles were chosen. Accordingly, links 0 and 3 are used for a square whilst links 1 and 2 are handwired into a pipe, Fig. 2. A different arrangement will be needed if more workers are available.

De-bugging: The system is arranged so that the lower transputers can always send messages and key data up; and entire workspaces can be displayed using special code.

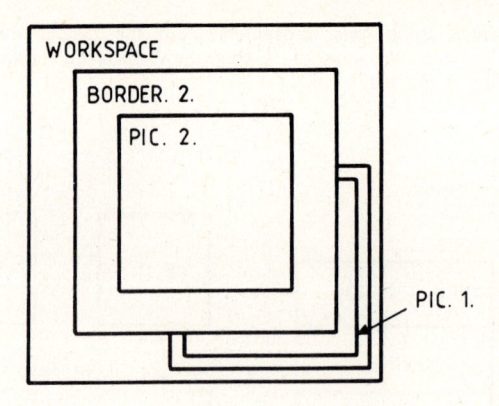

Fig. 3. Workspace. If necessary, Pic.1 is inserted first in an offset position and its borders are extended; then it is overwritten by Pic.2, whose borders are then extended in turn.

Data handling: Various image formats must be used. To save trouble, separate procedures are written for each format, and the whole image is read into the executive transputer before processing begins. The time taken depends on the complexity of the original format, and, if required frequently, images are reformatted before use. Meanwhile, all workspaces on the other transputers are initialised. Consideration was given to dividing the data between four arrays on the executive and using a PAR and two links to feed the workers in two short pipes; but no advantage was seen in this, and the data is simply piped through the workers into the display. This takes 30 seconds regardless of whether bytes or integers are passed; the delay is in the display.

At present, images are 512 x 512 pixels x 256 grey levels. Each worker processes 256 x 256 pixels; but provision is made for 128 pixel borders. Thus, the workspace is 513 x 513. Auxiliary workspaces 256 x 256 are also used if necessary.

To save trouble, each worker receives its own quarter picture, then two-pixel-wide borders are swapped. This was to be offset from the centre of the workspace, so that it can be safely overwritten with θ stored centrally, Fig. 3; but see below. U is immediately displayed over the original picture as a check on the calculation. Borders are then swapped again ready for mapping; but θ is not overwritten, because recalculation of the map with different parameters is necessary when optimising the parameters.

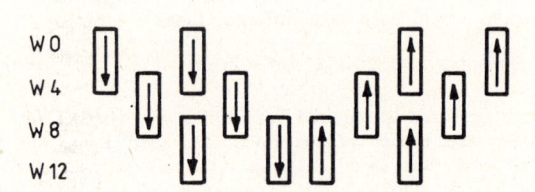

Fig. 4. Proposed timing diagram for a vertical swap of two rows for first column of a sixteen-transputer matrix. Each action is a transfer of one row. Steps 3 and 8 are parallel transfers.

When passing data and results, there is a choice between packet switching and counting in and out. The latter requires strict control. The former involves testing the delivery address. Both methods are used here depending on which is most appropriate.

Using a 5x5 filter to find the intensity gradient leaves a 2-pixel wide strip unprocessed around the outer edge of the image. If necessary, forward difference formulae could be found to process up to the edges (see Smart + Tovey 1988); 25 different formulae would be required. More importantly, using a 20-pixel radius filter for mapping originally left 15 % of the image unmapped, and this despite the fact that the area covered by the image was small. However, the multi-transputer system has enough memory for the image of coded directions to be reflected in its outer edges, so the mapping is now extended over the whole image.

Post-processing: When mapping is complete, the data is passed to a proprietary image analysis system, in which the mapped features are treated as particles and analysed accordingly. Surprisingly, no ready-written code has yet been found to do this on the transputers. Since feature analyses require different arrangements to field analyses, it is at this stage that the workers might be rebooted before continuing. In addition, field analyses are now made by the transputers for the mapped areas, Table 5.

Table 5 Apparent void ratios for areas mapped in Plate 1

Direction:	horizontal	down-left	vertical	down-right	random
Void ratio:	0.686	0.686	0.698	0.698	0.722

Future developments: The image storage requirements can be analysed by writing the equations (for an improved analysis) as:

$$
\begin{aligned}
U &\leftarrow\!\!- D+ \\
A &\leftarrow\!\!- D+ \\
T &\leftarrow\!\!-\!\!- A++, U++ \\
H.T &\leftarrow\!\!-\!\!-\!\!- T \\
B &\leftarrow\!\!- D, T+ \\
F &\leftarrow\!\!- D, A, U, T
\end{aligned}
$$

The arrow means 'is calculated from'. The increasing lengths of shaft indicate: pixel-by-pixel; small filter; large filter; whole image. + and ++ indicate small and large borders respectively, with the corresponding workspaces 260x260 and 513x513 say. A++ and U++ each require 513x513 integers x 4 bytes/integer = 1 MB. Alternatively, the values could be retyped to bytes for storage and retyped back to integers every time they are used; or A and U could be compressed into one image:

$$X = A + 1000\ U.$$

Both courses would complicate the code and delay execution, increase both development and running costs. Installing 4 MB per transputer would be safer and cheaper.

Practical points: It would be helpful to be able to run the Occam executive process on the 80386 processor and to give this process full access to the host computer's facilities. Greater flexibility of arranging the system and data links would be helpful; for example, switching the workers' pipehead to link 0 would enable the pipehead to accept a slow link without penalising the rest of the system. Larger cards would enable larger and more flexible transputer arrays to be incorporated within the desktop box; putting 4 no. 19-inch cards horizontally would enable 3 x 16 transputer arrays to handle red, green, and blue images of 1024 x 1024 size under the control of an executive card, which would have, say, an 80486 host, a small array of transputers, three digital signal processors, two or three graphics chips, a camera input, and communication chips.

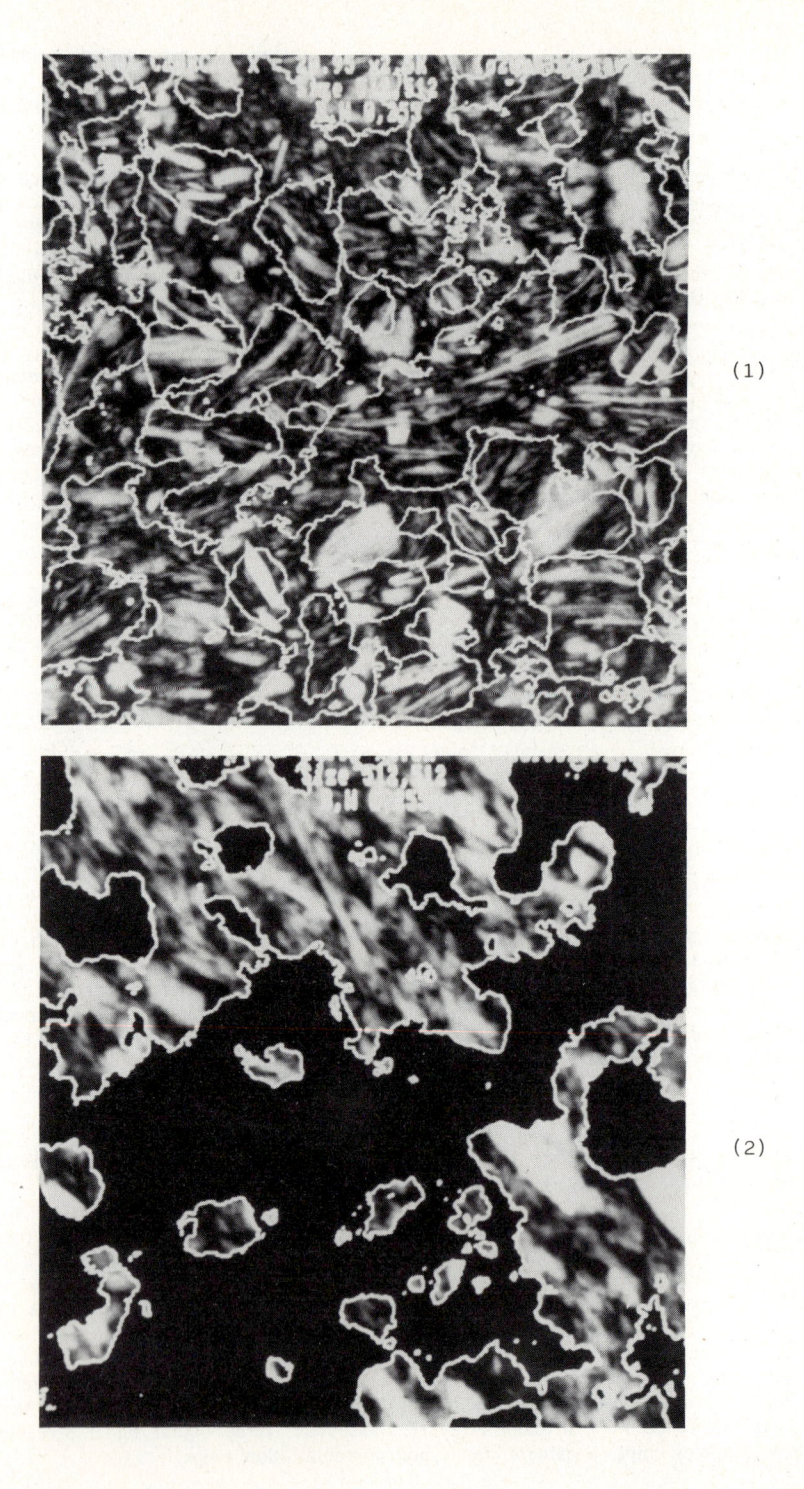

(1)

(2)

Conclusions

1. A medium cost transputer based image analysis system can process images at a convenient speed for an operator making routine visual checks.
2. The system must be designed from the start for ease of de−buggung.
3. The processor requirement is 16 workers/MMP, (1 MMP = 1 million monochromatic pixels); master, graphics, and control transputers are also needed..
4. The memory requirement is 4 MB/transputer.

Acknowledgements

The work is supported by US AFOSR Grant 87.0346 and SERC TR1/099. The original image for Plate 1 was supplied by Drs. N.K. Tovey and M.W. Hounslow of the University of East Anglia; that of Plate 2 by Mrs. X. Bai. We have also received helpful advice from Dr. H. Webber of RSRE.

References

P. Smart. 1988. Vector gradients in coloured images. Internal Report.
P. Smart + N.K. Tovey. 1988. Theoretical aspects of intensity gradient analysis. Scanning 10. 115−121.
P. Smart et al. 1988. Automatic analysis of microstructure of cohesive sediments. NORDA Workshop on Muds and Shales. Springer, New York. In press.

Plates

1. Electron micrograph mapped by the system described in the text. The mapping discriminates areas of local preferred orientation and areas of local random orientation. Four directions of preferred orientation were used: horizontal, down−right, vertical, and down−left.

2. Down−right areas extracted from a second electron micrograph ready for post−processing except that a border has been added for clarity.

VU3 SOTON90

IMAGE ANALYSER OF CARBON FIBRE ORIENTATIONS IN COMPOSITE MATERIALS

A.R. Clarke, N. Davidson and G. Archenhold
Instrumentation Group, Department of Physics, University of Leeds

Abstract. An image analyser is being developed to study fibre orientations in injection moulded thermoplastics by reflection microscopy. Thousands of circular and elliptical images must be decoded efficiently. An initial design using four transputers is described. By splitting the video frame into three equal areas and extending the network to nine transputers, an optimal design will be achieved. Future plans involve recording absolute fibre positions and true 3D orientations by pattern matching images on different planes.

1. Introduction

For the past few years, colleagues in the Polymer Group at the University of Leeds have been working on the properties of short fibre reinforced thermoplastics produced by injection moulding. In particular, carbon fibres (mean length = 120 μm and diameter = 7 μm) in PEEK(polyether ether ketone). The physical properties of these materials are very dependent upon the fibre lengths and the fibre orientation distribution.

The ultimate aims of this study are
   (a) to predict the fibre orientation in real mouldings - this demands a study of actual distributions for simple geometries and different moulding conditions
   (b) to predict the mechanical properties e.g. fracture and elastic constants of reinforced materials from a knowledge of the phase properties and fibre orientations.
   (c) to study subtle, though important, effects such as fibre - fibre interactions
A number of techniques have been developed to determine the spatial distribution of fibres:
   (a) Scanning electron microscopy [1]. The 3D visualisation of a localised region of a fracture surface certainly shows fibre orientation, but extensive quantitative orientation measurements would be difficult. Hence this technique is only really useful for determining the bond strength between fibres and the matrix.
   (b) Contact microradiography [2]. The technique depends upon a variation of X-ray absorption between the matrix and the fibres. Thin (50 - 150 μm) sections are cut from the moulding and a photographic plate of sufficiently high resolution to enable a magnification of x 500 is used. It has been used extensively for glass fibre reinforced thermoplastics, but is useless for investigating carbon fibres in most matrices (since both are carbon based).
   (c) Optical diffraction of radiographic images [3]. This technique is interesting because the researchers have attempted to significantly speedup the data acquisition time by passing laser light through a radiographic plate and onto a slit in a rotating screen. A photodetector measures the light intensity through the slit as a function of rotation angle which is a measure of the light diffracted by all of the fibres of a particular orientation in the sample. The technique does not work well for fibres perpendicular to the plane of the sample and cannot be used to investigate fibre-fibre interactions.
   (d) Transmission optical microscopy [4]. Once again, thin sections are prepared using microtomy or a diamond edged slitting saw. When the fibres are different in colour from the matrix, they can be seen directly in transmitted light.(Hence this works well for carbon fibres, but not for glass fibres.) However, the technique assumes that all fibres have identical lengths and there are major problems of fibre image unscrambling if the fibre density is high.
   (e) Reflection microscopy of polished surfaces [1]. This is one of the earliest techniques where a cross-section of the moulding is carefully polished down with 0.5 μm alumina powder and the polished section is observed by reflected light in an optical microscope.

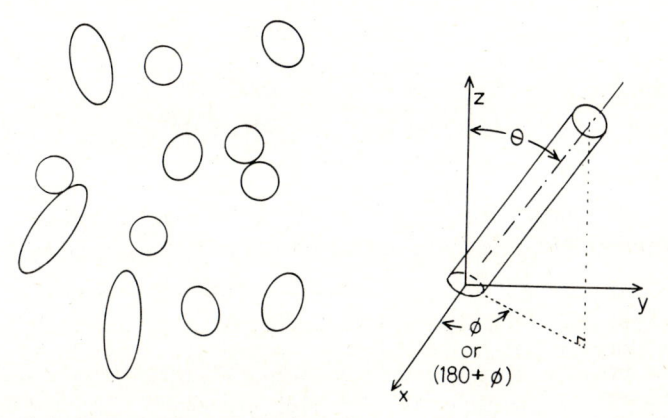

Figure 1. Typical Images in Reflection Microscopy

The cylindrical cross-section fibres form elliptical images on the polished surface and measurement of the elliptical parameters of each image may be used to deduce orientation distributions. There are three main drawbacks of the reflection microscopy technique. Firstly, the polishing process could damage the surface, but with care this problem can be overcome. Secondly, it is tedious. Only a small proportion of fibres are seen and manual estimates of the elliptical parameters is time consuming. Thirdly, there is a 180° ambiguity in determining the orientation of the fibre to the polished measurement plane.

Despite the apparent drawbacks, the reflection microscopy technique has been the preferred route for our polymer colleagues. The tedium of analysing the thousands of fibre images to generate fibre orientation distributions has been circumvented by using the COSMOS facility at the Royal Observatory Edinburgh [5]. The COSMOS (CO-ordinates, Sizes, Magnitudes, Orientations and Shapes) measuring machine is a high speed automatic scanning microdensitometer developed primarily for astronomical research [6],[7]. It was originally designed to analyse astronomical Schmidt plates and is currently being upgraded into 'SUPER COSMOS' [8] by the addition of transputers and extra input facilities. In order to derive the fibre orientation distributions, a photographic plate is taken of the magnified polished section on a microscope and the plate is sent to the ROE. The raw positional and ellipticity data for thousands of fibre cross-sections are returned on magnetic tape for further processing by the main Amdahl mainframe at the University of Leeds. This study is continuing, but the typical turnaround time is three weeks and it has become clear that a dedicated image analyser system attached to a standard laboratory microscope would be desirable! Also, significant inaccuracies could be introduced when the photographic plate is developed e.g. in the determination of the absolute positions and the ellipticities of the fibre images [9].

Recently, a number of research groups have adopted a computer based strategy to automate the decoding of the thousands of fibre images [10]. We are developing an economical image analyser incorporating a network of transputers which has the potential to speedup the turnaround time of this 'composites' research project to approximately 1 hour per sample. In this time, it will have archived all of the ellipticity parameters for each fibre image and will have graphically displayed the required fibre orientation distributions. We believe that the quality of the results will match those from the COSMOS machine because of the more direct technique of measurement.

2. Description of the Equipment

2.1. The Hardware

The current system is shown in figure 2. The image analyser consists of a Transtech TMB04 motherboard with a T800 host and a Quintek "Harlequin" frame grabber (which incorporates a T800) fitted into a Tandon microcomputer. The Tandon has the OCCAM transputer development system software running on it.

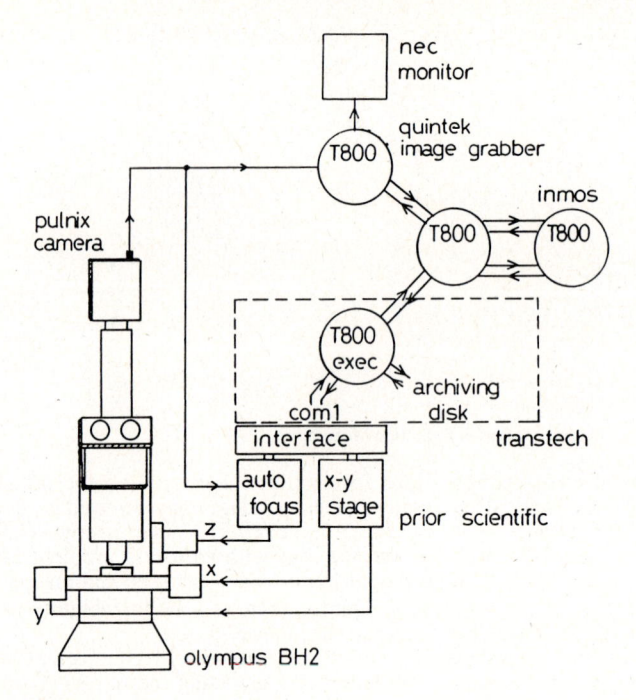

Figure 2. The Image Analyser

Initially, we had considered integrating a M212 and Winchester disk drive into the network in order to archive the data and to achieve a standalone microscope analyser, but simple economics forced us to scrap the idea. An INMOS B003 'ring of 4 transputers' provides another two T800's, but in a final system two T800 TRAM's would be inserted into the TMB04 motherboard. We have also tried to find a TRAM which could interface the network, via a RS232 link, to the microscope X-Y translation stage and autofocus unit, but without success. Therefore we conclude that the TDS Tandon microcomputer with internal transputer motherboard and TRAMs and frame grabber, RS232 port and built in Winchester provides us with the most economical system.

The microscope is an Olympus BH2 with a Prior Scientific Instruments X-Y translation stage and autofocus attachment. The X-Y stage gives better than $\pm$ 1 µm repeatability of positioning over the range of travel 104 mm x 65 mm. A joystick controller allows the user to manually define the starting point for the X-Y stage. The PEEK samples that are being scanned are approximately 10 mm x 2 mm and, for ease of handling and microtoming, are embedded in a thick resin base. An objective of x50 is used to give an overall magnification of x 135 and a 64 µm x 53 µm field of view results. At the moment, an economical Pulnix camera (TM 565M) with non square pixel elements is fitted on a parfocal mount on the microscope. Clearly, as we are observing a thick sample rather than a thin sample on a microscope slide, it is essential to maintain the focussing over a large cross-sectional area. Fortunately, our polymer colleagues require only 1 or 2 mm square areas to be sampled. The Prior Scientific Instruments autofocus attachment determines the position of maximum contrast across the field of view by cycling through progressively finer steps. The autofocussing takes approximately five seconds. If one considered that it was unnecessary to focus on every frame, an alternative strategy could be as follows: before the scanning mode is initiated, the X-Y stage could be driven to three points at different positions across the sample and the best position of focus could be determined for each point. By interpolation, the best focus settings for any X - Y position could be calculated and refocussing during scanning could be minimised.

2.2. *The Software*

As we ultimately intended to compare our results with those of COSMOS, we decided to use the same 'moments' technique that COSMOS uses to compute the elliptical parameters of the images [11]

$$M_x = \sum_i x_i w_i / \sum_i w_i = \bar{x} \qquad M_y = \sum_i y_i w_i / \sum_i w_i = \bar{y}$$

$$M_{xx} = \sum_i (x_i - \bar{x})^2 w_i / \sum_i w_i$$

$$M_{yy} = \sum_i (y_i - \bar{y})^2 w_i / \sum_i w_i$$

$$M_{xy} = \sum_i (x_i - \bar{x})(y_i - \bar{y}) w_i / \sum_i w_i$$

The centroids of the images are given by $\bar{x}$ and $\bar{y}$; the semimajor axis, a, and the semiminor axis, b; the orientation of the ellipse in the plane, ϕ, and the angle to the vertical, θ, are given by

$$\phi = \frac{1}{2}\tan^{-1}[2M_{xy}/(M_{xx}-M_{yy})] \qquad \theta = \cos^{-1}\left(\frac{b}{a}\right)$$

$$a = \sqrt{2(M_{xx} + M_{yy}) + 2[(M_{xx} - M_{yy})^2 + 4M_{xy}^2]^{\frac{1}{2}}}$$

$$b = \sqrt{2(M_{xx} + M_{yy}) - 2[(M_{xx} - M_{yy})^2 + 4M_{xy}^2]^{\frac{1}{2}}}$$

This 'single pass' moments technique is of interest because it could be used with both linear CCD sensors or, as we are using, CCD cameras in either slowscan mode or image grabbing mode. The weighting factor, w_i may be set to '1' if the pixel intensity is above threshold and '0' if below a preset threshold. In our application, there is little point in weighting in proportion to the pixel intensity for the bulk of each image, but a better ellipticity fit can be achieved by intensity weighting the edge pixels. Unlike the astronomical images that COSMOS has to unscramble, the fibre images are very regular, filled-in shapes which may touch neighbouring images but which do not overlap with each other.

We have therefore devised a simple 'image sort' process which tests for the connectivity of 4 neighbouring pixels in order to decide whether the current pixel intensity
 (a) is part of a new line segment (and hence a new image)
 (b) is part of a line segment in an existing, incomplete image
 (c) is below threshold and indicating that an image is now complete

The 'image sort' process running on a T800 is very fast, because it is essentially a set of nested IF constructs in OCCAM. We have ensured that the time for implementing the 'image sort' process is within the 64 μsec line scan period which defines a slowscan intersampling time. The program also keeps track of the 'space' between two neighbouring image line segments to check whether this space is decreasing and hence predicting and handling merged images. Using a short 'pipeline' configuration of transputers, the x-y pixel coordinates, weights and 'flags' (to characterise the status, (a), (b) and (c) of the line segments and identifying merged images) are

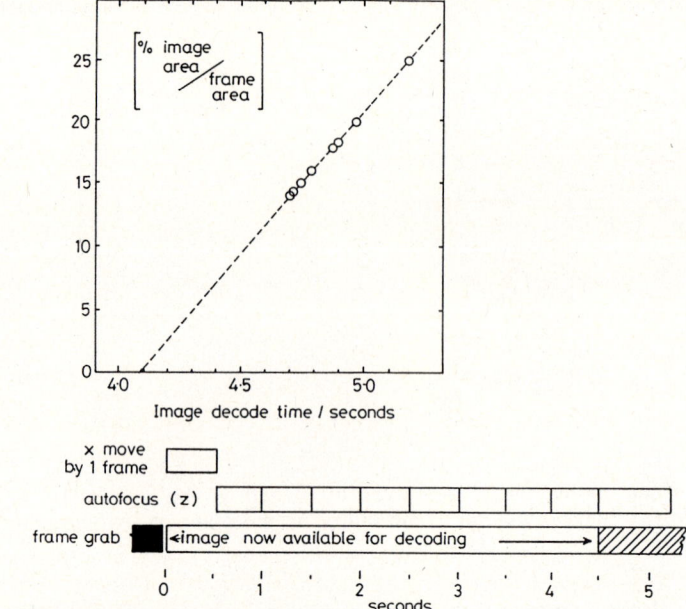

Figure 3. Timings for the 4 Transputer Network

communicated to another T800 and the moments calculation is performed while the next pixel intensity is being sorted. When the complete frame of data (512x512 pixels) has been analysed, the elliptical parameters are passed back down the pipeline for archiving on the Tandon hard disk.

2.3. System Performance

Clearly, in this scheme, we are not exploiting the parallelism that is possible when a fast, frame grabber is incorporated into an image system e.g. short 'pipelines' of transputers - each one decoding part of the frame - could significantly reduce the computation time of the 'moments' algorithm - but the parallelism would not reduce the overall timescale for analysing all of the images in this application. The dynamic performance of the autofocus is the main limitation of this technique. If an autofocus is required each new frame, it would be pointless to explore ways to speedup the image decoding.

We have effectively matched the time taken to complete the analysis of a full frame with the time to move the X-Y translation stage, autofocus and grab the next frame of data. This synchronism cannot be exact because the 'moments' algorithm takes longer to complete when more fibre images are in the field of view - see figure 3. Hence, with this combination of mechanical attachments, we consider that we have the near optimal design when an autofocus is required every frame.

3. Extending the Network

The four transputer system described works well for determining the ellipticities and hence the orientations of the carbon fibres provided the images do not intersect the edge of the field of view. At first sight, it might appear to be a trivial task to merge a partial image on one frame with the rest of that image on the neighbouring frame. Although the repeatability of the X-Y translation stage is to approximately 1 pixel, the precision of the lead screw determines the actual distance travelled when a certain number of pulses are sent to the stepper motors. By identifying images in the field of view and recording the movement of their centre coordinates when the same number of pulses were sent to the X stepper motors, the X displacements were plotted as shown in figure 4.

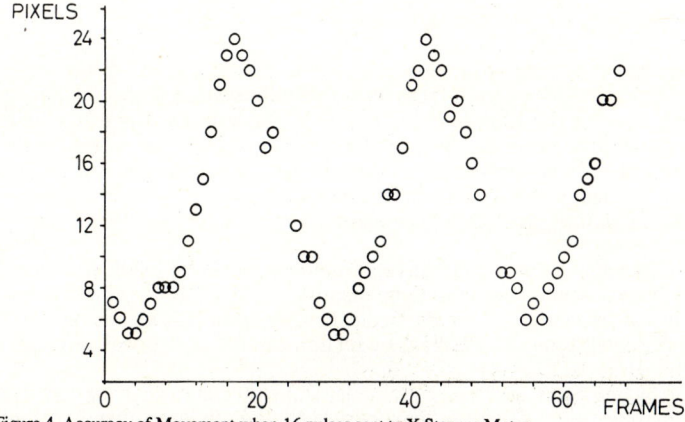

Figure 4. Accuracy of Movement when 16 pulses sent to X Stepper Motor

The peak to peak amplitude of this movement is 2.5 μm and the cycle length is approximately 800 μm. A similar plot is seen for the Y movement. Therefore, if fibre images between neighbouring frames are to be correctly merged, some scheme has to be devised to ensure 1 pixel registration *or* the X movement must be less than a frame width so that edge images will be recorded on the next frame and the actual distance travelled may be deduced.

At the time of writing, our preferred route is to extend the network, as shown in figure 5. By incorporating three short pipelines and splitting the video frame into three equal areas, we shall reduce the image decoding time to approximately 2 seconds. This time is comparable with the time to move in X, to grab another image ready for decoding and to make an interpolated correction to the focussing.

We shall probably move in X by just over two thirds of a frame width. The T800 denoted 'merger' will identify images from the previous 'first pipeline' dataset with the images in the current 'third pipeline' dataset in order to follow the absolute distance travelled by the stage. The two direct links between 'moments' transputers allow easy calculation of images at boundaries.

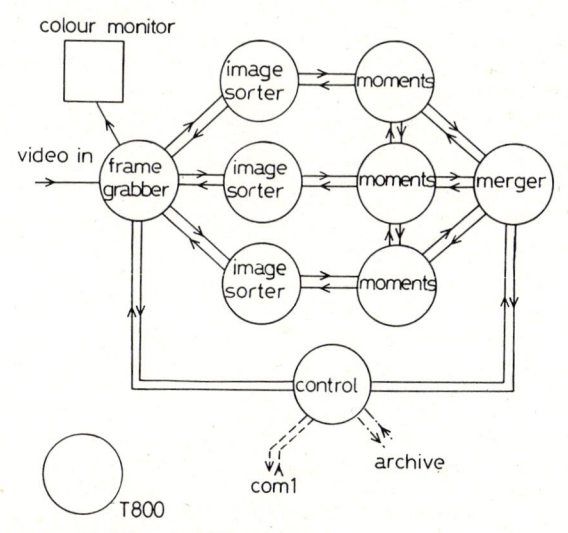

Figure 5. The Extended Network of 9 Transputers

4. 3D Reconstruction by Pattern Matching

A further refinement that we are investigating would be to either polish or microtome away, say a 20 μm layer of material from the surface of our sample, reanalyse the surface images and, by pattern matching, resolve the 180° ambiguity of fibre orientations. There is another bonus if the pattern matching can give image centre coordinates to an accuracy of a few pixels. Whereas the error in the fibre angle to the normal to the measurement plane increases to 10 degrees or more when the images are near circular, the identification of the corresponding fibre image on a plane separated by 20 μm would yield an independent, more reliable estimate of this angle from the centre coordinate values.

Successive removals of such surface layers would enable a true 3D distribution of fibres to be built up and the fibre length distribution to be recorded. We are aware of recent research into the 3D reconstruction of serial sections for biomedical engineering [12] and the use of 'control points' to find the best fit registration of two images with translational, rotational and scaling differences for satellite reconnaisance [13].

As we are analysing many thousands of circular and elliptical images for each crosscut through the composites sample, our problem is "how best to handle the large quantity of information per crosscut in order to deduce the optimal registration of two image planes?" Potentially, there will be a thousand or so circular and near-circular images which represent fibres perpendicular to the measurement plane and, if all of these are to be incorporated in the pattern matching algorithm, the computational requirements might be thought to be prohibitive. Also, because the fibres are physically short (approximately 120 μm in length) a significant number of fibres which appear in one image plane will not appear in the other image plane! However the resolution of this problem is eminently suitable for algorithmic and geometric parallelism strategies using a number of transputers.

At the time of writing, we have made a start with the pattern matching. A set of thousands of random image centre coordinates has been created and subjected to a displacement in both X and Y together with a rotation in the X - Y plane to create a second dataset. Using just one T800, we have performed timings on a program which searches for the displacements and rotation of the second dataset necessary to give the minimum least squares deviations of the new image centres with the original dataset. Figure 6 shows that a single transputer only takes a few minutes to define the displacement in X and Y to the nearest pixel and the angular rotation to within 0.1 degrees of the true value.

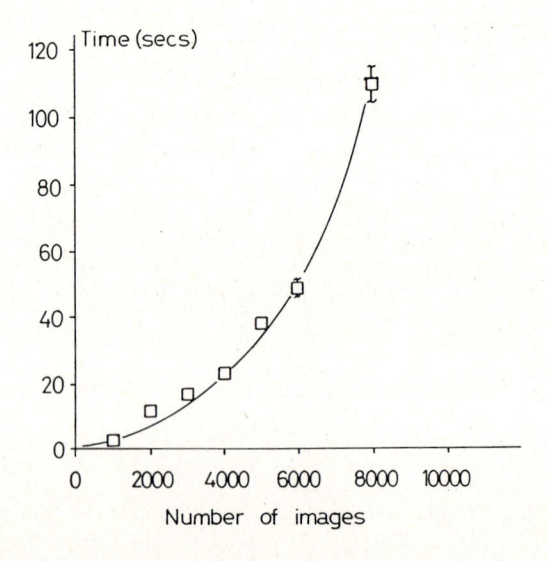

Figure 6. Single Transputer Timings for Pattern Matching Algorithm

5. Conclusion

Data will be presented at the MICRO 90 conference [14] comparing the quality of the results from COSMOS and those from our image analyser system. Preliminary results for the pattern matching will be presented at this conference. The pattern matching algorithm that we are developing on 1 transputer could be mapped onto the 9 transputers in the network (if necessary). Once the image decoding for the 1 or 2 mm square sample area had been completed, the transputer network would take only seconds to establish the correspondence between circular and near circular images on neighbouring planes. Within a few minutes therefore, the 180^0 ambiguity associated with all images would be resolved, improvements made to the fibre orientation estimates and fibre orientation distributions plotted.

The image analyser design should become a powerful tool for polymer research and will enable new studies to be performed within reasonable timescales.

6. Acknowledgements

We would like to thank members of the Polymer Group for stimulating discussions, especially Dr. R. A. Duckett and Dr. P. O'Connell. The research work is sponsored by the Quality Assurance Division of the Ministry of Defence and one of us (ND) is supported by an ICI CASE studentship. GA is taking his third year out, as required, from his BEng(Hons) course in Engineering Systems at Polytechnic South West to gain work experience.

7. References

[1] Thomas, K. and Meyer, D. (1976) Plastics and Rubber: Processing, pp 99 - 108 'Study of Glass Fibre Reinforced Thermoplastic Mouldings'
[2] Folkes, M. and Russell, D. (1980) Polymer, **21**, pp 1252 - 1258 'Orientation Effects During the Flow of Short Fibre Reinforced Thermoplastics'
[3] Polato, F., Parrini, G. and Gianotti, G. (1980) Advances in Composite Materials, **2**, pp 1050 - 1058 'A New Technique for the Measurement of Glass Fibre Orientations in Composite Materials'
[4] Darlington, M. and McGinley, P. (1975) J. Mat. Sci., **10**, pp 906 - 910 'Fibre Orientation Distribution in Short Fibre-Reinforced Plastics'
[5] Duckett, R.A. and O'Connell, P. (1988) Proc. Third Int. Conf. "Fibre Reinforced Composites" at Liverpool, March 1988 pp 27/1 - 27/9 'Fibre Orientation & Impact Behaviour of Injection Moulded Carbon Fibre in PEEK Composites'
[6] MacGillivray, H. and Stobie, R. (1985) Vistas in Astronomy **27** p 433 'New results from the COSMOS Machine'
[7] Stobie, R. (1986) Pattern Recognition Letters **4**, pp 317 - 324 'The COSMOS Image Analyser'
[8] Paterson, M., Cormack, W., Herd, J. and Beard, S. (1989) Proc. Int. Conference on Acoustics, Speech & Signal Processing (Glasgow) May 1989 pp 1528 - 1531 'An Astronomical Imaging Application Using Transputers'
[9] van Haarlem, M., Le Poole, R. and Katgert, P. (1989) Digitised Optical Sky Surveys Newsletter no. 1, pp 13 - 17, Royal Observatory Edinburgh 'Photometric and Astrometric Fidelity of Glass and Film Copies of a UK Schmidt IIIa - J Plate'
[10] Fischer, G. and Eyerer, P. (1988) Polymer Composites **9**, no. 4, pp 297 - 304 'Measuring Spatial Orientation of Short Fibre Reinforced Thermoplastics by Image Analysis'
[11] Stobie, R. (1980) Journal of British Interplanetary Society, **33**, pp 323 - 326 'Analysis of Astronomical Images Using Moments'
[12] Merickel, M. (1988) Computer Vision, Graphics and Image Processing, **42**, pp 206 - 219 '3D Reconstruction: The Registration Problem'
[13] Goshtasby, A., Stockman,G. and Page, C. (1986) IEEE Trans. Geoscience, & Remote Sensing, **GE 24**, no.3 pp 390 - 399 'Region-based Approach to Digital Image Registration with Subpixel Accuracy'
[14] Clarke, A.R., Davidson, N. and Archenhold, G. (1990) MICRO 90 Conference Proceedings in Transactions of the Royal Microscopical Society, **1**, 'A Multitransputer Image Analyser for 3D Fibre Orientation Studies in Composites' - in preparation

MONTE CARLO SIMULATIONS OF BIOMOLECULAR SYSTEMS USING TRANSPUTER ARRAYS

Douglas M. Jones and Julia M. Goodfellow,
Department of Crystallography,
Birkbeck College,
Malet Street,
London WC1E 7HX, UK.

Abstract:

This paper describes the implementation of a Monte Carlo method for the simulation of biomolecular systems upon a transputer based parallel computer. These simulations use the free energy perturbation method to estimate hydration related free energy changes in the system being studied. Such methods involve the repeated calculation of the intermolecular energy and are very computationally intensive. We have written a program that allows a Monte Carlo simulation to be implemented upon transputer arrays of variable size and returns results identical to those of the equivalent sequential program. Alternative algorithms are described which seek to minimise the limiting effects of interprocessor communication. In addition we have produced a much simpler program that parallelises the simulation by allocating each processor a short, independent simulation, and the implications of this approach are discussed.

Introduction:

As part of an SERC funded program to develop parallel-computer based applications for the study of macromolecular interactions, we have already implemented parallel code for the calculation of iso-energy contours around biomolecules (Goodfellow et al, 1990; Jones and Goodfellow, 1989; Goodfellow and Vovelle, 1989) and we are now developing parallel versions of a Monte Carlo simulation (Fortran) program. This program, BERNAL, has been written at Birkbeck College and uses the free energy perturbation method to estimate hydration related free energy changes in biomolecular systems (Goodfellow et al, 1989; Saqi and Goodfellow, 1990).

Such calculations are an important development of the basic Monte Carlo (or molecular dynamics) simulation techniques as they allow the estimate of the more relevant free energy change (rather than the traditional potential energy change) associated with, for example, amino acid substitutions in proteins or the relative binding of two related drug molecules (Wong and McCammon, 1986). Thus, they are directly relevant to both protein engineering and drug design experiments.

The motivation for adapting our original program was to discover whether parallel architectures could successfully be applied to this computationally intensive problem. They potentially offer a computing resource whose performance and memory capabilities can be expanded as larger and more complex systems need to be studied.

Methods:

The original sequential Fortran code was implemented on a single processor of the Cray

X-MP at ULCC. The parallel architecture for which the new version was written is a transputer based MIMD network of a variable number of processors. Specifically, the parallel code has been run on a small in-house Meiko Computing Surface and also on the much larger networks provided by the Edinburgh Concurrent Supercomputer Project.

The program uses a standard Metropolis algorithm to evaluate ensemble average properties. To test the code we use a simple reference system consisting of one molecule of methanol surrounded by 216 water molecules in a periodic cubic box of length 18.65Å. The Metropolis method generates a sequence of trial configurations for the system, with a probability distribution dependent on a Boltzmann distribution, so that the energy values we are interested in can be sampled over this ensemble of configurations.

Figure 1 illustrates the basic algorithm, with the labelled boxes representing the main subroutines.

At the beginning and end of each simulation, the total energy between all interacting pairs of atoms has to be calculated (E1). This is an $O(N^2)$ calculation, where N is the number of atoms in the system. The algorithm then progresses by taking the system through up to several million configurations. Each new configuration is generated by making a random move of a randomly selected water molecule (MC1). The change in the energy of the system is then evaluated by calculating the interaction energy of the moved molecule with all other atoms in the system (E2). The move is then accepted or rejected according to certain criteria (MC2): if the move reduces the potential energy of the system, then it is automatically accepted. If not, then a decision is made, based upon a Boltzmann factor which depends on the energy change and the temperature of the ensemble. The size of the random move is usually set so that about 50% of trial configurations are accepted.

Calculating the energy change is an $O(N)$ operation, but the number of iterations required means that it will always dominate the CPU usage for any size of system. Hence, in parallelising the algorithm we have concentrated on this section.

Monte Carlo

Fig 1

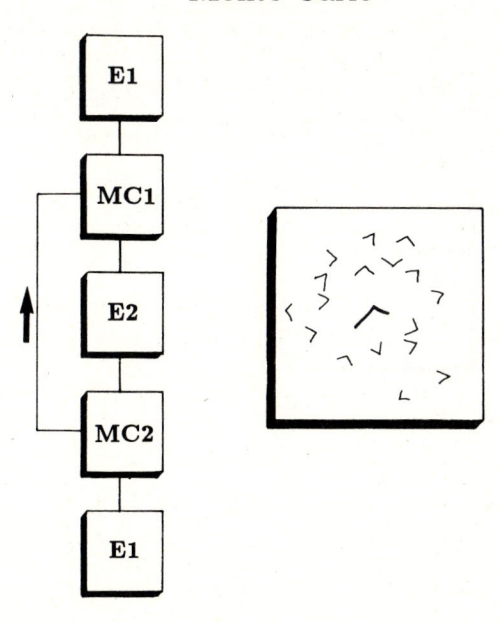

Repeatedly conducting the same set of calculations for a large number of elements, the atoms, makes parallelism a logical approach, but the task is complicated by the method's requirement for knowledge of the state of the whole system after each new configuration, and therefore a potentially high need for interprocessor communication.

Results:

A processor farm has been the standard model for our parallel applications in which the original code is divided into master and slave tasks. The master program runs on one processor and is responsible for the flow of data and control, whilst the slave program is allocated the repetitive calculations and is replicated on all the other processors in the network (Figure 2). Communication between processors is provided by a harness program written in occam 2. In order to implement the Monte Carlo program, we have written our own harness, which has enabled us to examine ways of optimising the communication process. The occam code runs in parallel with the Fortran programs and intrinsic routines are added to the Fortran to allow messages to be passed between the two. Whilst the original Fortran has to be expanded upon and modified in places, all of the calculation routines remain the same, so that updates to the sequential version can easily be incorporated into the parallel program.

Version 1. Data & Control flow

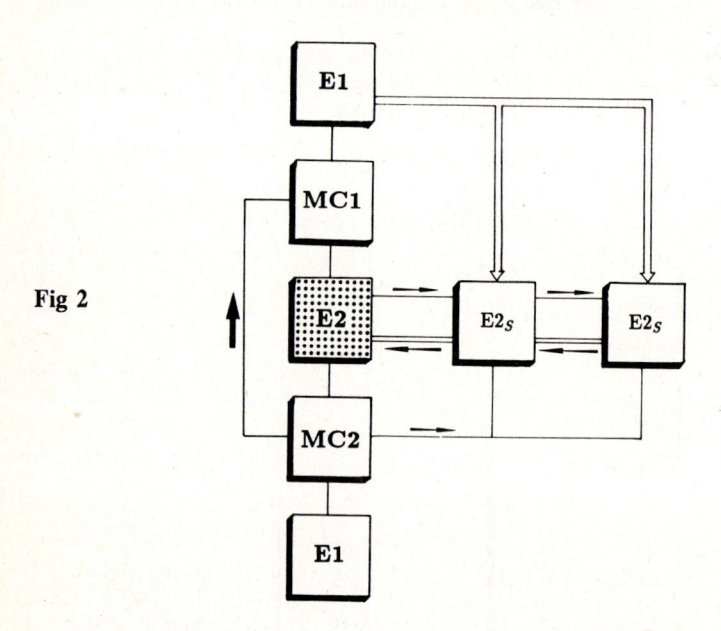

Fig 2

In our first implementation, the master program reads in the steering parameters and data, then performs the initial energy calculations, before broadcasting the starting data to the slaves. The subsequent workload of calculating the energy changes is divided up geometrically (Hey, 1988), that is, each slave is allocated a fraction of the data and carries out the same set of operations upon it as the other slaves. Here, data are shared out by giving each slave a number of specific water molecules to calculate for, rather than by allocating each a region of space. This method is more easily implemented and reduces load imbalance when a cut-off distance for calculating atomic interactions is used, since each share of the molecules is distributed throughout the system, rather than concentrated around the randomly chosen molecule.

Each processor holds the information for its part of the system within its 4 Mbytes memory. For each configuration, a random move is generated and the number and new coordinates of the chosen molecule are distributed to the slaves. Each slave processor calculates the interactions of its allocated fraction of molecules and sends these results back to the master program. Once the results are collected from all slave processors, the new energy of the system is determined and the decision made as to whether to accept or reject the move. This decision is then broadcast to the slave processors so that coordinates can be updated where necessary.

Figure.3.

Speed (Configurations per Hour)

——— hand-shake
– – – freeflow
············ +buffer

Number of Slave Processors

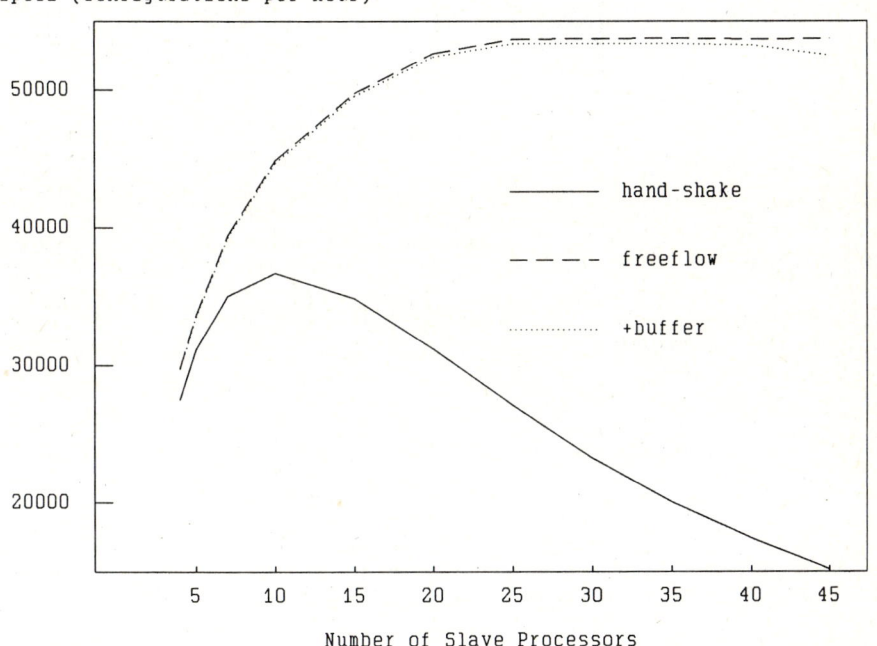

Figure 3 demonstrates the performance of the first versions of the program. Initial attempts to improve this concentrated on the communications harness. The original version used a 'hand-shaking' method to collect in results, where each slave sent back data only when requested by the master. This was replaced by a 'free-flow' harness where each slave sends back a labelled packet of results as soon as it has finished its calculation. A considerable gain in performance and efficiency resulted from this, where efficiency is a measure of the proportion of run time each slave processor spends on useful calculation.

Other changes have been less successful. Introducing buffers between communicating processes has only slowed the program down slightly. Binary and ternary tree configurations have been adopted for the processor network to reduce the average distance travelled by any message, but the minor improvements in performance are attributed to the presence of 2 or 3

Version 2. Distributed random number generation

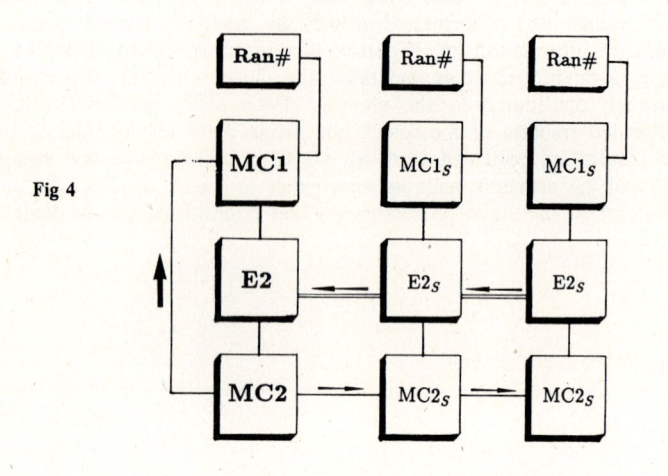

Fig 4

Version 3. Overlapping random number generation & communication

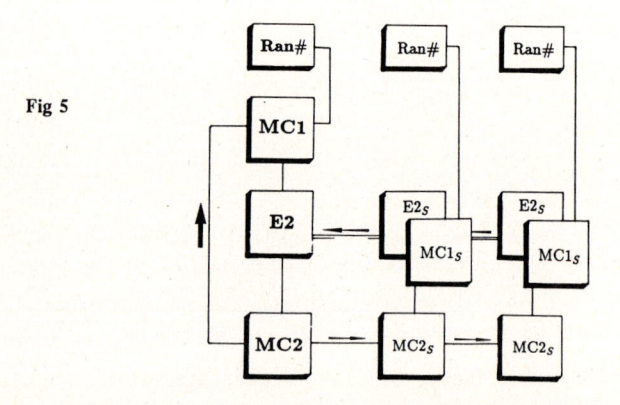

Fig 5

physical links to the master processor allowing a queue of messages to be dealt with more quickly. Other parallel programs written in the department therefore use a fixed configuration, general communications harness, such as FORTNET (Allan, DL) or F77farm (Taylor, Meiko). These allow distributed Fortran programs to communicate with each other without the need for the programmer to write the intervening occam routines.

Algorithmic improvements have also been made to the program. A random number generator is used to produce a new move for each iteration. This generator functions by producing a deterministic pseudo-random sequence from an initial seed. If it is replicated on each processor and identically seeded, its determinism can be exploited to provide the slaves with the information about the random move without having to communicate with the master processor (figure 4). A greater degree of parallelism is then possible, by freeing the slaves to generate the next random move whilst the master collects in the results and decides whether to reject or accept the current move (figure 5).

The relative performance of these algorithms is shown in figure 6. As a comparison, the equivalent sequential code runs on a Cray X-MP at a rate of 275000 configurations per hour of CPU time. While this figure can be considerably enhanced by careful vectorisation of the code and the use of Cray specific algorithms, the effective turnaround from such a multi-user machine can be slow due to multi-tasking. The available memory on the Cray is also limited to 4Mbytes.

Figure.6.

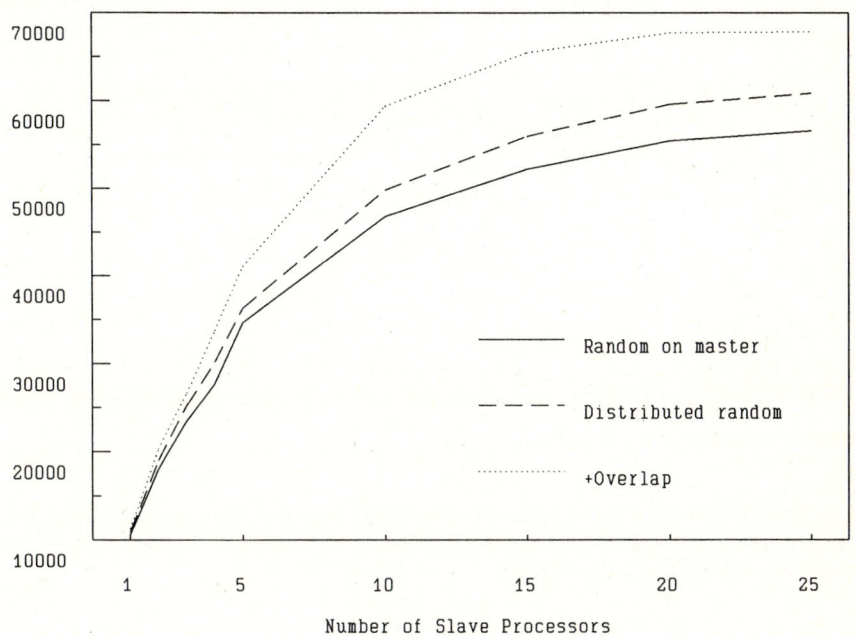

Speed (Configurations per hour)

[Graph showing speed vs Number of Slave Processors (1 to 25) for three algorithms: Random on master (solid line), Distributed random (dashed line), +Overlap (dotted line). Values range from about 10000 to 70000.]

Number of Slave Processors

The limiting effect of communication on the program can be seen from the diminishing gain in performance obtained from each extra processor. However, this effect appears most strongly only when the number of molecules per processor, and so workload between having to communicate, is very low. Hence the program is flexible enough to provide acceptable performance for small systems, but the larger the system, the more efficiently the program will run across larger networks of processors, and the better the performance will be relative to a sequential version.

An alternative approach to parallel Monte Carlo is to adapt the application to the limitations of the architecture by avoiding interprocessor communication. The simplest way to achieve this is to replace a simulation of length C, where C is the number of configurations, by x independent simulations of length C/x. The results can then be pooled in order to obtain similar precision in the calculation of ensemble average properties.

Problems quickly arise with this approach, though, as all simulations require an initial equilibration period, which for macromolecular systems can be very large. Over half the length of a simulation may be regarded as an equilibration period. Since all independent simulations have to be equilibrated in the same way, only a fraction of the original simulation can effectively run in parallel.

If the same system is being repeatedly studied, it may be possible to start each simulation from an equilibrated data set to avoid this overhead. Figure 7 shows the results of dividing such a simulation across 5 processors.

Figure.7.

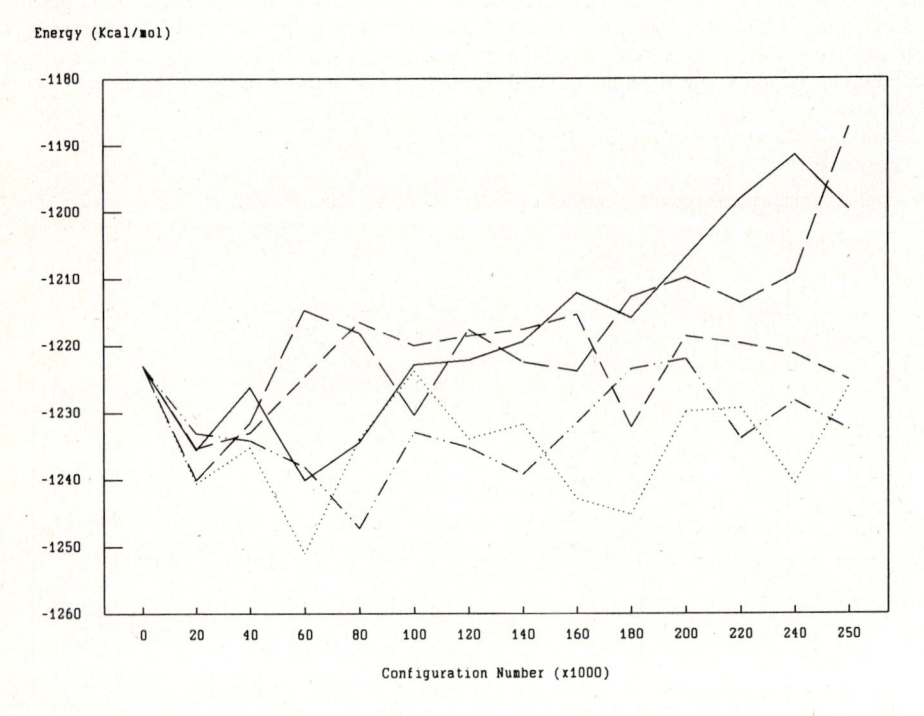

Energy (Kcal/mol)

[Figure: Line graph plotting Energy (Kcal/mol) from -1260 to -1180 versus Configuration Number (x1000) from 0 to 250, showing five simulation traces.]

Configuration Number (x1000)

It can be seen that the 5 short simulations have to run for a large number of configurations before they lose their correlation and can be regarded as independent. Hence a fixed overhead still remains, making this an inefficient method for parallelization.

Summary:

A parallel algorithm for a Monte Carlo simulation has been devised that provides acceptable performance and is adaptable with respect to both the size of system being investigated and size of processor network available. The program retains the basic structure and the routines of its sequential parent so that the calculations performed can be modified by future workers with little experience of parallel programming.

Acknowledgements:

We thank the SERC for a studentship to D.M.J. and for support under project grants GR/E72737 and GR/D86683. We also thank the Edinburgh Concurrent Supercomputer Project for use of their transputer array.

References:

RJ Allan and L Heck. (1989) in 'Applications of Transputers' (Eds Freeman and Philips).

JM Goodfellow and F Vovelle. (1989) Eur. Biophys. J. 17, 167.

JM Goodfellow, DM Jones, RA Laskowski, DS Moss, MAS Saqi, N Thanki and R Westlake. (1990) J. Comp. Chem. 11, 314-325

JM Goodfellow, MAS Saqi, N Thanki, JO Baum and JL Finney. (1989) in 'Theoretical Chemistry and molecular Biophysics' (eds DL Bevereidge and R Lavery), Adenine Press, NY.

Hey, AJG (1988) Phil. Trans. R. Soc. Lond. A 326 395

DM Jones and JM Goodfellow (1989) in 'Applications of Transputers' (Eds Freeman and Phillips).

MAS Saqi and JM Goodfellow (1990) Prot. Eng. In Press.

CF Wong and JA McCammon (1986). J. Am. Chem. Soc. 108, 3830-3832

Transputer Molecular Dynamics with Electrostatic forces

S. Miller, D. Fincham, R.A Jackson and P.J. Mitchell

Department of Chemistry, and Computer Centre, University of Keele, Staffordshire, ST5 5BG, UK.

Abstract

The implementation of a molecular dynamics program using the traditional Ewald sum and approximations to it to evaluate the electrostatic forces is described. The performance characteristics of these are presented, in terms of accuarcy and parallel efficiency.

1 Introduction

Molecular dynamics simulation is computationally intensive because of the need to evaluate many inter-particle interactions on each time step. It is very suitable for parallel processing on processor arrays and multi-computers and the techniques used have been reviewed by Fincham[1], who has also recently produced a bibliography of the field [2]. In the multicomputer case, with systems of a moderate number of particles (say around 1000) algorithms of the systolic loop type [3] are employed. These moderate sized systems are suitable for many problems in solid and liquid state physics.

In systolic loop algorithms particle data circulate around the processors in such a way that every particle meets every other on some processor, so that their mutual interactions can be evaluated. The algorithms have been studied in detail, using a Transputer implementation, by Raine, Fincham and Smith [4]. They have shown these to be efficient, both in terms of load balancing and low communication overheads, providing the number of particles per group exceeds about 10.

The particular systolic loop method we use is called SLS-G and is described here for the sake of completeness; further details can be found in [4]. The processors are connected in a chain and consist of a Head and a number of Segments (figure 1). Particles are divided into groups which at the beginning of each time step, are allocated to their "home" processor, one group in Head, and two groups in each Segment. Particle

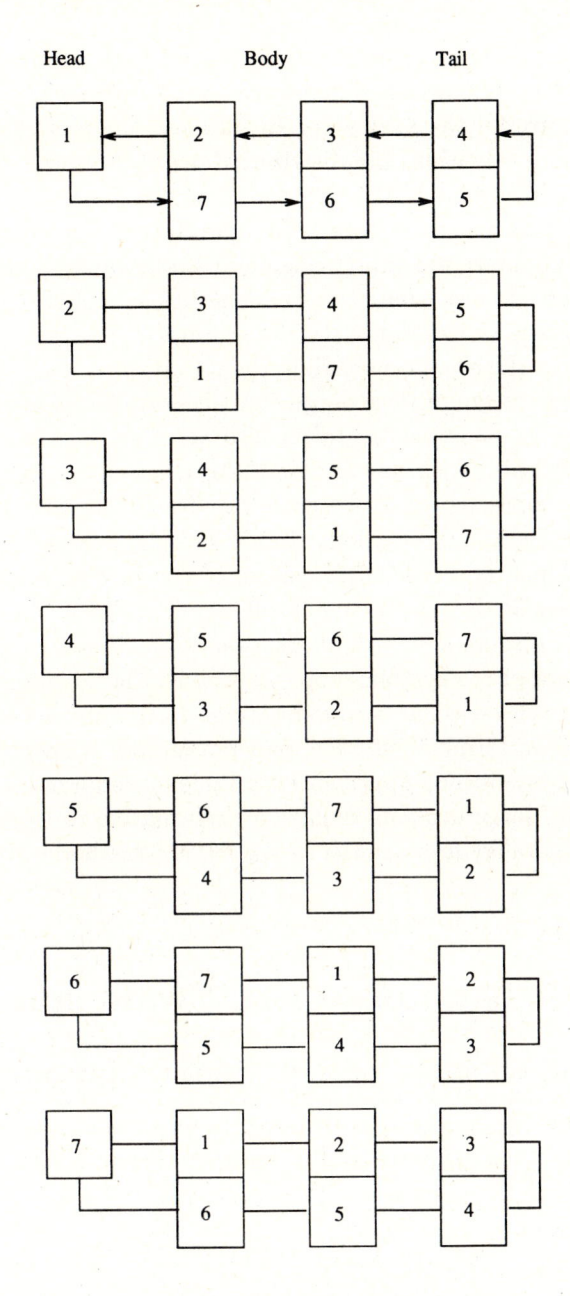

Figure 1: The SLS-G systolic loop algorithm

data then circulate in a series of "pulses", as shown in figure 1. On each pulse the segment processors evaluate all interactions between the particles in the two groups, while Head evaluates interactions between the particles within its current group. After the last pulse, particles return to their home processor. The forces section of each particles data array now contains the total accumulated force acting on it so its motion can be integrated, ready for the next step. In this way the motion, integrations and interaction evaluations are distributed over processors, resulting in a scaleable algorithm.

Previous applications of these techniques have been to molecular systems where the forces are short range and the periodic boundary conditions employed in such simulations can be implemented very simply by the nearest image convention (see, for example, the book by Allen and Tildesley [5]). With ionic materials the situation is very different: the electrostatic forces are of long range and the contribution of all the periodic images must be explicitly taken into account by a full lattice sum. In the standard approach due to Ewald [6] the slowly convergent direct lattice sum is converted into two more rapidly convergent parts: a "real space" part in which interactions are of short range and a "reciprocal space" part which is a sum over vectors of the lattice reciprocal to the periodically repeated computational cell.

This paper discusses the parallelisation of the Ewald sum within the basic framework of the systolic loop. As well as the full sum we will consider an approach based on approximations to it, introduced by Adams and Dubey [7], in terms of effective pair potentials. It should be emphasised that the systolic loop approach is suitable for moderate sized systems only; studies of large systems require an alternative to the electrostatic as well as short range forces, such as the PPPM method of Hockney and Eastwood [8].

2 Parallelisation of the Ewald sum

2.1 Using effective pair potential approximations

The full Ewald sum can be approximated in terms of effective pair potentials. The energy of the periodically repeated system has the form.

$$\psi = \frac{1}{2}\left(\sum_{i=1}^{N} q_i\right)^2 s + \sum_{i<j} q_i q_j \overline{\psi}(\mathbf{r}_{ij}) \qquad (1)$$

where $\overline{\psi}(\mathbf{r}_{ij})$ is an effective pair potential. It is worth noting that for a neutral system the first term vanishes. There are a series of approximations for $\overline{\psi}(\mathbf{r}_{ij})$. The first three are isotropic and are as follows.

$$\overline{\psi}_1(\mathbf{r}) = \frac{1}{r} \qquad (2)$$

$$\overline{\psi}_2(\mathbf{r}) = \frac{1}{r} + A_2 r^2 L^{-3} \tag{3}$$

$$\overline{\psi}_3(\mathbf{r}) = \frac{1}{r} + b_2 L^{-3} r^2 - b_4 L^{-5} r^4 + b_6 L^{-7} r^6 \tag{4}$$

The fourth is anisotropic.

$$\overline{\psi}_l(\mathbf{r}) = \frac{1}{r} + A_2 r^2 L^{-3} +$$

$$\sum_{n=4,6,\ldots}^{l} \left(L^{-(n+1)} A_n K H_n(\mathbf{r}) + (L^{-(n+1)} B_n K H_n(\mathbf{r}) \right) \tag{5}$$

For $4 \leq l \leq 20$, l even, and $B_n = 0$ except for $n = 12, 16, 18, 20$ and where $L = V^{\frac{1}{3}}$. Full details and values of the coeffiecients can be found in [7]. The forces on the ions are obtained from these expressions by differentiation. It is important that $\mathbf{r}$ is the separation between a pair of ions after the nearest-image transformation, and that the interactions between all ion pairs must be included, without the use of a spherical cut-off.

These approximations as well as being simple and easy to program, have a particular attraction for parallel computing because they involve pair potentials, albeit anisotropic in some cases, and they can be incorporated directly in a systolic loop program as an additional term in the potential. A possible disadvantage lies in the fact that all pairs must be evaluted, which may make the method rather slow unless the system is small.

2.2 Using the full Ewald sum

In the form the Ewald sum as usually used in molecular dynamics the real space, or error-function, contribution to the total energy is,

$$\sum_{i<j} q_i q_j \frac{\mathrm{erfc}(\alpha r_{ij})}{r_{ij}} \tag{6}$$

where erfc is the complementary error function and where $\mathbf{r}_{ij} = \mathbf{r}_i - \mathbf{r}_j$ but with the application of the nearest image transformation. The reciprocal space, or Fourier contribution is,

$$\sum_{\mathbf{k} \neq 0} A(\mathbf{k}) \left| \sum_j q_j e^{i\mathbf{k}\cdot\mathbf{r}_j} \right|^2 \tag{7}$$

where

$$A(\mathbf{k}) = 2\pi \frac{e^{\left(\frac{-k^2}{4\alpha^2}\right)}}{V k^2} \tag{8}$$

and $\mathbf{k} = 2\pi(l, m, n)$ is a reciprocal lattice vector in crystallographic units. The parameter α is adjustable, and controls the rate of convergence: increasing α increases the rate of convergence of the real space part, but decreases that of the reciprocal space part. Normal practice is to choose α so that the error function term becomes negligible at the same separation as the non-Coulombic interaction. It can then be evaluated along with the latter interactions. This part of the calculation then parallelises directly by means of the systolic loop method, exactly as in the case of the all pair potential approximations. However, in the present case, because of the decay of the complementary error function, it is possible to apply a spherical cut-off.

It remains to consider the reciprocal space term. Looking at the expression above we find that they involve, for each reciprocal lattice vector, the global sum over particles $\sum_j e^{i\mathbf{k}\cdot\mathbf{r}_j}$. The approach we adopt is to perform sub-sums on each processor involving the home particles of that processor. These are passed to the Head processor for accumulation, and the totals broadcast back to the Segment processors. The Head processor can then can calculate the total energy, and all the processors the forces on their home particles. The evaluation of global sums on a single processor of course involves a communication overhead and results in an algorithm which is not scaleable with processor number. In the next section we discuss how to minimise this overhead.

3 Implementation and results

The previous paper[4] employed Occam and the algorithms were tested on the Edinburgh Concurrent Supercomputer. The present work uses our own MEiKO in-Sun Computing Surface which has 28 Transputers, and programs written in Fortran or C. The MEiKO "svcs" software allows flexible allocation of a domain of processors to an individual job; user controlled wiring of the Transputer links; and loading of user processes onto individual processors. Communication between processes achieved by means of calls to the "cstools" library of message passing routines. The main difference between such a message-passing system and Occam is that messages may be sent between processes which are not directly connected, with routing of the messages by system software, transparent to the user program. There is a slight performance penalty in that there is a larger start-up time for communication than is the case with Occam. In our system we have found that a message of n bytes can be passed between directly connected processors in a time of approximately $(250 + 1.0n)\mu$ s.

It is a feature of the system software that the topology of communications established within the user program is independent of the hardware

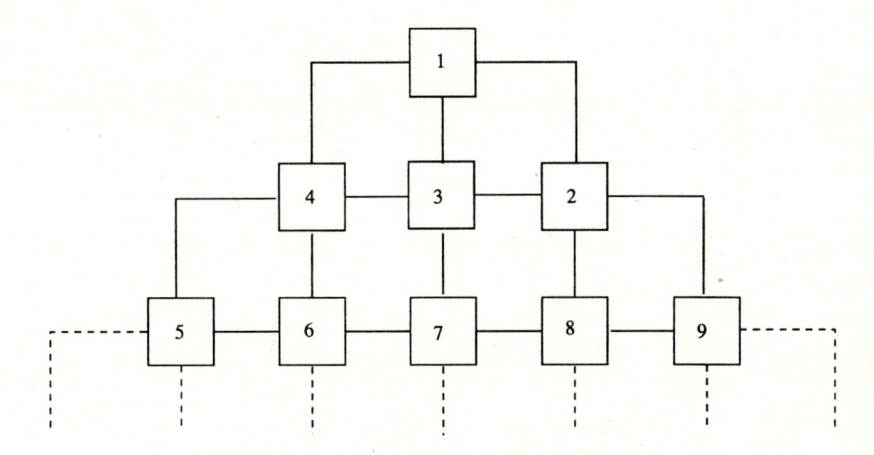

Figure 2: The pyramid topology used in SIMION. Processor 1 is Head; other processors are numbered down the chain used in the SLS-G algorithm. The chain can be continued indefinitely.

topology: changing the latter affects only the program performance, not the behaviour. The basic systolic loop requires only that the processors be connected in a chain, utilising two links per processor. We use the extra links to speed up the communications to the Head processor, particularly necessary in the full Ewald sum, by adopting the pyramid topology shown in figure 2.

We have written a molecular dynamics program called SimIon for the simulation of ionic materials. It utilises crystallographic coordinates so that it can be applied to materials of any lattice structure, and calculates radial distribution functions as well as thermodynamic quantities during the course of the run. The pair potential approximations, and the real-space part of the Ewald sum, utilise the SLS-G algorithm.

The Fourier space part involves a triple loop over the l, m, and n components of the **k** vector. Within this loop the $\sum_j e^{i\mathbf{k}\cdot\mathbf{r}_j}$ has to be evaluated i.e for every l, m, and n. Each processor forms the partial sum over its own group of particles and sends this to Head, receiving back the global sum over all particles. It would be inefficient to do this individually for eack **k** vector, i.e within the inner loop, because this would result in $O(lmn)$ short messages. This is reduced to $O(l)$ messages by storing the partial sums for all m and n components and grouping them into larger messages. Memory limitations prevent the grouping of partial sums for all the **k** vectors into a single message.

Our first task was to test the accuracy of the pair-potential approximations for molecular dynamics of ionic materials, since the original tests

	Ewald	ψ_{10}	ψ_2
Temperature (K)	1281.68	1276.83	1649.15
Total Energy (kj/mol)	-674.8374	-673.2180	-725.2362
K.E (kj/mol)	31.9686	31.8476	41.1342
P.E. (kj/mol)	-706.8045	-705.0534	-766.3710
Total time	5476.6960	5306.7950	2623.6020

Table 1: Results from a constant energy M.D. run of 216 ions of NaCl 5000 steps, with equilibration for the first 800, using 9 processors.

in [6] were for Monte Carlo Simulations of the one component plasma. A test job using the Ewald sum on a *CsCl* lattice containing 866 ions yielded a Madelung constant of 1.76267 and took 33.88 s in a sequential implementation (using our Sequent mainframe). The isotropic approximation $\overline{\psi}_2(\mathbf{r})$ took 10.65 s but gave a very inaccurate Madelung constant of 3.11380. The anisotropic approximations gave a greater accuracy. Using ten coefficients gave a Madelung constant of 1.75815, but took 34.82 s. This is marginally slower than the full Ewald sum but is not surprising in view of the all-pairs nature of these approximations and the fact that 866 ions already constitutes a rather large system.

In molecular dynamic simulations using SimIon we reached similar conclusions. The isotropic pair-potential approximations are not sufficiently accurate and do not give a stable simulation. The ten coefficient approximation gave a reliable simulation with acceptable accuracy, though not quite as good as the full Ewald sum. Some typical results are shown in Table 1.

It is interesting to compare the efficiency of parallelisation of the two methods. The efficiency is defined as the ratio of the sequential time to p times the time taken on p processors. Results are shown in figure 3. The systolic loop algorithms are known to give high efficiency as long as the ratio of particle numbers to processor number is sufficiently large. The example shown is for a small system of only 216 ions and the fall in efficiency as the number of processors increases can be seen. The $\overline{\psi}_{10}$ is better than the $\overline{\psi}_2$ case because of the higher ratio of calculation to communication. In the case of the full Ewald sum the efficiency falls off more quickly with large number of processors because of the bottleneck caused by the need for Head to receive subsums from all the other processors and broadcast the global sums.

4 Conclusions.

The pair potential approximations parallelise well (figure 3) using a di-

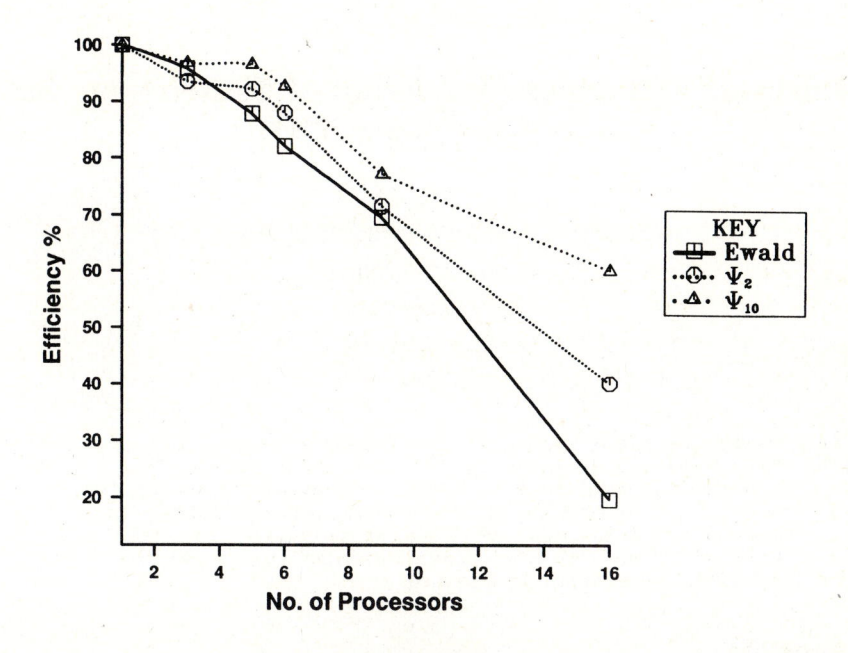

Figure 3

Parallel Efficiency

216 ions

rect systolic loop approach, although a large number of terms must be taken to give acceptable accuracy. For 216 ions the two methods have a comparable accuracy and speed on 9 processors. For larger number of ions the pair potential approximations become slower than the full Ewald sum because it is not possible to apply a spherical cut-off. For larger number of processors the Ewald sum becomes less efficient because of the global accumulation required in the Fourier part. In our work on the simulation of materials we typically use 500 ions on 10 processors and either method can be used successfully to produce high performance cost-effective computing. A major advantage of our local MEiKO facility, compared with the use of remote supercomputers, is its integration into our local area network which enables researchers to interface their programs to workstation graphics on their desk and watch the simulations as they progress.

Molecular Dynamics Simulation of Proteins on an Array of Transputers

A. R. C. Raine
Cambridge Centre for Molecular Recognition
Department of Biochemistry
Tennis Court Road
Cambridge
CB2 1QW

Abstract. Extensions to the systolic loop methods of Raine, Fincham and Smith, for the molecular dynamics simulation of liquids, are presented. These allow the simulation of complex molecules such as proteins. Additionally, a method for parallelising the SHAKE algorithm for constraining bond-lengths is described. Performance figures are given for an implementation for a Meiko Computing Surface, which demonstrate that the program retains the efficiency and scaling behaviour of the original methods.

Introduction

Molecular dynamics simulation is a powerful computational technique which allows the calculation of structural, dynamic and thermodynamic properties of atomic and molecular ensembles. It involves the integration of the equations of motion of the particles comprising the system of interest, generating a trajectory of the conformation of the system through time.

The study of proteins, their structure, and their interactions with other molecules is fundamental to our understanding of biology at the molecular level. Molecular dynamics simulation of protein structure allows the investigation of phenomena not accessible to conventional experimental techniques. In addition, molecular dynamics can be used as a tool to aid the determination of protein structure from x-ray diffraction [1] and two-dimensional nuclear magnetic resonance data [2].

Although molecular dynamics simulation can tell us a great deal about a system, it is an expensive technique. The equations of motion are integrated using a finite difference method such as that of Verlet [3], where the coordinates (r_i) and velocities (v_i) of the particles are stepped through time using the equations:

$$r_i(t+\Delta t) = r_i(t) + \Delta t \, v_i(t+1/2 \, \Delta t)$$

$$v_i(t+1/2 \, \Delta t) = v_i(t - 1/2 \, \Delta t) + \Delta t \, a_i(t)$$

and

$$m_i a_i = - \partial/\partial r_i \, E$$

where E is a function representing the potential energy of the system, and m_i is the mass of particle i

In order for this approach to be valid, the time-step (Δt) must be shorter than the period of the fastest motion present in the system, usually this is between 1-10 fs. This means that very many time-steps will be required to bring the system into thermal equilibrium. Furthermore, if the inter-particle interactions are significant at separations comparable to the size of the system, the number of pair-wise interactions that have to be evaluated at each time-step will be 1/2 N(N-1). Thus an efficient parallelisation of the molecular dynamics algorithm, to run on a transputer based parallel computer would be of great value.

In an earlier paper [4], efficient methods for performing molecular dynamics simulations of simple fluids on a ring of transputers was described. This paper describes how these methods have been generalised to accommodate the features of larger molecules, and hence allow efficient simulation of protein dynamics.

Systolic loop methods

As an example of the systolic loop methods, one (termed SLS) is described:

Consider a system of seven particles, interacting via pair-wise forces. The data representing the coordinates, and the forces acting upon each particle can be distributed over four particles in the following manner (figure 1):

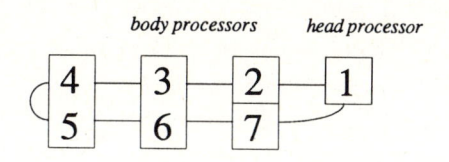

Figure 1. Distribution of particles over processors for the SLS method

The pair-wise forces 4-5, 3-6, and 2-7 can be evaluated in parallel. If the coordinates and forces are rotated around the processor ring, then interactions 3-4, 2-5 and 1-6 can be evaluated. If the data movements are repeated then, after seven such systolic pulses, all the pair-wise interactions will have been evaluated, and the data will have returned to their original processors (figure 2). The time taken for the calculation will be a third of the time that a single processor would take, but the total elapsed time will include the time taken to rotate all the data once round the loop.

This scheme can be extended for the case where there are many more particles than processors. Consider a system of twenty one particles, distributed over the same four processors (figure 3)

3	2	1	7
4	5	6	

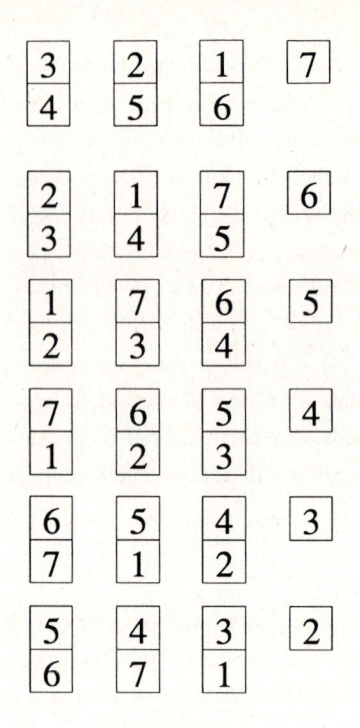

2	1	7	6
3	4	5	

1	7	6	5
2	3	4	

7	6	5	4
1	2	3	

6	5	4	3
7	1	2	

5	4	3	2
6	7	1	

Figure 2. Data movements for the SLS method

```
12 11 10      9 8 7       6 5 4        3 2 1
13 14 15     16 17 18    19 20 21

      9 8 7       6 5 4        3 2 1     21 20 19
     10 11 12    13 14 15    16 17 18

                       etc
```

Figure 3. Distribution of data, and data movements for the SLS-G method

If the data are moved as groups of particles rather than individually, then the *body* processors can evaluate forces between groups of particles, while the *head* processor can evaluate the forces between particles *within* each group. Furthermore, as the time taken for the calculation is proportional to the square of the size of the groups, while the communication time depends only on the total number of particles in the system, the calculations become more efficient as the size of the system increases. In practice it was found that, for a simulation of the Lennard-Jones fluid, optimum efficiency (close to 100%) was obtained when the group size exceeded 16 particles. For a simulation of 256 particles, a systolic loop program running on 30 T800 processors was equivalent to a conventional program running on a CRAY 1S.

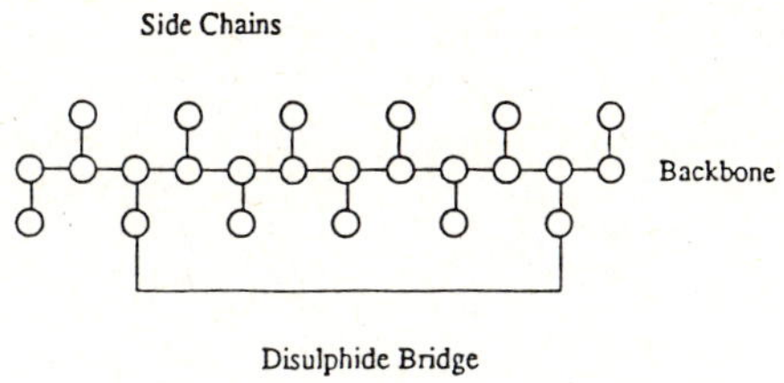

Figure 4. Cartoon of protein topology. Proteins have a long chain backbone, with different side-chains branching from it. Some side-chains can form covalent bonds with one another, creating closed cycles.

Protein structure

Proteins are long chain molecules, having a polymeric backbone with different side-chains branching from each backbone unit (figure 4):

In their biologically active form most proteins fold into a compact globular conformation. Some side-chains can then form additional chemical bonds, and thus cross-link the backbone.

Flexible covalent bonds are customarily modelled using two- three- and four-body forces (figure 5):

$$E_{bond} = \sum_{bonds} \frac{1}{2} k_b (r - r_0)^2$$

$$E_{angle} = \sum_{angles} \frac{1}{2} k_\theta (\theta - \theta_0)^2$$

$$E_{torsion} = \sum_{torsions} k_\phi \{1 + \cos(n\phi - \phi_0)\}$$

The systolic loop methods only guarantee that every pair-wise interactions taken into account, although some multi-body interactions could be evaluated within and between some groups. In order to use a systolic loop algorithm for protein simulation, some way must be devised to ensure that all the three- and four-body interactions occur

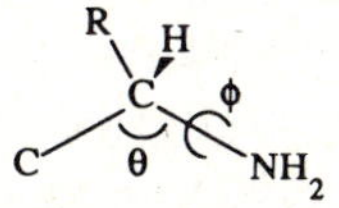

Figure 5. Bond geometry is defined by 2 (bond length), 3 (bond angle, θ) and 4 body (torsion angle, ϕ) relationships.

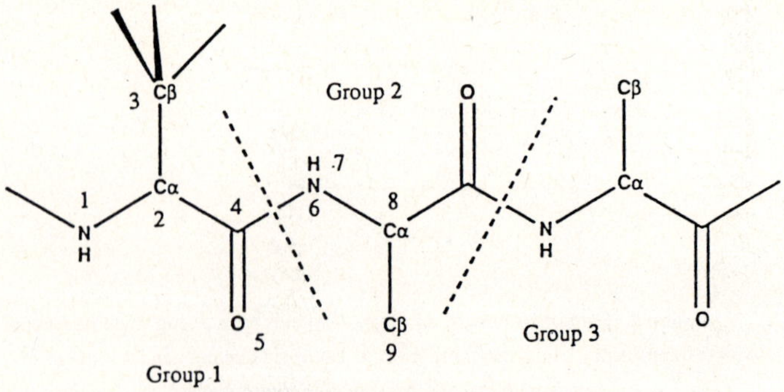

Figure 6. Division of atom into groups. No atom is allowed to contribute bonds to more than one group. Thus all the three- and four-body interactions are accommodated within the original systolic loop scheme.

between atoms within at most two groups. In practice, a simple rule can be applied when dividing the atoms into groups, which will enforce this condition.

Atom division rule

Group boundaries will necessarily cut atom-atom bonds (protein molecules are so large that there will always be more processors than molecules). If, however, atoms which participate in cross-boundary bonds are chosen such that none contributes to more than one such bond, then all the three- and four- body interactions will be limited to at most two groups as required.

This allows the systolic loop methods to be used unchanged to simulate *any* flexible macromolecular system.

Bond length constraints

As mentioned above, the time-step of a simulation is limited by the period of the fastest characteristic motions of the system being investigated. In systems with flexible chemical bonds, the fastest motions will be bond stretching vibrations. As these are not closely coupled to the other degrees of freedom of the molecule, an increase in the usable time-step can be achieved by fixing the lengths of bonds, without significantly affecting the dynamics of the system as a whole. For large molecules this is most often done using the SHAKE method [5], in which the coordinates of atoms are adjusted to satisfy the bond-length constraints after an unconstrained time-step has been made:

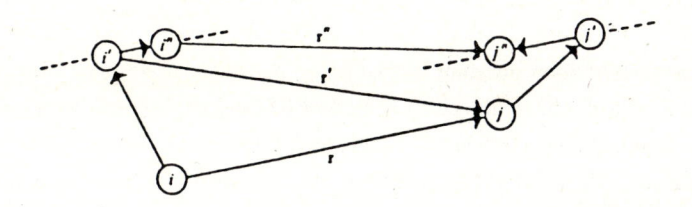

Figure 7. Vector relationships involved when satisfying a bond-length constraint using the SHAKE method. i and j are the atoms before the time-step, i' and j' are the atoms after the unconstrained time-step and i" and j" are the atoms after the SHAKE correction has been applied. The corrections dr_i and dr_j are calculated:

$$dr_i = -g \frac{r_{ij}}{m_i}$$

$$dr_j = g \frac{r_{ij}}{m_j}$$

$$g = \frac{(|r_0|^2 - |r'_{ij}|^2)}{2M \, r_{ij} \cdot r'_{ij}}$$

$$M = \frac{1}{m_i} + \frac{1}{m_j}$$

Where m_i and m_j are the masses of atoms i and j respectively. This process is iterated over all constrained ij pairs until all the constraints are satisfied.

Using SHAKE to constrain bond-lengths allows the time-step to be increased by a factor of 2-3, so an efficient implementation within the systolic loop scheme is desirable.

Because satisfying one constraint may well cause another to be violated, and because some bonds are split over processor boundaries, each iteration of the SHAKE algorithm is potentially as expensive in communication time as a full force evaluation. However, as was noted in [5], the shortest period motions in protein structures will be those of bonds involving hydrogen atoms. Constraining just these terms using SHAKE allows an increase of the time-step by a factor of two. Hydrogen atoms are monovalent, and therefore bonds involving hydrogens need never cross group boundaries. If this is the case, then the constraints within one group will be independent of those in other groups, and so SHAKE can be applied to all groups in parallel with no communication penalty at all.

Implementation

A systolic loop program (SLS-PRO) for molecular dynamics simulation of proteins has been written, in occam 2, for MEIKO and INMOS hardware. SLS-PRO uses the potential function from the established protein simulation suite GROMOS [6], and reads and writes GROMOS format files. Thus input data can be prepared using the appropriate programs from GROMOS on a conventional computer, and simulations run using SLS-PRO on transputers.

Performance

The performance of SLS-PRO was assessed by comparing simulations of crambin (a small protein, ~ 400 atoms per molecule) on three, five and twelve processors, with equivalent simulations run using GROMOS on a microVAX 3600. The results are shown in table 1:

As can be seen, for the simulations taking all pair-wise interactions into account, the speed-up is more or less linear. When a 1.0 nm cutoff is applied to the interactions (reducing the number of terms evaluated by a factor of three), the the time taken for inter-processor communication is more significant, and the efficiency drops. Overall, a T800 transputer gives a realizable performance equivalent to 1 - 1.5 microVAX 3600 processors for these calculations.

Conclusion

The work described in this paper set out to find a generalisation of the systolic loop methods to allow molecular dynamics simulation of proteins. It was found that simple rules governing the data decomposition of the problem allowed the many-body terms of the potential function, and the SHAKE method of applying bond-length constraints, to be accommodated without changing the original scheme.

The computer program (SLS-PRO), which was written applying these rules,

	Time per 100 steps (1.0 nm cutoff)	Speedup relative to VAX	Time per 100 steps (all pairs)	Speedup relative to VAX	Average group size
microVAX 3600	705	1.0	2045	1.0	400
3 T800s	215	3.3	450	4.5	80
5 T800s	165	4.4	260	7.9	44
12 T800s	60	11.8	125	16.4	17

Table 1. Performance of SLS-PRO for a simulation of crambin

performs effectively for typical simulation problems. Running on a twelve processor machine, SLS-PRO gives performance equivalent to a mini super-computer such as an Alliant or Convex. The generalised systolic loop method is not limited to protein structure, however, but is appropriate for simulations of *any* large flexible molecular system.

Acknowledgements

This work was performed while the author was a graduate student of the Department of Chemistry at the University of York, UK. The author is grateful for the support of Dr. R. Hubbard at York, and Dr. D. Fincham of the University of Keele, and W. Smith of SERC Daresbury laboratory for their help and advice. The author also thanks Polygen Corporation for the provision of equipment.

References

[1]   Brünger A. T. *et al. Science* **235** 458-460 (1987)
[2]   Clore G. M. and Gronenborn A. M. *Crit. Rev. Biochem.* **24** 479-564 (1989)
[3]   Verlet L. *Phys. Rev.* **159** (1967)
[4]   Raine A. R. C., Fincham D. and Smith W. *Comp. Phys. Chem.* **55** 13-30 (1989)
[5]   Ryckaert J. P. *et al. J. Comp. Phys.* **23** 327 (1977)
[6]   van Gunsteren W. F. *et al. PNAS USA* **80** 4315 (1983)

Prediction of protein secondary structure using transputers

Roman A Laskowski, Mark B Swindells, Janet M Thornton,
& David S Moss

Department of Crystallography,
Birkbeck College, Malet Street
London WC1E 7HX, UK.

Abstract. We are using a transputer-based parallel computer to investigate a new method for predicting the secondary structure of proteins. The method uses a simple pattern-matching strategy to search for patterns of amino acid residues that are consistently associated with particular secondary structures in a database of proteins of known structure. Successful patterns can then be used for prediction on protein sequences of unknown structure.
We have implemented the method on our in-house Meiko Computing Surface as the pattern-matching is CPU-intensive, particularly for more elaborate patterns. Using 3 slave transputers we have obtained approximately 6-fold speedups over our microVAX II computer.
Our preliminary results give a prediction accuracy of just under 59%, which is comparable with existing prediction methods, and we discuss proposed improvements.

1. Introduction

Prediction of the three-dimensional structure of protein molecules is one of the central problems of modern biocomputing. Knowledge of a protein's structure is important because it determines the protein's biological function and activity.

Currently, structures are determined experimentally, using methods such as X-ray crystallography and nuclear magnetic resonance, but these are time-consuming and expensive. As a result, only about 400 structures have been experimentally determined.

Often an alternative is to build a model of an unknown protein structure using a related protein of known structure. This works well only if the relationship, or homology, between the two sequences is high.

It would be extremely useful, therefore, given the known structures, to be able to predict those which are unknown from the sequence information alone - particularly as nearly 20,000 proteins have now been sequenced. After all, it is known that the sequence of amino acid residues is usually sufficient to determine three-dimensional, or tertiary, structure, so there should be a way of finding the relationship between the two.

2. Secondary structure prediction

Any complete prediction method is likely to be computer intensive. A stepping-stone towards this is the prediction of secondary structure. This describes the conformation of local regions along the protein's chain and is often restricted to just three classes: helical (H), extended (E), and random coil (C). (The second of these, the extended structure, is also called β-strand; several β-strands, arranged parallel or anti-parallel to one another, form β-sheets).

A standard method of automatically assigning secondary structure is provided by the DSSP program of Kabsch & Sander [1] which identifies the different elements from the three-dimensional coordinates of the protein atoms. Thus all proteins of known structure

TABLE 1

1-letter symbol	3-letter symbol	Name	%-tage	Order	1-letter symbol	3-letter symbol	Name	%-tage	Order
A	Ala	Alanine	8.85	1	M	Met	Methionine	1.85	19
C	Cys	Cysteine	2.08	18	N	Asn	Asparagine	4.59	11
D	Asp	Aspartate	5.78	8	P	Pro	Proline	4.53	12
E	Glu	Glutamate	5.51	9	Q	Gln	Glutamine	3.52	15
F	Phe	Phenylalanine	3.63	14	R	Arg	Arginine	3.89	13
G	Gly	Glycine	8.53	2	S	Ser	Serine	6.95	5
H	His	Histidine	2.31	17	T	Thr	Threonine	6.08	7
I	Ile	Isoleucine	4.97	10	V	Val	Valine	7.28	4
K	Lys	Lysine	6.83	6	W	Trp	Tryptophan	1.39	20
L	Leu	Leucine	7.92	3	Y	Tyr	Tyrosine	3.51	16

Table 1. Codes and names of the 20 amino acids found in proteins. The percentages show their frequency of occurrence in our database of known structures. The order column indicates their ranking order from the most frequently occurring to the least.

can be described in terms of these secondary structure elements. Attempts can then be made to see how the primary structure - ie the sequence of amino acid residues - is related to this secondary structure and how one might predict the latter from the former.

There are a number of methods, developed over the past 20 years or so, which aim to do this. The best known is that of Chou & Fasman [2]. This uses statistically derived propensities for each of the amino acid types to be in a particular structure.

Another commonly used statistical method is the GOR method which uses information theory [3,4]. Of the non-statistical methods, the major ones are that of Lim [5], which is based on the stereochemical properties of the different amino acids, and that of Levin [6,7], which assumes that similar subsequences will have similar secondary structures.

The one thing that all the methods have in common is that none has yet achieved a high degree of accuracy. Typically they are around 60% correct, which is above the random level of ~40%, but is still far from ideal.

3. Prediction based on pattern-matching

In this paper we report on our use of a transputer-based parallel computer to investigate a new prediction method. The method is based on a simple pattern-matching strategy originally proposed by Rooman & Wodak [8], involving patterns of amino acid residues.

The patterns are defined by two parameters: the maximum length of the pattern, and the number of amino acids specified within it. For example, given a maximum length of 5, with three residues specified, a total of 48,000 patterns can be generated, of which some examples might be: G--AQ, EHT--, and F-G-L. Here the letters represent different amino acid residues (see Table 1), and the dashes act as wild cards, allowing any residue type at that position.

The aim of the Rooman & Wodak study [8] was to look for patterns that are consistently associated with a given secondary structure. In their work they searched their database of known structures and accepted or rejected patterns as good predictors according to a set of acceptance rules. Each accepted pattern was then tested on a known structure, which could either be included in the database or excluded from it. This allowed the success of each pattern as a predictor to be assessed.

Our aim is to actually apply the accepted patterns to the business of predicting protein structure, rather than just look at their success rates. Because many individual patterns are involved, each residue position in the test sequence will be spanned by several patterns giving possibly conflicting predictions. Thus some means is required of resolving these conflicts.

4. Pattern-acceptance rules

The original pattern-acceptance rules are as follows. Wherever the pattern occurs in the database, a record is made of the secondary structure at each position along its length, L. Also noted is any secondary structure that occurs at least m times within that length, where $m = 1$ for $L \leq 4$, and $m = L/2$ for $L > 4$. The pattern is then accepted if:

1. It has occurred at least 3 times in the database.
2. It has some predictive property, as follows:

    2a. A structure type has occurred at a particular position in at least 80% of the cases.
    2b. A structure type has occurred at least m times within the pattern's length in at least 80% of the cases.

We have used these rules, but have also tried a set of rules based on probabilistic considerations. Here, rather than use a simple 80% criterion, we calculate a probability associated with each observation and make use of that. For example, if a pattern has occurred 5 times and a given structure is observed at a given position in 4 of those 5 cases, the 80% criterion would accept this pattern. However, this is much more likely to happen if the secondary structure involved is random coil (C) than if it is β-strand (E) which is far less common. The observed percentages are: random coil (C) at 51.16% of the residues, helix (H) at 29.88%, β-strand (E) at 18.96%. Under the old rules, this results in patterns that predict random coil far outnumbering all others.

Under the new rules, we calculate the probability of obtaining a given observation (eg the probability of observing a helix at position 1 in four or more instances of a pattern that occurs five times). This is then be used to accept or reject the pattern depending on whether the probability is above or below some cutoff value, the P-value. By amending the P-value cutoff, the acceptance rules can be made stricter or more loose. The new rules can also accept patterns that occur only twice in the database.

5. Using patterns for prediction

When the accepted patterns are used for prediction of an unknown structure, each residue position in the target sequence will have a large number of overlapping, and often contradictory, predictions made about it. The simplest way of deciding between them is to count the predictions for each type and take whichever is the most numerous.

However, predictions of random coil tend to dominate over all others, simply because of the higher frequency of this structure type. Thus some form of weighting of the counts needs to be introduced.

The weights can be determined empirically, but we prefer to use a method based on conditional probability. This gives similar results but does not require optimisation of the weights. The method makes use of "pattern success counts" obtained in the jack-knife procedure described below.

6. Testing prediction accuracy: the jack-knife test

The jack-knife test is the standard method of testing the accuracy of a prediction method. It involves using a database of sequences of known structure and removing each one in turn for use as a test sequence. Because the structure of each test sequence is known, the prediction accuracy can easily be found once all sequences have been cycled through.

In our method, this procedure is used in a two-step process. Firstly it is used for determining the "pattern success counts". These are simply counts of the number of times a structure was predicted as p_i when it was actually s_j, where $i, j = C, E$, or H. This gives a single 3 x 3 matrix of counts at the end of the first jack-knife procedure. From this can be obtained the probability of any pattern predicting a particular structure, say C, given that the actual structure is say E. In other words, we have nine conditional probabilities, $P(p_i|s_j)$ for $i, j = C, E$, or H.

The jack-knife procedure is now repeated. This time the predictions made for each residue in each test sequence are stored. Say that a particular residue is spanned by four accepted patterns, of which two predict coil (C), one predicts β-strand (E), and one predicts helix (H). The probability of observing this set of predictions (ie C, C, E, H), given that the residue is coil, say, can now be calculated from the conditional probabilities, $P(p_i|s_j)$, derived before. It is just:

$$P(O_{CCEH}|s_C) = \frac{4! P(p_C|s_C)^2 P(p_E|s_C) P(p_H|s_C)}{2!1!1!} \quad (1)$$

Similar expressions apply for $P(O_{CCEH}|s_E)$ and $P(O_{CCEH}|s_H)$.

Now, because we know the relative frequencies of the three structure types in our database, $P(s_C), P(s_E)$, and $P(s_H)$, we can use Bayes' theorem to calculate the probability of the residue being of a particular structure, s_j, given the observed predictions made for it. That is,

$$P(s_j|O_{CCEH}) = \frac{P(O_{CCEH}|s_j) P(s_j)}{P(O_{CCEH}|s_C) P(s_C) + P(O_{CCEH}|s_E) P(s_E) + P(O_{CCEH}|s_H) P(s_H)} \quad (2)$$

The final prediction is whichever of these $P(s_j|O_{CCEH})$ probabilities is the highest. Ideally, the value should also give a measure of the certainty of the prediction.

In the jack-knife test, this final prediction can, of course, be checked and the overall predictive success of the method assessed.

7. The database used

As mentioned above, only about 400 structures have been determined experimentally. However, not all can be included in our database as we need to exclude proteins that are related to one another to guard against biasing certain patterns. Also, the quality of the structures varies. Thus our database has been selected using the following two criteria. Firstly, that the resolution of each protein's structure be 3Å or better, and secondly that no two proteins should have a sequence homology greater than 20%.

Our resulting database holds only 76 of the 400 proteins, comprising 14,947 residues in the proportions shown in Table 1.

8. Parallel running

The pattern searching procedure is CPU-intensive not only because of the large number of patterns that need to be searched for in a database of 14,947 residues, but primarily because of the jack-knife test which requires that the whole operation be repeated 76 times. The CPU time increases further as more elaborate patterns are tried, and this is what makes parallel running so attractive. Typical run times on our microVAX II are around 2 hours 40 minutes for the fairly simple patterns we have tried so far, and this run time can be reduced significantly by parallel running.

We have thus written the program to run on our in-house Meiko Computing Surface. Our machine currently has a single quad-board of four T800 transputers, one T800 file-server, and one T414 host. We hope to get more transputers shortly.

The parallelisation was fairly quickly and simply achieved using the Meiko F77farm Fortran harness which handles all the communication between the master processor and the slaves via simple Fortran calls. On our machine we can have up to three slave processors. The time spent converting to parallel running has now been fully recouped in terms of the reduced run-times that we obtain.

We chose to adopt a fairly coarse-grained parallelisation of the program to start off with as the central routines are continually being modified as various minor amendments to the prediction method are made. The program works by having each slave processor perform the prediction on a different test sequence. The master processor initially distributes the

TABLE 2

Machine	Time	Factor faster	Speedup
μVAX II VMS 5.2	34m 37s	1.00	-
VAX workstation 3100	9m 3s	3.82	-
Meiko Computing Surface			
1 slave T800	16m 53s	2.05	1.00
2 slave T800s	8m 34s	4.04	1.97
3 slave T800s	5m 50s	5.93	2.89

Table 2. Timings for a test prediction run on two VAX computers and the Meiko Computing Surface with 1 to 3 slave transputers. The run was a full jack-knife procedure on all 76 proteins using patterns of maximum length 10, with 2 residues defined (ie 3600 patterns in all). Note that the timings show *elapsed* times for the Meiko machine, and CPU times for the VAX computers. The factor on the right gives the performance relative to the μVAX II, while the speedup is that obtained for parallel running on more than one slave transputer.

TABLE 3

Max Length	Residues Specified	No. of patterns	Ratio increase	Time	Factor longer
10	2	3,600	-	5m 50s	-
10	3	288,000	80	27m 2s	4.63
10	4	13,440,000	3733	10hrs 28m 3s	107.67

Table 3. Effect of number of patterns on run length. The timings are for pattern types of maximum length 10, having 2, 3, and 4 residues specified. The "ratio increase" shows the increase in the number of patterns, while the "factor longer" shows the increase in run time. All timings were made on the Meiko Computing Surface using 3 slave transputers.

entire database to each slave and then allocates the test sequences on a task-farming basis, processing the results as they are returned.

Good load balancing is achieved by sorting all the sequences into descending order of length at the start of the program. This ensures that the most time-consuming work is farmed out first, and that the shortest sequences are left till last.

Of course, such a coarse-grained parallelisation means that the program is limited to running on 76 transputers or less. However, once the prediction algorithm has been refined, a finer-grained parallelisation will be made so as to improve scaleability. Indeed, when used for the real work of predicting unknown structures, there will be no need for having the jack-knife procedure in operation.

9. Timings

Table 2 shows the timings obtained for a sample pattern type of maximum length 10 with 2 residues specified. The timings were performed on two of our in-house VAXes, and on our Meiko Computing Surface with 1 to 3 slave transputers. Overall, the speedup achieved has not been as great as hoped for, being a factor of just under 6 for 3 slave transputers when compared with the microVAX II. We had hoped for something like a 9-fold speedup. This suggests that the program requires some optimisation for the transputer, such as unrolling some of the innermost loops.

Nevertheless, even a factor of 6 is significant, particularly for the more elaborate patterns that we intend to investigate. And, of course, when we get more transputers, the situation will improve further. Table 3 shows how increasing the number of specified residues in the pattern increases the running time on our current machine.

TABLE 4

Method	Predicted C (%-tage) (51.16)	Predicted E (%-tage) (18.96)	Predicted H (%-tage) (29.88)	Random (38.70)	Correct	Diff
Pattern-matching (3 in 10)						
Orig. rules	52.69	13.57	33.74	39.61	58.39	18.78
Prob. rules (P=0.2)	37.60	29.89	32.51	34.62	55.41	20.79
Prob. rules (P=0.6)	44.22	22.47	33.31	36.84	58.88	22.04
GOR method	36.00	23.88	40.12	34.93	57.70	22.77
Lim method	55.82	17.67	26.51	39.83	58.45	18.62
Levin method	62.38	13.37	24.25	41.69	63.80	22.11

Table 4. Results of secondary structure prediction using the pattern-matching algorithm and three standard methods. The first three columns of figures show the percentages of secondary structure predicted by each method (the true proportions are given in brackets). The next column gives the results expected from random prediction based solely on these percentages. The final two columns show the correct percentage obtained and the difference between this and the random result. The results from the pattern matching algorithm are for patterns of maximum length 10 with 3 residues specified. The rules used were: the original rules, and probabilistic rules for P-values of 0.2 and 0.6.

10. Results

In preliminary trials we have tried both the original pattern acceptance rules and the probabilistic ones, described above. The results obtained have been compared with three of the existing methods already mentioned: that of Lim [5], Garnier, Osguthorpe, & Robson [3,4], and Levin [6,7]. The Chou & Fasman method [2] was omitted as it often gives an ambiguous prediction.

Table 4 gives the successes of the method for patterns of maximum length 10 with 3 residues specified. The original pattern-acceptance rules give an accuracy of 58.39% overall and compare favourably with the Lim and GOR methods.

Using the probabilistic rules with a P-value cutoff of 0.2 a poorer performance is obtained, with success dropping to 55.41% and the β-strands being massively overpredicted at the expense of the more common random coil. However, the probabilistic rules achieve higher accuracy for higher P-values. The best result is 58.88%, obtained for P=0.6 (see Table 4).

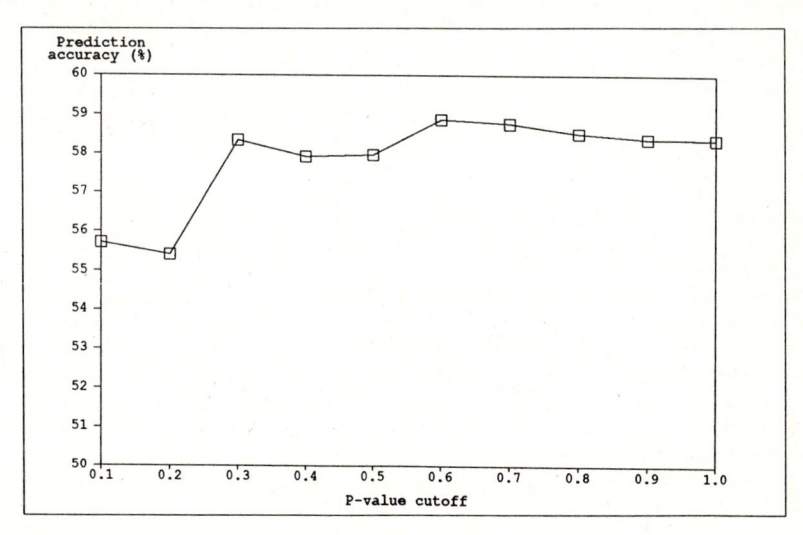

Figure 1. Prediction accuracy over all 76 proteins as a function of the P-value cutoff.

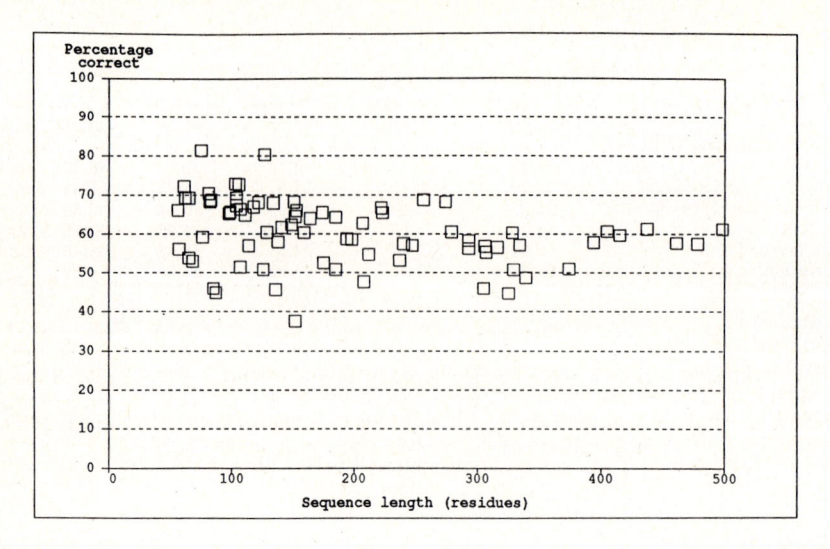

Figure 2. Percentage of protein correctly predicted as a function of the sequence length.

This is an improvement on the Lim and GOR methods, but still some way short of the Levin method which is the best at 63.80%.

Figure 1 shows how amending the P-value affects the prediction accuracy. The maximum occurs at P=0.6, though above P=0.2 the accuracy varies little. Figure 2 shows the distribution of prediction accuracy as a function of protein length for P=0.6. It can be seen that the success on short proteins is variable, while that on longer proteins tends towards the overall average. This is what one might expect as longer proteins are more likely to have a mixture of secondary structures that more closely resembles the overall distribution.

Figure 3 shows a fairly typical example of a secondary structure prediction.

11. Future work

Future amendments proposed to the prediction algorithm include considering amino acid properties, rather than just specific amino acid types, within the patterns. This should generate more patterns each of which will occur more frequently in the database. We expect these to be better predictors.

We also intend to investigate *pairs* of patterns as predictors. The separation allowed between each pattern in the pair would be variable, though kept within specified limits. The aim here is to include longer-range interactions and see what effect these have on predictive properties.

Another line of enquiry concerns patterns that are rejected simply because they do not occur often enough. It is very likely that many of these contain useful information. But which are the good ones, and which are the noise? One assumption that can be made is that the useful patterns will be those which occur often in nature. Thus, by looking at the database of 20,000 known protein sequences, one can identify those patterns which occur more frequently than one would expect by chance. It would be interesting to see whether these patterns are better predictors.

All these enhancements will make the program more CPU-intensive and will thus benefit even more from parallel running.

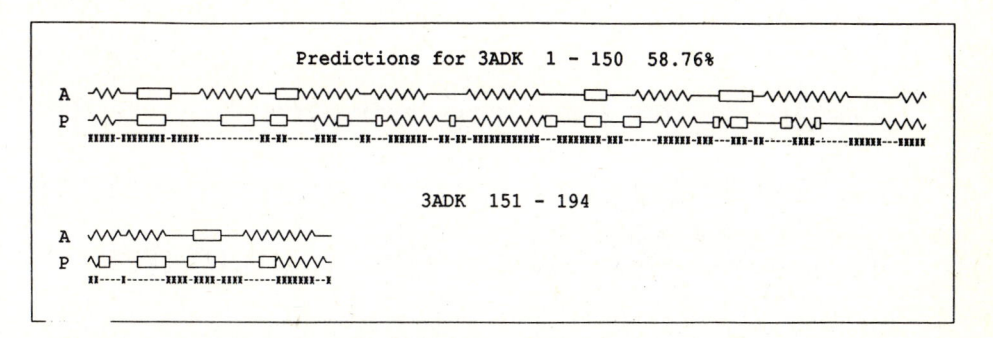

```
              Predictions for 3ADK   1 - 150    58.76%
A  ─ᴧᴧᴧ─▭──ᴧᴧᴧᴧ──▭ᴧᴧᴧ──ᴧᴧᴧ────ᴧᴧᴧᴧ───▭──ᴧᴧᴧ───▭──ᴧᴧᴧᴧ──ᴧ
P  ─ᴧᴧ──▭────▭─▭─ᴧᴧ▭─▭ᴧᴧᴧ─▭─ᴧᴧᴧᴧ▭──▭─▭─ᴧᴧ──▭▭──▭ᴧ▭───ᴧᴧ
   ‖‖‖‖‖-‖‖‖‖‖‖‖‖-‖‖‖‖‖----------‖‖-‖‖-----‖‖---‖‖‖‖----‖‖‖‖‖‖--‖‖-‖‖-‖‖‖‖‖‖‖‖‖---‖‖‖‖‖‖‖-‖‖‖------‖‖‖‖‖-‖‖‖---‖‖‖-‖‖----‖‖‖‖-‖----‖‖‖‖‖‖---‖‖‖‖‖

                      3ADK   151 - 194
A   ᴧᴧᴧᴧᴧ────▭──ᴧᴧᴧᴧᴧ──
P   ▭▭─▭──▭──▭────▭ᴧᴧᴧ─
    ‖----‖-------‖‖‖‖-‖‖‖‖-‖‖‖------‖‖‖‖‖‖--‖
```

Figure 3. A sample secondary structure prediction giving an accuracy comparable to the overall value obtained. The protein is porcine adenylate kinase whose actual structure is shown at A, and predicted structure at P. Coil is indicated by the single line, helices are shown as jagged lines, and strands as boxes. Correctly predicted regions are asterisked.

Acknowledgements

We would like to thank Dr Mark Johnson and Mr David Smith for assistance in deriving the database used here. R A Laskowski is supported by a SERC CASE studentships and is part-sponsored by Meiko Ltd; M B Swindells is a SERC CASE student with Wellcome Biotech.

References

[1] KABSCH W, & SANDER C (1983). *Biopolymers*, **22**, 2577–2637.
[2] CHOU P Y, & FASMAN G D (1978). *Adv. Enzymol.*, **47**, 45–148.
[3] GARNIER J, OSGUTHORPE J D, & ROBSON B (1978). *J. Mol. Biol.*, **120**, 97–120.
[4] GIBRAT J-F, GARNIER J, & ROBSON B (1987). *J. Mol. Biol.*, **198**, 425–443.
[5] LIM V I (1974). *J. Mol. Biol.*, **88**, 857–894.
[6] LEVIN J M, ROBSON B, & GARNIER J (1986). *FEBS Lett.*, **205**, 303–308.
[7] LEVIN J M, & GARNIER J (1988). *Biochem. Biophys. Acta*, **995**, 283–295.
[8] ROOMAN M J, & WODAK S J (1988). *Nature*, **335**, 45–49.

Preemptive process scheduling and meeting hard real-time constraints with TRANS-RTXc on the Transputer.

Eric Verhulst,
Intelligent Systems International nv/sa
Interleuvenlaan 62, 3030 Leuven, Belgium
Tel.(32)16.290128. Fax.(32)16.208057
Hans Thielemans
K.U.Leuven/PMA
Celestijnenlaan 300B, 3030 Leuven. Belgium.

Abstract. While the Transputer is an ideal hardware component for building distributed systems, there is a need for preemptive scheduling to support system designers of real-time systems. This is now available as a feature of a proven real-time kernel RTXC which was ported by ISI to the Transputer under the name TRANS-RTXc. Several design features as well as the benefits from using TRANS-RTXc are discussed.

1. Using Transputers for process control.

Transputers have very attractive features for using them as building blocks in distributed control systems. As a component, the Transputer is a complete computing system consisting of a processor with its local memory, an on-chip floating point unit and an on-chip network interface. In addition, the programming model, derived from the CSP (Communicating Sequential Processes [1]), reflects very well the nature of most control systems. This enables easier and safer software development and easier remapping when the system needs to be modified. If no hard real-time constraints are to be satisfied, the overhead due to the use of communicating processes is relatively low as the Transputer provides support in microcode for process scheduling and for communication. If however hard real-time constraints are to be satisfied, the designer is faced with a major difficulty, as the microcoded scheduler is FIFO scheduler. Whereas this scheme was chosen for simplicity and performance, a FIFO scheduler cannot guarantee the scheduling of a process within a known time interval. With the FIFO scheduler, a process can be worst case delayed for a time-interval equal to $(2*N - 2)*TS + TSCH$. TS being the timeslice (1 ms), N the number of processes in the low priority queue and TSCH being the time interval to the next descheduling point. [2],[3],[9]. The net result is that the Transputer FIFO scheduler enables fast throughput but results in unpredictable interrupt service response intervals. This problem has been identified by various authors. See [3],[4],[10].
To illustrate the problem, Table 1 represents typical lower and upperlimits of the interrupt service response interval (ISRI) in microseconds when 5 respectively 10 processes are in the FIFO queue. For Tsch, it was assumed that a normal distribution was valid with an upperbound of 100 microseconds. These figures are to be compared with the results obtained when using TRANS-RTXc on a 25 MHz Transputer.

	without TRANS-RTXc		with TRANS-RTXc		direct switch
ISRI limits	lower	upper	lower	upper	
5 processes in queue	1	8100	36	140	6
10 processes in queue	1	18100	36	140	6

Table 1. Typical ISRI limit values.

2. Using multiple priorities.

To be correct, the Transputer has features that enable to meet hard real-time constraints, provided one is willing to give up most of the benefits of the CSP model. The Transputer knows two priority levels, each with its own process queue. Whereas a low priority process will be descheduled by a higher priority process at the next instruction, a high priority process cannot be interrupted. A feasible design methodology is then to let a high priority processes accept the interrupt ("interrupt handling") and forward the actual handling to a low priority process for "interrupt servicing". However to achieve timely execution, the resulting program will consist of a short high priority process with at most one low priority process. The unpredictable timing of the multi-tasking program is avoided by implementing a single-task program. Hence, the designer is back at sequential programming and processor cycles will be wasted. More complex programming techniques are possible, such as artificially shorten the hardware fixed timeslice using a cyclic timer. The net result is once again more complex programs. The worst side-effect however is that the problem is solved in an application dependent manner. See [12] for an example.

A general solution consists in using multiple priorities. This was demonstrated by various authors. See [4], [5], [6], [7]. The use of multiple priorities and the use of an appropriate scheduling algorithm can guarantee, under the right conditions, the timely execution of all processes. As such, the determination of the priority of each process is application dependent. On a single processor a rate monotonic scheduler where the priorities are inverse related to the periodicity of the processes, will result in a feasible scheduling order if the workload is under 70 %. An algorithm that better deals with aperiodic events is the earliest deadline. This can guarantee the scheduling of all processes even if the workload is close to 100 %. [7]. In general, the problem in known to be NP-complete, especially if all factors such as aperiodic events and common resources are taken into account. In these cases, a priority inheritance mechanism is advisable [5],[11]. Fortunately, the general case is often an exception so that most applications can be implemented using simpler algorithms.

3. Design considerations for embedded real-time systems.

Embedded real-time systems have a number of characteristics that enable the designer to relax some of the conditions to be met :

- often the application will be static;
- input and controlling actions are known in great detail, including their duration as well as their timing;
- most of the code will be cyclic;
- the application is often stand-alone.

As such, most of the program will be spent in a periodic loop, while aperiodic events (such as alarm conditions) are relatively rare.

Hence, such a control program will consist of a number of tasks, each with its own static priority. The designer will assign highest priority to the critical aperiodic events, while the periodic tasks receive an application dependent priority.

Various real-time kernels are on the market that provide these services. In an era where processing technology is changing at a very rapid pace, a portable kernel, written in a high-level language, is essential. RTXC from A.T. Barret (Houston, USA) is such a kernel. RTXC is the result of years of experience in designing embedded real-time systems. It is mostly written in standard C and available for a wide range of processors. The latter is a benefit for porting applications to various target processors. As a consequence, ISI decided to port RTXC to the Transputer. As the Transputer is a processor with real parallel processing capabilities, multi-processor kernel calls in addition to multi-language support were added. The result is TRANS-RTXc, the first true real-time kernel for the Transputer.

4. Preemptive scheduling : the key issue.

Porting the kernel code written in C was a straight-forward. However for the processor dependent low level routines, written in assembler, two major obstacles had to be overcome. The first was to find the algorithm that converted the FIFO scheduling mechanism into a preemptive scheduling mechanism. The second was how to implement the kernel in such a way that user tasks could safely interact with the special I/O hardware of the Transputer. Both problems were solved in a satisfactory way using occam and Parallel C with a minor amount of assembler inserts. In addition we were happily surprised to find that the implementation on the Transputer is one of the fastest available when compared with other processors running at the same speed.

In order to understand the importance of this key issue, it is worthwhile to have a closer look at the actual Transputer mechanisms. On the Transputer, the compiler will generate for each user defined process a "startp" instruction. In order to start, a process needs to be initialised with its Workspace Pointer (Wptr) and its Instruction Pointer (Iptr). Whenever a new process is started (normally from within the first started process), a FIFO process queue, implemented as a linked list, is build up. This is achieved by adding the new process at the back of the queue. Figure 1 illustrates the FIFO-list on the Transputer. S is executing while P, Q and R are awaiting to be scheduled.

Once started, a process can be descheduled for the following reasons :
- because it has to wait on a communication with another process, via an external link, via a soft channel in memory, or via the event pin;
- because it has to wait on a timer event.
- because of an interrupt from a high priority process which is ready to execute;
- because its timeslice has expired and a descheduling point has been reached.

In both queues all processes are executed in the order they received when placed in the queue. Parallel processing on a single Transputer is then emulated through the time-slicing mechanism. Note that not all processes all present in the queue at all time. Only those processes that are ready to execute will be.

Hence to completely know the state of an executable process on the Transputer, one needs to know the following elements [2]:
- Wptr;
- Iptr;
- Areg, Breg, Creg;
- Ereg and the process status, if appropriate;
- FAreg, FBreg, FCreg;
- the place in the queue.

Fortunately, these elements can be known be exploiting the fact that when a low priority process is interrupted by a high priority process, its elements are saved in the lower memory locations. Once

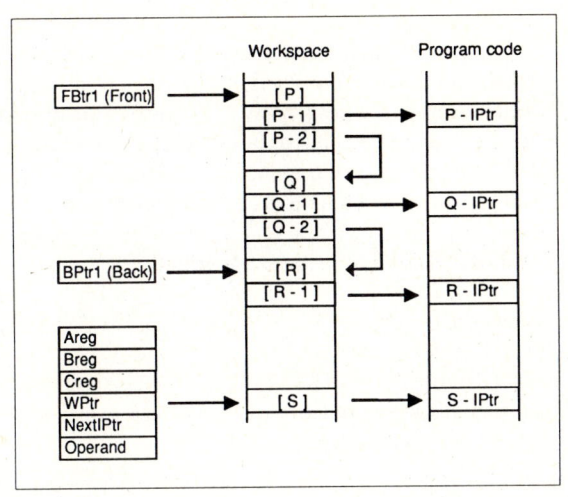

Figure 1. Transputer FIFO queue as a linked list.

these elements are known, it is possible to rearrange the linked list of the process queue such that, using a look-up table, the highest priority process is always in front of the queue. Care has to be taken that the linked list structure is not broken at any moment, especially as the Transputer may start to manipulate the queue, independently of the currently executing instruction [8].

5. Letting the user tasks communicate.

In essence there is no difference between a user task communicating with the outside world or with a process having a different priority. Both will result in a process being removed from the current process queue, hence breaking the linked list continuity as known by the kernel. Therefore, all tasks are implemented as low priority processes while these tasks can communicate among each other via the kernel running at high priority.

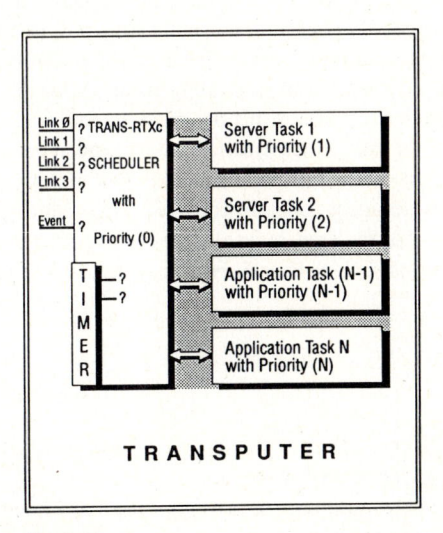

Figure 2 : TRANS-RTXc on a Transputer

For this reason, TRANS-RTXc contains some Transputer specific calls, such as rtxc_linkin and rtxc_linkout. On the other hand, if within a user defined task of a given priority several processes are started that communicate with each other, the Transputer hardware still takes care of the linked list continuity. The final result is that at each priority level, the normal interprocess communication facilities are available. This is primarily of interest as it simplifies the software design. The kernel itself is not resident but forms an integral part of the application program that is linked with the task code. Figure 2 gives a schematic overview of TRANS-RTXc running on a single Transputer.

6. Support provided by TRANS-RTXc (See also appendix).

6.1. Single processor services.

These services are identical to those found in RTXC. These include task manipulation, communication and synchronisation services, timer functions and resource management. They are activated through a protocol based message to the kernel.

6.2. Multi Transputer support.

Following the CSP paradigm, there is no logical difference between processes running on the same processor or running on different processors. In real-time situations, there might be a different behaviour of the system as timing characteristics change. Most of the time, as interprocessor communication takes less time than a process to execute, placing tasks on different processors will result in better through-puts and hence faster interrupt servicing. For this reason, remote invocation of the kernel essential services is supported. In a first release, the programmer will need to supply the processor identifier and the link to be used for routing the call. This mechanism is fast and sufficient for embedded applications. In a second release, we investigate the usefulness of handling this in a transparent way so that all remote invocations are seen by the programmer as normal kernel calls. This however will result in more memory usage and slower invocations.

6.3. Additional benefits from using the Transputer.

As was already indicated, the user can still use the normal Transputer mechanisms within each priority level. We exercise complete control over the Transputer from within the TRANS-RTXc kernel. As such, we are able to provide programming services usually not available for the Transputer programmer. First of all, we are able to monitor each scheduling event, so that the programmer knows exactly what has happened during the execution of his program. In addition, we are now in a position to manipulate the execution of the tasks at the instruction level and at the task level. This enables us to single step through the user tasks while providing a direct link with the original source code. At the time of writing, the latter development under the form of a single step debugger was not finished yet. The support for the CSP model on the Transputer also means that through the use of interface libraries, tasks written in other languages such as Pascal, Fortran, Modula-2 and occam can make use of the kernel calls.

7. Performance results.

In order to manipulate the process queue explicitly, it was necessary to use additional instructions. Nevertheless, the resulting performance is excellent.
The native Transputer interrupt response can be fast (typically 1 to 3 microseconds) [9], but in reality this is the lower limit as to the actual scheduling of a specific process, one has to take account of the

queue "latency", often resulting in tens of milliseconds of reaction times. In the occam version and in the Parallel C version, we obtained basic switching times of 6 microseconds on a Transputer running at 25 MHz and using the internal RAM. This means that the actual penalty is less than 5 microseconds, while we gain the certainty that the process will be scheduled within a known interval. The actual TRANS-RTXc call takes longer as the kernel has to verify all pending messages, timers and the priority. Typically, a kernel call will take a minimum of 22 microseconds on a 25 MHz Transputer using 3 cycle external memory and in absence of floating point code. When the FPU is in use, the times obtained are increased with 16 microseconds (64 bit reals). Below, a summarising table taken from the provided demo program, gives performance details for the current version of TRANS-RTXc. These compare favourably with the figures obtained with other processors.

8. Designer utilities.

As was already mentioned, with TRANS-RTXc, we are in a position to fully control the execution of processes on the Transputer. The original RTXC already contained a debugging facility operating at the task level. This is actually a normal task that runs at the highest priority and can be invoked when connected to a terminal. As mentioned, we have been able to extend the functionality by providing logging facilities and single step capability at the instruction level.

TRANS-RTXc also contains a system generation utility. This is a program that interactively let the designer specify all his tasks, their priorities, the semaphores, the system resources, etc. The program then generates all system tables in source form. The only thing left to do is to write the task code, debug and fine-tune the system.

9. Are the objectives met ?

The first objective was to achieve preemptive scheduling with multiple priorities on the Transputer. The objective was clearly met. As far as we are aware of other developments, this is the first time this was achieved.

The second objective was to achieve portability across current and future target processors. At first this seemed not so obvious as the Transputer has a totally different architecture, richer in many aspects, but lacking the traditional interrupt support. After a first Transputer specific implementation, we found that a generic port was possible. This means that the same source code will run with almost no modifications on all processors supported by RTXC. Even console and screen I/O are supported with exactly the same calls via the afserver. This was tested on a PC-host as well as on a VME based system running UNIX/V. Besides the portability issue, we benefit from the fact that the major part of RTXC

Minimum TRANS-RTXc kernel call	22 µs
average allocate and deallocate	33 µs
enqueue 1 byte	39 µs
dequeue 1 byte	37 µs
enqueue 4 byte	38 µs
dequeue 4 byte	36 µs
signal semaphore	26 µs
average lock and unlock resource	29 µs
enqueue 1 byte to a waiting higher priority task	167 µs
send message to a higher priority task and wait for acknowledgment	179 µs
send message to lower priority task and wait for acknowledgement	153 µs
signal/wait + wait/signal handshake between two tasks	173 µs
send message over link to lower priority task with fpu swap	192 µs
send message over link to lower priority task without fpu swap	176 µs

Table 2. Performance figures TRANS-RTXc services (at 25 MHz)

is written in a high level language and has been proven for many years. As such we could concentrate our efforts on the Transputer specific part, wich is relatively limited.

One could argue that by manipulating explicitely the process queue, security has been lost. This is not the case as long as the user tries not to manipulate any of the process variables and communicates only between tasks using the kernel calls. Moreover, we found that as we have total control over the scheduling, we are in a much better position to debug user programs. As anyone knows who is experienced in writing parallel programs, while one wins in the design phase by the ability of defining processes, one looses during the debugging phase, due to the absence of control over the FIFO scheduler. It is sometimes easier to debug a program distributed over different processors as to when the same program is run on a single processor. With TRANS-RTXc, the user is in a position to monitor each scheduling event as well as all pending messages and timer events. So all benefits from writing parallel programs are retained while at the same time total control, usually only available on purely sequential systems, is provided as well.

10. Future work.

TRANS-RTXc is now available from ISI in conjunction with RTXC for use on other processors. We intend to support TRANS-RTXc with different compilers as well as with different host systems. User input is actively sought to further improve the product. The application of the preemptive scheduling algorithm for a fault-tolerant kernel as well as for a more general purpose real-time operating system is under investigation.

CONCLUSION.

TRANS-RTXc is the first true real-time kernel on the Transputer enabling to meet hard real-time constraints without the need of application specific code. The performance is better than on most other processors. Moreover, the designer gains by having total control over the Transputer while retaining the advantages offered by it. In addition, as use is made of a proven and portable kernel, this solution provides for future-proof real-time applications.

Bibliography.

[1]. Hoare C.A.R. Communicating Sequential Processes. Prentice Hall, 1985.
[2]. INMOS, T800 Engineering Data, 1989.
[3]. Törngen Martin, Transputer and occam based control systems in electronic control of machines. OUG Newsletter Nr. 12. January 1990.
[4]. Burns Alan, Wellings, A.J., Occam's priority model and deadline scheduling. OUG 7. Grenoble. September 1987.
[5]. Burns Allan, Wellings. A.J., Real-time systems and their programming languages. Addison Wesley, 1990. Chapter 12.
[6]. Liu C.L., Layland James W. Scheduling Algorithms for multiprogramming in a hard real-time environment. Journal of the ACM. Vol. 20, No 1, January 1973.
[7]. Zhao wei, Ramamritham Krithi, Jhon A. Stankovic, preemptive scheduling under time and resource constraints. IEEE Transactions, Vol. C-36, No. 8, August 1987.
[8]. INMOS, The Transputer instruction set : a compiler writers guide. 1988.
[9]. INMOS, Communicating Process Architecture. Prentice Hall, 1988. Chapter 2 & Chapter 8.
[10]. A. Bakkers and J. Van Amerongen, Transputer based control of Mechatronics Systems. University of Twente, 1989. Private preprint copy.
[11]. Alan Burns, Distributed hard real-time systems : what restrictions are necessary ? Real-time systems, theory and applications. North Holland, 1990.
[12]. Welch P, Managing hard real-time demands on Transputers. OUG 7. Grenoble, 1987.

Appendix. Kernel calls available with TRANS-RTXc

Task Management
  block(from_task_nr,to_task_nr)
  reset(task,to_condition)
  resume(task)
  suspend(task)
  terminate(task)
  unblock(from_task_nr,to_task_nr)
  execute(task)

Memory and Resource Management
  alloc(mem_partition)
  allocw(mem_partition)
  dealloc(memory_partition,block)
  inqmap(partition)
  lock(resource)
  unlock(resource)

Intertask Communication and Synchronisation
  wait(sema)
  wait_any(semalist)
  signal(sema)
  signalm(semalist)
  pend(sema)
  pendm(semalist)
  send(message,task)
  send_wait(message,task,sema)
  receive_next([sender_task])
  dequeue(queue,destination)
  enqueue(queue,source)
  defqueue(queue,width,depth,body)
  inqqueue(queue)
  purgqueue(queue)

Timer support
  delay(task, timer)
  elapse(counter)
  set_timer(task,sema,timer)
  wait_timer()
  purge(task,[sema])

Special
  nop()
  user_func(function,arglist)

Transputer specific
  rtxc_linkin(link,size,message)
  rtxc_linkout(link,size,message)
  rtxc_event(result)

Distributed Processing Specific
  remote_block(processor,link,from_task_nr,to_task_nr)
  remote_reset(processor,link,task,condition)
  remote_resume(processor,link,task)
  remote_suspend(processor,link,task)
  remote_terminate(processor,link,task)
  remote_unblock(processor,link,from_task_nr,to_task_nr)
  remote_execute(processor,link,task)
  remote_wait(processor,link,sema)
  remote_wait_any(processor,link,semalist)
  remote_signal(processor,link,sema)
  remote_signalm(processor,link,semalist)
  remote_pend(processor,link,sema)
  remote_pendm(processor,link,semalist)
  remote_send(processor,link,message,task)
  remote_send_wait(processor,link,message,task,sema)
  remote_receive(processor,link,[sender task])
  remote_dequeue(processor,link,queue,destination)
  remote_enqueue(processor,link,queue,source)
  remote_defqueue(processor,link,queue,width,depth,body)
  remote_inqqueue(processor,link,queue)
  remote_purgqueue(processor,link,queue)

Distributed Programming on Transputer Networks – An Object Oriented Interface to the Helios Operating System

Alan Tully

Computing Laboratory, University of Newcastle upon Tyne,
Claremont Road, Newcastle upon Tyne, UK. NE1 7RU.
Tel: +44 91 2227873. Fax: +44 91 222 8232.
E-Mail A.Tully@uk.ac.newcastle.

Abstract: This paper considers the implementation of a C++ interface to Helios clients and servers. The interface consists of a number of C++ class types from which application classes may be derived. Together they provide an abstract view of Helios which hides the complexities of client/server creation and communication.

1 Introduction

The Transputer has established itself as a leading component in the construction of massively parallel computers for numerically-intensive applications. The use of crossbar switches allows the physical architecture to be configured for a given application. However, the permissible architectures are limited by the number of Transputer links and the size of the switches.

More general applications, whose process architecture cannot be directly mapped onto a physical configuration of the hardware, require additional communication software; to multiplex inter-process channels over physical links and to forward messages between processes not resident on adjacent processors. For small applications, the programmer can produce this software. However, for larger applications, a more standardized form of inter-process communication service is needed. The Helios [1] operating system provides such a service.

Helios supports the client/server model for the structuring of application programs [2]. When applications are written in a high-level object-oriented language such as C++ [3], an abstract view of this model which hides the complexities of client/server creation and communication would be beneficial to the programmer. This paper considers the implementation of such an abstraction as a number of C++ class types from which application classes may be derived.

2 The Helios Operating System

A Task as defined by Helios is a self-contained program unit which has been separately compiled and linked. A task may be multi-threaded but all threads share the same data space and are constrained to run on the same processor.

An application may be structured as a set of tasks (task force) which communicate using facilities provided by Helios. True concurrency may then be obtained by distributing the task force over several processors.

There are three distinct ways in which a task force may be structured; using pipes, using the Component Distribution Language (CDL) and using clients and servers. In general, the choice of method for a particular application must balance the flexibility of the solution against the complexity of it's implementation.

Both pipes and CDL use streams (*stdin, stdout etc.*) for inter-task communication and produce static software architectures. Clients communicate with named servers using Helios primitives. So an application program using clients and servers provides a more dynamic software architecture.

Helios itself is based on the client/server model. Server tasks are provided by Helios to control access to system resources such as screens, keyboards and disks and usually reside on the processor closest to the resource that they manage. Application programs act as clients to these servers by sending requests and receiving replies (Remote Procedure Calls [2]) and may be located anywhere in the processor network. A client task may send requests to many servers during it's lifetime, so the structure of the Helios + application task force is continually changing under the direct control of the application.

Passive part which also has access to the Data Part distinguishes a server from any other task. Whenever a request is received from a client a new thread (Passive Part) is spawned by Helios to deal with it. The Passive part is thus provided by the application but invoked automatically by Helios and may be thought of as a Remote Procedure Call (RPC) handler. In general, the passive part will continue to exist after completion of the RPC, remaining dormant until a further request is received from the same client. When the client has no further use for the server, the connection is broken and the RPC handler destroyed. If requests are received from a number of clients, a separate RPC handler is spawned for each client.

The sequence of actions which comprise a typical client/server interaction are shown by Figure 2. The name of the new server (screen) is passed by the Active Part to the name server along with a port descriptor, then a dispatcher process is spawned to listen on that port. Thereafter, a locate request issued by a prospective client returns the server's port descriptor. On receipt of an open request, the dispatcher spawns a new Passive Part which returns a unique port descriptor to the client, to be used in all future requests. A remote procedure call is implemented using two messages; a request from client to server followed by a reply from server to client. When the client has no further use for the server, a special kill message causes the Passive Part to terminate.

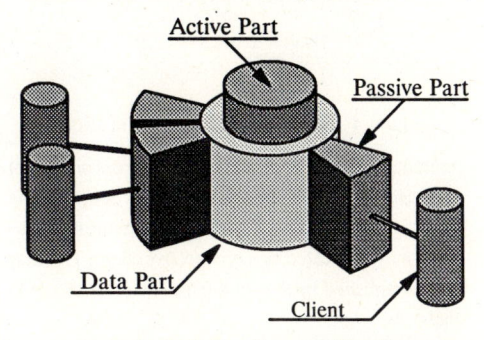

Figure 1 A Helios Server with Clients

Fortunately, all the mechanisms used by Helios to provide the client/server framework are also made available to application task forces. There are three main parts to a typical server as shown in Figure 1. The Active part corresponds to the main body of a conventional single-threaded task. It continues to execute during the lifetime of the server. The Data part corresponds to the data space of the task. The

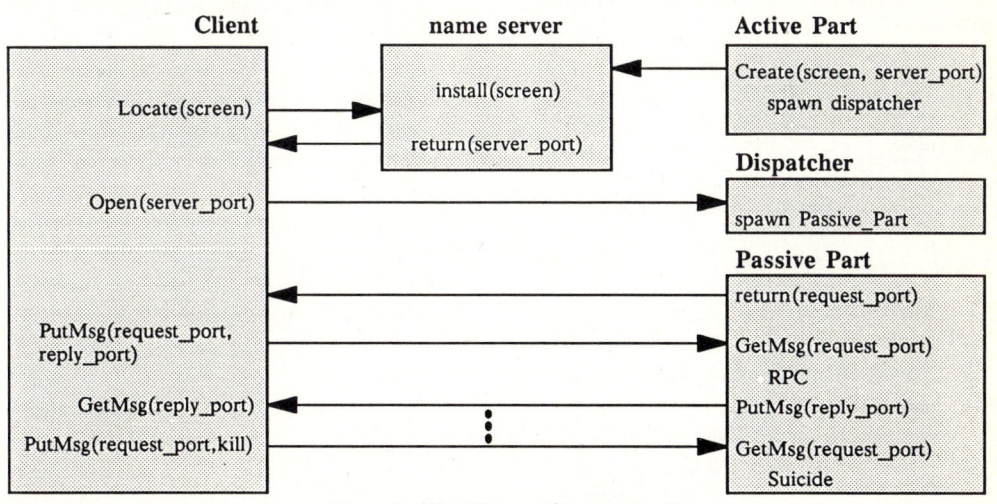

Figure 2 Client/Server Communication

3 A C++ Interface to Clients and Servers

The Helios Server of Figure 1 may be implemented in C++ as a task which declares an instance of a class. The Data Part is represented by the private class data members and the Passive Part by a private class member function. The Active Part is represented by the body of the task, accessing the Data Part via public class member functions.

In a typical application there will be a need for several distinct server types. Although their functions may vary widely, their basic structure is identical. It makes sense therefore to encapsulate this structure into a `Base_Server` class from which individual server class types may then be derived. Similarly, the mechanisms by which a client may connect to and communicate with a server may be encapsulated within a `Base_Client` class.

3.1 The Base Classes

The base classes are responsible for making, maintaining and breaking the client/server connection. The interface between the base classes and the derived classes consists of a single well-defined operation in each case (RPC_call, RPC_handler) with a consistent parameter (message block, of Figure 3). The derived classes are responsible for the mapping of individual procedure calls onto this interface). In addition the derived server provides the target procedures which implement the server passive part of Figure 1.

```
typedef struct {
    unsigned short    DataSize;
    unsigned char     ContSize;
    word              *Control;
    byte              *Data;
} Message_Block;
```

Figure 3 Message_Block

3.1.1 The Base_Server Class

The `Base_Server` class declaration is shown in Figure 4. The class data elements comprise all that is necessary to maintain the server and are hidden from the derived class. The public interface specifies that the derived class must supply two functions; the `RPC_handler` and `give_block`. The function `do_open` must be public for reasons explained later in this Section.

To establish a server, two actions must be performed. Firstly, a dispatcher process must be

```
class Base_Server
{   typedef struct UserDispatchInfo {
        DispatchInf  info;
        Base_Server  *that;};
    ObjNode        objnode;
    NameInfo       nameinfo;
    UserDispatchInfo userinfo;
    struct Object *server_obj;
public:
    Base_Server(char *);
    ~Base_Server();
    void do_open(ServInfo *);
    virtual void    RPC_handler
        (Message_Block *) = 0;
    virtual Message_Block
        *give_block() = 0;}
```

Figure 4 The Base_Server Declaration

created to spawn a new Passive Part process on receipt of an Open request from each new client. Secondly, the server must identify itself to the Helios name server so that it may be located by a prospective client. This may be accomplished by the class constructor as shown in Figure 5.

Consider first the action of identification. The server name, as passed to the constructor, is entered into the Helios name table by a call to Create. One of the parameters to Create is a nameinfo structure. One of the elements of nameinfo is a port descriptor called NamePort. This port descriptor, which corresponds to server_port in Figure 2, is passed back to the client in response to a Locate server request. The same port descriptor is passed to the dispatcher process as the ReqPort element of the Info structure.

The Dispatcher is created by forking a process. The function table within the Info structure tells the dispatcher which function to call on receipt of a particular type of request such as Open, Rename, Link, etc.. The entry for Open requests points to a function called Inter_do_open which must implement the Passive Part.

Interpretation of RPC's and generation of replies is the responsibility of the derived class. However, lower-level functions such as the reception, interpretation and transmission of Helios messages may be handled by the `Base_Server` to contain unnecessary detail.

The `Base_Server`'s Passive Part is implemented by the `do_open` class member function. Unfortunately, class member functions cannot be called directly by Helios (a 'C' world) as it has no way of initializing the implicit this pointer parameter. Instead, the this pointer is passed to Inter_do_open (a 'C' function)

```
Base_Server::Base_Server(char *name)
{
    /***************************************/
    /*   Prepare information for the dipatcher   */
    /***************************************/
    InitNode(&objnode, &(name[0]), Type_File, 0,
                                            DefFileMatrix);
    DispatchInfo *info    = (DispatchInfo *)&userinfo;
    Info->Root            = (DirNode *) &objnode;
    info->ReqPort         = NewPort();
    Info->SubSys          = SS_NullDevice;
    info->ParentName      = NULL;
    info->PrivateProtocol.Fn       = NULL;
    info->PrivateProtocol.StackSize = 0;
    for (int l=0; I<IOCFns; I++)
    {   info->Fntab[i].Fn = (VoidFnPtr)InvalidFn;
        info->Fntab[i].StackSize = 2000;
    };
    info->Fntab[0].Fn        = (VoidFnPtr)inter_do_open;
    info->Fntab[0].StackSize = 5000;
    info->Fntab[2].Fn        = (VoidFnPtr)DoLocate;
    info->Fntab[3].Fn        = (VoidFnPtr)DoObjInfo;
    userinfo.that            = this;
    Fork(2000, (VoidFnPtr)Dispatch, 4, info);
    /***************************************/
    /*  Enter the server into the Heliosname table */
    /***************************************/
    nameinfo.NamePort    = info->ReqPort;
    nameinfo.Flags       = Flags_StripName;
    nameinfo.NameMatrix  = DefFileMatrix;
    nameinfo.LoadData    = NULL;
    struct Object *sysroot =
                Locate(Null(struct Object), "/");
    server_obj = Create(sysroot, name, Type_Name,
                sizeof(NameInfo), (byte *)&nameinfo);
    Close((struct Stream *)sysroot);
}
Base_Server::~Base_Server()
{
    FreePort(nameinfo.NamePort);
    Delete(server_obj, "");
}
```

Figure 5 The Base_Server Class Constructor and Destructor

```
void    Base_Server::do_open(ServInfo *servinfo)
{
    /***************************************/
    /*   Reply to 'open' command                   */
    /***************************************/
    MsgBuf  *r           = New(struct MsgBuf);
    FormOpenReply(r,servinfo->m, (struct ObjNode *)
                        userinfo.info.Root,Flags_Server,
                        servinfo->Pathname);
    Port request_port    = NewPort();
    r->mcb.MCBMsgHdr.Reply = request_port;
    PutMsg(&r->mcb);
    Free(r); UnLockTarget( servinfo );
    /***************************************/
    /*  Continue to direct RPC requests        */
    /***************************************/
    MCB           mcb;
    word          function_code;
    Message_Block *mb     = give_block();
    mcb.Timeout           = -1;
    mcb.Control           = mb->Control;
    mcb.Data              = mb->Data;
    mcb.MCBMsgHdr.Dest    = request_port;
    while ((GetMsg(&mcb) >= 0)
        && ((function_code = mcb.MCBMsgHdr.FnRc
                        & FG_Mask) != FG_Close))
    {   mb->ContSize= mcb.MCBMsgHdr.ContSize;
        mb->DataSize= mcb.MCBMsgHdr.DataSize;
        if (function_code == FG_Write)
        {   RPC_handler(mb);
            mcb.MCBMsgHdr.ContSize
                                = mb->ContSize;
            mcb.MCBMsgHdr.DataSize
                                = mb->DataSize;
            mcb.Control         = mb->Control;
            mcb.Data            = mb->Data;
            mcb.MCBMsgHdr.Dest
                        = mcb.MCBMsgHdr.Reply;
            PutMsg(&mcb);}
        mcb.MCBMsgHdr.Dest    = request_port;}
    FreePort(request_port);delete(mb->Control);
    delete(mb->Data);delete(mb);
    return;
}
```

Figure 7 The Base_Server Passive Part

explicitly by casting an additional element to the info structure (userinfo.that in Figure 5). This pointer can then be extracted from the servinfo parameter (by casting) to call the do_open member function of the appropriate class instance as shown in Figure 6. To the do_open function, this indirection is invisible.

```
void inter_do_open(ServInfo *servinfo)
{
    ((((UserDispatchInfo *)servinfo->info)
            ->that)->do_open)(servinfo);
}
```

Figure 6 Calling a Class Member Function

The do_open function, as shown in Figure 7, begins by returning the request port descriptor to the client.

It then continues to direct RPC requests (function_code = = FG_Write) to the handler and returns RPC replies to the client until a terminating message is received (function_code = = FG_Close). It then commits suicide. The call to get_block is to allow the size of the first message block to be determined by the derived class. Note that the message block which is returned by the handler containing the RPC reply is re-used to store the following RPC request. It is the responsibility of the derived class to ensure that the size of this block is sufficient to contain the largest possible request.

3.1.2 The Base_Client Class

The `Base_Client` class declaration is shown in Figure 8. The class data elements comprise all that is necessary to maintain the server connection and are hidden from the derived class. The public interface consists of a single function (`RPC_call`). When a client calls this function with a given message block the `RPC_handler` of the server is invoked with that block. Any reply generated by the server is returned to the client caller in the same block.

```
class Base_Client
{
    Port                reply_port;
    struct Stream       *server;
    MCB                 mcb;
public:
    Base_Client(char *);
    ~Base_Client();
    void RPC_call(Message_Block *);
};
```

Figure 8 The Base_Client Declaration

To connect a client to a server, two actions are necessary. Firstly the server must be located, secondly an Open request must be sent to the server to spawn an `RPC_handler`. This may be accomplished using the class constructor as shown in Figure 9. The server port descriptor is contained within the `severobj` structure returned by the Locate request. The request port descriptor is contained within the server structure returned by the Open request. The latter is maintained as a class data element for the use of private member functions.

To break a client server connection, a special message must be sent to kill the server Passive Part for that particular client (function_code == FG_Close). This may be accomplished by the class destructor, also shown in Figure 9.

Generation of an `RPC_call` and interpretation of the reply is the responsibility of the derived class. However, as with the `Base_Server`, low-level message passing may be handled by the `Base_Client`.

The `Base_Client` class provides an `RPC_call` function to send an RPC request using the FG_Write function_code then return the RPC reply to the caller, as shown in Figure 10. Note that the message block

```
Base_Client::Base_Client(char *name)
{
    /*******************************/
    /*   Find the server.          */
    /*******************************/
    struct Object *sysroot;
    struct Object *serverobj;
    sysroot     = Locate(
                    Null(struct Object), "/");
    serverobj   = Locate(sysroot, name);
    Close((Stream *)sysroot);
    /*******************************/
    /*   Open a connection to the serve*/
    /*******************************/
    server      = Open(serverobj,
                    Null(char), O_ReadWrite);
    reply_port  = NewPort();
    Close((Stream *)serverobj);
}

Base_Client::~Base_Client()
{
    InitMCB(&mcb, MsgHdr_Flags_preserve,
        server->Server, reply_port, FG_Close);
    mcb.MCBMsgHdr.DataSize   = 0;
    mcb.Data                 = NULL;
    mcb.MCBMsgHdr.ContSize   = 0;
    mcb.Control              = NULL;
    PutMsg(&mcb);
    Close(server);
    FreePort(reply_port);
}
```

Figure 9 The Base_Client Constructor and Destructor

which contains the RPC request is re-used to store the RPC reply. It is the responsibility of the derived class to ensure that the size of this block is sufficient to contain the largest possible reply.

```
void Base_Client::RPC_call(Message_Block *mb)
{
    InitMCB(&mcb, MsgHdr_Flags_preserve,
        server->Server, reply_port, FG_Write);
    mcb.MCBMsgHdr.DataSize   = mb->DataSize;
    mcb.Data                 = mb->Data;
    mcb.MCBMsgHdr.ContSize   = mb->ContSize;
    mcb.Control              = mb->Control;
    PutMsg(&mcb);
    mcb.MCBMsgHdr.Dest       = reply_port;
    GetMsg(&mcb);
    mb->DataSize = mcb.MCBMsgHdr.DataSize;
    mb->Data     = mcb.Data;
    mb->ContSize = mcb.MCBMsgHdr.ContSize;
    mb->Control  = mcb.Control;
}
```

Figure 10 Making a Remote Procedure Call

3.2 The Derived Classes

An implementation of an example Text class pair is now presented to illustrate the use of the base classes.

```
typedef struct Queue_Obj
{       List        list;
        Semaphore   access;
        Semaphore   not_empty;};
```

Figure 11 The Queue Object

The `Queue_Obj` (Figure 11) employs the Helios structured types, List and Semaphore. The access semaphore is used to control access to the List to prevent a conflict between the active and passive parts of the server. The not_empty semaphore allows the active part to wait for data without consuming processor time. This technique should be used wherever a data structure must be shared between the active and passive parts of the server.

Both the Text_Client and Text_Server rely on the constructors and destructors of the base classes for server and connection creation and management. They need only create and manage their own data structures, as shown in Figure 12.

```
Text_Server::Text_Server
        (char *name):Base_Server(name)
{       InitList(&queue_obj.list);
        InitSemaphore(&queue_obj.access, 1);
        InitSemaphore(&queue_obj.not_empty, 0);}
Text_Client::Text_Client
        (char *name):Base_Client(name)
{       mb      = new(Message_Block);}
```

Figure 12 The Derived Class Constructors

The text example implements two RPC's; reverse and push. They are encoded into a message by the client, as shown for push in Figure 13. They are then

```
void Text_Client::push(char *message)
{       word rpc= RPC_Push_Text;
        mb->ContSize    = 1;
        mb->Control     = &rpc;
        mb->DataSize    = strlen(message)+1;
        mb->Data        = message;
        RPC_call(mb);}
```

Figure 13 Encoding the RPC

decoded by the server to vector control to the appropriate function as shown in Figure 14.

```
void Text_Server::RPC_handler(Message_Block *mb)
{       word    rpc = *(mb->Control);
        if (rpc == RPC_Reverse_Text)
            reverse(mb->Data);
        else if (rpc == RPC_Push_Text) push(mb->Data);
}

typedef struct Entry
{       Node    node;
        char *message;};

void Text_Server::push(char *message)
{       Entry *next_entry = new(struct Entry);
        int length      = strlen(message)+1;
        next_entry->message = new(char[length]);
        sprintf(next_entry->message,"%s",message);
        Wait(&queue_obj.access);
        AddHead(&queue_obj.list, &next_entry->node);
        Signal(&queue_obj.access);
        Signal(&queue_obj.not_empty);}

void Text_Server::reverse(char *message)
{       int length      = strlen(message);
        for (int i = 0; i < length/2; i++)
        {
            char hold;
            hold = message[i];
            message[i] = message[length - i - 1];
            message[length-i-1] = hold;
        }}
```

Figure 14 Decoding and Performing the RPC

The RPC reply is generated by allowing the function to directly manipulate the data part of the message block via the message pointer it receives as a parameter.

A pop function is provided for the use of the Active Part of the server (Figure 15). Note that in the case of a non-empty queue, the Active Part is forced to wait on a semaphore to avoid consuming processor time.

```
char *Text_Server::pop()
{       struct Entry    *next_entry;
        char            *message;
        Wait(&queue_obj.not_empty);
        Wait(&queue_obj.access);
        next_entry      =
            (struct Entry *) RemTail(&queue_obj.list);
        Signal(&queue_obj.access);
        message     = next_entry->message;
        Free(next_entry);
        return(message);}
```

Figure 15 Active Part Access Function

4 Using the C++ Interface

A Text_Server is created by declaring an instance of the Text_Server class as shown in Figure 16. The body of this program implements the server active part. Messages which have been placed in the queue in response to a push RPC are removed by the pop function and displayed on the screen. The name of the server (to be entered in the Helios name table) is derived from the command line used to invoke the program (argv[1]).

```
int main(int argc, char *argv[])
{
    if (argc != 2) {printf("Illegal
            number of parameters\n");return(0);};
    Text_Server  screen(argv[1]);
    char        *message;
    do
    {
        message   = screen.pop();
        printf("Message is %s\n",message);
    }
    while (strlen(message) > 1);
}
```

Figure 16 A Text Server

A Text_Client is created by declaring an instance of the Text_Client class as shown in Figure 17. The name of the server to which the client must be attached is derived from the command line used to invoke the program (argv[1]). A string derived from the second command-line parameter is sent to the server, reversed, then sent again. This causes the string to be displayed twice on the screen associated with the server; once as normal and once reversed.

```
int main(int argc, char *argv[])
{
    if (argc != 3) {printf("Illegal
            number of parameters\n");return(0);};
    Text_Client  screen(argv[1]);
    char         *message = new(char[20]);
    sprintf(message, "%s", argv[2]);
    screen.push(message);
    screen.reverse(message);
    screen.push(message);
}
```

Figure 17 A Text Client

5 Conclusions

The base classes provide a convenient interface which encapsulates the application-independent aspects of Helios servers. The application programmer need only be concerned with the server data structures and their manipulation through RPC's as shown in the text example of Section 3.2.

Although at present the client/server structure is expicitly defined in the form of two separate programs (see Section 4), it may in future be derived automatically. A standard C++ program will be processed by a stub generator [4] which will convert classes into servers and map invocations of class member functions onto calls to member functions of a corresponding client class. This would allow an arbitrary C++ program to be distributed across a network of processors running Helios.

6 Acknowledgements

This work has been supported in part by a grant from the U.K. Science and Engineering Research Council and from the European Community ESPRIT-II reasearch programme project P2252 (DELTA-4). My thanks go to Dr Graham Parrington for his comments during the preparation of this paper.

7 References

[1]   Perihelion Software Ltd. "The Helios Operating System". Prentice Hall International (UK) Ltd. 1989. ISBN 0-13-386004-3.

[2]   A. D Birrell and B. J. Nelson. "Implementing Remote Procedure Calls", ACM Transactions on Computing Systems Vol 2. No 1 1984 pp 39–59.

[3]   Stanley B. Lippman. "C++ Primer", Addison-Wesley Publishing Company 1989. ISBN 0-201-16487-6.

[4]   Graham D Parrington. "Reliable Distributed Programming in C++: The Arjuna Approach", Digest of papers, Second Usenix C++ Conference, San Francisco, April 1990.

The Metrobridge - an Application of Transputers in Transparent Bridging

B. Robertson M. Chopping K. Zielinski D. Milway
Olivetti Research Limited, Cambridge

Abstract. This paper describes the Metrobridge project - a distributed switch for connecting PC cards via a high-speed backbone network. The paper outlines the communication and management functions that are provided, and describes the hardware and software modules that make up the system. Finally, the advantages and disadvantages of using the transputer are discussed.

1 Introduction

The Metrobridge is a distributed switch for the connection of PC cards via a high-speed backbone network, with Ethernet bridging as the first application. Unlike many conventional bridges, it can connect up to sixteen LANs at once, and provides for both local and remote bridging. The backbone network runs over optic fibre, so bridged LANs may be physically separated by considerable distances.

At an early stage in the Metrobridge project, several major decisions were taken:

1. The 75 Mbps Cambridge Fast Ring (CFR) [4] was chosen to act as the backbone network. Much experience had been gained in its use in previous projects at ORL, and it was the only high-speed network freely available when the project began.

2. The INMOS transputer [5] was chosen as the processor, because of the ease with which it can be incorporated into embedded systems and its fast context switching.

3. It was decided that a standard PC card would be the LAN interface. A PC bus had to be used to communicate with this card, imposing a performance bottleneck. However, the bus gave access to a wide range of PC cards, and allowed for future development of the project (e.g. bridging other types of LAN) without significant hardware changes.

The decision to use transputers in the system led to the choice of OCCAM [6] as the programming language, as a high level language was desired to ease debugging and maintenance of the software. Also, a parallel language should allow the exploitation of the parallelism inherent in a community of independent communicating entities.

2 Metrobridge general structure

The Metrobridge may be divided into two basic domains. The first represents a general communication subsystem whose main goal is to pass information from a source system to a destination system, and the second covers all management aspects.

The logical structure of the communication subsystem is shown in Fig. 1. This subsystem consists of a number of identical logical units, called bridge nodes, connected together by a backbone. Each bridge node may be split into the following logical entities:

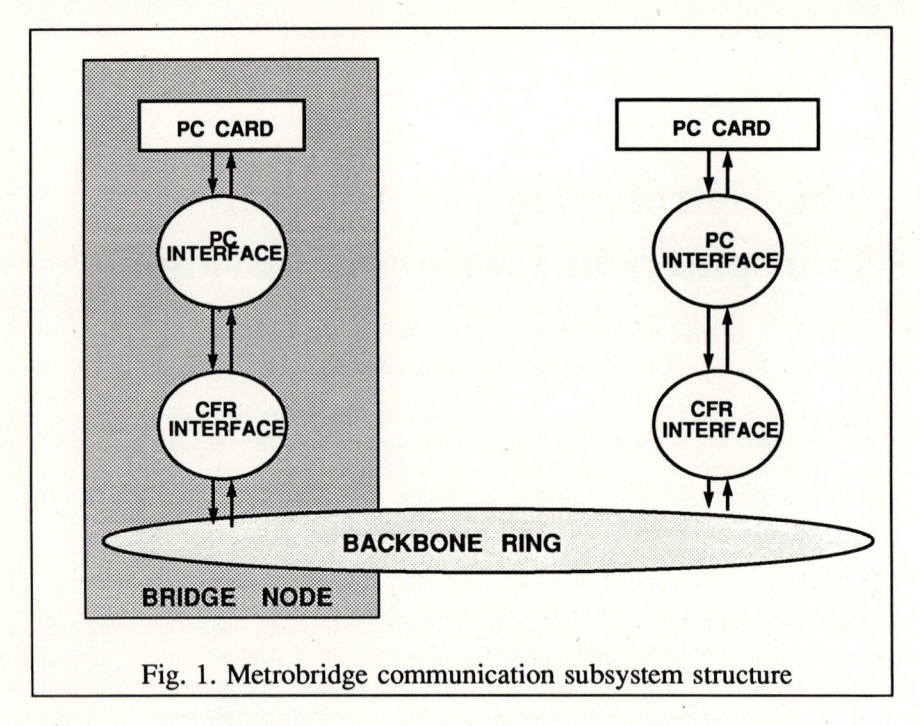

Fig. 1. Metrobridge communication subsystem structure

PC card - a standard PC LAN card used for transmitting and receiving LAN packets.

PC interface - responsible for providing the PC bus signals for the PC card, and performing access/routing control (ARC) [7] on all packets passing through the bridge node.

CFR interface - responsible for transmission and reception of minipackets containing the data carried by the CFR to/from the backbone ring.

The logical structure of the Metrobridge management subsystem is shown in Fig. 2. For management purposes, the bridge nodes are organised in groups of up to four. Each group is housed in a Metrobridge box and controlled by a management module. The boxes may be distributed over considerable distances and connected by a serial CFR ring. Inside a box the CFR is parallel, with the conversion between serial and parallel format being performed by special hardware. Hence a box may be used as a standalone module, or be connected to other boxes via the backbone ring as part of a distributed system.

For the distributed version of the Metrobridge, a centralised management structure was chosen. One of the boxes is set up as the master, with all other boxes being referred to as remote; the master box is the only one which can download new versions of software and ARC data. The entire system configuration may be viewed from the master box, whereas remote boxes can only inform the user of their own local configuration.

The box management unit can be split into two entities - the box supervisor and the box memory. The box supervisor is responsible for monitoring bridge nodes, loading them with code and ARC tables when appropriate, gathering statistics, and communicating with other supervisors in the system via the CFR. The box memory provides an intelligent file store for bridge code and tables, and the user interface to the system.

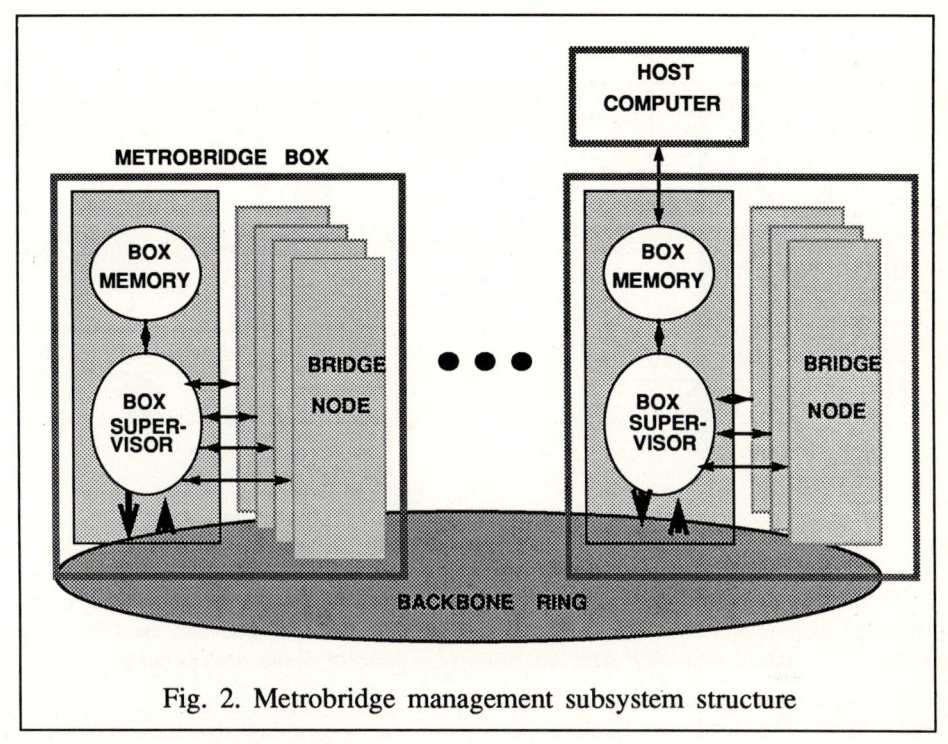

Fig. 2. Metrobridge management subsystem structure

3 Metrobridge hardware structure

The logical entities outlined in the previous section make up the modules of the system. With the exception of the PC card, each module has its own dedicated INMOS transputer.

3.1 Communication subsystem hardware structure

A bridge node contains two independent transputer-driven modules, as shown in Fig. 3. The first module is the PC interface, consisting of a T222 transputer, 16K static memory, a 256 x 48-bit Content Addressable Memory (CAM) [1], and a simple state machine to implement PC XT/AT timing.

The T222 was chosen instead of a more powerful transputer because an 8/16-bit wide PC bus was to be used, and we did not require a large address space for storing code or buffering packets (too many buffers lead to unacceptable latency [3]), so a 16-bit processor was considered adequate.

The transputer directly controls the PC LAN card via the PC Bus, and the performance of the whole module is largely dependent on the speed of access to the PC card's memory. After comparing various commercial offerings, the WD8003EBT card was chosen [8], [9].

Other time-critical operations of the PC interface module are routing, filtering and ARC. For the Metrobridge, a source routing scheme [2], [10] was chosen. To increase the efficiency of routing and filtering a CAM was used. With this hardware assistance, filtering can be performed completely transparently.

Fig. 3. Bridge node hardware structure

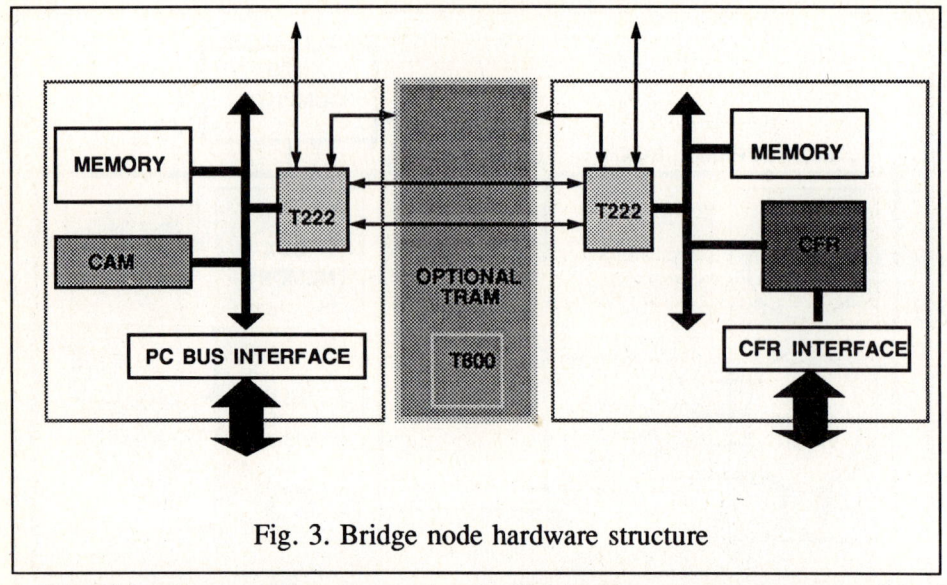

The PC interface module is connected to the CFR interface using two transputer links. It is possible to plug a standard 2 slot Transputer Module (TRAM) between the PC interface and the CFR interface to provide extra processing (e.g. protocol conversion) or buffering.

The CFR interface module contains a T222 transputer, 16K static memory and CFR interface logic. The transputer is used to perform the fragmentation/reassembly operation between 32 byte CFR minipackets and Ethernet packets, and to control transmission and reception of the CFR minipackets.

3.2 Management subsystem hardware structure

Fig. 4 shows the structure of the management subsystem hardware. The box supervisor card contains a T222 transputer which controls two CFR chips. The first of these is called the CFR station, and is used for communication with remote box supervisor cards using the backbone ring. The second, called the CFR monitor, is only used in the master box, where it maintains the structure of the backbone ring. The transputer present on this board may communicate with bridge nodes in the box using three of its transputer links. The fourth link is used for communication with the box memory card.

The box memory card contains a T425 transputer, 1 Mbyte DRAM, EPROM, EEPROM, a deadman's handle circuit, and connections to a keypad and 24 x 2 LCD. The T425 is connected via one of its links to the box supervisor card, and one of the remaining links may be used for communication with a host computer system.

4 Metrobridge software

Each of the hardware modules is controlled by a set of processes, which communicate via OCCAM channels or the backbone ring. This section briefly describes the communication subsystem algorithms, before discussing the management issues, which may be of more general interest to those using transputers.

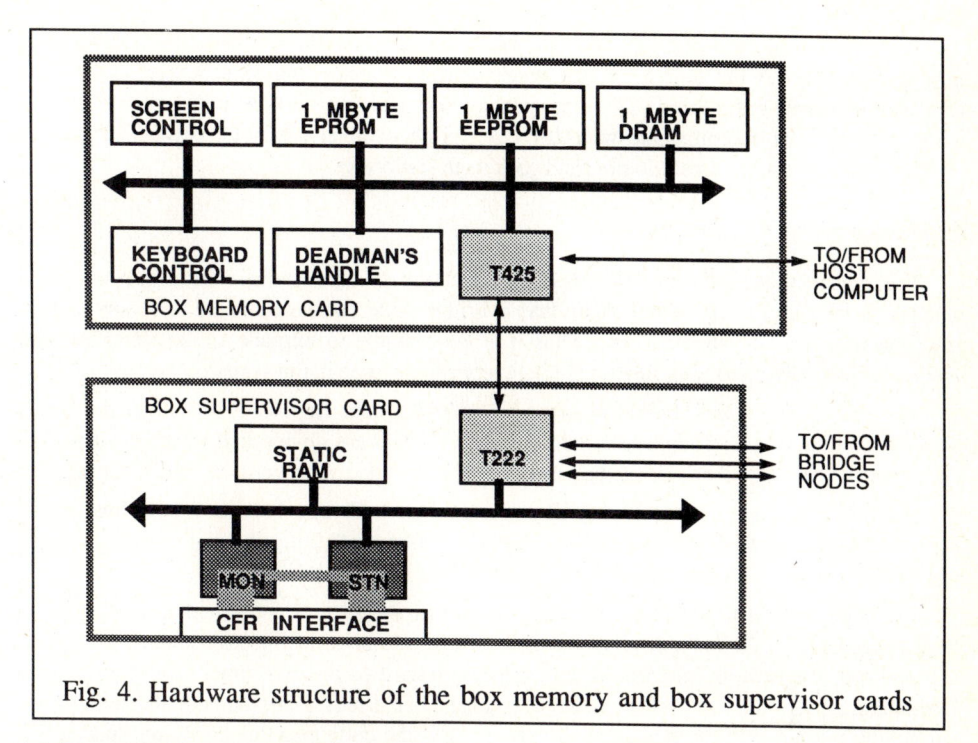

Fig. 4. Hardware structure of the box memory and box supervisor cards

4.1 Communication subsystem software

Several tasks must be performed when forwarding a packet from LAN A to LAN B:

1. *Packet reception on LAN A* - the packet must be detected by the PC interface transputer. Interrupts were tried, but did not give acceptable performance (see section 5).
2. *Filter/forward decision* - the packet's source and destination are checked. If the packet is to be forwarded, the destination LAN must be determined - this could be one LAN if the destination is known, or all LANs if it is unknown or a multicast.
3. *Transmission of the packet on the CFR* - as the CFR uses 32 byte minipackets, the LAN packet must be fragmented into 28 byte chunks (4 bytes per minipacket are used by protocol headers to allow reassembly) before transmission.
4. *Reception of the packet from the CFR* - the minipackets arriving at the bridge node connected to LAN B are reassembled to form the original LAN packet.
5. *Transmission of the packet on LAN B* - the packet's header is checked to ensure that it may be transmitted on LAN B. If permitted, the LAN card transmits the packet.

Bridge nodes learn source addresses using an asymmetric scheme; all packets from the local LAN have their source addresses stored in the CAM, but remote packet source addresses are only stored if their destination address is in the CAM. This stops the CAM from filling up with the addresses of remote stations that never communicate with a local station. An LRU algorithm is employed for deleting entries that are no longer in use.

Packet filtering can occur for two reasons; either because the destination is known to be on the same LAN as the source, or as a result of management filtering schemes - e.g. do not forward broadcasts from this LAN. This management filtering may be performed at the network level (do not communicate with LAN A), protocol level (do not receive TCP packets from LAN A), or station level (do not send packets to station A).

4.2 Management subsystem software

The management software tries to ensure that the system recovers from power cuts or glitches. It also gives the system flexibility; a bridge node can be rebooted with any code at any time from the management box. Thus it is very simple to upgrade to the latest software version without having to plug EPROMs into every bridge node in the system.

The box memory and supervisor cards in each box boot from EPROM when the box is powered up and start a deadman's handle - this is a hardware device that must be hit periodically by the software, otherwise the box memory and box supervisor cards will be rebooted.

The box supervisor card is connected to each bridge node in a box via a reset link, allowing it to detect a crashed bridge node and reboot it without affecting the rest of the system. A node is also booted if it stops communicating with the box supervisor card.

The code and ARC tables for all bridge nodes in the system are stored in EEPROM on the management box's box memory card. When a bridge node in the management box needs to be booted, the code is sent from the box memory card to the box supervisor, then down a transputer link to the card. When a remote bridge node needs to be booted, the remote box will submit a request to the management box, be sent the code over the CFR, and load it into the bridge node in the normal way. When a bridge node has been booted, it is sent appropriate ARC tables from the management box's EEPROM via the CFR.

As there are only three data links available on the box supervisor card, any box containing four bridge nodes cannot use the conventional link connection scheme shown in Fig. 5. A pure daisychain scheme was tried, but this can impose too high an overhead on the bridge at the head of the chain which has to pass all messages in both directions. It also requires that three bridges be working if communication with the fourth is to be possible, and forces all link timeouts to be longer, as messages may have to pass through many transputers.

Therefore, we adopted the mixed link connection scheme: data for the fourth bridge node must be sent through the PC and CFR interfaces of another bridge node. All statistics returned by the fourth node must travel the same route in reverse. This has the advantage that in a box with up to three bridge nodes everything works as for the conventional scheme, with daisychaining only being used when necessary.

A Metrobridge system comprising of more than one box must ensure that remote boxes have the same view of the system as the management box. Each remote box only knows its local configuration, as it has no need to know about other boxes. The configuration information, concerning the code and ARC tables to be loaded into each bridge node, is stored in non-volatile RAM on the box supervisor card.

When a box is brought into a new system or has to be reconfigured the non-volatile RAM must be updated. This is done over the CFR by the management box, whose non-volatile RAM contains the configuration information for the entire system. Remote boxes periodically inform the management box of their configuration to ensure consistency.

The EEPROM on the box memory card provides a simple file system for the Metrobridge. It consists of 512 byte sectors which can only be written to a few hundred times, so it is difficult to maintain a directory in EEPROM. Therefore, each file has a header sector specifying file type, name, size, and the location of all sectors in the file, allowing a directory and sector map to be constructed in RAM during initialisation. A garbage collector can be run to recover any sectors lost during erroneous writes e.g. writes aborted by a power cut. .

5 Transputer-related problems

The following transputer features have added latency or required software fixes:

1. *Long interrupt service time* - the transputer has only one interrupt, the event channel. This means that the box supervisor must combine the interrupts from its two CFR chips, and then distinguish between them in software. It also prevents hardware support for interrupts, with each event raising a different interrupt.
2. *Memory saturation* - Ethernet packets are copied directly from the PC LAN card's memory via a transputer link to the internal memory of the CFR interface transputer at a rate of approximately 5 Mbps. The obvious way to increase this throughput would be to use two transputer links and do the copy operation in parallel. However, this reduces the overall throughput of a bridge node. This is because the links and processor gain access to the bus using a round-robin scheduling scheme; hence the slow memory accesses performed by the links slow down the processor, preventing adequate response to real-time events, such as LAN packet reception interrupts.

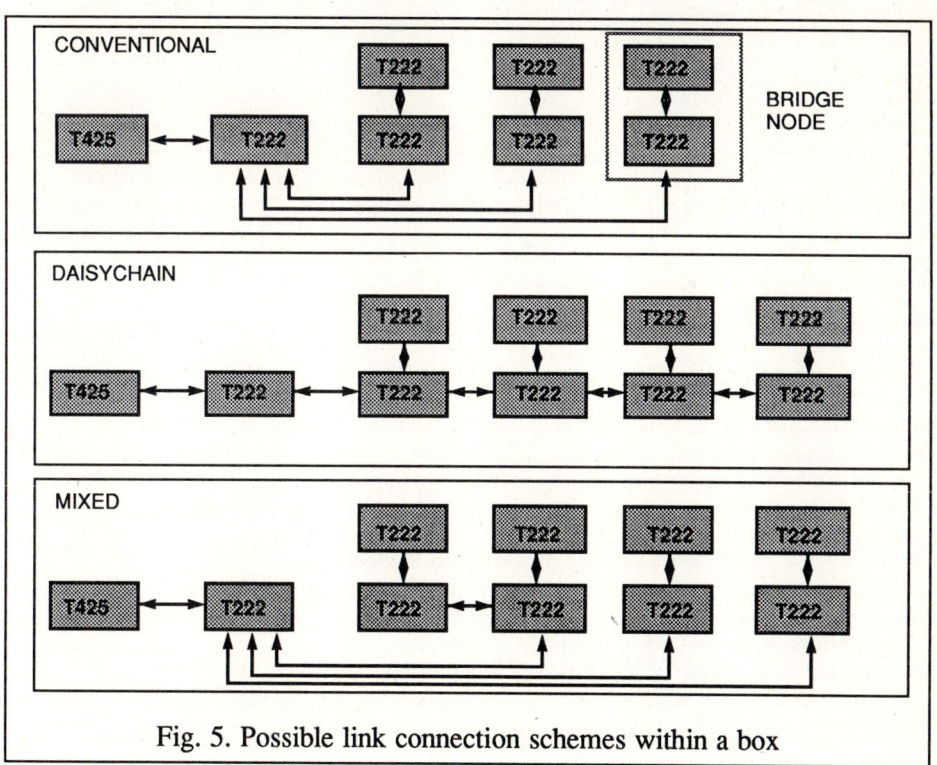

Fig. 5. Possible link connection schemes within a box

As this problem can also occur on a single bidirectional link, the strategy for dealing with LAN packet reception had to be altered: if a bridge is not processing a packet it waits for a LAN interrupt in the normal way. However, when a packet has been received, receive interrupts are not reenabled. Instead the packet is processed, then the packet buffer is checked to see if further packets have been received. If so, the next packet is processed. This process continues until no more packets can be found in the buffer, at which point receive interrupts are reenabled.

3. *Block copy bug* - block copying of data to/from FIFOs must not be interrupted, as the copy operation restarts at the last successful item copied, causing loss or duplication of data. The solution is to ensure all such block copy operations run at high priority.

6 Conclusion

The Metrobridge's performance has been satisfactory in its two prototype installations, both in terms of speed and reliability. The first external installation was in the Cambridge University Computing Service, bridging three LANs (one of which contains over 120 active stations). The second test was a link between the University Computer Laboratory and ORL using an optic fibre backbone. Video and voice traffic were using the backbone at the same time as the Ethernet traffic was being bridged, yet there were no major problems. End-to-end throughput has been measured at 5 Mbps.

The transputer is ideal for use in prototyping systems as it requires little support hardware, has good context-switching times, and can be programmed in a high-level parallel language well suited to exploit its capabilities. The TDS provides an adequate environment, with the debugger an excellent tool for locating software bugs in embedded systems.

Acknowledgements

We would like to thank all the members of ORL and the University who helped with this project. They include A. Hopper for contributions throughout the course of the project, I. Wilson and J. Porter for their invaluable advice on using the CFR, D. Garnett for constructive comments, and A. Morris and M. Johnson for their willingness to provide a test site for the system.

References

[1] Chisvin L., Duckworth J., *Content-Addressable and Associative Memory : Alternatives to the Ubiquitous RAM*, COMPUTER, July, 1989.
[2] Hamner C.M., Samsen G.R., *Source Routing Bridge Implementation*, IEEE Network, Vol.2., No.1, 1988.
[3] Heath J., *Analysis of Gateway Congestion in Interconnected High-Speed Local Networks*, IEEE Transactions on Communications, Vol.36, No.8, August 1988.
[4] Hopper A., Needham R.M., *The Cambridge Fast Ring Networking System*, IEEE Transactions on Computers, Vol.37, No.10, October 1988.
[5] INMOS Limited, The Transputer Databook, Second Edition, Redwood Burn Ltd., 1989.
[6] INMOS Limited, Occam 2 Reference Manual, Prentice Hall Int., Series in Comp. Sci., 1988.
[7] Karhuse R., Whipple J., *IEEE 802.6 Security Features and Enhanced Security Service*, Third IEEE Workshop on MANs, San Diego, California, March 28-30, 1989.
[8] *Survey: LAN Adaptor Cards*, Communications, January 1989.
[9] *Western Digital Wins, LAN Magazine Network Drag Race*, LAN Magazine, July 1988.
[10] Zhang L., *Comparison of Two Bridge Routing Approaches*, IEEE Network, Vol.2, No.1, 1988.

The Application of Transputers as a Network 'Compute' Server

I.D. Hardy   A.P.H. Jordan

Department of Computer Science & Applied Mathematics,
Aston University, Birmingham, B4 7ET.

Abstract. This paper considers the use of Transputer system as a *'compute'* server in a heterogeneous network. A prototype system, the *Aston Networked Transputer System* (ANTS) is described. We show that this can provide an efficient service to multiple simultaneous users.

1. Introduction: Why a 'Compute' Server?

There is now approximately five years of experience in the use of Transputer based parallel computers. Many systems have been produced that have successfully exploited a number of Transputers. Transputer systems have been shown to provide a cost effective, high performance solution for many problems. The series of Occam User Group Conferences and the 1989 Transputer Applications Conference [1] have provided plenty of evidence for this.

However Transputer systems remain a specialized processing resource for several reasons, most of which are unlikely to change in the foreseeable future. Applications have to be written for a parallel architecture, this involves either rewriting them in a parallel language such as Occam or modifying them to a parallel version of a conventional language such as C or Fortran. In either case a substantial amount of effort is required to make maximum use of the available parallelism.

Many problems only contain sections of code that can be rewritten to make effective use of a parallel computer. The effect of this is illustrated by Amdahl's law [2], that effectively states that if code representing only 9/10th of the serial execution time can be converted to parallel code that the maximum speed up possible for that application will be 10, assuming an infinite parallel computer. In addition it is often found that >90% of the execution time of an application involves less than 10% of the applications source code. There is therefore a large potential advantage to be gained in terms of development expense by only porting suitable, computationally intensive, sections of code to the Transputer system. The remainder of the application can then be executed on the host computer system.

A large Transputer system remains a relatively expensive resource. It is therefore desirable that it should not be dedicated to a single user for long periods of time, particularly if, as is likely, the user only exploits its power for a small proportion of the available time. A solution to this problem is for a Transputer system to provide a number of commonly used computationally intensive services to users of a computer network. This solution is considered by Peel [3], who suggested that the processing of 'troff' document interpretation could be handled by a dedicated Transputer, saving a large amount of processing time on existing computing facilities.

We have developed a system, the *Aston Networked Transputer System*, ANTS, that allows a multiple Transputer system to provide a number of services to users of a computer network. The design, implementation and testing of this system is described in this paper.

2. Network Access to Transputer Based Services

The calling of a service provided by the ANTS system falls naturally into the so called client-server model of communication. In this model a client process sends a message to a server process requesting that it perform some operation. After performing the operation the server sends a message containing the results of the operation back to the client. This exchange of messages can be conveniently hidden from the programmer by extending the procedure call mechanism found in most programming languages. In a *Remote Procedure Call* (RPC) system the passing of messages between client and server is handled by stub routines; the client views the accessing of a remote service as a simple procedure call. The issues raised in providing and using RPC mechanisms are discussed in a paper by Wilbur & Bacarisse [4].

One widely available RPC system is the *Network Computing System* (NCS) developed by Apollo Computers [5]. NCS is intended to operate in a heterogeneous environment, that is between computers of different types. A protocol specification of NCS has been published [6] and

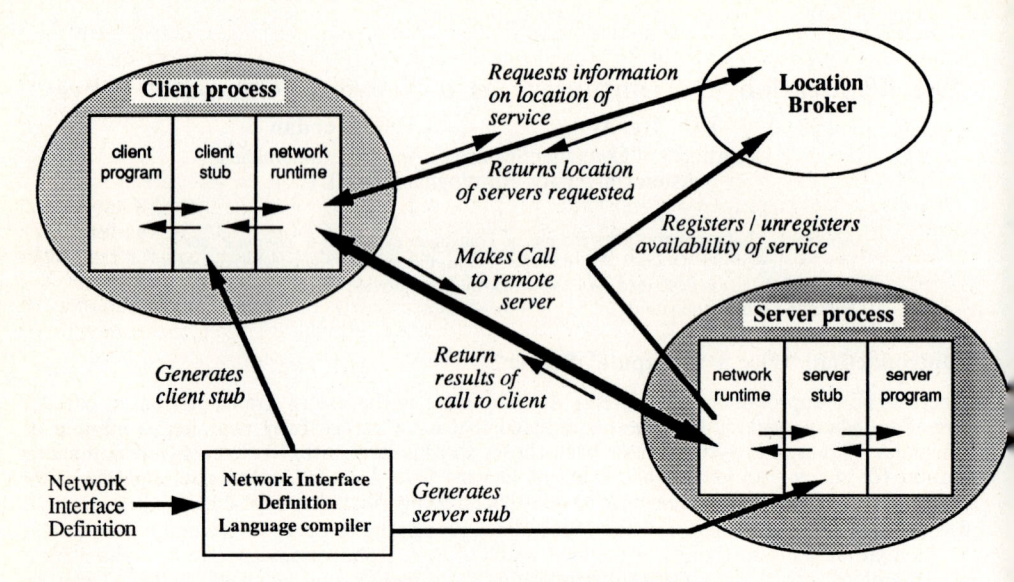

Figure 1. Components of NCS

implementations exist on a range of platforms including Unix, DEC, Cray and IBM computers as well as Apollo workstations.

NCS includes several tools that aid the development of RPC based distributed computing systems. A *Network Interface Definition Language* compiler generates the client and server stub files from a C or Pascal based description of the procedures exported by the server. The NCS run time system automatically handles the conversion of data when a call is made between computers with different data representations. NCS also introduces the concept of *Location Brokers*. A client process can request from the location broker information on the location of servers providing particular services. The components of NCS are illustrated in figure 1.

The location brokers allow for an object oriented style of programming, in which the service required is specified and not a particular server implementation. A client is not bound to a server implementation until run time. Servers may therefore be developed independently from clients. For example a new faster implementation of a server may be introduced into a network with no modification to the client program.

3. Considerations in the Design of ANTS

3.1. Support for Multiple Simultaneous Users

An early consideration in the design of ANTS was support for multiple users. Any resource providing a service on a computer network is potentially available to any user of the network. It was therefore necessary to consider how to deal with multiple simultaneous requests for access to the server. To reject calls when the server is in use would place an unacceptable responsibility on the client process to locate a free server. Different calls to the server may have different processing requirements ranging from milliseconds to minutes and upwards, it would therefore be inappropriate to queue calls for later processing. Our preferred solution was for the ANTS system to be able to process multiple simultaneous calls.

3.2 Requirement for Efficiency and Fairness

A system for processing multiple simultaneous calls on a Transputer system was therefore required. Two primary goals were set for the development of this system. First it had to result in an efficient utilization of processing resources. Efficiency may not be of paramount importance in a single user system, provided that a required absolute performance is obtained. However in a multi-user system processor cycles not required in the processing of one job can potentially be used in the processing of another. The reason for using a Transputer system is, after all, to obtain the highest possible performance. The second goal was to provide each active call with a fair share of the available processing power. These two goals led to the requirement for a system that could dynamically adapt its allocation of processing resources to user calls as new calls entered the system and calls completed their processing.

3.3. Development Environment

Of secondary importance were considerations regarding the ease of development of application code for the system. While this aspect of the system is obviously important, it was felt that a substantial amount of effort has been put into the development of programming tools for Transputer systems compared to that put into the development of efficient run-time systems. However ANTS is designed to provide a framework in which code may be structured, easing the development of efficient parallel code. In addition ANTS allows server application code to be developed independently of the configuration of the target hardware.

3.4. A Component of a General Purpose Computing System

ANTS is intended as a component of a general purpose computer system, not as a complete general purpose system. NCS provides the '*glue*' with which different specialized processing resources can be used to form a general purpose computer system. Indeed it is envisaged that other Transputer based systems may be developed and used alongside ANTS, providing a different style of operation and being therefore suitable for different tasks.

4. A Multi-User Processing Paradigm

Three basic programming paradigms are used in the programming of multiple Transputer systems [7]: algorithmic parallelism, geometric (data) parallelism and processor farming. All three paradigms can produce good results in the processing of certain types of problems.

4.1 The Processor Farm Paradigm

The processor farm paradigm has received a considerable amount of attention due to its ability to achieve a near 100% processor utilization for a range of computationally intensive problems. The basic principle of this paradigm is for a *controller* process to split the problem into a large number of sub-problems that can be processed independently. These sub-problems are then allocated to a number of *worker* processors as these processors become available. The high processor utilization obtainable is due to two factors:-

(1) *Good load balancing* - if the number of sub-tasks is large compared to the number of processors, no processor will have allocated to it at any time a significant proportion of the total processing load. Apart from for short start and finishing periods all the processors can be kept busy.

(2) *Overlapped processing and communication* - if each worker processor is allowed to buffer a sub-task in addition to the one that it is processing then it will always have work ready for processing. This allows advantage to be taken of the ability of Transputer processors to perform processing and communication concurrently. There is therefore very little cost associated with the communication of sub-tasks.

In addition a processor farm is easily modified to run on systems containing different numbers of processors. It is also possible to produce a harness that handles all the required communications: an application then consists simply of two sequential processes to perform the controller and worker functions. As an example the Fortnet [8] system provides a harness that allows the controller and worker functions to be coded in Fortran.

4.2 A Multi-User Processor Farm Paradigm

For ANTS we have adapted the conventional processor farm paradigm, to form a *Slot Based Processor Farm* paradigm. This new paradigm is illustrated in figure 2. Each worker processor provides a number of *slot* processes, each of which is able to process a sub-task. Unlike a conventional processor farm [9], sub-tasks are sent to specific worker processors and to a specific slot process within that worker. The controller processor contains a number of controller processes, each of which is responsible for the processing of a different call. Associated with each slot process is a *slot token*; a controller may only send a sub-task to a slot process if it holds the token for that

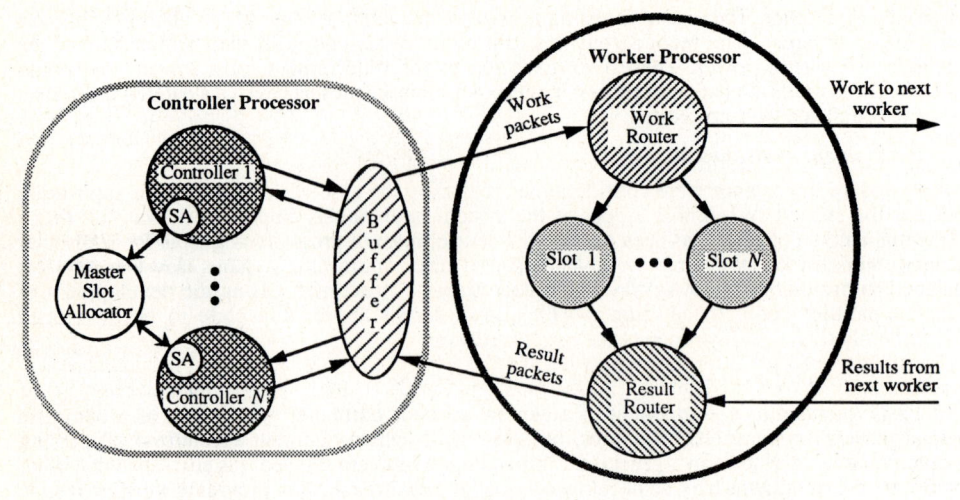

Figure 2: Structure of Slot Based Processor Farm Paradigm

slot. When a controller process dispatches a sub-task it also sends the slot token, therefore a slot process can only have one sub-task allocated to it at any time. This prevents the system from becoming congested with undeliverable sub-task messages.

The slot tokens are distributed among the currently active controller processes by a *Master Slot Allocator* (MSA) process. The MSA process is responsible for obtaining the efficiency and fairness of operation discussed in section 3.2. The MSA achieves these objectives by following the policy outlined below:

(1) Each active controller should have an equal number of slots allocated to it;
(2) The slots allocated to an active controller should be evenly distributed among the worker processors;
(3) Each active controller should have as many slots allocated to it as possible, subject to a maximum of 'Max_Slots_Per_Worker' on any one processor.

The first rule is intended to obtain an even allocation of processing resources among the active controllers. The second rule ensures that efficient use can be made of all of the worker processors, even if an active controller temporarily ceases producing sub-tasks. The final rule ensures that all of the worker processors are kept busy whenever one or more controllers are active. The limit of 'Max_Slots_Per_Worker' is based on the premise that this number of slots is sufficient to keep a worker processor busy; allocating more slots to a single controller would have no performance benefit and would introduce additional overheads in reallocating resources should another controller become active.

Slot tokens allocated to a controller are managed by a *Slot Allocator* (SA) process. Each controller process has its own local SA. Before sending a sub-task to a worker a controller obtains a slot token from its SA, this token identifies the address to which the sub-task is sent. When the results of the processing of a sub-task are returned the controller returns the slot token to its SA process.

When a controller process becomes active through a new call being received by the ANTS system, the controller sends a request to the MSA process for an allocation of slot tokens. The MSA first looks to see if it is holding any slot tokens that are not currently allocated to a controller; such slots are allocated to the new controller provided that the allocation policy is met. If this does not locate sufficient slots then the MSA process looks for slots to reallocate to the new controller. When the MSA decides to reallocate a slot it sends a message to the SA of the controller where the slot is currently located, requesting the return of the slot token. The MSA maintains a note of the new 'assigned' location of the slot token, enabling it to be sent to its new controller when it is returned. The SA processes are obliged to return requested slots to the MSA immediately, if the slot is not currently in use, or as soon as the slot completes processing its current sub-task.

When a controller process finishes processing a job it signals this fact to the MSA process and returns all of its slot tokens. On receiving a termination message the MSA reassigns all of the slots held by the terminated controller to any remaining active controllers.

The MSA in collaboration with the individual SA's therefore maintains dynamically an even allocation of processing resources, slots, to the currently active controller processes. The process scheduler incorporated in the instruction set of Transputer processors ensures that the slot processes running on a particular processor each receive a fair slice of the CPU's time.

4.3. Multiple Services

Several different services can be supported within a slot based processor farm system by including a *service-id* field in call or sub-task messages. An Occam CASE statement in the controller and slot processes is then used to select the appropriate operation.

4.4 Multiple User Processes on a Single Processor

The slot based processor farm paradigm breaks one of the widely accepted rules in the development of Transputer systems, in allowing processes belonging to more than one user to run on a single processor. This is normally regarded as undesirable due to the lack of support for memory protection on Transputer processors. We justify this decision with the argument that our system is intended to run developed, well tested code. Application code provided in the system should be regarded as being *'trusted'*. The concept of *trusted* servers is analogous to that of supervisory or privileged modes in a conventional operating system. In addition some protection is provided through the use of Occam, which supports array bound checking and *usage checking* of data [10]. It is also possible that future Transputer processors will provide support for memory protection.

5. ANTS Implementation

5.1. A Workstation Hosted Transputer System

ANTS has been implemented using an Apollo DN3000 workstation to host a Transputer system. The decision not to connect the Transputer system directly to a computer network was made due to there being a lack of Transputer networking products during the early stages of this project. The development of networking products was considered to be beyond the scope of this project.

The Apollo DN3000/4000 series of workstations contain an IBM PC compatible expansion bus, which allows standard Transputer boards such as the Inmos IMS B008 to be used. A *Transputer Software Environment*, CD-TSE, for use with Apollo hosted Transputer systems is available [11]. The CD-TSE software consists of two components. The first, CD-TDS, is a port of the standard Inmos *Transputer Development System* to the Apollo environment. The second component, CD-CPS, provides a co-processor mechanism. This allows a process running on the host Apollo workstation to invoke a program on the Transputer system and to communicate with it using communication channels.

5.2. A Surrogate Server

A process, which we call the *surrogate* server, because it appears to a client to be the process providing the service, executes on the host workstation. This process contains a stub procedure for each service exported by the ANTS system. It is the job of these stub routines to listen for NCS calls to the ANTS system, to forward the parameters to the ANTS system and to forward the return parameters to the client having first input them from the Transputer system.

The NCS run-time system generates a light-weight task running a stub routine for each call received. A mutual exclusion lock (*mutex*) is used to ensure that only one task gains access to the channels to the Transputer system at any time. An additional *Input Guardian* task reads from the Transputer system the identity of calls that are completing and awakes the appropriate stub task using an event count (*ec2*) so that it can read the return parameters.

The surrogate server process is also responsible for registering the services provided by the ANTS system, acquiring and booting the Transputer system and dealing with error conditions. The structure of this process is shown in figure 3. The experience of developing this process in C using system calls to provide the required parallelism and synchronization mechanisms has illustrated to the authors the superiority of Occam, which was used for the rest of the system.

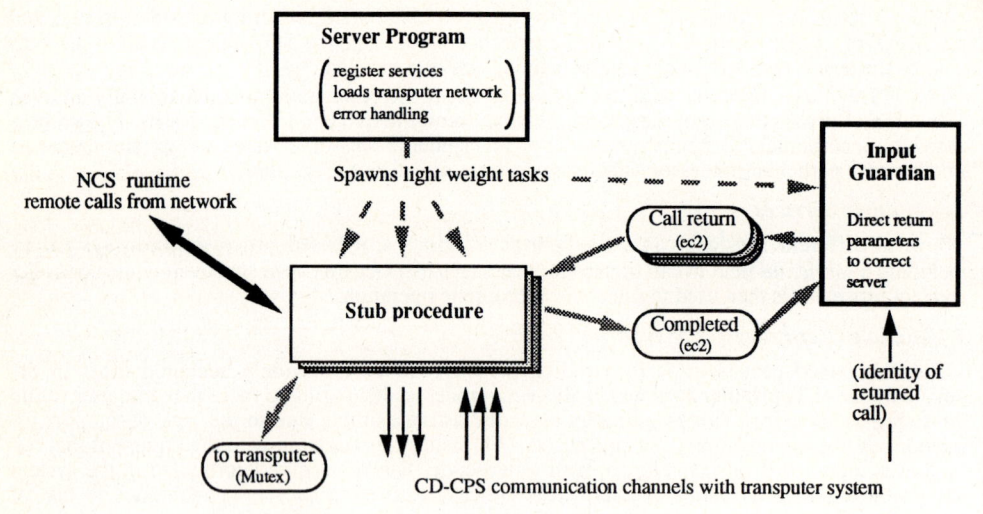

Figure 3. Structure of surrogate server

5.3. The 'Transputer System Manager'

On the Transputer side a buffer process reads in the call parameters and forwards them to a *Transputer System Manager* process. This process schedules the call on a controller process for processing using the slot based processor farm paradigm described in section 4. If there is not a free controller process then the Transputer system manager places the job on a FIFO queue of jobs waiting to be processed. The Transputer system manager is also responsible for forwarding the results of a call back to the surrogate server process via an output buffer.

5.4. Transputer Configuration

The overall configuration of the ANTS system is shown in figure 4. The input/output buffers, Transputer system manager and controller processes are placed on the *root* Transputer. In the current implementation the worker processors are arranged in a linear topology. It is envisaged that future implementations may use a binary or tertiary tree topology in order to increase the bandwidth available between the controller and worker processes. A single, switchable, slot process is also implemented on the root processor to ensure that this processor can be kept fully utilized in small systems.

6. Results

The ANTS system has been tested using up to eighteen Transputers (2 T800's and 16 T414's).

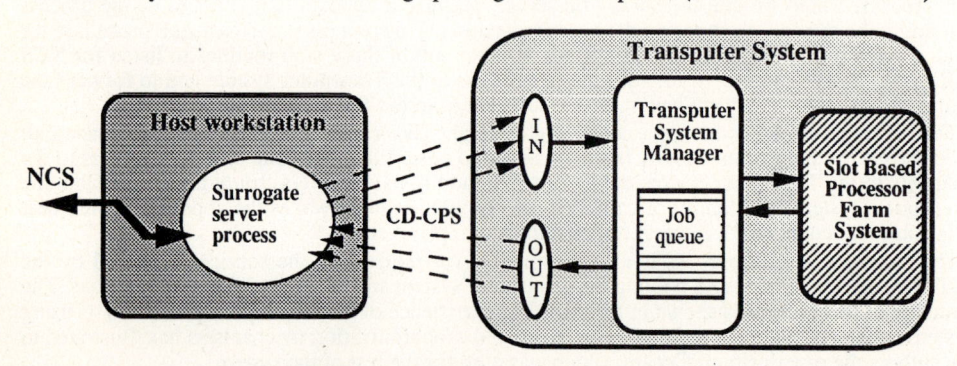

Figure 4. Structure of ANTS system

6.1. A Synthetic 'testbed' Server

To evaluate the general performance of the ANTS system a synthetic '*testbed*' server has been developed. This server simulates an application by generating a number of sub-tasks. Each sub-task is processed by a worker slot. The processing of a sub-task involves a number of iterations of a tight loop. Parameters to the server include the number of sub-tasks to be generated, the number of iterations per sub-task and the size of the sub-task packets. The output is the time that elapsed in the processing of the call as viewed by the controller process.

Tests have shown that for processing loads with a sufficiently high processing to communications ratio an almost linear speed increase can be obtained with increasing numbers of processors. These tests have shown that there is a negligible performance penalty due to the use of the slot based processor farm paradigm.

The performance of ANTS in the processing of multiple simultaneous calls has also been tested. A number of *long lasting* client calls were made. A further client call was then made with the same processing requirement per sub-task, but with fewer sub-tasks. This additional, *reference*, call completes before any of the long lasting client calls. It is the time taken to process the reference call that is shown in figure 5. Line (a) of this graph shows that the time to process a call increases linearly with the number of active calls as expected. The graph is not completely straight, as the total number of slots is not always exactly divisible by the number of active calls; in such cases a new call is favoured with the allocation of an extra slot process.

In general the time taken by a client call is the sum of the processing time and the average time taken to obtain a slot. If there are no free slot processes on a worker processor when a new client call is received slots must be reallocated. A slot process cannot be reallocated until it has completed the processing of its current sub-task. Therefore if the processing requirement per sub-task for the long lasting calls is increased, the time to process the reference call increases. This is shown by the lines (b) and (c) of figure 5, in which the processing requirement per sub-task of the long lasting calls is 50 and 100 times respectively that of the processing requirement for the sub-tasks of the reference call. In general a client call will receive a poor response from the slot based processor farm paradigm if its total processing requirement is small compared to that of the individual sub-tasks of existing client calls.

The 'Max_Slots_Per_Worker' policy can remove the delay involved in the reallocation of slots to a new client call. This is shown in the graph of figure 5. In these experiments each worker processor provided six slot processes and 'Max_Slots_Per_Worker' was set to two. The first three calls to the system each received two slots and no slot reallocation was necessary: the time taken for

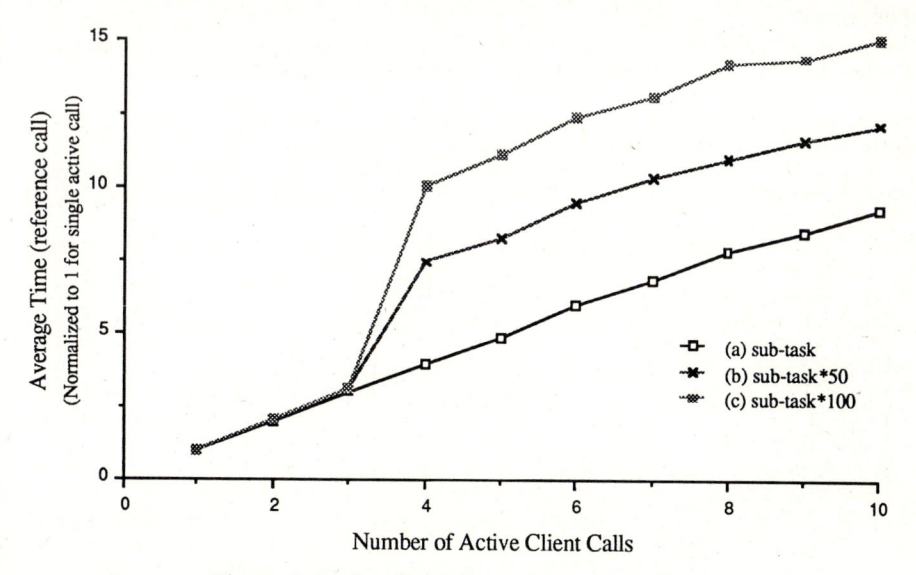

Figure 5. Performance when processing multiple client calls

the reference call was therefore independent of the processing requirement of the sub-tasks of existing calls. However there are no remaining free slots when the fourth and subsequent calls are received and a delay is introduced while slots are reallocated. If the 'Max_Slots_Per_Worker' policy was not used then slots would also have had to be reallocated for the second and third client calls received.

6.2 A Mandelbrot Server

We have also implemented a server that calculates pixel values for a single display line of the Mandelbrot set. This server was designed to be compatible with an Apollo NCS demonstration program that calculates a Mandelbrot image by distributing the processing of display lines to a number of computers. This application has demonstrated the transparency with which an ANTS based server may be used, as no modifications were necessary to the client program. It also demonstrates the potential processing power of such a server; each T800 processor used was found to provide processing power equivalent to approximately four Apollo DN3000 or two DN3500 workstations, which use Motorola 68020 and 68030 processors respectively.

7. Conclusions and Discussion

In this paper we have discussed the rationale for using a Transputer system as a 'compute' server in a heterogeneous computer network. We have described the design, implementation and testing of a prototype system, ANTS. This system has shown that a Transputer system can be used to provide efficient computational services to multiple users of a computer network.

As well as providing application specific services we also envisage that ANTS systems may be used to provide libraries of commonly used computationally intensive routines. It would have the advantage over existing Transputer library mechanisms such as that used in the NAG numerical library [12] in that it would be available to applications running on conventional computers. It would therefore not be necessary to port entire applications to a Transputer system.

Acknowledgements

The work described in this paper was supported by a SERC studentship.

The support of Apollo Computers (now part of Hewlett Packard) in supplying some of the hardware and software used in this is project is also gratefully acknowledged.

References

[1] Freeman L. & Phillips C. (eds.), *Applications of Transputers 1*, Proceedings of the First International Conference on Applications of Transputers, 23-25 August 1989, Liverpool, UK, IOS Press, Amsterdam, 1990.

[2] Amdahl G.M., "Validity of the single-processor approach to achieving large scale computing capabilities", *AFIPS Conference Proceedings*, Vol. 30, AFIPS Press, pp. 483-485, 1967.

[3] Peel R.M.A., "Using Transputers in an Ethernet Environment", in *Developments Using Occam* (proceedings of the 8th Technical Meeting of the Occam User Group), Kerridge J. (ed.), IOS Press, Amsterdam, pp. 167-172, 1988.

[4] Wilbur S. & Bacarisse B., "Building Distributed Systems with Remote Procedure Calls", *Software Engineering Journal*, 2(5), pp.148-159, 1987.

[5] Apollo, *Network Computing System (NCS) Reference*, Apollo Computers Inc., Order No. 010200, 1987.

[6] Apollo, *Network Computing Architecture (NCS) Protocol Specifications*, Apollo Computer Inc., Order No. 010201-A00, 1989.

[7] Hey A.J.G, "Reconfigurable Transputer Networks: Practical Concurrent Computation", in Elliot R. & Hoare C.A.R. (eds.), *Scientific Applications of Multiprocessors*, Prentice Hall, pp. 39-54, 1989.

[8] Allan R.J. & Heck L., "Fortnet: a parallel FORTRAN harness for porting application codes to transputer arrays", in [1], pp. 82-89.

[9] Atkin P., *Performance Maximisation*, Technical note 17, Inmos Ltd., Bristol, 1987.

[10] Shepherd R., *Security aspects of occam 2*, Technical note 32, Inmos Ltd., Bristol, 1987.

[11] Cresco Data, *CD-TSE Transputer Software Environment*, Reference Rev. 1.0, Cresco Data A/S, Øresundsvej 148, DK-2300 Kbh S., Denmark, 1989.

[12] Brown N.G., Delves L.M., Howard G., Downing S., Phillips C., "Numerical Library Development for Transputer arrays", in [1], pp.103-112.

An Environment for the Development of Large Applications in Parallel C

Chris Brown and Michael Rygol
Artificial Intelligence Vision Research Unit
University of Sheffield
Sheffield S10 2TN
Tel: +44 742 768555 Xtn 6551
email: chris@aivru.sheffield.ac.uk

Abstract. The limitations of 3L Parallel C for large projects are discussed, and the various components of a software environment we have built to overcome these limitations are described. This environment greatly enhances the productivity of 3L Parallel C for the development of realistically sized applications. We also describe a novel and low-cost approach to connecting transputers to desktop workstations.

1. Introduction and Overview

3L's parallel C product includes a Transputer C compiler with its associated run-time libraries, and a collection of simple tools for building and loading multi-tasking applications into a transputer network. There is also the so-called *alien file server* (afserver) program which runs on the host and makes the filesystem and console I/O facilities on the host machine available to the network.

These tools perform well, as far as they go, and are sufficient to distribute, say, half a dozen 1000-line tasks around three or four processors. However, when the volume of code and the number of processors have both risen by a factor of 10, these tools become inadequate. Furthermore, the afserver provides no mechanism to access any multi-tasking or inter-process communication (IPC) mechanisms on the *host* computer. This is not surprising, as this server was written for the single tasking PC/DOS environment.

In this paper we describe a run-time environment and a set of development tools which we have constructed using 3L parallel C, which support convenient and efficient development of large applications, and which allow access to the multi-tasking and IPC mechanisms of the Sun Workstation which hosts our transputer network, and to the entire local area network of Suns to which the host machine is connected. This environment has supported the development of a large 3-D machine vision application[2], comprising some 35,000 lines of code, split amongst 10 tasks, most of which are replicated across an array of 25 transputers.

Details of the hardware architecture (called *MARVIN*) on which this environment runs have been reported elsewhere [1]. Essentially MARVIN is a mesh-connected rectangular (3 rows, 8 columns) array of T800 transputers connected via an additional *root* transputer to a Sun-3 workstation. MARVIN has other frame-rate digital video data paths, which are important for the performance of the machine in our own application area (machine vision), but which are not required to run the software described here.

2. The Host File Server

Our *host file server* (hfs) program for the Sun is derived from the Inmos *afserver* code. We have removed those protocols which were specific to the DOS environment, such as the generation of DOS interrupts. We have written a unix device driver to support the link adaptor which connects the host to the root transputer. This is used to field

---

This work was funded by the SERC ACME Directorate under Grant No. GR/E 64497 awarded to Prof. J.P. Frisby and Dr. J.E.W.Mayhew, with industrial sponsorship from GEC.

interrupts so that hfs can 'sleep' whilst waiting for input, rather than burning CPU cycles in a polling loop.

New protocols have been added to permit the creation of additional unix processes on the host, (or other workstations on the network), and to communicate with them. These facilities are described further in section 7.

3. Store-and-Forward Message Routing

The IPC model directly supported by 3L Parallel C resembles the occam model. In particular, if two tasks are to trade data, there must be a direct channel between them; either a *soft* channel (implying that the tasks are on the same processor), or a *hard* channel, requiring that a transputer link is dedicated to the connection. We have found this too limiting for building large applications. One needs the freedom to address messages to any task, without regard to its physical placement on the network.

To achieve this we have implemented a 'store and forward' message routing system. A *routing* task (instantiated on every processor) interprets destination address information in a small header prepended to every message, forwarding the message via the appropriate transputer link to a neighbouring processor if necessary. In this scheme, application tasks connect *only* to the router on their own processor, and only the routers have access to the transputer's links. This scheme is shown in Fig. 1

The destination address consists of a processor I.D. number and a task I.D. number. Each router builds, at run-time, a table mapping processor ids onto link numbers ("Processor 14 is west of here"). The routing algorithm assumes a rectangularly-connected mesh topology with wrap-around connections. (It would be straightforward to rework the algorithm for other regular network topologies, such as a tree or a hypercube). The algorithm is essentially "Go vertically to the right row, then go horizontally to the right column". There is no attempt to dynamically adjust the routing to balance the message traffic, so messages are guaranteed to arrive in the order in which they were sent. To build the routing table, the router needs to know the number of rows and columns in the array, and the number of the processor on which it is running. (The processors are numbered in a simple raster-scan order). This information is made available by a trick — a dummy input port is allocated to the router, which has assigned to it, in place of the usual channel word address, a 32-bit value made up from the 3 items of data required. This is accomplished through statements of the following form appearing

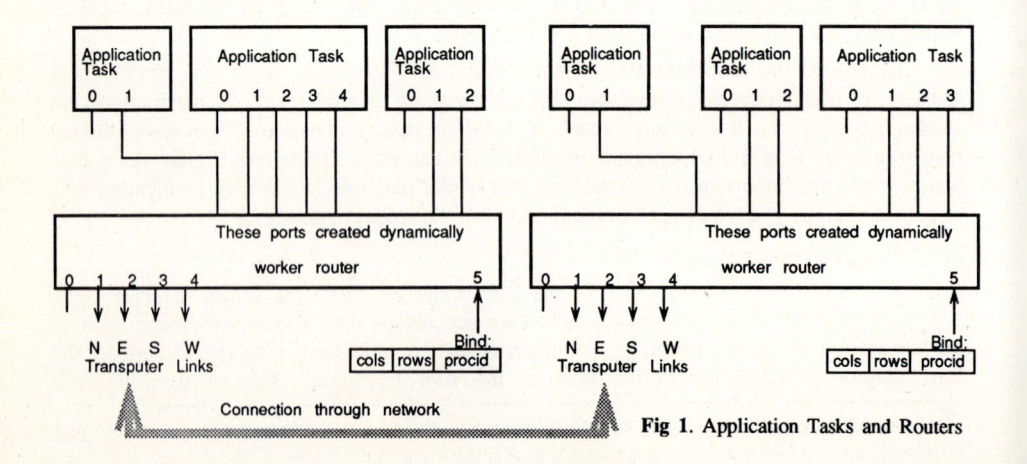

Fig 1. Application Tasks and Routers

in the configuration file:

```
bind input wrouter1[5] value = &0800301
```

To deliver messages destined for *this* processor, the router builds a second table which maps task ids onto internal 'soft' channels. Entries are made in this table at run time in response to *registration messages* sent to the router by the application tasks themselves. Tasks *must* register in this way so that the router knows what their task ids are. A task can register more than one id if it wishes. By building these routing tables at run-time, the routers avoid compiled-in assumptions about which processor they are running on, and what configuration of application tasks are present on that processor.

This routing scheme leads to a very simple view of the world for the application tasks. Each task simply has one (or more) connections to its local router, and need only know the task and processor id of the intended recipient of a message in order to send it.

4. System Configuration Language

```
ROWS 3 COLS 8

wirefile /marvin/parc/wiring.3by8

task stgeom         ins=2   outs=2   STACK=4K  HEAP=14K
root_task postman   ins=14  outs=14  STACK=28k HEAP=200K
task join_task      ins=3   outs=3   STACK=12K HEAP=600K
task tmax           ins=4   outs=4   STACK=14K HEAP=280K
task minteg         ins=3   outs=3   STACK=14K HEAP=60K
task tracker        ins=2   outs=2   STACK=8K  HEAP=440K
task tina           ins=9   outs=9   STACK=18K HEAP=1580K

on 0 1 2 3 4 5 6 7 8 9 10 11 12 13 14 15 16 17 18 19 20 21 22 23
put stgeom

on 0
put join_task

on 1 2 3 4
put minteg

on 0 1 2 3 4 5 6 7
put tracker tmax

on   8 9 10 11 12 13 14 15 16 17 18 19 20 21 22 23
put tina

on root
put postman
```

Fig 2 Example of MCL configuration language

The message routing scheme also leads to a highly regular arrangement of connections between tasks and routers, and between routers themselves. Also, since the same collection of tasks is usually replicated on several processors, we find identical patterns of internal channel connections repeated many times throughout the network. However, the configuration language provided by 3L is totally 'flat' — there is no way to describe the tasks and their interconnections in a hierarchical fashion, and in particular, there is no way to express the notion of *task replication*. Every task on every processor, and every channel, has to be separately and explicitly named and described. This gives rise to large configuration files which are tedious to build by hand. Conceptually simple changes, such as adding an additional task to the top row of processors, require extensive changes which extend throughout the configuration file.

To simplify the configuration process we devised a higher level configuration language (called *MCL*), which requires the user to describe each task (once!), and then simply to list which processors that task is to be instantiated on. A translator (written using the unix utility *awk*) reads the *MCL* description and generates a (much longer) 3L configuration file, automatically generating the channels connecting the application tasks to the routers. This scheme dramatically increases the speed at which one can experiment with different task configurations on the network. Fig. 2 shows an example of the MCL language. This example generates a *900-line* 3L configuration file.

5. Tditool - The Poor Man's Debugger

Version 2.0 of 3L Parallel C has no run-time debugger. In the absence of such facilities, programmers generally resort to 'signpost' debugging by judiciously sprinkling *printf()* calls into the code. Even that approach is not usable here, because only one task in the entire network can call directly on hfs to perform console I/O.

We have provided primitive signpost debugging through a function *net_printf()* which provides a subset of printf's format capability, and automatically routes the output to the host. A separate program *tditool*, running on the Sun, receives these messages. Tditool runs under the SunView window system, generating a small window for each column of processors in the network. (This choice is merely expedient; there are too many processors to have a window each!) Messages received from calls to *net_printf()* are de-multiplexed out to the appropriate window, depending on the processor from which they came. Tditool also has a facility to enter a message and despatch it back to a specified processor and task in the network. This allows the user to hold interactive conversations with any number of tasks in the network, for example to manually control dataflow in the system. As tditool communicates with the network through a separate link, a front end may easily be added by providing a thread with a known id on the root processor to accept asynchronous messages from the user via tditool. Fig 3 shows how tditool appears on the screen.

In these days of mouse-driven symbolic debuggers, it is astonishing (not to mention embarrassing) to even report the development of such a tool. Nonetheless, this "lifeline to the outside world" provided for tasks through *net_printf()* and *tditool* has been an invaluable aid to our software development effort.

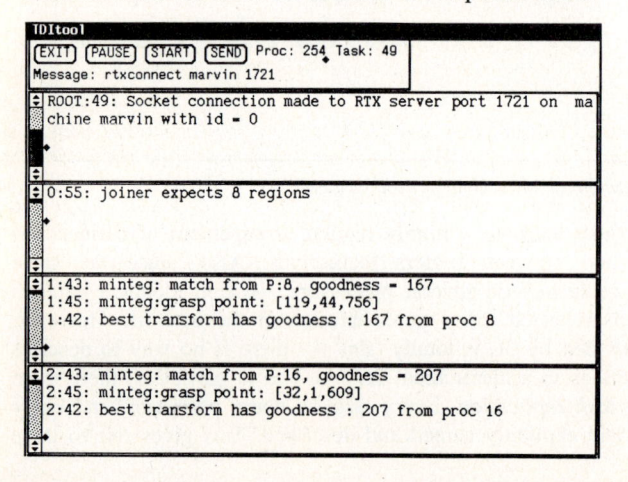

Fig 3. Example of tditool.

Four of the eight windows are shown. Each has a scrollbar. The panel and buttons at the top provide the input facility.

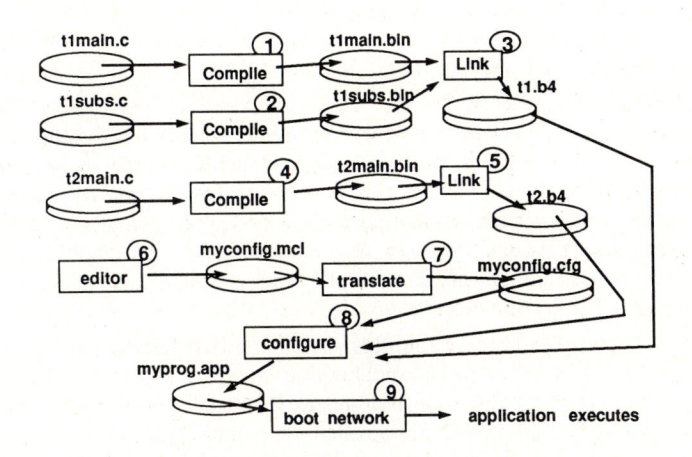

Fig. 4 shows the original approach to building and executing an application. Task t1 is built from two source files *t1main.c* and *t1subs.c*, which are compiled (steps 1,2) and linked (step 3) to create a task image *t1.b4*. Task t2 is built similarly - in this case from a single source file. (Steps 4,5). A 3L configuration file *myconfig.cfg*, describing task placement and interconnection, directs operation of the configurer (step 8) to build an application file *myprog.app* using replicated copies of the task images. The *.cfg* file was originally created tediously by hand. Later, a higher-level configuration language *MCL*, and a translator (step 7) were designed to automate this process. Finally, the application file is booted into the network and executed (step 9).

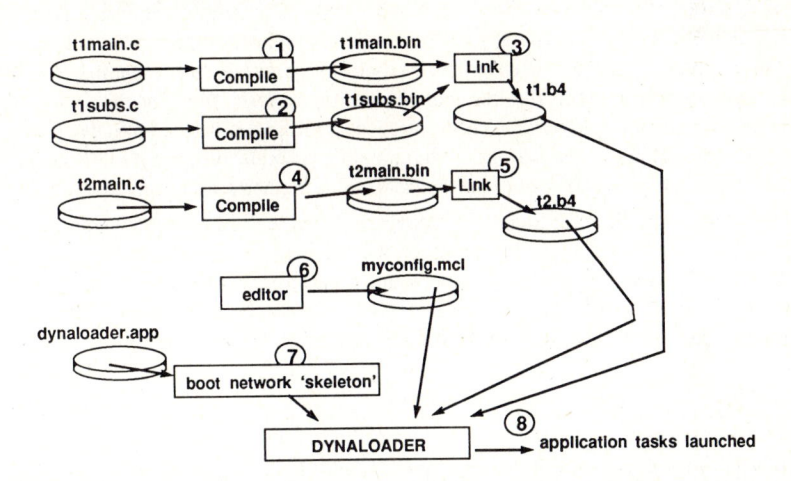

Fig 5 shows the approach currently in use. The task image files *t1.b4*, *t2.b4* are created as before (steps 1 to 5). To run the application, the dynamic loader 'skeleton' application file *dynaloader.app* is booted into the network (step 7), and reads the high-level configuration file *myconfig.mcl* to determine which task images to read in and launch as application tasks. The time-consuming configuration step, and the use of the 3L configuration language, are eliminated entirely, except for the one-off job of building the dynamic loader skeleton.

6. Dynamic Task Loading

The *configurer* utility provided by 3L combines a number of separately compiled and linked *task* files, together with bootstrap code, into a single *application file* which can be downloaded into the network and run. This is the mechanism by which multi-tasking applications are executed. The configurer does not support the notion of *task replication*.

If a task is to be loaded onto, say, 16 processors, then 16 separate copies of that task's code are included in the application file. This makes the application files extremely large (4 Mbytes), slow to load (55 seconds), and very slow to build (4 minutes — these figures are for our current application).

To address these problems we developed a mechanism for *dynamic task loading*, which works as follows. First, a 'skeleton' application file is built which consists of the routers only, plus a *dynamic loader* task which resides on the root transputer. This skeleton is small (about 15 Kbytes per processor), and quite generic. It needs rebuilding only if the physical network topology has changed or if the routers themselves are modified. The routers are enhanced to accept *task instantiation messages*, which are converted into running tasks on receipt.

When an application is to be run, this skeleton is first booted into the network. The name of the *MCL* file describing the configuration is passed as a command-line argument to the dynamic loader on the root transputer. By reading the *MCL* file, the loader determines which tasks are to be instantiated on which processors. For each task, it reads the task file (once!), and builds a task instantiation message. This consists of a header detailing the task's memory and port requirements, (this data is obtained partly from the task's entry in the *MCL* file and partly from the task file itself) followed by the code and static data areas of the actual task (read from the task file). This message is then transmitted to each processor on which that task is to run. When a router receives a task instantiation message, it allocates memory from its own heap for the task's code, stack, and heap; creates new ports for itself, binds them to the task's ports, then launches the task as a thread. (In the skeleton, all free memory is initially allocated to the router's heap).

The dynamic loader uses two threads to overlap the sending of the task instantiation messages with the reading of the next task file. In this way, the huge application file, and the time-consuming step of building it, are eliminated entirely, and loading is substantially speeded (For example, 55 seconds reduced to 20 seconds). Figs 4 and 5 illustrate the old and the new methods of building and executing applications.

These changes have dramatically reduced the time taken to iterate around the edit-compile-test cycle. In a heavily development-oriented environment such as ours, the benefits are enormous. Note that although the mechanism allows new tasks to be added into the network "on the fly", we do not currently exploit this capability. Instead, all tasks are launched immediately upon booting the network.

7. Unix-based IPC

We have added extra protocols into the host file server to allow the creation of a new unix process on the host machine, and to obtain connections to the standard input and/or the standard output of that process. Any number (up to some compiled-in limit) of such processes may be started.

Further protocols are provided to request the host file server to create a *socket*, and make a connection to a remote *server* process running elsewhere on the local area network. (A *socket* is an end-point of a two-way communication channel and is the underlying mechanism for most IPC in Berkeley Unix. It is roughly analogous to a *port* in 3L Parallel C, except that connections between sockets are created and destroyed dynamically, and the connection is asymmetric: a *server's* socket listens for and accepts connections from a *client's* socket). The following code fragments illustrate the use of these facilities:

```
int pipe_id, socket_id;
char buffer[100];
...
pipe_id = pipeline_open("sort", PIPE_OUT_MODE);
pipeline_write(pipe_id, "rat\ncat\ndog\n", 12);
...
socket_id = socket_open("zaphod", 1066);
                /* Machine name and port number */
socket_read(socket_id, buffer, 50);
...
```

Although these services can only be requested directly from hfs by a task on the root processor, we have provided *pipe server* and *socket server* tasks on the root to extend these facilities to any task on the network.

These simple mechanisms have greatly improved the usability of the system. They provide a 'generic' way of adding extra functionality into hfs as required for specific applications. For example, we have written a (unix) program called *dcube*, which is spawned to provide control of the Datacube frame grabbers and frame stores, which form part of our system, but which are mapped into the host Sun's VME address space, and so cannot be controlled directly from the transputer network. More recently, we have written a robot arm driver program which runs on another Sun, and which is controlled via socket-based IPC from the transputer network.

8. Sun - Transputer Interface

Most commercial transputer hardware available for in-Sun use requires a VME backplane in the Sun to accommodate a motherboard or root processor, often with dual-ported memory. MARVIN itself is connected in this way (though it has no dual-ported RAM). However, the price premium paid for Suns with VME backplanes (as compared with the single-board diskless desktop machines such as the Sun-3/60) is large. To provide a cheaper way of connecting transputer networks to diskless Suns we have designed a link-adaptor interface which plugs into the (unused) SCSI port on the Sun. This provides an extremely low-cost connection, with moderate bandwidth (150 Kbytes/sec). The SCSI port is simply used ('abused' may be more honest) as a bi-directional 8-bit data port with a collection of control lines which are pressed into service as register-select and strobe signals. No attempt is made to use the proper SCSI protocol. Consequently, true SCSI peripherals cannot co-exist with the link adaptor interface.

We have used this to provide two 'development' systems of 8 (soon to be 16) processors each. An alternative version of hfs is required for this configuration, but the run-time environment and the application tasks may be moved between the VME and SCSI connected machines without change.

9. Other Ideas

Further ideas for the development of this environment remain to be implemented as and when the need for them arises:

Firstly, we plan to add some form of 'instrumentation' to the routers, enabling them to log (at some specified level of detail) the message traffic. *Logging control messages* sent to the routers would control the level of detail of the log, (including turning it off completely), and request a dump of the logged data to the Sun. A program on the Sun would then permit a post-mortem analysis of the message traffic in tabular or graphical form. If the logging were to record *individual* messages with time-stamps (rather than just statistical or cumulative summaries), then some form of graphical 'action replay' of the message traffic in the system may be possible. Such a tool may help visualise the operation of the machine and identify communication bottlenecks.

Secondly, the logical completion of the dynamic task loading work would be to provide for the dynamic termination and destruction of a task, freeing its memory resources for use by other tasks. This should not be too difficult; and in principle it would allow the 'skeleton' application to stay permanently resident, rather than being repeatedly rebooted into the network. If this were done, the environment might perhaps justifiably be called an operating system. Whether such a development would actually be useful is not clear.

Thirdly, an extension to the debugging utility *tditool* has been proposed, to permit more flexible control of the demultiplexing of messages into windows. For example, menus associated with each window might allow selection of precisely which processor's (and which task's) messages should appear in that window.

10. Summary of Benefits

The work described here greatly enhances the productivity of 3L Parallel C for the development of realistically sized applications by:
- Making it much easier to change the task configuration
- Dramatically shortening the edit-compile-test cycle
- Allowing interactive I/O (for debugging) from any task on the network
- Allowing access to multi-tasking and IPC facilities on a unix host

It would be wrong to imagine that this environment was designed "up front" in its entirety. On the contrary, each piece evolved in order to fix whatever we perceived to be the biggest problem at the time. We have not attempted to build tools to automate the parallelisation of our algorithms. We view this as a fundamentally intellectual effort which is nowhere near sufficiently principled to automate. It is also fun. Neither have we attempted to automate the distribution of the code amongst the computing resources. Once a method of partitioning the workload has been chosen, it is generally fairly easy to visualise and roughly quantify the pattern of data flow. This usually leads to one or two obviously 'sensible' task configurations. We do not feel the need to have the computer help us in these areas.

11. References

[1]   Marvin — Multiprocessor Architecture for Vision
      Chris Brown and Michael Rygol, Proceedings of the 10th Occam User Group Technical Meeting, Enschede, 3-5 April 1989.

[2]   Marvin and Tina: A Multiprocessor Vision System
      Michael Rygol, Stephen Pollard, Chris Brown, and Jennifer Kay,
      Transputer Applications '90.

Transputer Environment to Support Heterogeneous Systems in Robotics

M. Martins-Barata, José C. Cunha, A. Steiger-Garção
Universidade Nova de Lisboa
Departamento de Informática
2825 Monte de Caparica
Portugal

Abstract. This paper describes the design and implementation of an environment for transputer-based systems that is being used for experimentation in robotics. After an introduction to the application domain we describe its basic requirements and the structure of a suitable environment, emphasizing the heterogeneity issue. The environment layers are discussed and a Computerized Control Machine (CNC) monitoring application is described.

1. Introduction

Robotics is a field where a very rich set of research and technical developments have been being concentrated. The Flexible Manufacturing System (FMS) concept brought a challenge about future manufacture and by that reason lots of scientific works were and are being done around it. Recent research done by the Intelligent Robotics Group [8] provides as a preliminary result the need of integrating several programming paradigms. These encompass both symbolic and numeric processing and the capability of addressing real time control issues.

The applications we are addressing in Robotics (namely monitoring and prognosis experiments) involve systems of heterogeneous agents at distinct levels [8]: physical sensors and controllers, sensor integration and virtualization [2], user interfaces with graphics, simulation and Artificial Intelligence knowledge based expert systems. A parallel and distributed architecture is suitable to support the above environment: (i) it provides the required processing power (meeting efficiency requirements); (ii) it fits well into the distributed nature of the applications, regarding multiple specialized agents spread over distinct processing nodes. This architecture can be implemented on a transputer network.

A low-level software architecture for this environment should offer suitable execution mechanisms towards the support of those high-level paradigms, and their mappings onto a real parallel and distributed architecture. It should support the implementation of agents as a set of transputers tasks, but accessing services and resources that may be available through other non transputer based processors (IBM PC, workstations, etc.). The communication facilities offered by the architecture should provide an uniform way of programming systems of cooperating agents.

In order to provide a satisfactory programming environment for an in-house developed transputer network [1], a basic communication network package was developed. It permits communication between tasks using virtual channels. A set of utility modules were also developed so that a network task may have access to general services such as file I/O, user communication with a window and graphics facilities.

Symbolic processing capabilities are supported through the Prolog language, and numeric ones are supported in C [9]. While the low-level services are directly accessible to C programs, we still needed to provide a clean interface for each Prolog agent. This was achieved by extending an existing Prolog interpreter, C-Prolog [6], with a set of communication predicates, and by implementing them on top of the low-level architecture. Each transputer node currently supports multiple Prolog interpreter instantiations, depending on the locally available memory.

2. Environment for heterogeneous multiple agents systems

The research we are doing in robotics, monitoring and prognosis can rely upon systems of specialized agents, each providing a specific service to a global application. The requirements of each specific application are met by defining suitable sets of specialized agents, e.g. the monitoring of a specific process requires sensors, controllers, simulations and user interfaces agents. The global application is supported through the cooperation of its agents, executing in parallel, and coordinated by a supervisor process.

Currently agents' heterogeneity in robotics exists due to multiple reasons: i) the broad spectrum of encompassed subjects, ii) distinct programming paradigms and tools must be used at each level of abstraction, and iii) most of the currently existing tools are compromised with specific machines (hardware and operating systems). Sensorial processing illustrates item i): depending on the physical principle used (vision, tactile, frequency signal analysis, etc.) a different hardware architecture is used. According to the goals we have in mind and the nature of the problem, we consider the use of procedural and symbolic / logic programming paradigms. Finally, case iii) exists because many software houses started developing specific applications to be explored using some of the popular machines (personal computers, workstations, etc.). Mainly these applications are specialized tools meant to be used on specific fields (Knowledge Base Shells, CAD System, Graphics Stations, etc.).

The design of an application in our environment comprises the following steps: i) identification of all necessary agents and their functionality to fit the application needs; ii) individual agent's implementation and iii) agents' mapping on the required machines. To make possible this approach, all the machines and related tools must be integrated in spite of their heterogeneous nature. The integration can be understood as an abstract layered system where each abstract layer corresponds to the integration of the several similar but heterogeneous layers of each component system. Fig(1) illustrates the integration of three different hardware and software systems: a personal computer, a workstation and a transputer network. The inner layer supports hardware integration by means of an InMos Links based network [5]. InMos Links provide high-speed dedicated communication channels, and allow a very simple use by a non InMos computer: it only needs an IMSC011/012 link adaptor based board. At system level the integration is done by adding the necessary device drivers and exporting the

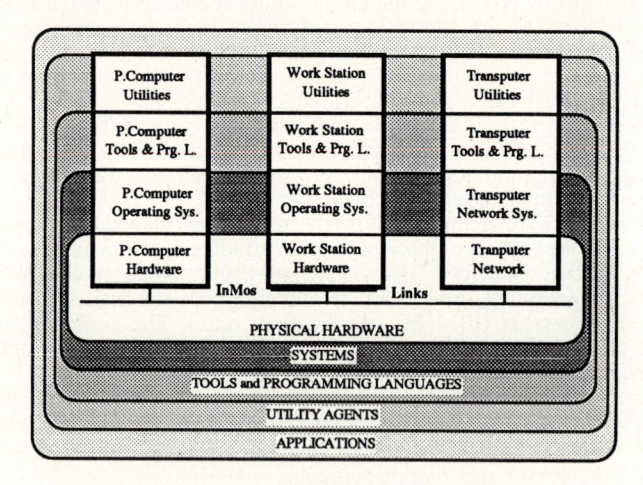

Fig(1)
Integration of Heterogeneous System Layers

provided services to the upper levels. The integration must also be done at the next level by incorporating into the existing tools and programming languages suitable mechanisms to access the lower level services. Programming language integration is done by making the imported services accessible to the programmer. User configurable tools can also be integrated by a similar procedure. An utility agent is a program developed by an integrated tool or programming language. It can run on the local machine as a process and still be accessible for communication from the overall system.

3. A low-level software architecture for transputer networks

3.1 Why transputers have been used

Since the beginning we aimed at the development of testbeds for experimentation in robotics. We found out that several distinct tools available in our laboratory machines could be used to support the required processing agents. Thus we started with an heterogeneous system based on personal computers (PCs) and workstations. The workstations were interconnected by a local Ethernet network and the PCs were directly connected to them through RS232 serial lines. Typical agents running on the workstations were AI shells, relational data bases, solid modelling CADs and graphics. PCs were mainly used as sensor and machine controller interfaces. The several heterogeneous agents were integrated by means of the existing network of workstations.

The decision about the use of transputers was mainly based on two factors: i) the possibility of designing high performance systems at reduced costs; ii) their communication channels permit the development of more efficient interprocess communication mechanisms (specially at sensor processing levels [2]). The simplicity of transputer based hardware design was assessed by the development of a transputer network [1]. The development of an operating system like layer was necessary because most of the available systems are too much hardware compromised, being less suitable to be integrated into specific environments. Additionally, owning an in house developed system will make future configurations or refinements easier.

3.2 Network hardware structure

In order to preserve software compatibility, the developed network has a functional structure like the IMSB008 boards. While IMSB008 boards are meant to be installed inside

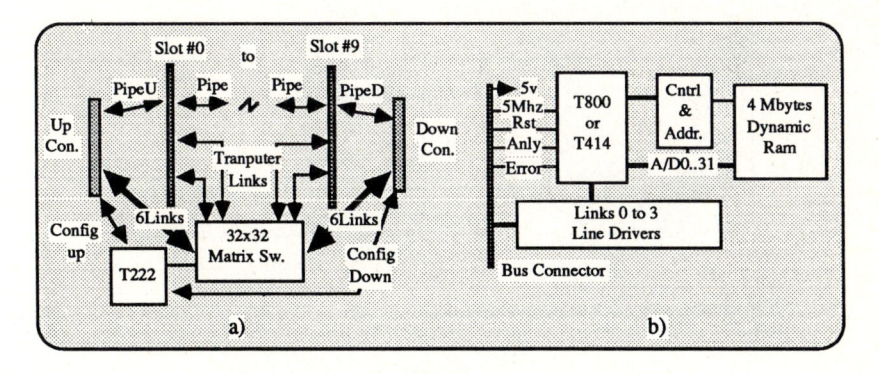

Fig(2)
Transputer network hardware structure:
a) links, matrix switch and processor slots; b) processor modules

PCs, we have decided for an autonomous structure providing the necessary power supply for the installed CPU boards and the necessary signal buffering to external link connections. The network can grow easily because new modules can be inserted into the chain [1].

Network and processor diagrams are presented in Fig(2). It is divided in two sections: a) presents the communications physical hardware links and processor slots; b) presents the internal processor module block structure. Each processor module is configured to boot from link, and it can only communicate by means of its four links. When it is inserted in one slot, two links are used by the physical chain and the remaining two are directly connected to the local matrix switch. An extra processor T222 is used to support a secondary matrix switch control network. Besides the Pipe Up and Down channels, each module can communicate with 6 Up and Down additional links. Network control and error supervising is done by chaining the Error, Reset and Analyze Up and Down lines (not shown in the figure). These lines are connected to the host system: an IBM AT equipped with an IMSB004 compatible board.

3.3 Network system logical structure

To integrate the transputer network in an heterogeneous system a proper layer must be available. The network software that was developed provides basic operating system services to each running task, namely file I/O and interprocess communication. It provides the same functionality of a multi-tasking operating system.

All the processors in the hardware architecture presented in Fig(2) are connected as a ring network by closing the loop through the Up and down pipe links. This ring supports the system level services. After being booted, each transputer works as exemplified in Fig(3). In both cases there is a *Network Task* taking care of the message routing between all processors. Situation a) illustrates the case of a general processing node: two tasks *Task a* and *Task b* are running concurrently. Because these tasks need to access file I/O services, they are connected through an internal channel to a *File I/O Task* which in turn routes the requests to a network *File Server Task*. The extra two hard link channels are used by each task. These links are directly connected to the matrix switch, and they can of course be used to establish a direct communication with another network task. Another mechanism for task communication is supported by the *Network Task* : the connection between *Task b* and *Network Task* permits the communication of *Task b* with any other task somewhere in the network.

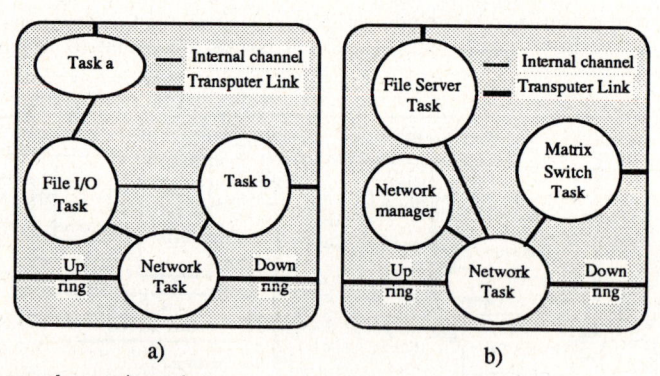

a) general processing node
b) file server, network manager and matrix switch tasks.
Task File I/O in a) routes all requests to task File Server in b)

Fig(3)
Network task organization

Case b) corresponds to a special processing node where the management tasks have been concentrated (it is not mandatory to concentrate all of these tasks in one single node). An external file server computer, like an IBM Pc/At or a workstation, must be directly connected through an hardware link to the File *Server Task*. This task routes all network file I/O requests to the external file server. More than one external file server can be used if we instantiate the *File Server Task* in more processor nodes and connect it to the corresponding file server computer. The *Network manager* task must be unique and it manages the necessary network global data structures to support message routing and virtual channels (presented in 3.4). Finally, the *Matrix Switch Task* controls the matrix switch sub-network. After booting, it sends the necessary commands to the matrix switch in order to establish default connections. At run time, it can receive requests for new connections / cancelations from the network.

3.4 Virtual channels

It is well known the impact of current limitations on the physically available transputer links upon the execution environment of occam programs and any distributed application. Several approaches may be followed towards the removal of the above limitation, as far as a high-level program is concerned (be it an occam [10] program or another parallel programming language).

A possible approach to the above problem is referred in section 3.5, relying on a dynamic transputer link reconfiguration scheme. This guarantees no loss of efficiency in the communication as a new direct (non-buffered) connection is established according to the run-time needs of the application processes. The penalty to be paid comes from the need to define a switching service, which must be responsible for the management of the link connections between transputers (cf. section 3.3 *Matrix Switch Task*).

In this section, we discuss a distinct approach corresponding to the virtualization of the connections, and relying on a system layer that is responsible for message routing and buffer processing. A criticism may be stated here that this does not retain the occam synchronous communication model, as well as its direct mapping on the transputer-based hardware, loosing on efficiency. Regarding the programming model we offer primitives for asynchronous and synchronous interprocess communication, and so there is no limitation on the high-level model. Regarding efficiency the criticism may be true but one gains in getting more flexible communication schemes.

The *Network Task* provides the basic interprocess communication mechanism: the virtual channel. It implements a port-based message-passing mechanism supporting communication schemes with one consumer and many producer processes. The consumer creates a global named port by issuing a request to the *Network manager*. Similarly, any producer makes a connection to a named port by requesting an open operation that establishes a virtual channel connection. The term *virtual* means that the producer has no need to take care of the consumer physical location and any necessary intermediary routings. Virtual channels enable the communication between heterogeneous tasks that may be running on the network: the only thing that must be previously defined is the message protocol.

This strategy allows us to run servers, e.g. the *File Server Task* and *Matrix Switch Task*, that provide specialized services to the network. Each server creates a port that can be opened by any network task needing these services. New services servers can be added in the same way.

Because virtual channels are high-level services, being supported by the *Network Task* and the transputer's physical links, buffering is required at each node. Also, at the consuming task node messages are stored in a local FIFO buffer. Thus there is an indefinite delay between the transmission and the reception of a message. A synchronous message transmission implies no buffering at the consumer node and it relies upon the return of an acknowledge message. This mechanism can be used to synchronize tasks.

The main services that the *Network Task* offers to an user task are: initialization, global port name management, port creation and opening, asynchronous message send, synchronous message send, reception of message from a port, and reception of a message from any port (non-deterministically selected) in a specified set of ports (presented in 4.).

Deadlock avoidance related to asynchronous buffered communication is also handled by the *Network Task*. Additionally, the underlying transport system preserves the message arrival order between a pair of processes in the network.

3.5 Services and Servers

A basic strategy for heterogeneous agents integration is the use of the *Server* concept. The *Server* agent is visible in the network through a named port, and is able to execute specialized services. The requests for services are sequentially processed by each server. These messages must follow a pre-defined service protocol. Fig(3) b) presents two server agents: a *File Server Task* and a *Matrix Switch Task*. In the first case, the actual server is running on a non transputer machine (Pc or workstation), and the *File Server Task* supports its interface to the transputer network. In the second case the server is itself running as a transputer task; it receives matrix switch connection requests and translates them to the matrix switch network.

4. Language interfaces

The design of new agents or the integration of existing ones can be made easier if the programming language offers mechanisms to access the previous described system services.

4.1 System access from C

The interface libraries implemented for C programmers are: i) *Network Interface* and ii) *File I/O*. This makes all of the system layer facilities accessible to the C programming level. Space limitations preclude us from further discussing the details of the corresponding C functions, but some of them are presented in Fig(4).

4.1 System primitives access from Prolog

Prolog programs can be executed in the transputer-based architecture as tasks, by configuring multiple instances of a Prolog interpreter, and mapping them into multiple processor nodes. Each Prolog process on a transputer node possesses private program clauses (consulted during an initialization phase, by requests made to the File Server Tasks) as well as workspace memory areas, allocated from the locally available memory in each node.

This interpreter is mostly written in C and its integration in the network is similar to any C program. However, a clean interface must be offered to the Prolog programmer, allowing the specification of systems of cooperating agents written in Prolog.

```
short int create_port(char *Port_name)
short int open_port(char *Port_name, int mode)
int async_send(short int Port, char *Message, int size)
int sync_send(short int Port, char *Message, int size, Time)
int message_input(short int Port, int Time, char **Message_ptr)
int message_any(int Time, char **Message_ptr, int nPort, short int Port1, ... )
```

Fig(4)
Main C system communication primitives. See also Fig(5)

```
create_port( Port_Name, Port )              open_port( Port_Name, Mode, Port )
asynchronous_send( Port, Message )          synchronous_send( Port, Time, Message )
receive_message( Port, Time, Message )      receive_any( List_of_Ports, Time, Message )

            Port_Name : Name of the virtual channel
            Port : Internal identifier for the virtual channel
            List_of_Ports : List of internal channel identifiers
            Message : Message text ( a Prolog term )
            Mode : one of (forever, no_wait)
            Time : Time-out specification,
                   one of (forever, no_wait, time_count)
```

Fig(5)
Prolog system built-in communication predicates.
*Note: arguments in italic must be uninstantiated variables
on input and are bound on output to a return value.*

On defining the communication model we are aware of the intensive current research on novel parallel Prolog dialects, which is still an open issue. So we decided to provide a lower-level interface of a Prolog task to the system layer environment [3] meeting two basic requirements: i) access to file I/O services, and ii) interprocess communication facilities. Prolog processes communicate through ports by sending and receiving Prolog terms (i.e. the fundamental structure handled by Prolog programs). Port-based interprocess communication generalizes the I/O interface of a conventional Prolog process, relying on the built-in predicates shown in Fig(5) (whose names hint their functions). By using this model it is possible to build systems where multiple agents cooperate, some of them being specified in Prolog while others are specified in C, or any other language having an interface to the system layer. This is briefly illustrated in the following section for an example application.

5. An application

FMS systems use computerized numerical controlled machine tools. In order to increase their productivity and work quality a suitable monitoring and prognostic system is required. Due to the contextual nature of the evaluation of the relevant parameters, sensorial data interpretation and resulting actions should be done by having in mind specific working conditions: machine to be used, machined material type, desired accuracy, tool wear permitted, etc.

The overall monitoring system structure is presented in Fig(6). It shows three levels of detail: the physical process under monitoring (CNC Lath [4]) and related sensors; the transputer network and non transputer processors (Pc/At); the system and application tasks. The tasks mapping into the physical processors and their logical interconnections are highlighted. The application is to characterize and monitor one of the CNC machine working conditions, namely its sound characteristics. The sensed characteristics are contextually interpreted according to the CNC program being executed. Starting with an user command (issued through the user interface task) a CNC program sequencer is activated as a transputer task. This task is responsible for the update of the knowledge base (managed by a Prolog task) with the current machine status: CNC instruction being executed, current tool, etc.

Each time a new CNC program is introduced into the system, a learning phase is required in order to determine the normal behaviour patterns (for each CNC instruction) and register them in the knowledge base. Once trained, the monitoring tasks evaluate the actual sensed patterns against the previously learned ones, and report to the user about the system behaviour. The tasks shown in Fig(6) fulfil the application requirements by relying on the services provided by the previously described system and language layers. The cooperation between the application tasks and the specific servers was easily programmed under this environment.

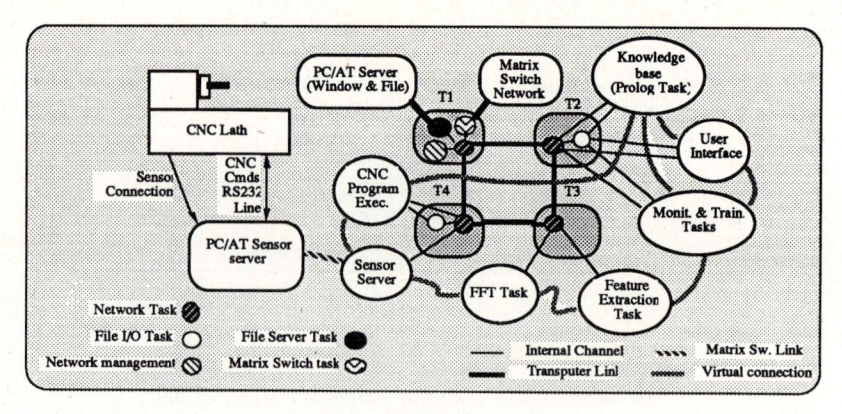

Fig(6)
Logical and physical structure of the example application

6. Conclusions and Future work

Regarding the presented approach for the environment, we found out that we have achieved a reasonable degree of support for heterogeneous systems. Additionally, the features that have recently been announced by Inmos [7] for the forthcoming H1 transputer will allow a more efficient implementation of our system layer.

The presented application is being incrementally enriched with new sensors and dedicated transputer based acquisition modules, in order to do experiments with monitoring and prognosis in a wider sensorial environment. We believe this will be possible on top of the developed environment, due to its inherent modular characteristics.

Acknowelegements. To Luís Silva and João Cabral for their work on the system level implementation. To colleagues of the Intelligent Robotics Group of UNL.

References

[1] Barata M. M., *Transputer Based Multiprocessor System*, UNL DI 49/88, Lisbon, 1988.
[2] Barata M. M.; Steiger-Garção, A., *Sensor Environment for Prognosis and Monitoring Systems Support*, presented in 3rd ISRAM'90 Conference (International Symposium on Robotics and Manufacturing), British Columbia, July 18-20 1990.
[3] Cunha, J. C.; Medeiros, P. ; Carvalhosa, M., *Interfacing Prolog to an Operating System Environment: Mechanisms for Concurrency and Parallelism Control*, UNL DI 15/87, Lisbon, April 1987.
[4] DENDFORD Computerized Machines and Systems, *Starturn Programming Instruction & Maintenance Manual*, UK 1988.
[5] InMos Limited, *The Transputer Data Book*, InMos, 1988.
[6] Pereira, F.(ed.) , *C Prolog User's Manual*, DAI Edinburgh University, 1983.
[7] Pountain, D. , *Virtual Channels: The Next Generation of Transputers*, Byte Magazine, April 1990.
[8] Steiger-Garção, A.; Barata, M.M.; Gomes, Luís F.S., *Integrated Environment for Prognosis and Monitoring Systems Support*, UNIDO 1st Workshop, Lisbon, September 1989.
[9] 3L Ltd, *Parallel C User Guide*, Peel House, Scotland.
[10] InMos Limited, The occam 2 Reference Manual, Prentice-Hall, 1987.

Numerical Algorithm Libraries for Multicomputers.

R.J.Allan
Advanced Research Computing Group, S.E.R.C., Daresbury Laboratory,
Warrington, WA4 4AD, U.K.

Abstract. A new strategy is described for interfacing numerical routines to parallel computers, in the form of a library of algorithms which handle data distributed across many processors. This data may be computed in situ by the parallel application which has access to underlying communications using the Fortnet paradigm to provide portability and performance and tools. Data passing in the library is implicit. One library is implemented as a set of algorithms providing the functionality of VecLib to allow use of automatic vectorisation tools to produce parallel code. Some examples of using the parallel routines illustrate a generally useful programming style.

1. Introduction

The work described in this contribution forms part of an ongoing development using the Fortnet programming environment [1] and extends its use to the area of parallel numerical algorithm libraries. During this work a number of strategies for global communications are being investigated, the final one used will depend on the hardware available. We present just one approach which has been tested here.

It is possible to remove message passing from numerical programs by formulating the latter in terms of elementary numerical operations with distributed data and operations which redistribute data in an optimum fashion. The vector formulation is well understood and lends itself to automatic vectorisation tools (*e.g.* VAST-2 [2]) which may also be used for automatic parallelisation when the library is internally parallel. Whilst hand optimisation by putting explicit communications into individual routines will always yield higher performance, we aim for "programmability" using an environment which has skeleton subroutines, rather like special purpose harnesses, to acess globally defined variables for rapid applications development. This kind of approach is also familiar, and many grid-type applications have been written in a similar structured way, for instance by Suprenum [3]. This is consistent with the coarse-grained nature of current work on multicomputers, and their use of high performance floating-point engines, although it also permits implicitly fine-grain programming.

The library is written to use the Fortnet message passing environment to achieve some portability. Fortnet is a multi-layered system of subroutines, each being largely independent of the previous one providing calling conventions are adhered to. Independent optimisation is possible in each layer. The structure of Fortnet is now:

1) Occam-2 communication harness, or other low-level harness (such as 3L parallel FORTRAN) to pass messages between transputers in a controlled fashion: provides point to point communications, accesses front-end file-store, prints diagnostic messages to the screen, and does bookkeeping.

2) A layer of FORTRAN-77 subroutines called as an interface to the Occam or other subsystem. These incorporate a protocol to verify the transmission of messages and warn of any problems. Whilst novel handshaking and blocking is used which differs from other systems, the routine calls are superficially similar to those on hypercube machines such as the Intel iPSC. This layer provides a portable interface and is described in detail in [1].

3) Active profiling is in general the only way to test performance of a parallel algorithm. This, and graphical replay of parallel execution, are now built into stage 2 and discussed in [4].

4) Development of a generic set of global–memory operations is in progress. This is the main subject of this contribution.

5) The highest layer of the environment would directly call these global routines to do numerical tasks. Standard VecLib calls have already been implemented in this way for distributed data, and matrix algorithms are being adapted. These are not fully described here as space does not permit, but are documented and compared with other work in a longer report [2].

Fortnet can be had for use with the following low–level routing software and compilers and from several sources:
i) Meiko Computing Surface Occam–2 and FORTRAN–77
ii) Meiko CSTOOLS
iii) Intel iPSC FORTRAN–77
iv) 3L Parallel FORTRAN–77
v) UNIX sockets

2. Fortnet Distributed Library Strategy

Several strategies have been adopted to write parallel algorithm libraries. They should rely on some underlying global communications scheme rather than ad hoc solutions for each routine. The reason for this is twofold; firstly there is a multiplication of effort in writing communications into each algorithm where the job can be done once, secondly there is the question of data placement. Programmability arises through hiding the communications routing altogether inside convenient packages which carry out certain actions on globally distributed data. Assumptions must be made in doing this, but first what are the essential actions?
i) distribute data across global memory (scatter) from local variables
ii) collect data from global memory to local (gather)
iii) move data in global memory
iv) transform data in global memory

Item (iv) is the global algorithm which is the goal of our work. Items (i) to (iii) may be steps towards it. Other operations are identical to those on sequential vector computers such as local gather, scatter, copy and vector algorithms and might even be implemented in hardware as on the Intel [2] or Suprenum [3]. We would however like to consider global data motion in a MIMD computer to be expressible in the same way as vector operations in a vector computer.

2.1. Sequential or parallel calling program

A decision has to be made which is: will data be moved to processors before the operation of each numerical routine which is called from a serial host program, or: will data be acted upon no matter where it is in the computer by routines called synchronously by all processors?

The first of these solutions has been widely used, for instance in the Liverpool software [5] and treats the array as an attached numerical engine. My own experiments mainly employed the second, which permits parallel programming of an application together with parallel library calls. Both these approaches permit the following:
i) routing may be optimised, eventually in hardware
ii) global communications may be optimised, possibly in hardware
iii) algorithms may map on to shared–memory architectures or vice versa
iv) Communications can be tested once and for all and proved to be deadlock free
v) Programmer free to concentrate on applications rather than difficult problems of data movement
vi) most programs spend a lot of time generating expensive data "in situ" and a true parallel programming paradigm is essential (this is easier in the second approach)
vii) portability can be assured by modifying only communications layers
viii) Analysis and performance tools may be built into well–defined communications layers (such as Fortnet).
ix) automatic parallelisation tools are possible which employ well defined mathematical objects (the library routines)

As the communication speed of parallel computers increases redistribution of data can be carried out so that algorithms may be made simpler and given data with an optimum placement. In adapting some existing parallel algorithms to the Fortnet library interface this has already been done, and a set of routines is provided which, for instance, redistribute matrix data to storeage by whole columns on processors.

2.2. Local and Distributed Data Types

In working with parallel distributed-memory computers two types of data emerge: those which are needed only locally and those which must be globally accessible. We have therefore made explicit use of these two types in designing the interface. Local data types are just those defined within a program on a single processor, and within a single process. They are protected from access by any other process except by explicit message passing, which is generally the most problematic area for programming. We have therefore made areas of data accessible to any processor by calls to the library, in which each routine must be called synchronously by all processors in order to perform internal communication. Global data is referenced in the calling sequences by a number of symbolic variables. Data may be put into memory pointed to by these variables, moved between them and operated on by algorithms, but the user need have no knowledge of how the communications is carried out.

The symbolic variables are treated as contiguous distributed vectors (although some of the routines access them as square matrices). Any other form of matrix can be mapped on to them by calculating offsets. In practice performance is critically dependent on data placement for a particular kind of algorithm. Often storage of matrices with a complete column per processor is preferred. Some routines therefore rearrange the data if there is sufficient memory before beginning numerical work. We emphasise that this is only necessary to gain maximum performance.

3. Fortnet IOSUP library

The Fortnet IOSUP global communications library differs significantly from other developments and depends fundamentally on, firstly the set of global symbolic variables which reference real data somewhere in the multicomputer's memory as just described, and secondly, on a set of routines which control completely parallel overlapped communications and allow movement of data between these variables.

During the course of our work it has been possible to identify a small number of communication patterns which are frequently met. These involve operations with one, tow, three or more vectors and an equivalent number of processors, or less, may need to communicate. Systematic work can be done to parallelise these patterns, as described in section 4, and a number of "skeleton" routines have been written. These routines are in the form of harnesses to which the user can supply a function name that performs a particular numerical operation, which may be very complex in coarse-grained scenarios. This is described in section 3.2. Simpler routines are provided to find which elements are on a given processor, the next element on that processor from a given one, or which processor holds a given element. Other routines assign space, put and fetch real data from the symbolic storage, perform gather, scatter and more complex operations, these are now described.

3.1. Global communications routines in the IOSUP library

assign('a',nbytes) — assign nbytes of local memory for storage of data in symbolic variable 'a' (up to eight characters) on the rocessor which calls it. Enter 'a' into the symbol table for this processor. This is a "monadic" routine (i.e. executed on each processor with no communications).

put(iproc,x,offx,stepx,'a',offa,stepa,n) — copy n elements of data from real variable x defined locally on processor iproc into globally defined memory referenced by symbol 'a'. Offsets for start of data and strides are given. Communications are internal and 'a' is defined in previous assignment calls. A distributed scatter operation.

fetch(iproc,'a',offa,stepa,x,offx,stepx,n) — reverse of above. A distributed gather operation.

gather0('a',offa,stepa,'b',offb,stepb,n) — on the processor on which this is called, takes all available elements of 'a' starting from the given offset and with the given stride and attempts to store them in given elements of 'b' if such are in local memory area. This is a monadic routine.

scatter1(i,j,'a',offa,stepa,n) — finds all available elements of 'a' as described which are present on processor i and attempts to send them as a single message to processor j. This is a "dyadic" operation (i.e. pairs of processors communicate).
gather1(i,j,'b',offb,stepb,n) — receives a message from processor i on processor j and attempts to store the data into 'b' in local memory. A dyadic operation.

Gather1, scatter1 and gather0 are not usually called by the user. They do however form the elementary basis of higher routines. They are very powerful and quite novel in their behaviour. They carry out masking so that only elements which can actually be stored in local memory on j are sent, the message contains only the "intermediate" or "compressed" vector b_j^i, and is preceeded by protocol as follows:
protocol index
number of index bytes
index bytes
number of data bytes
data

The protocol index is
0 — no data available, abort
1 — data as requested
2 — partial data, single offset and stride description
3 — partial data, separate offset sent for each element

gather2(j,'a',offa,stepa,'b',offb,stepb,n) — collects data referenced by symbol 'a' from all processors, including processor j, and attempts to store it in 'b' on processor j. It build up the sum of compressed vectors $b_j = \sum_i b_j^i$ into the jth "segment" of b. As an example we illustrate how that can be done in terms of the simpler routines:

```
    subroutine gather2(j,'a',offa,stepa,'b',offb,stepb,n)
    ...
c dyadic part
    do i=1,nproc
    if(i.eq.inode.and.i.ne.j)
 1  call scatter1(i,j,'a',offa,stepa,n)
    if(inode.eq.j.and.i.ne.j)
 1  call gather1(i,j,'b',offb,stepb,n)
    end do
c monadic part
    if(inode.eq.j)
 1  call gather0('a',offa,stepa,'b',offb,stepb,n)
    end
```

We see that this example has a simple structure, starting with communication between pairs of processors and finishing with the remaining local operations. This observation has been found to be quite general and forms the basis of our algorithmic work described below.

3.2. Skeleton Routines

Some of the global communication primitives use to build the library are now listed:
global1('a',offa,stepa,n,fun) — computes the vector a=fun(a) elementwise
global2(c,offc,stepc,a,offa,stepa,n,fun) — computes the vector c=fun(a) elementwise
global3(c,offc,stepc,b,offb,stepb,a,offa,stepa,n,fun) — computes the vector c=fun(b,a)
global1a('a',offa,stepa,n,fun,alpha) — computes the vector a=fun(alpha) elementwise
global2a(c,offc,stepc,a,offa,stepa,n,fun,alpha) — computes the vector c=fun(alpha,a) elementwise
global3a(c,offc,stepc,b,offb,stepb,a,offa,stepa,n,fun,alpha) — computes the vector c=fun(alpha,b,a)

4. Covering Scheme.

An important requirement of global communications is that they should work in parallel. The skeleton routines require communications between constituents of all pairs of processors (e.g. in a vector copy), or of all sets of k processors in an array of nproc processors. It is possible to optimise the parallelism in this by "covering" the machine's nproc processors with as many independant k-fold connected subsets as possible, and allow communications within each to be concurrent with the others, and then use another covering with different connections and so on until all possibilities have been exhausted.

For pairs we have written a function ncover=dyadic(nproc) and for triads ncover=triadic(nproc). Higher schemes are possible. Of course if nproc is large, then ncover is *very* large illustrating a fundamental difficulty of global communications schemes – the inflation in data movement. This will not occur in current machines with high compute to communicate ratios (coarse grain).

To use the above covering schemes a "connection matrix" can be accessed.
   common/cover/connect(nproc)
the nth entry of this indicates that processor connect(n) should talk to processor n.

The matrix is filled by calling
   covering(i,k,nproc) — for the ith k-fold covering of nproc processors.
These routines are written in C and are monadic.

The worst algorithm for a multicomputer is a matrix transpose because it is all communications with no computation. We illustrate part of one as follows

```
    subroutine mtrans(...)
    ...
    common/cover/connect(nproc)
c dyadic part
    m=dyadic(nproc)
    do i=1,m
     call covering(i,2,nproc)
     do k=1,nproc
      k2=connect(k)
      if(inode.eq.k.or.inode.eq.k2)then
c swap all elements of matrix and its transpose between procs k and k2
       ...
      end if
     end do
    end do
c do remaining monadic part
    ...
    end
```

5. Vector Libraries

To date a number of the simpler routines replacing calls to the VecLib [2], MathAdvantage, Linpack, Eispack and CRAY libraries have been programmed. The number of routines included will be extended as required and as experience in optimising them grows.

We do not list the routines in the library, but provide an example of a gaussian elimination program to show their use:

```
    subroutine gauss(n,a,ia,ndim)
    implicit real*8(a-h,o-z)
    character*8 a
c switch on broadcasting mode for functions
    call br$all('ON')
    do i=1,n
c find offset in global vector for element i,i of square matrix
     ioff=index2d(n,i,i)
c find index of global vector with largest element (requires broadcasting)
```

```
          j=idamax(n-i+1,a,ioff,1)
          joff=index2d(n,j,i)
c swap rows of global a
          call dswap(n-i+1,a,ioff,n,a,joff,n)
c find element ioff of global vector a and broadcast it into local variable t
          t=fetch$a(a,ioff)
          do j=i+1,n
          joff=index2d(n,j,i)
          s=fetch$a(a,joff)
          v=-s/t
c scale row and add to another row
          call daxpy(n-i+1,v,a,ioff,n,a,joff,n)
          end do
          end do
          call br$all('RESET')
          end
```

6. Acknowledgements

Part of the practical work in developing Fortnet and its parallel algorithm library was carried out on a Meiko M10 Computing Surface which is on loan from the SERC/DTI Transputer Initiative loan pool. The work on Fortnet was done in collaboration with Dr. Lydia Heck of Durham University. My thanks are due to her for many valuable discussions on parallel computing.

7. References

[1] R.J.Allan, L.Heck and S.Zurek "Parallel FORTRAN in scientific computing: a new Occam harness called Fortnet" Computer Physics Communications (1990) in press and R.J.Allan and L.Heck "Fortnet: a parallel FORTRAN harness for porting application codes to transputer arrays" in "Transputer Applications 1" Proceedings of the 1st International Conference on Applications of Transputers, Liverpool 23-25 August 1989, ed. T.L.Freeman and C.Phillips (IOS Press: 1990)
[2] Intel Scientific Ltd. "iPSC/2 User's Guide" and "iPSC/2 Programmer's Reference Manual" Intel Scientific Ltd. (March 1989)
[3] Suprenum GmbH special issue Supercomputer 6 (March 1989) 1-57 and R.Hempel "The Suprenum communications subroutine library for grid oriented problems" user manual GMD (Gesellschaft fuer Mathematik und Datenverarbeitung: Sankt Augustin: 1989)
[4] R.J.Allan "Numerical Libraries for Parallel Computers" D.L. Technical Memorandum (1990) in preparation
[5] NA Software Ltd. "The Liverpool Parallel Transputer Libraries" (NA Software Ltd.: Liverpool: 1989)

ECCL
A general communications harness and configuration language.

Dr. Mike Surridge

Department of Electronics and Computer Science
University of Southampton
Southampton S09 5NH

Abstract

Transputer applications tend to be successful when there is an obvious mapping between the application and a processor topology. In other cases, the problem of implementing message passing along with the application is too great. The detailed topology can be hidden by the use of suitable through-routing software. Such an abstraction offers a considerable increase in the versatility of transputer arrays. ECCL is such a router and abstraction device. A configuration language allows the physical network and the user's logical process network to be specified separately. The ECCL compiler converts this to an occam configuration which incorporates the routing software. Some performance measurements for the system are reported.

ECCL is available from the SERC/DTI Transputer Initiative's Parallel Software Library at Liverpool Transputer Support Centre. It is currently being used at Southampton University in the implementation of AND-parallel Prolog.

1 Introduction

The transputer has now been with us for five years. In this time, it has been used successfully to construct parallel processing arrays which provide high-performance computing resources at a low cost.

To a large extent, however, applications have to be tailored to the particular topology of the transputer array [1, 2]. The problem of handling communications between processors which are not physically connected is typically too complex to be dealt with easily by an applications programmer. Only in a few, well known cases can through-routing of such messages be incorporated easily into an applications program, such as applications exploiting farmed event parallelism [3].

One solution to this problem is the use of totally reconfigurable transputer arrays. One may then be able to realise a topology appropriate for each problem, although the restricted number of links still limits the amount of connectivity which can be used [4]. Another approach which exploits this type of hardware is to reconfigure the network during run time, to provide connections between processors when required [5].

The other solution to the problem is to accept a sparsely connected processor array, and to build a software router capable of handling any required traffic. By moving the issues relating to message forwarding into the domain of the system software, one releases the applications programmer from the difficult and time consuming business of dealing with routing. One can also widen the range of possible applications by introducing some abstraction away from the physical processor network.

The Eulerian Channel Configuration Language (ECCL) is such a software router and abstraction device. The routing issues (livelock, deadlock, operating efficiency, etc.) have been studied over a period, and ECCL incorporates a router which provides solutions to all these well known problems [6]. The user is presented with a consistent picture of the transputer array, irrespective of the topology chosen [7].

2 Deadlock.

The most major issue which faces a programmer using a transputer array is deadlock. It is possible whilst engaging in communications between several processors in a network to enter a state from which no further progress is possible.

One response to the possibility of deadlock is to ignore it. This may be satisfactory in non-critical (eg. scientific) applications, since deadlock tends to arise in a non-deterministic fashion, and so might be expected not to occur in every execution of a program. The author does not accept this approach, which seems to be a form of capitulation with respect to more serious, or critical applications.

There are two ways in which deadlock can occur. The first case can be thought of as a "user-deadlock", in that it arises because of the behaviour of the processes served by the routing system. Figure 1 shows this sort of deadlock in the context of traffic moving in a road system.

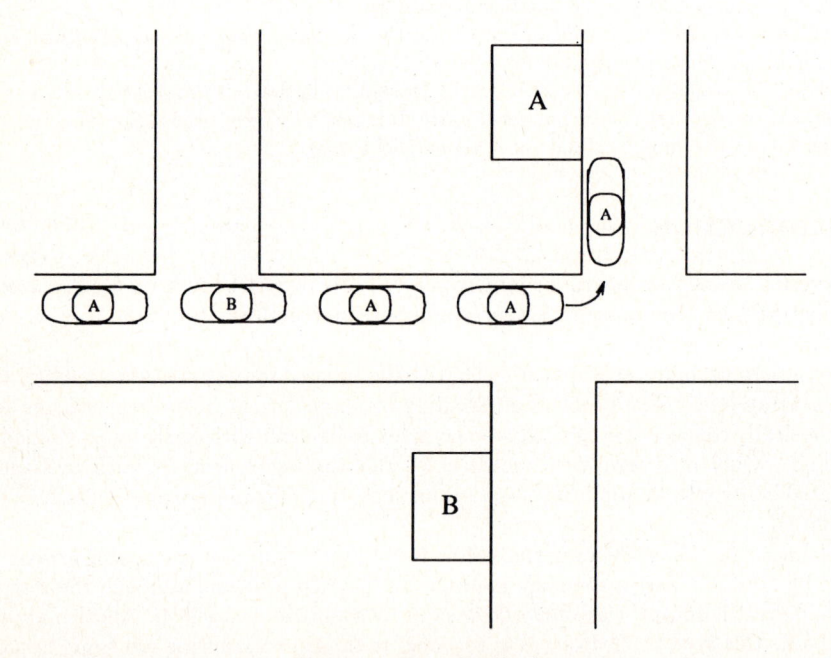

Figure 1: User deadlock.

The system has reached a state where no further progress is possible because location 'A' has begun to refuse inputs. The router (the roads) are now congested with traffic destined for 'A'. Note that because of this congestion, traffic destined for other locations may become blocked (as has happened in this case with respect to location 'B'). In this sense, the router is a shared resource, and can be compromised with respect to all its clients by a single aberrant process.

The second form of deadlock which must be considered is "router deadlock". This occurs when the router itself enters a deadlocked state. The analagous traffic jam is shown in Figure 2.

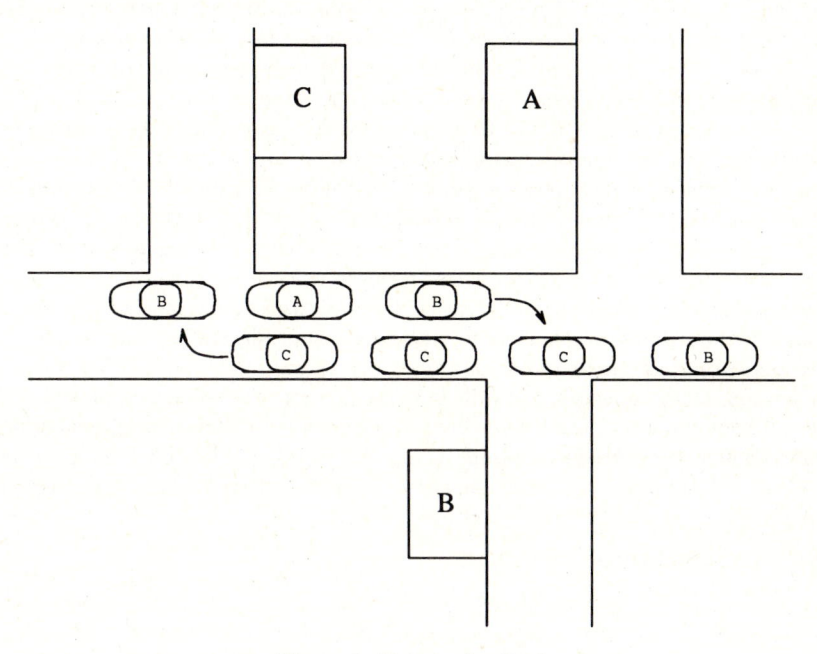

Figure 2: Router deadlock.

A through-routing system should have some strategy for avoiding both these deadlock situations. In practice, the second form of deadlock is more easily avoided, since it arises only in the router and can be eliminated by an appropriate design. The first form "user deadlock" is more difficult, as the various techniques depend to an extent on the user.

3 Communications models.

In order to prevent "user deadlock", it is necessary to place some restrictions on the applications processes (the user). If these rules are of a local nature (ie. the validity of the user's behaviour can be determined without global information about the network), they may be enforced by the routing software.

These rules may be thought of as a "communications model" within which a user should operate. The choice of communications model involves making certain compromises between universality and raw efficiency.

3.1 Eager readership.

The most primitive communications model is formed by requiring all processes served by the router to be "eager-readers" of messages. This requirement simply states that no process may refuse a message indefinitely — it must at some stage read any message presented to it by the router.

From the viewpoint of router design and implementation, eager-readership is a very attractive model to choose. Its primary advantage is that no flow-control protocol is required, since one may at any stage transmit a message knowing that it will eventually be read. This means that the router can deliver messages very efficiently in a single transaction.

Unfortunately, the corresponding disadvantage is that processes cannot synchronise with each other in a controlled fashion. This is because a process is not allowed to wait for a message from a chosen source (it has to be prepared to read any message). In general, this inability may prevent the construction of some programs.

In practice, eager-readership is never imposed in its pure form directly on the user. Instead, one imposes a bound on the number of messages which the router may ever have to store. Typically there will be several message types, each with their own set of storage buffers, to facilitate selective reading of messages where required.

This type of model "eager-within-bounds" is very expensive in terms of memory requirements, as one has to build in significant message-storage capacity into the router. Furthermore, the amount of buffering required on each processor may depend on the precise topology of the underlying processor array, and will typically increase with the size of the array. Finally, the applications programmer is left with the sometimes very difficult task of remaining within the specified bound (or perhaps of finding an appropriate value for this bound). It does not provide a particularly elegant abstraction away from the underlying hardware, therefore.

3.2 Occam channels.

The communications model represented by occam-channels is almost diametrically opposed to the eager-reader model. Here, all communications are synchronous, removing the need for a router to store messages. It is still possible for a program to deadlock, but this kind of user-error will not prejudice the operation of the router with regard to uninvolved processes. This allows (say) diagnostic output messages to continue being transmitted from processes which are not in deadlock.

Unfortunately, it is impossible to build a router which will cater for such a communications model directly. This is because the model allows for highly un-eager behaviour by the applications processes, such as committing to input (or output) on a given channel and refusing all messages on other channels pending completion of this communication.

Instead, one implements the occam-channel model by using a flow-control protocol (handshaking) between processes which are specified as full eager readers. This handshaking introduces extra latency into communications whilst the flow control tokens are crossing the network.

Just as in the eager-reader model, one is not stuck with all the bad features of the occam model. Here too, one can introduce extra layers of software to alleviate the overheads. Providing a buffer on each input to a process allows the extra latency to be hidden from the applications process, but at the cost of some cpu cycles and memory, for example. Another approach is to incorporate redundant parallelism into a program, so that message latencies are spent productively in some other execution thread [8].

3.3 ECCL Communications.

ECCL adopts a communications model very close to the occam channel model. This choice represents a compromise to efficiency (raw throughput times for messages). The advantages of the model are that it represents a high level of abstraction from the underlying hardware, makes no global restrictions on the user, and can be implemented using very little memory.

This last advantage eventually proved to be crucial during the development of ECCL, as the transputer systems available came with just 256 kBytes of memory per processor.

Finally, with the development of the H1 transputer, one can anticipate that at least some of the capabilities of the routing software will be provided by hardware in future. The signs at present are that Inmos continues to favour the "clean" occam-channel model of communication [9]. It makes sense to use this model in ECCL and other pre-cursors to the H1. As well as providing continuity of the programming model which the user will employ, it is possible that some insights will be gained into the ways in which programmers will exploit total connectivity. These may be of value in the construction of the H1 and associated operating system software.

4 The ECCL router.

The ECCL router adopts a novel algorithm for ensuring that no router-deadlocks appear within it. The algorithm was designed to keep memory requirements (for through-routing buffers) to a minimum, and to be applicable to a wide range of network topologies.

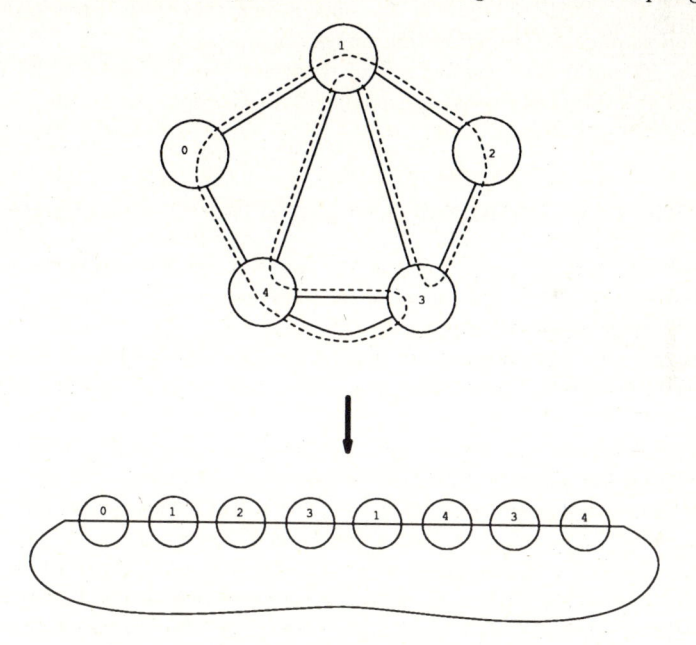

Figure 3: Linearisation by finding Eulerian Circuit.

The ECCL routing algorithm depends on the linearisation of the physical network, to provide a simpler topology on which to construct a deadlock-free routing algorithm. This is done by finding an eulerian circuit through the network, as shown in Figure 3. An eulerian circuit traverses each link of a network once [10].

Eulerian circuits exist if and only if all nodes in the network are of even valence. Since transputers have four links (an even number), this can always be achieved for a network of transputers by joining together any odd-valent nodes in pairs, using "spare" links. If such a circuit exists, it is easy to find one for a given network [11].

Having obtained a linearised network in this way, the simple routing algorithm due to Roscoe is used [12]. This has the property that the number of buffers required is fixed (being proportional to the number of links on each node). The proof of deadlock freedom is trivial.

Since the linearised network is so simple, one can set up a distance function on it which can be affordably evaluated at run-time, so eliminating the need for large routing tables to store the best output link for each possible message destination at each node.

Of course, routing around the linearised network (a ring) alone would give rise to rather long message paths as the number of nodes in the network increases. To avoid this problem, a short-cut mechanism has been introduced, based on the run-time evaluation of the best output link for a through-routed message in transit (using the linearised distance function).

Committing to such a short-cut could in principle deadlock the Roscoe routing algorithm. However, it is possible to determine whether this is the case soley on the basis of local information - no extra messages need be introduced to check the security of a short-cut. In practice, one queues a message on both the default and the short-cut link, committing to neither output until the link is no longer busy. The message goes out on the first link to become free, thereby introducing some non-determinism into the actual route taken across the network. This has the side-benefit of spreading the load of a single channel over several paths in the network.

Finally, due to the simple structure of the routing algorithm on the linearised network, one can envisage performing some compile-time analysis of a program in relation to the hardware. This may allow for automatic distribution of processes over the network to minimise the amount of through-routing required, for example. ECCL does not attempt to do this at present.

5 The Eulerian Channel Configuration Language.

The final component of ECCL, which gives it its power as an abstraction device, is a configuration language designed to facilitate use of the underlying router.

ECCL was first developed to automate the process of finding an eulerian circuit for a given physical network, labelling the nodes according to the linearised structure, and forming message headers for each of the occam-channel-like communications links specified by the user.

Subsequently, it grew into a device for constructing a static occam configuration incorporating the router, for a process distribution and physical network specified by the user. Linearisation of the network and message header formation are components of this process, which is achieved by the use of a pre-processor (the ECCL compiler).

The syntax is very explicit, being based on occam and on the "wiring diagram" syntax produced by the occam compilers. However, the arrangement of an ECCL program (the block structure) is designed with a view to separating out the various issues in forming a configuration for execution on a transputer network.

In the following example, it is assumed that the TDS-compatible version of ECCL is used. The notation uses the folded presentation familiar from TDS to hide un-necessary detail.

5.1 Overall structure.

The general form of an ECCL program is

```
... user procedure declarations
PROGRAM
    ... network
    ... harness
    ... placement
```

The first fold will contain the user's processes, in the form of SC procedure declarations. These must be written in occam (in the TDS-compatible version of ECCL). The form of the procedural interface is fixed

```
PROC my.proc ([expr]CHAN OF ANY OUTPUT,
              [expr]CHAN OF ANY INPUT,
              VAL INT PROC.ID,
              VAL []INT FLAGS,
              ...)
  :
```

The user's processes must be valid occam procedures. In practice this is ensured by introducing the requirement that the SC foldsets containing them must be compiled (relying on the TDS fold attributes to maintain validity of the user's code).

The folds below the PROGRAM statement contain the ECCL specifications of the physical network, the communications channel connectivity which the harness is to support and the placement (calling) of procedures on each of the processors in the network.

5.2 The network.

The **network** description contains a wiring diagram for the physical processor network. The syntax follows that for the wiring diagrams produced by the Inmos occam configurers. For example

```
NETWORK SIZE = n + 1
  PAR
    PAR i = 0 FOR n
      CONNECT PROCESSOR i LINK 2 TO PROCESSOR (i+1)\n LINK 3
    CONNECT PROCESSOR n LINK 2 TO PROCESSOR 0 LINK 0
```

This corresponds to the simple network of Figure 4.

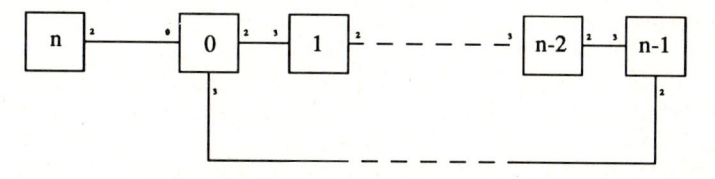

Figure 4: A simple network.

Note that integer expressions are allowed involving the operators +, -, *, /, \. Replication is also permitted, but at present arrays are not implemented in the TDS ECCL.

5.3 The harness.

The `harness` fold uses a similar wiring diagram syntax. It specifies the channels which the user requires, and so constitutes a specification of the logical as opposed to the physical network. The channel connections specified will be supported by an ECCL router incorporated into the occam configuration produced by the ECCL compiler.

For example, full connectivity between all processes can be specified as

```
HARNESS
  PAR i = 0 FOR n
    PAR j = 0 FOR i
      PAR
        CONNECT PROCESSOR j OUTPUT i-1 TO PROCESSOR i INPUT j
        CONNECT PROCESSOR i OUTPUT j TO PROCESSOR j INPUT i-1
```

This separation of the physical and logical network specifications constitutes an important objective of ECCL. In the present version, no attempt is made to automate the mapping of one of these networks onto the other (placement), so the processor numbers must correspond between the two. Apart from this, they are completely decoupled, and alteration of (say) the hardware can be accomodated by adapting just one section of the ECCL program.

5.4 The Placement.

The `placement` section is where the user calls a procedure on each processor. As such, it forms part of the logical network description.

In addition to the actual procedure call, each processor statement can incorporate declarations of variables or channels not arising from the ECCL For example, one can declare TDS interface channels, or indeed channels to be placed on unused links. These extra declarations form "gateways" between the ECCL configuration and other pieces of software which may be running elsewhere.

```
PLACED PAR
  PROCESSOR n T4
    PREDEF CHAN OF INT keyboard :
    PREDEF CHAN OF ANY screen :
    CHAN OF ANY from.graphics, to.graphics :
    PLACE from.graphics AT link.1.in :
    PLACE to.graphics AT link.1.out :
    host (keyboard, screen, from.graphics, to.graphics)
  PLACED PAR i = 0 FOR n
    PROCESSOR i T4
      worker ()
```

The final configuration produced by the ECCL compiler from the example description would contain a router. It is encapsulated in Figure 5.

5.5 Applications.

Unlike many other routers (such as TINY), ECCL was not developed on the back of some applications program[1]. It is partly for this reason that ECCL has evolved into a fully-fledged

---

[1] The first version was funded by a SERC/DTI Transputer Initiative Extra-Mural Research contract

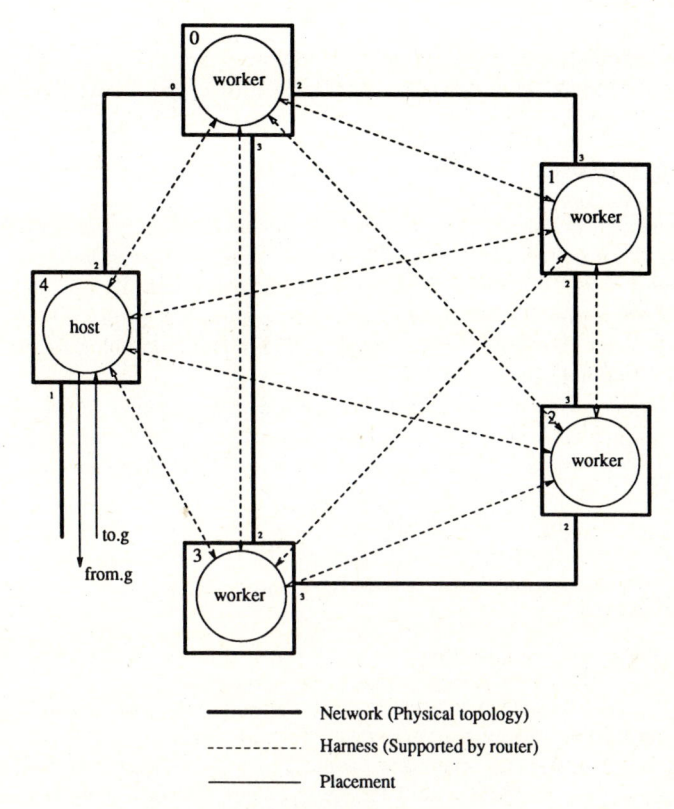

Figure 5: An ECCL-generated configuration.

configuration language with a well-defined communications model, as opposed to a less elegant system such as might have resulted from a more application-driven project.

Since the first release, ECCL has been used to implement parallel Prolog over a network of transputers at Southampton University. This system exploits so-called 'restricted AND-parallelism', which is derived statically at compile-time. The Warren Abstract Machine (WAM) [13] with extra instructions provides the basis for parallel execution. The system has a WAM on each processor, which can hand out tasks dynamically to idle processors. The sequential implementation is described in [14] — the parallel version will be described in detail later this year [15].

The aim of this research is to reduce the overheads of and-parallel execution, and to improve on the parallelism detected statically at compile-time. This latter objective is being addressed by exploiting the run-time distribution of variable-bindings and loads in the decision to 'fire' dependent subgoals.

The implementation uses occam and the in-line GUY assembler, under the TDS. ECCL is used to provide all-to-all connectivity between the WAM processes, so that any process can spawn child tasks to any other process. A controller process is used to maintain status information for each WAM in the system and to provide support for i/o, also via the ECCL.

Buffers have been placed at each ECCL input channel to the WAM so that tasks can be stored locally in anticipation of the WAM becoming idle. This has to be done by the user in the current version of ECCL — an example of explicit breaking of the ECCL channel communications model to conceal the message latency due to synchronous communication from an application process.

The system was distributed over a transputer network in less than 2 days, starting from an implementation of the WAM suited to incorporation into a (non-distributed) occam program.

6 Performance.

ECCL was developed primarily as an abstraction device to remove the details of the physical hardware from the user's domain. As such, the emphasis has been on constructing a clean, easily understood model of communications, and a suitably friendly user-interface.

The underlying router is nevertheless quite fast, comparing quite well with other fast "research oriented" through-routing systems such as TINY [16], and being superior to operating-system oriented products such as Helios [17].

The router was optimised during its construction using a small (5-processor) network as a test-bed for performance measurement. This allowed the local behaviour (raw speed across a link) to be highly optimised. The large-scale behaviour and heavy-loading behaviour could not be measured easily using the test hardware.

More recent tests using a Meiko M10 Computing Surface with 32 T800-20 processors show that, although room for further optimisation exists, ECCL still performs very well under most circumstances. Figures quoted below are derived from these tests.

6.1 Single Channel Testing

The first test involves passing messages along a single ECCL channel, firstly across a single link and then across two links via a through-routing processor.

By varying the length of the messages passed along the channel (see Figure 6), the setup time for a message (the time for a zero length message) could be determined, and also the channel bandwidth (excluding the setup time). In the two-link case, the CPU overhead at the intervening processor was measured as the increase in time taken to perform a standard work-loop (Figure 7).

In order to make comparison with other routers possible, the performance of the underlying router was extracted (ie. allowing for the handshaking overheads deriving from the communications model supported). The message latency can then be parameterised using

$$T = A + Bd + Cl + Dld \tag{1}$$

d is the distance travelled (number of links) and l the length of the message. The parameters A, B, C and D can be related to the performance of various components of the system (the user interface, through-routing, etc.).

This equation is valid only for messages which can be sent in one packet (up to 256 bytes in ECCL). Beyond this, overlapping between input and output on intermediate processors occurs, and a more sophisticated model is required to deal with this. Figure 6 shows this effect clearly for d = 2.

The values obtained for the parameters A, B, C and D (Table 1) are comparable with those quoted for TINY [18]. In fact, when TINY was subjected to the same test program as ECCL, its performance was considerably worse than this. At the time, up-to-date documentation for TINY was unavailable, and it is believed that this discrepancy may have been due to misuse of TINY in the test programs [19].

Table 1: Performance parameters (μs)

Parameter	ECCL	TINY
A	29	33
B	26	24
C	0.0	0.2
D	0.7	0.7
CPU	32 / 47	—

6.2 Bouncing messages.

The next test was to bounce a message around the network. This was done by selecting a random destination for the message. Thereafter, on arrival at a destination, the next destination was generated randomly and the message re-transmitted.

The purpose of this test was to investigate the routing algorithm as the network size changed. The ECCL algorithm is based on a linearised network with short-cuts, and it was not known whether its performance would scale well for increased network size. Each network was a grid of size $N(N+1)$, for $N = 2, 3, 4, 5$. The average latency per bounce was plotted against message length, Figure 8. Again, the advantages of splitting up a longer message (over 256 bytes) is clear.

To see how changing the size of the network affected performance, a log-log plot of message latency against network size was made (Figure 9). The network diameter is also shown, shifted so as to fit on the same plot. Unfortunately, this graph does not give a clear indication as to whether latency scales as the network diameter (parallel to the diameter plot) or network size (a steeper curve). Interestingly, TINY gave curves with the same kink in this test [19], despite being based on a different routing algorithm where no linearisation was expected. On this basis, one may conclude that short-cutting is effective in countering the underlying linearity due to Roscoe's routing algorithm.

6.3 Heavy loading.

In the last test, the output of messages occurs continuously at every node, destinations being chosen randomly. This most stringent test causes saturation of the network, and at last ECCL begins to exhibit linearisation (as can be seen from the log-log plot, Figure 10).

It is not surprising that ECCL fails to perform as well under these conditions, as the test hardware available during its development did not permit such a test as this, and consequently no optimisation for these conditions was performed.

7 Future developments.

At the time of writing (April 1990), a new version of ECCL is under development. This will be targetted at the Inmos Stand-Alone Occam configurer, and will cater for embedded C anf Fortran user-processes.

The router itself will be further optimised during this process, with more consideration given to its behaviour under heavy loads. In particular, the system will be optimised with respect to the last test described in the previous section.

The ECCL language itself will continue to develop. The objectives at present are the introduction of higher-level constructs for network description, using a declarative style which builds on the simple combination of connections using PAR. The linearisation of the physical network will be exploited where possible to introduce the maximum amount of automation in the placement of processes within the network. The issues which will be addressed include

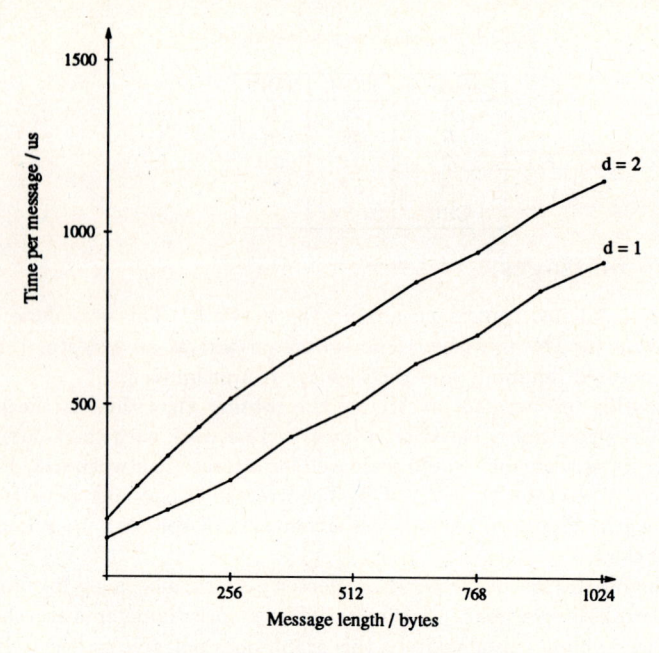

Figure 6: Message latency vs. Message Length

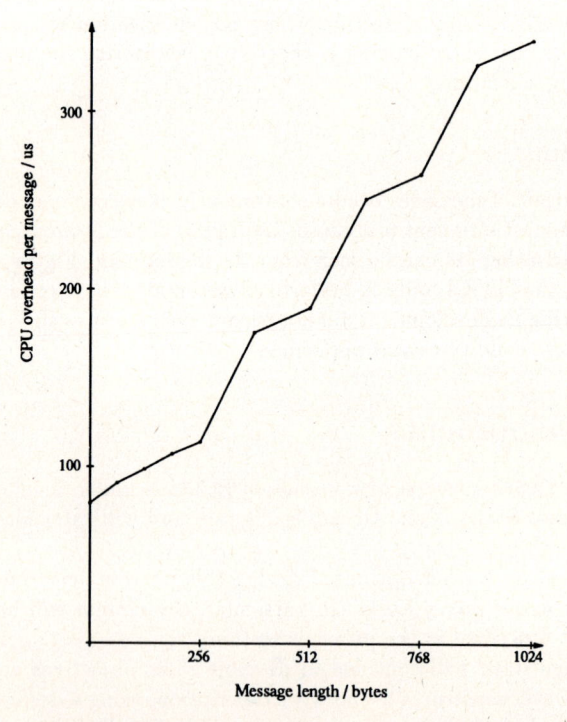

Figure 7: CPU overhead vs. Message Length

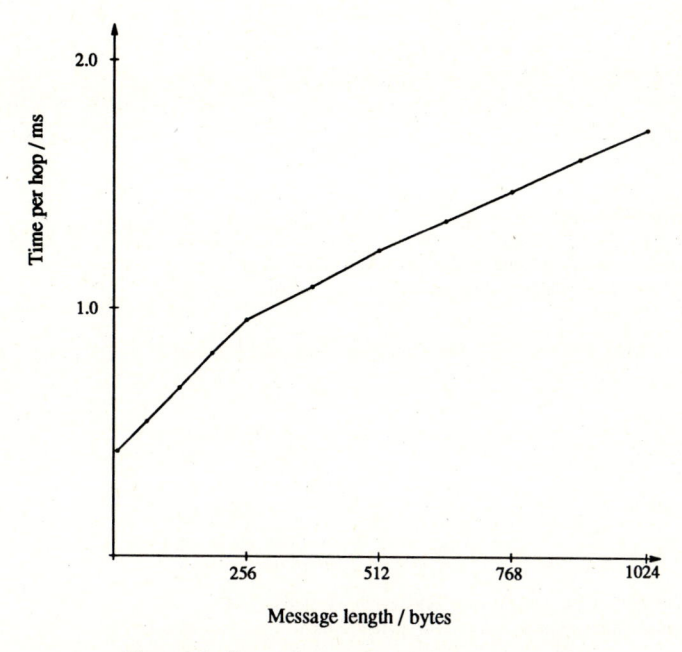

Figure 8: Bouncing a message on 5 x 4 grid.

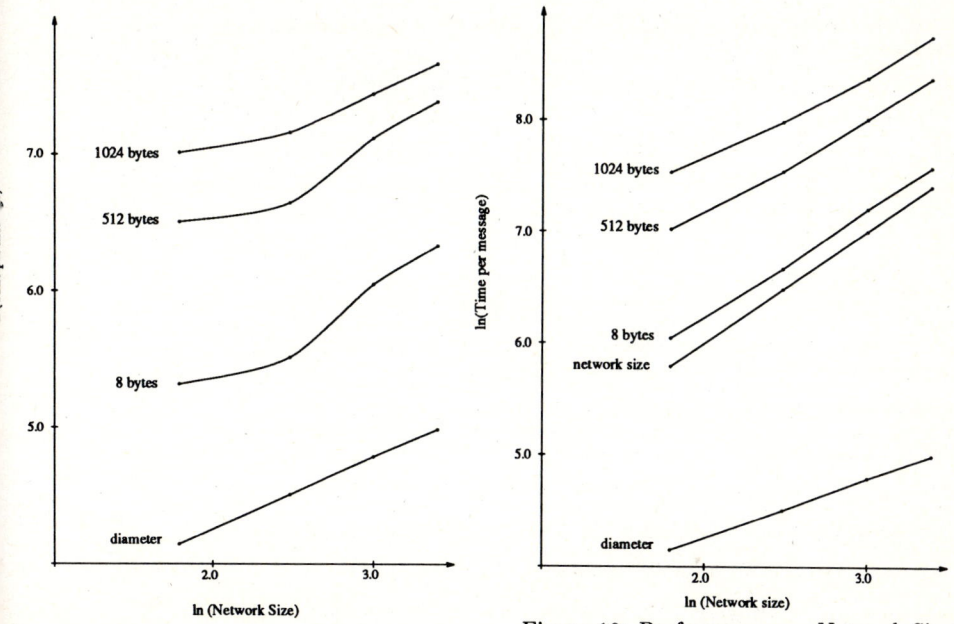

Figure 9: Performance vs. Network Size.

Figure 10: Performance vs. Network Size (saturation conditions).

the minimisation of through-routing for the declared harness channels.

Finally, ECCL will continue to be used to explore the problems associated with programming non-local networks (which the H1 will soon make possible) via a process model with synchronous communications. In this sense it will act as a "probe" to help establish the requirements of users of such networks.

References

[1] A.J.G.Hey, C.R.Jesshope, and D.A.Nicole. High performance simulation of lattice physics using enhanced transputer arrays. In L.O.Hertzberger and W.Hoogland, editors, *Proceedings of the International Conference on Computing in High Energy Physics, Amsterdam*, pages 363–369. Elsevier, July 1985.

[2] C.R.Askew, D.B.Carpenter, J.T.Chalker, A.J.G.Hey, D.A.Nicole, and D.J.Pritchard. Simulation of statistical mechanical systems on transputer arrays. *Computer Physics Communications*, 42(1):21–26, 1986.

[3] I.Glendinning and A.J.G.Hey. Transputer arrays as fortran farms. *Computer Physics Communications*, 45:367–371, 1987. International Conference on Computing in High Energy Physics.

[4] A.J.G.Hey, D.J.Pritchard, and C.Whitby-Strevens. Multi-paradigm parallel programming. In B.D.Shriver, editor, *Proceedings 22nd Hawaii International Confernce on System Sciences, Volume II*, pages 716–752. IEEE Computer Society Press, January 1989.

[5] S.Baker. Dynamic reconfiguration on the supernode, including link switching and process migration. Technical report, Royal Signals and Radar Establishment, January 1990. Memorandum 4340.

[6] M.Surridge. The eulerian channel configuration language and message-passing system. Technical report, S.E.R.C./D.T.I. Transputer Initiative, October 1989. Report for E.M.R. Contract N2A-8R-1756 (Phase II).

[7] M.Surridge. *The eulerian channel configuration language and communications system, user guide.*, February 1990.

[8] L.G.Valiant. Optimally universal parallel computers. *Philosophical Transactions of the Royal Society*, A 326:373, 1988.

[9] D.May. Implementing full occam. Technical report, ESPRIT, February 1990. PUMA Working Paper 2.

[10] L.Euler. *Commentarii Academiae Scientiarum Imperialis Petropolitanae*, 8:128, 1736.

[11] D.A.Nicole, E.K.Lloyd, and J.S.Ward. Switching networks for transputer links. In J.Kerridge, editor, *Proceedings of 8th Technical Meeting of the Occam User Group.*, Mar 1988.

[12] A.W.Roscoe. Routing messages through networks : an exercise in deadlock avoidance. In T.Muntean, editor, *Proceedings of 7th Technical Meeting of the Occam User Group.*, Sept 1987.

[13] D.H.D.Warren. An abstract prolog instruction set. Technical Report Techical Note 309, Artificial Intelligence Center, SRI International, August 1983.

[14] A.Verden, A.King, and W.Hall. An implementation of prolog for the inmos t800 transputer. In *Proceedings of the 1st North American Transputer User Group meeting, Salt Lake City, Utah.*, 1989.

[15] A.Verden. And-parallelism in a prolog evaluator. in preparation.

[16] L.J.Clarke. *TINY, Version 1.0, Discussion and User-Guide*, May 1989.

[17] Perihelion Software Ltd. *The Helios Operating System.* Prentice Hall, 1989.

[18] L.J.Clarke, July 1989. Figures quoted by D.Wallace in private communication.

[19] M.Surridge. Comparison between tiny and eccl. Unpublished working paper, January 1990.

A disk accessing library utility for 3L compilers.

Jon Kerridge and Geraint Huw Jones

National Transputer Support Centre
Sheffield Science Park
Sheffield S1 2NS
United Kingdom

Abstract

This paper concerns itself with work related to porting applications using transputer disk controller hardware (Transtech TMB05). The paper reports on an apparent lack of direct support for the 3L compiler environment and considers an idea for a low cost porting solution based on minimal transputer hardware.

1. Introduction

With recent hardware developments relating to disk conroller boards the bottleneck of accessing large volumes of data via the slow afserver/link adaptor circuitry has been breached. This document discusses an add on product for the 3L compiler series which facilitates access to data stored on disk via a suite of callable library routines and file management utility. The paper concludes with a brief discussion of an industrial application where this software is currently being used as a porting tool.

2. Porting Applications

One of the principal headaches in parallel programming is one of distributing data over a transputer network topology so that optimum data processing can occur. Although algorithm design is important, for example the incorporation of buffering, a system requiring access to megabytes of mass storage data will ultimately be slowed down by the relatively slow path to the data if the path is via the host/bus/link adaptor circuitry as compared to a transputer/transputer link communication. A preferable approach would be for a transputer to directly access mass storage data without going through the afserver bottleneck.

Hardware now exists that supports this. A board such as the Transtech TMB05 disk controller provides a motherboard platform for four 2MByte TRAMS plus a winchester disk (ST506/412 compatible) having a format capacity of either 20 or 55Mbytes. The root transputer communicates to the hard disk via an IMS M212 disk conrolled device. This chip is actually an IMS T212 with additional disk controller firmware.

Transtech provide software which allows the board to be configured as an additional DOS drive (ie D:/E:/F:). This environment makes the movement of files between the two systems totally transparent. Support for applications accessing data off disk is provided through TDOS. TDOS provides a software platform on top of which user applications can be written in C, Fortran, Pascal or occam. Basically TDOS resides on the transputer module which has a link to the M212 and in the case of TDS intercepts requests made to the TDSserver and relays them onto the M212. In the case of the 3L compilers support is provided by a protocol converter which has to be dynamically loaded by an application, as a 3L unsupported task, since no driver has been directly written using the 3L compilers.

This last point is significant. Since most porting work is undertaken in either C or Fortran the 3L compilers are used extensively as parallel development platforms. It would be useful to extend this range of tools to include an M212 driver written specifically to support the 3L range of compilers and providing optimum access to disk. This philosophy treats the winchester as a mass storage card directly attached to the transputer network so avoiding the additional software required to make the card seem like an another DOS drive and also, in the context of an application, precludes the need for software required to dynamically spawn the intermediate protocol task. The system would be serviced via a utility enabling the general file maintenance of the winchester. The utility would also facilitate experimentation with different format parameters to allow the user to find the optimum format structure for the data being accessed or written.

3. The TBIOS Utility

The TBIOS utility is a M212 driver written by the authors in 3L Parallel C Version 2.1. The utility provides :-

1) A format/reformat facility allowing the user to experiment with different combinations of format parameters (ie interleave, skew, sector size, cylinders)

2) A flat sequential filing system.

3) A suite of functions allowing the copying from the host, reading, writing, renaming and deletion of transputer winchester based files.

4) A defragmentation utility to reorganise files on the disk for optimal disk usage.

The driver software has been written under mode 1 operation (ref. 2) which utilises software residing in the M212 on chip ROM to interface to the winchester circuitry. Logical addressing has been selected as mode of sector access.

Using this tool the user can experiment with different format permutations :-

1) Number of Cylinders :- the number of cylinders on the disk.

2) Interleave :- the spacing set between contiguous sectors during a read or write. It can be optimised so that the controller is always ready.

3) Skew :- provides an offset from the first logical sector.

4) Sector size :- The size in bytes of each sector.

The filing system basically keeps track of the file name and the contiguous sectors it resides over. A new file is always placed at the start of the last logical sector plus one.
A simplified operating system has been implemented in order to keep code size down and also to keep the operating system function to a minimum in terms of run time execution. This is particularly relevant to the TBIOS software kernel where data throughput has to be maximised. An unnecessarily complex operating system would slow things down.

4. TBIOS software kernel

This code provides the intermediate interface between a user written application and the M212 disk controller. The code is compiled as a standalone unsupported 3L task which may be incorporated into the user written application via the 3L configuration syntax. As the 3L binaries are compatible across the compiler series the kernel may be incorporated into Parallel Pascal and Parallel Fortran applications.

Currently a set of library function calls is used which as far as possible is functionally equivalent to the standard C file handling functions but accesses data on the transputer winchester. These library functions are callable from 3L Pascal/Fortran.

The equivalent C file handling functions available include :-

tbios_open()	- Opens a file
tbios_read()	- Reads a file
tbios_write()	- Writes to a file (overwrite, append)
tbios_close()	- Closes a file
tbios_delete()	- Deletes a file
tbios_exists()	- Tests a file exists
tbios_seek()	- moves file pointer
tbios_tell()	- tells present postition of file pointer

5. Software architecture of system

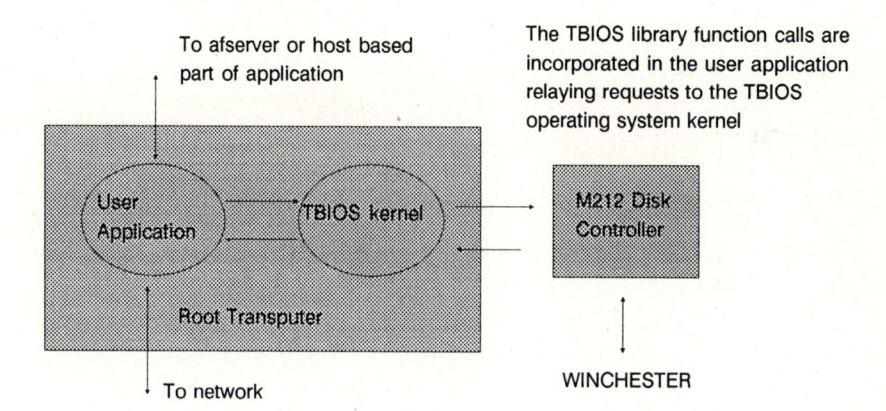

The TBIOS library function calls are incorporated in the user application relaying requests to the TBIOS operating system kernel

6. Performance information

The following benchmark timings on various file sizes and format permutations.

Sector size = 8K, Interleave = 1, skew = 0

filesize (bytes)	Transputer ticks (low priority)	read/write	transfer rate
54844	3565	w	234K/sec
49152	3203	w	235K/sec
32768	2379	w	210K/sec
40960	2935	w	212K/sec
54844	3797	r	210K/sec
49152	3617	r	207K/sec
32768	1948	r	256K/sec

Sector size = 4K, interleave = 2, skew = 0

54844	5028	w	167K/sec
49152	4616	w	162K/sec
32768	2663	w	164K/sec
40960	3860	w	161K/sec
54844	5237	r	159K/sec
49152	4637	r	162K/sec
32768	2538	r	172K/sec

Sector size = 2K, interleave = 3, skew = 0

55296	5451	w	155K/sec
49152	5273	w	142K/sec
28672	3170	w	138K/sec
40960	4424	w	141K/sec
55296	5443	r	155K/sec
49152	5245	r	143K/sec
28672	3018	r	145K/sec

Sector size = 1K, interleave = 4, skew = 0

55296	7063	w	119K/sec
48128	6779	w	110K/sec
28672	4080	w	107K/sec
40960	5699	w	109K/sec
55296	7401	r	114K/sec
48128	6599	r	113K/sec
28672	3904	r	112K/sec

The results show that data throughput varies considerably depending on how the winchester disk is formatted and where the file is physically situated on disk in relation to the read/write heads of the disk controller. However, throughput seems to be significantly higher than results obtained using the Transtech 3L protocol converter software where the maximum data rates peaked at around 100K/sec.

7. Dynamic Task Loader for 3L unsupported tasks

This section briefly discusses an application where the TBIOS software is currently being used in response to the industrial needs to accelerate a quotation system currently running on a PC platform.

When porting an application onto a parallel hardware platform at least two considerations need to be addressed. Firstly, in what language to develop the parallel side of the application ? Since most software has been written in FORTRAN or C it would seem logical to use the same language compiler to develop the software on the transputer. This would then circumvent the need to rewrite and debug code written into occam. The port could then concentrate on the parallel design aspects of distributing code and data over multiple processors, in itself a non trivial task. Secondly, what is the optimum hardware transputer platform that is right for the job. This boils down to a function of performance against cost in the context of the end user market for the application. This is of fundamental importance since any incremental cost will ultimately be passed onto the consumer.

With these points in mind a dynamic task loader kernel has been developed in 3L parallel C as a porting tool built on a low cost hardware platform employing a single 2MByte TRAM and a transputer disk controller controlled via TBIOS. The idea behind the system is that instead of throwing more TRAMS at particular problem, which is fine if money is no object, it is possible to use a single TRAM with software that is clever enough to maintain the tranputer at optimum performance whilst also accessing data/programs off the transputer winchester disk.

This software architecture was derived because the industrial application used a suite of overlay programs to work out various quotations against data entered by the user. These overlays could have been hard coded onto a transputer network topology. However such an approach would have rendered the system too expensive for the end user market.

8. The software architecture of the dynamic task loader

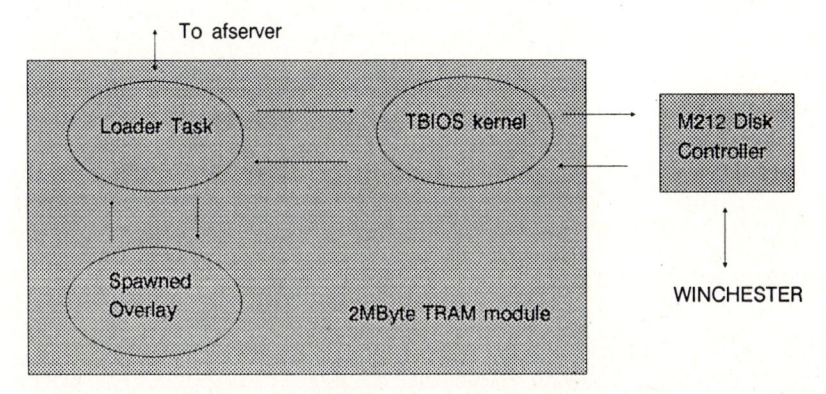

The loader task is responsible for reading the compiled 3L standalone task from the transputer winchester. The loader then dynamically spawns the task providing channel access to it. When completed the loader destroys the task's memory model and proceeds to read the next task from disk. Communication between the loader and spawned task is achieved by channel communication only. This means that any spawned task must be relieved of any runtime IO functions (printf, scanf, file IO etc) which have to be replaced by corresponding channel communications. The loader task which has access to the runtime library functions can convert these requests into equivalent IO functions and relay them on to the afserver. As an extension to this point, if a spawned task does not contain any IO the user must add a communcation at the end of the task computation to inform the loader it can go ahead and destroy the memory model ready for the next task.

In order to spawn a task the loader has to :-

1) Allocate memory for the task.
2) Load the task from its task file into memory.
3) Arrange channels for the child's communication.

In order to allocate memory the loader must interrogate the task file stripping out any secondary/primary bootstrap information. Bootstrap information is added by the 3L linker unless the /c switch is used. The file header contains information concerning code size, workspace size and code offset in bytes. This information is used to build the memory model for the task and then is passed into the 3L function thread_start() which then dynamically starts executing the task as a thread.

At the time of writing the system has successfully spawned standalone tasks up to 1.5MBytes in size read off the winchester disk.

Currently work is in progress to relieve a number of the application overlays of runtime IO which will give some indication has how the system performs against the 80286 based product.

References

1. Transtech TMBO5 User manual. Transtech Devices Ltd.

2. IMS M212 disk processor, Inmos product data.

3. 3L Technical Note 5, Loading and Running Tasks from Parallel C.

RADIATION TOLERANCE TESTING OF T425 TRANSPUTER IN SUPPORT OF THE SOHO SATELLITE MISSION

J.P. Nicholls, Satellites International Limited, Newbury, England

Abstract. The T425 transputer has been identified by Satellites International Limited (SIL) as a suitable processor for the Command and Data Handling System (CDHS) for the Coronal Diagnostic Spectrometer (CDS) on the Solar and Heliospheric Observatory satellite (SOHO), due to be launched in 1995. This paper describes the SOHO satellite mission, the CDS and the CDHS. It outlines radiation tolerance testing performed on the T425 transputer in December 1989 at the European Space and Technology Centre (ESTEC), presents the results of that testing and concludes that the device is suitable for use in the expected radiation environment of the SOHO mission.

1. Introduction

1.1 The SOHO Space mission and the Coronal Diagnostic Spectrometer.

Solar activity has a significant impact upon terrestrial weather systems; the Solar-Terrestrial Science Programme (STSP) is an international venture to examine solar activity and its effect upon the Earth's environment. The SOHO Space mission is a joint undertaking between ESA and NASA and forms part of STSP. The objective of the SOHO mission is to gather information concerning the solar corona, solar wind and the solar interior.

SOHO will be placed in orbit around the Lagrangian 1 position - the point at which the gravitational fields of the Earth and the Sun are equal and opposite. SOHO is due to be launched in early 1995 and to fly for a period of 2.5 to 6.5 years. It will carry a payload of 11 experiments, one being the Coronal Diagnostic Spectrometer (CDS), an instrument designed to measure the intensities of emission lines in the ultraviolet spectrum at very short wavelengths. Such data are required to produce models of the transport of mass, momentum and energy within the heliosphere so that the mechanisms of plasma heating and solar wind acceleration can be fully understood [1]. Overall responsibility for the CDS is with the Rutherford Appleton Laboratory (RAL).

A Command and Data Handling System (CDHS) is required to control and monitor the CDS, to process the science data and to communicate with the satellite. Satellites International Limited (SIL) is designing a suitable CDHS, under contract to the Mullard Space Science Laboratory (MSSL). The chosen design for the CDHS uses multiple redundant processors (for reliability) sharing a common bus interface to image capture memory boards [2].

A suitable processor was required for the CDHS, and a processor trade-off study was performed. The transputer was selected - it offers a high performance at relatively low power; it is ideally suited to the preferred architecture of the CDHS; it is European sourced; and preliminary tests (see below) indicate a good radiation tolerance. The T425 was chosen because:

- the memory interface is more flexible and efficient than the T2xx series;
- it supersedes the T414 in both military and commercial variants;
- it consumes less power than the T800 series;
- the floating point capability of the T800 series is not required.

In addition to providing processor redundancy, multiple transputers may be configured to offer a system of high processing power, which may be used to increase the data throughput. A multiple transputer design for the CDHS has been finalised and a breadboard is currently under test, leading to flight electronics in 1992.

Tests on the T414 [3, 4] had indicated that it would be radiation tolerant to approximately 30krad (greater than the expected mission environment). However, in 1989 doubts were raised about the suitability of the transputer in the light of more recent tests performed on the T800 [5], although these tests were made on a single sample with the internal RAM of the transputer enabled (which is not the case in the SIL design). Since no radiation data were available for the T425 it was decided that SIL would undertake testing of this device (with internal RAM disabled) with support and assistance from INMOS and ESTEC.

1.2 Radiation Testing

1.2.1 The Space Environment

The radiation environment in space is considerably more severe than that found on the Earth's surface. In the vicinity of the Earth, the main sources of radiation are the radiation belts which surround the planet (trapped protons and electrons). Further out, background radiation is predominant (high velocity charged particles e.g. electrons, protons, gamma rays and cosmic rays); nearer to the sun, the influence of the solar wind and solar flares becomes significant (solar protons, ultra-violet and X-rays).

The interplay between these various radiations is complex, and the actual conditions experienced by spacecraft depends upon their orbit. SOHO will encounter radiation from the radiation belts during the orbit injection phase, but the main radiation source will be the solar wind and solar flares once the spacecraft is at the Lagrangian 1 point. Simulations of the total radiation dose which may be expected to be experienced by the SOHO mission have been generated and a figure for total dose extrapolated from this - approximately 9 krad after 6.5 years. To allow a margin of safety, the baseline total dose for the CDHS has been taken to be 12 krad.

1.2.2 Radiation Effects on Electronics

The three main effects experienced by electronic devices as a result of radiation are as follows:

1) Single Event Upset (SEU) - or "soft error" occurs in memory cells or latches where a bit becomes flipped by a high energy particle. Normally not catastrophic since the memory can be re-written with the correct value, although clearly it can cause operational problems.
2) Latch-up - potentially a catastrophic device failure caused by a very high energy particle or cosmic ray inducing a parasitic thyristor in the device, leading to thermal destruction. Protection can be provided by detecting the current surge and then removing power. When power is re-applied the device behaves normally.
3) Total Dose Failure - the gradual shift in threshold voltage of a CMOS device caused by the total accumulated radiation dose causes it to fail completely. This is a permanent effect, although annealing may occur if the device is removed from the radiation environment or if it is powered down.

1.2.3 Terrestrial Simulation of Radiation Environment

The radiation source used to test the T425 was Co60, a radioactive isotope of cobalt which decays with the emission of gamma rays of energy 1.17 and 1.33 MeV. Although this does not simulate the full radiation environment, previous work [see reference 6] has shown that irradiation by gamma rays provides a useful simulation of all radiation in the space environment, and Co60 is therefore widely used for radiation testing of this nature. The testing performed by SIL was that necessary to determine the Total Dose (TD) to failure.

2. Radiation Testing of T425

2.1 Test Chamber

The test facility at ESTEC uses a collimated Co60 source. The 2m x 4m test chamber is screened from the outside world by 1m concrete walls, heavy steel doors, etc. Test boards to be irradiated are placed in front of the source, and the distance from the source may be varied in order to adjust the radiation dose rate. A dosimeter was placed next to the board to allow the radiation dose to be measured. Cables carrying power supplies, control and data signals were passed from the test chamber to a control room. This contained the following test equipment: a dedicated test box; a PC running the current monitoring software; a PC with a B004 transputer card running the INMOS Transputer Development System (TDS); and a dose rate monitor displaying the dose rate and total dose accumulated.

2.2 System Hardware

The test board (Figure 1) consisted of four separate modules, each having one T425 transputer, SRAM and associated logic. A C004 link switch connected all transputer links from each transputer and the B004. The transputers were grouped near the centre of the board and all other components sited at the periphery to facilitate shielding as shown in Figure 1. The test board was held vertically in clamps, standing upon a movable trolley in front of the source with the memory and associated components protected by 100mm of lead.

The external test box contained five regulators supplying regulated power and which sensed the 5 volts rail. Vcc1 - Vcc4 supplied the transputers, Vcc5 supplied all the memory, clocks and other components. Links from the B004 and all subsystem signals were brought to a connector at one side of the box and passed to the test board via ALS244 buffers and a 5m twist-and-flat shielded cable. The box also contained debounced manual Reset/Analyse switches and LED indicators; these signals could be provided manually or via the B004 with their status indicated by the LEDs.

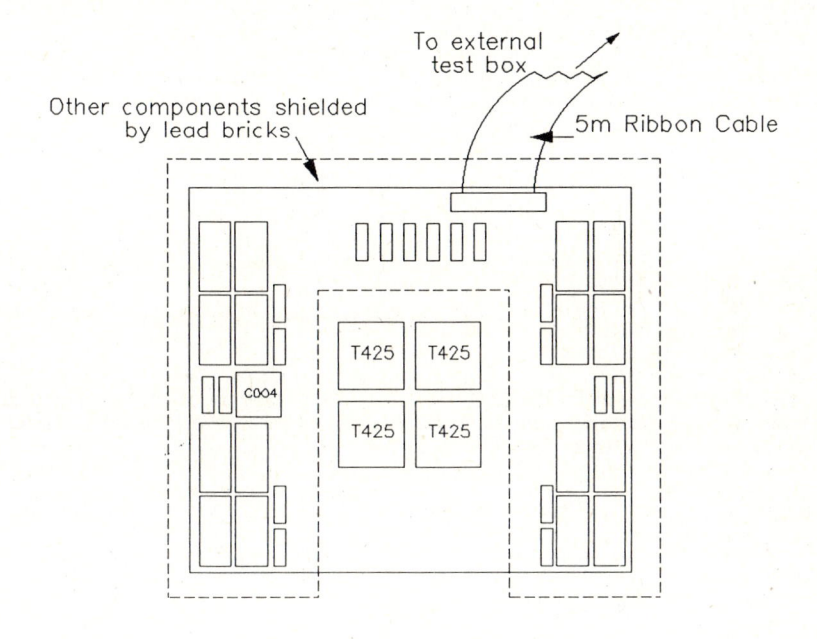

Figure 1 - Transputer Test board

2.3 System Software

The system software was written as two separate programs - control software running on the B004/PC, and test software running on each of the four transputer modules.

2.3.1 Software on each module

The test software was designed to ensure that most of the T425 hardware and instruction set were exercised. The software running on each module is outlined in the flow diagram in Figure 2 - note that link communications with parallel processes (in this case the controlling software) are shown as a double-headed arrow.

2.3.2 Controlling Software on the B004

The program running on the individual transputer modules and described above was written and compiled within the INMOS TDS. The disassembler supplied with the TDS was then used to generate a table of bytes of transputer code from the program, and this table imported into the controlling program for loading into the modules. An outline of the controlling software running on the B004 is given in Figure 3.

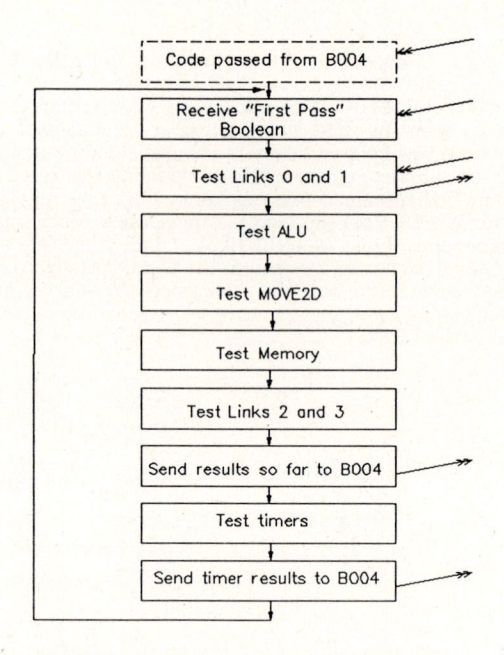

```
┌─────────────────────────┐
│ Code passed from B004   │
└─────────────────────────┘
            ↓
┌─────────────────────────┐
│  Receive "First Pass"   │
│       Boolean           │
└─────────────────────────┘
            ↓
┌─────────────────────────┐
│   Test Links 0 and 1    │
└─────────────────────────┘
            ↓
┌─────────────────────────┐
│        Test ALU         │
└─────────────────────────┘
            ↓
┌─────────────────────────┐
│      Test MOVE2D        │
└─────────────────────────┘
            ↓
┌─────────────────────────┐
│      Test Memory        │
└─────────────────────────┘
            ↓
┌─────────────────────────┐
│   Test Links 2 and 3    │
└─────────────────────────┘
            ↓
┌─────────────────────────┐
│ Send results so far to B004 │
└─────────────────────────┘
            ↓
┌─────────────────────────┐
│      Test timers        │
└─────────────────────────┘
            ↓
┌─────────────────────────┐
│ Send timer results to B004 │
└─────────────────────────┘
```

Figure 2 - Software running on each module

2.3.3 Current Measuring Software

Each power supply had a 2W 0.5R series resistor for the purpose of current measurement. A Burr-Brown data acquisition system measured the voltage across these resistors at intervals, and filed them in a spreadsheet-readable format for later analysis.

2.4 Parts Tested

Twenty of the twenty-one transputers tested were supplied by INMOS. Fifteen came from batch number 8933, whilst five were from batch number 8930. The odd transputer was a part purchased by SIL and was marked batch number 8918.

2.5 Test Sequence

The tests performed were as follows:

Test A High Dose Rate test, 2.15 rads^{-1} for 8 hr up to 66 krad, powered.
Test B High Dose Rate test, 2.14 rads^{-1} for 17 hr up to 140 krad, powered (same test as above with different batch).
Test C High Dose Rate test, 2.15 rads^{-1} for 25 hr up to 193 krad, unpowered, powered-up occasionally for testing (for approximately 5 minutes every 30 minutes while the experiment was attended).
Test D Medium Dose Rate test, 0.68 rads^{-1} for 17 hr up to 41 krad, powered.
Test E Low Dose Rate test, 0.18 rads^{-1} for 94 hr up to 59 krad, powered.
Test F High Dose Rate test, 2.12 rads^{-1} for 5 hr up to 38 krad, unpowered (as above with one device).

3. Results and Analysis

3.1 Results

The results are summarised in Table 1 below:

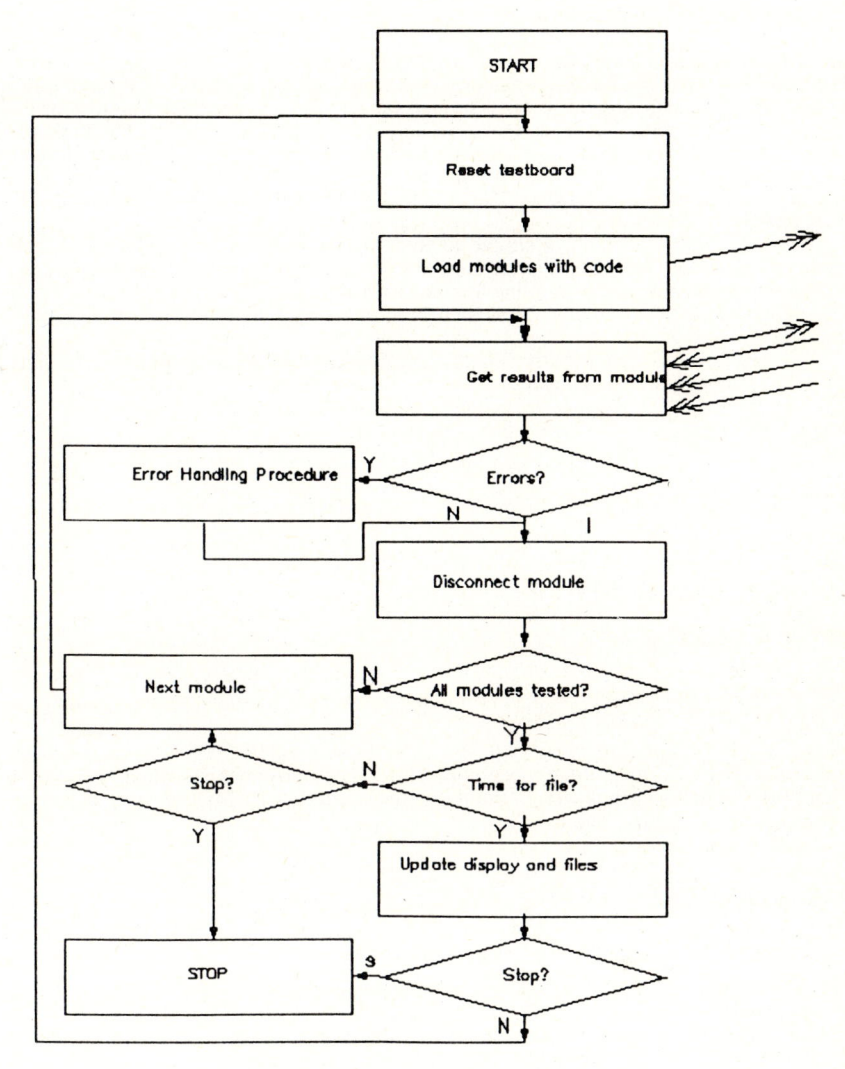

Figure 3 - Software running on B004

Table 1 - Results of Radiation Testing

Dose Rate		Number Of Devices		Failures (krad)
		Batch N° 8933	Batch N° 8930	
High	2.18 rads^{-1}	4	4	A: 28, 28, 56, >66 B: 13, 14, 14, 16
Medium	0.68 rads^{-1}	4	-	A: 29, 36, 40, >41
Low	0.18 rads^{-1}	3	-	A: 44, >59, >59 (also TEST, >59)
High (unpowered)	2.18 rads^{-1}	4	1	No processor failed (A >193, B >38)

3.2 Statistical Analysis Of Results

These tests were not intended to characterise the T425 completely, but to provide reassurance that the device is suitable for use in the expected environment of SOHO, and some tests were therefore terminated before all processors had failed. Furthermore, the number of devices tested is still quite small. For these reasons a detailed statistical analysis cannot be performed on these figures - a basic "worst case" analysis is more relevant. It was also assumed that those devices which had not failed by the end of a test were about to do so, for example in Test E Processor 1 is considered as having a TD at failure of 59 krad, although it did not actually fail during testing.

From the data obtained, a simple analysis of the mean TD at failure for each test appeared to show no dose-rate dependence, and so figures for the larger batch marked 8933 were considered as a whole. Assuming a normal distribution, the number of processors in the whole batch with a TD at failure of less than 12 and less than 9.1 krads has been derived (see section 1.2.1).

It is acknowledged that the statistical derivations below are of limited validity since the number of samples tested was small.

Batch number 8933:

Test A	Mean:	44.5	Standard Deviation:	19.49
Test D	Mean:	36.5	Standard Deviation:	5.45
Test E	Mean:	54.0	Standard Deviation:	8.66
Whole Batch:	Mean:	44.2	Standard Deviation:	13.80
Percentage of batch with TD to failure < 12 krad:				0.99%
Percentage of batch with TD to failure < 9.1 krad:				0.55%

Batch number 8930:

Test B	Mean:	14.4	Standard Deviation:	1.52
Percentage of batch with TD to failure < 12 krad:				5.90%
Percentage of batch with TD to failure < 9.1 krad:				0.03%

No statistical analysis is possible for the unpowered tests since no parts failed. Previous work [6] has shown that when unpowered, the radiation tolerance of CMOS devices increases and these results support those findings.

4. Conclusions and Future Work

4.1 Conclusions

1) No processor failed at less than 13 krad compared with the 2 - 3 krad total dose failures observed with internal RAM enabled.
2) Although no dose-rate dependence was established conclusively by this testing, the results for the low dose rate test suggest that this is a possibility.
3) Radiation tolerance is increased when a processor is powered down - it is therefore recommended that processors are powered down when possible.
4) Results for batch 8933 were consistently better than those for batch 8930 in terms of total dose to failure, but either batch would be acceptable for the SOHO mission.
5) In the light of these results, SIL will use the T425 transputer in the CDHS design.

4.2 Future Work

1) SIL is using the transputer in other space designs including an on-board Data Compression Unit and other on-board data handling applications.
2) SIL has been contacted by several other agencies requesting information about transputer-based space systems.
3) ESA are considering the transputer as one of the recommended processors for use in space - space qualification of INMOS assembly lines is being investigated with INMOS/SGS-Thomson.
4) Further characterisation of T425/T800 is being performed by SIL under ESA contract to investigate possible effects of process variation on radiation tolerance (position on wafer, inter-batch correlation, etc).

References

1. *CDS for SOHO EID Part A*, CDS Experiment Interface Description, ESA document PLP/410S/EID
2. *SOHO CDS - Proposal for the design and build of the Command and Data Handling System*, Satellites International Ltd, June 1989, SIL CP90612
3. *The Final Report On A Programme To Evaluate Occam And The Transputer For Use In Orbit*, Smith Associates Ltd, 1987, TR-87/161
4. *The SEU And Total Dose Response Of The INMOS Transputer*, J. Thomlinson et al, IEEE Transactions on Nuclear Science, December 1987
5. *Total Dose Radiation Tests on INMOS T800 - Final Report*, M. Lopez Cotarelo and B. Johlander, ESA report, September 1989
6. *The Radiation Design Handbook*, ESA document PSS-01-609 (DRAFT), October 1989

A Transputer Radar ESM Data Processor

R. D. Beton, J. B. Kingdon, C. Upstill

Plessey Research Roke Manor Ltd, Romsey, Hampshire, SO51 0ZN

A parallel radar ESM data processing system using occam and transputers is presented. High-level software solutions for radar ESM to run on multiple transputer systems were investigated, capable of expansion, to achieve higher throughputs cost-effectively. The system was intended as a vehicle to support further algorithm research and to permit performance benchmarking. A novel technique is described for improving the load balancing of algorithmically-decomposed parallel systems.

An Introduction to Radar ESM

Radar Electronic Support Measures (ESM) are concerned with monitoring the radar wavebands, and deriving useful information from the millions of radar pulses that can be detected. No active source of radar pulses is included - the objective is to determine the identity and bearing of surrounding radar emitters, and perform the functions of area surveillance and threat detection. Modern radar ESM systems usually obtain real-time performance using algorithms implemented in dedicated hardware, or programmed in assembler running on fast microprocessors or dedicated bit-slice processors. Our aim was to investigate high-level software solutions to run on multiple transputer systems, capable of expansion, to achieve higher throughputs cost-effectively.

The functional units of a generic radar ESM data processor are shown in figure 1. Connections to other systems (for example, active radar systems, weapons control systems, and Electronic Counter-Measures systems) were not part of the work and have been omitted from this diagram. The shaded functions are the ones covered in this paper.

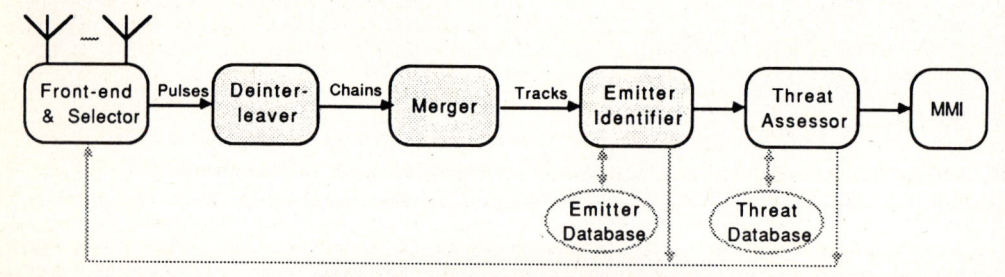

Figure 1 Radar ESM Data Processor

In order to operate in real-time, ESM processors are required to be capable of processing radar pulse densities of up to 10^5 pulses per second, after front-end filtering. Pulses are received by a multi-antenna front-end capable of Instantaneous Frequency Measurement (IFM). The relative amplitude of the signal in a number of the antennae is used to assess the Direction of Arrival (DoA) of the pulse. The characteristics of the pulse are then passed on to the front-end processing equipment in digital form. A pulse is typically characterised in terms of DoA, Time of Arrival (ToA), frequency, amplitude, and Pulse Width (PW). This typically occupies about 100 bits of information. Thus a total data rate of around 10^7 bits per second can be expected at the input to the deinterleaver.

An important processing stage in the algorithms is to assemble individual radar pulses, that are similar according to some criteria, into pulse chains. This process is termed deinterleaving (because the pulses arrive in an interleaved form), and if carried out successfully will enable individual emitters to be identified and tracked. The performance of the deinterleaver in processing complex radar waveforms in a high-pulse-density environment is fundamental to the reliable operation of the entire ESM system.

Each of the deinterleaved chains is used to build up a table of tracks (believed emitters) - a task called merging, or chain association. This table is cross-checked against the known characteristics of real emitters - a task called emitter classification or identification. This yields the operator a display of the real emitter scenario, with each emitter annotated by type, heading, etc. Figure 1 shows the relationship of these tasks.

Note that the main data flow from the antennae to the operator's console is a simple pipeline (with a feedback path to the pre-filter to allocate and define the pre-filter windows). In order to present the operator with a manageable amount of information, data reduction must be performed at each stage of the pipeline. This pipeline is emphasised in figure 1: data flows from the receiver to be deinterleaved, merged, emitter identified, and then to the console, via post-processing as necessary. Essentially the same pipeline exists in the implementation. Within each stage of the pipeline, we shall see how different architectural approaches - farms, geometric parallelism, and algorithmic parallelism (these are described in [1] and [2]) - are appropriate at a more local level.

Deinterleaving

Deinterleaving forms the most crucial (and computationally intensive) part of the ESM system. A deinterleaver typically operates in four stages on batches of several hundred pulses. Firstly, pulses are sorted into clusters formed from the basic pulse measurements. Secondly, the time differences between pulses in each cluster are used to form a histogram. Thirdly, peaks are located in the histogram - these correspond to particular Pulse Repetition Intervals (PRI - the interval between successive pulses from a radar). The pulses in that peak are extracted from the histogram, and output as a characterised pulse chain; several iterations of the histogramming process may be required to detect all pulse chains. Fourthly, any pulses left over (called dregs) are collected together and reapplied for further deinterleaving; this ensures the extraction of chains with very long PRI.

Merging

The merger receives deinterleaved chains which need to be matched together across time. A track table is built up, comprising the set of emitters which are currently believed to be sending pulses towards the ESM system. Each chain is matched with the current tracks, and if a match is found, that track is updated accordingly. If a match is not found, a new entry is put into the track table. Tracks are deleted from the table if they are not updated for a long time.

Emitter Identification

This is also a pattern matching task, where detected emitters are compared with a database of known emitter types (e.g. Aircraft A, Missile B, Ship C). The emitter identifier has a table of currently believed emitters similar to that of the merger, with additional information added from an external database. For each new emitter registered, the database must be searched and a match found. For subsequent emitter updates, the database only needs searching again if sufficient uncertainty has arisen regarding the previous match, otherwise a fresh search need not be performed. Each update is output to the console with relevant information appended.

Implementation

The target equipment was a Meiko Computing Surface, with over 60 T800 processors. The overall architecture of the system is pipelined. However, the architecture within each stage varies according to the specific requirements of that stage - this hybridisation is described more fully in [3]. Figure 2 shows more detail of the architecture. The deinterleaver consists of a farm with a rectangular or planar topology (as shown in figure 2), or a double ternary tree (see figure 4 and discussion below). It includes a dregs handler to sort leftover pulses. The merger is a distributed database across which the track table is dynamically shared. It includes a post merger, described below. The emitter identifier requires only a single processor.

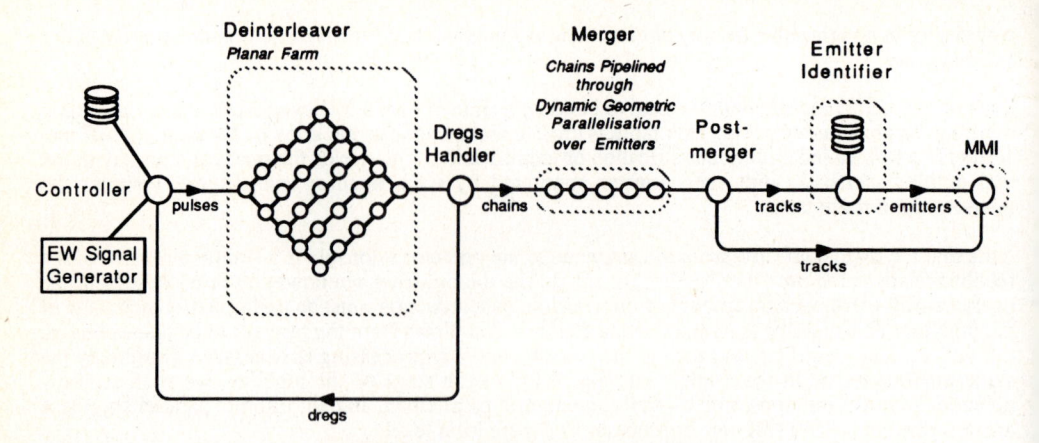

Figure 2   Transputer Architecture

For this research system, data can be generated by a special programmable signal simulator, or recorded data can be read from disk. The source control processor can run a buffer process to accumulate large amounts of pulse information (several megabytes) in RAM, in order to smooth the accessing of pulse data from disk. Further development will involve feeding live data from a receiver.

Deinterleaver Farm

Our strategy was to reformulate an existing state-of-the-art sequential deinterleaver into a parallel form capable of efficient execution on a large array of transputers. The deinterleaving algorithm used was originally developed in Pascal to run on a Vax computer. A step-by-step method was adopted for the transition from serial Pascal code with fixed-point arithmetic, to parallel occam code. Initially, the existing algorithms were converted almost line by line directly into occam, to run on only one processor. This was relatively straightforward to do, in spite of the recursion and record structures used in the Pascal.

The coarse parallelism inherent in the problem was then identified and a process farm was implemented, in order to achieve efficient load sharing between processors. A farm is desirable for the deinterleaver because it is easy to implement, it provides automatic load balancing, and it is inherently scalable. An algorithmic decomposition was rejected because it is inherently unscalable. A geometric decomposition was rejected because it is not easy to implement in this instance. Only the farm offers automatic load balancing - important in a deinterleaver, where the computation requirement can vary widely between different data.

In the initial version a very simple bidirectional (one-ended) farm consisting of a linear chain of processors was used (figure 3). This was then developed into a more efficient unidirectional farm, for which the two alternative topologies developed were the planar topology (figure 2), and the double ternary tree (figure 4). The planar and double-tree farms have several advantages over the linear farm, especially lower latency. (The double-tree has a higher symmetry than the (single) tree, which makes it easier to describe in occam.) The planar farm is essentially a sideways concatenation of several linear farms, and is implemented such that it can be configured with any number of processors, because the linear parts do not need to be of equal size. From a topological point of view, we have found little to choose from between the planar farm and double ternary tree farm. Our communications software is more complex in the planar farm, offering higher flexibility to the user, at a slight cost (about 2%) in efficiency.

The final phase was to re-code the algorithms using floating-point arithmetic to take advantage of the T800s and to increase the accuracy. In this phase, algorithmic optimisations were also sought.

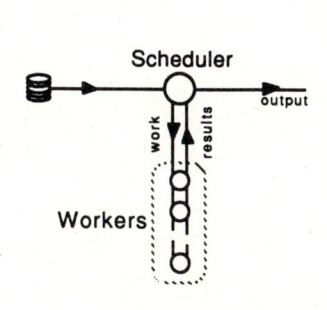

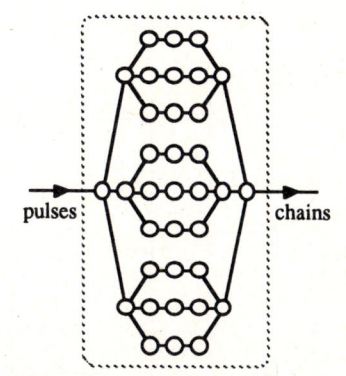

Figure 3   Simple Bidirectional Linear Farm   *Figure 4   Double Ternary Tree Farm*

To achieve high efficiency in a processor farm it is necessary to consider very carefully the characteristics of the scheduler in relation to the number of processors under its control and the time taken to process each batch of information. Farms of the type shown in figure 3 normally require some *valve* scheduler [4]. Our scheduler was of the form:

```
PAR
    ... buffer data from disk
    WHILE running
        SEQ
            proc.free ? processorID
            from.buffer ? work.packet
            work.out ! processorID; work.packet
```

which proved to limit the farm to around 15 processors, because it communicated explicitly with specific processors. This is to be avoided. The two-ended (unidirectional) farm sidesteps the problem in our application by removing the need for a valve entirely. Workpackets are supplied whenever they are available; workpackets are consumed whenever there is an available processor. This approach yields nearly 100% processor utilisation with over fifty processors.

Merging

Merging was implemented in three phases, termed *pre-merging*, *merging*, and *post-merging*. All three contribute to the merging of deinterleaved pulse chains into a track table, but the bulk of the work is handled by the main *merger*.

The preliminary phase, *pre-merging*, is possible because the farmed deinterleaver operates on blocks of pulses. Each pulse block processed typically produces several chains. These chains may or may not be mergeable with each other - the pre-merger determines this and merges chains together where possible. This will typically reduce the data rate being sent to the main merger, and hence the workload that the merger has to bear. *Post-merging* concerns the possible merging of tracks in the track table with each other. This is necessary because complex emitters, noisy signals, or input drift can cause false splitting of an emitter across two or more track table entries.

The three phases are distributed: pre-merging is farmed along with deinterleaving, because this automatically extracts maximum parallelism and provides automatic load balancing. The main merger consists of a parallel database engine configured in a linear-topology pipeline, described below. Post-merging is handled in a separate processor which is tightly coupled to the merger output.

Parallel Database Engine Merger

The merger was implemented as a linear processor structure (figures 2 and 5). It is unusual because the emitter table is shared dynamically between the workers. Associative searching is performed in a parallel and pipelined manner by all the processors in the merger for each incoming chain. Figure 5 shows the structure of the merger. Chains from the pre-merger are converted to prototype tracks, which are passed along the pipeline of matchers, each of which possesses an approximately equal portion of the track table.

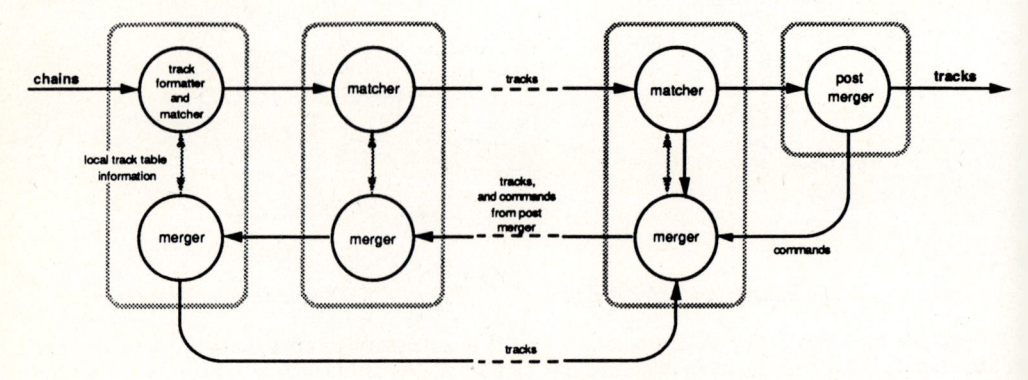

Figure 5   Process Structure for the Merger

After passing through every matcher, the track information enters the merger loop (bottom of figure 5), around which it circulates until it has been merged into the track table. The updated track table information (held by the matchers) is passed to the post-merger. Each processor has a loading manager (not shown in figure 5). The loading managers are configured in a ring to form a distributed dynamic load balancing system. They allocate new tracks to whichever processor is least loaded. The computational load on the merger is about an order of magnitude lower than that of the deinterleaver, primarily because the input data rate is much lower. Typically, fewer than 10 processors are required in the merger, and a linear topology has proved adequate.

Post-Merger

The post-merger continually checks the track table supplied by the merger for pairs of tracks which could be merged together, which it achieves with an identical matcher to those in the main merger. Whenever it finds a pair of similar tracks, it instructs the merger to attempt to merge them together. A simple control substructure permits the post-merger to send commands to the main merger, effectively placing the post-merger in overall supervision of the merger.

A key feature of the post-merger is the decoupling of the communications rate from the processing rate. The benefit of this is that the post-merger is able to cope with a wide range of throughput rates, without affecting the track throughput of the merger, or indeed the pulse throughput of the deinterleaver. The decoupling is achieved using a decoupling table, i.e. all input is placed in a table (the emitter track table) as soon as it arrives. Computation is performed on entries in the table when no new input is arriving. This can be shown simply thus:

```
SEQ
    ... initialise work indicies
    WHILE running
      PRI ALT
        in ? trackID
          SEQ
            ... input new information into the table
            ... output new information to the emitter identifier

        TRUE & SKIP
          SEQ
            ... do some computation
            ... adjust work indicies for next time round
```

The 'computation' performed by the post-merger is the attempt to merge two entries in the track table. The key parameter to ensuring that this technique is successful is the maximum permissible cycle time, T_{max}, for checking the whole of the track table, which contains N entries, each to be checked against all the others once per cycle: by inspection, there are w checks to be performed, where

$$w = \sum_{i=1}^{N} i = \frac{N(N-1)}{2} \quad (1)$$

When the post-merger is in a steady state such that it finds no merging to be done, N is constant; merging will cause the value of N to fall. If the processor spends a fraction x of its time doing 'work' (i.e. following the TRUE & SKIP guard) for which each check takes p seconds, and it spends a fraction y = 1-x doing overhead for communications (i.e. following the in ? trackID guard), then total cycle time T is

$$T = \frac{wp}{x} = \frac{wp}{(1-y)} \quad (2)$$

p can be estimated by measuring T when x is known to be 1 (i.e. no input is being received). We must ensure that $T < T_{max}$, i.e.

$$x < \frac{wp}{T_{max}} \quad (3)$$

This sets an upper bound on the permissible track throughput rate for the post-merger. For our merger, x is typically greater than 0.95, which indicates that the computation is efficient.

Emitter Identifier

The emitter identifier is implemented on a single processor with a small database. Each incoming track is placed in a track table, which thus reflects the track table in the post-merger. With its remaining cpu time, the emitter identifier takes each track in turn and performs what is essentially a branch-and-bound search through the emitter database looking for matches, of which it may find several. This list of matches is sorted into confidence order, then sent to the graphics display.

As with the post-merger, a decoupling table is used to prevent the emitter identifier from being a bottle-neck to the whole system. The structure is similar to that for the post-merger, except that the results are output whenever work has been done, thus:

```
SEQ
  ... initialise work indicies
  WHILE running
    PRI ALT
      in ? trackID
        ... input new information into the table

      TRUE & SKIP
        SEQ
          ... do some computation
          ... output new information to the MMI
          ... adjust work indicies for next time round
```

The estimation of the maximum cycle time is similar to that for the post-merger, except that in equation (1) w is simply equal to N.

The difference between the decoupling used for the post merger and for the emitter identifier is important. The post merger inputs and outputs data at the same rate. Hence what is achieved is a decoupling of communications rate from processing rate. The emitter identifier, on the other hand, inputs information at one rate, and performs computation and output at a separate rate. Hence what is achieved is a decoupling of input communications rate from both processing rate and output communications rate, without any loss of integrity (except under pathological conditions), preventing the emitter identifier from slowing down earlier elements of the ESM pipeline.

Load Balancing

Efficient use of a multiple transputer system depends upon careful balancing of the work to be done by each of the processors in the network, to ensure the time that processors spend idle is minimised. The most obvious approach is to use a farm, where the work is shared out dynamically, taking care to ensure that the scheduler does not limit overall throughput.

Efficiency also depends upon consideration of the communications requirement and the ability to obtain 'free' communications in parallel with computation. In work described elsewhere [5], we have developed a method for reducing the limiting effect of the transputer link bandwidth when farming computationally undemanding tasks. Normally, transputers cannot be used efficiently when computation takes less time than communication, but if a farm can be supplied with work packets which take a long time to compute (relative to the communication time) interleaved with work packets which are computationally undemanding, then the communications limited operations are essentially hidden. We call this technique *heterogeneous work packet mixing*.

The top-level architecture of our radar ESM data processor is a pipeline - i.e. algorithmic parallelism is used. Each stage therefore requires manual load balancing by varying the numbers of workers. In circumstances where performance is data dependent, care must be taken not to tune a system against test data which does not properly represent the characteristics of real data.

We have found a simple technique invaluable for reducing the dependence of the parallel system on a pre-determined static load balance. This is the decoupling table, which in our radar ESM application is implemented as a track table. This has been built into both the post-merger and the emitter identifier, as described above. The essential feature is the high-priority input and storage of data, allowing earlier pipeline stages to continue at full speed. Data is taken off the table and processed in the remaining node cpu time. This technique is limited to applications such as radar ESM, where the overall aim is the data-reduction of the input stream to produce some table of current state.

Note that this is not the same as using an over-writing buffer - another decoupling technique involving the non-deterministic discarding of data. This is useful at certain phases of the development process when data degradation is less important than performance degradation; indeed, we have found empirically that an over-writing buffer does not seriously affect the results produced by the ESM system, because of the repetitive nature of the input data.

A simple tool has aided us significantly in the load balancing of our system, both within each of the pipeline stages, and at the higher level. This is a processor idle-time monitor - a bar chart of processor activity is displayed on the graphics screen in real time. This is implemented using two processes: one runs at low priority in parallel with the main work, the other at high priority in parallel with the communications harness. It is described in more detail in [6].

Performance Measurements

The crucial performance assessments in the ESM system are for the deinterleaver and for the merger.

Deinterleaver

As the deinterleaver is the computational centre of ESM, it is useful to compare the deinterleaving performance of the transputer and Vax implementations. This was investigated using several different test data sets, representing different types of radar scenario and also representing different computational tasks for the program.

A single T800 transputer, running at 20MHz with 4-cycle memory, executes the optimised occam deinterleaver between 30 and 41 times faster than a single Vax 11/750 executes the original Pascal. Of this, a factor of between 1.4 and 2.8 (according to data set) is accounted for by optimisations we have made to the deinterleaver algorithm, such as the in-lining of crucial procedures. The deinterleaver farm has been found to have excellent linear scalability. In summary, for 50 transputers, performance up to 2000 times the Vax has been observed, with either 10 Mbit/s or 20 Mbit/s links.

Merger

The characteristics for throughput versus data set are quite different for the merger compared to the deinterleaver. The effect of this widely varying loading between the two, e.g. 2 merger processors can support the throughput of between 10 and 45 deinterleaver processors, according to scenario. This represents better than the state-of-the-art in commercial mergers. For more than 4 processors the scalability of the merger is sub-linear, with 16 processors reaching about 35% of projected linear efficiency, supporting between 28 and 125 deinterleavers, according to scenario.

Input

The deinterleaver input communications link, which handles pulse data at 20 Mbit/s, would only be a bottle-neck above 10^5 pulses per second - beyond this, special hardware would have to replace the controller processor (figure 2) to permit input into more than one deinterleaver farm, i.e. along more than one link. Such special hardware would probably distribute the pulses by buffering them into blocks in the same way that the present transputer controller does, then distribute the blocks between the links to the various deinterleaver farms. An alternative strategy would be to partition on RF or bearing, but the parameters tend to be very non-uniformly distributed.

Conclusions

This work has shown that a multi-transputer implementation of a radar ESM data processing system is a practicable possibility. The system embodies a software solution useful for further development and enhancement of the algorithms. The comparison of deinterleaving performance with the Vax shows a valuable and exceedingly cost-effective speed-up of three orders of magnitude, for a medium sized farm of 50 transputers. The parallel database engine merger offers high performance, without sacrificing accuracy. Our technique of using decoupling tables permits different stages in the system to operate at full speed, without the whole system running at the speed of the slowest module.

Acknowledgement

This work has been carried out with the support of Procurement Executive, Ministry of Defence.

References

[1] *Communicating Process Computers*, D. May, R Shepherd; Inmos Technical Note 22 (1987)

[2] *Practical Parallelism Using Transputer Arrays*, D.J. Pritchard, et al.; Parallel Architectures and Languages Europe, Vol. 1, Springer-Verlag (1987).

[3] *Hybrid Architecture Paradigms in a Radar ESM Data Processing Application*, R.D.Beton, S.P.Turner, C.Upstill; Microprocessors and Microsystems Vol.13 No.3 (1989).

[4] *Performance Maximisation*, P.Atkin; Inmos Technical Note 17, (1987).

[5] *Using Transputers to Simulate Optoelectronic Computers*, I.Cramb, C.Upstill; Procs 12th Occam User Group; IOS (1990).

[6] *A State-of-the-Art Radar Pulse Deinterleaver*, R.D.Beton, S.P.Turner, C.Upstill; Procs 9th Occam User Group; IOS (1988).

DICARPS Transputer Signal Processing System.   Extended Abstract

City Computing Ltd.
Surrey House,
Surrey Street,
Croydon.

Authors:
Tel.
Fax

J.M. Little.
C.M.H. Klimpke.
J.P. Madar.
0737 557412
0737 557761

A DICARPS VHS recording system stores time series data collected from operational sonar systems. This paper describes a Transputer based system used to process and display raw sonar data output from a Dicarps recorder. Display data generated by the processing system can be fed into an already existing shore based sonar simulator using high speed network services. The Transputer sonar system (TSS) receives digitised acoustic data from a ship based Dicarps recorder. The time series data is processed, using a variety of algorithms from FFTs to specialised data compression and normalisation routines, into a form ready for display on high resolution graphics monitors (typically 1280 x 1024 x 256 brightness levels). The data from Dicarps encapsulates information from up to 400 channels with a data flow rate of 125 Kbytes/sec. This data is fed into a network of 11 transputers for signal processing, display conditioning and data base storage. The Transputer sonar system is hosted by a single PC to give a very portable system with minimal duplication costs. The Transputer based sonar processing and display system has proved to be successful and reliable. It is currently in use within MOD research divisions.

A display system similar to 2031Z (TADS) is used to perform the display functions of 2031Z. The TADS system works with data represented in terms of normalised Amplitude - Frequency spectra. As data from the DICARPS system is complex time series information, FFT processing is required to transform the complex time series into Amplitude - Frequency spectra.

The Transputer sonar system will also operate in stand alone mode whereby operator interaction with the system is achieved using a Transputer based graphics display running a Windowing system to provide data and control windows. The operators use either a mouse or a tracker ball for interaction with the displayed windows.

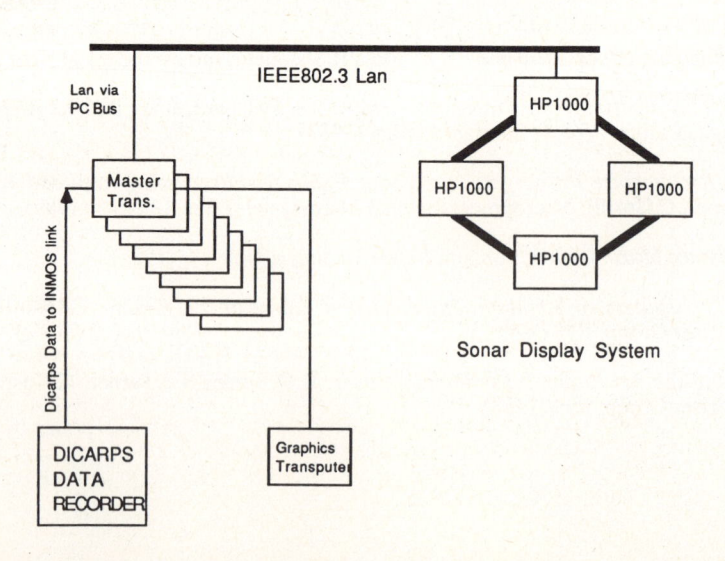

Operators using the system are able to set up sonar processing options. For surveillance data, operators are only able to control the data generation rate. However for vernier options operators are able to specify the update rate, centre frequencies and bandwidths. The TADS system expects FFT'd information corresponding to the options set up by the operators. As there are numerous different vernier processing configurations, generation of the total possible data set would prove to be extremely expensive in terms of required processing power and data transmission rates. For these reasons Time series data obtained from the DICARPS system should be analysed (FFT) according to the requirements of the TADS system as chosen by the sonar operators.

Data received by the HP1000 A-series computers over the LAN (IEEE802.3) is fed into the already existing software system using the CityNet communication system.

CSP design techniques have been adopted. Careful design and an implementation of the critical processing routines have important consequences with respect to the number of Transputers required to achieve Real Time performance. This is particularly important when the Transputer Sonar system is to duplicated in any quantity. Efficient implementations cut duplication costs. For example the FFT algorithm, written in transputer assembler, has produced one of the fastest transputer based FFT algorithms currently available for the T800 processor (see below).

The TSS consists of five distinct modules.

o   PC interface.
o   Initial time series data store.
o   FFT engine.
o   Normaliser.
o   Man machine interface.

A short summary of the functionality and important design features of each of these is given below.

Dicarps data interface.

The system accepts input from DICARPS via a Transputer link adaptor interface card. The time series data is acquired by the top level transputer (master) using one of the links and is passed out to the chain of slave transputers. Each slave processor is responsible for selecting its own data for processing from the data as it passes by.

Commands for changes in the processing rate and selection of verniers are received from a LAN card on the PC which is networked to the main TADS HP1000 A series processors. This information is passed, via the PC Bus, to the master transputer processor and then onward to the slave processors.

Processed data (FFT results) is fed back from the slave processors to the master which normalises the data (see below) and sends the resulting data to the PC Bus using a standard PC link adapter. Server software resident on the PC forwards this data to TADS via the LAN (IEEE802.3). A sustained data rate exceeding 150kBytes per second has been achieved between a PC and an HP1000 A series computer.

Initial time series data store.

Each of the transputers has to store data for a certain number of beams for each octave. Each packet of Dicarps data from the master processor will contain a number of datums which need to be collected. Each datum point is used twice for surveillance channels (50% overlap processing) and once for vernier channels. Each datum point is discarded when it is no longer useful and the space occupied is released to the system. The time series data store provides an efficient global memory resource within each transputer which optimises the storage requirements by reclaiming recently freed memory blocks. The time series data is transmitted to the FFT engine following the receipt of timing control commands from the master transputer. As the time series data is forwarded to the FFT engine it is windowed.

FFT engine

The FFT engine consists of 2 implementations of the Cooley-Tukey complex FFT algorithm optimised for both radix 2 and radix 4 transforms. The appropriate version is selected depending upon the number of points requested for processing. Careful design and an implementation of the kernel code in GUY (transputer assembler) form has produced one of the fastest transputer based FFT algorithms currently available for the T800 processor.

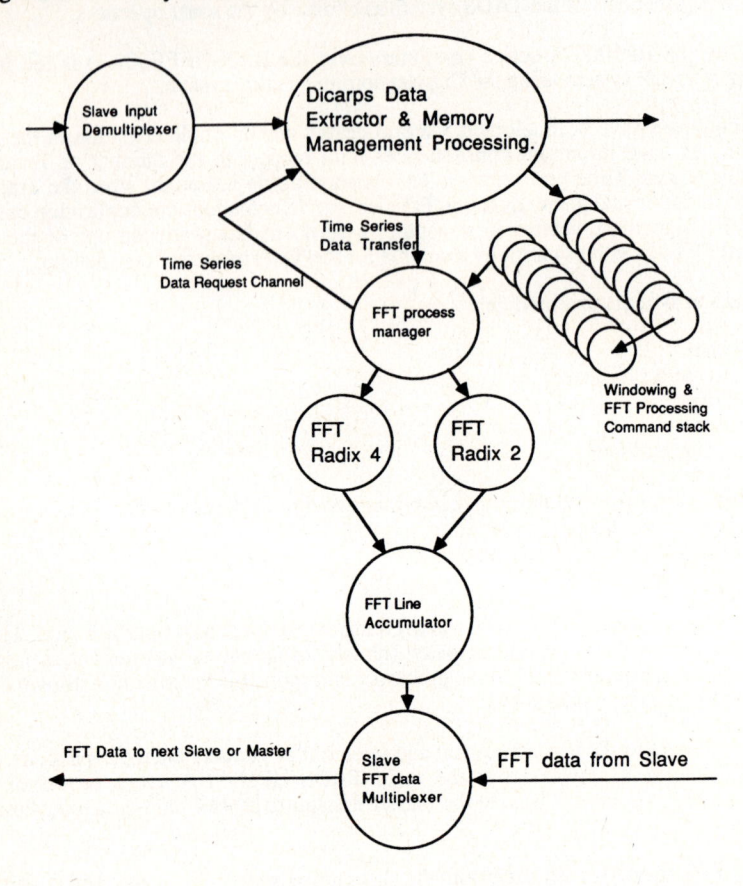

Software Structure of Slave FFT processing

Normaliser

Data output from the FFT system must be normalised before transmission to the display system. At present two different normalisation algorithms are available. One of the major advantages of the Transputer system design is that the structure of the normalisation process can be extended to any degree of complexity. It is no longer necessary to *hard wire* certain algorithms to achieve real time performance.

Software Structure - Master TPR

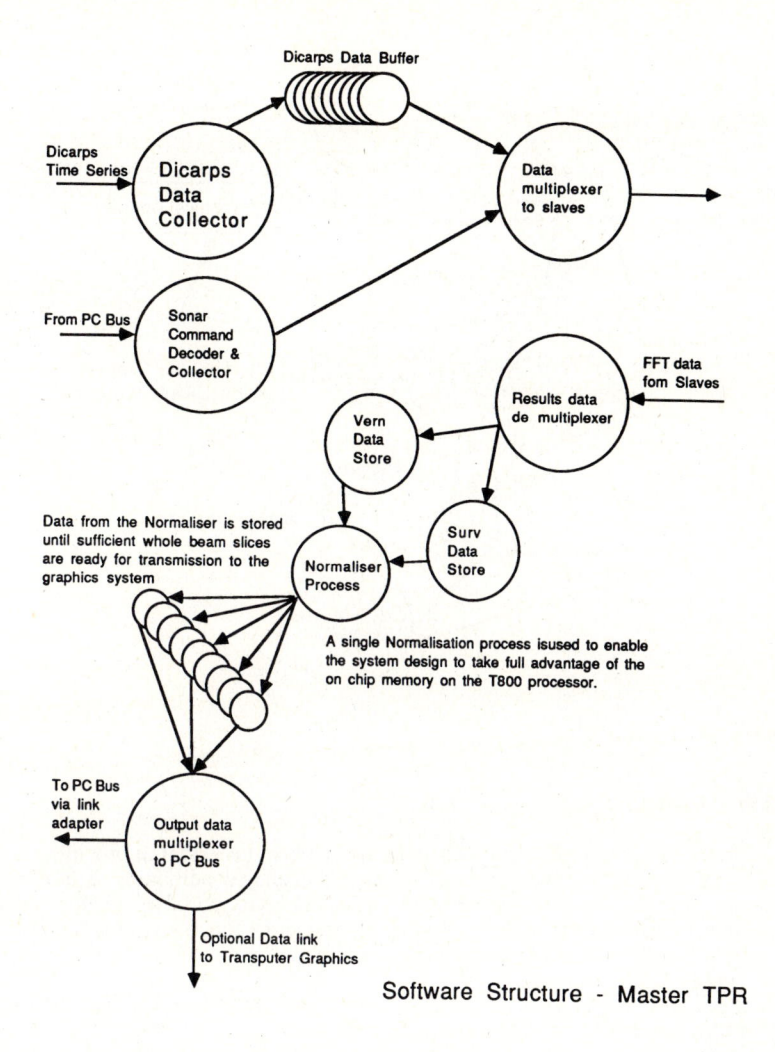

(Diagram description labels:)
- Dicarps Data Buffer
- Dicarps Time Series → Dicarps Data Collector
- Data multiplexer to slaves
- From PC Bus → Sonar Command Decoder & Collector
- FFT data from Slaves → Results data de multiplexer
- Vern Data Store
- Surv Data Store
- Normaliser Process
- Data from the Normaliser is stored until sufficient whole beam slices are ready for transmission to the graphics system
- A single Normalisation process is used to enable the system design to take full advantage of the on chip memory on the T800 processor.
- To PC Bus via link adapter ← Output data multiplexer to PC Bus
- Optional Data link to Transputer Graphics

Man machine interface.

The MMI for the TADS/DICARPS system is also transputer based. The interface provides a graphical WIMPS style interaction which closely models the appearance of a standard sonar array operator's console. The entire interface is written in OCCAM and runs on one transputer. Each request is considered to be a separate event. This is queued up by the window manager and passed as a message to the windows, each of which is a separate parallel process.

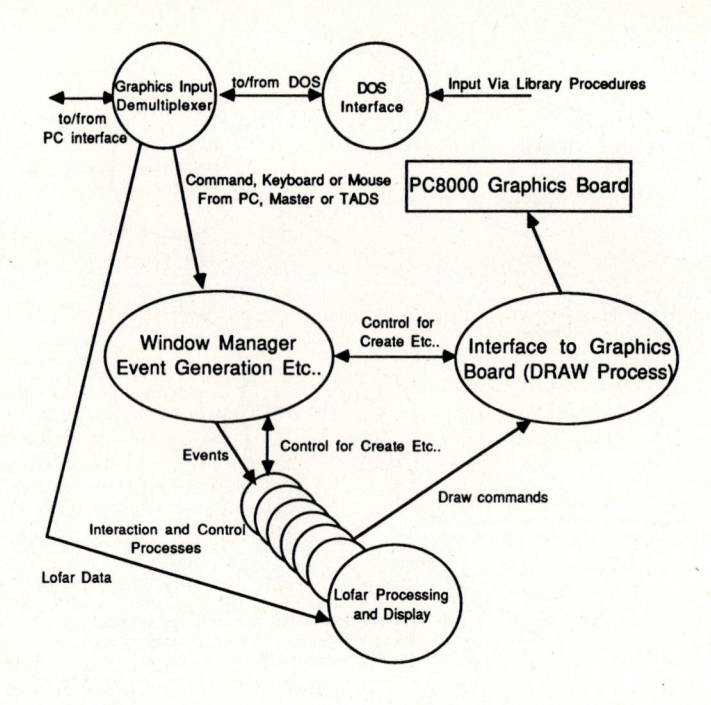

Stand Alone System.

The transputer based signal processing system has been very successful in providing a very cost effective means for performing the signal processing and display conditioning required to feed the sonar simulator. As this sonar display simulator (TADS) is not portable, depends on specially constructed operator switch hardware and is very expensive the functionality of the sonar display system has been installed on a transputer graphics system.

To achieve this Transputer graphics are being incorporated into the already existing transputer based processing system to provide a fully functional portable sonar system. All operator interaction being made via either mouse of tracker ball used in conjunction with screen based menus.A windows type of display methodology is being employed. The resolution of the transputer graphics system, being 1280 x 1024 x 8 bits is sufficient to display two conventional data display formats concurrently. This effectively reduces the four screens currently used by two sonar operator to two screens. The system is capable of driving four such operator stations.
To make efficient use of memory a dynamic memory allocation and efficient data base subsystem were designed to give excellent operator response/performance at a fraction of the cost of the real sonar system. The Transputer Sonar System has shown that it is no longer necessary to *hard wire* certain algorithms to achieve real time performance.

The major advantages of such a system are:

o   Increased reliability brought about by using only standard commercially available hardware.

o   Reproduction systems costs are low due to the low cost of the processing hardware.

o   Portable processing systems with high computational performance and low electrical power consumption.

A Versatile Sonar Transmitter Signal Generator

by

J.W.R.Griffiths, D.B.Payne, T.A.Rafik, W.J.Wood and J.Zhang

University of Technology, Loughborough

For some years now our group at Loughborough have been developing and experimenting with versatile Sonar Transmitters e.g. references 1,2. The basis of these systems is that a set of waveforms are generated digitally and then after analog to digital conversion are separately amplified and fed to the staves of a transducer array. A schematic diagram is shown in figure 1. Two main systems have been built and in the high power system the power in each channel is 1 kW giving a total power output of 16 kW. The flexibility of the generation allows many different types of sonar signal to be transmitted and opens up many new lines of research. However when the basic digital signal generation section was built micro processors were not so powerful and memory not so cheap. With the continuing rapid development in microelectronics it was decided to have a fresh look at the method of generation.

There are two basic methods of digital signal generation which can be used, the direct and the indirect methods. In the direct methods the signals are generated from a software program and transmitted as they are generated. In the indirect method an intermediate step is used, in that the signals are stored in digital memory before transmission.

The advantage of the first method is simplicity, greater versatility and there is virtually no limitation on the duration of the transmitted signal. However when a large number of channels are required the speed of operation of the basic processor limits the highest frequency of operation.
On the other hand the indirect method requires a significant size of memory to enable long pulses to be stored and for accuracy of the waveform the resolution has to be quite good e.g., at least 12 bits.

As stated earlier it was decided to design a new generator taking advantage of the significant reduction in the cost of memories and the improvements in the power of microprocessors. A number of processors were considered including the TMS320 series, the Motorola 56000 and the INMOS transputer. This paper describes the system based on the transputer.

The generator was to be designed to be suitable for a number of sonar transmitters but the highest frequency required was of the order of 50kHz. In theory a sampling frequency of 100kHz would have been sufficient, but this would require very tight tolerances on the output filters after the D/A converters and would introduce possible transient problems arising from the sharp cut-off. Instead it was decided to be reasonably conservative and to use a sampling frequency of 250kHz. A fourth order Butterworth filter then provides satisfactory performance.

The basic word size in the transputer is 32 bit which is far more than is required for the signal generator. A 12 bit word giving a dynamic range of over 70dB would probably have been sufficient but as a 16 bit A/D converter able to operate at the required sampling frequency was available cheaply it was decided to use a 16 bit word. This choice was also convenient for the memory and a single chip provided enough memory for 1 channel (64K samples) making a very compact system. With the sampling frequency of 250 kHz this gives a maximum pulse length of about 260 ms which is more than adequate for the intended applications.

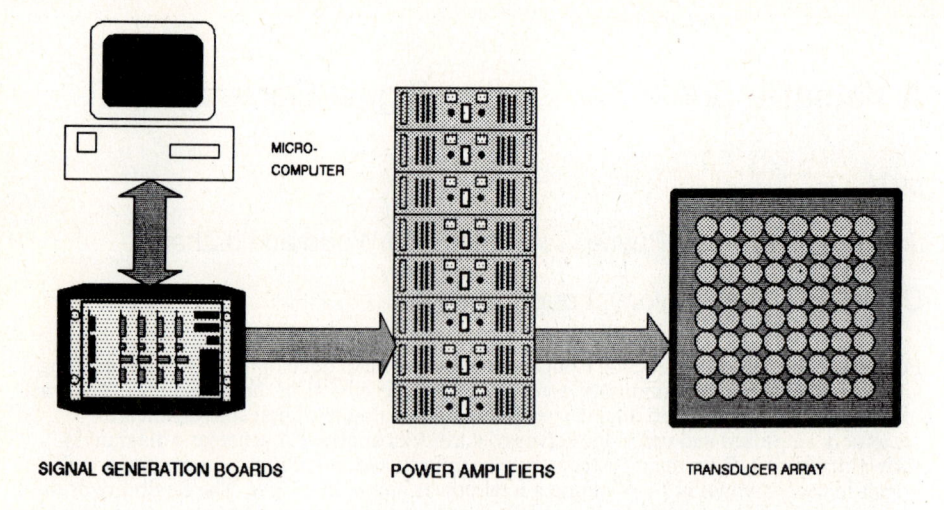

Fig 1. GENERAL SCHEMATIC OF VERSATILE TRANSMITTERS

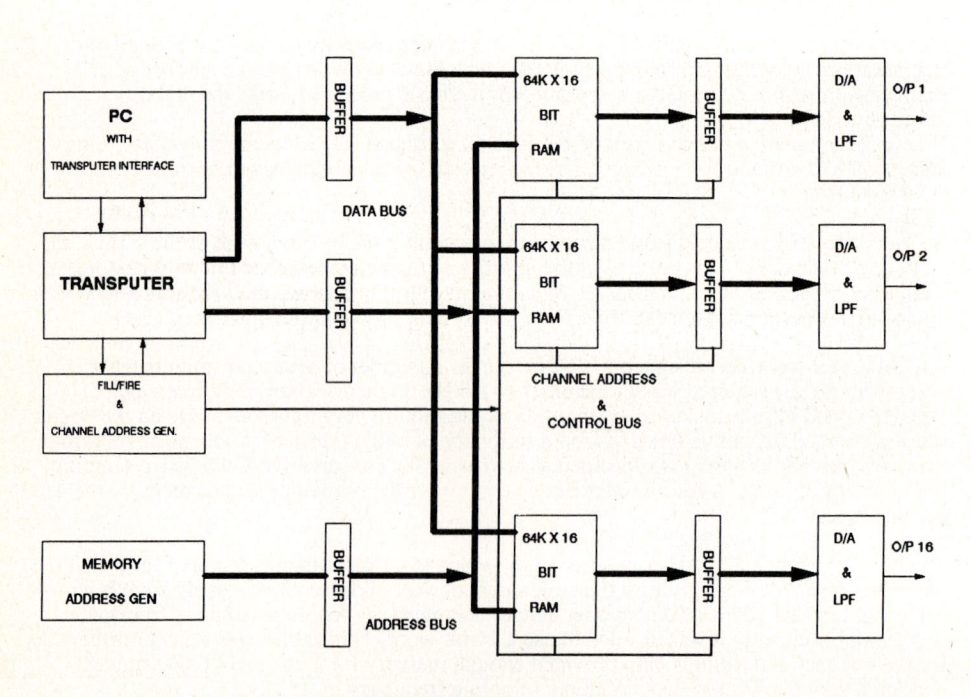

Fig.2: System Block Diagram.

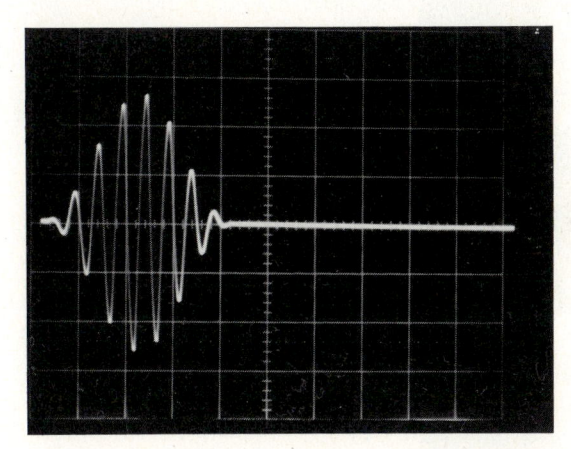

FIG. 3: Weighted Pulse
Frequency = 4 kHz
Time scale = 0.5 msec/Div
Amplitude scale = 2 V/Div

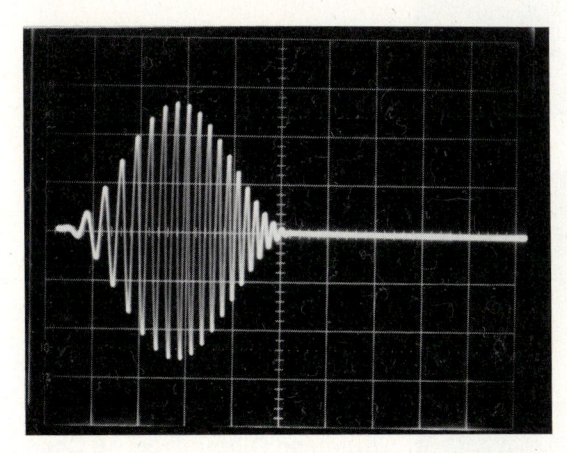

FIG. 4: Weighted FM Pulse
Lower Frequency = 2 kHz
Upper Frequency = 6 kHz
Time scale = 1 msec/Div
Amplitude scale = 2 V/Div

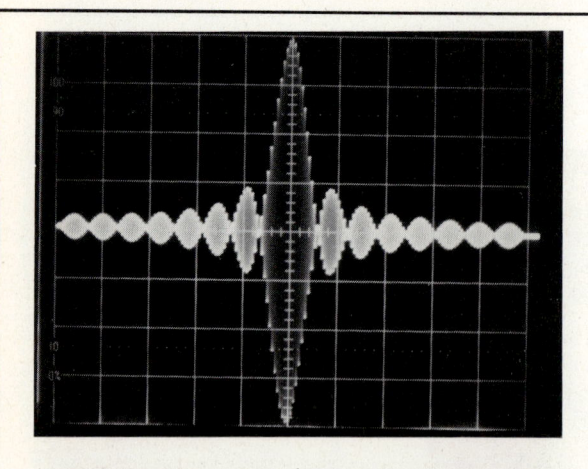

FIG. 5: Swept Beam
Frequency = 40 kHz
Pulse Length = 4 msec
Sweep Frequency = 250 Hz
Summed Output

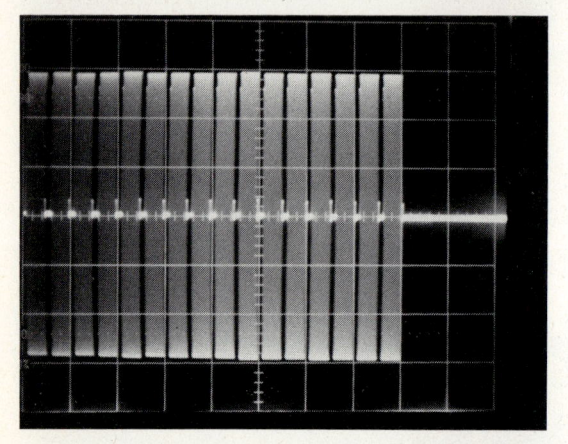

FIG. 6(a): Amplitude Test
Frequency = 40 kHz
Time scale = 2 msec/Div
Amplitude scale = 0.1 V/Div
Summed Output From 16 Channels

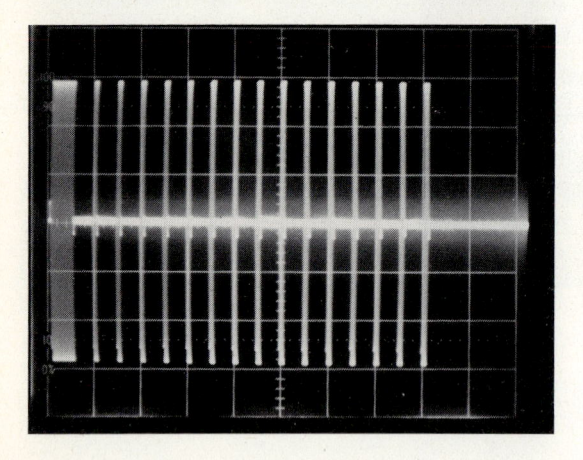

FIG. 6(b): Phase Test
Frequency = 40 kHz
Time scale = 2 msec/Div
Amplitude scale = 0.1 V/Div
Summed Output From 16 Channels

Figure 2 shows a block diagram of the system. The memory is part of the transputer memory but is isolated from the transputer during transmission by buffers controlled by software from the transputer as can be seen from the block diagram. For convenience the transputer is controlled by a micro-computer and an Acorn Archimedes is being used at the moment since it offers some advantages over the commonly used IBM/PC clone.

Some typical results are shown in figures 3 and 4. Figure 3 shows a simple sonar pulse with a raised cosine amplitude modulation and in Figure 4 a similar pulse but with the carrier frequency modulated.

An output is available from the unit which is the addition of all the channel outputs. This provides an estimate of the waveform which would be received in the far field of an array in a direction normal to the plane of the array. Figure 5 shows the waveform at this point when each of the elements has a waveform different from its neighbour by a constant frequency. The effect of this is to cause the beam to sweep across rapidly at the difference frequency and so produce an electronic sweep as is seen in the figure.

Figure 6 show two test waveforms. In 6(a) each of the channels is switched on in turn so checking the equality of the amplitudes. In 6(b) channel 1 is on for the whole pulse while the other channels are switched on in turn but in opposing phase. This allows the accuracy of the phasing of the channnels to be checked.

References

1 Goodson A.D. et al. "A High Power Flexible Sonar Transmitter" Proc. I.E.R.E Conf. 'Electronics in Oceanography' Edinburgh March 1987.

2 Wood W.J. et al. "A Low Frequency Versatile Sonar Transmitter" Proc IOA Conf. 'Sonar Signal Processing', Loughborough, Dec 1989.

PARALLELIZED 2D-DISCRETE HARTLEY TRANSFORM BY USING IMS A100 DEVICES

G. D'Angelo, L. Fortuna, G. Muscato, G. Nunnari

Istituto di Elettrotecnica ed Elettronica, Università di Catania
viale A.Doria 6, 95125 Catania, Italy

Abstract. In this paper new results regarding the implementation of a 2D-DHT parallel algorithm, by using a mixed Transputer and DSP IMS A100 architecture, are reported. The relationships between the 2D-DHT and 2D-DFT are introduced and an original parallel computation scheme is proposed. In order to evaluate the suitability of the described parallel implementation of a 2D-DHT a comparison with a 2D-DFT is shown.

1. Introduction

The Discrete Hartley Transform (DHT) is a procedure, recently introduced by Bracewell [1], suitable for computing the Discrete Fourier Transform (DFT) of real data sequences. The main advantage of the DHT consists in manipulating real data only, so that it requires one half of the computations needed in the case of complex data.

In this paper the generalization of the DHT algorithm in two dimensions is proposed and the relationships between the 2D-DHT and 2D-DFT are introduced. The 2D-DHT algorithm is particularly appropriate to perform Nuclear Magnetic Resonance (NMR) data processing. In order to speed-up the 2D-DHT algorithm a computation scheme, which is also described in the paper, is studied. A parallel architecture based on a T800 Transputer and a B009 card, containing a T212 Transputer which drives a chain of four IMSA100 DSPs, is adopted.

2. The Discrete Hartley Transform

Let $x(n)$ ($n = 0, 1, \ldots, N-1$) be a real data vector of length N. The Discrete Hartley Transform of the sequence $x(n)$ is:

$$H(k) = \frac{1}{N} \sum_{n=0}^{N-1} x(n) \, \text{cas}\left(2\pi \frac{nk}{N} \right) \quad (1)$$

where $\text{cas}(.) = \cos(.) + \sin(.)$.
The DFT of $x(n)$, indicated as $F(k)$, can be derived from $H(k)$ via the expression:

$$F(k) = Ev(k) - j\, Od(k) \quad (2)$$

where $Ev(k)$ and $Od(k)$ indicate respectively the even and odd parts of $H(k)$:

$$Ev(k) = [H(k) + H(N-k)] / 2$$
$$Od(k) = [H(k) - H(N-k)] / 2 \quad (3)$$

By using the Hermitian property of DFT algorithm [2] for real data sequences, N complex values of F(k) can be computed from N real values of H(k). Based on the expression of a 1D-DHT, the definition of the 2D-DHT of a given real data matrix, $x(n_1,n_2)$, can be given as follows:

$$H(k_1,k_2) = \frac{1}{N_1 N_2} \sum_{n_1=0}^{N_1-1} \sum_{n_2=0}^{N_2-1} x(n_1,n_2) \, \text{cas}\left(2\pi \frac{n_1 k_1}{N_1}\right) \text{cas}\left(2\pi \frac{n_2 k_2}{N_2}\right) \quad (4)$$

From the expression (4), well-known in literature, we introduce here the relationships between the 2D-DHT and 2D-DFT as follows:

$$\text{Re}[F(k_1,k_2)] = \frac{H((N_1-k_1),k_2) + H(k_1,(N_2-k_2))}{2}$$

$$\text{Im}[F(k_1,k_2)] = \frac{H((N_1-k_1),(N_2-k_2)) - H(k_1,k_2)}{2} \quad \forall k_1, k_2 \neq 0$$

$$(5)$$

$$\text{Re}[F(0,k_2)] = \frac{H(0,k_2) + H(0,N-k_2)}{2}$$

$$\text{Im}[F(0,k_2)] = \frac{H(0,N-k_2) - H(0,k_2)}{2} \quad \forall \, k_2 \neq 0$$

Analogous expressions can be given for the case when $k_2 = 0$; $k_1 \neq 0$.

3. Algorithm Implementation

In order to compute both the DHT and the 2D-DHT an architecture consisting of a T800 Transputer and a B009 card, containing a chain of four IMSA100 devices, is used. This chain allows to calculate the correlation of 128 points in 128 steps. In fact the peculiarity of each IMSA100 device is due to its internal transversal filter architecture consisting of 32 multipliers and 32 delay-and-add stages. Such a characteristic is fully employed in the implementation of the 2D-DHT algorithm.
It is possible to show, by appropriate manipulations of expression (4), that a 2D-DHT of a $N_1 * N_2$ matrix x can be obtained in two steps:

1. evaluating N_1 1D-DHT corresponding to the rows of the x matrix;
2. evaluating N_2 1D-DHT corresponding to the x matrix columns.

Each individual 1D-DHT is computed by using the IMSA100 chain,

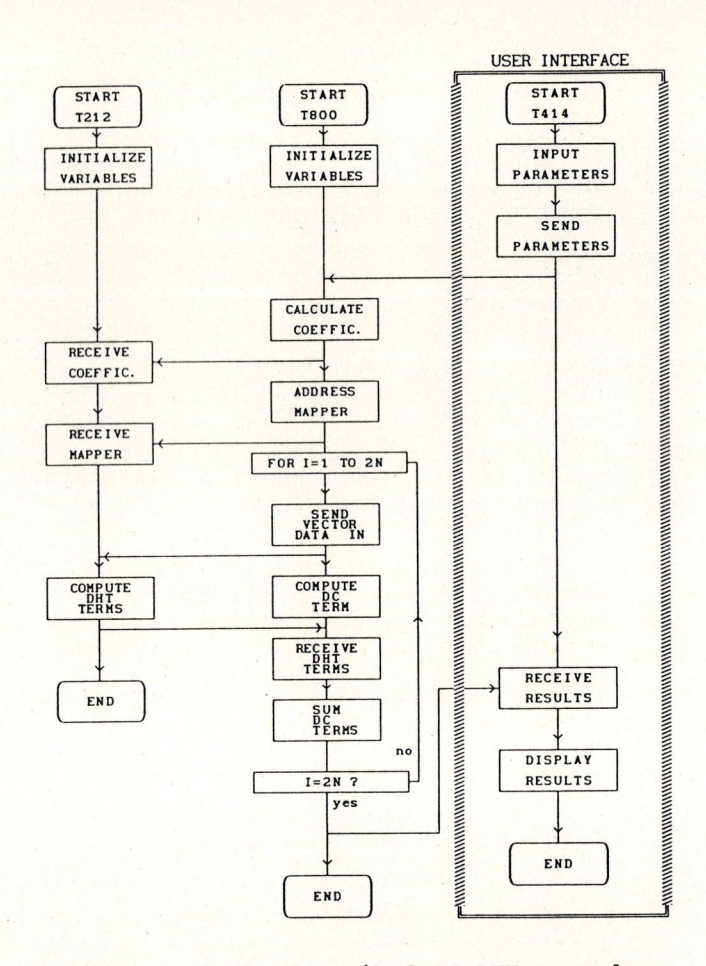

Fig. 1 - Flow-chart of the described 2D-DHT procedure.

after arranging the DHT coefficients cas(.) and the elements of the input sequence in a circular correlation, in order to further speed-up the computations.

The mapping algorithm used for this purpose is the Rader's Prime Number Transform (PNT) [3] which is here briefly summarized in order to illustrate the DHT implementation.

Let N be a prime number, a permutation {v} of a sequence {v} = 0,1,2,...N-2 can be computed via the expression :

$$v = (r^w) \bmod N \qquad (6)$$

where r is the primitive root of N.
The DHT expression (1) can be also written as follows :

$$H(0) = \sum_{n=0}^{N-1} x(n) \; ; \quad H(k) - H(0) = \sum_{n=1}^{N-1} x(n) \; cas\left(\frac{2 \pi n k}{N}\right) \qquad (7)$$

Assigning:

$$n = (r^m) \mod N \quad \text{and} \quad k = (r^1) \mod N \qquad (8)$$

it is obtained:

$$H\left[(r^1) \mod n\right] - H(0) = \sum_{n=1}^{N-1} x\left[(r^m) \mod N\right] \cas\left(\frac{r^{(1+m)}}{N}\right) \qquad (9)$$

The expression (9) represents a circular correlation between the input data sequence and the coefficients cas(.).
The flow chart of the described 2D-DHT computation scheme is shown in Fig. 1 and is illustrated below.

- The T800 processor computes the coefficients of the DHT and the permutation sequences which are sent to the A100 chain and to the address mapper respectively. Successively the input matrix is decomposed in 1D sequences which are sent to the IMSA100 chain in order to evaluate the corresponding DHTs.

- The A100 chain, receives the sequences of data, appropriately permuted by the address mapper, which is a hardware device contained into the IMS B009 board, performs the correlation and sends the results to the T800 Transputer. Concurrently, the Transputer T800 evaluates the DC terms which are then added to the data received from the DSPs.

In this framework the T414 Transputer is used for running the user interface program.
A schematic representation referring to a DHT of a 7x7 point matrix row is shown in Fig.2.

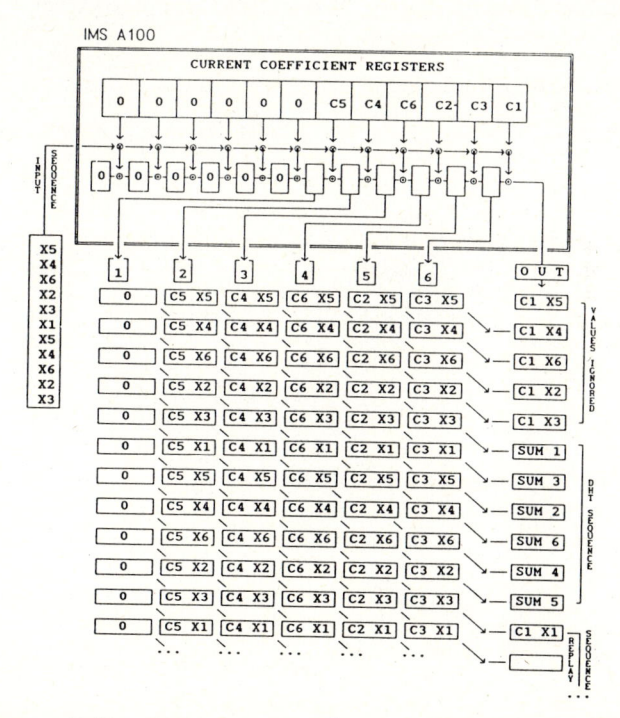

Fig.2 - Scheme of the DHT computation by using A100 devices.

The sequence of discrete input data, appropriately permuted, is sent to the DSP chain. Step by step each element is presented to the A100 chain input, where is multiplied by the coefficients cas(.) which are stored in the CCR (Current Coefficient Registers).The value obtained after each individual multiplication is added to the content of the previous register and the result is stored in the next register. After N-2 cycles the DHT elements begin to be available at the output of the A100 chain. These elements will be then ordered in the correct sequence by the address mapper.

4. Results and Conclusions

Nowadays in many scientific applications fast 2Dspectral analysis is required [4]. In particular our team is interested in Nuclear Magnetic Resonance data processing, for molecular modeling; in this area the need of high computation rates is due to the considerable amount of data to be processed. A revision of classical algorithms, in conjunction with the use of appropriate parallel architectures, allows us to obtain high performance at a low cost.

Execution times concerning the implemented 2D-DHT are reported in Table I, for different matrix order data set. In particular the 2D-DHT execution times obtained by using two different hardware configurations are shown.
By using A100 DSPs drawbacks arise due to the 16-bit word length which could limit the precision. To overcome such problems the coefficients cas(.) and input elements can be appropriately normalized. In the presented architecture this operation is performed by a Transputer.The obtained speed-up versus the point number is shown in Fig.3 for three different cases:

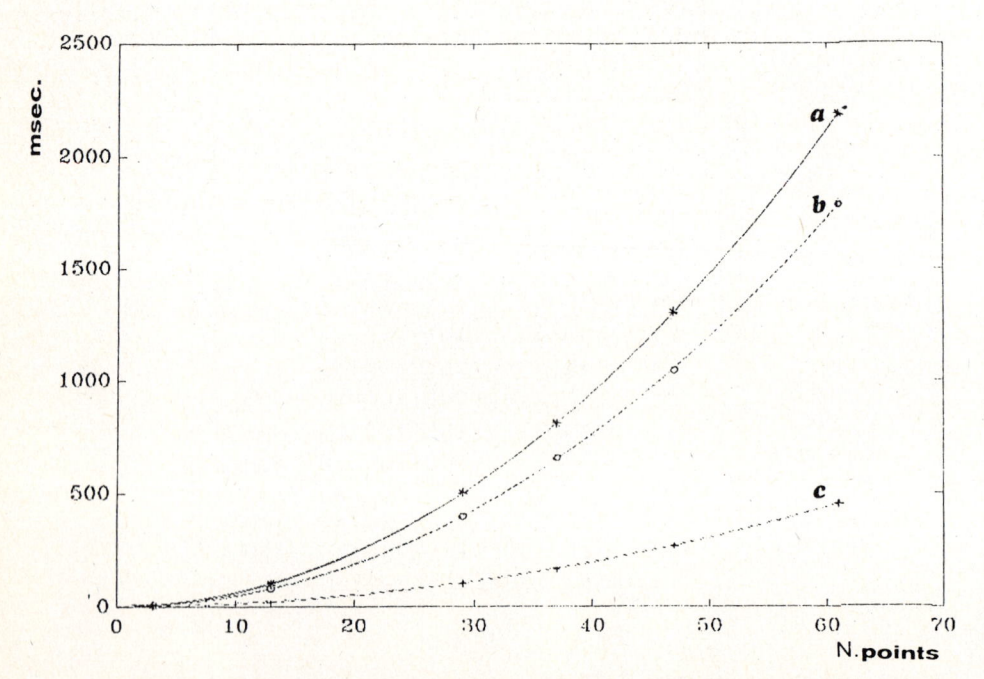

Fig.3 - Execution times versus the number of points.

a) 2D-DFT by using the IMSA100 chain and a T414 Transputer;
b) 2D-DHT by using the same architecture as in a);
c) 2D-DHT substituting the T414 processor with a T800 one.

From the results reported in Table I it appears evident that the described 2D-DHT runs faster then the corresponding 2D-DFT;

TABLE I

N × N POINTS	2D-DFT	2D-DHT (T414) mSec.	2D-DHT (T800)
3×3	5.601	3.681	1.275
13×13	99.648	62.462	20.105
29×29	499.021	305.517	102.655
37×37	805.690	500.096	166.561
47×47	1288.112	805.848	268.160
61×61	2187.324	1356.223	451.102
128×128	-	4579.341	1483.215

References

[1] R.N. Bracewell, "*Discreted Hartley Transform*", J.Opt. Soc. Am., Vol. 73, No.12, December 1983.
[2] R.A. Roberts, C.T. Mullis, "*Digital Signal Processing*",Addison Wesley 1987.
[3] H.Yassaie, "*Discrete Fourier Transform with IMS A100*" , INMOS A100 Application Note 2, 1986.
[4] I. D'Antone,L. Fortuna,A. Gallo,G. Nunnari 1989 "*A Cascadable Signal Processor Architecture for the Implementation of On-Line Recursive Identification Algorithms*",In Proceedings of the 1989 Summer Computer Simulation Conference (Austin,Texas,July 24-27), pp.211-216.

Fast Digital Parallel Processing module

FDPP

D. Crosetto

CERN
CH-1211 Geneve 23
Switzerland

Abstract. The FDPP [1] is a modular system implemented in an industry standard package, the TRAnsputer Module (TRAM), to allow the realization of a reconfigurable parallel processing system, oriented principally toward fast data acquisition and analysis. The FDPP it integrates the computing power of the DSP with the communication facilities of the Transputer. This flexibility supports efficient data acquisition and data reduction operations and enables rapid topological reconfiguration, under program control for load balancing and/or fault tolerance. The Transputer serial links permit highly varied and economic network-type connections. The presence of DSP processors, with fixed and floating point instructions and with the capability of fetching data at high speed through DMA I/O ports, makes the system suitable for Real time data acquisition systems. TRAM modules can function on motherboards inserted into different buses (VME, IBM PC/AT, etc.) Programming languages include: Occam, C, Fortran, and Pascal for the Transputer, C and assembler for the DSP32C.

1. Structure of the FDPP parallel processing system.

The structure of the FDPP module, which combines a Transputer and a Digital Signal Processor [2] on a single boards, gives it the following characteristics:

1.1. Tightly coupled interconnecting scheme inside the node between the two processors.

There is a tightly coupled communication between the DSP and the Transputer residing on the same FDPP board. This communication is supervised by a small software module residing in the DSP and a larger one in the Transputer. This solution provides on the one hand serial communication between the DSP and the Transputer and on the other a tight, very high speed block type parallel communication through dual port memories.

1.2. Loosely coupled interconnecting scheme among nodes.

The easy interconnecting among Transputers in a loosely coupled scheme using message passing is ideal for building a scalable architecture, to execute parallel processing programs in high level languages (ADA, Pascal, FORTRAN, C, etc.), with the possibility also to reconfigure the topology of the system by means of programmable crossbar switches.

1.3. Multiple Instruction Stream, Multiple Data Stream (MIMD) multiprocessor model.

The characteristics described above, allowing to have instructions partitioned into independent streams and each instruction stream to have its own data stream, make it possible to build systems of the MIMD type.

This structure gives the possibility to build special purpose as well as general purpose machines.

Fig. 1 shows the Processing Element FDPP Fast Digital Parallel Processing module.

Fig. 2 show how the basic FDPP building block can be used to synthesize an array of communicating signal processing nodes.

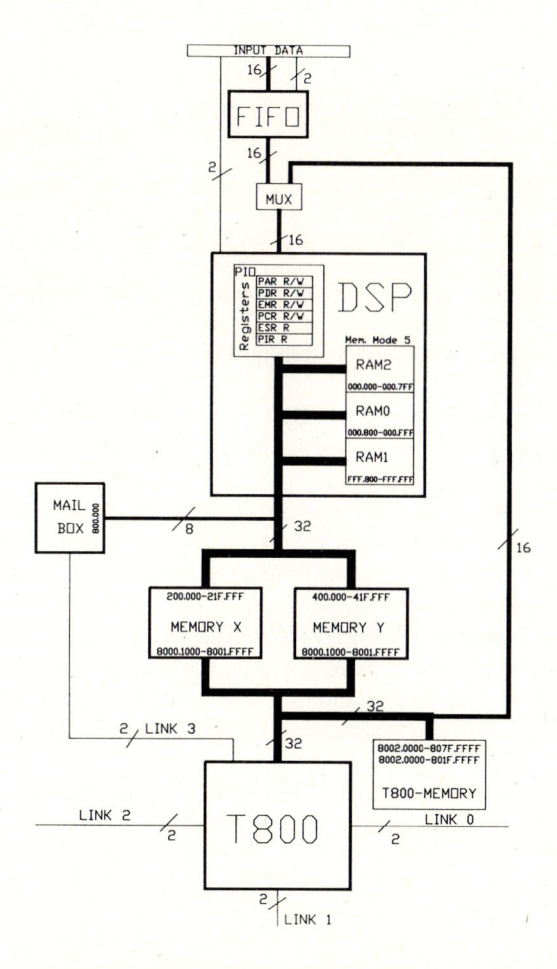

Fig. 1   FDPP   block diagram.

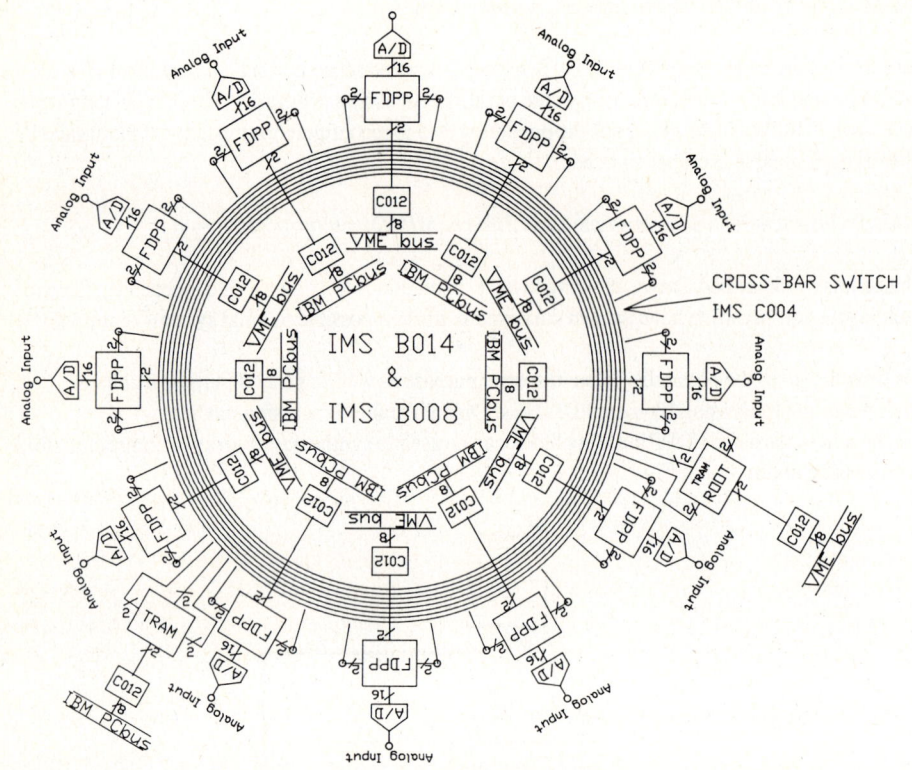

Fig. 2 Transputer cluster of FDPP with reconfigurable interconnection.

2. What kind of applications can the FDPP handle the best ?

The above characteristics of the multiprocessing FDPP system make it specifically targeted at applications whose throughput requirements are so large that they demand multiprocessing and/or specialized topologies.

The presence of the fast DSP processor, with fixed and floating point instructions and with the capability of fetching data at high speed through DMA I/O ports, makes the system ideal for Real time data acquisition systems, whereas the presence of the Transputer gives a powerful means to correlate these data in a scalable, reconfigurable system.

The FDPP can find applications in High Energy Physics Experiments [3], [4] where huge detectors are used to track elementary particles and it is extremely important to be able to make decisions, based on information of thousands of signals in real time as fast as possible. It can be used in an intelligent programmable trigger decision and also to treat analog signals in a data acquisition system to perform data compaction.

The applications that are well matched to the FDPP parallel processing system architecture are all the ones requiring the execution of the following types of algorithms:
- pattern recognition,
- track finding, peak finding
- parallel matching of incoming data to a stored lookup table
- image processing
- scientific computing and numerical analysis

- solving linear systems of equations
- and, of course, signal processing as supported by the algorithms listed in the AT&T DSP32C Library.

The best use of the DSP32C on the above applications is to perform the computationally intensive algorithms on large amounts of data which are entered from the external input for on-line applications, or from the Transputer side for off-line ones. In both cases the DSP programs can continue, without interruptions, their execution while new input data and output results are transferred by DMA from the input port or by the Transputer through the dual port memory.

2.1. FDPP architecture evaluation for real time High Energy Physics algorithms.

As reported in [5] and [6] some typical High Energy Physics real-time algorithms have been identified which can be used as benchmarks for triggering and data compaction applications on FDPP.

Figure 3 illustrates a parallel architecture containing 256 FDPP for "Generic Peakfinding" and "Cluster analysis" algorithms.

This parallel architecture can calculate the "Generic peakfinding" algorithm as described in [5] in 125 usec in an array of 100x100 channels. Each FDPP module analyses 36 (6x6) channels out of 100 (10x10) read-in, corresponding to an overlap of 4 channels with each neighbor. The same architecture is then also feasible for the "Cluster analysis" algorithm that is being benchmarked and results are planned for presentation at this conference.

In the generic peakfinding algorithm [5] a peak is defined as a centerpixel greater than the average of the nearest neighbors by a given threshold, if also the average of the nearest neighbors is greater than the average of the next nearest neighbors by another threshold and the centerpixel is a local maximum. If these three conditions are true, the centerpixel is set to one, otherwise to zero. To be a local maximum, a pixel must be equal to or greater than the maximum value of the pixels in a 3 by 3 neighborhood.

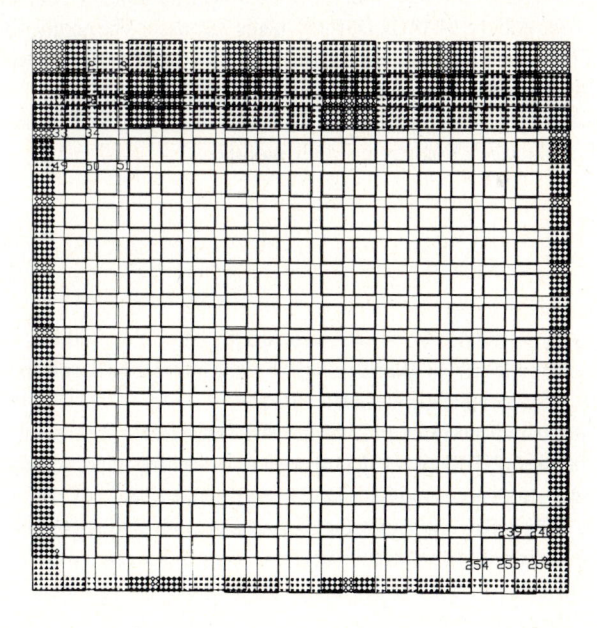

Fig. 3   Parallel architecture of 256 FDPP.

In the generic peakfinding algorithm [5] a peak is defined as a centerpixel greater than the average of the nearest neighbors by a given threshold, if also the average of the nearest neighbors is greater than the average of the next nearest neighbors by another threshold and the centerpixel is a local maximum. If these three conditions are true, the centerpixel is set to one, otherwise to zero. To be a local maximum, a pixel must be equal to or greater than the maximum value of the pixels in a 3 by 3 neighborhood.

```
             GENERIC PEAKFINDING
                     0
                   0 I 0
                 0 I C I 0
                   0 I 0
                     0
```

The Calorimeter Cluster-analysis [5], a simple jet/electron finder algorithm, finds the center pixel with the highest intensity among the pattern of neighborhood shown in figure 3.

```
           SIMPLE JET/ELECTRON FINDER
                   0 0 0 0 0
                   0 I I I 0
                   0 I C I 0
                   0 I I I 0
                   0 0 0 0 0
```

2.2. Q-measurements at SPS accelerator.

Since April 1990 an FDPP inserted as a TRAM in a IMSB014 [7] VME board in the BOSC VME system crate is making Q-measurements of the SPS beam. The measurement can be activated from the SPS control room and has the following performances. While the Transputer is uploading results of FFT (n-1) from dual-port memory X and downloading new data for FFT (n+1) into the same memory, the DSP32C is converting integer inputs to floating, executing 256 point FFT (n), calculating the power spectrum and converting DSP32C floating to IEEE floating in dual-port memory Y. For these operations the Transputer takes 6 msec and the 50 MHz DSP32C takes 2.1 msec. The acquisition programs, on the Motorola 68030 CPU of the BOSC system and on the Apollo workstation, used to send and retrieve results from the IMSB014 VME board have been adapted by S. Hunt.

Figure 4 illustrates in the lower sections the digitalized input signals from the SPS beam and in the upper ones, the results of the FFT done by the FDPP module.

3. FDPP features.

The FDPP features are illustrated in Fig. 1 and Fig. 2.

a) The FDPP is packaged in a 4 unit TRAM board [8]. This allows adding the FDPP to existing TRAM based Transputer systems with the advantage of using all existing development software (Occam 2 toolset) and Operating System (Helios; Unix like) [9], [10].

b) The FDPP uses of two processors, a 25 MHz T800 Transputer [11], [12] and a 32-bit floating point AT&T DSP32C processor (25Mflops) [13], [14] at each node of the multiprocessor system.

c) The Transputer shares access with the DSP to two memory banks of 124Kbytes each of 30 nsec SRAM which can be switched by the Transputer between the two processors in 100 nsec.

d) The FDPP incorporates two mechanisms for passing data between the Transputer and DSP:
- short messages are transferred using one of the Transputer Links. The synchronization and buffering is provided by the IMS C012 chip automatically in a loose coupling scheme.
- large blocks of data are transferred using the switchable memory banks in a tight coupling scheme.

e) Incoming data from a parallel input port are stored in the FIFO by an externally generated write signal, (the FIFO can also be reset externally). Data can then be transferred between the FIFO and the

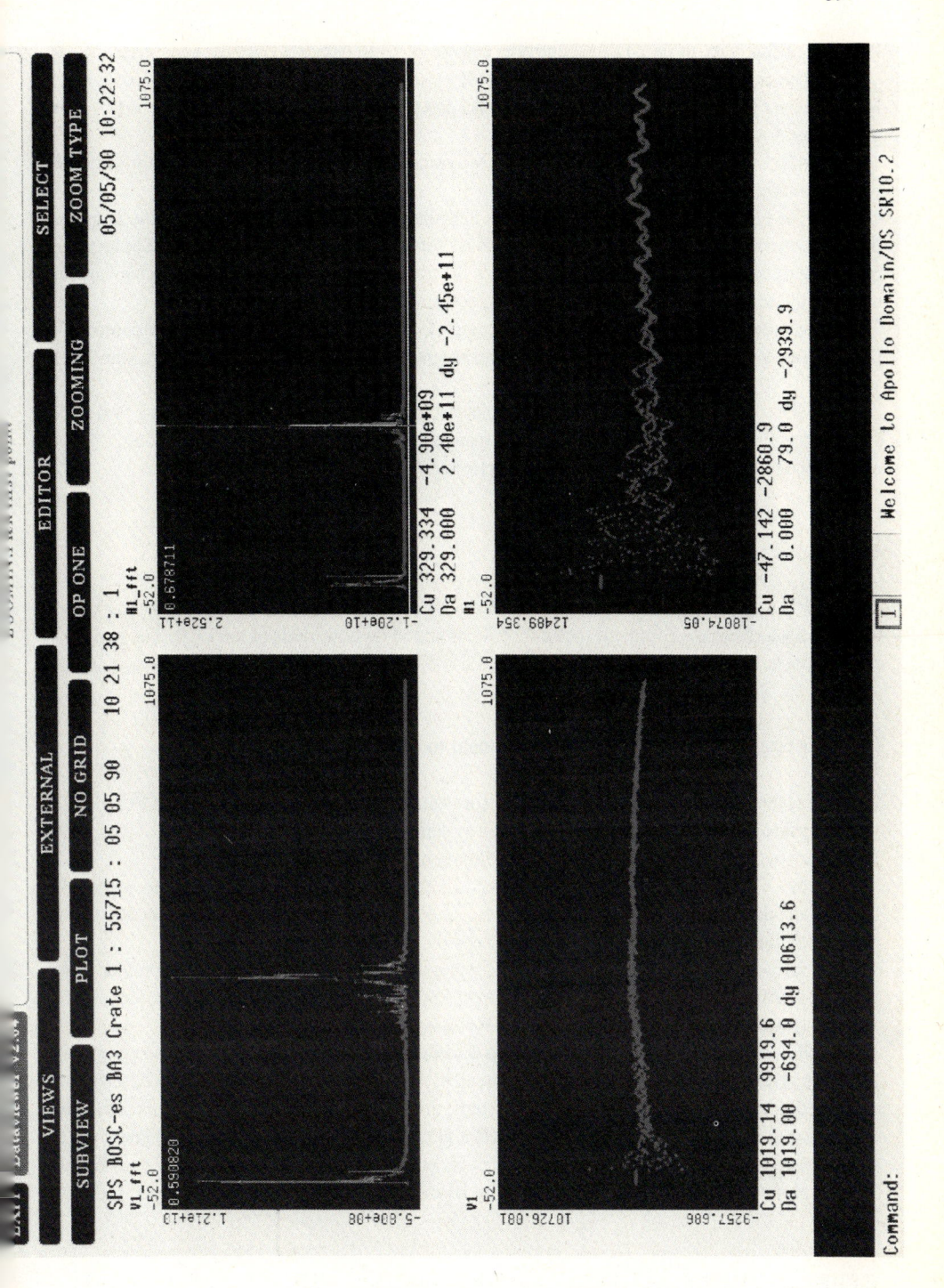

Fig. 4 Q-measurements of the SPS beam.

DSP memories by its on-chip DMA controller at a rate of 10 Mbytes/sec.

f) The maximum external input rate is 50 Mbytes/sec for 2048 consecutive 16-bit words and 10 Mbytes/sec for larger bursts of data from the parallel port whereas it is 2.4 Mbyte/sec bidirectional on any of the three remaining Transputer Serial Links.

g) A Transputer at each FDPP node has 8 Mbyte of local DRAM maximum for storing complex programs and events.

h) The FDPP nodes can be configured in a network either by manually connecting the Transputer links or dynamically by programming the crossbar switch located on the mother board. The latter also provides a reconfigurable interconnecting between the nodes that gives the possibility of achieving fault recovery by isolating and routing around faulty processing nodes.

The Transputer always acts as the master processor. It can reset the DSP under program control. The DSP I/O port is used by the Transputer for loading programs into the DSP and monitoring/controlling its activity.

The DSP is not usable as a co-processor to implement specific instructions, but rather to off-load certain computationally intensive algorithms like matrix manipulation, peakfinding, track finding, cluster finding, pattern recognition, filter and FFTs, from the Transputer, which remains the master.

4. Hardware packaging.

The FDPP is a ten layer printed circuit board 9.29 cm x 11 cm with normal dual-inline IC's, pingrid array IC's and SMD (Surface Mounted Devices) IC's mounted on both sides of the PCB. The density of components is 109 equivalent IC's per dm^2.

5. Commercially available software development tools.

Software is developed for the FDPP parallel processing system primarily on the IBM PC and then downloaded to the real time multiprocessor array system.

There are two environments to allow the development of the software on the IBM PC:

a) the OCCAM 2 toolset [9] for transputers which is a complete cross development system for building and debugging occam [15] and mixed language programs for transputers. (The same software, occam 2 toolset, is available also for VAX and SUN3)

b) software tools for the DSP32C running under the MS-DOS Operating System provide a crossassembler, a link editor, simulator, utilities, a support software library and a "C" Language compiler (The same software tools run also under the UNIX Operating System).

To build a multi-transputer program one must describe the distribution of procedures over processors. In OCCAM this distribution is explicit in the so called 'configuration' description. This description is processed by a tool called the configurer. The configurer creates all necessary bootstraps and routing information to load the entire network, and stores this, along with the compiled code, in a program file. The server is used to load programs on to transputer networks. Once loaded, the programs start automatically. The server supports access to the host terminal and file system from the transputer network. [10], [16], [17].

6. FDPP project software.

A monitor has been developed that can download, start, stop, and upload user programs. As well it can be used to examine and modify register and memory contents.

At power on a series of programs which test the FDPP module, first from the host Transputer and then from the FDPP Transputer, are performed.

The FDPP hardware TROUBLE SHOOTING programs, together with a two channel oscilloscope, provide a means to test the module completely in an interactive way and to find faults derived from erroneous assembly, short circuits or missing connections. The criterion for the ordering of the tests is based upon the assumption that nothing works before being tested and that only tested parts are used to generate functions to test the other parts. Besides indicating faults, the messages associated with the various tests, indicate signals to be checked with the oscilloscope in order to better localize the problem.

Applications on the DSP32C Digital Signal Processor can be easily developed and run:

- a kernel residing on the Transputer which activates execution of programs ("command code" through the MAILBOX) on the DSP32C and provides a means of communication between the user and the DSP32C.

- a kernel residing on the DSP32C which handles requests from the associated Transputer at its node.

- a library of standard routines for many commonly used functions.

Some characteristic system times are the following:

- to send a one byte message from the Transputer and to receive an acknowledgment from the DSP32C takes 1.4 usec.

- to start a routine (among a maximum of 256) by sending a one byte message from the Transputer, which must be interpreted and acknowledge by the DSP32C kernel, takes 1.7 usec. Thus the execution times listed in the AT&T subroutine library must be increased by this amount for the FDPP case.

Acknowledgements

This project has been funded by CN and by SL Divisions. I especially thank P. G. Innocenti for his active and generous support.

I would like to thank S. Hunt for his collaboration and A. Burns and L. Vos for their support. A special thanks to the student S. Buono for his significant contribution to the basic software development.

I would like to thank A. Werbrouck and C. Verkerk for proof reading this document and for their precious suggestions and support.

References

[1] D. Crosetto. FDPP Fast Digital Parallel Processing module. CERN - DD /89 - 33(AC) Dec. 1989.
[2] David A. Mindell "Dealing with a Digital World". Byte magazine, August 1989, pp. 246-256.
[3] V. Roveda and A. Werbrouck, Cluster Analysis with Fast Microcomputer. Microprocessing and Microprogramming, 22(1988) 347-351.
[4] D. Crosetto, FDDP Fast Digital Data Processor. CERN-EP/87-151, 25 August 1987.
[5] W. Krischer, Commercial Highly parallel signal processors on-line ?. Computer Physics Communications 57 (1989) 121-128. North-Holland
[6] S. Lone et all, Fine-grain parallel computer architectures in future triggers. CERN-EP/89-116.
[7] INMOS Technical note 49, Module motherboard architecture.
[8] Paul Walker, INMOS Technical Note 29, Dual Inline Transputer Modules (TRAMS) INMOS, 1987.
[9] INMOS, OCCAM2 TOOLSET manual, 1989.
[10] PERIHELION SOFTWARE "The Helios Operating System", Prentice Hall 1989.
[11] INMOS "The Transputer Data Book" Nov. 1988.
[12] INMOS, The Transputer Applications notebook System and Performance, First edition 1989.
[13] AT&T WE DSP32C Digital Signal Processor Information Manual
[14] WE DSP32C Digital Signal Processor Data Sheet.
[15] INMOS OCCAM2. Reference Manual, Prentice Hall 1988.
[16] INMOS Technical note 05, Program design for concurrent systems
[17] INMOS The Transputer development and iq systems databook.

A TRANSPUTER ARCHITECTURE FOR PARALLEL PROCESSING OF POLYGONAL REGIONS

C. Montani*, A. Tomasi+

* Istituto di Elaborazione dell'Informazione
Consiglio Nazionale delle Ricerche
Pisa, Italy

+ Istituto di Informatica - Facoltà di Ingegneria
Università di Ancona
Ancona, Italy

Abstract. The growing interest in computer graphics has to be faced with the great complexity of many practical applications, as for example digital mapping. This paper discusses a solution in the field of parallel management of polygonal regions. The proposal is designed according with an integrated approach towards the definition of a data representation scheme suitable to be processed by parallel algorithms and its implementation on a parallel architecture programmed by a concurrent language.

The proposed solution is based on DPCS, a distributed version of a data representation scheme called PCS. Data processing operates on partitioned data structures, and a transformation method is defined by a parallel algorithm to convert data represented as vectorial information to and from DPCS.

The DPCS system is implemented on a Transputer ring, by now composed of five Transputers, but easily extendible. The processing and communicating facilities of the Transputer permit to exploit the maximum degree of parallelism, not only when processing the partitioned data, but also during the inherently sequential operations of data conversion.

1. Introduction.

The development of ever more complex graphic applications as, for example, in computer aided design, digital mapping, scientific visualization or graphical analysis of natural phenomena has pointed out the need for efficient tools for the manipulation, processing and display of spatial data.

In digital mapping, for instance, the operations on geometric data reach easily exponential complexity with respect to the number of regions represented by the maps, thus enforcing the research needs towards efficient representation schemes and solutions based on parallel algorithms.

In this paper, a hardware/software integrated approach to the problem of manipulation and processing of polygonal regions is presented. The proposed solution starts from the definition of a data representation model suitable for efficient processing. A set of parallel algorithms are derived from a previously defined sequential solution [1], leading to a parallel computational model. The implementation on a distributed architecture reflects the parallel computation approach adopted, with the aim of efficiently supporting the computation/communication tradeoffs.

The distributed architecture is implemented by a ring connecting a set of Transputers [2]. The computational model and the architecture features of Transputer meet well with the conceptual design of the proposed system.

The basic logical information of our system is given by a set of planar regions representing a binary map (for example, a theme of a thematic map, the regions of a plane with identical characteristics with respect to some parameters, etc.). Each region (or interior hole) of a binary map can be represented by the description of its boundary in vectorial form; the scheme adopted is the Freeman's chain, where a region boundary is represented by the coordinates of a starting point and a list of movements along a reference regular grid [3].

The chosen computational model is the classical processor farm architecture: a controller node gives commands and assigns data to p slave nodes; each slave node sends the results of the requested operations to a collector node which provides to the manipulation and display of the received data.

Our hardware/software integrated proposal is not restricted to the distribution of the vectorial data among the processing nodes by means of a load balancing technique: the boundaries of the input regions are converted, in a parallel way, into a new representation scheme, the Distributed Parallel Connected Stripes (DPCS). This coding scheme allows to parallelize the boolean operations between different maps (rather than between different regions) with a degree of parallelism which is proportional to the number of slave processors of the architecture. The results of the operations on the maps are reconverted, by a parallel algorithm, into the vectorial representation and sent to the collector node. A brief presentation of DPCS scheme is discussed in section 2.

The DPCS coding scheme (which is the extension of the PCS coding scheme [1]) lends itself to subdivide the maps to be processed into large horizontal stripes: each stripe is manipulated and processed by a single slave node of the system. This data partitioning technique shows a logical straight correspondence between the processing nodes and the spatial correlation of the regions represented in a map.

The processing and communicating facilities of the Transputer support an efficient implementation of the proposed solution, not only while processing the partitioned data, but also during the inherently sequential operations of data conversion. The main features of the implementation are presented in section 3.

2. DPCS: the data representation scheme

A convenient data representation constitutes the starting point in order to exploit the maximum degree of parallelism. The proper design of data structures has been pointed out as the basis for the implementation of efficient algorithms, even according with a sequential solution [1].

The PCS (Parallel Connected Stripes) coding scheme, fully described in [1], has been defined for representing polygonal regions efficiently. A brief example shows the main features of the PCS scheme.

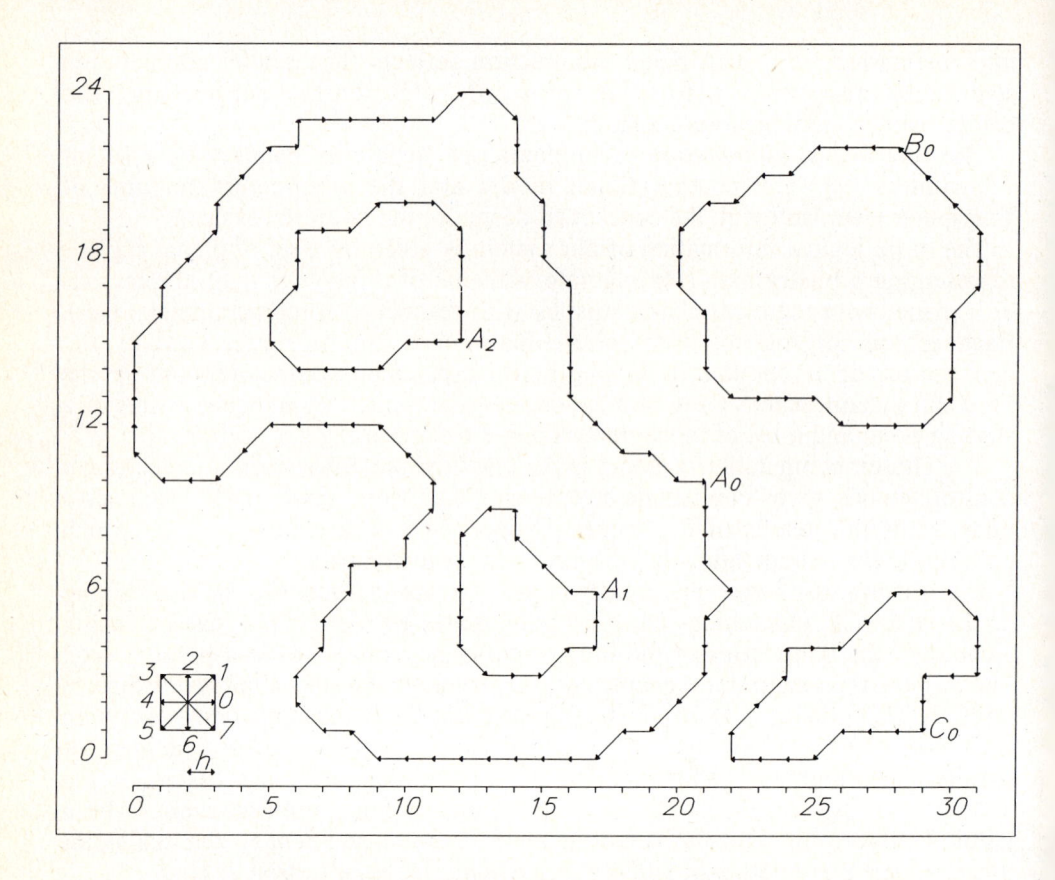

Fig. 1 - Freeman's chains representation of the region boundaries in a map.

In Fig. 1 a binary map including three polygonal regions is represented. Each polygonal boundary is described by a Freeman's chain; the starting points of the chains are denoted by A_0, A_1, A_2, B_0, C_0.

If the map is cut along the horizontal lines of the ideally superimposed regular grid, the stripes representation of Fig. 2 is obtained. The PCS scheme describes a map as a set of stripes, each one being composed of trapezoidal substripes represented in the form of $[Y, X_w, T_w, X_e, T_e]$, where Y is the ordinate of the stripe, X_w and X_e are the abscissas of the west and east sides of the substripe, T_w and T_e the side type (one of three possible inclinations) of the west and east sides.

The PCS representation is obtained from the Freeman's chains observing that:

(a) the horizontal links (movements on the regular grid) of the chain describing the boundaries of the map are not recorded in the data structure;

(b) the west and east sides of each substripe correspond to links being in odd and in even position scanning the stripe from left to right, respectively.

Thus the vectorial representation is encoded into the PCS form simply reordering the non-horizontal links according to their absolute coordinates.

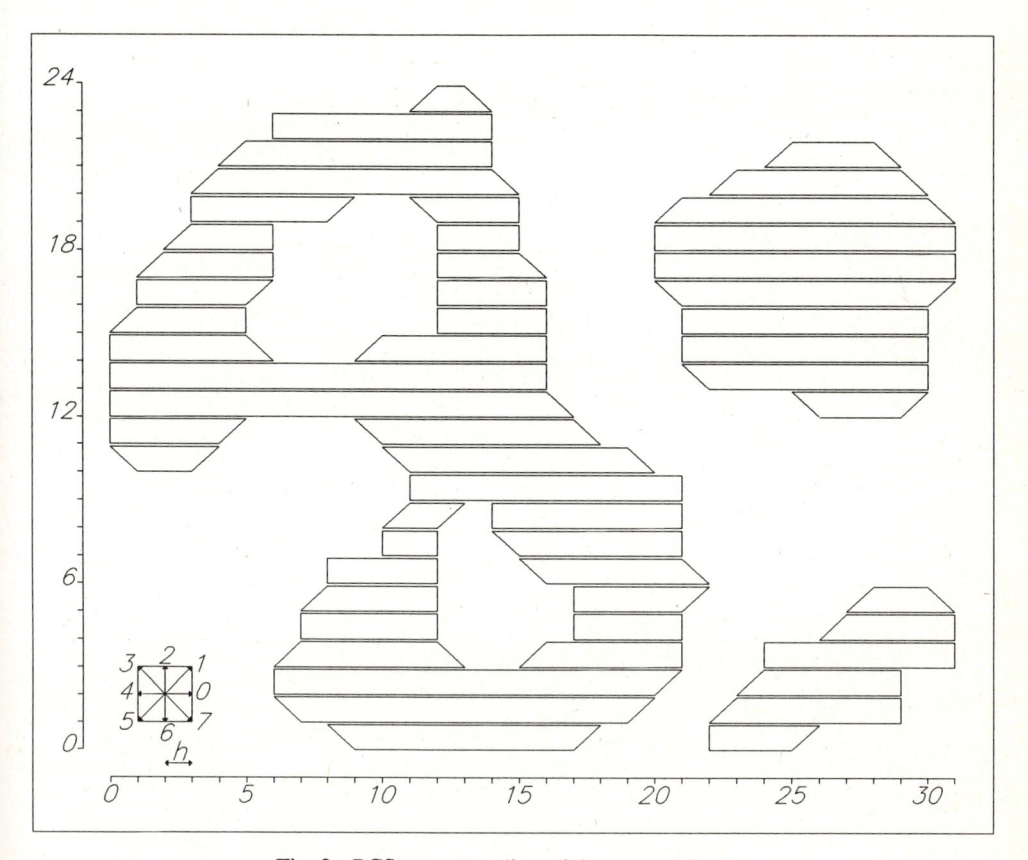

Fig. 2 - PCS representation of the map of fig. 1.

The conversion from PCS to vectorial representation is obtained "walking" from one substripe to another if they are connected (i.e. if they have one base or part of it in common or they have a third substripe connecting them) and returning the boundaries of the regions clockwise and the boundaries of the holes anticlockwise, as shown in Fig. 3.

The logical operations, mainly the union, intersection and difference of two maps, are performed on the PCS data structure with a parallel scanning method. An operation on two PCS's consists of iteratively analyzing the stripes of identical ordinate and the corresponding substripes therein.

Although in sequential form, the algorithms implementing boolean operations works on disjoint sets of stripes. As a consequence, the parallel processing of PCS can be achieved without transformations of the data structure. The partitioning of PCS data between the processing units (i.e. DPCS, Distributed PCS) permits the activation in parallel of more copies of the same program.

More careful considerations have to be stressed when applying parallel algorithms to the scheme conversion operations. The vectorial representation is inherently sequential, because each point is obtained moving from the previous one.

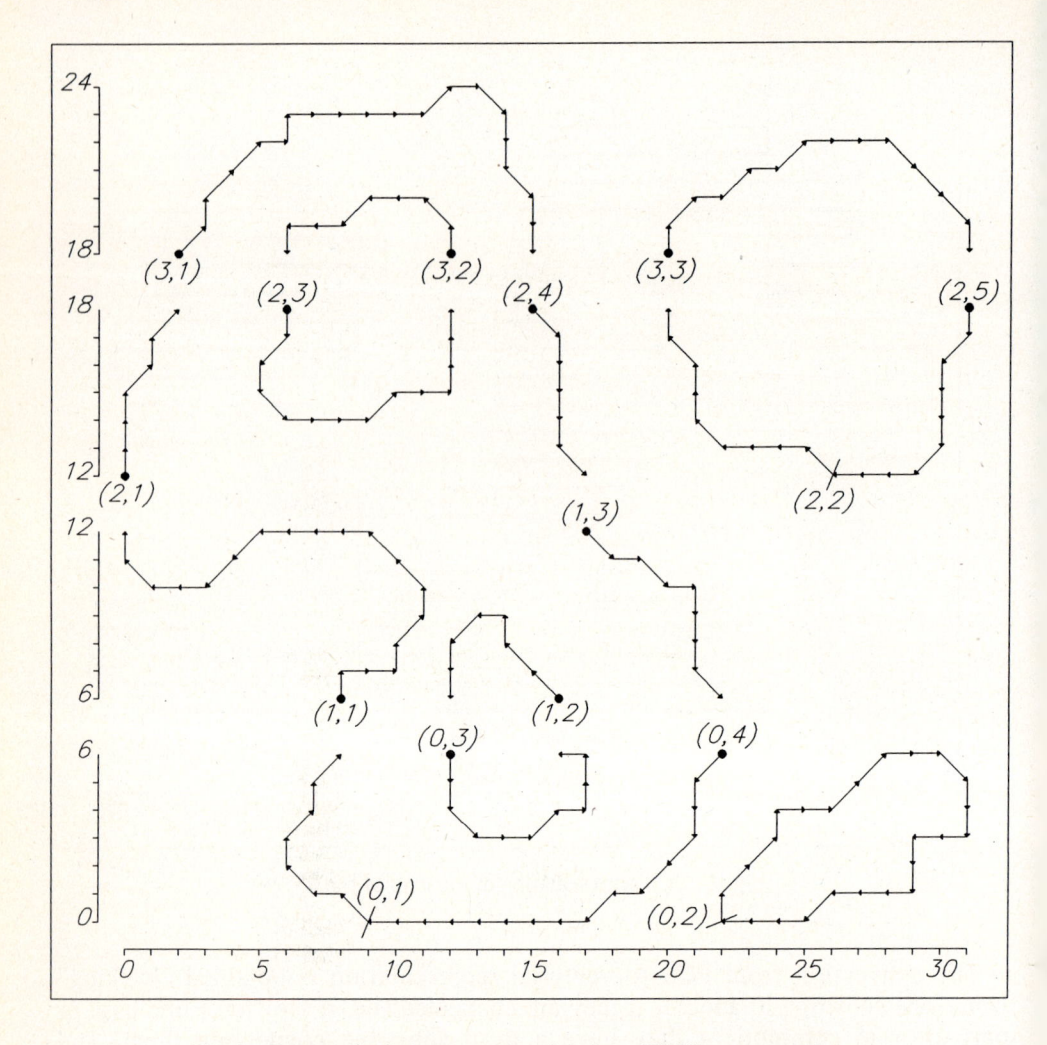

Fig. 3 - Freeman's chains reconstruction from DPCS representation.
In parentheses the node name and the reconstruction sequential ordering.

The parallelism is exploited in our proposed solution activating more copies of the conversion program and processing in parallel distinct chains belonging to the same region or to different regions. According with the DPCS data partitioning, a single chain is pipelined through the system, and the conversion operations are performed on the chain segments or on the corresponding stripes owned by each processing node.

The sequential algorithm implementing the conversion operations has to be extended with communications between nodes operating on the segments of the same chain. In Fig. 3 four processing nodes are illustrated during the reconstruction of the chains of Fig. 1. The communications are not shown in the figure.

3. The implementation on a Transputer ring

The DPCS model has been implemented on a parallel architecture consisting of a bidirectional ring of Transputers; the first implementation is constituted by five nodes (Fig. 4). The node denoted as T_0 interfaces the system with a personal computer (Host) supporting the file system, the graphic unit and the user interface.

Each node T_i is devoted to processing a set of stripes determined by equally partitioning the interval of ordinates for the represented maps. The logical and scalar operations on the maps are performed independently by the various Transputers.

The messages containing data to be processed or requesting the execution of operations flow round the ring in both directions, starting from T_0, so that communication time can be optimized.

The communications between T_0 and the other nodes can be directed to a particular node, as it happens during the conversion from vectorial to DPCS representation, or can be diffused to each node, as in requiring the executions of the operations. The other communications between nodes are all point-to-point communications between a node T_i and one of the two adjacent nodes in the ring. The ring connection of the Transputer nodes results to be well suited to the communications circulating in the system.

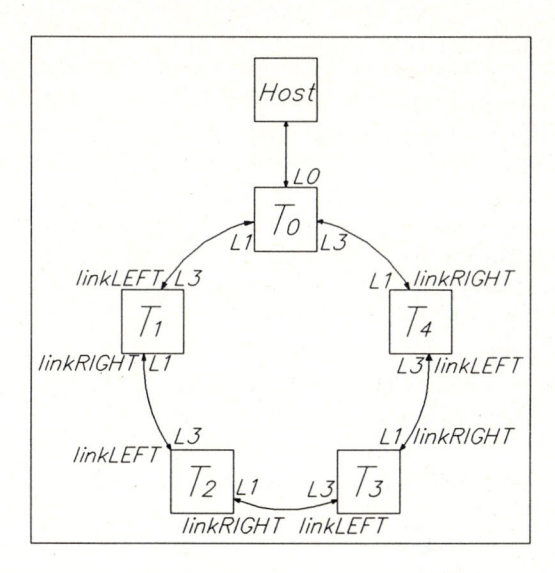

Fig. 4 - The Transputer ring implementation.

The parallel implementation of DPCS introduces additional processing load caused by the communications occurring between the nodes cooperating during the computation; moreover the distribution of processing activities among the nodes requires load balancing functions in order to optimize processing times.

With regard to the logical operations performed on DPCS data, only communications of starting operation are needed and the load processing distribution can be assumed balanced if the polygonal regions are homogeneously distributed on the maps.

The critical operations, from the point of view of optimizing the parallel execution, are the conversions of data from vectorial to DPCS representation and viceversa.

The vectorial data to be converted are sent by T_0 to the node T_i owning the stripe which includes the starting point of the chain under examination. When the conversion algorithm generates a point outside the range of stripes in T_i, the remaining part of the chain is sent to the adjacent node, and T_i is available for processing a new chain, or part of a chain. In this way, during the data conversion, different nodes process in parallel distinct chains or different parts of the same chain.

The reconstruction of Freeman's chains from DPCS is started by a communication diffused to all the nodes from T_0. Each node applies the reconstruction algorithm, producing segments of chains (or complete chains in the best cases): a segment looks like a Freeman's chain, added with the coordinates of the starting point and the ending one. The segments are communicated to the node T_0, which proceeds to the linking of the whole chains comparing the coordinates of the segment's extents.

Under the assumption that the polygonal regions are homogeneously distributed on the maps, and hence on the processing nodes too, the load distribution of the conversion functions can be considered well balanced.

The communication overload is reflected by the structure of the processing programs (Fig. 5). A set of processes is replicated on each node T_i :

i) a communication control process (CONTROL_COM) interfaces the ring, implementing a simple routing algorithm. The messages circulating on the ring and directed to other nodes are sent in parallel with the processing activities; the messages requiring operations to be performed on the node itself are sent to the corresponding operating process. The CONTROL_COM process implements the communication buffers and schedules the activities of the node, interacting with the operating processes by means of local communications.

ii) a set of processes execute the required operations on DPCS partitioned data.

iii) The DPCS data structure is incapsulated into a manager process (PCS_MANAGER); the reading or writing operations on DPCS data can be requested by the various processes of the node. Requests coming from the adjacent nodes during the conversion processing are sent to PCS_MANAGER directly from CONTROL_COM.

With respect to the sequential solution, it can be noted that the parallel algorithms obtains an improvment proportional to the number of nodes. The cost in communications does not affect the performance considerably, providing that the communications management is performed by the CONTROL_COM process in parallel with the other processing activities.

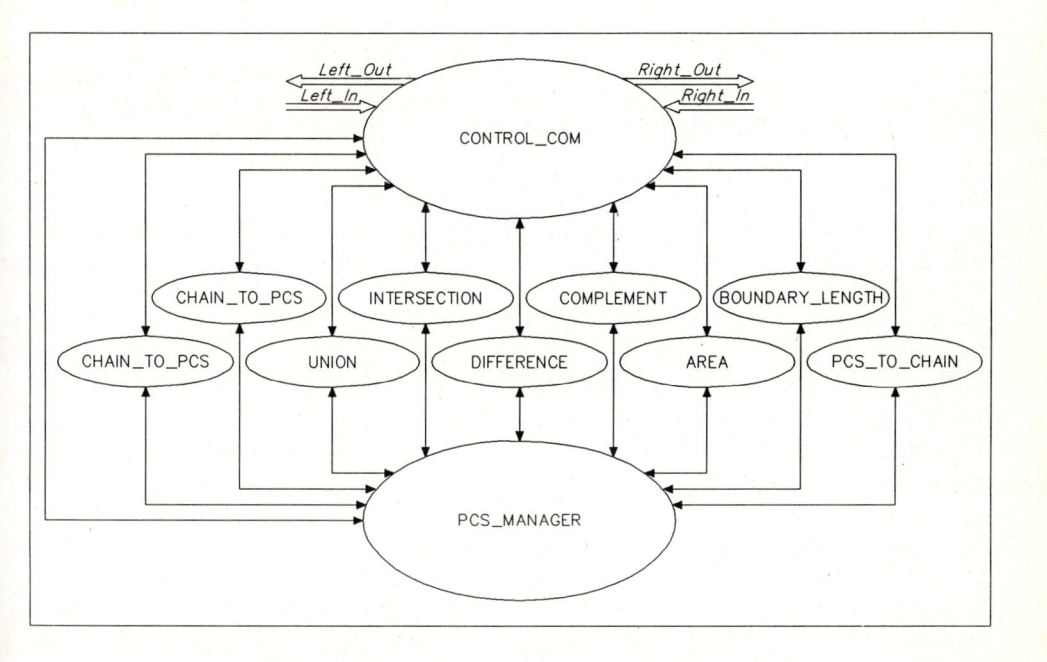

Fig. 5 - Parallel processes on a generic Transputer node.

It should be stressed that the design of the proposed solution adopts the computation/communication model of the Transputer in order to exploit the maximum degree of parallelism.

The parallel solution described in this paper has been implemented in Occam and Parallel C, starting from the sequential algorithms already implemented in C language.

By now the implementation of monitoring facilities integrating the processing and communicating functions [4] is in progress in order to evaluate the overall system.

References.

[1] C. Montani, Region Representation: Parallel Connected Stripes, Computer Vision, Graphics, and Image Processing, 28, 1984, 139-165.
[2] D. May, Communicating Sequential Process: Transputer and Occam, in Future Parallel Computers, Lectures Notes in Computer Science, 272, Springer & Verlag, 1987.
[3] H. Freeman, Computer processing of line-drawing images, ACM Computing Surveys, 6, 1974, 57-97.
[4] R. Pompei, M. Sciortino, A. Tomasi, An Occam development environment for parallel architectures based on Transputer, (in italian), AICA Annual Conference, 1989.

Product Label Inspection using Transputers

Majid Mirmehdi.
Department of Computer Science,
City University,
London EC1V 0HB.

email: majid@uk.ac.city.cs

Abstract.

A product label inspection system implemented on a transputer network is described. Two data routing algorithms are considered, one for a general MxN array and one for a customised setup of transputers. Data transfer results for various image sizes are provided. Reliable and fast label inspection algorithms are described for rectangular, acute-angled and oval-shaped product labels, and their implementation on both the general and the customised networks are discussed. Simulated test results are provided to illustrate the present capability of the system for inspecting large numbers of labels per second.

1 Introduction

As an industrial requirement for perfect quality control, visual inspection of products is carried out by either machines or humans at various stages of manufacture. The stage involving the detection and verification of labels stuck on products, and sometimes the inspection of the print on the label, is generally termed *label inspection*, and is often the final task in the manufacturing process.

To keep in step with the production line, the inspection task must be carried out in real-time, thus introducing the need for the use of the most advanced and yet affordable technology. This investigation considers the use of a small network of transputers, for the computing power of a reasonably priced inspection system.

To begin with, the transputer is introduced. Next, it is shown how images may be mapped onto simple networks of transputers, and the distribution and collection phase of image data is outlined. This is be followed by a description of the methods used to inspect various labels, and their implementation on the network. Finally, results are shown to illustrate the capabilities of the system.

2 The Transputer and Occam

The Inmos IMS T414 transputer is a 32 bit microcomputer with 2Kbytes on-chip RAM for high speed processing, a configurable memory interface, and all necessary system services such as reset and clock. It can directly access a linear address space of 4

Gbytes, and running at 20MHz achieves a throughput of 10 million instructions per second [Inmos 86]. It has four synchronised communication links operating at 20Mbits per second which offer simple, cheap, and direct point to point connection to other transputers with no external logic. Thus, the transputer can be used as a building block with other transputers to construct extremely high performance computing networks (Figure 1).

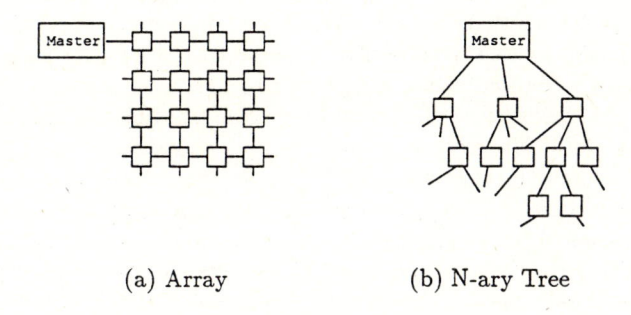

(a) Array   (b) N-ary Tree

Figure 1 - Typical Network Topologies.

Occam is a concurrent programming language designed especially for the transputer. In Occam, processes can be mapped directly onto a number of processors for sequential or parallel execution. They can communicate via memory-to-memory data transfer on a single transputer or via the standard links on different transputers. The combination of the transputer and Occam can produce very powerful SIMD and MIMD systems.

3   Image Processing on Transputer Networks

The structure of an array network of transputers lends itself well to low level image processing applications [Mirmehdi 87]. An image can be split equally to produce similar matrices for each node of the network. Thus, running virtually the same processes (similar operation on data, slightly different routines for message passing), one may be said to have set up a SIMD system. This is adequately demonstrated with a processor performance comparison for the Sobel Edge Operator and the Median Filter [Chapman, et al 86].

For real time applications, the sequences involving the distribution and collection of raw data from the network must require minimum processing time. A very flexible method would also allow future expansion of the network to accommodate a larger array of transputers. Two methods are now considered.

The first method consists of a general distribution and collection algorithm flexible enough to map any PxQ image over an array network of MxN transputers (where, $4 <= P,Q <= 512$, and $2 <= M,N <= P/2, Q/2$, and P/M, Q/N yield integers). This method has been used to implement the label inspection algorithms, as well as a number of various image processing routines. It is useful for implementation on systems where the number of transputers in the system may increase. Secondly, a customised image distribution and collection method will be considered. This was developed solely for the purpose of label inspection on an affordable system with the fixed number of five transputers.

The general distribution and collection method is an adaptation of a proposed method [Morrow, et al 88]. They define a tidy method for distributing image data over a square array, passing edge information after the distribution operation. In this improved implementation, the image can be spread over rectangular arrays, and the edge information is included in the distribution phase, thus requiring less code development. Also, the image is passed around in larger chunks and therefore less time is required for setting up fewer link transfers. The method is as follows. With reference to *Figure 1(a)*, the master transputer communicates only with the top-left transputer, transmitting and receiving all image information through the connecting channel. The top-left transputer transmits information to its neighbours on the top row of transputers until they all contain their own appropriate image section. Then the data for the rest of the rows is distributed down each column. The image is distributed a row at a time, and the reverse process of data collection follows the opposite path of distribution.

For *PxQ* images on an *MxN* array network, given the aforementioned conditions, the following can be derived for distribution and collection of image data:

Total Number of Link Activations =

$$2(\frac{Q}{N} + 2)((M + 1)\sum_{a=1}^{N}(N - a) + (2N - 1)\sum_{b=0}^{N}(N - b))$$

Total Data Transfer across Network =

$$2(\frac{P}{M} + 2)(\frac{Q}{N} + 2)((M + 1)\sum_{a=1}^{N}(N - a) + (2N - 1)\sum_{b=0}^{N}(N - b))$$

Ignoring image size limitations, the data distribution method would suffice for any transputer array sizes.

However, despite its speed and flexibility, the method was not fast enough for this real-time label inspection application due to the number of link activations and total data load necessary during communications, and a new customised method was developed to maximise data routing efficiency, and thus improve overall performance.

The new method was implemented in the configuration shown in *Figure 2(a)*, which represents the total hardware system necessary for this label inspection exercise. (In the existing development system the frame grabber is a separate PC-board and is not directly connected to the transputer memory. This introduces delays in image acquisition for the master transputer, although there are PCB configurations where the main transputer has direct access to the frame buffer.)

FIGURE 2

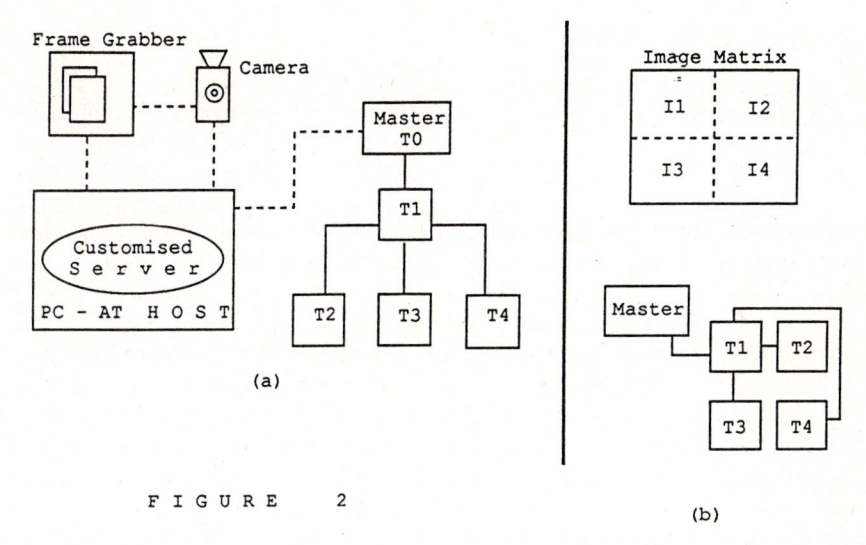

(a)

(b) Direct Mapping: In <==> Tn

The method works as follows. The 2D image array is spread out into a single 1D vector which is subsequently squirted, in whole, from the main transputer to T1 (*Figure 2(a)* or *2(b)*). Transputer T1 extracts I1, I2, I3 and I4 from the vector, retains I1, and passes the rest to T2, T3 and T4 (as vectors) respectively. At this stage, each transputer has its own image section and will be working on the data. Using the Occam RETYPE capability, there is no need for actual hard-coded translation of 2D to 1D to 2D vectors, and therefore no time is wasted on those operations. Hence, the image will have been communicated in only eight *parallel* link activations, plus the throughrouting.

The image can then be gathered similarly in the opposite direction. Table 1 shows the timings for the distribution and collection of image data using the two methods described above, when applied to various image sizes on similar number of transputers. The differences may seem insignificant, but when intending to inspect several labels per second, every microsecond counts. The results shown in *Table 1* amount to less for the label inspection exercise since post-processing results will occupy a few bytes only and there is no necessity for gathering the resultant image.

Image Size	Flexible Method	Dedicated Method
bytes	*seconds*	
512x512	1.03	0.76
256x256	0.30	0.19
128x128	0.07	0.05
64x64	0.02	0.01

Table 1

4 Label Inspection Methods

There are numerous approaches for tackling this problem ranging from Template Matching [Fang, et al 83] to Hough Transforms [Casasent 88]. However, the methods used are generally not fast enough for a real-time environment, unless the bottle-necks involved are hardwired (e.g. cosine/sine evaluation by look-up table). Here, some simple and efficient algorithms are proposed that will detect some very common defects such as those classified in *Figure 3*.

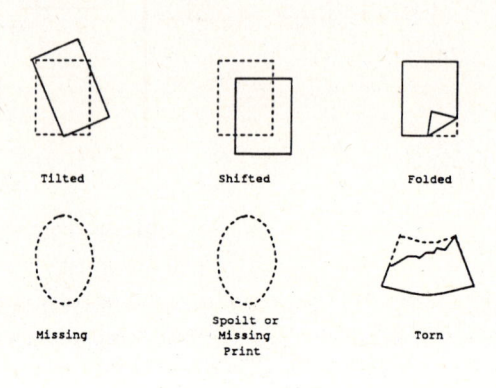

Figure 3

The main principle involved in the following algorithms is the detection of corner points. Again, many expensive techniques exist such as in [Kitchen 82], but here we are concerned with known corners that must be present in certain areas of an image. Their presence is checked for, essential measurements are made and compared with a known perfect model, and if the results are within an acceptable threshold, the label is passed.

4.1 Rectangular Labels
For this example, the dedicated and the general systems will be discussed, both of which use similar algorithms. Initially in either case, some features of a perfect model of a label are specified by the user. This set of measurements, including a histogram of the label, are stored and used in the process of inspection.

4.1.1 Dedicated 5 Transputer System
To detect a rectangular label, the master transputer distributes the current image frame over the four transputers in the network, as shown in *Figure 2(b)*. Each transputer would then have a part of the image which it will threshold into a binary representation prior to scanning it pixel by pixel. The method and direction of scanning for each transputer is different and is shown in *Figure 4(a)*.

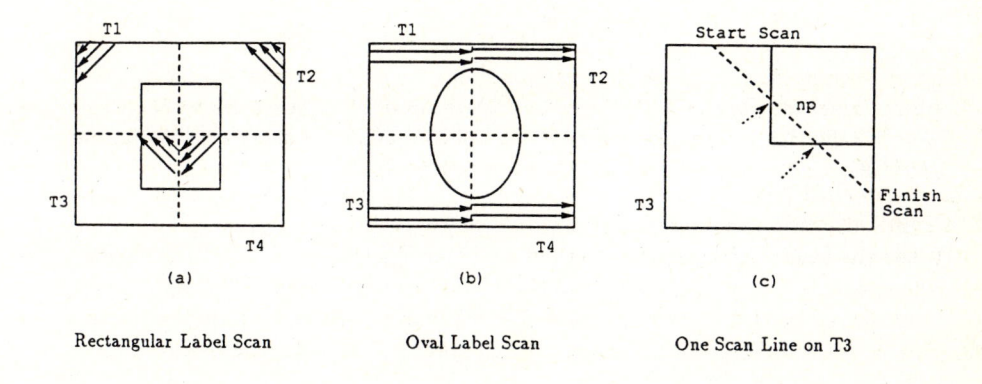

Figure 4 (a) Rectangular Label Scan · (b) Oval Label Scan · (c) One Scan Line on T3

Figure 4

The direction of scanning is always orthogonal to the expected corner point, and the first scanned line found to satisfy the following conditions is accepted as the line touching a corner point:

- the start pixel value must be the same as the final pixel value,
- the pixels scanned must show a change of state at least once,
- the number of image pixels *(np)* must satisfy $0 < np <= L$, where L is dependent on the general quality of image registration. (*Figure 4(c)*)

Similar code runs on T1 and T4, and also on T2 and T3. Each transputer then returns either the address of the pixel which it has found to be the corner point, or an indication if no corner point has been found.

4.1.2 General, Flexible System

In this system, each transputer will receive a part of the image which may be any one of the possibilities illustrated in *Figure 5*. *Figure 5(a)* shows the outline of an image and the rectangular regions processed by each transputer. *Figure 5(b)* shows the possible contents of each transputer with black for label and white for background. (Since edge information is passed, there are no complications if the image falls exactly on the border of two transputers.)

(a) Image across transputer array · (b) Possible distribution per transputer

Figure 5

The search strategy is more complex. Each transputer has to scan the whole of its own image section from all directions, stopping only when a possible corner or the end of scan is reached. Hence, with the extra distribution time, this method is considerably more costly. An alternative method would be to split the array into 4 quadrants to allow the same search pattern as the dedicated method.

While the transputers in either method are returning the corner pixel addressess to the master transputer, they are ready and receiving the next image. The master transputer sorts the returned information and decides if the inspected label (il) is perfect or faulty. This is determined by using a user-defined label (ul) as a template and checking the following against it for each corner:

$$ABS(ul\ Corner\ Address - il\ Corner\ Address) < Allowance\ Threshold$$

This condition will indicate if the label is shifted, tilted, missing, folded, or torn at the corners. To detect the presence and legibility of the print on the label, we compute the following,

$$Max(\frac{|F_i - F_i'|}{F_i})$$

where F_i is the linear histogram of the user-defined label and F_i' is the linear histogram of the label under inspection, and both are functions of intensity i, (i ϵ [black..white]) [Batchelor 79]. The computed value is then compared to a predefined tolerance parameter, which is set heuristically by the system. These calculations are performed only on a predefined area of the label called the *print check* area.

4.2 Oval Labels
For Oval labels, two *corner points* are searched for. These are the peak point and the base point of the label, and are found by tracing downwards on transputers T1 and T2, and tracing upwards on transputers T3 and T4 (*Figure 4(b)*). Similar comparisons to those used for a rectangular label are used to pass or fail oval labels.

4.3 Acute-angled Labels
As for rectangular labels, there are four distinctive corner points to search for. The search involves a normal downward scan for transputers T1 and T2 and a vertical left to right scan for transputers T3 and T4. Once the points are returned to master processor, the defects, if any, are detected using the same comparison methods as those used for a rectangular label.

4.4 Other Labels
The same philosophy can be used to develop the software to detect most other types of labels.

5   Inspection Results
The algorithms were tested using 128x128 and 256x256 images of 256 gray levels, with print check areas of various sizes. The average distribution and processing times, in seconds, are shown below for various configurations. *Table 4* indicates a fast rate of inspection using the customised network configuration.

Label Type	Image Size	Check Area	Average/Label	Labels/Sec
Rectangular	256x256	60x110	0.514	1
	128x128	30x60	0.160	6
Oval	256x256	95x155	0.487	2
	128x128	40x80	0.144	6
Acute-angled	256x256	30x125	0.535	1
	128x128	30x60	0.170	5

Table 2 - Results for a single transputer

Label Type	Image Size	Check Area	Average/Label	Labels/Sec
Rectangular	256x256	60x110	0.432	2
	128x128	30x60	0.111	8
Oval	n/a	n/a	n/a	n/a
Acute-angled	256x256	30x125	0.382	2
	128x128	30x60	0.097	10

Table 3 - Results for a 2 x 2 Array

Label Type	Image Size	Check Area	Average/Label	Labels/Sec
Rectangular	256x256	60x110	0.214	4
	128x128	30x60	0.054	18
Oval	256x256	95x155	0.199	5
	128x128	40x80	0.049	20
Acute-angled	256x256	30x125	0.239	4
	128x128	30x60	0.061	16

Table 4 - Results for the customised system

The major bottleneck for implementing a general real-time image processing system on transputers is the data communication load, and perhaps with the availability of more links on future transputers this problem would be overcome. However, as a unit in an embedded, customised architecture, the transputer has been repeatedly and successfully implemented in a number of commercial products.

The customised label inspection system presented here uses a fast image distribution algorithm, thresholding, directed scanning based on a *priori* knowledge, and simple feature evaluation methods. It has been constructed to aid development in label inspection research, and is designed with an easy-to-use menu interface. The system forms the basis of an affordable and efficient inspection system, using one of the world's most advanced processors as its basic building block.

6 Acknowledgements

This work has been carried out at the City University. The author would like to thank Dr. Geoff Dowling for his advice, and Transtech Devices Ltd. for their contribution and consultancy service.

References

[Inmos 86]   Inmos Ltd., *The IMS T414 Data Sheet*, December 1986

[Mirmehdi 87]   Mirmehdi M., *Parallelism in Image Processing*, City University Internal Report, TCU/CS/1987/13, 1987

[Chapman, et al 86]   Chapman R., et al, *Image Processing Strategies on Transputer Arrays*, Signal Processing III: Theories and Applications, Elsevier Science Publishers B.V., 1986

[Morrow, et al 88]   Morrow P.J., et al, *A Comparison of Two Notations for Programming Image Processing Applications on Transputers*, OUG7 Proceedings, pp. 1-9, 1988

[Inmos 88]   Inmos Technical Notes no. 72-TCH-017-00, *Performance Maximisation*, 1988

[Casasent 88]   Casasent D. and Richards J., *Industrial Use of a Real-time Optical Inspection System*, Applied Optics, Vol. 27, No. 22, 1988, pp. 4653-4659

[Fang, et al 83]   Fang T.J. et al, *An Experiment in Label Inspection Using Template Matching*, Proc. of Int. Conf. on Systems, Man and Cybernetics, 1983, Vol. 1, pp. 192-196

[Kitchen 82]   Kitchen L. and Rosenfeld A., *Gray Level Corner Detection*, Pattern Recognition Letters, 1982, Vol. 1, pp. 95-102

[Batchelor 79]   Batchelor B.G., *Interactive Image Analysis as a Prototyping Tool for Industrial Inspection*, Computers and Digital Techniques, 1979, Vol. 2, No. 2, pp. 61-70

On the Solution of some Classical Scheduling Problems Using Parallel C

Nick Bailey[φ], Alan Purvis[φ], Peter D Manning[♯] and Ian Bowler[♯]
DURHAM MUSIC TECHNOLOGY[†]

φ: School of Engineering and Applied Science,
Durham University Science Laboratories,
South Road,
Durham DH1 3LE.
UNITED KINGDOM.

♯: Department of Music,
Palace Green,
Durham DH1 3RL.
UNITED KINGDOM.

Abstract

This group has already addressed the problem of increasing the speed of MIT's CSOUND[*] direct music synthesis program by parallel execution after suitable pre-processing of the "score" file. This paper describes in detail some of the problems of implementing the multi-processor version of the program, concentrating upon the multi-threaded buffer and multiplexor/demultiplexor algorithms designed to execute as efficiently as possible in the Transputer C environment. Whilst the paper takes its examples from the CSOUND package, the principles which are discussed are likely to be applicable wherever a large piece of software is being transported onto a multi-Transputer machine.

CSOUND with Multiple Processors

It has already been shown that the speed of execution of CSOUND can be considerably enhanced by running the program on an INMOS Transputer$^{(TM)}$, simply by virtue of this processor's proficiency in general purpose, floating point calculation[1]. Using only one T800 floating point, 20MHz Transputer, the speed of execution is some 24 times as great as a desktop P.C. based on a 68000. An approximate load-balancing algorithm for mapping standard scores onto multi-processor arrays has also been presented, and a pipeline topology which avoids communications bottlenecks to a large extent for many digital signal processing algorithms is available and tested[2]. There are two major data-flow paths through the parallel CSOUND system: the dissemination of score and orchestra information along the pipeline, and the collection of the resultant sound samples flowing in the opposite direction.

Conventional CSOUND expects score data to appear from stdin. In the parallel environment, however, there is no direct attachment of any of the CSOUND threads to the host file system, so the usual file system support calls to read or write information are not allowed. Additionally, the score data has been prefixed by an allocation program to indicate the destination of each line of data: the prefix is either an '!' which indicates that the line should be sent both to CSOUND and to the rest of the pipeline, or '#⟨d⟩#' where ⟨d⟩ represents the destination processor number.

The score demultiplexor has to run concurrently with the main synthesis code, and without any significant overhead in terms of processor time. In practice, this implies that any waiting should be performed using either a semaphore or channel I/O calls, and that "busy waiting", or polling, must be avoided. The demultiplexor must perform three functions: read input lines from the host and mark them according to their destination; send the necessary lines of the score to the rest of the pipeline; strip the prefix characters and send the raw score data to the CSOUND thread. In this Transputer implementation, these functions are, broadly speaking, mapped onto three separate threads executing in parallel.

First In, First Out buffers for single thread environments are well understood[5] and several optimised algorithms exist for their implementation, but the solution of the above problem requires that multiple

---

* CSOUND is modified with the kind permission of Barry Vercoe, Department of Music, MIT.
† All of the above-named are members of the inter-disciplinary *Music Technology Group* at Durham

Fig. 1: The Score Demultiplexor & Buffer

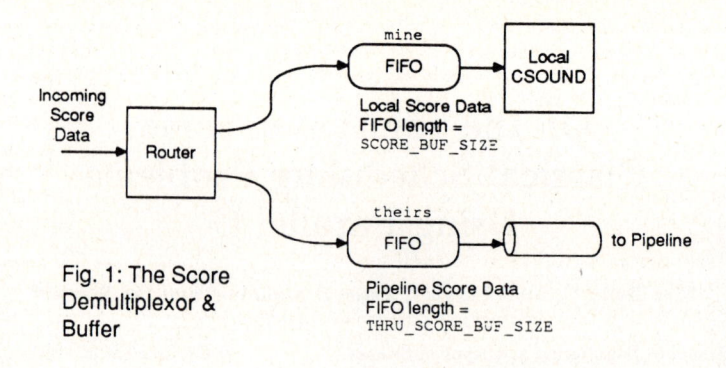

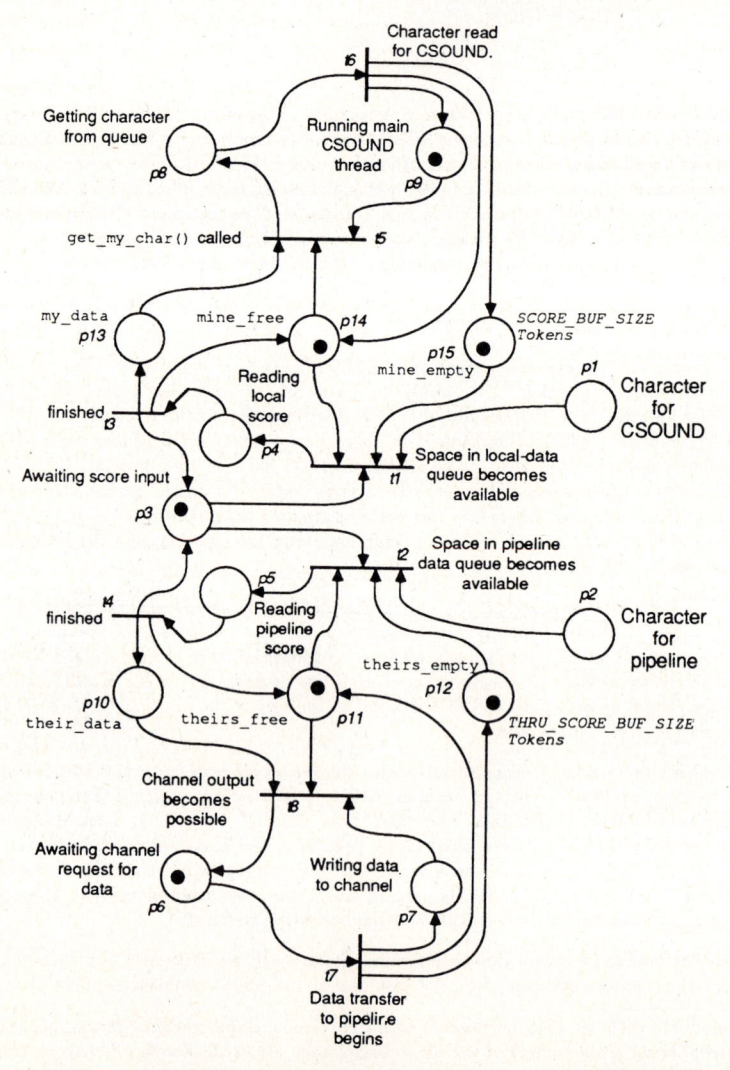

Fig. 2: A Petrinet of the Score Buffer with Initial Marking

threads share a common data structure. The use of FIFO buffering for both local and egressant data is mandatory; this avoids the processor waiting for score simply because pipeline communications are not available, and likewise avoids the starvation of the pipeline when the local CSOUND does not require any score data. Unfortunately, if a single FIFO buffer were used, whilst the resulting algorithm would be deadlock free because it is topologically free choice*[6], it would be possible for either the pipeline or the local main thread to be suspended unnecessarily because of the order in which the data arrive. It is possible to avoid such inefficiency without the use of multiple FIFO queues by use of the "Coloured Ticket" algorithm[7] but this introduces an (albeit minor) increase in processor overhead, and requires a non-trivial investment in writing the necessary code in Transputer-C.

The solution arrived at for the score buffering module (Fig. 1) implements two autonomous FIFO queues: these are labelled mine for data destined for the local CSOUND thread, and theirs for data to be transmitted along the pipeline. After the command line arguments and orchestra have been transmitted, the only data flow away from the host machine is score data**; consequently no complex transport protocol is necessary and the score data is simply output as words along the hardware links. Further, the size of theirs need only be small in comparison with mine; exiting data will be read quickly by the next processor in the pipeline unless its score buffers are full. Fig. 2 shows a Petrinet[8] representation of the concurrent score buffer algorithm, excluding the decision process concerning the destination of the characters as they arrive. This may be determined by a simple state machine which feeds the input places with the correct number of tokens, corresponding to the number of characters read, as each input line is presented.

The Petrinet (Fig. 2) clearly demonstrates the interaction between the three threads. The novel aspect of the control of the FIFO buffers is that instead of relying upon the more usual pointer comparisons to determine the presence of data within the queue, this test is performed using their associated semaphores. Taking the pipeline output buffer as an example, the related semaphores would be theirs_free, theirs_empty, and their_data. The initial values of these semaphores are respectively 1 (True), THRU_SCORE_BUF_SIZE, and 0 indicating that the pipeline output buffer is available (i.e. not being accessed by another thread), has THRU_SCORE_BUF_SIZE free locations, and contains 0 items of data.

A thread writing to the queue first suspends until empty space is available by waiting on theirs_empty. It then locks access to the queue and its associated pointers by waiting for theirs_free. When permission has been granted, the character is placed at the head of the queue according to the traditional algorithm, and its presence signalled on their_data. Finally, the queue is unlocked by signalling theirs_free. Conversely, a thread requiring input from the queue waits for their_data before locking the structure, removing a character, signalling on theirs_empty and finally unlocking it. Since similar operations appear as primitives in the Transputer assembly language instruction set, the processing overhead which accompanies this algorithm is marginal. Also, there is a saving in that it is no longer necessary to test for buffer overflow explicitly as this test is inherent in waiting on the theirs_empty semaphore; neither is any busy waiting required.

If the avoidance of starvation is important in the case of score routing, then for the temporary storage of sound samples it is doubly so. A fundamental requirement for the significant increase in speed of this application is that processors which are less loaded for a given section of the score may "rush ahead". Such processors store their output data locally in a large FIFO queue until such time that data from the rest of the pipeline can be added in to produce the required output. Similarly, data emerging from the pipeline must, if space permits, be read and stored locally if the processor falls behind as the score becomes particularly computationally intensive; failure to do so would block any other messages from the pipeline, and may even result in a CSOUND main thread becoming suspended. Whilst the score sorting algorithm takes steps to distribute the workload evenly, there is inevitably some imbalance which must be absorbed by local buffering. The conceptual interrelation of the three executing threads, the buffer space, and a notional access permission arbitrator is shown in Fig. 3.

Because of the relatively large size of the data items involved (sound samples are computed in buffers of 8KB length in the current implementation), it is unacceptable to use to discrete buffers as for the score buffering example. Instead, FIFO queues are built from 8KB blocks of RAM using three lists. Because of

---

* For every possible data item appearing at its output, there is a transition (or event) which can (eventually) remove that item.
** This places some restrictions on the functionality of the CSOUND package.

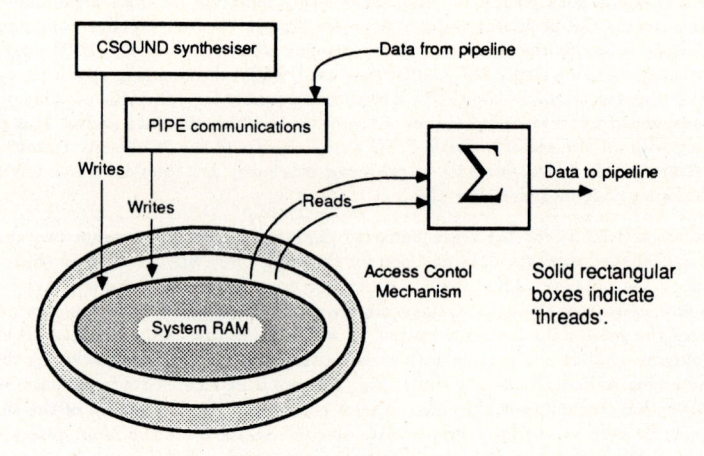

Fig. 3: The Sound Sample Recombination Processes

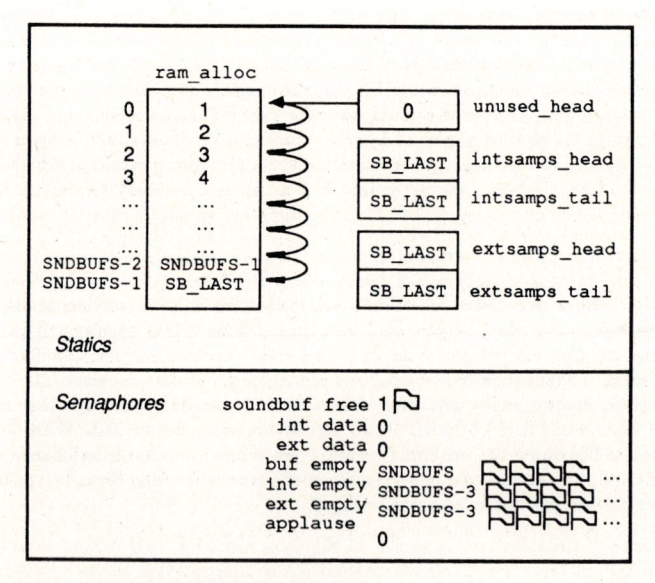

Fig. 4: The Sound Buffer Data Structure with Initial Values

the close analogy to the operation of a simple disk filing system, these 8KB blocks of RAM will be referred to as *sectors*. The data structure and its initial contents used for sound buffering is shown in Fig 4. All operations on this structure are performed by routines in the module SNDBUF.C. As in the case of the score demultiplexor, there are three threads to support this algorithm: one reads data from the pipeline and enqueues them; one reads data from the local processor and enqueues them; a third dequeues a sector of data from each queue, performs a vector sum of their contents and sends the result towards the host.

The word array ram_alloc contains three interleaved lists of integers representing the two FIFO queues and a LIFO (Last In First Out) stack within which a free sector list is maintained. Data present and space present conditions are flagged by semaphores following a similar naming convention to the score buffering module: int_data and ext_data flag the presence of sectors containing respectively internally or externally generated samples; int_empty and ext_empty are raised if space exists for more samples; buf_empty is raised if there are free sectors in the buffer. The entire structure is locked using the semaphore soundbuf_free to prevent interference between concurrent threads attempting simultaneous access. All of the semaphores are shown in the Petrinet description of the sound buffering module in Fig 5.

There is a potential deadlock situation in the sound buffer module which cannot occur in the demultiplexor. Suppose the local processor has raced ahead of the processors further up the pipeline and filled all of available RAM. The sample output thread cannot output a sector of samples because it has no sectors from the pipeline in RAM with which it may perform its vector summation (ext_data is lowered). The thread which reads samples from the pipeline is suspended waiting for space in the external data queue to become available; this will never occur, however, because data from the pipeline must be written into a buffer before this can happen (the "dining philosophers" problem[3,10]). The solution implemented in SNDBUF.C, without resorting to polling, is to introduce two further semaphores, one for each writing process. For a process to be allowed to allocate a sector of RAM, is must have either int_empty (for local data) or ext_empty (for remote data) *and* buf_empty raised. Noting the initial values of the semaphores in Fig. 4, this effectively extends the preconditions for writing to "There is at least one empty sector in RAM and not more than SNDBUFS − 3 sectors are occupied by data from this source".

Analysis of the Petrinets

Figs. 2 & 5, the Petrinet models of the score and sound buffering modules, permit a further insight into how the three threads interact dynamically; in particular, they present concisely the resource sharing system. Consider the simpler score buffering module (Fig. 2), the initial marking yields the following interpretation: place p_{15} (mine_empty) has one token for each character of free space in the local score buffer; likewise, p_{12} (theirs_empty) has a token for each empty location in the pipeline forwarding buffer. The presence of a token in p_{14} or p_{11} represents the availability of the buffers and their associated pointers for access; these are the mutual exclusion semaphores. Tokens in p_3, p_6 and p_9 represent the program counters associated with the three buffering threads; their relocation represents execution of the associated code.

When an input character becomes available, the routing algorithm will make a decision about its destination and place a token in one of the input places p_1 or p_2. The data input thread may then proceed via the firing sequence (t_1, t_3) if the data is destined for the local CSOUND, or via (t_2, t_4) if the item is to be passed along the pipeline. Following the token around this route gives an indication of the conditions necessary for execution to proceed by observing the labels associated with the transitions and their input places. The pipeline output thread circulates through transitions (t_7, t_8) as data is transmitted along the pipeline; similarly, the CSOUND service routine get_my_char* enables the sequence (t_5, t_6). By following the execution tokens around these transitions, the movements of the memory resource tokens between the "data" and "empty" semaphores may also be observed. A required property of the memory resource tokens is that they are conserved; that is to say, the amount of memory which they represent is constant. Conservation with respect to storage is now demonstrated formally, using the matrix definition of the Petrinet.

Let the Petrinet of Fig. 6 be defined by the quadruple $C_1 = (P, T, D^+, D^-)$ where $P = \{p_i\}$, the set of places in the Petrinet, $T = \{t_i\}$, the set of transitions. D^+ and D^- are matrices defined by the forward and backward reachability functions as follows:

---

* An additional character input function provided for use within parallel CSOUND, similar to getchar() in standard C.

Let $\#(p_i, I(t_j))$ be the multiplicity of place p_i with respect to the input function of transition t_j. This takes a non-negative integer value equal to the number of arcs connecting p_i to t_j. Also, let $\#(p_i, O(t_j))$, the multiplicity with respect to the output function, be the non-negative number of arcs between t_j and p_i. Define

$$D^-_{j,i} = \#(p_i, I(t_j))$$

and

$$D^+_{j,i} = \#(p_i, O(t_j))$$

Further, define the composite change matrix $D = D^+ - D^-$. The Petrinet C_1 is conservative with respect to a weighting vector $\vec{w}$ if and only if

$$D.\vec{w} = \vec{0}$$

Element i of this vector, w_i, is referred to as the weight of place p_i.

The appropriate weighting for each place in the network will now be considered. A token in theirs_empty, their_data, my_data or mine_empty is a direct representation of a memory location; hence assign $w_{10} = w_{12} = w_{13} = w_{15} = 1$. Data storage locations are also "possessed" by tokens outside these places for the duration of the execution of the critical sections of code. These places must also be considered in the weighting vector, because the buffer space which they use is returned to the global buffer pool when the critical section of the code completes. Thus we also assign $w_4 = w_5 = w_6 = w_8 = 1$. D is a fairly sparse matrix; the non-zero elements are listed below:

$$D_{1,4} = D_{2,5} = D_{3,13} = D_{4,10} = D_{5,8} = D_{6,15} = D_{7,12} = D_{8,6} = 1$$
$$D_{1,15} = D_{2,12} = D_{3,4} = D_{4,5} = D_{5,13} = D_{6,8} = D_{7,6} = D_{8,10} = -1$$

Direct substitution into the equation of conservation yields:

$$D \cdot \vec{w} = \begin{pmatrix} D_{1,6} + D_{1,8} + D_{1,10} + D_{1,12} + D_{1,13} + D_{1,15} \\ D_{2,6} + D_{2,8} + D_{2,10} + D_{2,12} + D_{2,13} + D_{2,15} \\ \vdots \\ D_{8,6} + D_{8,8} + D_{8,10} + D_{8,12} + D_{8,13} + D_{8,15} \end{pmatrix}$$

Substitution of the values from the above lists shows directly that
$$D \cdot \vec{w} = \vec{0}$$

A similar procedure may be followed for the sound sample recombination buffers, although in this case there is the added complication imposed by the deadlock avoidance strategy.

7. Conclusion

The use of a pipeline architecture with distribution of sound generation tasks followed by signal superposition has been shown to be an efficient approach to real-time synthesis. This architecture is suitable for CSOUND provided that acceptable routing and allocation algorithms are available, and that the communications protocols do not place undue extra processing load on the chosen processors.

Inmos Transputers perform particularly well in a multi-processor machine, even when the software package is written in a language with poor support for concurrent processing. The algorithms presented here have been shown to be secure and efficient in the day-to-day use of the package.

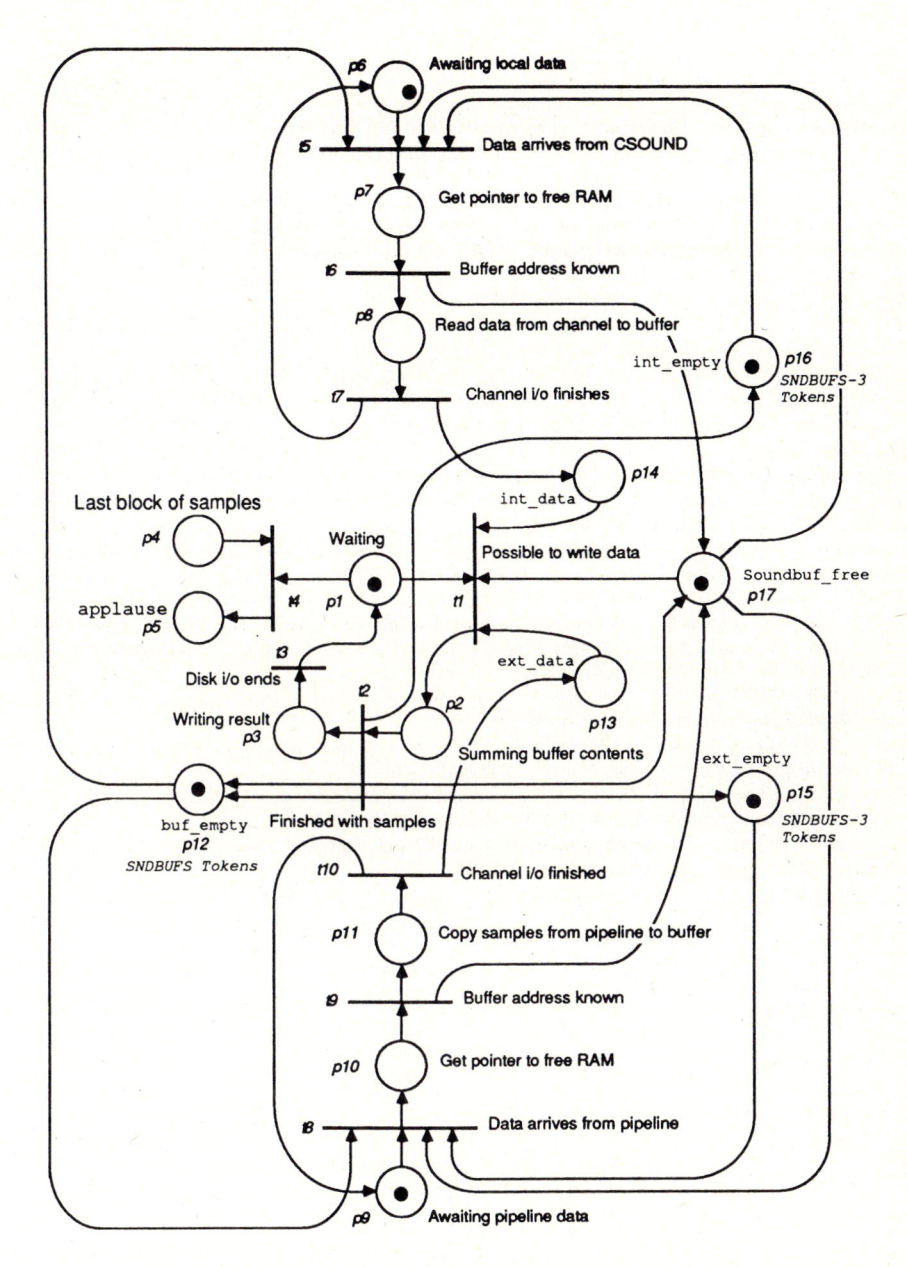

Fig. 5: A Petrinet of the Sound Buffer with Initial Marking

References

[1] **Bailey,N.J., Purvis,A., Bowler,I.W. and Manning,P.D** *'An Implementation of CSOUND on the Transputer'*. Proceedings of the International Conference on the Applications of Transputers. University of Liverpool, 1989.
[2] **Bowler,I.W., Manning,P.D., Purvis,A. and Bailey, N.J.** *'A Transputer-Based Additive Synthesis Implementation'*. Proceedings of the International Computer Music Conference, Ohio 1989.
[3] **Dijkstra,F. (in 'Programming Languages' ed. Genuys,F.)** *'Cooperating Sequential Processes'* New York Academic Press (1968) pp34-112
[4] **Vercoe,B.** *'CSOUND Reference Manual'*, MIT Press, 1986.
[5] **Knuth,D.E.** *'The Art of Computer Programming vol. 1: Fundamental Algorithms'* Sec. 2.2 pp234 et seq., Addison-Wesley (1968) Lib. Cong. Cat. No. 67-26020
[6] **Finkel,A., Choquet,A.** *'FIFO Nets Without Order Deadlock'* Acta Informatica 25(1) (1986) pp15-36
[7] **Fischer,M.J., Lynch,N.A., Burns,J.E. and Borodin,A.** *'Distributed FIFO Allocation of Identical Resources using Small Shared Space'* ACM Transactions on Programming Languages and Systems, 11(1) pp90-114
[8] **Peterson,J.L.** *'Petrinet Theory and the Modeling of Systems'* Prentice Hall (1981) ISBN 0-13-661983-5
[9] **Courtois,P., Heymans,F. and Parnas,D.** *'Concurrent Control with 'Readers'and 'Writers'* Communications of ACM 14(10) (Oct. 1971) pp667-668
[10] **Cooprider,L.** *'Petrinets and the Representation of Standard Synchronisations'* Dept of Computer Science, Carnegie-Mellon University, Pittsburgh, Pensylvania (Jan. 1976)
[11] **Clarke,J.M., Manning,P.D., Berry,R. and Purvis,A.** itsans 'VOCEL: New Implementations of the FOF Synthesis Method' Proceedings of the 14th International Computer Music Conference, Cologne, 1988
[12a] **Clarke,J.M.** *'A Tutorial on FOF Synthesis in CSOUND'* The Composers' Desktop Project, Ltd., Unit 7, 35 Hospital Fields Road, Fulford Industrial Estate, York, U.K.
[12b] **Clarke,J.M.** *'FOF Synthsis on the Atari ST'* The Composers' Desktop Project, Ltd., Unit 7, 35 Hospital Fields Road, Fulford Industrial Estate, York, U.K.
[13] **Holme,F.** *'Frequency Scheduling: Real-time Scheduling in Multi-tasking Systems'* Proceedings of the International Computer Music Conference, Ohio, 1989. pp127-130
[14] **Orlarey,Y. and Lequay,H.** *'A Real-time Multi-tasks Software Module for MIDI Applications'* Proceedings of the International Computer Music Conference, Ohio, 1989. pp 234-237
[15] **Walker,W.F.** *'KIWI: A Parallel System for Software Sound Synthesis'* Proceedings of the International Computer Music Conference, Ohio, 1989. pp328-331

Transputer Based Pin Compatible i80287 Accelerator Board

D. Wong, Cheer Target Co. Ltd., Hong Kong.
Y.K. Chan, Electronic Eng. Dept., City Polytechnic, Hong Kong.

Abstract. This paper describes a "pin compatible" i80287 add-on card for AT-compatible motherboard. When compared like with like, the add-on card yields better floating point performance than i80287 or IIT-C287 "IIT"[1]. The add-on card is also designed to support the execution of "small chunks" of T800 native code within an i80286 tight loop for maximum performance gain.

1. Introduction

In engineering and scientific applications, response and throughput is largely governed by floating point performance rather than integer performance.

In a uniprocessor environment, a T800 is known to be a good "FORTRAN engine" with a good Dhrystone performance and excellent Whetstone performance. On the other hand, an i80286 has an adequate Dhrystone performance and yet the Whetstone performance of an i80286/i80287 pair is disappointing.

The objective of the prototype, an AT add-on card, is that it can be used in two ways. One of which is to boost floating point performance of an i80286 based system to a more respectable level. The other usage is T800 native code execution to harness the maximum floating point performance of a T800.

Photo 1: Prototype Accelerator Board

2. Hardware Description

The current wire-wrapped prototype occupies the area of about twice an AT-compatible full size add-on card. The core of the board consists of a T800, 8K bytes SRAM, an attached ribbon cable with an i80287 pin-compatible plug. The prototype has about 110 TTL components. The prototype needs a 16-bit slot on the motherboard with the cable securely plugged into the i80287 socket on the motherboard.

A photograph of the prototype board in a vertical position is shown in Photo 1. A ribbon cable on the right hand side connects the board to the i80287 socket. A floppy disk drive on the left hand side partly obscures the i80286 mother board.

3. Software Aspect of the Prototype

The amount of T800 code/data for i80287 emulation currently takes up to 4K bytes of T800 internal RAM and 8K bytes of external SRAM. The emulation code is developed using a "home brew" tiny assembler.

As expected, most often executed i80287 instructions are stored in the internal RAM.

Current implementation of the transcendental functions is a super set of i80287 transcendental function. For example, the T800 prototype has SIN, COS and EXP implementation which is not available in i80287.

AT-compatible power-on reset raises the hardware reset as well as the execution of the script-file "AUTOEXEC.BAT" which transparently boots up the prototype via a C011 like serial link implemented by TTLs. The prototype is then fully compatible with the i80287.

4. i80287 execution behaviour

The i80287, as a stack architectural extention to the register oriented i80286, consists of a Bus Interface Unit "BIU" and a Numeric Execution Unit "NEU".

The control signals "PEREQ" and "PEACK" provides "handshaking" for the data transfer between i80286 and i80287; while the activation of the "BUSY" signal line informs the i80286 that the "NEU" of the i80287 is processing the data. In otherwords, the "BUSY" signal is used for synchronization. (To guarantee that the previous instruction is error free and to ensure that the two processors access the memory operands in the proper sequence, just as they would be accessed by a single processor with no concurrency.)

While "BUSY" is active, the i80286 can execute the succeeding instruction only if it is not an floating point "ESC" instruction.

5. Concurrency design for the prototype

The prototype provides buffering for the instruction pointers "IP", data pointers "DP", opcode as well as the operands. Consider two successive ESC instructions, "FDIV memory" (single precision) and "FMUL memory" (single precision), the prototype will behave as the follows :

(i) the i80286 processes the ESC instruction and calculates the effective address "EA" of the source.
(ii) the i80286 issues the opcode to the prototype. In response to the opcode, the prototype asserts the "PEREQ" to signal the i80286 for data transfer. The "BUSY" is activated once the i80286 transfers the opcode to the card.
(iii) IP, DP and the operands are transferred to the card's buffer. The operands (transferred as 16-bit each time) are assembled to be 32-bits operand

by the T800 time the last transfer has taken place. The T800 can now divide the T800 top-of-stack "TOS" by the source.
(iv) at the same time, "busy" is deactivated. i80286 detects that "BUSY" is inactivated and begins to process the next ESC instruction ("FMUL memory") while the T800 performs division in 64-bits precision.
(v) step (ii) is repeated. IP, DP and the operands are transferred to the card as usual, but at this time, the T800 has not yet finished the floating-point division and will not retrieve the source from the operand buffer. In this case, "BUSY" remains active and step (iv) cannot proceed until T800 finishes processing the "FDIV" instruction and takes up the source from the operand buffer.

The 12MHz i80286 and the T800-20 is a balanced system in the sense that "T800-20 internally maintained 64-bits calculation" and "i80286 effective address calculation and bus activity" takes about the same amount of time. Performance is increased when using 16/20 MHz i80286 and T800-25/30.

6. Compatibility issue with i80287

i80287 supports the IEEE-P754 floating point standard for 32-bits and 64-bits precision. It also supports temporary-real format with the 80-bits precision. Internally, the i80287 always maintains the full 80-bits precision for operands of single (32bits), double(64bits) and temporary-real(80bits).

The prototype supports full i80287 instruction set including 80-bits related instructions. The prototype always maintains 64-bits precision. When compared with the 80-bits precision, a theoretical discrepancy of about $1.0*E-16$ percent is possible. Put it in another way, an error of about 1.0 cent out of 100 trillion dollars is possible.

A comparison[2] of accuracy based on the "SAVAGE" benchmark clearly indicates that, when operands are 64-bits double precision data type, 80-bits internally maintained accuracy has no advantage over 64-bits internally maintained accuracy.

The range for 64-bits is $(1.0*E-308, 1.0*E+308)$ and for 80-bits is $(1.0*E-4932, 1.0*E+4932)$ respectively. With most compilers supporting only 32-bits and 64-bits data types, the range capability of 80-bits is an advantage that cannot be reflected in real life applications.

7. Transcendental function: Range and Performance

The prototype supports direct full range transcendental instructions such as SIN, COS, EXP which is not available in i80287. IIT has better range coverage than i80287. The prototype has the most comprehensive range coverage that is only limited by "exponents" in 32-bits and 64-bits representation. For example, the ranges of TAN for

        i80287 :   I I T   : Prototype   are
$0 \leq TAN \leq \pi/4$: $0 \leq TAN < \infty$: $-\infty < TAN < \infty$ respectively.

Below is the performance of i80287, IIT and the prototype respectively in micro-seconds.

It should be noted that SIN, COS, EXP and indeed other transcendental functions can be performed as "in line code" instead of" library functions" due to the prototype's full range capability.

8. Raw speed, Benchmark and Application Performance.

Some preliminary raw performance is tabulated in Table 3.

TABLE 2: Transcendental functions timing comparison in μs

	i80287**	IIT**	Prototype*
SIN	272	130	45
COS	271	130	47
EXP	332	180	44

* Proprietary maths. library for Turbo-C
** Standard Turbo-C maths. library

TABLE 3: Raw speed comparison in μs

expression	12 MHz i80286 motherboard		
	8MHz i80287	IIT 8MHz	T800-20 prototype
A = B	36.8/ 42.9	8.9/ 12.4	6.2/ 7.3
A = B + C * D	97.9/124.6	20.4/ 26.6	13.8/ 16
ST(0)=ST(1)*log2ST(0)	119/ 119	30/ 30	19/ 19
internal precision	80 bits	80 bits	64 bits

ST(0) = Top of i80287 stack
SP/DP = Single Precision/Double Precision

TABLE 4: Whetstone benchmark in units of kilo-Whetstones

	i80287	IIT	Prototype
QAPLUS V2.69 *	319.0	489.7	611.4
Double precision Turbo-C with standard maths. library **	221.0	408.0	592.0

* Compiler not stated; precision not stated
** C version of the OCCAM[3] Whetstone program

Table 3 indicates that for short arithmetic expression, gain in performance relative to a 8 MHz i80287 is about 7.5 times. The gain is higher if the expression is longer or the expression consists of division.

Preliminary Whetstone benchmark for the prototype and comparisons with other systems are tabulated in TABLE 4. It should be noted that if proprietary library were used, the prototype performance should be around 700KW.

When executing Turbo-C double precision 4X4 matrix multiplication 20,000 times, the time taken for i80287:IIT:Prototype are 58.9sec.:26.8sec.:16.9sec., respectively. The program is of the form

```
       ┌─── k = 1, 20000
       │    i = 1, 4
       │    j = 1, 4
       │    a[i,j] = b[i,1]*c[1,j] +
       │             b[i,2]*c[2,j] +
       │             b[i,3]*c[3,j] +
       │             b[i,4]*c[4,j]
       └─── loop k
```

For AutoCAD regeneration, such as St.Paul's Cathedral, Columbia, mparts, etc., the execution time ratio is about 1.6:1.15:1

9. Conclusion

The prototype accelerator board, at the present stage of inmaturity, outperforms i80287 and IIT. Application performance is enhanced for productivity gain that is totally transparent to the users. Full power of the T800-20 can be harnessed by system developers. (e.g. small chunks of T800 native code for ray-tracing and orthogonal transform).

The prototype can be reduced to a half-size AT-compatible add-on card using a few thousand gates ASIC.

10. References

[1] "In Search of a Faster 80287", Rick Grehan. Page 206, Byte. September 1989.
[2] "SAVAGE" benchmark, Page 267, The Transputer Application Note Book, 1st ed., 1989.
[3] "Source of the OCCAM Whetstone program", pp. 269-272, The Transputer Application Note Book, 1st ed., 1989.

11. Acknowledgement

The authors would like to thank Dr. Andrew Layfield for presenting this paper in the TA'90 International Conference.

HIGH PERFORMANCE RELATIONAL DATABASE SYSTEMS ON TRANSPUTERS

C.H.C Leung, H.T Ghogomu, K. L. Mannock

Computer Science Department
Birkbeck College, University of London
Malet Street, London WC1E 7HX

Abstract. *This paper presents strategies necessary for realising a high performance parallel database system. These strategies include the transformation of SQL transactions into efficient parallel execution plans consisting of relational algebraic operations. Models are also included to efficiently allocate processors to the execution plan to optimise performance.*

1. Introduction and Overview

In many large database applications, the flexible retrieval and intelligent correlation of data are often inhibited because of the excessive demand such activities placed on the processing component of the system, even though the required information is available either directly or indirectly via deduction. In this paper, the reduction in database processing speeds through suitably exploiting processor parallelism is studied. Such a reduction will substantially enhance the performance efficiency of large database systems, and permit the intelligent processing of database information, which at present do not appear to be feasible on any significant scale.

This work forms part of a project supported by ESPRIT under the Parallel Computing Action Initiative. The hardware used is a stand alone machine, with 20 transputers, each with an on board 4Mbyte of main storage. Our system environment can be set up according to a number of pre-defined domains, each with a number of software reconfigurable transputers. These domains form the working environments, one to each user. User SQL queries are accepted by a query reconstruction subsystem. These queries, after appropriate transformations, are converted into parallel query execution plans consisting of relational algebraic operations. Each execution plan consists of a number of phases; each phase, in turn, comprises a set of parallel operations that will have to be physically mapped to the available transputers within a user domain. As shown in Figure 1, the subsystem consists of an SQL translator, a parallel plan generator, and a processor allocator. The allocator makes use of a cost model to map the execution plan to the available transputers.

```
  SQL  →  translator  →  par-plan     →  processor   →
                          generator       allocator
```

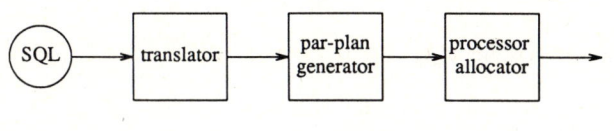

Figure 1

2. Query Reconstruction

This process involves query translation, parallelism detection, and parallel query plan generation.

3. Translation of an SQL Query into Relational Algebra

As SQL is fast becoming a standard query language for relational databases, it is adopted as the user interface for our system. Translation of SQL queries have been covered by several authors [1,2,3,4], and the approach adopted here is an extension of [2]. The approach in [2] is syntax directed; translation rules are associated with the grammer productions, each production corresponding to a particular type of SQL query. Our extensions include the formalization of further rules for detecting algebraic operations and intra-query parallelism. The methodology is hierarchical in structure. The first step performed by the reconstruction subsystem is to translate the SQL query into a relational algebraic equivalent. To ensure completeness, the translation must be capable of taking care of all the expressiveness of the SQL language. A typical SQL query has the following basic structure:

SELECT [distinct] ....{target relations}

FROM.......{source relations}

WHERE......{search predicate}

[GROUP by FIELD(s)[HAVING predicate] [ORDER by FIELD(s)]

For brevity we shall only deal with the primary structure i.e *SELECT...FROM...WHERE* to illustrate how it is transformed in the process. Four main query types exist.
1. Simple Query :- these are requests based on a single key with value specified.
2. Range Query :- these are requests based on a range of values on a single key.
3. Functional Query :- in these requests, some function of key values in the relation is specified e.g average, median etc.
4. Boolean Query:- a Boolean query contains a Boolean combination of the the earlier three using logical operators of *AND,OR,NOT*.

As can be seen , the major difference in the above queries arises from the complexity of their search predicates and/or functions involved. Otherwise any complex query can be seen as a relationship between one or more simple queries, and can be expressed as such. In this approach, we demonstrate that every query in the basic form irrespective of its complexity can be translated stepwisely in a heirarchical fashion in terms of simple queries. The basic SQL structure below is used as an illustration.

SELECT aaaa
FROM xxxx
WHERE yyyy

A heirarchic analysis of this begins by evaluating the " select.. from" block to determine which algebraic operation it translates to. The target relations and the source relations (intermediate or base) would provide enough information to determine the algebraic operation for producing the output. The next step relates the source relation specification with the *WHERE* clause to produce further translations. The clause could consist of simple, or a Boolean combination of simple predicates, or could further specify a subquery. In the case of the predicate consisting of simple comparisons or a *join* predicate, the translation process will terminate there; otherwise it iterates on the subqueries. This process is bottom-up in terms of the output or dataflow. The following primitive algebraic operations will be used for illustration:
restriction, projection, and product. The *join* operation though not primitive is often used and will be included. How do we determine when each of the above is present in an SQL expression? The following are rules for detecting their presence.

3.1. Projection

Unlike in relational algebra, the presence of algebraic operations in SQL is not explicit. Hence these rules are necessary for their extraction. The result of the projection of one or more tuples always yields a vertical subset of the attributes of the relation. The target attributes are explicitly defined. The relation on which the projection is performed can either be a base relation, or an intermediate relation from another query. Hence an evaluation of the target relation(s) specification against the source relation specification will determine if a projection is involved in the SELECT..FROM... step.

3.2. Restriction

Restriction is used here to avoid confusion with the select which is used in SQL queries as a generality. The resultant tuple of a restriction operation has exactly the same qualified attribute names as the source relations. So a restriction is determined from the result specification and the restriction predicate. The restriction predicate in a general sense consist of an arbitrary Boolean combinations of simple comparisons e.g R WHERE c1 AND c2 etc.

3.3. Cartesian Product

This is often used as part of a more popular operation, the *join* operation.

3.4. Join

A join operation as often used in SQL is a combination of a cartesian product and a restriction operation. The θ-join of a relation A and B is the set of tuples in the product of A and B satisfying a join predicate a.x θ b.y . There must be more than one source relation and the join predicate must involve more than one relation.

We shall illustrate the overall translation process with a comparison using an example from [2]. Let us consider the relational schema:

S(SNUM, NAME), storing supplier's name, and number.
SP(PNUM,SNUM), storing supplier and part number for a supply.

The query below retrieves the name of suppliers who do not supply product "p2".

```
SELECT NAME
FROM S
WHERE "p2"<> ALL

SELECT PNUM
FROM SP
WHERE SNUM=S.SNUM
```

The ALL keyword is used to select all supplier part numbers that are not equal to "p2". That same query can also be written as

```
SELECT SNAME
FROM S
WHERE NOT EXISTS
  (SELECT *
  FROM SP
  WHERE SNUM=S.SNUM
  AND PNUM = 'p2').
```

A translation from [2] produces

(PJ[S.SNAME] S) DF (PJ [S.SNAME] ((SL [SP.PNUM='p2'] S) JN [SP.SNUM = S.SNUM] SP)).

Five relational algebraic operations are involved here, PJ for projection, DF for difference, SL for selection, and JN for join. This same query can easily be done with four operations thus:

step 1:
SELECT SNAME
FROM S

This translates to (PJ[S.SNAME]S).

We are now left with the *WHERE* clause which is a subquery. This subquery involves SP and the predicate uses S.SNUM. This implies a join is involved (SP.SNUM=S.SNUM). The logical AND implies a restriction on SP for PNUM=p2.

step2
(PJ[S.SNAME] S)
WHERE NOT EXISTS
(SL[SP>PNUM='p2'] JN [SP.S3=S.SNUM] SP))

NOT EXISTS is a keyword and is translated using the grammatical rules and not facts about the relations and predicates. In a sequential fashion the operation can be ordered into a query tree. Using precedence/dependence between the operations, alternative query plans can be derived.

4. Detection and Generation of Parallel Query Plan

The parallelism to be detected involves identification of all operations that can be executed concurrently either producing a single output or feeding their results to succeeding operation(s). The following are situations under which such possibilities occur.
1. When there are more than one source relations to operate on.
2. The predicate in the where clause is an exlusive Boolean combination of simple comparisons. Assuming a schema

DEP(D-NUM,DEPTYPE,DEPHEAD), storing department number,department type, and the head of that department.
EMP(E-NUM,E-SAL,E-NAME,D-NUM), storing employee number,name , salary and department number. Now consider the query

SELECT E-NUM
FROM DEP, EMP
WHERE   DEPHEAD = manager OR E-SAL > 20k.

There are two algebraic operations here i.e. restriction and projection. The logical OR in the restriction predicate and the fact that there are two independent source relations implies that the restriction can be done concurrently. The two restrictions could well apply to the same relation and we only have to eliminate duplicates.

The other parallelism is the splitting of costly operations in to smaller units that can be processed concurrently. This however does not require detection [5].

In generating the parallel plan, it is necessary to determine the precedence and dependency between the various operations. The dependency are of two types. A loose dependency and a strict dependency. A loose dependency between two operations is one where the operation sequence may be altered or reversed while still producing the required output e.g the dependency between a Select-Join operations (in that order) is loose; the join can be performed before the select still producing the same result. The dependency could also be a strict one, in which case the operation sequence has to be strictly maintained in order to produce the required output e.g. the dependency between a restrict-project operations in that order, will in most circumstances affect the result if the sequence is reversed. This is because some columns may be lost through projection and these columns may be required for the restriction predicates. This implies that the dependency must be closely examined if an operation leads to a reduction in the number of attributes or columns of a tuple.

A parallel query execution plan can then be constructed. This will allow a step by step generation of a set of ordered parallel operations. Each set of parallel operations form an execution phase. This phase oriented approach maintains the simplicity of sequential processing while taking advantage of parallel processing. This approach ensures that all operations within a phase are executed within an equal amount of time: the phase elapsed time.

With such a plan, the key consideration is to so distribute the transputers to the operations as to minimise both the individual phase completion time, and the total elapsed time for the completion of the execution stream.

As illustrated in the example query tree in Figure 2, operations 1,2, and 3 form the first phase of the query execution stream and are executed in parallel. In the same manner 4 and 5 form phase 2, and 6 forms phase 3.

Figure 2

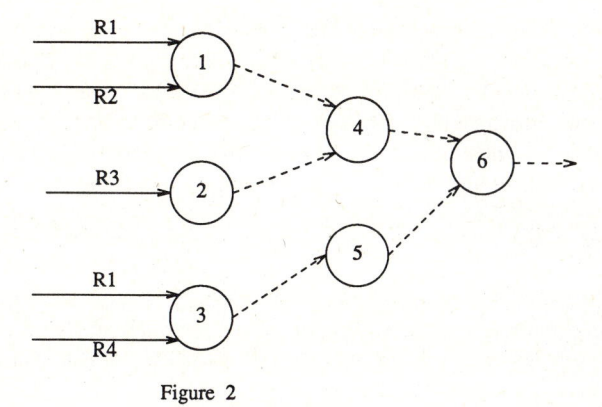

5. Allocation of Processors

The key consideration in the allocation model is the characteristics of each algebraic operation: the cost of the different implementation algorithms, parameters and statistics of the relations involved, and the degree of repetition inherent in nature of the operation.

We first concentrate on the allocation procedure for a given phase. We start with an estimate of the time required for each operation within a phase, assuming each operation is carried out using a single transputer. The shortest time so obtained can be regarded as a goal which other operations aim to achieve through the acquisition of additional transputers, after which a new shortest time is obtained. The process would continue until all the available transputers have been allocated. Loosely speaking, our allocation model uses a strategy whereby each phase is allocated transputers in such a way that all operations within it take the same amount of time to execute, which equals to the time necessary to complete the shortest operation in that phase. If this is not possible, as can occur if the number of transputers are limited, they then assume a mean phase elapsed-time. As a result, there is no critical path in the whole query plan. It can be demonstrated that under certain circumstances, this method produces the highest performance possible through parallelism.

For a resident database, our model considers two situations for the transputer network; the first one is when the number of reconfigurable transputers within a domain are large enough to be considered a virtual machine, and the second case is one with a finite and limited number of transputers.

In principle, if an operation takes t seconds to execute on a single processor, then it will take t/n seconds to execute on n processors in parallel. In practice, this is limited by the topology adopted. In general, if K represents the number of operations in a given phase, and if a given operation K_i in that phase takes t_i seconds to execute on a single transputer and that the shortest operation K_s takes t_s seconds to execute, then for $i = 1$ to K, the number of transputers required by operation K_i is:

$$\frac{t_i}{t_s}$$

This applies to a case of unlimited number of transputers. The phase elapsed time t_s is thus the CPU time to complete the given phase. As indicated above, this process can actually be iterated to reduce the shortest phase elapsed time and further improve the overall execution time.

An iteration will result when the cost t_s of the shortest operation is too costly for a single processor. In such a situation, functional decomposition [5] is applied to the shortest operation.

For a given phase suppose we have $k_i...k_n$ operations with $t_i...t_n$ costs respectively. We first select the minimum and the maximum operations in terms of their costs. Min$(t_i...t_n)$ gives us t_s. Also Max$(t_i...t_n)$ gives us t_{max}. We apply the general principle to t_s and t_{max}. Every time k_s is decomposed we have a new shortest operation, and this process continues until when further decomposition will not achieve any saving in processing time.

In a situation where the above specified allocation is not possible due to, for example, the limited number of transputers, we have to use the statistical mean to allocate transputers to operations. Now, the total uniprocessor time for a given phase equals:

$$T = \sum_{i=1}^{K} t_i$$

This can then be averaged to give the mean operation time

$$\overline{T} = \frac{T}{K}$$

Thus, the number of transputers needed by operation K_i is :

$$\frac{t_i}{\overline{T}}$$

This ensures that all operations in that layer converges on the mean time $\overline{T}$.

The approach adopted in this paper is configuration independent, and any transputer can be allocated to any operation. It also assigns transputers to operations using a model which seeks to equalise the minimum execution time over all operations for any given phase. This ensures that the resources are efficiently utilised in any given phase and thus give rise to a high query processing rate.

6. Conclusion

We have described techniques for deriving parallel relational algebraic query execution plans from SQL queries. We have also developed algorithms to optimally allocate processors to an execution plan. A phase-oriented technique is a particularly efficient way of executing the parallel plans for high transaction rates. All the methods described have been combined into a coherent strategy for the efficient parallel processing of relational databases on transputers.

References

[1] G. V. Bultzingsloewen, "Optimizing SQL queries for Parallel Execution," *SIGMOD RECORD,* Vol. 18, No. 4, Dec. 1989.
[2] S. Ceri, and G. Gottlob "Translating SQL into Relational Algebra: Optimization, Semantics and Equivalence of SQL Queries," *IEEE Trans. S.E, April 1985, pp. 324-345.*
[3] C. Le Viet, "Translation and Compatibility of SQL and QUEL Queries," *Journ. Inf. Proc.* Vol. 8, No. 1, 1985, pp. 1-15.
[4] U. Dayal, "Of Nests and Trees: A Unified Approach to Processing Queries That Contain Nested Subqueries, Aggregates, and Quantifiers," *Proc. 13th Int. Conf. on VLDB,* Brighton, Sept. 1987, pp. 197-208.
[5] T. Baba, S. Bing Yao, and A. Hevner, "Design of a Functionally Distributed Multiprocessor Database Machine Using Data Flow Analysis," *IEEE Trans on Computers* vol. c-36, No.6,June. 1987, pp. 650-665.

THE APPLICATION OF TRANSPUTER BASED SCALAR SUPERCOMPUTERS IN FINANCIAL RISK MANAGEMENT

Philip Bond   Simuledge SA   May 1990.

INTRODUCTION

Financial modelling is a field in which transputer based scalar supercomputers can offer substantial price / performance benefits compared to vector processors of equivalent power. Two major areas of interest to researchers in Investment Banking are computer aided asset allocation and risk management. The Arbitrage Pricing Theory is an example of asset allocation techniques requiring the inversion of very large non-sparse covariance matrices. Term Structure Models (TSM 's) are a class of model used in the pricing and hedging of interest rate sensitive instruments such as bonds, futures and options. Such models have proved valuable in risk management. However, Investment Banks typically require that the models run in soft real time which is not possible using existing work station or mainframe processing rates. The present paper aims to demonstrate that such models are easy to parallelise and that transputer based machines offer the levels of performance required at a very low cost.

TERM STRUCTURE MODELS

A TSM aims to describe as succinctly as possible the observed structure of interest rates in the bond markets. It is possible to borrow a certain amount today with the promise that the sum of one pound will be repaid at a future date. This promise implies a certain rate of interest on the loan, which we call the spot rate for the period. Different periods have different interest rates associated with them, and we call the spot rate vs. maturity curve the Term Structure of Interest Rates.

The price of bonds, futures and options are equal to the present value of the future cash flows generated by the instruments. Hence prices are calculated by multiplying the future cash flows of a financial instrument by a discount factor which depends on interest rates.

In the case of default free Government Treasury Bonds (Gilts) the future cash flows are known with certainty, whilst the discount factors are unknown. In the case of options, the future cashflows are also unknown. Corporate bonds add ' signature risk ', which is simply the risk that the company will be unable to pay its debt. Mortgage backed securities have the risk of prepayment. The aim of the models is to incorporate the major risk factors and subsequently determine the expected present value of the future cashflows of a financial instrument. In the present paper we will consider a model with two factors which provides an adequate description of default free bonds and options. To build the model we write stochastic differential equations describing the evolution of empirically significant state variables. Application of the Ito calculus then gives us a Partial Differential Equation (PDE) from which we can deduce the price and hedge ratios of interest rate sensitive instruments.

It turns out that the main difference between various classes of instruments is the initial condition imposed on the PDE. This allows a single model to describe essentially all bonds, futures and options and leads to the idea of 'Global hedging' of securities in which the factor sensitivities of all securities in a portfolio are combined to give the total risk exposure. Analyses of the factor sensitivities are crucial for banks managing large bond and option positions.

At the practical level the use of multi factor models poses a number of problems. As the number of factors is increased so the theoretical power of the models improves. However, it is important that precise estimates of the model parameters are obtained, a task which becomes increasingly difficult as degrees of freedom increase. Explicit solutions have rarely been found for models with more than one factor so that numeric resolution is required, leading to increased run times.

Parameter estimates are obtained by minimising the difference between observed and theoretical prices using global minimisation techniques. Large numbers of parameters lead to excessively long estimation times As an example, a large US investment house recently required one week on a large IBM mainframe in order to estimate a three factor bond model. Mortgage backed securities require five or more factors and consequently need substantial computer resources. Fitting the two factor model considered here requires around twelve hours of run time on a work station using a finite difference scheme.

THE DIFFERENTIAL EQUATION FOR BOND PRICING

We present an example of a coupled set of stochastic differential equations used in financial modelling.

Let r be the short term interest rate , and l be the long term rate which serves essentially as a proxy for inflation, which is precluded in most practical models due to the non-observable nature of the variable.

Let $dr = K(l - r) dt + \beta r\, dz(1)$

Let $dl = \alpha l\, dt + \sigma l\, dz(2)$

and let the coupling be expressed by $dz(1) \cdot dz(2) = p \cdot dt$ where p is a correlation coefficient.

β and σ are volatility terms (the standard deviation of changes in interest rates).

K is a mean reversion rate.

α is the expected return on the long term interest rate.

Let Γ be a risk premium term.

Let $B(r, l, T)$ be the price of a zero coupon bond maturing at time T ie : a default free promise of one pound at time T.

The basic problem we will consider is to price the zero coupon bonds for every value of r, l and t.

Applying Ito's lemma, and Girsanov's theorem we can write the bond price as follows :-

$$\tfrac{1}{2} \beta^2 r^2 (d^2B/dr^2) + \tfrac{1}{2} \sigma^2 l^2 (d^2B/dl^2) +$$
$$\beta \sigma p r l\, d^2B/(dr\, dl) +$$
$$[\, K(l-r) - \Gamma \beta r\,]\, dB/dr +$$
$$[\, \sigma^2 + l - r\,]\, l\, dB/dl - rB + dB/dt = 0$$

Ito's lemma essentially enables us to Taylor expand stochastic differential equations and keep only the correct terms. Girsanov's theorem provides a convient method of adjusting asset returns for risk, and accounts for the Γ term which appears.
The initial condition (IC) is the payout of the financial instrument so that a zero coupon bond paying one pound at a future date will have an IC of 1.0 , whereas an option on interest rates with a strike S will have the boundary condition max(0 , r - S).

The first and second order differentials are known in the financial literature as the delta and gamma respectively, whilst the values $1/B\, dB/dr$ and $1/B\, dB/dl$ are known as the stochastic duration terms. These values characterise the relative sensitivities of financial instruments and are used in hedging portfolios. The deltas are also known as hedge ratios. A portfolio with a net delta of zero is known as a delta hedged portfolio. Generally, such a portfolio will have non-zero second order derivatives (Gamma) and is thus said to have residual gamma. In essence, a delta hedged portfolio is insensitive to changes in interest rates and is hence relatively free of interest rate risk. The portfolio remains sensitive to parameter changes (in the volatilities β or σ for example) so that simulation of the impact of time varying parameter values is important in risk management.

RISK MANAGEMENT USING TERM STRUCTURE MODELS

To use the model it is necessary to estimate the parameters. The simplest method is to discretise the stochastic differential equations and perform a linear regression using historic values of the observable state variables ie: the interest rates. In practise we use this method to obtain a first order estimate only. To increase the precision of the estimator we then use market prices of bonds and options so as to compute the expected rather than historic parameter values. This is achieved by minimising the difference between the theoretical prices obtained using the model, and market prices. The Generalised Method of Moments estimator provides a way to tighten the model fit by using multiple orthogonality conditions and provides excellent parameter fits as well as test statistics.

Having determined the parameters, the model can be used both to price and hedge financial instruments. By resolving the pricing PDE numerically we are able to determine the price, delta, gamma and stochastic duration of the instruments in a portfolio and hence the number of bonds and options that must be bought and sold in order to adjust portfolio interest rate risk exposure.

The PDE can be resolved in a number of ways. The Alternating Direction Implicit (ADI) Finite Difference schema of Mitchell and McKee is an efficient method for parabolic differential equations in two dimensions with mixed derivatives. For path-dependent pricing problems it is necessary to recast the problem as a path integral and use Monte Carlo methods to solve the pricing problem as an expectation. The necessary theorem is due to Feynman and Kac. The advantage of such methods is their simplicity. Furthermore, they lend themselves to efficient parallel implementation on transputer networks using a straightforward farming technique. The disadvantage of Monte Carlo techniques is that they give poor estimates of the delta and gamma, and are hence more useful for pricing than hedging.

It is essential in practise that model parameterisation is fast and that the models themselves can be run in soft real time. Whilst the finite difference scheme can be solved using either vector or parallel scalar machines, the Monte Carlo methods are a natural candidate for parallel implementation at low cost. Indeed, Monte Carlo simulations are the method which, par excellence, demonstrate the advantages of parallel scalar supercomputers as the computation speed is essentially linear in the number of processors, and the memory requirements are minimal.

THE USE OF TRANSPUTERS IN FINANCE

Transputers can be used to solve the kind of financial modelling problem above very easily. The range of processor power required for soft real time pricing with sufficiently high resolution for practical purposes is around 100 M Flops. This can achieved using a 64 transputer T Node with 4 M Bytes dynamic RAM per processor to store the look up tables for the difference scheme.

Monte Carlo methods run extremely well on 250 K Byte static RAM machines. Such machines offer a cost effective alternative to the current offerings of vector supercomputer vendors in the financial marketplace which include real time modelling of bond and option prices as well as simulation facilities for volatility effects.

THE MONTE CARLO APPROACH TO ASSET VALUATION.

Details of the monte carlo scheme follow :
Let $B(r, l, t)$ be the price of a zero coupon bond.
(1)
Taylor expand the differential of the price dB :

$$dB = (dB/dt) \, dt + (dB/dr) \, dr + (dB/dl) \, dl$$
$$+ \tfrac{1}{2} (d^2B/dr^2) \, dr^2 + \tfrac{1}{2} (d^2B/dl^2) \, dl^2$$
$$+ (d^2B/drdl) \, drdl \, .$$

(2)

For the risk-adjusted process the expected bond price change is the riskless rate times the asset value ie: $r.B.dt$

We want to compute the stochastic differencial equations needed for the Monte Carlo simulation. These are the risk adjusted versions of the original stochastic equations

$$dr = K(l - r) \, dt + \beta \, r \, dz(1)$$
$$dl = \alpha \, l \, dt + \sigma \, l \, dz(2)$$

which are not however the appropriate equations for monte carlo simulation as they fail to correctly adjust for relative asset risk. We can directly obtain the correct form of the equations by applying the rather technical theorem of Girsanov, but a simpler but equivalent method is to state that under a Girsanov transform all assets have the same expected return, which is the riskless rate, and demonstrate the result by construction. This leads to the

Theorem :

The risk-adjusted processes are given by :-

$$dr = [\ K(1-r) - \Gamma \beta r\ ]\ dt + \beta r\ dz(1)$$
$$dl = [\ \sigma^2/l^2 + l^2 - rl\ ]\ dt\quad + \sigma l\ dz(2)$$

Demonstration :

(a) Compute dB using the risk adjusted process.

$$\begin{aligned}dB = &\ (dB/dt)\ dt + (dB/dr)\ [\ K(1-r) - \Gamma \beta r\ ]\ dt \\ &+ (dB/dr)\ \beta r dz(1) + (dB/dl)\ [\ \sigma^2/l^2 + l^2 - rl\ ]\ dt \\ &+ (dB/dl)\ \sigma l dz(2) \\ &+ \tfrac{1}{2}(d^2B/dl^2)\ \sigma^2 l^2 dt + \tfrac{1}{2}(d^2B/dr^2)\ \beta^2 r^2\ dt \\ &+ \tfrac{1}{2}(d^2B/drdl)\ \sigma\beta prl\end{aligned}$$

We have applied Ito's lemma which simply states that terms in dt^2 or $dz.dt$ are ignored in stochastic calculus, whilst $dz^2 = dt$.

(b) Compute E[dB], the expectation of the risk adjusted bond prices :

$$\begin{aligned}dB = &\ (dB/dt)\ dt + (dB/dr)\ [\ K(1-r) - \Gamma \beta r\ ]\ dt \\ &\ (dB/dl)\ [\ \sigma^2/l^2 + l^2 - rl\ ]\ dt \\ &+ \tfrac{1}{2}(d^2B/dl^2)\ \sigma^2 l^2 dt + \tfrac{1}{2}(d^2B/dr^2)\ \beta^2 r^2\ dt \\ &+ \tfrac{1}{2}(d^2B/drdl)\ \sigma\beta prl\end{aligned}$$

We have used the fact that E[dz] = 0, ie : The brownian motion is a martingale.

(c) Set the expected return equal to the riskless rate :

dB = r.B.dt , giving

$$\begin{aligned}&+ \tfrac{1}{2}\sigma^2 l^2\ (d^2B/dl^2)\ + \tfrac{1}{2}\beta^2 r^2\ (d^2B/dr^2) \\ &+ \tfrac{1}{2}\sigma\beta prl\ (d^2B/drdl) \\ &+ [\ K(1-r) - \Gamma.\beta.r\ ]\ (dB/dr) \\ &+ [\ \sigma^2/l^2 + l^2 - rl\ ]\ (dB/dl)\ - rB + dB/dt = 0\end{aligned}$$

which is recognisably the PDE we announced initially. Hence, we need to simulate the following processes :

$$dr = [\ K(1-r) - \Gamma \beta r\ ]\ dt + \beta r\ dz(1)$$
$$dl = [\ \sigma^2/l^2 + l^2 - rl\ ]\ dt\quad + \sigma l\ dz(2)$$

There are a number of schemes for reducing simulation error. The Milshtein discretisation provides minimal errors when we want to compute the expectation of a function of a stochastic process. This schema can be succinctly presented as follows.

Let P(t) be a stochastic process given by :-

$$dP = b(P)\ dt + \sigma(P)\ dz(t)$$
$$P(0) = Po.$$

Let tk be a series of 1..N discrete steps.
Let h be a small time step such that Nh = T, the total time.
Let G() be a normalised gaussian random variable.
Then

$$P(t_{k+1}) = P(t_k) + \{b - \tfrac{1}{2}\sigma \, d\sigma/dP\}\, h + \sigma\sqrt{h}\, G() + \tfrac{1}{2}\{\sigma \, d\sigma/dP\}\, h\, G()^2 + \qquad 3/2$$
$$[\tfrac{1}{2} b \, d\sigma/dP + \tfrac{1}{2}\sigma \, db/dP + \tfrac{1}{2}\sigma \, d\sigma/dt + \tfrac{1}{4}\sigma^2 d^2\sigma/dP^2]\, h +$$
$$[\tfrac{1}{2} b \, db/dP + \tfrac{1}{2} db/dt + \tfrac{1}{4}\sigma^2 d^2b/dx^2]\, h^2$$

By performing the appropriate calculus we obtain the Milshtein scheme for the r(t) and l(t) processes.

At this stage we know the PDE for pricing the bonds, we know the risk adjusted diffusion processes which correspond to the PDE and we have a suitable discretisation scheme. We now need to know how to solve the pricing problem using monte carlo. There are at least two methods available. One would be to use a grid in a similar way to a finite difference approach and let particles wander 'at random' inside the grid, with the transition probabilities given by the usual difference approximation. Another approach, which we will consider here, directly simulates the paths of the stochastic processes dr and dl, using the Milshtein scheme above. However, our main interest is the pricing of bonds so we need to relate the interest rate paths to bond prices. To do this we make use of a theorem due to Feynman and Kac which was originally used in perturbative quantum field theory, and enables us to write the solution of a PDE (in our case, the bond pricing equation) as a functional integral, or expectation of a path integral :

THE FEYNMAN-KAC THEOREM

1) Define the infinitesimal generator of a markov family X_t as

$$\lim (1/t)\, E[\, f(X_t) - f(x)\,] = (Æf)(x)$$

for all $x \in R$, and for suitable test functions $f \in C^2$.

E[] is an expectation operator.

The operator Æ is given by :

$$(Æf)(x) = \tfrac{1}{2} \sum_{i=1}^{d} \sum_{k=1}^{d} a[i,k](x)\, d^2 f(x)/dx(i)dx(k) + \sum_{i=1}^{d} b[i](x)\, df/dx(i)$$

a = a[i,k] is known as the diffusion matrix, whilst b = b[i] is the drift vector of the differential operator.

2) **Theorem (Feynman, Kac)**

Suppose that $P(t,x) : [\ 0,T\ ] \times R^n \rightarrow R^n$ is $C(1,2)$ and satisfies the Cauchy problem :

$- dP/dt + k.P = Æ(P) + g\ ;\ P(T,x) = f(x)$

P is said to be the solution to the Cauchy problem for the backward heat equation with potential k and lagrangian g. Then $P(t,x)$ admits the stochastic representation :

$$P(t,x) = E[\ f(Xt)\ \exp\{\ -\int_t^T k(\theta,X(\theta))\ d\theta\ \}$$
$$+ \int_t^T g(s,Xs)\ \exp\{\ -\int_t^s k(\theta,X(\theta))\ d\theta\ \}\ ds\ ]$$

Furthermore, the solution is unique. This is generally necessary as a feature in finance, as the same asset should have only one price at any given time in an efficient market.

3) We can see that in the present case the Cauchy problem is given by the bond pricing PDE. Hence bond prices $B(r,1,t)$ have a stochastic reprentation with unique solution. The Lagrangian of the problem is zero, so that the representation simplifies to :

$$B(r,1,t) = E[\ \exp\{\ -\int_0^T r(s)\ ds\ \}\ ]$$

where the expectation is with respect to the risk adjusted (martingale) probability measure.

4) We can thus price a bond by computing the expectation of the path integral given above. The path integral is computed by simulation, and the expectation by averaging over large numbers of paths. The simulated path of the interest rate r is computed using the Milshtein approximation. The code required to generate the individual paths is small enough to fit on the on-chip static RAM of a T800 transputer, so that very large numbers of paths can be generated fast. The farming paradigm provides a simple means to parallelise the work ; each processor computes seperate paths, yielding approximately linear performance even with very large numbers of processors. In this way we can

achieve very high performance for multi-factor models. The monte carlo method is approximately linear in computation time vs. state variables, unlike finite difference schemes, so that large state spaces can be modelled with little effect on performance, opening the way to more realistic models using more factors, such as stochastic volatility terms. The simulated moments estimator of Bossaerts and Hillion can be used to compute the model parameters.

A similar approach can be for the pricing of interest rate option contracts such as caps and floors.

In order to test the performance of transputer based parallel machines for financial modelling both the finite difference and monte carlo schemes were programmed in the C programming language and run on a number of different machines at the TTS supercomputer center. The comparison machine was a 25 MHz 80386 based PC using an 80387 numeric co-processor and the efficient MetaWare HighC compiler, which produces native 32 bit 386/387 code running in the processor protected memory mode.

References :

Simulation Estimators of Optimal Early Exercise : Peter Bossaerts
                                                 Carnegie Mellon.

Brownian motion and stochastic calculus : Karatsas and Shreve,
                                          Springer Verlag.

VLSI Design Stations Using Transputers

Stephen Christian
INMOS Limited
1000 Aztec West
Almondsbury
Bristol
Avon BS12 4SQ

The development of a Transputer based workstation to support the INMOS design community is discussed. The emphasis is on the practical application of multiple CPU technology to the solution of a specific problem and the advantages that Transputers bring to such a system development. The more general use of Transputer arrays for the acceleration of CAD algorithms is facilitated by the use of facilities within this workstation.

1. INTRODUCTION

This paper presents the approach taken, within INMOS, to development of a new workstation to support the needs of its VLSI design community. It describes, in effect, a bootstrapping of technology---using the components designed by one generation of the CAD system to facilitate the implementation of the next. The new workstation is now being used for the design of the next generation of components, including advanced Transputers. To some extent the development started off as an advertisement for the versatility and coherence of the system model embodied by the Transputer and related INMOS products, but it is also a fully practical approach to the provision of sophisticated design tools to more than one hundred engineers, as well as a versatile platform for our future tool development. It is felt that a semi-dedicated workstation design can more fully exploit the concurrency apparent in the support of real applications and achieve significant performance and offer significant cost advantages over more general purpose designs.

2. THE REQUIREMENT

The last few years has seen a significant increase in the number and quality of tools for VLSI design work available in the marketplace. This is especially true for tools that incorporate the concept of an integrated design database. Quite a few years ago now, INMOS recognised the need for a coherent, cooperating set of design tools and, because no suitable vendor/workstation combination existed at that time, set about developing a set of such tools that incorporated, and specialised in, support of the design methodologies employed by its engineers. The result of this intensive development is a large legacy of source code written in the BCPL language (a forerunner of C) that represents a significant investment, and a worthwhile refinement of the design and production process, which cannot be lightly discarded. The original code was hosted on a 68000 based system supported by some dedicated graphics hardware. The requirements of any new development included the need to be able to re-host the existing code while providing significantly enhanced performance, better workstation networking and higher speed, higher resolution graphics operation. There was also a secondary need to converge CAD developments with the software products supplied by INMOS so that future code development could exploit newer and better recognised languages and interfaces. Since a suitable BCPL compiler existed for the Transputer, it was felt that an assembly of Transputer based products could be employed to fulfil the immediate requirement and provide a convenient platform for subsequent significant parallel algorithmic developments.

3. DESIGN APPROACH

The arrangement of the workstation is a very familiar one---separate alphanumeric and graphic terminals, a three button mouse and alphanumeric keyboard. The majority of workstations are diskless nodes on a network, where the filing system is provided by conventional Microvax or Sun machines. The database of design information on these commercial platforms is then potentially shareable between INMOS tools and those tools which are externally developed or purchased. The workstations are not just terminals for the host operating system environment, but themselves contain significant software support and computational power for interactive simulation and layout---our design system is highly interactive in nature and this requires fast response at all levels of operation. Also included was the ability to host standard INMOS program development tools since much high level modelling and analysis is done in the C and Occam environments. Although the application code itself does not currently exploit multiple CPUs, the system support for these applications can very readily be provided in a networked fashion by providing specialised hardware and software components to support each function. Above all the environment was designed to act as a vehicle into which could be added other modular functions at a very low incremental cost, the most important of these being the ability to host parallelised CAD algorithms----in effect adding arbitrary amounts of application CPU power to each desk.

A fundamental decision was made at an early stage not to "host" each workstation Transputer network on a standard machine such as a PC, but to make a largely stand-alone approach possible and so create a Transputer only box. This may seem to some to have been a somewhat masochistic approach given the amount of "free" support that is obtained when working in conjunction with a standard platform, but it is not technically difficult in concept and certainly worthy of the effort .

To satisfy the design criteria, and to minimise the design time required for the system as a whole, a modular approach was adopted. This, as it turned out, amounted to nothing more than a decision to utilise INMOS development boards (TRAMs) in their standard forms as far as possible and supplement them with specially designed components, where required, designed in a compatible way. The INMOS TRAM architecture is described more fully in standard INMOS publications (technical notes referenced below), but is well suited for constructing arbitrary networks of processors, especially when there is a control hierarchy embedded within the configuration.

The Transputer itself is, of course, still one of the worlds fastest, most highly integrated processor chips. What was envisaged here was to initially use one or more Transputers dedicated to the running of applications alone and back them up with the services of several more dedicated to particular kinds of system support. The partitions of machine functionality were drawn on fairly conventional boundaries:

-Dedicated graphics service also using an INMOS colour video controller component
-Transputer link based communications network
-Dedicated peripheral handling modules

with the overall structure of the workstation being drawn up as shown in Figure 1. It may seem extravagant to use so many modules within a single workstation but, since each module is simple in design (the Transputer requires very little in the way of glue logic chips) the cost of such an approach is not exorbitant. We can construct a full configuration machine, as shown, with 8MB of application dedicated memory for $12000. In addition, the full computational power of the application Transputers can be effectively dedicated to the application code itself. This is a significant consideration where intensive networking and interface activities would otherwise be competing for CPU cycles.

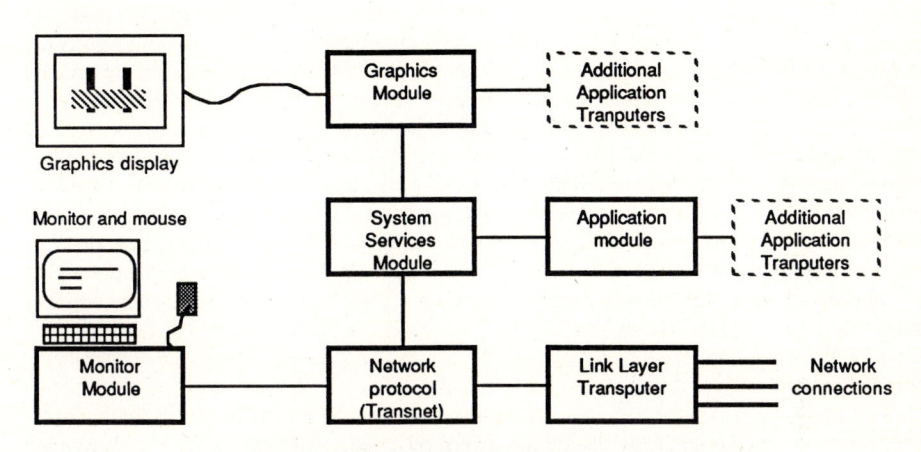

Figure 1 Workstation modules and interconnect

4. HARDWARE AND SOFTWARE COMPONENTS

4.1 System bootstrap

The problems of initialising a network based machine present technical difficulties quite unlike those of any single CPU design. In particular, there is a tightrope to be walked between commiting too much of the system level inter-processor protocols into relatively difficult to maintain EPROM form, and the alternative of designing and debugging the network startup when there is a process of setting up, and clearing down, various different levels of communication protocol. A secondary problem is that of the much larger core of hardware components that must be functioning correctly (and connected correctly) for startup to succeed. There is an effort made to hide these complexities from the ordinary user by making as much of the process as possible occur in an automatic sequence.

An EPROM based low level initialisation and bootstrap system forms the first level of this system, and it runs entirely on a monitor (or root) Transputer board, nominally in control of the rest of the workstation components and also able to communicate with the user through an attached terminal port. Within the EPROM is also a core network communication module, which can be propagated across the other transputer modules, and sufficient network and/or file system support code to be able to access files containing the final system and a description of how this is placed within the workstation modules. During the lifetime of the application code, the hardware facilities on the monitor board are made available to the rest of the system at a peer level, and the initialisation code only regains control in the event of an error condition being detected.

The monitor Transputer code also supports a network form of diagnostic test facility, designed to give confidence in the connectivity and operation of the rest of the modules. Variations in hardware configurations are dealt with by storing description parameters within an area of battery-backed RAM.

4.2 Transnet communications

Transputer links form a serial communication system operating at a basic rate of 10 or 20 Mbits/sec. on a point to point basis. Using differential RS422 drivers the connection of links at distances of up to 30m become quite possible, and it was felt that this represented a means of creating a viable local area network with an intrinsically high bandwidth. By imposing a software packet based protocol over the basic link connections, it has been possible to create an ISO standard link layer service, and then to base a Network service on that in turn. The application support functions make use of this to implement a distributed file system. Files systems accessed using this function are typically resident on only one node (the host) of the network, but multiple file systems are supported and networks can be interconnected to provide more or less transparent access to several machines. The Network service, named Transnet, supports dynamic re-routing of messages and various configurations of network based around a ring with cross connections. A Sun or Vax machine becomes part of the network by installing a Transputer module and running on that module network service software that transfers all addressed requests to host resident resources.

4.3 Graphics support

The high resolution display in the workstation is driven by a dedicated Transputer module running a layout oriented graphics service. The module also features an INMOS G300 Colour Video Controller device and so is an unusually compact and versatile design. The window and graphics management software contains many algorithms to optimise the display of the colour plane oriented service and uses to good effect the specialised instructions of the T800 device. A mouse input is provided, albeit via a remote RS232 port, but this is easily sufficient for the rapid response desired. The keyboard input is associated with the alphanumeric terminal port.

5. SYSTEM SOFTWARE

5.1 Local service support

All modules of system software and system services can communicate with one another within the workstation network using a highly optimised version of Remote Procedure Calls. The services are accessed using a set of Run Time Library calls that translate language specific requests into a defined common protocol. In this way we have provided the link between the existing BCPL code and the newer system code, which has been written in Occam. Requests and responses are routed in a predetermined optimal way between servers and requestors such that the scope of the network can easily be increased without altering the established configuration. Since the service actions can be offered in syncronous or asyncronous form, almost complete concurrency can be achieved in, for instance, drawing operations, between the requestor operation and the service of CPU intensive request. Services offered within the support environment (and extended to the application) include RS232 read and write (two ports are spare and available for printers etc), IEEE 488 for control of plotters and instrumentation, screen graphics, clock, non-volatile RAM, file operations and a multi-windowed textmap There is also a generalised executive service for the startup and control of multiple applications. The protocol used for (assumed reliable) communication within the tightly coupled workstation environment is simply extended over the longer haul communications medium by the addition of a fault tolerant software layer. This provides an efficient and elegant symmetry between the two levels of service communication, and a possible extension of application operation between workstations. An indication of some performance figures is given in Table 1.

Table 1. Communications performance

	Message Latency	Overall circuit bandwidth
Within workstation	0.5 mS	500 kB/s
Transnet communication	30 mS	80 kB/s

5.2 Unreliable applications

The development of the techniques of subdivision of the workstation environment into its modular components gives us, by way of a bonus, a completely reliable way of trapping application errors and recovering from them without damage to the system support structure. This is achieved as a by product of the dedication of a Transputer module or modules to the exclusive use of the application. This exclusivity, of course, gives total memory protection in the hardware sense. It must, however, be accompanied by some form of software support for correctly terminating all the applications outstanding activities at the point at which any error occurred. By introducing a fault tolerant software layer in-between the request made by the application and the services that are requested, all state changing activity can be reliably tracked and, when an abnormal termination takes place, the protection mechanism can be invoked to close down the service operations in a controlled manner. Multiple applications, in either BCPL or Occam, can be run within the same workstation on multiple Transputer subsystems if performance and security are paramount.

5.3 Command Line interpreter

The user interaction with the workstation is via a simple CLI, offering a range of utility commands for file manipulation, data editing and workstation control. A logical name translation service is extensively used to provide both file abbreviations and command similes. Both BCPL and Occam applications originally written for CAD use can be invoked from this CLI. It is also possible to use standard INMOS development tools and applications (in C for instance) via a specially ported version of the iserver task.

6. CAD APPLICATIONS

Two modes of parallism can potentially be employed by the applications---the local networks of closely coupled processors, and the use of multiple workstations. The second is at present the more frequently employed within INMOS (greatly accelerating the fracture process, for example) as algorithms for supporting highly concurrent CAD activities are still very much under development. One multiple Transputer accelerated simulator was of course described by Dyson(1987), and a port of SPICE was described in an INMOS technical note. Further developments will be greatly assisted by the availability of a platform on which to easily integrate the sequential and parallel components of the design cycle as a whole.

7. PLANS FOR THE FUTURE

The future work planned on this project involves a re-assessing of the systems view of the CAD activities and fully realising the the ability to use commercial standard tools in close conjunction with, even on the same screen as, those from in-house developments. The integration of some standard software environments to support this will be a priority. To reduce the distance between INMOS data formats and those of commercial packages, we are considering the integration of a standard CAD database, offering access to its contents by means of another networked service. Increasing amounts of work are also being scheduled for parallel DRC implementations, routing packages, timing analysers and more versatile simulators.

REFERENCES

INMOS Limited, "Module and Motherboard architecture", *Technical note 49*
INMOS Limited, "Porting SPICE to the T800 Transputer", *Technical note 52*
INMOS Limited, "A high resolution graphics system using the G300", *Technical note 62*
Dyson, C and Gray,A., "Mixed Mode Simulation on Transputers", *Hardware Accelerators*, Adam Hilger 1988.

A VLSI Routing System on Configurable Multi-transputer Hardware

V.K. Sagar and R.E. Massara
CAD Research, Electronic Systems Engineering, University of Essex
Colchester CO4 3SQ, UK.
Tel: (0206) 872902, Fax: (0206) 873598, email: sagar/rob@essex.uk.ac

Abstract. This contribution describes a novel parallel routing system based on configurable multi-transputer hardware. It concentrates on the evaluation of the performance of various multi-transputer topologies for use in the parallel routing system for VLSI design. The routing system is aimed at general cell VLSI circuits such as those designed using full-custom or standard cell approaches although it can be adopted for other approaches as well. The suite has been developed around the processing and communicating abilities of the transputer. Another feature of the multi-transputer hardware on which the parallel routing system is based is to do with reconfigurability of the hardware. For maximum speedup it is important to be able to configure the hardware into different topologies. This paper presents performance evaluation of several multi-transputer topologies for use in SPHIR.

1. Introduction

This contribution describes a novel parallel routing system based on configurable multi-transputer hardware. It concentrates on the evaluation of the performance of various multi-transputer topologies for use in the parallel routing system for VLSI design. The parallel routing system, known as SPHIR is aimed at general cell VLSI circuits such as those designed using full-custom or standard cell approaches although it can be adopted for other approaches as well. The SPHIR suite has been developed around the processing and communicating abilities of the transputer. Another feature of the multi-transputer hardware on which SPHIR is based is to do with reconfigurability of the hardware. For maximum speedup it is important to be able to configure the hardware into different topologies. This paper aims to evaluate performance of several multi-transputer topologies for use in SPHIR using Transim.

Transim is a tool developed by the Polytechnic of Central London to simulate the behaviour of an application program running on a network of transputers. Transim will simulate a single transputer or a complex network of transputers. Parallel execution, alternation, channel communication, timeslicing, priorities, interrupts, concurrent operation of transputer links, effects of external memory and so on are taken into account [1]. The main advantage of using Transim in this research was that it allowed for easy experimentation with communication protocols and of different transputer topologies for use in the parallel routing system.

With the coming of age of CAD workstations based on parallel hardware and the increasing need to accelerate CAD tools whilst maintaining the integrity of current automatic CAD systems for VLSI design, there is a demand to exploit parallelism on general-purpose parallel hardware rather than build expensive dedicated hardware to achieve speedup. There is a need to not only accelerate the routing phase of the VLSI design cycle in an integrated environment but other phases as well. Hence it was recognised that there was a need for a system based on a general-purpose architecture which could be configured to speed up other phases of the VLSI design cycle. It was with this in mind that SPHIR was proposed for VLSI design on a CAD workstation based on parallel hardware.

Previously, research carried out in trying to speed up routing has been directed towards single phase search routers, mostly applicable to PCB routing. This has often resulted in expensive dedicated pieces of hardware to achieve speedup. The routing process in VLSI design is different from routing in PCB designs in that it is usually broken up into two phases: global routing and detailed routing. In keeping with this, the newly proposed SPHIR suite performs routing in two stages. The optimum technique to exploit parallelism in each stage is different.

2. Parallel Programming Techniques for VLSI Routing

There exist several parallel programming paradigms for multi-transputer systems: algorithmic parallelism, geometric parallelism and task farming. For optimal speedup, geometric parallelism is used in global routing [2] and task farming [3] is used for detailed routing.

Parallel architectures are application sensitive and it is equally true that applications are architecture sensitive. An architecture well suited for one application, may be less suited for others. So the multi-transputer hardware is reconfigured through software to match each of the routing stages. To understand the use of different multi-transputer architectures and the use of different parallel programming paradigms in each of the stages it is important to know about the routing and layout process in VLSI design.

3. The Layout Process in VLSI Design

The layout process takes up a very large part of the time required to design a circuit, and involves placement [4] and routing. The starting point for a layout is thus a set of functional modules represented by rectangular blocks which may be hierarchically decomposed into sub-blocks. Their external connections (pins) are at fixed positions around the peripheries of the blocks. Routing is performed in the area of the layout not occupied by the blocks. The routing area is divided into rectangular areas referred to as channels. The global routing phase determines the nets that are to pass through each channel. The detailed or fine routing, which involves the exact positioning of the tracks within each channel, is done channel by channel. Due to the fact that any particular channel can feed into another channel, there is usually a preferred order in which channels are routed. This preferred order can best be expressed by a 'channel routing order graph' [5]. When all the channels have been routed the layout is complete. However, there are many systems where placement and routing are iterative processes. Several iterations are often required before the final design is completed.

4. SPHIR Suite

Figure 1 shows that the System for Parallel Hierarchical Routing, SPHIR, comprises three modules: PGRM [2], CHATOBOX [6] and PDRM which process the placed blocks in that order.

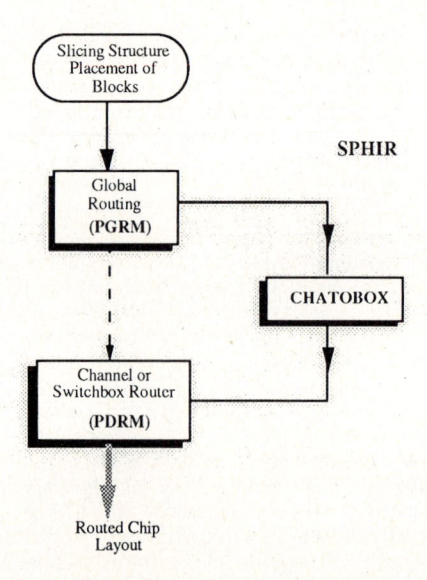

Figure 1 - SPHIR

The task of *PGRM*, the **P**arallel **G**lobal **R**outing **M**odule is to assign nets to channels, after which detailed routing (*PDRM*) is required to assign the nets to track positions within the channel. In an automatic routing system for full custom or standard cell designs, a routing channel order graph is constructed so that the channels which feed into other channels are routed first. The channels are then routed in sequence following the order of the graph. The use of the channel order graph is important in order to obtain a good routing result [5]. However, to exploit parallelism in the detailed routing phase, i.e. to route the channels in parallel, the detailed routing phase needs to be freed of the channel routing order. The routing areas can then be regarded as totally independent and can then be routed in parallel on separate processors. The method depends for its success on the ability of CHATOBOX to provide this conversion successfully. In this context, success is interpreted as a functional conversion without an increase in silicon area. Research has been carried out on how to make the channels independent without sacrificing much of the quality of the routing result in terms of area. The CHATOBOX algorithm sensibly fixes the pins at the ends of the channel taking into account the adjacent channels to achieve this.

The parallel routing model is presented with detailed placement information (a slicing structure) which is passed on to the global routing process. In the parallel software model, each of the blocks are implemented as separate modules. The system is interfaced to the British Telecom automatic floorplanner (*AFP*) [4]. The AFP generates hierarchical floorplans which have associated slicing structures. The hierarchical floorplan, which has its pins fixed around its periphery as well as around the blocks at lower levels of hierarchy, is than presented to PGRM.

4.1. Parallel Processing for SPHIR

The SPHIR suite is implemented in 'Parallel C' instead of Occam for a number of reasons. Parallel C supported dynamic data structures and recursion which was needed for implementation of SPHIR. The hardware on which SPHIR has been implemented is a transputer card (TSBO4-2) linked to a multi-transputer (TSMB-16) rack system. The logical structure of the hardware is as shown in Figure 2. The Inter-Node Switches enable the transputers to be configured into different topologies through software.

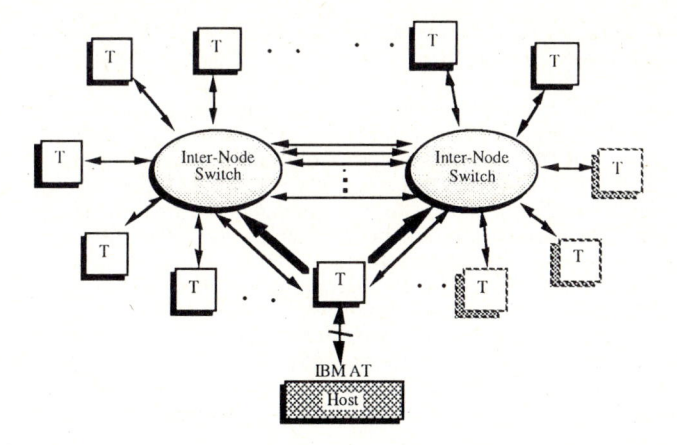

Figure 2 - Re-configurable hardware for SPHIR

As already mentioned the techniques for exploiting parallelism in each of the routing stages are different. Parallel processing of the global routing problem is achieved by exploiting the structural hierarchy of the layout. It was natural to map the hierarchy to a tree type architecture which had processors at each node of a tree. The detailed routing stage requires that the inter-dependent routing areas be made independent of the channel routing order graph before task-farming parallelism can be exploited. For PDRM, task farming was possible using several different topologies (architectures). The topologies of interest were a tertiary tree and linear chain. It was found that the linear chain was not only more convenient to use but it also performed marginally better than the tertiary tree topology. Due to saturation of communication links, there was a maximum throughput that could be obtained from the linear chain or tertiary tree for detailed routing. The bandwidth of the communication links prevented any further increase in performance.

5. Use of Transim in Evaluating SPHIR

As parallel applications are architecture sensitive, it was important to be able to choose an optimal topology (architecture) for the different parts of SPHIR. Reasons for using certain topologies in SPHIR are discussed in the paper. For example why a tree topology was chosen instead of a linear chain for PGRM and why a linear chain was chosen instead of a tree or array for PDRM. The determination of suitable topologies for use in SPHIR was carried out using Transim simulations.

The Research evaluated the parallel programming paradigms and topologies used in each of the routing stages. This was carried out with the use of Transim and a limited amount of transputer hardware. Initially, the use of Transim was useful, in that it allowed for experimentation with communication protocols and transputer topologies with ease. In later stages of the research, Transim proved useful in evaluating the multi-transputer topologies and techniques used in SPHIR. The simulation models set up using Transim were very realistic and the results obtained from Transim corresponded with the those from the actual system using real transputer hardware. In Transim, a parallel application is described using pseudo-occam code and map statements to specify the mapping between processes and processors. It is possible to simulate long pieces of sequential code by way of a SERV(cpu cycle) statements.

A results file produced by Transim describing the utilisation of each processor and link in the hardware enables measurements such as speedup and throughput to be made to evaluate the SPHIR suite. These figures are often used and quoted by engineers and designers of parallel processing systems. Speedup is the most commonly used figure and is self-explanatory. Throughput, which is the rate that results may be produced by a system, is defined more exactly for multi-transputer systems by Pritchard [7]. This figure can be defined as an aiming point at the start of any multi-transputer design and so is the most useful piece of information from an engineering point of view as it is often the case that one wants to achieve a certain rate of results production.

5.1. Evaluation of PGRM

The simulation runs were done with a view to obtaining more information on the performance of PGRM than was available from real multi-transputer hardware. Before simulation of PGRM could be carried out, the average time required to perform global routing on a standard size floorplan (of one level of hierarchy) on a single transputer had to be measured and the average number of bytes required to transfer actual floorplan data to a transputer in the tree had to be estimated. Using Transim it was possible to measure the time to distribute the global routing problem, the time do the computation, and the time to return the results to the host for varying amounts of transputer hardware (see Figure 3). In the simulation model the time taken to load each of the different size binary trees was approximately equal. This is probably attributable to the fact that floorplan data was sent to each of the processes as single byte data and no matter what the size of the tree of processors, the driver processor would have had to perform the same number of setups for communication. In this case, T_{setup} would have been greater than T_{com} ($T_{setup} = 4.1\mu s$ and $T_{com} = 1.125\mu s$) and the cpu would have had to perform more setups to transfer a single sub-floorplan.

In addition to total processing time (speedup), throughput was measured for routing a floorplan on different sizes of processor tree. The throughput was observed to increase as the number of processors in the tree were increased from 1 to 7. This is shown in Figure 4.

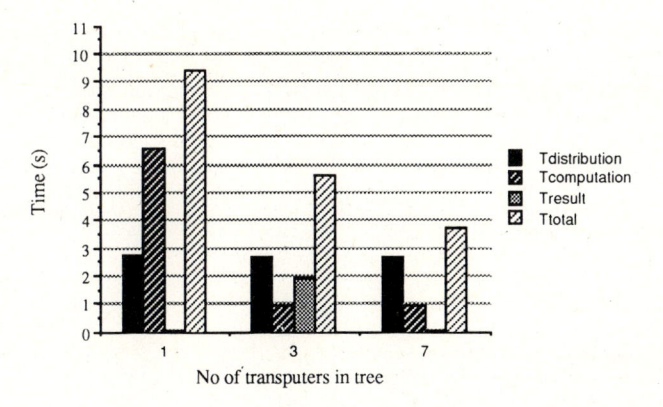

Figure 3 - Routing a floorplan DTMN1.1 on binary trees of different sizes

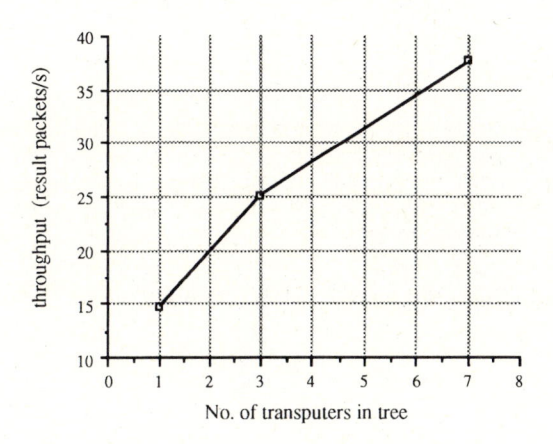

Figure 4 - Throughput in routing a floorplan on different size trees

5.2. *Evaluation of Topologies for PDRM*

Linear chain and tertiary tree topologies were set up using Transim. Timing measurements of various switchbox routing problems were carried out on transputer hardware and fed into the Transim simulation. The Transim simulations modelled the actual setup in hardware by incorporating the same protocols for inter-processor communication. Instances of the switchbox routing algorithm solving routing problem were modelled by SERV statements. Timing measurements were taken for typical-size switchbox routing problems being solved on a transputer using the internal timers of the transputer. These measurements were averaged and used in the SERV statements to simulate the execution of the switchbox router.

The simulations of PDRM had two purposes: firstly the intention was to compare the performance two proposed architectures for PDRM (linear chain and tree); secondly, it was intended to evaluate the performance of PDRM. The simulation results presented were obtained through Transim and concentrate on performance measures such as throughput and speedup (execution time).

Figure 5 shows how the throughput of a linear chain farm and tertiary tree farm increase for PDRM as the number of transputers increase. The critical number of processors (N_c) for a tree is reached at 21 and for a linear chain at 13. This is the point at which the communication links will saturate and data flow through them cannot be increased any further. For a smaller number of processors the tertiary tree performs marginally better than the linear chain but as the farm size increases for both, the throughput of the tertiary tree increases less rapidly than that of the linear chain and becomes less than the linear chain. The maximum throughput is reached at a farm size of 13 processors; this corresponds to a tree depth of 3.

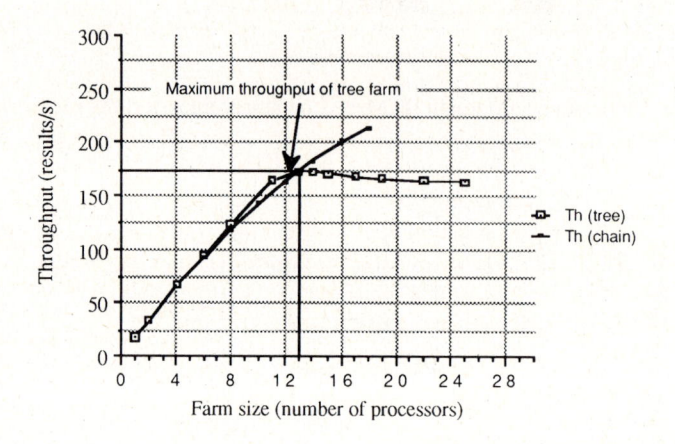

Figure 5 - Throughput of tertiary tree and linear chain as farms for PDRM

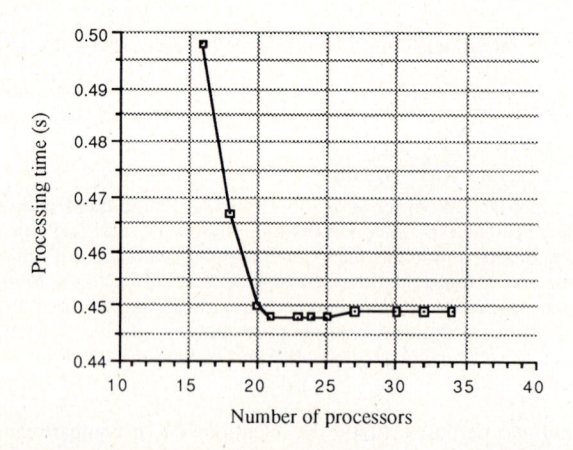

Figure 6 - Decrease in processing time with increasing farm size (linear chain)

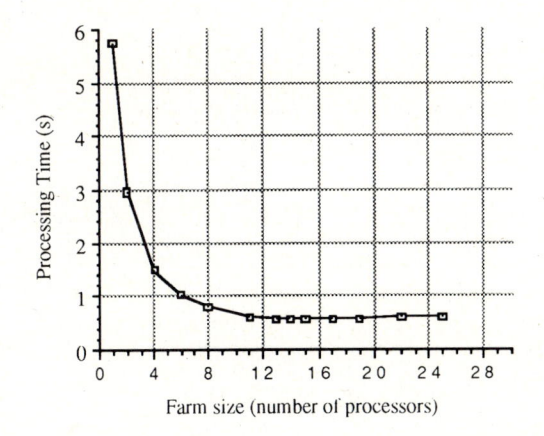

Figure 7 - Decrease in processing time with increasing farm size (tertiary tree)

Figures 6 and 7 show the decrease in processing time for a linear chain and tertiary tree structure as the number of of processors is increased. These results for processing time are depicted as speedup figures in Figures 8 and 9. Figures 8 and 9 show how the speedup increases as the number of processors increase. The maximum speedup possible is achieved with 21 processors in a linear chain and 13 processors in a tertiary tree; any further processors added to the farm will not increase the speedup factor any further. Beyond a size of 25 processors the speedup factor of the linear chain actually begins to fall. A similar observation can be made for the tertiary tree. Speedup increases until the the links become saturated and as a result any more processors added to the chain or tertiary tree will not be able to receive the data packets or return result packets. It must be noticed that the maximum speedup possible, is greater for a linear chain than a tertiary tree. This is attributable to the extra overhead of routing the data packets to the free processors in the tertiary tree farm.

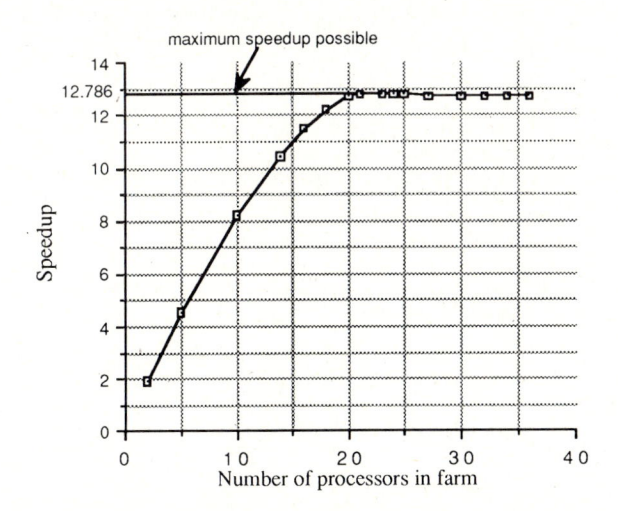

Figure 8 - Speedup with increasing farm size (linear chain)

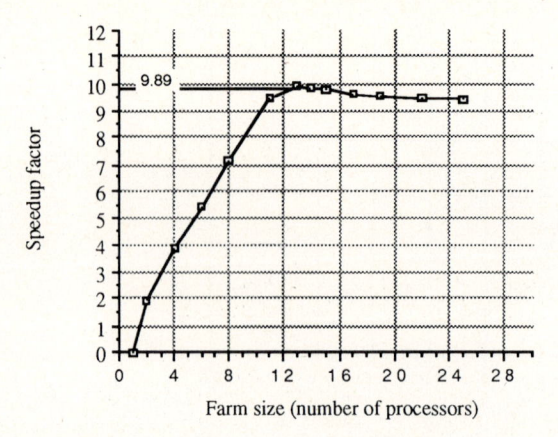

Figure 9 - Speedup with increasing farm size (tertiary tree)

6. Conclusion

The evaluation of the SPHIR suite showed that there is significant speedup to be gained from exploiting parallelism in the routing process for VLSI design. Each stage can be speeded up optimally by using different parallel processing techniques and different topologies.

The PGRM stage was speeded up using tree topology which mapped well on to the geometric parallelism present in the global routing problem. For PDRM the technique used to exploit parallelism in the detailed routing problem is the task farming technique and the two multi-transputer topologies considered for this purpose were the tertiary tree and linear chain. Although for farm sizes less than 12 the tertiary tree had marginally higher throughput, the maximum throughput acieavable was possible with the linear chain structure.

Transim facilitated the fine-tuning of the communication protocols as well as debugging of the communications framework. Transim was found to be a very useful tool for not only evaluating the performance of SPHIR, but for evaluating the possible topologies for use in SPHIR.

References

[1] Parker Y. and Hart E., *"Transim User Manual"*, Polytechnic of Central London, London, England, 1989.

[2] Sagar V.K. and Massara R.E., 'SPHIR - A System for Parallel Hierarchical Routing', *Proc. 32nd Midwest Symposium on Circuits and Systems*, IEEE/University of Illinois, Urbana, USA, September 1989.

[3] Sagar V.K. and Massara R.E., 'Task Farming of the Detailed Routing Problem', submitted for publishing to *33nd Midwest Symposium on Circuits and Systems*, IEEE, Canada, September 1990.

[4] Massara, R.E., Nadiadi, Y., and Winder, C.L., 'Silicon compilation in analog and digital custom VLSI design', in *Progress in Computer-Aided VLSI Design*. G.W. Zobrist (Ed.) Ablex, 1989.

[5] Preas, B.T. and Van Cleemput, W.M., 'Routing Algorithms for Hierarchical IC Layout', *Proc. 1979 ISCAS*, p482-485.

[6] Sagar V.K. and Massara R.E., 'Exploiting Parallelism in Routing for a Hierarchical VLSI Design Environment', *Proc. 1989 European Conference on Circuit Theory and Design*, IEE, Brighton U.K., September 1989.

[7] Pritchard D. J., "Mathematical Models of Distributed Computation", *Parallel Programming of Transputer Based Machines* - Proc. 7th Occam User Group Technical Meeting, 14-16 September 1987, Grenoble, France, Ed.: T. Muntean.

ONDA : a river modelling system

H K F Yeung

SERC Rutherford Appleton Laboratory
Chilton, Didcot, OXON OX11 0QX

This paper describes the effort required in porting the ONDA river modelling package, the runtime environment in which the system operates, and the lessons learned from the exercise. There should be no doubt that application software written ten or twenty years ago is unlikely to be thrown away overnight because of the advent of parallel computers, and so while new programs are being developed for the new architectures, there will be many old programs to be adapted.

The argument for protecting software investments is a persuasive one, which can be extended to hardware in our organization where workstations are widely used for scientific and engineering applications. It is therefore an obvious decision for us to choose the workstation as the host for the transputer system rather than the PC. After making that decision, our effort is then concentrated on exploiting the capabilities of both machines rather than relegating the host to a dumb terminal and/or file depository as in the case of the PC. The design of our runtime environment is thus very much dominated by the need to present a transparent interface to the application spanning across the two architectures.

Our experiences have shown that porting dusty deck programs from a sequential machine to the transputer is no harder (or easier) than to another sequential machine. We have also demonstrated that such tasks can be carried out by someone with little prior knowledge of the application. The primary lesson is that any modifications to the program being ported must be kept to the absolute minimum, which, in our opinion, is clearly feasible, and the speed-up comes naturally by simply exploiting the parallelism inherent in the application. Looking into the future, we are optimistic that the task can only be easier with better tools, compilers, runtime environment, and hardware which are improving all the time.

An Overview of the Application

Onda[1] is a typical dusty deck Fortran package written more than 10 years ago but still widely used by the Water Authorities. It was developed and supported by the Water Division of the international civil engineering consultancy company, Sir William Halcrow and Partners, and runs on a range of machines including IBM 3090, Sequent, and Whitechapel workstation. Without the simulation tools such as that provided by this application, many of the investigations in river management would be difficult, if not impossible. For example, the cost in testing a new flood alleviation scheme in real life could be prohibitive, not to mention the problems it might cause to people living nearby. Similarly, a poorly designed and constructed drainage system or river course diversion would be expensive to put right again. Within the system, a river is represented by many thousands of different units (eg. weir, sluice, junction etc.) and each unit is governed by an equation of the appropriate type, which together describe the behaviour of the complete model. At each time step, the equations are solved and the results fed back for the next time step. The computation time therefore depends on the number of units specified and the number of time steps required, both of which are normally huge.

There are three main modules in the system : the specification module, the simulation module, and the display module. A simple user friendly interface is provided for the details and initial conditions of a river to be defined. The information is then stored in a file to be used by the simulation module. It is obvious that the specification module is normally run independent of the other modules, and typically there will be many such data files (for different rivers, or even the same river with different initial conditions) maintained in the system. The specification process is very i/o intensive, and while we believe it is not a good candidate for parallelization on the transputer, it is, of course, a natural choice for the workstation. This, in fact, is the main essence of our approach in porting existing applications, emphasising the computational intensive parts of the application for the transputer treatment. There is a conscious effort in not putting the whole program onto the transputer for putting there sake, whether it is suitable or not. In the final analysis, one has to take into account the capability of the underlying system, the current state of the technology, the cost of development, the performance overhead, and the user convenience (for example, by providing the user interface on the workstation, one can thus make use of a familiar workstation environment for the user).

Results of the simulation are presented graphically. This includes graphs of various entities (eg. velocity, water level) at locations (nodes) of the river requested by the user. By utilizing the X Window Management System, more than one graphs can be displayed simultaneously in separate windows. The decision of whether to implement the display module on the transputer or on the host is a matter of choice. There are transputer cards (eg. IMS B419 Integrated Graphics TRAM) which support high quality graphics and so could be used by the display module. However, it is also conceivable that a workstation is already in use for other parts of the application, and the traffic of the output data is such that it is not unreasonable for the workstation to be used for the display purpose as well. We have adopted the latter approach. In arriving at that conclusion, we are very much conscious of the number of transputer related hardware and software products already available on, for example, SUN, Apollo and PS/2 workstations, which indicates the demands for such combined systems.

Porting the Application

Our porting effort, therefore, is concentrated on the simulation module. The computation is divided into two parts. In the first part, the independent variables of the system equations are calculated. In the second part, the unknowns, or dependent variables, are evaluated by the MA28 [2] sparse matrix solver. The amount of processing in the two parts is divided in the ratio of 7 to 3 (measured in execution time). Schematically, the complete river model is described by a set of equations as shown below :

$$a_{1i}q_i + a_{1j}q_j = b_1$$
$$a_{2s}q_s + a_{2t}q_t = b_2$$
$$---$$
$$a_{nx}q_x + a_{ny}q_y = b_n$$

where,

n : number of equations in the system
i, j, s, t, x, y : any number between 1 and n
a's, b's : independent variables
q's : dependent variables from which other quantities can be calculated

Here we are not concerned with how the independent variables (a's and b's) are calculated apart from the observations that :

- they are calculated from quantities that are derived from the q's in the previous time step (or initial values for the first iteration) as well as from the initial conditions

- their values can be calculated independently from those of other equations

- the matrix obtained from the set of equations is sparse

Although we shall restrict ourselves to the discussion of river simulation in this paper, it is worth mentioning that what we have said so far with regard to setting up the system equations and solving the resulting matrix is common to many applications, for example, applications using linear programming, finite element, and boundary element techniques.

The fact that it takes 70% of the total computation time to set up the system equations for the river simulation module and each equation can be processed independent of each other provides an excellent opportunity for parallelizing this application. Provided the work is divided evenly among the transputers at the outset, load balancing is achieved with no extra effort because all the processors can proceed without any communication until the end of the assembling phase when the intermediate results are assembled. As the amount of processing required differs significantly between equations of different unit types (eg weir, sluice), it is unwise to distribute the units as they appear in the specification data file, so some re-ordering is required to ensure equations of similar unit type are grouped together for distribution. The programming effort for the change here is small but is necessary to maintain an equal workload on all slave transputers. Another change, which again involves only a small effort, is to modify the pointers in the data file so that each transputer is sent only the relevant data instead of the complete set. The third change we have to make is to ensure the equations returned by the transputers are re-assembled in the same order in every time step.

Workstation/Transputer Interface

A transputer network of four T800 housed on a single Transtech TSB44-4 board provides most of the processing power for the project. This is connected to an IMS B004 board with one T414 serving as the root transputer. The workstation in this case is an IBM 6150 which features a RISC architecture, AIX (and everything that comes with the Unix system), high quality graphics, and a PC bus interface which allows both boards to be plugged into the system expansion slots. It is optional whether the second board is on the workstation or not as long as it is connected to the first board via the standard transputer links, and in fact, for a larger network, an expansion box (eg. the INMOS ITEM Rack) may be required. A schematic view of the structure is shown in diagram 1.

The run time environment that we would like to establish for our applications in this workstation/transputer combined system is that it should allow a free flow of data and/or commands between the two systems so that both can be employed simultaneously for the execution of the applications. For example, we may have a scenario that a part of an application (eg. the i/o intensive part) runs on the workstation and the rest (the compute

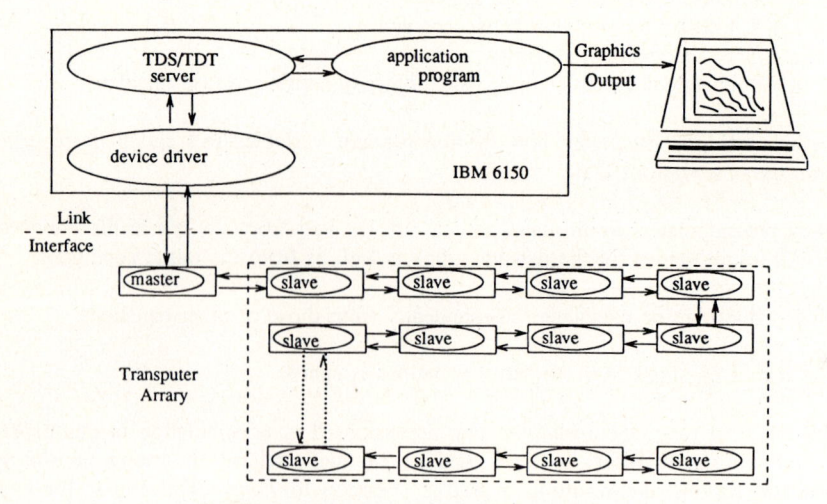

Diagram 1 : Schematic view of the system structure

intensive part), working in parallel with it, run on the transputer. This mode of operation is different from the day (which is not long ago) when the host was used simply as a dumb terminal and a filestore, but the advent of software products such as Express, Genesys etc. have certainly added a new reality into the co-working of workstation and transputer (it is also noted that this is a standard mode of operation on the Intel iPSC/2 hypercube).

As a part of the project, we have also looked into the basic mechanism involved to facilitate such workstation/transputer interface and experimented with the designs. On a host workstation running an Unix (or clone) system, all that is required is for the host-part of the application (HA) and the server (eg. the Inmos afserver) to run as separate processes. Some changes to the standard Inmos afserver is necessary for two reasons :

- to allow the server to recognise messages from the transputer-part of the application (TA) which are destinated for HA and to deliver them accordingly

- to allow the server to communicate with HA using standard Unix Inter Process Communication (IPC) facilities. The System V Message queue IPC is chosen for most part of the project, but we have also experimented with the BSD sockets. There is an added advantage for using the socket mechanism in that HA can actually reside on any workstations on a Local Area Network, and thus exploiting the afserver as a more conventional Compute Server. We have experimented with the latter approach using the Transputer Development Toolkit (TDT) to compile, link, and execute simple programs remotely. For this to become a useful service, we believe the issues of security, integrity, and performance have to be scrutinized more stringently. It is no doubt that such provision is useful in our environment because some of our workstations are not expandable (which means there is no spare system slot for any extra card), and even for the workstations which are expandable, there is still a case for sharing resources (for example, a large network of more than a thousand transputers).

From the user point of view, sending data and/or commands between HA and TA is accomplished by invoking the appropriate routines provided in the libraries. The presence of the afserver acting between the two parts is completely transparent to the user. Obviously an

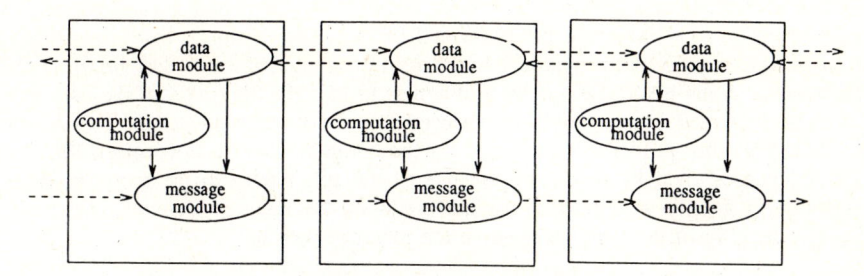

Diagram 2 : schematic view of the links and modules

i/o handler and/or harness is required on the transputer to complete the interface needed, and this separation of the communication and application code is important in order to minimize changes to TA.

Transputer Implementation

The transputer implementation of Onda consists of three modules : the data module, the computation module, and the message module. Internally, the modules are connected with each other via software channels. Externally, both the data and message module are connected to their respective counterparts on the neighbouring transputers via hardware links. The relationship of the three modules is shown in diagram 2.
The computation module consists mainly of the original Onda routines. A main program is added which maintains the threads of execution within the module. Typically the flow of the main program follows the sequence outlined below :

(a) initializes data
(b) receives data/instruction from the data module
(c) calls on one of the Onda routines to execute the instruction
(d) returns results to the data module
(e) repeats steps (b)-(e)
(f) terminates

It is by providing a similar interface to the routines as in the original sequential code at step (c) that allows the code to be ported to the transputer almost un-modified. The main program is also a natural place to implement anything that deviates from the original program.

A number of routines (eg. CHANOUTWORD, CHANINMESSAGE) are provided for channel communications. These are used exclusively within the main program for passing data to and from the data module. The interface is rather primitive, and is based on bytes irrespective of the data type, for example, one can read an array of 100 integers with the following statement (assuming IA is an array of 100 or more elements)

   CALL CHANINMESSAGE(ichannel, IA, 400)

where *ichannel* is one of the channels passed to the module when it is initiated, and 400 is 100 integers in bytes. In addition to the data channel, such as ichannel, there are two reserved channels allocated to the module.

The reserved channels are used by the Fortran library to implement, for example, standard i/o routines. There are two practical problems in handling even a simple instruction such as the *write* statement in a Fortran program running on a transputer network. The first problem is to return the data to the host. The second problem is to identify the origin of the data especially if it is to be displayed on the terminal (or stored in a file for later inspection on the terminal). Unfortunately neither problem is addressed by the compiler used in the project. The problems are in fact glossed over by restricting the use of the full library to the root transputer only. Our solution is simply to take over the other end of the reserved channels and arrange the routing and tagging of the data ourselves in the message module.

The message module can be extended to handle not just the data/message generated by the Fortran library routines in the computation module, but also those from the data module, and in fact any other modules to be added in future. As the fan-in channels are declared as a vector of channels, the index to the vector can be conveniently used to identify the process which generates the data. Together with the processor id, each message can therefore be uniquely identified. There is only one fan-out channel which links the message module to the message module on the neighbouring transputer (except on the root transputer where the message module is linked to the i/o handler). Therefore the message module is also called a message multiplexor. It is, of course, possible to combine the data and message modules into a single module, but we believe that would confuse the purpose of the two modules and certainly does not add to any clarity in the design.

The main purpose of the data module is to act as a courier for the computation module. It is essentially an Occam ALT construct polling continuously for data arriving on its channels. For data coming from its own computation module, this will be passed on unchanged. In a chain topology the routing strategy is not an issue, and the direction in which the data is transferred is simply determined by the type of the data. For data coming from the neighbouring transputer, there may be an additional information specifying the destination of the data. It is our intention to keep this part as simple as possible, and in the longer term, to replace it by a *standard* harness.

Matrix Solver

The design of MA28 is documented in [2] and [3]. It is convenient for our discussions here to divide the solver into two parts rather than three as described in the two papers (or four if one includes block triangularization). There is little to be gained from carrying out the block triangularization process on Onda because apart from a number of small blocks (with only a single element), the resulting matrix is almost the same size as the original one. The two parts we are interested in are

    (a) the analyzer which determines the pivots and the associated permutations.
    (b) the Gaussian forward elimination and backward substitution

For the Onda application, it is reasonable to assume that the sparsity of the matrix and the position of the pivot elements would not change significantly during the simulation. This means in an ideal case, it is only necessary to analyze the matrix once and the results can be re-used in subsequent time steps. (Should there be significant changes, MA28 would arrange for part (a) to be called automatically). This raises the question of whether it is worthwhile to parallelize part (a) if it is to be used only once comparing with part (b) which may be called hundreds and thousands of times. Part (a) involves a lot of data shuffling and so imposes a cap on the speed-up that can be achieved when executed in parallel. Our conclusion is that it should be left as it is, bearing in mind it is only used sparingly, so there should be few effects on the overall performance.

The parallel Gaussian operation is described in [4]. A simplified version of the algorithm implemented in one of our earlier projects [5] is shown below

```
for i = 1 to n   -- n is the order of the matrix
{
    if (i) is the column held on this transputer
    then
      send the column to other transputers
    else
      wait until the column is received
    endif
    for j = i to n
    {
        if (j) is the column held on this transputer
        then
          do the elimination as in the serial case
        else
          do nothing
    }
}
```

Similarly, the backward substitution can also be coded in the style outlined. Apart from the control structure (eg. the loop and the tests), the code is largely retained from the serial program. It is not difficult to see that the scheme works more efficiently with larger matrices because this will increase the ratio of computation to each pivot vector communicated. We choose to send the whole vector instead of the multiplying factors in order to minimize the idle time on the transputers not holding that column. Of course the multiplying factors will have to be calculated on all transputers once the vector is received. An alternative is to calculate the factors on the machine holding the pivot column but that will delay the availability of the required information, and thus increase the communication overhead.

Compared with our previous implementation, there are minor differences in the way MA28 handles this part in that the multiplying factors are calculated and stored in the lower part of the matrix prior to the forward elimination. If the block triangularization process is applied in the earlier stage, then the off diagonal blocks will also have to be dealt with at the substitution step. However, these are minor details and can be handled easily within the scheme outlined.

Performance Monitoring

We are interested in monitoring the performance not just to show how much speed-up is achieved, but also to gain further insight into the parallelization process. There are tools which provide information on elapsed time, cpu utilization, link usage and etc., but one can also obtain useful data by reading the timer at strategical places. In fact, the latter method, crude as it is, can be finely tuned to meet our specific requirements. It can be argued that the measurement would be affected by the extra code added, but that is important only if we are interested in the absolute performance. Very often, we are only interested in the relative performances, for example, the performance of one transputer compared with that of n transputers, or the ratio between compute and communication time. Depending on the analysis one would like to do, a simple time measurement with the stop watch may be just as meaningful as that produced by an elaborate tool. It is useless to generate a large set of numbers without any idea of how to interpret them (for example, what useful conclusion can one make with a statement such as 80% cpu utilization). We use the timer for monitoring the performance because of its flexibility and *interpretability* (the interpretation comes naturally from the reason why the timer is placed at a particular spot).

In the discussions below, an one letter code (A, B ...) is used to denote the point where the timer is read. The time between two points is given by X-Y. The locations where the timer are placed are described first :

A : this is placed at the beginning of each time step and is measured on the root transputer only

B : this is placed at the point where the root transputer is ready to receive results from the slave transputers. It should be noted that between A and B, the root transputer can be busy communicating with the host, and thus executing in parallel with the slave transputers. Once this point is reached, the root transputer is effectively idle, but on the other hand, we certainly do not want other transputers to be held up because the root transputer gets here too late.

C : this is placed at the point where the first packet of the result is returned by one of the slave transputers.

D : this is placed at the point where the last packet of the result is returned by the slave transputer. The number of packets to be returned should be the same as the number of slave transputers on the network.

E : this is placed at the point where all the results from the slaves are received. It is also the point where the matrix is to be evaluated by the solver.

F : this is placed at the point there the matrix is to be assembled. It is measured on all the slave transputers. Useful observations can be made by comparing the values of Fs, B and A, for example, if B is much smaller than Fs, there is probably not much overlap between the root and the slave transputers because the former is already idle before the latter start to work! On the other hand, if the values of the Fs differ a lot, there is probably a lot of delays in routing the *start* command.

G : this is placed at the point where the matrix assembling phase is completed. It is measured on every slave transputers. The measurement includes the time to pass the result from the Fortran program to the occam harness.

Though a lot can be read in each individual measurement, or in comparison with other measurements, there are time ranges which are also worth examining, for example,

A-A : the time for one iteration of the simulation

A-B : the time for the root transputer to be ready to receive results from the slaves

B-C : the time between the root transputer is ready to receive the results and the arrival of the first packet

C-D : the time between the arrivals of the first and last packet of results on the root transputer.

F-G : the time required to assemble the matrix. This is the only part which represent the code that is parallelized, and hence of particular interest in comparing the speed-up.

Some of the measurements for different number (2-4) of transputers are illustrated in diagrams 3, 4, and 5.

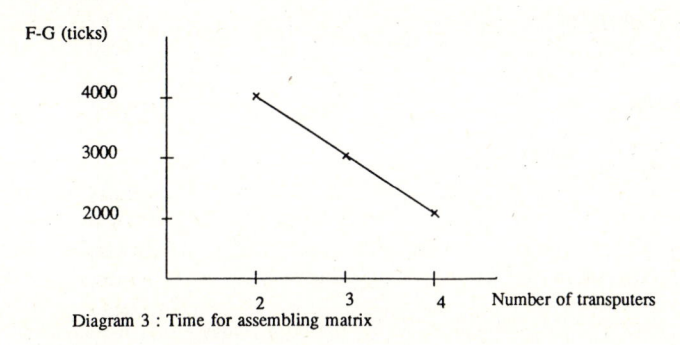

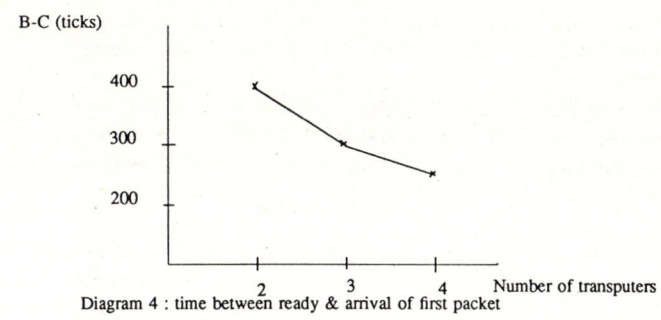

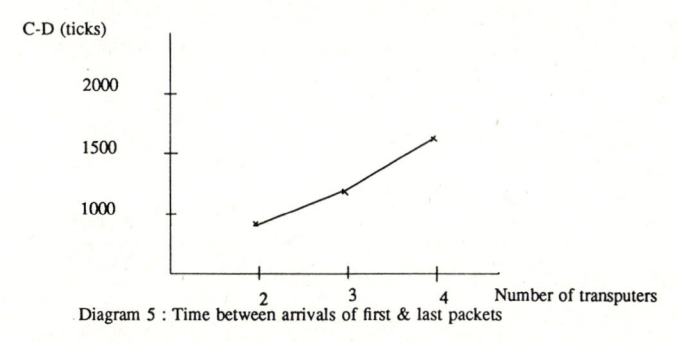

Diagram 3 : Time for assembling matrix

Diagram 4 : time between ready & arrival of first packet

Diagram 5 : Time between arrivals of first & last packets

A number of observations can be made from the graphs above :

(a) There is a good speed-up in the parallelized code (F-G) as shown in diagram 3. This is precisely what we have expected because, as already described in earlier section, there is no communication required between the transputers once the calculation starts.

(b) The time between the root transputer is ready to receive the results and the arrival of the first packet (B-C) decreases when the number of slave transputers increases. This is because the size of the data packet is smaller with larger number of transputers.

(c) The time between the arrival of the first and last packet of results increases with the number of slave transputers (C-D). This is due to the increase in the number of packets transferred.

Obviously one is not limited to the observations above which are simply examples for the purpose of this paper. Taking everything into account, we are in general happy with the speed-up achieved, but we are also concerned about the rather slow transfer rate between the host and the root transputer.

Future Developments

The current implementation is restrained by the size of the memory available on the slave transputer. If implemented in full, we would need in excess of one MByte of memory which is beyond what we have at the moment. As a result of that, the solver code has not been parallelized in order to reduce the memory requirement. We would clearly like to complete the implementation when more memory is available.

There are a number of ways we could improve the data transfer rate between the host and the transputer, for example, using the dual ported shared memory. A better solution may also be developed as a result of the work at the European Microprocessor Initiative.

Wherever possible, we would like to adopt *standard* methodology and/or tools in future applications. However, with so many products available, for example, in the runtime environment alone, there are Express, Strand, Genesys, CSTool and etc., which leaves the average users with little help but confusions.

It would be useful to the application writers if mathematical libraries with standard interface are generally available as on sequential machines. However any suggestions that the libraries would have the monopoly use of the transputer system are unlikely to be acceptable to us because apart from the mathematical routines, there are other parts of the application which could be parallelized (eg. setting up the equations) as well and the Onda application is a good example of this.

Conclusions

Our work has shown that it is possible to inject new lives into dusty deck Fortran programs. However, a lot still have to be done before we can see a massive exodus of applications from the supercomputers to parallel machines. Some issues have already been addressed in the recent SERC/DTI workshop on Standards for MIMD Parallel Systems and we hope the recommendations will be implemented without delay. We are also looking forward to a successful outcome from the European Microprocessor Initiative, and in particular advances in transputer based high performance workstations. Porting existing applications is only the first step in applying parallel systems which, in a sense, is a confidence boosting exercise. The next step is to re-think how we should address scientific and engineering applications in the future. Computer users are very good in adapting to whatever constraints hardware and software engineers place on them. But if we can do the job with the wrong tool (solving parallel problems with sequential machines and languages), then we should be able to do a better job with the right tool, and that will be the real success of parallel systems!

Acknowledgements

I would like to thank IBM for providing the 6150 workstations for the Joint Study Project, Sir William Halcrow & Partners for the Onda software, the London & SE Regional Transputer Centre of the SERC/DTI Transputer Initiative for their support, Mark Roberts for contributing to the IPC and harness work, and Chris Wadsworth for the discussions and comments on the paper.

References

[1] Evans, E : The design of Onda software. Private discussions.

[2] Duff I.S.; MA28 - A Set of Fortran Subroutines for Sparse Unsymmetric Linear Equations; AERE Report R.8730; November 1980.

[3] Duff I.S., Reid J.K.; Some Design Features of a Sparse Matrix Code; ACM Transactions of Mathematical Software, Vol 5, No.1, March 1979.

[4] Wray F W; Who needs supercomputers and why?; Evaluating Supercomputers, Unicom; June 1988.

[5] Bryant C.F., Roberts M.H., Trowbridge C.W.; Implementing a Boundary Integral Method on a Transputer System, Proc. of Compumag Conference, Japan, 1989.

Spectral Element Methods for Computational Fluid Dynamics on Transputer Arrays

Russell Watts
Concurrent Computation Group
Dept of Electronics and Computer Science
University of Southampton

Spectral Element methods are high order techniques for the solution of partial differential equations, such as those encountered in Computational Fluid Dynamics. The computational domain is divided into elements within which the variables are approximated by Nth order polynomial expansions.

The decomposition of the computational domain into elements provides a natural basis for distribution onto a parallel architecture. The high order, and so computational intensity, of the spectral approximation within each element compared to the communication of only edge data and the relatively few global inner products enables high efficiencies to be obtained on MIMD parallel architectures.

Keywords

Spectral, Spectral Element, Stokes, Navier-Stokes, Domain Decomposition, Transputer, MIMD, Parallel, Conjugate Gradient

1. Introduction

Spectral methods

In a full spectral method, variables are expanded in terms of an expansion basis. The basis chosen is usually Chebychev polynomials, so allowing use of the efficient FFT algorithm. Convergence to an analytic solution is achieved by increasing the order, say N, of the expansion.

Such high order techniques are required to resolve to sufficiently small length scales to model transition to turbulence, for example. However, the computational domain must be rectangular and hence conformal transformations are required to handle complex geometries.

Finite element methods

A finite element method approximates the variables in terms of low order polynomials, usually quadratics, within a number, say K, of elements. Convergence of the numerical approximation is achieved by increasing the number of elements.

Since these elements can be organised in an unstructured manner, complex geometries can be handled without the need to resort to conformal transformations.

Spectral element methods

Spectral element methods [1],[2] are a combination of the two methods, using high order polynomial approximations within a number of elements. For such an approximation, we define a discretisation pair h=(K,N) where, as above, K is the number of elements and N the order of the approximation.

If K=1 the method is a spectral method of order N.
If N=2 it is finite element method with K elements.

Spectral element methods have K ~ 10-100 and N ~ 8.

They are particularly suitable for distribution onto medium-grained parallel architectures by virtue of the tightness of the coupling within elements compared to the sparsity of the communication between elements.

2. Application to Navier-Stokes Equations

The spectral element method is applied here to Computational Fluid Dynamics, specifically to the steady and unsteady Stokes equations and the incompressible Navier Stokes equations.

$$\frac{D\mathbf{u}}{Dt} = \mathbf{F} - \nabla p + \nabla^2 \mathbf{u}$$

and

$$-\nabla \cdot \mathbf{u} = 0$$

where
  $\mathbf{u}$ is the velocity field
  p is pressure
  $\mathbf{f}$ is body force
  $\frac{D}{Dt} = \frac{\delta}{\delta t} + \mathbf{v} \cdot \nabla$ is the convective derivative

An iterative implicit Stokes solver handles the viscous parts of the Navier-Stokes equations, with the non-linear convective terms being treated by an explicit Adams-Bashforth scheme.

3. Poisson solver

3.1. One-dimensional

Consider a one-dimensional Poisson equation on a region $]-1,1[$ with homogeneous Dirichlet boundary conditions,

$$-\frac{\delta^2 u}{\delta x^2} = f \quad \text{and} \quad u(-1)=u(1)=0$$

The associated variational form of this equation is,

$$a(u,v) = (f,v)$$

where

$$a(u,v) = \int \frac{\delta u(x)}{\delta x} \frac{\delta v(x)}{\delta x} dx$$

and

$$(f,v) = \int f(x) v(x) \, dx$$

$v(x)$ is the arbitrary test function of the variational method and $u(x)$ and $v(x)$ are restricted to function spaces satisfying the boundary conditions.

The spectral element discretisation decomposes the domain in K subdomains within which the variables are approximated by Nth order polynomials. Functions restricted to this approximation space are denoted by a suffix h, referred to as the discretisation pair, $h = (K,N)$.

The global inner products of the variational form are numerically integrated by N+1 point Gauss-Lobatto quadrature (suffix GL) within each element.

$$(f,v)_{h,GL} = \frac{b}{2} \sum_{k=1}^{K} \sum_{n=0}^{N} \rho_n f(\varepsilon_n^k) v(\varepsilon_n^k)$$

$$a(u,v)_{h,GL} = \frac{b}{2} \sum_{k=1}^{K} \sum_{n=0}^{N} \rho_n \frac{\delta f(\varepsilon_n^k)}{\delta x} \frac{\delta v(\varepsilon_n^k)}{\delta x}$$

where ρ_n and ε_n^k are Gauss-Lobatto Legendre quadrature weights and points respectively.

The functions are approximated by Lagrangian interpolants through the N+1 Gauss-Lobatto Legendre quadrature points.

$$u_h(x) = \sum_{p=0}^{N} u_p^k h_p(r)$$

Approximations for u(x), v(x) and f(x) are inserted into this discrete inner product equation. By making the trial function v(x) unity at each *global* grid point in turn a discrete matrix equation is produced. Global this is expressed as

$$Au = Bf$$

The desirable consequence of the approximation and the quadrature being performed on the same grid points is that the elements couple only through the globally shared grid points, that is those located on the elemental boundaries. This relatively weak coupling between elements is the essence of the method from a parallel point of view.

3.2. Two-dimensional

$$-\nabla^2 u = f \quad \text{and} \quad u = 0 \text{ on } \delta\Omega$$

The discretisation for the two-dimensional Poisson equation proceeds in much the same manner as the one-dimensional. The inner products are now integrated with two-dimensional Gauss-Lobatto integration,

$$a(u,v)_{h,GL} = \frac{b}{2} \sum_{k=1}^{K} \sum_{n=0}^{N} \sum_{m=0}^{N} \rho_n \rho_m \, \nabla f(\varepsilon_n^k \varepsilon_m^k) \cdot \nabla v(\varepsilon_n^k \varepsilon_n^k)$$

The approximation basis is tensor-product Lagrangian interpolants,

$$u_h(x,y) = \sum_{p=0}^{N} \sum_{q=0}^{N} u_{pq}^k \, h_p(r) \, h_p(s)$$

Again a matrix equation, $Au = Bf$, is produced. However, when considered globally, this matrix equation is very large and sparse. For a small problem, eg 2-dimensional, 16 elements, order N=8 the operator A would be a 1024 x 1024 matrix. Direct solution of the matrix, or even its formation, is hence impractical, especially in parallel. Hence, an iterative method is used.

4. Parallel Conjugate Gradient

Iterative conjugate gradient is used to solve for the positive-definite symmetric Laplace operator.

$$
\begin{aligned}
r_0 &= Bf - Au_0 \, ; \, q_0 = P^{-1} r_0 \, ; \, s_0 = q_0 \\
a_m &= (r_m, s_m) / (q_m, Aq_m) \\
u_{m+1} &= u_m + a_m q_m \\
r_{m+1} &= r_m - a_m Aq_m \\
s_{m+1} &= P^{-1} r_{m+1} \\
b_m &= (r_{m+1}, s_{m+1}) / (r_m, s_m) \\
q_{m1} &= s_{m+1} + b_m q_m
\end{aligned}
$$

The operations required to implement this conjugate gradient are,

4.1. Simple local matrix operations

$u_{m+1} = u_m + a_m q_m$ for example. These require no communications.

4.2. Pre-conditioning (P^{-1})

A diagonal pre-conditioner (diag A) is used, and so this stage requires only local calculation and no communication. A more efficient pre-conditioner (in terms of convergance) is likely to require communication.

4.3. Laplace operator (Aq_m)

The operator is first evaluated locally in each element (since it can be evaluated as a tensor-product, a reduction in the order of the computation required is possible). Then the global 'direct stiffness summation' is performed.

This operation contains most of the communication of the method. It requires that the values of local grid points corresponding to the same global grid point are summed and redistributed.

Various methods have been considered for the direct stiffness summation.

Orthogonal

One common method is to swap and sum boundaries first in the x direction and then in the y direction. This has two disadvantages. Firstly, certain elemental configurations will produce incorrect results at corners of elements (eg an internal corner shared between 3 elements). Secondly, only half of the link bandwidth is used at any one time.

Through-routed edges

Another method is to perform all of the edge swaps simultaneously, and then send corrections for the corners. This utilises the link bandwidth better, but requires the introduction of short messages.

4.4. Global inner products (r,s)

The global sum, used in inner product calculations, is a sum of a value from each element and is simple to implement. The only precaution is that the value received by each element must be *exactly* the same. Different round-off errors caused by summation along each vertex of a hypercube in turn, for example, will cause problems since the results are used for decisions on convergence of the iterative method.

5. Partitioning of elements onto processors

The efficient partition of a general set of nearest-neighbour communicating entities onto an architecture is a research topic in its own right, especially when the architecture can be reconfigurable.

So far concentration has been on the implementation of the CFD rather than in depth consideration of this problem. A simple geometric distribution of one element per processor with a Parsys Supernode suitably configured for nearest (processor) neighbour stiffness summation has proved highly efficient and totally suitable for test problems.

6. Steady Stokes Solver

Now consider the steady Stokes equations (non-dimensionalised such that the viscosity is unity).

$$-\nabla^2 \mathbf{u} + \nabla p = \mathbf{f}$$
$$-\nabla \cdot \mathbf{u} = 0$$
$$\mathbf{u} = 0 \quad \text{on } \delta\Omega$$

The variational form is,

$$a(\mathbf{u},\mathbf{v}) - b(p,\mathbf{v}) = (\mathbf{f},\mathbf{v})$$

and

$$b(q,\mathbf{u}) = 0$$

where all inner products have been previously defined, except for

$$b(p,\mathbf{v}) = \int p(x) \nabla \cdot \mathbf{v} \, dx$$

The discretisation proceeds as with the Poisson equation, except that the pressure variables are approximated and numerically integrated on a grid with N-1, not N+1 points. This is necessary to avoid spurious pressure modes, and eliminates problems associated with representing the infinite pressure found at sharp corners.

A discrete matrix equation is produced,

$$A\mathbf{u} - D^T p = \mathbf{g}$$
$$-D \cdot \mathbf{u} = 0$$

The Uzawa algorithm is used, decoupling the problem into a solve for pressure and then poisson solves for the velocity with the pressure gradient as an augmented force.

$$A\mathbf{u} - D^T p = \mathbf{g}$$
$$S p = -D \cdot A^{-1} \mathbf{g}$$

where

$$S = -D \cdot A^{-1} D^T$$

This pressure solve requires inversion of the operator, S, on the pressure grid. As with the Laplace operator, direct inversion is impractical, and so conjugate gradient iteration is used to solve this system.

However, each iteration requires operation by S. Since S involves the inverse of the laplacian operator, A^{-1}, it is neither practical to from nor to operate directly with S. So nested conjugate gradient solves are used to operate with A^{-1}.

$$y = D^T p$$
$$Az = y \quad \text{(nested conjugate gradient solve)}$$
$$Sp = -D.z$$

The use of a nested conjugate gradient solve is not prohibitive since the matrix S is very well conditioned, and converges in order unity iterations. It is important, for reasons of efficiency, to ensure that the inner iterations are performed only to the accuracy required for the outer solve to converge to the attainable pressure accuracy for the order N of the solution.

The pressure gradient operators (**D**) are local to each element, and so it is only through the inner poisson solves that the elements are coupled. The same poisson solver is then used to calculate the velocity field once the pressure gradient is established.

From the point of view of inter-element communication, the Stokes problem is in this manner reduced to the simpler poisson problem, requiring only the implementation of the Laplacian operator and vector products at a global level.

7. Unsteady Stokes and Navier-Stokes

The unsteady stokes problem is solved in a very similar manner to the steady stokes, with the important difference that while the steady operator S is very well conditioned, its unsteady version, S_t is very *poorly* conditioned.

Conjugate gradient iteration of the Uzawa algorithm is no longer suitable, and so a Richardson scheme is used. This involves inversion of S, as in the steady stokes problem, but only operation by S_t, in which the conditioning is not important.

Extension to the incompressible Navier-Stokes equations is achieved by explicit treatment of the convective term by use of an Adams-Bashforth scheme. The contribution from this term appears as an augment to the body force in the unsteady Stokes algorithm.

8. Conclusions

The spectral element method is highly suited to distribution onto an array of transputers. The inherent parallelism enters the derivation of the algorithm at a very early stage.

The computational demand of the high order approximation within the elements compared to the edge-only communication requirements yields high efficiencies, even with very simple parallel implementations.

References

1. Patera, A.T., "A spectral element method for fluid dynamics : Laminar flow in a channel expansion," J.Comp.Phys., 54, 1984, p.468.

2. Maday, Y. and Patera, A.T.,"Spectral element methods for the incompressible Navier-Stokes equations", 1987.

Time Evaluation of a Transputer-Based Model of the Ventricle

K.E. TEHRANI*, C.M. SHAPCOTT**, J. ANDERSON*

Northern Ireland Bio-Engineering Centre, University of Ulster, Jordanstown, N.Ireland.
**Department of Computing Science, University of Ulster, Jordanstown, N.Ireland.*

Abstract. The implementation on a transputer network of a finite-element model of conduction processes within the ventricular heart chamber is described. Interactions between adjacent cell segments in the ventricle are modelled by simple neighbourhood rules. The graphical interface to the model is also described. Parallel execution is achieved by dividing the cylinder of elements into surface patches, each patch being allocated to a different processor. The transputer implementation used between one and four surface patches. It was found that the speed of execution scaled linearly with the number of processors, and that this linear speed-up could be achieved with much larger numbers of processors. The graphical interface acted as a constraint on output and would need to be modified to keep pace with calculations. Advantages and drawbacks of the transputer in this application are discussed.

1. Introduction

There is currently much interest in producing computer-based models of the heart in order to eliminate the need for animal experiments in research into heart dysrhythmias, following the early work of Moe[1]. This paper describes the implementation of a transputer-based model of the behaviour of the ventricular heart chamber. This is a simple finite-element model of ventricular conduction processes that explicitly incorporates spatial dispersion of refractoriness. Output of the model consists of a conventional electrocardiogram (ECG)[2] and of a visual display of the current state of the elements in the grid. In this paper we describe the implementation of the model on transputer networks.

The paper is organised as follows. In sections two and three we give a brief description of the model, and describe the algorithm used to implement it, including an outline of the user interface which has been implemented as a separate process. Parallelism is introduced in section four and experiments and results are described in section five. In section six we analyse the results. Section seven consists of a discussion of the advantages and drawbacks of the transputer for this application and we conclude in section eight.

2. Physical Model

The goal of the modelling approach is not necessarily to develop a model that closely represents the detailed electrophysiology of ventricular conduction and its ionic currents, but rather to develop the simplest possible model that retains the key features of the problem and explicitly includes spatial dispersion of refractory times.

We have used a finite element model of ventricular conduction. The neighbourhood model is represented as a two-dimensional rectangle of elements of linear dimensions. A cylindrical shell model is taken as a first order approximation to the ventricular geometry.

Each element in the rectangle can exist in one of four discrete states :

i) Quiescent (at rest).
ii) Depolarised (excited).
iii) Absolute refractory (depolarised and unexcitable).
iv) Relative refractory (depolarised and excitable with sufficient stimulus).

In the excited state an element has the ability to excite any quiescent neighbours. At the end of the excited phase a cell becomes refractory. An element in the absolute refractory state can not excite or be excited, and will remain in that state for the duration of its pre-assigned refractory period, after which it will change to a relative refractory state in which it can be excited with sufficient stimulus from its neighbours. The refractory periods are randomly assigned to each element according to a Gaussian probability distribution with a mean refractory time and a standard deviation input by the user.

Each element is taken to be conductively linked to eight of its adjacent neighbours, four on the sides (north, east, south and west) and four on the diagonals (north-east, north-west, south-east and south-west). The spread of depolarisation is controlled by a simple conduction scheme in which an element is depolarised if two conditions are met:

i) the time since its last depolarisation exceeded the element's refractory period, and
ii) one or more of its neighbours is depolarised.

3. Algorithm

In the implementation of the model the cylindrical mesh of elements is represented by an array, the contents of each member of the array representing the current excitatory state of the corresponding element. The eight nearest neighbours of each element are easily defined with the elements at the end of each row in the array defined to be neighbours, and the top and bottom rows of the cylinder having no neighbours above or below them respectively. Initially all elements are assumed to be quiescent except for a single element at the top of the cylinder which is excited.

3.1 Computation

In essence the algorithm consists of the computation of the contents of the array at successive time steps. For each time step and for each member of the array the current state of the element and of its neighbours are used to compute the state of the element at the end of the time step. Pseudocode for this computation is on the next page. Note that the variable *time.changed* is the time at which the element last changed its excitatory state, and may be used to determine whether a state change is possible. Also, the contribution by the element to the total ECG is computed.

```
new.state(element, time)
    CASE current.state[element]
        quiescent
            If (any neighbour is excited)         {new.state := excited; time.changed := time}
            else                                   {new.state := quiescent}
        excited
            If (time - time.changed) > Excitation.period
                                                   {new.state := absolute.refractory; time.changed := time}
            else                                   {new.state := excited}
        absolute.refractory
            If (time - time.changed) > Absolute.refractory.period[element]
                                                   {new.state := relative.refractory; time.changed := time}
            else                                   {new.state := absolute.refractory}
        relative.refractory
            Compute net effect of neighbours
            Compute current excitation threshold
            If (net.effect > threshold)           {new.state := excited; time.changed := time}
            else if (time - time.changed > total.refractory.period)
                                                   {new.state := quiescent; time.changed := time}
            else                                   {new.state := relative.refractory}
```

Next we show the algorithm, *ventricle()*, for the complete grid of elements, where the initialisation step has been shown explicitly.

```
ventricle()
    initialise()
    time := 0
    WHILE TRUE
        time := time + conduction.period
        SEQ element = 0 FOR no.of.elements
            new.state(element, time)
            compute ecg of element
            total.ecg := total.ecg + ecg[element]
```

3.2 User Interface

As presented so far, the algorithm takes no account of the user interface. This can be developed conveniently by introducing a second process, *display()*, which communicates with the user by the channels *keyboard* and *screen*, and with ventricle() via the channels *to.ventricle* and *from.ventricle*. Parameters for the model input by the user are accepted by display() and forwarded to ventricle(). Results from each time step are passed from ventricle() to display() and presented to the user. The algorithm has been elaborated to allow the user to interactively enter codes while the model is executing. If the user presses a key, display() recognises this and passes on the appropriate instruction to ventricle(). These instructions are responsible for functions which simulate dysrhythmias and change values of the parameters for predefined subgroups. At the beginning of each loop display() must send an extra message which tells ventricle() which key (if any) has been pressed. The following code fragments indicate how this is done.

```
display()
    keyboard ? parameters
    to.ventricle ! parameters
    from.ventricle ? results
    WHILE TRUE
        PRI ALT
            keyboard ? key
                to.ventricle ! key
            clock ? time
                to.ventricle ! key.not.found
        process(results)
        screen ! results
        from.ventricle ? results
```

```
ventricle()
    to.ventricle ? parameters
    WHILE TRUE
        ... compute new state of grid
        from.ventricle ! results
        to.ventricle ? key
        if (key is key.not.found)
            continue
        else
            act.on.key(key)
```

4. Parallelism

There are two main sources of parallelism in the model. We have already implicitly allowed for the first in separating out the functions of user interaction and actual computation of the model. Hence, it is possible to place display() and ventricle() on separate processors.

However, because the display of results to a user is basically a sequential process, the potential for parallelism is limited. In contrast the second available form of parallelism arises naturally from the nature of the model itself. Because each element interacts only with its nearest neighbours it is straightforward to implement a version of domain (i.e. geometric) parallelism[3]. The grid of elements is divided into surface patches, which overlap only along their boundaries, and each of which is allocated to a single processor. Apart from boundary elements each processor operates autonomously. Boundary elements are the only ones which require interprocessor communications between adjoining patches. The array of elements can be subdivided both horizontally and/or vertically. For the north, east, south and west neighbouring patches the state of the top, rightmost, bottom and leftmost elements of a patch must be sent at the beginning of a time step, and the corresponding elements must be received from the neighbouring patches. The corner elements must be sent to the north-east, south-east, south-west, and north-west patches and the corresponding elements from these patches received.

The following pseudocode illustrates the case where the cylinder has been divided horizontally. Each patch needs to communicate its second topmost and second bottommost rows with its two neighbouring patches via channels *to.north* and *to.south*. Similarly it must receive the state of the corresponding bordering rows from the neighbouring patches via *from.north* and *from.south* to obtain the topmost and bottommost rows. The interactions with the display process are also straightforward, except that the individual contributions of each patch to the overall electrocardiogram (ECG) vector must be summed. Each patch is logically connected to display() by its own communications channel, to.ventricle and from.ventricle being replaced by arrays of communication channels.

```
vent.patch(p)
    ....
    WHILE TRUE
        PAR
            to.north ! second.row.from.top
            to.south ! second.row.from.bottom
            from.north ? top.row
            from.south ? bottom.row
        compute next state of inside of patch
        from.ventricle[p] ! results
```

display()
    ...
    WHILE TRUE
        PAR p = 0 FOR P
            from.ventricle[p] ? results[p], ecg.vector[p]
        total.ecg.vector := SUM(ecg.vector[p])
        process(results)
        screen ! results; total.ecg.vector

5. Experiments and Results

The equipment used consisted of an IBM PC-AT acting as a host machine, and between one and five transputers, one of which, the *root* transputer, interfaced directly to the host, and the others of which were connected to the root transputer. The host was equipped with an Enhanced Graphics Adaptor, controlling an Enhanced Colour Display.

Development work was carried using the Transputer Development System[4] supplied by INMOS, all code executing on the transputers being written in OCCAM [5].

The functions of the user interface are divided between two processes - the process on the root transputer, which acts as a conduit between the computational transputers and the host and a process on the host machine which receives data from the user and which actually drives the EGA adaptor. For simple interactions between user and transputers it is possible to use a server process provided by INMOS[4], but for more complex applications it is necessary to add extra functionality to the server. The activity of the model was represented graphically in two ways (Figure 1). Firstly, the simulated ECG was displayed as a series of points on the screen. Secondly, the grid was displayed graphically, the colour of each point on the grid corresponding to the current excitatory state of the corresponding element. To achieve adequate speed for the display of the grid it was necessary to modify the server directly. This proved to be quite easy, except for the intricacies of programming the EGA.

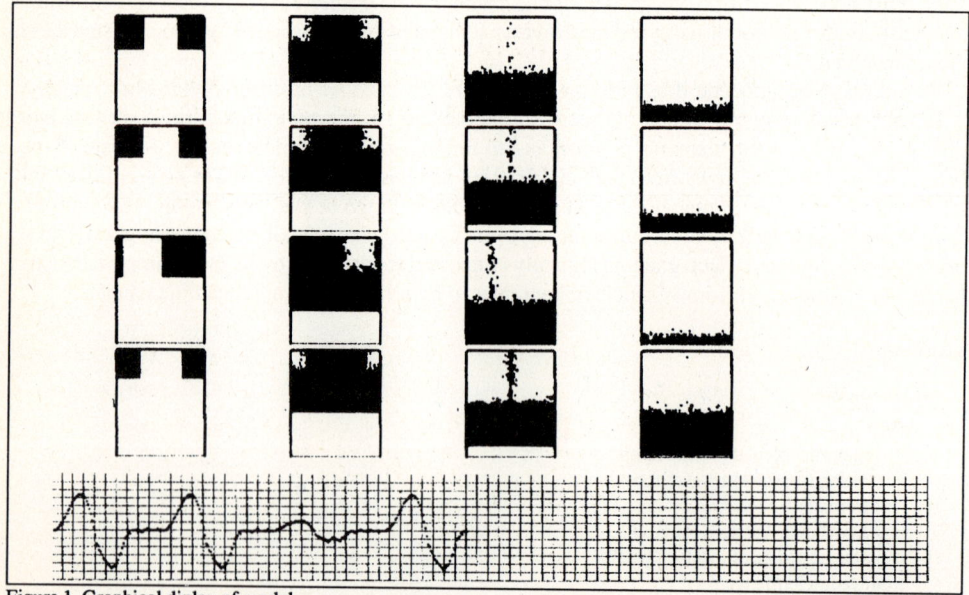

Figure 1. Graphical diplay of model.

The model itself was tested in five different configurations. In the first configuration display() and ventricle() are located on the same transputer, in the second, they are placed on two different transputers. In the third, fourth and fifth configurations the grid is divided into two, three and four surface patches respectively. Results from configurations (1) and (2) indicated that for small numbers of processors such as those considered here the computation time required for a time step would dominate the communication time required to exchange rows, given the speeds of the hardware links between transputers. Hence, for simplicity the grid has been divided horizontally in configurations (3), (4) and (5). Because each transputer has four bi-directional communications links this configuration leaves two links on each computational transputer free for communications with the display, and simplifies the software. Only in configuration (5) which had four computational transputers was

Table 1. Time required for 64 time steps.

Number of elements		Configuration including display of grid				Configuration excluding display of grid				
		(1) DP	(2) D+P	(3) D+2P	(4&5) D+3(4)P	(1) DP	(2) D+P	(3) D+2P	(4) D+3P	(5) D+4P
1024	32x32	5.9	5.6	4.5	4.5	5.9	5.2	2.8	2.1	1.3
2048	32x64	11.4	10.3	8.4	8.4	11.3	10.2	5.4	3.9	2.6
4096	64x64	22.1	20.8	16.0	16.0	22.2	20.5	10.7	7.6	5.1
8192	64x128	42.8	41.2	30.9	30.9	42.2	40.8	20.9	14.6	9.6
16384	128x128	84.9	80.4	60.5	60.5	83.6	81.5	41.8	29.1	19.2

it necessary to share a physical link between north/south channels and display channels. This was because the display transputer has one link dedicated to communications with the host and hence only three physical links available for communicating with the computational transputers.

Table 1 and Figures 2 and 3 summarise the results of runs of the model for the five different configurations. The times in left section of the table refer to runs in which all the graphical output was produced on the screen, whereas the times in the right half of the table are for runs in which only the points of the ECG were plotted. Each time is actually the total time required for 64 time steps. It is clear from comparing the left and right sides that the time required to display the grid is a bottleneck on the total performance for more than one or two computational transputers. However, if the display of the state of the grid is omitted the time taken varies inversely with the number of patches - the time taken per element remains constant. Relatively little improvement was obtained by allocating the display() and ventricle() processes on separate transputers, because the screen update on the host PC was acting as a bottleneck.

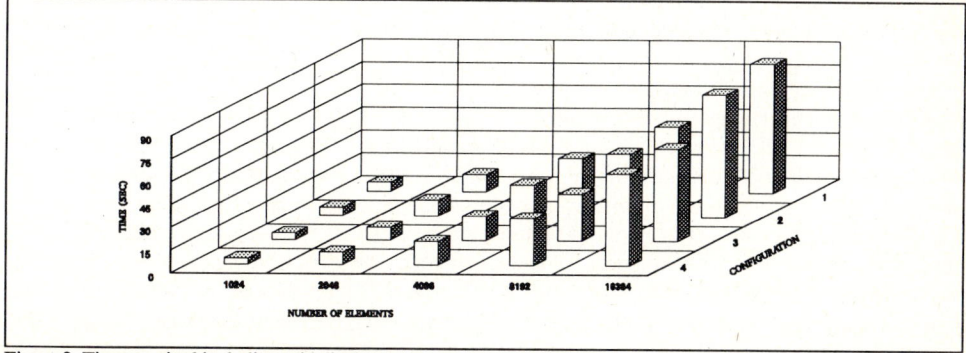

Figure 2. Time required including grid display.

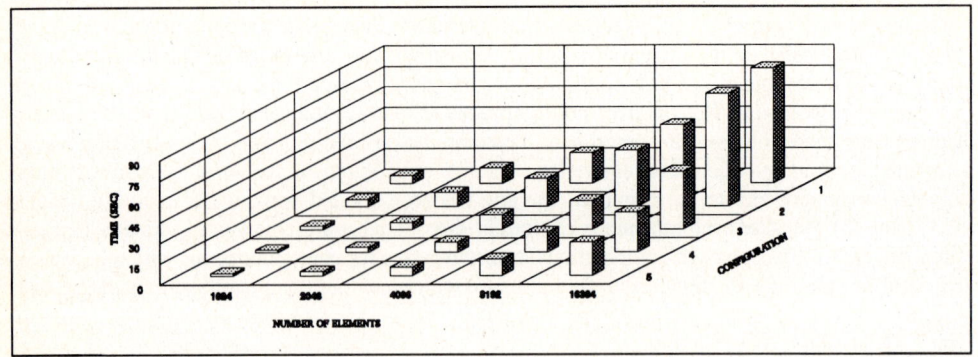

Figure 3. Time required excluding grid display.

6. Analysis

The results obtained in the previous section can be used to predict the behaviour of the model on larger transputer networks. Assume that t_{cpu} is the average time required to compute new.state() for a single element, and that t_d is the average time required to transfer the state of a patch to a neighbouring patch, and that there are w^2 elements in a square grid. Then, if there are P surface patches, arranged as horizontal stripes, the total time, T, required to compute newstate() is :

$$T = t_d w + t_{cpu} w^2 / P$$

For large values of P the communications time, which is a constant for constant w, will dominate the total time. Using a conservative value of t_d of 2.0×10^{-6} sec, and a measured value of 7.3×10^{-5} sec for t_{cpu} we find that for w=1024, the communications cost and the cpu cost become comparable only when P is greater than 38,000 - not yet a realistic option - so that there would be no need to use vertical banding as well as horizontal banding to define the patches in the model.

7. Discussion

One of the earliest computer models is Moe's model of the atrial[1]. The elements are arranged hexagonally in a flat sheet following similar neighbourhood rules. Up to 999 "tissue units" could be used. Malik [6] presented a similar model, developed on a NORD-100 minicomputer, using NORD-FORTRAN. Six seconds of real time required between five and fifteen minutes of CPU time. Another paper by Malik[7] describes the use of an ICL-4/72 computer. The simulation of a complete heartbeat with a total of about 6,000 elements required about 50 second of CPU time. Ahlfeldt[8] described a rectangular grid of 115 elements, implemented on a PDP-11/44 in which 10ms of real time was simulated in three to eight seconds. Auger [9] constructs a model of cardiac activation and conduction using the Hodgkin-Huxley model[10]. The system was implementd as an array of 10,000 elements on an HP 9836 computer, but there is no mention of the simulation time. The experiments presented here represent a considerable improvement over all these cases, and the parallel implementation allows for the possibility of further improvement by the use of more transputers. As we have already remarked the fact that interactions between elements in the model are purely local makes the model very suitable for application on a transputer network. The programming model supplied with the transputer development system requires the user to write his or her own software for moving data between remote processors, so communications which are solely between neighbouring processors are much simpler to implement and the resulting system is less prone to deadlock than systems which require complex routing processes to be written. In addition the cost of moving data between processors has proved to be relatively low in comparison with the computational cost and this has allowed us to further simplify the implementation by dividing the grid horizontally (rather than both horizontally and vertically). The performance of the model is close to real-time for 1024 elements.

On the negative side, the performance of the graphics interface was a little disappointing. This could be obviated in two ways. Firstly, faster hardware could be used. Secondly, the system could update the grid display less often than once per time-step - just often enough for the user to feel comfortable about the display rate. In any case, for very large grids, the time-steps are actually shorter, and the need to display the grid on every time-step is less obvious. Apart from the graphics performance, the main drawbacks encountered in the implementation process were mostly to do with the limitations of the process model we were using rather than with hardware. The model itself was straightforward to implement, but it would have been even easier if we had only to think about the placement of processes and not had to consider for example, the multiplexing of screen communication, and the details of the INMOS configuration language. At times the synchronous nature of communication in OCCAM complicated the implementation - for example it would have been useful to have had a 'send and forget' facility for screen output whereby the data would have been deemed to have been sent even if it had not physically been sent.

8. Conclusions

We have presented a simple finite-element model of ventricular conduction processes incorporating the concept of spatial dispersion of refractoriness. The purpose of the simulation was to introduce parallel processing into a model in which a physical model incorporates the most minimal features of ventricular conduction needed to represent spatial dispersion of refractoriness; in order to generate a variety of re-entrant disturbances of rhythm.The model was quite straightforward to implement on transputer networks and the high-efficiency parallelism was obtained. The use of multiple transputer chips opens the way for a program which is capable of running in times close enough to real-time.

As well as work into speeding up the sequential parts of the basic algorithm work is already under way to enhance this model into a four chamber heart model.

References

[1] Moe, G.K., Rheinboldt, W.C., Abildskov, J.A. "A Computer Model of Atrial Fibrillation". American Heart Journal, 1964. pp 200-220.

[2] Plonsey, R. "Bio-Electric Phenomena". 1969. McGraw Hill, New York.

[3] INMOS Limited. "Some Issues in Scientific Language Porting and Farming Using Transputers". In "The Transputer Development and iq Systems Databook". 1989. INMOS Limited. U.K.

[4] INMOS Limited. "Transputer Development System". 1988. Prentice Hall International (UK). Hemel Hempstead.

[5] INMOS Limited. "OCCAM-2 Reference Manual". 1988. Prentice Hall. Hemel Hempstead.

[6] Malik, M., Cochrane, T., Camm, A.J. "Computer Simulation of the Cardiac Conduction System". Computers and Biomedical Research. 16, 1983. pp 454-468.

[7] Malik, M., Cochrane, T. "Shell Computer Model of Cardiac Electropotential Changes". Journal of Biomedical Engineering. 7, 1985. pp 266-274.

[8] Ahlfeldt, H., Tanaka, H., Nygards, M-E, Wigertz, O. "A Mathematical Model of the Cardiac Conduction System Including External Pacemakers". Computers in Cardiology. 1985. pp 397-400.

[9] Auger, P., Lorente, P., Bardau, A., Degonde, J., Saumont, R. "A Model of Reentry Based on Huyghens Construction Method". Computers in Cardiology. 1984. pp 467-470.

[10] Noble, D. "A Modification of the Hodgkin-Huxley Equations Applicable to Purckinje Fibre Action and Pacemaker Potentials". Journal of Physiology. 160, 1962. pp 317-352.

Non-local Cluster Update Algorithms for Spin Models

Paul D. Coddington and Clive F. Baillie
Caltech Concurrent Computation Program,
California Institute of Technology,
Pasadena, CA 91125, USA
email: paulc@wega.caltech.edu

Abstract

Parallel computers are ideally suited to the Monte Carlo simulation of spin models using the standard Metropolis algorithm, since it is regular and local. However local algorithms have the major drawback that near a phase transition the number of sweeps needed to generate a statistically independent spin configuration increases as the square of the lattice size. New algorithms have recently been developed which dramatically reduce this "critical slowing down" by updating clusters of spins at a time. The highly irregular and non-local nature of the clusters means that these algorithms are much more difficult to parallelize efficiently. Here we introduce some parallel algorithms for identifying and labeling clusters, which have been implemented on the Meiko Computing Surface and other MIMD machines using the Express parallel programming environment. These algorithms are also applicable to the problem of labeling connected components in image analysis.

1. Introduction

Computer simulations are extremely useful for the study of spin models in condensed matter physics. In these models the spins are usually set up on the sites of a d-dimensional hypercubic lattice of length L. The L^d spins form some configuration. The goal of computer simulations of spin models is to generate configurations of spins which are typical of statistical equilibrium and measure physical observables on this ensemble of configurations. The generation of configurations is traditionally performed by Monte Carlo methods such as the Metropolis algorithm [1] . One of the main problems with these methods in practice is that successive configurations are not statistically independent, but rather are correlated, with some autocorrelation time τ between effectively independent configurations.

A key feature about traditional (Metropolis-like) Monte Carlo algorithms is that the updates are *local*, that is, the new value of the spin at a given lattice site depends only on the spin values at local (usually nearest neighbor) sites. Thus in a single step of the algorithm, information about the state of a spin is transmitted only to its near neighbors. Now, in order for the system to reach a new effectively independent configuration, this information must travel a distance of order the (static or spatial) correlation length ξ. As the information executes a random walk around the lattice, one would suppose that the autocorrelation time $\tau \sim \xi^2$. However, in general $\tau \sim \xi^z$, where z is called the dynamical critical exponent. Almost all numerical simulations of spin models have measured $z \approx 2$ for local update algorithms.

For a spin model with a phase transition, as the temperature approaches the critical value, ξ diverges to infinity, so that the computational efficiency rapidly goes to zero! This behavior is called critical slowing down, and it has plagued Monte Carlo simulations of statistical mechanical systems, in particular spin models, at or near their phase transitions. Recently, however, several new algorithms have been introduced which decrease z dramatically by performing *non-local* spin updates, thus reducing (or even eliminating) critical slowing down and facilitating much more efficient computer simulations.

Parallel computers have been very successfully applied to the Monte Carlo simulation of spin models using the traditional algorithms such as that of Metropolis. These algorithms are easily and efficiently parallelized using domain decomposition of the lattice, since they are very regular, and thus perfectly load balanced, and only require a small amount of local communication between processors. The new cluster algorithms, on the other hand, are highly irregular and non-local, and are therefore much more difficult to parallelize efficiently. Here we introduce the cluster update algorithms, briefly explain some sequential algorithms for identifying and labeling connected clusters of spins, and then outline some parallel algorithms which have been implemented on a transputer array.

2. Cluster algorithms

The aim of the cluster update algorithms is to find a suitable collection of spins which can be flipped with relatively little cost in energy. The first such algorithm was proposed by Swendsen and Wang [2], and was based on an equivalence between a Potts spin model [3] and percolation models [4], for which cluster properties play a fundamental role. The Potts model is a very simple spin model of a ferromagnet, in which the spins can take q different values. The case $q = 2$ is just the well-known Ising model. In the Swendsen and Wang algorithm, clusters of spins are created by introducing bonds between neighboring sites with probability $1 - e^{-\beta}$ if the two spins are the same, and zero if they are not, where β is the inverse temperature. All such clusters are created, and then updated by choosing a random new spin value for each cluster and assigning it to all the spins in that cluster. This very simple algorithm can be shown to be ergodic and to satisfy detailed balance, which are the two basic requirements of any Monte Carlo update algorithm.

A variant of this algorithm, for which only a single cluster is constructed and updated at each sweep, has been proposed by Wolff [5]. The algorithm of Swendsen and Wang seems to be better suited for parallelization, since it involves the entire lattice rather than just a single cluster, so will we restrict our attention to their algorithm.

3. Cluster labeling

Cluster algorithms have in common the problem of identifying and labeling the connected clusters of spins. This is very similar to an important problem in image processing, that of identifying and labeling the connected components in a binary or multi-colored image composed of an array of pixels. The only real difference is that in the spin model case, neighboring sites of the same spin have a certain *probability* of being in the same cluster, while for neighboring pixels of the same color that probability is one. Unfortunately this is a large enough difference so that some algorithms which work in image analysis will not work, or require substantial changes, for spin models.

First we mention some sequential algorithms for labeling clusters of connected sites. Perhaps the most obvious method for identifying a single cluster is the so-called "ants in the labyrinth" algorithm. The reason for its name is that we can visualize the algorithm as follows [6]. An ant is put somewhere on the lattice, and notes which of the neighboring sites are connected to the site it is on. At the next time-step this ant places children on each of these connected sites which are not already occupied. The children then proceed to reproduce likewise until the entire cluster is populated. In order to label all the clusters, we start by giving every site a negative label, set the initial cluster label to be zero, and then loop through all the sites in turn. If a site's label is negative then the site has not already been assigned to a cluster, so we place an ant on this site, give it the current cluster label, and let it reproduce, passing the label on to all its offspring. When this cluster is identified we increment the cluster label and carry on, repeating the ant-colony birth, growth and death cycle until all the clusters have been identified.

An alternative method which is commonly used, especially for cluster identification in percolation models, is that of Hoshen and Kopelman [7]. We have found that 'ants' gives slightly better performance than this algorithm, and so we will not discuss it further.

Identifying and labeling clusters of connected sites in a lattice is a special case of the more general problem known variously as the set union, union-find, or equivalence problem, that is, given a list of equivalences between elements, sort the elements into equivalence classes. In the context of cluster algorithms, the list of equivalences is just a list of the sites which are connected together, and the equivalence classes are just the clusters. There are a multitude of algorithms for this problem [8]; we have used an elegant and easy to code method due to Galler and Fisher, the details of which are described in Ref. [9].

4. Parallel algorithms

As with the percolation models upon which the cluster algorithms are based, the phase transition in a spin model occurs when the clusters of bonded spins become large enough to span the entire lattice. Thus near criticality, which in most cases is where we want to perform the simulation, clusters come in all sizes, from order N (where N is the number of sites in the lattice) right down to a single site. The highly irregular and non-local nature of the clusters means that cluster update algorithms do not vectorize, and hence give poor performance on vector machines. On this problem one head of a CRAY X-MP is only about twenty times faster than a single transputer (the time for the CRAY is taken from Wolff [10]). Hence using the trivial parallelization technique of running independent Monte Carlo simulations on different processors, it is possible to do as well as a CRAY on a transputer array of only about twenty nodes. This works well until the lattice size gets too big to fit into the memory of each node, and in fact we have used this method to calculate the dynamical critical exponents of various cluster algorithms [11]. However in the case of the Potts model, for example, only lattices of size less than about 300^2 or 50^3 will fit into 1 Mbyte, and most other spin models are more complicated and more memory intensive. We therefore need a parallel algorithm where a large lattice can be distributed over many processors.

This can be easily and efficiently done for local update algorithms such as Metropolis, however for cluster algorithms it a much more difficult problem. The quality of non-locality which makes cluster algorithms so useful also makes them very difficult to parallelize efficiently, since this involves a large amount of non-local communication. Also the irregular nature of the clusters means that SIMD machines are probably not well suited to this problem, whereas for the Metropolis type algorithms they are perhaps the best machines available. It therefore appears that the optimum performance for this class of problem will come from MIMD parallel computers such as transputer arrays.

A parallel cluster algorithm involves distributing the lattice onto an array of processors using the usual domain decomposition. Clearly a sequential algorithm can be used to label the clusters on each processor, but we need a procedure for converting these labels to their correct *global* values. We need to be able to tell many processors, which may be any distance apart, that some of their clusters are actually the same. Thus we need to be able to agree on which of the many different local labels for a given cluster should be assigned to be the global cluster label, and to pass this label to all the processors containing a part of that cluster. We will discuss two methods for tackling this problem, "self-labeling" and "global equivalencing".

4.1. Self-labeling

We shall refer to this algorithm as "self-labeling", since each site figures out which cluster it is in by itself, from local information. We begin by assigning to each site i a unique cluster label S_i. In practice this is simply chosen as the position of that site in the lattice. At each step of the algorithm, in parallel, every site looks in turn at each of its neighbors in the positive directions. If it is bonded to a neighboring site n which has a different cluster label S_n, then both S_i and S_n are set to the minimum of the two. This is continued until nothing changes, by which time all the clusters will have been labeled with the minimum initial label of all the sites in the cluster. Note that to check termination of the algorithm involves each processor sending a termination flag (finished or not finished) to every other processor after each step, which can become very costly for a large processor array.

This is a purely SIMD algorithm, and when implemented on a SIMD machine such as the AMT DAP it gives very poor performance due to a large load imbalance, with most processors waiting for the few in the largest cluster which are the last to get the label for that cluster. However on a MIMD machine such as a transputer array, we can greatly improve this method by using a fast sequential algorithm, such as "ants in the labyrinth", to label the clusters in the sublattice on each processor, and then just use self-labeling on the sites at the edges of each processor to eventually arrive at the global cluster labels. The number of steps required to do the self-labeling will depend on the largest cluster, which at the phase transition will generally span the entire lattice. The number of self-labeling steps will therefore be of the order of the maximum distance between processors, which for a square array of P processors is just $2\sqrt{P}$. Hence the amount of communication (and calculation) involved in doing the self-labeling, which is proportional to the number of iterations times the perimeter of the sublattice, goes like L for an LxL lattice, whereas the time taken on each processor to do the local cluster labeling goes like the area of the sublattice, which is L^2/P. Therefore as long as L is substantially greater than the number of processors (which is generally the case) we can expect to obtain a reasonable speedup.

The speedups obtained on a 32 T800 Meiko Computing Surface for a variety of lattice sizes are shown in Fig. 1. The dashed line indicates perfect speedup (i.e. 100% efficiency). We can see that the algorithm performs poorly for the smallest lattice size, however this sized calculation can easily be done by running multiple simulations on each processor. The lattice sizes for which we actually need to use many processors for each simulation are of the order of 512^2 or greater, for which we obtain efficiencies of greater than 90% on 16 nodes (or by running multiple simulations of 16 nodes each). Using all 32 nodes gives an efficiency of only about 70%, however even this modest figure is enough so that the transputer array outperforms one head of a CRAY X-MP on this problem.

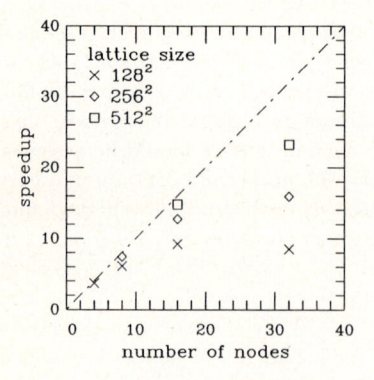

Fig. 1. Speedup for self–labeling.

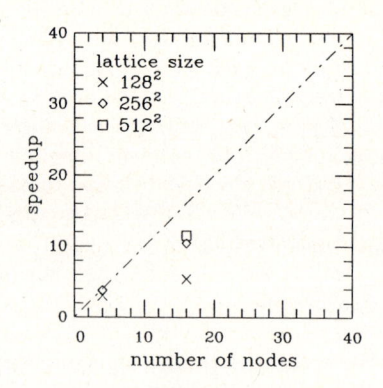

Fig. 2. Speedup for hierarchical equivalencing.

4.2. Global equivalencing

In this method we again use the fastest sequential algorithm to identify the clusters in the sublattice on every processor. Each node then looks at the labels of sites along the edges of the neighboring nodes in the positive directions, and works out which ones are connected and should be assigned the same cluster label. All the nodes send their list of equivalences to one of the nodes (or to the host processor), which uses them as input to the equivalence class algorithm of Fisher and Galler [9], performing a global matching of the cluster labels and then broadcasting the results back to all the nodes.

As stated above, the global equivalencing step is purely sequential, and is thus a potentially disastrous bottleneck on a large array of processors. What we have done instead is to distribute the creation of global equivalence classes by using a hierarchical divide-and-conquer approach. In this hierarchical equivalencing the processor array is divided up into smaller subarrays of, for example, 2x2 processors. Each subarray performs the global equivalencing algorithm on its section of the lattice. The results of these partial matchings are then combined on each 4x4 subarray, and this process is continued until finally all the partial results are merged together to give the global cluster values. In this way the number of processors performing the equivalencing step is $P/4$ for the first level of the hierarchy, $P/16$ for the second level, and so on, until the final stage is done on a single processor. However by that time most of the work has been done, so the bottleneck has been at least partially alleviated.

A very similar algorithm which uses the same hierarchical procedure has been implemented on a hypercube for the image processing component labeling problem by Embrechts et al. [12] . The hierarchical structure of this algorithm and the non-local communication required favor a hypercube connectivity rather than the mesh connectivity of a transputer array.

The speedups for hierarchical equivalencing are shown in Fig. 2. The results are rather poor, and much worse than for self-labeling, however this is a very preliminary implementation of an algorithm which is quite complicated and difficult to code, and there are many parts of the program which could be improved upon. We expect that an optimized version of this algorithm will do better than self-labeling, at least for large numbers of processors. Results are given only for 4 and 16 processors, since the algorithm requires the number of processors to be an even power of two.

4.3. Other algorithms

Currently the only other parallel cluster algorithm proposed for spin models is a parallel extension of the Hoshen and Kopelmann algorithm [7] due to Burkitt and Heermann [13], which has been implemented on a transputer array. Their algorithm is much more complicated, and less efficient, than the self-labeling algorithm, giving speedups for a 512^2 lattice of approximately 11.5 and 11.0 on 16 and 32 processors respectively.

There have been many different parallel algorithms proposed for the connected component labeling problem in image analysis. These algorithms are generally aimed at shared memory [14], SIMD [15] [16], or hypercube [17] architectures, but could probably also be implemented on transputer arrays. Further investigation is needed to see if these algorithms might be applied to the problem of producing a more efficient parallel cluster algorithm for spin models on large numbers of processors.

5. The Express programming environment

The two parallel algorithms outlined above have been coded in C using the Express parallel programming environment from Parasoft Corporation, which is a commercial version of the Crystalline Operating System (CROS) developed for the Caltech hypercubes. Express is basically a toolkit which provides utilities for debugging, performance monitoring, graphics, allocation of nodes, and simple I/O using the usual *printf* and *scanf* routines, as well as a library of subroutines for decomposing arrays onto processors, and communicating between processors. This greatly simplifies the writing of parallel programs, as anyone who has had to write their own I/O or communications routines can testify. A general communications routine, where messages may be sent between any two processors, was particularly useful for the hierarchical equivalencing algorithm, which requires a lot of non-local communication.

A major advantage of Express is that it is portable, so that we now have the same self-labeling cluster algorithm program running Potts model simulations on Caltech's 512 node NCUBE-1 and 192 node Symult S2010, as well as the 32 node Meiko Computing Surface. It is also portable between host machines, allowing you to edit, compile and run your code from, for example, a Sun, IBM PC, or Macintosh, using the standard operating system of the host machine.

Some performance is sacrificed for all this convenience, however. Although the throughput is very good, the latency for sending a message on the Meiko is substantially increased, to around $280\mu s$ [18]. This almost certainly affects the efficiency of our programs on the Computing Surface, since in these algorithms there is a lot of communication of fairly small amounts of data. This is not so noticeable for other machines, however, which generally have latencies much higher than that of the transputer.

6. Conclusions

Cluster algorithms can give orders of magnitude better performance than local update algorithms on large lattices, however simulating large lattices requires parallel or vector supercomputers, for which the local algorithms are much better suited. Due to the irregular and non-local nature of the cluster algorithms, it seems possible that these algorithms cannot be implemented efficiently on a large number of processors. However we have shown that it is possible to obtain good efficiencies on moderate numbers of processors, so that by running multiple independent Monte Carlos of around 16 or 32 nodes each, a large transputer array can be efficiently used for simulating spin models using the cluster algorithm of Swendsen and Wang.

References

[1] N. Metropolis et al., *J. Chem. Phys.* **21**, 1087 (1953).
[2] R.H. Swendsen and J.-S. Wang, *Phys. Rev. Lett.* **58**, 86 (1987).
[3] R.B. Potts, *Proc. Camb. Phil. Soc.* **48**, 106 (1952); F.Y. Wu, *Rev. Mod. Phys.* **54**, 235 (1982).
[4] D. Stauffer, *Phys. Rep.* **54**, 1 (1978); J.W. Essam, *Rep. Prog. Phys.* **43**, 830 (1980).
[5] U. Wolff, *Phys. Rev. Lett.* **62**, 361 (1989).
[6] R. Dewar and C.K. Harris, *J. Phys. A* **20**, 985 (1987).
[7] J. Hoshen and R. Kopelman, *Phys. Rev.* **B14**, 3438 (1976).
[8] R.E. Tarjan and J. van Leeuwen, *J. ACM* **31**, 245 (1984).
[9] D.E. Knuth, *Fundamental Algorithms*, vol. 1 of *The Art of Computer Programming* (Addison-Wesley,Reading,1968); W.H. Press et al., *Numerical Recipes in C; The Art of Scientific Programming*, (Cambridge University Press, Cambridge, 1988).
[10] U. Wolff, *Phys. Lett.* **B228**, 379 (1989).
[11] C.F. Baillie and P.D. Coddington, "A Comparison of Cluster Algorithms for Potts Models", Caltech Concurrent Computation Report C^3P-835, October 1989.
[12] H. Embrechts, D. Roose, and P. Wambacq, "Component Labeling on a Distributed Memory Multiprocessor", *Proc. First European Workshop on Hypercube and Distributed Computers*, F. Andre and J.P. Verjus eds., (North-Holland, Amsterdam,1989).
[13] A.N. Burkitt and D.W. Heermann, *Comp. Phys. Comm.* **54**, 210 (1989).
[14] R. Hummel, "Connected component labeling in image processing with MIMD architectures", in *Intermediate-Level Image Processing*, M.J.B. Duff ed., (Academic Press, New York, 1986).
[15] W. Lim, A. Agrawal, L. Nekludova, "A Fast Parallel Algorithm for Labeling Connected Components in Image Arrays" Thinking Machines Corporation Technical Report NA86-2.
[16] D. Nassimi and S. Sahni, *SIAM J. Comput.* **9**, 744 (1980).
[17] R. Cypher, J.L.C. Sanz and L. Snyder, *J. Algorithms* **10**, 140 (1989).
[18] R. Salvador, "Message passing benchmark for the NCUBE-1, Symult, Mark III and Meiko", in C^3P Technical Bulletin 19, November 1989.

The Numerical Solution of ODE IVPs in a Transputer Environment

Centre for Mathematical Software Research, University of Liverpool,
Liverpool, United Kingdom, L69 3BX

Abstract. In the paper we consider two different approaches to the numerical solution of ordinary differential equation initial value problems (ODE IVPs); one in a general setting and one in a specific. In the first case we report on the performance of a code based on Gragg's extrapolation algorithm for solving nonstiff ODE IVPs on a rectangular array of transputers; while in the second case we consider the solution of certain time-dependent parabolic partial differential equations by a Fourier-integration approach on a chain of transputers.

1. Introduction

The study of numerical methods for the solution of ordinary differential equation initial value problems ODE IVPs for implementation on a single-processor computers has resulted in a number of successful and efficient codes such as EPISODE [5], STEP [11] and DORP8 [10]. It would be desirable however, if similar codes could be developed for multi-processor computers because methods that are efficient in sequential environment are not necessarily efficient in a parallel environment.

As a first step towards developing parallel ODE solvers it is useful to consider the potential parallelism in single-processor ODE solvers. In general, parallelism can arise in such codes in two ways. Firstly, parallelism may exist in the solution algorithm independent of the ODE IVP. Secondly, parallelism can be dependent on the ODE IVP. Considering the first kind, we find that current sequential solution methods (excluding extrapolation methods) possess little parallelism. Thus if we wish to exploit this kind of parallelism new parallel solution methods will have to be developed. Turning to the second kind of parallelism, we find that typically, ODE IVPs which have more than one dependent variable offer the greatest scope for parallelism. This is because where explicit solution methods are used, as is the case for non-stiff ODE IVPs, the method can be applied to each equation without further partitioning.

In this paper we have adopted two different approaches. In section 2 we take an existing successful single-processor method based on Gragg's modified midpoint rule and try to exploit the natural parallelism which results from the fact that each low order approximation can be calculated in parallel. We report on the performance of a code PEXTRAP written in Occam2 running on a rectangular array of transputers in which the problem is partitioned across the rows of the array and the low order approximations and the extrapolation process are partitioned across the columns of the array.

In section 3 we consider specific application areas where parallelism can be more easily exploited than in a general setting. One such area is the numerical solution of time-dependent linear partial differential equations. By discretizing the spatial variables these PDEs can be transformed into a set of ODE IVPs with a time-dependent forcing term, for which the eigenvalue and eigenvector structure of the A-matrix is often well-known. Thus the problem can be decoupled into a number of independent quadrature problems, by an orthogonal transformation. These can then solved in parallel independently of one another and with minimal communication. In section 3 we report on the performance of an Occam2 code running on a linear chain of transputers which does this decoupling automatically. This uses an adaptive ten point Gauss, twenty one point Kronrod extension, to evaluate the independent quadrature problems and we compare it with the performance of a standard ODE IVP code (STRIDE [4]) running in FORTRAN 3L on a single transputer.

The work presented in the paper has been carried out as part of the *EEC Supernode II* project to develop a library of numerical codes for transputer array computers. Participants in the project include *The Centre for Mathematical Software Research* and the *Numerical Analysis Group*.

2. PEXTRAP - A Parallel Extrapolation code based on Gragg's Rule

2.1 Gragg's Rule

Extrapolation methods based on Gragg's Rule [8] have become a popular method for solving non-stiff ODE IVPs in recent years. Bench tests using sequential codes based on Graggs's rule show that the method performs best where high accuracy is required and the solution is 'smooth'. These methods calculate an approximation to the solution of the ODE IVP

$$y'(x) = f(x,y), \quad y(x_n) = u_n, \quad y, x \in \mathbf{R}$$

at $x_{n+1} = x_n + H$ by constructing the extrapolation tableau

$$\begin{array}{ccccc} P_{1,1} \\ P_{2,1} & P_{2,2} \\ P_{3,1} & P_{3,2} & P_{3,3} \\ \vdots & \vdots & \vdots & \ddots \\ P_{m,1} & P_{m,2} & P_{m,3} & \cdots & P_{m,m} \end{array}$$

where $P_{i,1}$, is calculated from **procedure gragg**

procedure gragg
  begin
    $\eta_0 = u_n$;
    $h_i = H/s_i$;
    $\eta_1 = \eta_0 + h_i f(x_n, u_n)$;
    for $j := 1$ step 1 until $s_i - 1$ do
      $\eta_{j+1} = \eta_{j-1} + 2h_i f(x_n + jh_i, \eta_j)$
    $P_{i,1} = \frac{1}{2}(\eta_{s_i-1} + \eta_{s_i} + h_i f(x_n + H, \eta_{s_i}))$
  end.

and $P_{i,j}$ is calculated from Neville's algorithm, modified to take into account the even-power expansion of $P_{j,1}$.

$$P_{i,j} = P_{i,j-1} + \frac{P_{i-1,j} - P_{i-1,j-1}}{\left[\frac{s_i}{s_{i-j+1}}\right]^2 - 1} \quad i = 1,\ldots,m, \quad j = 1,\ldots,i.$$

Note that in most extrapolation codes a modified form of Neville's algorithm is used to minimize rounding errors. To ensure the $P_{j,1}$ has an even-power expansion, the sequence $S = \{s_i\}$ used in Gragg's rule to calculate h_i must satisfy the following conditions:

(i) S is a strictly increasing sequence of natural numbers.
(ii) all the terms in S are either all odd or all even.

Further constraints are also placed on S so that the numerical efficiency and stability of the overall method are satisfactory. A popular sequence that meets these requirements is the *harmonic* sequence
$$S_{2H} = \{2, 4, 6, 8, \ldots 2n, \ldots\}.$$

The local error in Gragg's extrapolation method can be controlled by using the following expression for the *local truncation error*

$$y(x_n + H) - P_{i,j} = C_{i,j}(x_n)H^{2j+1} \qquad (2.1)$$

so that an estimate for the error in $P_{m,m-1}$ is given by

$$\varepsilon_{m-1} = |y(x_n + H) - P_{m,m-1}| \approx |P_{m,m-1} - P_{m,m}|.$$

Thus, a step is accepted if
$$\varepsilon_{m-1} \leq eps \qquad (2.2)$$

where eps is the *local error tolerance*. To improve accuracy the method proceeds to the next step with $u_{n+1} = P_{m,m}$ using *local extrapolation*. A suitable stepsize for the next step can also be estimated from (2.1) by finding the stepsize $\hat{H}$ such that $eps = C_{m,m-1}(x_n)\hat{H}^{2j-1}$, so that

$$\hat{H} = H \left(\frac{eps}{\varepsilon_{m-1}}\right)^{1/(2j-1)} \qquad (2.3)$$

In practice it is often necessary to scale eps to reflect the size of the solution. $\hat{H}$ is also multiplied by a small *safety factor* (about 0.9) to minimize the number of rejected steps. The stepsize is not increased if the step has been repeated for the same reason.

In sequential codes, Gragg's extrapolation method proceeds at each step by applying the test (2.2) as each row of the tableau is calculated. Thus if we are at the j-th row we only proceed to the next row if (2.2) has not been satisfied and we are confident that the tableau will converge. The rate at which the tableau is converging can be estimated by the ratio $\varepsilon_j/\varepsilon_{j-1}$. Thus if

$$\varepsilon_j \left(\frac{\varepsilon_j}{\varepsilon_{j-1}}\right)^{\bar{m}-j} > eps \qquad j = 2, \ldots, \bar{m} - 1 \qquad (2.4)$$

we repeat the step. Note $\bar{m}$ is the maximum tableau size (usually about 10). When a step is repeated a new stepsize can be calculated from $\hat{H} = shrink \cdot H$, where $shrink = 0.4$ is a typical value.

A number of strategies have been proposed for controlling the tableau size m, but for most ODE IVPs the following simple scheme is usually effective

$$\text{if} \quad m > \hat{m} \quad \text{then} \quad \hat{H} := 0.8\hat{H} \qquad (2.5a)$$
$$\text{if} \quad m < \hat{m} \quad \text{then} \quad \hat{H} := 1.2\hat{H} \qquad (2.5b)$$

where $\hat{m}$ is the 'optimal' tableau size. This is should be set as large as possible to maximize efficiency (assuming the solution is sufficiently smooth), but consistent with the need that the occasional overestimate of stepsize does not cause the step to be repeated. Setting $\hat{m} = \bar{m} - 2$ is a good compromise.

2.2 Parallelism in Gragg's Rule

A study of Gragg's rule will show that the calculation of each $P_{i,1}$, $i = 1, \ldots, m$ can be carried out in parallel. Since the amount of computation in $P_{i,1}$ is proportional to s_i, the maximum speedup β_S (i.e. ignoring any time taken for communication or synchronization) is given by

$$\beta_S(i) = \frac{\sum_{j=1}^{i} s_j}{s_i}. \qquad (2.6)$$

Thus for S_{2H} and $\hat{m} = 8$ we get $\beta_{2H}(8) = 4.5$. To achieve this speedup each $P_{i,1}$, $i = 1, \ldots, m$ would have to be assigned to a different processor. A speedup for the extrapolation can also be achieved by assigning the calculation of $P_{i,i}$, $i = 1, \ldots, m$ to a different processor. Then if $f(x, y)$ is sufficiently expensive to compute, $P_{m-1,j}$, $j = 1, \ldots, m-1$, will have been calculated before $P_{m,1}$ giving a speedup of $\approx m/2$.

So far we have we have only considered the parallelism in Gragg's extrapolation method which is independent of the ODE IVPs. Gragg's extrapolation method can also be used to solve ODE IVPs which have N dependent variables by applying Gragg's extrapolation method to each equation. However the $i-th$ equation can only be processed in parallel, provided the necessary y values to calculate $f_i(x, y)$ are available. If we ignore the time required to communicate these arguments the maximum speedup β_f is given by

$$\beta_f = \frac{\sum_{j=1}^{N} t_j}{\max_{1 \leq k \leq N} t_j} \qquad (2.7)$$

where t_i is the computation time for $f_i(x, y)$.

The PEXTRAP code tries to exploit both these types of parallelism by using a rectangular array of transputers, with the row dimension $R \leq N$ and column dimension $C \leq \bar{m}$. The computation of $P_{j,j}$ for the $i-th$ equation is assigned to the (k, l) transputer according to the integer arrays, row.start, row.end and col.start, col.end and the rules

$$\text{col.start}[k] \leq j \leq \text{col.end}[k], \qquad \text{row.start}[l] \leq i \leq \text{row.end}[l].$$

To allow the (k, l) transputer to calculate $f_j(x, y)$, $j = \text{row.start}[k], \ldots, \text{row.end}[k]$ it is necessary to include in the parameter list for the function subroutine the row.start and row.end values. In addition to this the subroutine also has to be modified so that only $f_j(x, y)$, $j = \text{row.start}[k], \ldots, \text{row.end}[k]$ are calculated. Because data propagates towards the transputer(s) assigned to the calculation of $P_{\hat{m},\hat{m}}$, these transputers are the first column of the array. Hence the columns are numbered from max.col - 0 whilst the rows are numbered from 0 - max.row.

The operation of PEXTRAP is as follows. After the initial conditions have been sent to each processor the (k, l) transputer starts by calculating $P_{\text{col.start}[l],1}$ for the row.start[k]-row.end[k] equations. Before each function evaluation the y-arguments are simultaneously shifted up and down a column so that every transputer has access to the arguments required. Since communicating these arguments can be expensive a bandwidth parameter can be set to indicate the maximum number of shifts required to communicate any y argument. For example, if the structure of the ODE IVP is tridiagonal then bandwidth = 1. As the values $P_{j,j}$, $j = 1, \ldots, \hat{m}$ are calculated the corresponding values ε_j are simultaneously shifted

up and down a column so that each transputer can find the maximum value for ε_j. Each transputer in the column then uses the tests, (2.2) and (2.4) to determine its subsequent actions. If we assume that the (k,l) transputer has found the maximum value of ε_j then three possible actions can occur.
1) (2.2) and (2.4) have not been satisfied. The step must be repeated so the status signal never.converged is sent to all transputer in the k-th row. A new stepsize is calculated from $\hat{H} = shrink \cdot H$.
2) (2.2) has not been satisfied but (2.4) has. If the $(k+1,l)$ transputer has calculated $P_{j+1,1}$ the status signal not.converged is sent to the $(k+1,l)$ transputer along with the values $P_{i,k}$, $i = 1, \ldots, j$ otherwise the (k,l) transputer calculates $P_{j+1,1}$ and then $P_{j+1,j+1}$.
3) (2.2) has been satisfied. The status signal converged is sent to all transputers in the $k-th$ row and along with the new stepsize (calculated from (2.3) and (2.5)) and the new initial conditions.

After 1) and 3) a new step can commence immediately. For 2) the (k,l) transputer waits for a status signal before starting a new step. When the new initial values reach the transputers in the max.col column they are shifted up to the (max.col,0) transputer where they are sent to the host.

2.3 Results and Conclusions

A number of different ODE IVPs have been solved to evaluate the performance of PEXTRAP. For comparison purposes the same ODE IVPs have been solved with a sequential extrapolation code (SEXTRAP) and the Prince and Dormand 7(8) Runge-Kutta method (DORP8). All the results were calculated in double precision using T8 transputers running with a 25Mhz clock. The programs were written in Occam2.

In the following tables *Time* refers to the computation time in machine units, *Fns* to the number of function evaluations used, *Steps* to the number of steps used, *Eps* to the local error tolerance and *Error* to the global error measured at the end of the interval.

Problem 1 $y'(x) = y(x)$, $y(0) = 1$, solved at $x = 60$ with $eps = 10^{-9}$. PEXTRAP was run on a 1×8 grid. The results are shown in table 2.1 and the figures on the right are as Problem 1 except a delay of 10 time units was placed in the function subroutine. The PEX* row are for PEXTRAP running on a pseudo-parallel 1×8 grid

Problem 2 Three body problem [1]. The results for SEXTRAP, DORP8, PEXTRAP (using a 1×8 grid) are shown in tables 2.2a, 2.2b, and 2.2c respectively.

Problem 3 A tridiagonal system of N equations derived from a parabolic PDE, Hull [9], solved at $x = 60$ with $eps = 10^{-9}$. PEXTRAP was run on a 9×1 grid. The figures on the left are for $N = 9$ whilst the those on the right are for $N = 900$. The same number of equations were assigned to each transputer.

From the results presented it is clear that PEXTRAP can not achieve any speedup when the computation time for the function evaluation is small. This is because the management of the communication and partitioning increases the overheads of PEXTRAP over SEXTRAP. The results for PEX* in table 2.1 show this. The time need to communicate between transputers is also significant when the function evaluation is cheap.

Another factor that can seriously reduce the expected speedup given by (2.6), even when the function evaluation is expensive is where the average tableau size is much smaller

Table 2.1

Method	Time	Fns	Steps	Method	Time	Fns	Steps
SEX	743	2300	34	SEX	23750	2300	34
PEX	836	–	34	PEX	6199	–	34
PEX*	1796	–	34				

Table 2.2a

Eps	Time	Fns	Steps	Error	Eps	Time	Fns	Steps	Error
10^{-6}	9369	1651	43	7×10^{-4}	10^{-9}	15735	2796	50	1×10^{-7}
10^{-12}	25630	4566	74	2.5×10^{-12}					

Table 2.2b

Eps	Time	Fns	Steps	Error	Eps	Time	Fns	Steps	Error
10^{-6}	8087	1360	76	2.2×10^{-6}	10^{-9}	17072	2872	160	7.4×10^{-10}
10^{-12}	27421	4622	350	8.9×10^{-13}					

Table 2.2c

Eps	Time	Steps	Error	Eps	Time	Steps	Error
10^{-6}	6663	43	7×10^{-4}	10^{-9}	7950	49	1×10^{-7}
10^{-12}	11230	74	2.5×10^{-12}				

Table 2.3

Method	Time	Steps	Method	Time	Fns	Steps
SEX	6365	45	SEX	982186	3376	60
PEX	4910	45	PEX	119779	–	60

than `col.start[max.col]`. This is because the minimum computation time must be greater than the time needed to calculate $P_{\text{col.start[max.col]},1}$. Since the effective solution of Problem 2 requires much changing of stepsize the average tableau size is small. However reducing `col.start[max.col]` does not give any improvements in this case because a large tableau size is still sometimes used, thereby causing the `max.col` transputer extra work.

To achieve a speedup close to (2.7) it is necessary that the ratio of computation time of the function evaluation to the time required to communicate the y-arguments is as large as possible. For Problem 3 the results show that this ratio is too small for $N = 9$. Increasing N to 900 however, does not increase the amount of communication but does increase the computation time for the function evaluation. Thus the ratio is increased by a factor of a hundred and this leads to a better speedup.

3. The solution of linear time-dependent parabolic PDEs

Consider the solution of the M-dimensional inhomogeneous diffusion-convection problem, in some region Ω, given by

$$u_t(x,t) = D\nabla^2 u(x,t) - Cu_x(x,t) + f(x,t), \quad t > 0 \qquad (3.1)$$

where $x \in \mathbf{R}^M$ and ∇^2 denotes the Laplacian operator. We note in the case that $C = 0$ that this represents purely a diffusion problem and that f can be considered as representing some internal heat source or sink.

A very popular and successful way of solving such a problem is by the process of semi-discretization in which only the spatial variables are discretized, thus reducing the problem to a system of ordinary differential equations of the form

$$u'(t) = Au(t) + \phi(t), \quad u(0) = u_0, \quad u \in \mathbf{R}^N. \qquad (3.2)$$

Here A is a constant matrix with a bandwidth dependent on the ordering of the equations and the dimension of the partial differential equation. Equation (3.2) can now be solved by a standard ordinary differential equation initial value problem (ODE IVP) integrator.

However, in order to be able to exploit the massive parallelism that is available through the technology of the transputer we should consider methods that minimise the amount of communication. The numerical solution of ODE IVPs is notoriously difficult in a parallel setting because communication is both global and extensive, instead we propose to solve (3.2) by decoupling the equations by finding the eigenvalues and eigenvectors of A, and hence reducing the problem to a set of independent quadrature problems. These can be solved in parallel efficiently on, for example, a linear chain of transputers (see Burrage [2] and Burrage [3]) with a minimal amount of communication. The integrator itself is an adaptive one based on the ten point Gauss, twenty one point Kronrod extension, and incorporating the extrapolation algorithm of Wynn and is coded in Occam2.

As we will see the eigenvalue and eigenvector structure of A is well-known for many classes of semi-discretizations, with the eigenvalues often being real and the transformation matrix being orthogonal. Thus in this case we can write

$$T^{-1}AT = \Lambda, \quad T^{-1}u(0) = z(0), \quad T^{-1}\phi(t) = g(t)$$

so that the solution of (3.2) is

$$u(t) = Tz(t)$$
$$z_i(t) = e^{\lambda_i t}z_i(0) + \int_0^t e^{(t-s)\lambda_i} g_i(s)ds, \quad i = 1, \ldots, N. \qquad (3.3)$$

As a particular example we consider the case of the 1-dimensional diffusion problem ($C = 0$.) If $\Omega = [0, L]$ and central differencing on a grid of $N+1$ equal subintervals is used with $u_k(t)$, $k = 0, \ldots, N+1$ approximating $u(x_k, t)$, $x_k = kh$, $h = L/(N+1)$ then the form of (3.2) depends on the initial conditions associated with (3.1). If Dirichlet initial conditions of the type

$$u(x, 0) = r(x), \quad 0 < x < L, \quad U(0, t) = p(t), \quad u(L, t) = q(t), \quad t > 0$$

are used then (3.2) becomes a system of N equations. Let (a, b, c) denote the tridiagonal matrix with b on the diagonal and a and c on the lower and upper subdiagonals, respectively. Then in this case

$$A = \theta(1, -2, 1), \quad \theta = \frac{D}{h^2}, \quad u_0 = (r(x_1), \ldots, r(x_N))^T$$

and

$$\phi(t) = (f(x_1, t) + \theta p(t), f(x_2, t), \ldots, f(x_{N-1}, t), f(x_N, t) + \theta q(t))^T.$$

On the other hand if the boundary conditions are derivative (Neumann) boundary conditions of the form

$$u(x, 0) = r(x), \quad 0 < x < L, \quad u_x(0, t) = p(t), \quad u_x(L, t) = q(t), \quad t > 0$$

then using a central difference formula to approximate the left and right boundary conditions it is readily seen that A has the same form as before apart from the $(1, 2)$ and $(N, N-1)$ entries which are 2θ. For both the Dirichlet and Neumann conditions the eigenvalue and eigenvector structure of A is well-known (see [6], for example). In the case of the Dirichlet conditions the eigenvalues are

$$\lambda_j = -2 + 2\cos\left(\frac{j\pi}{N+1}\right), \quad j = 1,\ldots,N$$

with corresponding eigenvector

$$v_j = \left(\sin\left(\frac{j\pi}{N+1}\right),\ldots,\sin\left(\frac{jN\pi}{N+1}\right)\right)^T;$$

while for the Neumann conditions the eigenvectors are

$$\lambda_j = -2 + 2\cos\left(\frac{(j-1)\pi}{N-1}\right), \quad j = 1,\ldots,N$$

with corresponding eigenvector

$$v_j = \left(1, \cos\left(\frac{(j-1)\pi}{N-1}\right),\ldots,\cos((j-1)\pi)\right)^T.$$

Furthermore, if the problem has a convection term, and has Dirichlet initial conditions, then A can be written in the form (a, b, c) and the eigenvectors and eigenvalues in this case are given by

$$\lambda_j = b + 2c\sqrt{\frac{a}{c}}\sin\left(\frac{j\pi}{N+1}\right), \quad j = 1,\ldots,N$$

with corresponding eigenvector

$$v_j = \left(\beta\sin\left(\frac{j\pi}{N+1}\right),\ldots,\beta^N\sin\left(\frac{j\pi N}{N+1}\right)\right)^T, \quad \beta = \sqrt{\frac{a}{c}}.$$

Thus for one dimensional equations of the form given in (3.1), central differencing in the spatial dimension leads to an eigenvalue and eigenvector structure of A that is well-known. This structure can be stored in an appropriate data structure within the program and is the approach adopted in this paper. The program that we have written runs in Occam2 on a linear chain of p transputers. If the system size is N then the first $rem(N/p)$ transputers each evaluate $1 + [N/p]$ equations with the remaining $p - rem(N/p)$ transputers each evaluating $[N/p]$ equations. This represents an attempt at some elementary form of load balancing. (Note that if $p > N$ we can split the interval of integration up into subintervals and compute approximations to the integral on appropriate subintervals in order to use all available transputers efficiently.) This approach leads to minimal communication. The work that each transputer performs is essentially the multiplication of a number of rows of a matrix by a vector of length N plus the appropriate number of quadrature problems. The user can input the nature of the partial differential equation to be solved (such as Dirichlet or Neumann boundary conditions or diffusion or diffusion-convection problems) and the program will choose the appropriate eigenvalue and eigenvector data structure for A, make the appropriate transformations and then evaluate the resulting integrals.

We have extended the program to include higher dimensional problems of the form given in (3.1). But in order to preserve the regular structure of A we have assumed that Ω is rectangular in $\mathbb{R}^M$, although the program can be modified so that the user's known eigenvalue structure of A can be used. To give some insight into how the eigenvalue and eigenvector structure of A changes as the dimension of the problem changes we give some results on the structure of A for 2-dimensional problems.

Suppose the rectangular region is $[0, (r+1)h] \times [0, (s+1)h]$ then if the problem is of Dirichlet type and a five point difference stencil is used with ordering from left to right and bottom to top then A can be written as an $rs \times rs$ block tridiagonal matrix $\theta(I, B, I)$, where I is the unit matrix of order r and B is the tridiagonal matrix $(1, -4, 1)$. In this case it is easily shown that the eigenvalues of A are

$$\lambda_{ij} = -4 + 2\left(\cos\left(\frac{i\pi}{r+1}\right) + \cos\left(\frac{j\pi}{s+1}\right)\right), \quad i = 1, \ldots, r, \quad j = 1, \ldots, s,$$

with corresponding eigenvectors

$$\left(\sin\left(\frac{j\pi}{s+1}\right)v_i, \ldots, \sin\left(\frac{js\pi}{s+1}\right)v_i\right)^T$$

where v_i is an eigenvector of B.

On the other hand if Neumann conditions are used Then A is as above but with $2\theta I$ in the $(1,2)$ and $(s, s-1)$ block position.

Imposed spatial constraints means that we will only give numerical results for a single one dimensional problem, although the results that we have obtained elsewhere for higher dimensional problems show similar behaviour to the results presented in this paper.

The problem is a one dimensional heat diffusion problem with Dirichlet boundary conditions (see [7], for example) which measures the temperature oscillations in a wall heated by a sinusoidal heat source given by

$$u_t = u_{xx} + \sin^2(\omega t), \quad u(x, 0) = 1, \quad u(0, t) = 0, \quad u(1, t) = 1 - e^{-t}.$$

Here ω is a parameter which can be varied. For this problem with differing discretization parameter h and frequency ω we present three tables. The first table gives the performance of a standard IVP code (STRIDE [4], a type-insensitive code based on certain high order Runge-Kutta methods) running in FORTRAN 3L on a single T800. These results indicate the performance of an "off the shelf" IVP code and no attempt has been made to exploit the nature of the problem. The second table again gives results on the performance of STRIDE but optimised for the class of semi-linear problems given by (3.2). This means performing only 1 Jacobian evaluation in the interval of integration and using linear algebra based on the LU factorization of a tridiagonal matrix rather than a full dense matrix as in the case of the results presented in Table 3.1.

The third table presents numerical results for our Fourier-integral program running in Occam2 on a SuperNode 1000Series consisting of up to 32 T800-20 slave transputers connected to a BOO4 board with a single T800 master transputer with interprocessing links running at 20Mb/sec. In each of the three cases the programs run in Double Precision mode and we request an absolute error accuracy of 10^{-6} in each component. The third columns in these tables represents the number of function evaluations taken and in Table 3.3 it represents the maximum number of function evaluations taken over all components. The times are given in terms of ticks of the computer clock. The results are as follows:

Comments and conclusions

First of all when comparing Tables 3.1 and 3.2 we see that the performance of "optimised" STRIDE is significantly better than the non-optimised version. At moderate values of ω the speedups for $N = 20, 40$ and 80 are approximately 1.5, 2 and 6, respectively. This is of course to do with the savings in the linear algebra costs and will become even more pronounced as N increases.

Table 3.1

N	ω	Fns	Time	N	ω	Fns	Time
20	1.0	581	74250	40	1.0	686	246211
20	20.0	976	147693	40	20.0	877	338567
20	100.0	1861	321950	40	100.0	2444	1141514
80	1.0	885	1431670	40	1000.0	15302	6471526
80	20.0	1389	2643054	80	100.0	1995	2985484

Table 3.2

N	ω	Fns	Time	N	ω	Fns	Time
20	1.0	562	49728	40	1.0	723	112594
20	20.0	801	80708	40	20.0	926	163975
20	100.0	1834	211525	40	100.0	2444	460858
80	1.0	827	251589	40	1000.0	16168	2721100
80	20.0	1197	398251	80	100.0	2320	872614

Table 3.3

N	ω	Fns	Procs	1	2	4	8	16	32
20	1.0	315	Time	34746	19590	10224	5384	3129	
20	20.0	315	Time	35890	19755	10295	5422	3147	
20	100.0	651	Time	39735	19788	10317	6793	5444	
40	1.0	399	Time	101592	55648	29366	15424	8414	5073
40	20.0	399	Time	103305	56097	29574	15534	8467	5099
40	100.0	651	Time	107604	56144	29603	15551	8481	6204
40	1000.0	5397	Time	155936	95386	69201	57509	51783	43425
80	1.0	483	Time	306427	163704	86229	45086	22721	12572
80	20.0	483	Time	318700	173362	92567	50522	31854	16989
80	100.0	651	Time	314665	164878	87199	45391	22873	12644

In terms of the performance of our Fourier-integration program as the number of transputers (P) increases we observe that for moderate values of ω (1, 20) the speedup is close to linear. For example, with 8 transputers there is a speedup of approximately 7 over 1 transputer, while for 16 this factor is 12 and for $P = 32$ it is approximately 20 (N=40) and 24 (N=80). As the frequency is increased, however, these speedups tend to fall away until in the case of $N = 40$ and $\omega = 1000$ there is a speedup of approximately only 4 with 32 transputers. These phenomena are easily explained. In the case of mildly oscillatory problems the individual components require approximately (within a factor of 3 or 4, say) the same number of function evaluations to get the requested accuracy. Consequently, the rudimentary load balancing strategy discussed earlier is quite effective. However, for highly oscillatory problems ($\omega = 1000$) some components require many more function evaluations than others so that our load balancing strategy becomes ill-balanced. We could overcome this difficulty by more sophisticated load balancing based on the oscillatory nature of the problem but, in general, for all but the most highly oscillatory of problems the above mentioned speedups are quite satisfactory.

Finally we compare the performance of our Fourier-integration program running in Occam2 with the optimized version of STRIDE running in FORTRAN 3L. The difference in running time between these two languages running the same problem of course varies but a very rough factor is a factor of 2 in the favour of Occam2. For $N = 40$ and 80 at mild values of ω the speedup with 32 transputers is in the range of 20 to 32, while for highly oscillatory problems the speedup with 32 transputers is approximately 70. Taking into account the difference between Occam2 and FORTRAN 3L the differences are still substantial. Furthermore, as the number of transputers are increased (up to the value of N) even larger speedups will accrue since the data in Table 3.3 suggests a graph of N versus

P will yield a rough straight line with gradient approximately 0.75, falling away slightly as $P \to N$. Another advantage of this approach is that rather than using a one-step method to step through in time with concomitant worries about stability and local versus global error behaviour, the adaptive quadrature approach is very robust in a global error sense.

In conclusion we have seen that for time-dependent parabolic PDEs which are discretized in the spatial dimensions and for which the eigenvalue and eigenvector structure of the A matrix is well known our Fourier-integral approach on a chain of transputers seems to be a very effective one. Of course for many problems (such as those defined on an irregular domain) the eigenvalue and eigenvector structure of A is not known. In this case we hope to tie in a parallel eigenvalue package, which produces the dominant eigenvalues and eigenvectors, with our existing program to produce numerical results for the dominant modes.

References

1. Bulirsh G. and Stoer A., *Numerical Treatment of Ordinary Differential Equations by Extrapolation Methods*, 1968, Numerishe Mathematik, vol. 8, pp. 1-13.
2. Burrage K., *An adaptive numerical integration code for a chain of transputers*, 1990 CMSR University of Liverpool.
3. Burrage K., *Routine Quad.Real, Liverpool parallel transputer libraray mark 2, Occam Implementation*, 1990, N.A.S. Ltd, Liverpool.
4. Burrage K., Butcher J.C. and Chipman F.H., *An implementation of singly implicit Runge-Kutta methods*, 1980, BIT 20, pp. 326-340.
5. Byrne G. and Hindmarsh A., *A Polyalgorithm for the Numerical Solution of Ordinary Differential Equations*, 1975 TOMS 1, pp. 79-96.
6. Duchateau P. and Zackmann D., *Applied Partial Differential Equations*, 1989, Harper and Row.
7. Dean G. Duffy, *Solutions of Partial Differential Equations*, 1986, Tab Books.
8. Gragg W.B., *On Extrapolation alogithms for Ordinary Initial Value Problems*, 1965, SIAM J. Numer. Anal., vol. 2b, pp. 384-403.
9. Hull T.E., Enright W.E., Fellen B.M. and Sedgewick, A.E, *Comparing Numerical Methods for ODEs*, 1972, SIAM J. Numer. Anal., vol. 9, no. 4, pp. 603-637.
10. Prince P.J and Dormand J.R., *High Order Embedded Runge-Kutta Formulae*, 1981, J. Comp. Appl. Math. 7, pp. 67-75.
11. Shampine L. F. and Gordon M., *Computer Solution of Ordinary Differential Equations*, 1975, W. H., Freeman and Company, San Francisco.

An Efficient Implementation of Search Trees on an Array of Transputers

A. Colbrook, C. Smythe
Department of Electronic & Electrical Engineering
& D.H. Pitt
Department of Mathematics and Computer Science
University of Surrey, Guildford, Surrey, GU2 5XH, UK.
Tel. 0483 571281 x2326

Abstract. A scheme for maintaining a balanced search tree on a transputer architecture is described. A general $2^{P-2}-2^P$ (for integer P≥3) search tree is introduced, which allows tree operations to execute concurrently. Several examples of these search trees have been implemented on the Supernode architecture using an array of transputers. Significant improvements in both query throughput and response time were demonstrated when moving from a sequential to a parallel implementation and the optimal search tree was identified. Applications of these structures include neural networks, parallel simulation systems, distributed database applications and the migration of sequential systems onto parallel architectures.

1. Introduction

Several techniques for the storage of large data structures in main memory have been proposed and, although none is optimal in every situation, tree structures have become a commonly adopted algorithm. A balanced binary tree structure [1] allows a uniprocessor system to perform operations in $O(\log_2 N)$ time, where N is the number of entries in the data structure. For a parallel algorithm the improvement in the response time for a single query can be logarithmic only in the number of processors used (for p processors the improvement in response time is $\log_2 p+1$). The suggested strategy for executing queries in a parallel system is to seek increases in throughput for a series of operations executing concurrently.

A $2^{P-2}-2^P$ search tree structure is introduced, which utilises an array of up to $[\log_2 N/(P-2)]+1$ processors to store N data elements. A $2^{P-2}-2^P$ tree [2] (integer P≥3) being a tree in which every vertex which is not the root or a leaf has between 2^{P-2} and 2^P children and every path from the root to a leaf is of the same length. The root has between 2 and 2^P children. A search tree is formed by associating a value with each tree node such that all the values at the same level in the tree are distinct.

Each processor in the array holds a level of the tree structure in local memory and the last processor stores the actual data items. The scheme requires $O(\log_2 N)$ time per tree operation, but allows

$O(\log_2 N)$ concurrency on the operations; one operation completes every $O(1)$ time.

The 2^{P-2}–2^P search tree is discussed in section 2 followed by an outline of the pipeline algorithm in section 3. The implementation of the structure on the Supernode architecture is described in section 4.

2. The 2^{P-2}–2^P Search Tree

A 2^{P-2}–2^P tree (integer P≥3) is a tree in which every vertex which is not the root or a leaf has between 2^{P-2} and 2^P sons and every path from the root to a leaf is of the same length. The root has between 2 and 2^P sons.

A 2^{P-2}–2^P search tree is a 2^{P-2}–2^P tree where associated with a node n is a value V(n) such that all the values at the same level in the tree are distinct. In addition, for all nodes (expect the root):
$$V(n) \geq V(fatherof(n))$$
where the function fatherof(n) returns the father of node n in the tree. Also, if n1 and n2 are any two nodes then:
$$(depth(fatherof(n1)) = depth(n2)) \wedge (V(fatherof(n1)) < V(n2)) \Rightarrow V(n1) < V(n2)$$
where the function depth(n) returns the level of node n in the tree.

Data elements are represented by the values of the leaf nodes. The searching operation for such a tree is the normal B+ tree search operation [3] and the insert and delete operations follow a top-down node-splitting scheme [4]. The insertion transformation is applied when an insertion operation encounters a node, other than the root, with 2^P sons. The node is split to form two nodes each having 2^{P-1} sons, as depicted in Figure 1. In this diagram the optional pointers are represented by the dashed lines and the search path pointer is indicated by the small filled circle. This transformation ensured that any future node splitting does not cause upward propagation in the tree structure. When a deletion operation encounters a node, other than the root, with 2^{P-2} sons one of the two general deletion transformations is applied. If the neighbouring node has less than or equal to 2^{P-1} sons then the transformation depicted in Figure 2a is applied, otherwise the transformation of Figure 2b is used. (Note, that the neighbour relationship used in the deletion algorithms relates a node to its left brother in the sub-tree or in the case of the leftmost node, to its right brother.)

When the transformations are applied to a root node, the insertion transformation converts a root node with 2^P descendants into a double 2^{P-1} node configuration and a new root node, increasing the height of the tree. The deletion transformation (I) converts a root node with 2 descendants into a new root node formed by the merging of the root's offspring, reducing the height of the tree.

Since the insertion transformation involves splitting a 2^P-node, it will maintain the tree structure provided that the parent of a 2^P-node is not itself a 2^P-node. Otherwise, a 2^P+1-node is created. Noting

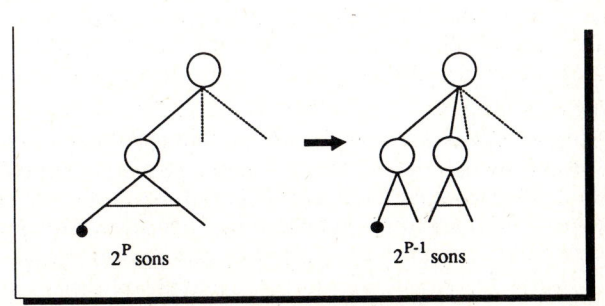

Figure 1 The Insertion Transformation

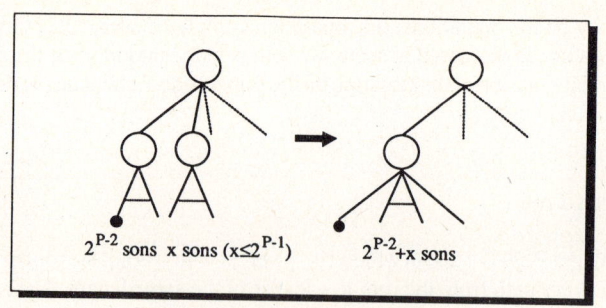

Figure 2a The Deletion Transformation I

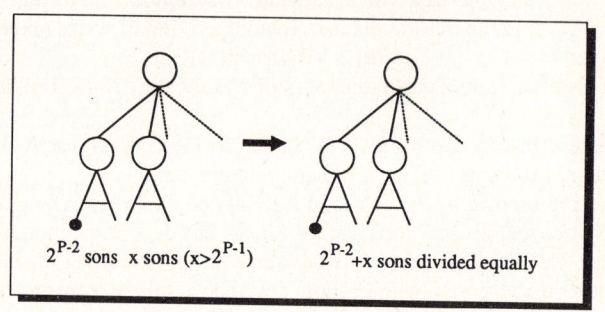

Figure 2b The Deletion Transformation II

that the insertion transformation would have already been applied (if it were applicable) to the father and proceeding by induction over the tree level, the transformation is shown to preserve the structure. Consideration of the deletion transformations follow this pattern since, if a father (which is not the root) is a 2^{P-2}-node it would be transformed prior to applying any transformation to its sons. Transformations applied to the root node result in expansion and contraction of the tree height. For the insertion transformation, the root node is left with less than 2^P sons and for deletion, the root node has more than 2 sons. This allows successive transformations to be applied to the next level of the tree without upward propagation.

It is possible to place bounds upon the maximum size of the data structure, S_{MAX}, which may be stored in a 2^{P-2}–2^P search tree of L levels. In such a case:

$$2^{L(P-2)} \leq S_{MAX} \leq 2^{LP} \quad (1)$$

Therefore, for a tree of N data elements, the maximum number of levels L required in the tree is given by:

$$L = \frac{\log_2 N}{P-2} + 1 \quad (2)$$

A further property of the 2^{P-2}–2^P tree is worth noting at this point. The insertion transformation for the 2-3-4 tree presented in [4] had a direct inverse in the deletion transformation. Oscillations occurred when insertions and deletions were applied in succession resulting in transformations and their inverses being applied to the tree structure. The behaviour of the structure under these conditions increased the processing time for a query and placed a strain upon the throughput of the system. A stabilising effect occurs in the 2^{P-2}–2^P tree since the insertion transformation leaves each node (which is not the root) with 2^{P-1} sons. Therefore, 2^{P-2} sons must be removed from such a node before a deletion transformation may be applied to it (since P≥3, 2^{P-2}≥2).

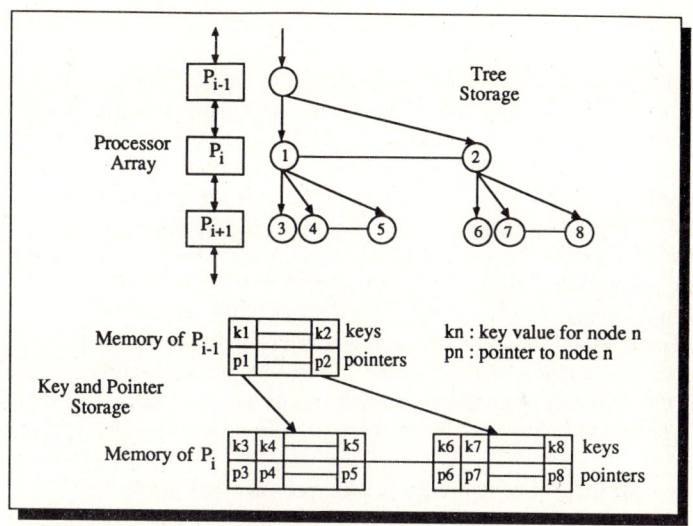

Figure 3 The Implementation of the Search Tree in a Linear Array of Processors

3. Parallel Search Trees

A 2^{P-2}–2^P search tree may be implemented in a linear array of $O(\log_2 N)$ processing elements in a similar style to that found in [5]. The number of processors required is $[\log_2 N/(P-2)]+1$ and as many as $([\log_2 N/(P-2)]+1)/2$ insertion and deletion operations may proceed in parallel.

In this section the three operations associated with this algorithm, Search, Insert and Delete, are considered. In a processor array of length K, processor P_i ($1 \leq i < K$) is an index processor and stores key values and pointers for processor P_{i+1}. P_i contains a list of the key values and pointers for the sons of each node in level i of the tree. Processor P_K contains data nodes. An example of this key and pointer storage is shown in Figure 3.

When a processor P_i receives a "Search(key n, using pointer p)" message it does the following:

Case 1 : P_i contains index nodes (it does not store the leaf nodes of the tree)
Using pointer p, the appropriate index node in local memory is found. Using the key value n, the appropriate pointer p' is selected. The message "Search(p',n)" is then sent to processor P_{i+1};
Case 2 : P_i contains data nodes (it stores the leaf nodes of the tree)
The data pointed to by p is searched to see if it contains n. If so, the data is sent out of the structure. If not, a message is sent indicating that the desired data was not found.

When processor P_i receives an "Insert(key n, using pointer p)" message it does the following:

Case 1 : P_i contains index nodes (it does not store the leaf nodes of the tree)
P_i follows the pointer p to the appropriate index node in local memory and selects the appropriate pointer p' from the key value n. Next it sends "Insert_Transform(p')" to processor P_{i+1}. P_{i+1} applies the insert transformation if it is applicable and sends the "Insert_Transform_Reply(m,np)" to P_i. This informs P_i of the new splitting key m and the new offspring pointer np. If np≠NULL then P_i increases the size of the index node pointed to by p. If a transformation occurred P_i uses n to select the appropriate path p'. Finally, P_i sends "Insert(n,p')" to P_{i+1};
Case 2 : P_i contains data nodes (it stores the leaf nodes of the tree)
If the data element is not already present in the tree it is installed in the data node pointed to by p.

When processor P_i receives an "Delete(key n, using pointer p)" message it does the following:

Case 1 : P_i contains index nodes (it does not store the leaf nodes of the tree)
P_i follows the pointer p to the appropriate index node in local memory and selects the appropriate pointer p' from the key value n. Next it sends "Delete_Transform(m,p',p'')" to processor P_{i+1}, where p'' is the neighbouring pointer to p' and m is the splitting key for p' and p''. P_{i+1} applies a delete transformation if it is applicable and sends the "Delete_Transform_Reply(m',np)" to P_i. This informs P_i of the new splitting key m'. The pointer np indicates which transformation, if any, was applied. If a transformation occurred P_i changes the index node pointed to by p and then uses n to select the appropriate path p'. Finally, P_i sends "Delete(n,p')" to P_{i+1};
Case 2 : P_i contains data nodes (it stores the leaf nodes of the tree)
If the data element is present in the tree it is removed from the data node pointed to by p.
Since the mode of operation of the pipeline is based upon a request/reply paradigm, half the processors in the array may be processing requests at any one time. The reason for this is that, until a processor P_i receives its reply from processor P_{i+1}, the keys and/or pointers in P_i may be incorrect.

Thus, the attainable level of concurrency in a k processor array is k/2.

4. Implementation on a Transputer Architecture

Examples of the search tree structure were implemented at Thorn EMI Central Research Laboratories on a Supernode. The basic single Supernode architecture consists of sixteen T800 worker Transputers each with 256Kb static RAM or 4Mb dynamic RAM local memory, a controller Transputer, one or two T800 processors acting as disc servers and caches, a link switching network and a number of external links and devices. A complete supercomputer may be formed by combining up to sixty four Supernodes with an appropriate outer switching network, controllers and devices [6]. The communication links between the processors were pre-set at 10M bits/s.

In any multi-processor architecture used for searching structures two critical criteria are the throughput and response time of the system. The throughput is the rate at which queries are executed and the response time is the time delay between sending a query and receiving the reply. The 2^{P-2}–2^P search tree structure is highly flexible as it allows variations in the throughput and response time to be achieved by simple changes in the processor architecture or the value of P.

Six tree structures were implemented:
- six level 2-3-4 tree
- four level 2-8 tree (P=3)
- three level 4-16 tree (P=4)
- two level 8-32 tree (P=5)
- two level 16-64 tree (P=6)
- one level 4096 tree (P=12)

It should be noted that the 2-3-4 tree was not a 2^{P-2}–2^P tree but will be assumed to have a value of P=2 in the results given herein. These structures were chosen because the maximum number of detail elements which could be stored in each was 4096 (except for the 8-32 tree in which could be stored only 1024 data elements). The physically limits of the storage available at processor prevented tree structures storing more elements being investigated.

Each structure was implemented on a linear array of Transputers and the length of the array was varied for each case. For example, for the six level 2-3-4 tree array lengths of one, two, three and six processors were used. This allowed the effect of assigning several levels of the tree structure to a single processor to be determined. Measurements were made for one hundred queries to the tree structures using random data keys, generated by the linear congruential method. The keys were five digit integer values. The measured values of the throughput and response time were normalised for each case. Since the search time for a given tree structure was proportional to $\log_2 N$, a normalising coefficient for each case was calculated as $[\log_2 N/(\log_2 N_{2-3-4})]$, where N is the number of elements in the tree prior to the one hundred queries being applied and N_{2-3-4} is this value for the 2-3-4 tree. Normalisation allowed comparisons between the values of throughput and response time for differing tree structures to be made without the need to consider the number of elements stored in each structure.

The throughputs and response times of the 2^{P-2}–2^P trees are shown in Figure 4. The value of L for a given search tree was the maximum array length used in the implementation of that tree. The throughput for the single processor case improved with increasing P as far as P=5, the 8-32 tree. This was due to the reduction in context switching between processes on a single processor. The results for the 16-64 tree (P=6) demonstrated the effect of increasing the size of the data structure allocated to each process so that the correspondingly long processing times caused a degradation in throughput. When the array length was increased to L processors an increase in throughput was seen on changing from a 2-3-4 (P=2) to a 2-8 (P=3) tree and then to a 4-16 (P=4) tree. The change to a 8-32 (P=5) and then to a 16-64 (P=6) tree resulted in a decrease in throughput. The response time followed a similar pattern with improvements being seen for increasing values of P until the 16-64 (P=6) tree was reached. Note that the response time decreased as additional processors were added for the 2-4 (P=2), 2-8 (P=3) and 4-16 (P=4) trees. However, for the 8-32 (P=5) and 16-64 (P=6) trees the response time increased as additional processors were used since very little of the processing for a single query ran concurrently in these cases. When the 4096 tree with a single processor was considered, the burden of the single computational intensive process was clearly demonstrated by the poor values for throughput and response time, 12.74replies/s and 78.47ms respectively.

It is worth considering why there should be, for the 2-3-4, 2-8 and 4-16 trees with random data, such a significant decrease in the response time for the tree architectures as the length of the processor array is increased. So far the process architecture has been described in terms of the pipeline paradigm mainly because this was the original classification made by Carey and Thompson [5]. For a processor pipeline, increasing the number of processors in the pipeline usually results in a degradation in the response time for a single query but an improvement in the throughput for several such queries. This

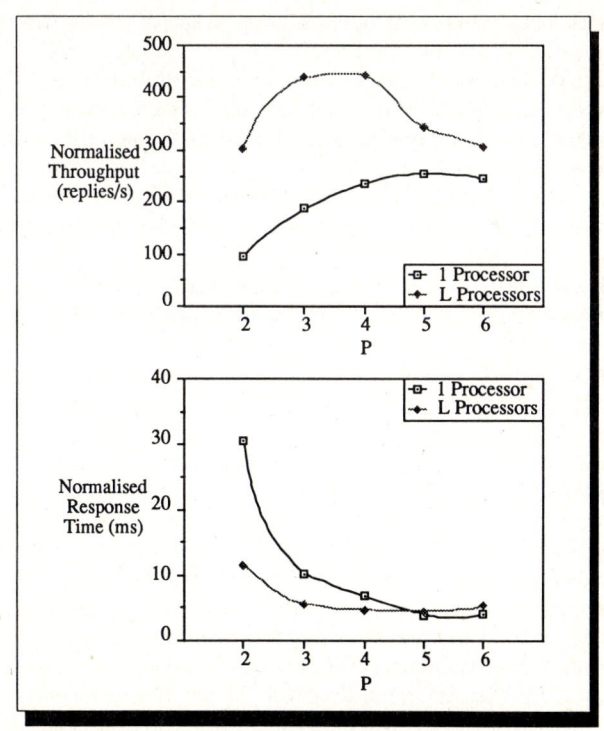

Figure 4 TheThroughputs and Response Times for Random Data

leads to the so called throughput/response time trade-off. However, in the results presented herein improvements are seen in both the throughput and the response time as the length of the processor array increases. Each process may be divided into two parts which are separated by communication between the process and its neighbours. The first (upper) part processes the transformations relevant to the parent level process. The second (lower) part processes information concerning the child level process. In most operations a transformation does not take place resulting in the second part of the process consuming the majority of the processing time. This leaves processes to run in an arrangement similar to a client-server structure where all processes may concurrently execute the same query. Hence, the response time for a single query improves as more processors are added to the structure.

These results demonstrate the flexibility of the 2^{P-2}–2^P search structure since both the value of P and the number of processors allocated to the search structure may be varied in order to achieve the desired throughput and response time. For the architectures considered, the 4-16 tree with three processors in the array may offer the best performance for random data. If a single processor was to be used, the 8-32 tree provides the greatest all round performance. The optimum search structure is largely dependent upon the speeds of the processor and the communication links between processors.

5. Conclusion

A top–down node–splitting scheme may be generally applied to a linear array of processes implementing a 2^{P-2}–2^P search tree structure (P≥3). In such a structure, an insertion transformation is applied when a node with 2^P branches is encountered by an insert operation. Similarly, a deletion transformation is applied when a node with 2^{P-2} branches is encountered by a delete operation.

A reconfigurable system of Transputer processors provides an architecture on which 2^{P-2}–2^P search tree structures may be implemented. In this system improvements in both query throughput and response time may be achieved by varying the value of P and/or the number of processors in the pipeline.

For other distributed memory systems based upon either differing processing elements and/or architectures the optimal search tree structure will vary and is largely dependent upon the speeds of the processor and the communication links between processors. However, these underlying properties of the 2^{P-2}–2^P tree search structure remain:

- Efficiency – at most $[\log_2 N/(P-2)]+1$ processors are required to store N data elements and as many as $([\log_2 N/(P-2)]+1)/2$ operations may be executing concurrently;

- Flexibility – variations in both the number of processors allocated to the array and the value of P allow the optimal search structure for a given architecture to be determined;

- Performance – improvements in both the query throughput and response time are achieved as additional processors are added to the array.

6. Acknowledgements

The authors should like to acknowledge the kind assistance of Professor S.A. Schuman, Department of Mathematics and Professor B. Cohen, Department of Electronic and Electrical Engineering, University of Surrey. This work was completed under a Science and Engineering Research Council Studentship and was undertaken during a period spent at Thorn EMI Central Research Laboratories, Hayes, Middlesex, UK. The authors should like to thank Dr J.S. Severwright and other colleagues at Thorn EMI Central Research Laboratories for their continuing support.

7. References

[1] Quinn M.J., "Designing Efficient Algorithms for Parallel Computers" McGraw–Hill, New York, 1987.

[2] Colbrook A., Smythe C., "Efficient Implementation of Search Trees on Parallel Distributed Memory Architectures", to appear IEE Proceedings Part E.

[3] Comer D., "The Ubiquitous B–Tree", Computer Surveys, 11(2), pp121–137, 1979.

[4] Guibas L.J., Sedgewick R., "A Dichromatic Framework for Balanced Trees", Proceedings 19th Annual IEEE Computer Society Symposium of the Foundations of Computer Science, pp8–21, 1978.

[5] Carey M.J., Thompson C.D., "An Efficient Implementation of Search Trees on [LgN+1] Processors", IEEE Transactions on Computers, C–33(11), pp1038–1041, 1984.

[6] Nicole D.A., "Reconfigurable Transputer Processor Architectures", Proceedings 22nd Annual Hawaii Conference on Systems Sciences, 1, pp365-374, IEEE, Washington DC, 1989.

Experimenting with Divide-and-Conquer algorithms on a parallel graph reduction machine

FETHI A. RABHI and GORDON A. MANSON
Department of Computer Science
University of Sheffield, Sheffield S10 2TN
United Kingdom.

Abstract. This paper is concerned with the implementation of functional languages on a parallel architecture, using graph reduction as a model of computation. Parallelism in such systems is automatically derived by the compiler but a major problem is the fine granularity, illustrated in Divide-and-Conquer problems at the leaves of the computational tree. The paper addresses this issue and proposes a method based on complexity analysis combined with run-time tests to remove the excess in parallelism. We report experiments on an prototype machine, simulated on several connected INMOS transputers. Performance figures show the benefits in adopting the method and the difficulty to automatically derive the optimum partitioning due to the different nature of the problems.

1. INTRODUCTION

Although designing and building multiprocessor systems has proceeded at a dramatic pace, the development of effective ways to program them has generally not. Conventional imperative languages are inadequate for programming parallel systems because they are inherently sequential. Extending these languages with parallel constructs has put a new burden on the programmer because not only has he to ensure that his program is correct but that it is also properly synchronized and deadlock-free. In contrast, functional programming languages (also called applicative languages) are better candidates for parallel computing because no matter what order of computation is chosen to evaluate a program, the result is always the same. A consequence is the possibility to design simple and powerful computational models in which parallelism arises from the nature of the language rather than from explicit programming by the user.

This paper describes an implementation of functional languages based on the graph reduction model and realised on a multi-transputer system. An interesting idea investigated is the possibility to control the granularity of the tasks generated by performing a complexity analysis on expressions, then delaying the creation of tasks for these expressions till run-time. Finally, some experimental results using Divide-and-Conquer algorithms show how the new method affect the overall performance of the machine.

2. REVIEW OF GRAPH REDUCTION AND PARALLEL IMPLEMENTATIONS

The graph reduction model [11] is a simple demand driven parallel model of computation suitable for functional languages. In graph reduction, a program is represented by a graph and the execution of this program consists of reducing the corresponding graph until the normal form (i.e the result) is reached. This process may be carried out in parallel since any sub-graph can be reduced independently from the others by a parallel task.

A task is to be executed by an evaluator, this task may create parallel sub-tasks so the run-time system is in charge of allocating tasks to evaluators. It also ensures the cooperation between tasks and provides an equal access to the computational graph by all the evaluators. For these reasons, many proposals adopted a shared memory architecture where the graph is equally shared by all the evaluators and where the active tasks are kept into a global queue. Whenever an evaluator is free, it evaluates the next task on the queue. Examples of such systems include ALICE [15], GRIP [12] and the $<v,G>$-machine [3].

The drawback in these architectures is the degradation in performance when the number of processors becomes large. This is mainly due to the shared memory which acts as a bottleneck. The distributed memory model offers a more flexible and extensible architecture. Falling into this category, a network of transputers has been given preference for the development of a prototype. The advantage of the transputer is that it offers a powerful processor associated with a large extensible memory and fast link speed. The latter property is crucial to reduce the delays due to communications. Other examples of distributed memory graph reduction machines are ALFALFA [8], ZAPP [10] and the HDG-machine [9].

There are techniques for generating code that will perform sequential graph reduction, most of them based around the G-machine [2]. The implementation described here uses a similar code called extended G-code because it contains constructs for the explicit creation of tasks and synchronisation between these tasks. For more details about the distributed computational model, see references [5] and [4].

3. IMPLEMENTING GRAPH REDUCTION ON A MULTI-TRANSPUTER SYSTEM

3.1. General description of the system

The system comprises a Host and a network of Reduction Agents (see figure 1). The host provides the user interface, file access and input/output. It also supports the compile-time system that produces the code, which is then distributed to the network.

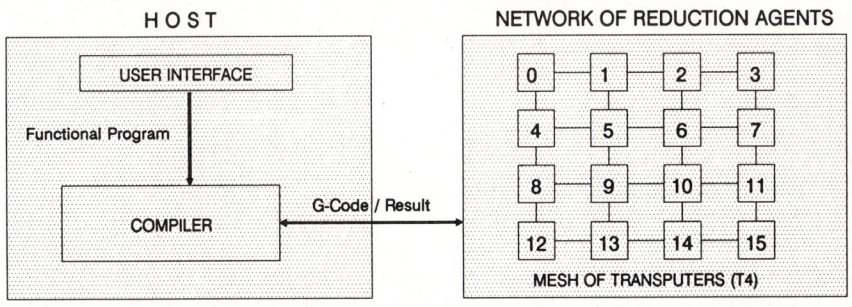

Figure 1 : Overall structure of the system

The network is in charge of executing the code and sending back the result to the host. The system is designed to work on any topology. In the experiments described, we used a wrap-around mesh of 16 transputers. Each transputer in the network supports a Reduction Agent.

3.2. Description of the Reduction Agents

A reduction agent consists of an Evaluator, a Graph Manager and a Router, all programmed using occam and running in parallel (see figure 2). The role of the Evaluator is to interpret the code produced by the compiler. The Graph Manager maintains the local portion of graph, responds to data requests from other processors, and also stores suspension records and reactivates tasks. The Router is the only module which "knows" about the topology of the network. It determines the appropriate route depending on the destination of a packet. The router runs as a high priority occam process.

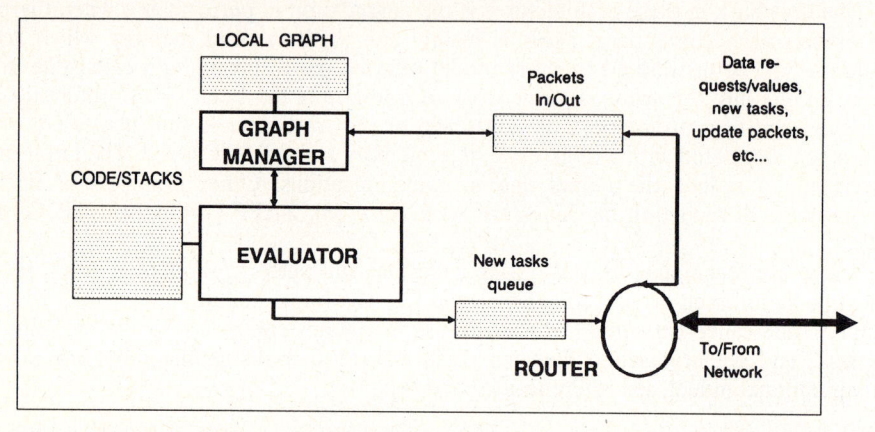

Figure 2 : Structure of a Reduction Agent

3.3. Data structures

In programmed graph reduction, the principal data structures are the stack and the graph. To avoid the space allocation problem, the stack is implemented on the heap as in recent projects ([3],[12]), but the Graph Manager and the Evaluator had to be integrated into a single process because there could be no shared data structure between two parallel processes in occam. This is illustrated by using an ALT statement instead of a PAR statement as shown by the piece of code below :

```
WHILE TRUE
  ALT
    ...              receive a message from the network
      GraphManager()         -- process the message
    evaluator.active & SKIP
      Evaluator()            -- one machine cycle
```

At the moment, there is no garbage collection and this limited the size of the problems tested. However, because we are comparing execution times, the inclusion of the garbage collection time would have altered the meaning of the results.

3.4. Tasks scheduling

We adopted a very simple tasks scheduling policy. Whenever a task is created, it is immediately exported to a neighbour processor i.e. a processor within a direct physical connection. In addition, the processor records the number of uncompleted tasks it has sent to each neighbour and the number of tasks it received from each neighbour. A new task is exported to the processor from which it has received or sent the lowest number of tasks.

Since we are restricting partitioning, we felt that there is no need to implement a sophisticated load balancing strategy. Recent experimental evidence [8] shows that there is not much difference between a simple inexpensive load balancing strategy and a complicated one providing a large number of tasks generated.

4. THE GRANULARITY PROBLEM

When running on a physical multiprocessor architecture, there are two major problems associated with graph reduction. First, some tasks are too tiny and take more time to be executed in parallel than sequentially, mainly because of the communication overhead. This problem occurs similarly in most systems which exploit implicit parallelism e.g. data-flow machines. The second problem is that often, too many tasks are generated, overwhelming the resources of the machine and causing a significant communication overhead.

That is to say, the granularity of the computation is too fine and there is a need to increase it to a level which yields the optimum performance. The solution adopted consists of performing a compile-time complexity analysis on the expression, then deciding to create a task for that expression only if its complexity is beyond a certain threshold determined by the characteristics of the physical architecture. Unlike in other approaches [7], the decision to create tasks is made only at run-time.

The advantage of this method is that complexity measures are more accurate because data values can be tested at run-time, which is not obviously possible at compile-time. The disadvantage is that it is not always possible to determine the complexity equation. In this case, an arbitrary cost is assigned to the corresponding expression. In addition, the run-time tests are very likely to introduce an extra-overhead in the computation. These issues are further explained in [13].

5. EXPERIMENTS

We tested some simple Divide-and-Conquer [1] algorithms because their implementations generally suffer from a rapid explosion of parallelism and a fine granularity more evident at the leaves of the process tree. The following functions have been selected : Fib(n) (Nth element of the Fibonacci numbers), Pfac(n) (Parallel factorial of a number n), Qsort(n) (Quicksort a list of n numbers) and Msort(n) (Mergesort a list of n numbers). The ML definitions of these functions can be found in [14].

A complexity analysis is first carried out on the functions, determining their complexity. Next, functions are compiled into extended G-code as in the standard way. Then code that computes the complexity of a function is inserted at the beginning of the corresponding function's body. There is a branch instruction which switches between the sequential and parallel version of the function depending upon the result obtained by computing the complexity function being below or beyond an arbitrary threshold.

When applying this method to Divide-and-Conquer problems, the execution tree expands in a breadth first manner (parallel evaluation) until the work becomes sufficiently small and then, the execution proceeds in a depth first manner (sequential evaluation). By using different threshold values, we can switch to sequential evaluation at different depths, generating different trees (hence partitions) for the same problem.

6. EXPERIMENTAL RESULTS

We run the examples through all possible partitions, recording the corresponding execution times. Figure 3 shows the general aspect of the results obtained, in this graph the partition into tasks is plotted on the horizontal axis (in logarithmic progression) and the execution time on the vertical axis. Starting from 1 task partition (sequential time), the execution time decreases as the problem is further divided. In most of the cases, it increases again as the maximum partition is reached. This confirms the intuitive belief that a partial partition is more effective than a complete one.

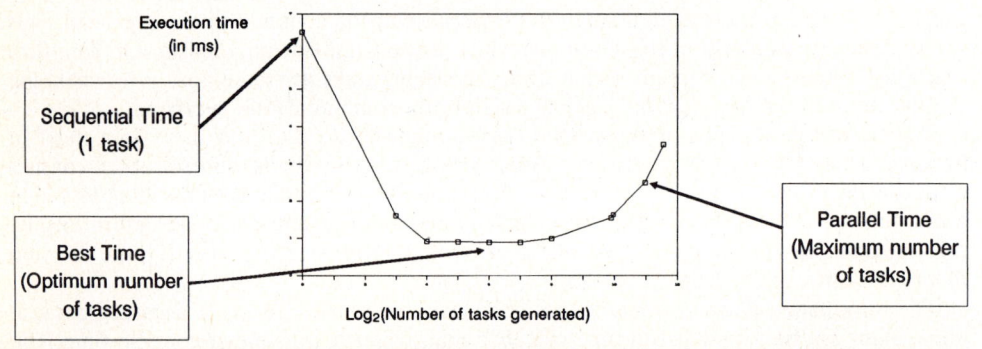

Figure 3 : General aspect of the execution time depending on the partition into tasks

We define the **optimum number of tasks** as being the partition corresponding to the best performance. In the rest of the paper, we show the different figures obtained for every problem. A more detailed analysis of the results can be found in [14].

6.1. Fib

The graph obtained for the Fib function is displayed in figure 4, it shows irregularities because the execution time depends on load balancing, which vary from one partition to another. The best partition (around 377 tasks, $\log_2(377) = 8.5$) corresponds to the one with the best combination of low communication overhead, high parallelism exploitation and good tasks distribution.

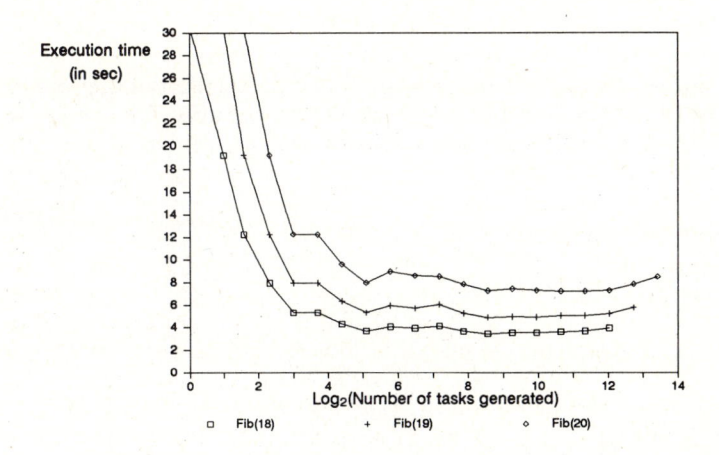

Figure 4: Execution times depending on the partition into tasks for Fib

6.2. Pfac

Pfac is an example of regular Divide-and-Conquer problem where a problem is always divided into two problems of equal length. The results shown in figure 5 indicate that the best partition corresponds to the one where 16 tasks are generated ($\log_2(16)=4$) and in which each task has been allocated to each processor. We will refer to such situations as the "exact match". This means that the best situation is when the generation of tasks stops at the depth where there is exactly one processor executing one task.

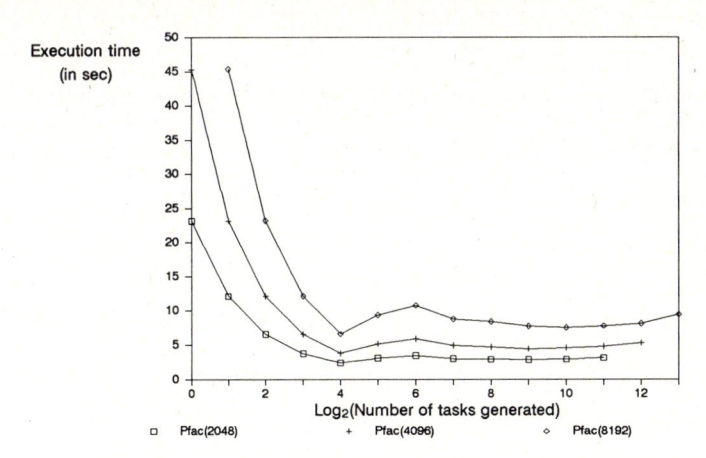

Figure 5: Execution times depending on the partition into tasks for Pfac

6.3. Msort

`Msort` is a regular balanced problem but with a high overhead during the divide and combine phases, due largely to copying of lists across processors. We can see in figure 6 that although there is an exact match (i.e. when 16 tasks are generated, $\log_2(16)=4$), it is not the optimum solution. This is an evidence that the exact match situation is not the optimum partition for all the problems.

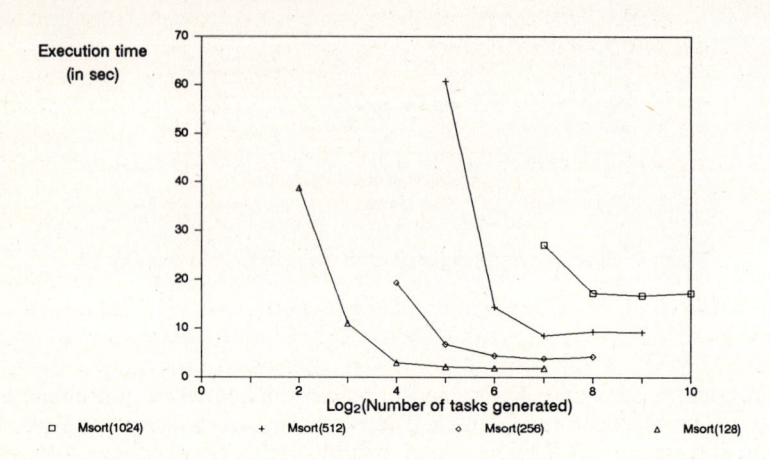

Figure 6: Execution times depending on the partition into tasks for Msort

6.4. Qsort

`Qsort` is an example of irregular unbalanced Divide-and-Conquer because the two lists sorted in parallel are of unequal length and because their length cannot be predicted. From the results in figure 7, we can see that load balancing is very irregular, explaining the ran-

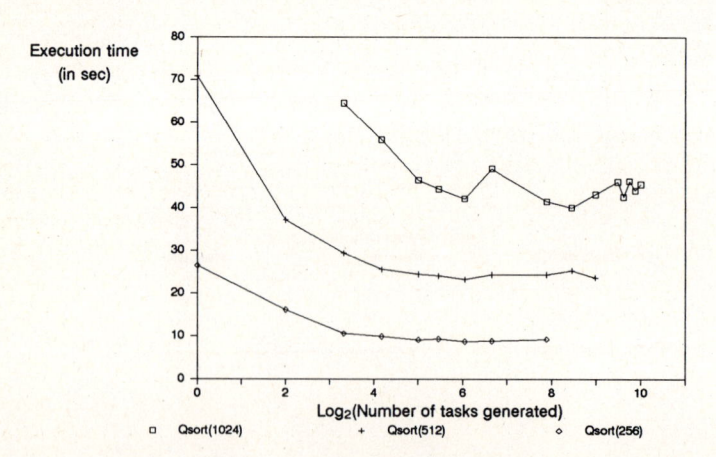

Figure 7: Execution times depending on the partition into tasks for Qsort

dom shape obtained. Unlike Fib, changing the size leads to a completely different optimum partition because the size of the sub-problems generated is data dependent, making hard any prediction.

7. CONCLUSIONS

In all cases, the results show that a better speed-up can be obtained by removing the small grains. For the particular case of Divide-and-Conquer problems, the results also show that for some problems, there is an optimum partition which corresponds to the best combination of even load balancing, low communication overhead and parallelism exploitation. (e.g. see figure 4 obtained for the Fib function). This suggests that for these problems, the system should concentrate on controlling the total number of tasks generated rather than the size of individual grains.

For regular and balanced problems with short delays (such as Pfac), it is unnecessary to create any more tasks when every transputer is already busy (exact match situation). The main difficulty is to design a load balancing strategy that would provide an exact match for any value of the branching factor (i.e. the number of branches for each node) on a network with any topology. In the system used, we could easily move from one strategy to another by modifying a table. This table contains the direction where to send tasks and the priorities when there is a choice between two directions. Implementing an exact match would switch between different tables depending on the branching factor, possibly supplied prior to starting the execution (e.g. when loading the code). In our case, tables were made relatively easily because of the small number of processors, but for larger configurations, more systematic placement strategies should be used (e.g. in [6]). Because the number of tasks with their relative complexity is known, static scheduling techniques [16] could also be used.

For problems with long divide and combine phases (Qsort, Msort), it seems that there is no gain implementing the exact match, the only profit that can be made is by controlling the grain size down to a certain limit

The results obtained are specific to this particular implementation. If the speed of sequential execution becomes faster, for example by directly executing the code rather than interpreting it, we should move more problems towards the best match situation because divide and combine delays are shorter, and also because the grain becomes finer. If the link speed increases, there is less penalty in creating tasks, then we should concentrate on controlling the grain rather than on the total number of tasks. The precise influence of the computation-communication ratio is still being investigated.

Using transputers has proved worthwhile for problems where the exact match was the optimum partition, adding more processors has significantly increased performance. However, for problems acting upon data-structures (e.g. Msort and Qsort on lists), the speed-up obtained was very poor due to extensive copying and a shared-memory system would have been more appropriate.

8. FUTURE WORK

Further investigations are required into different directions. First, there is the issue of automatically deriving the complexity of an expression, in the experiments described this was easily determined by hand but a method that could be incorporated into a compiler is required. Next, these equations have to be solved at run-time. Even if an equation is available, the compiler may choose not to solve it because it is either too complicated, or it may refer to a parameter whose value cannot be determined. Some changes in the implementation (such as data structure representation, abstract machine instruction set, etc,..) could be introduced to make the access to some parameters possible and within an acceptable time. There is also the issue of how to use effectively the complexity functions at run-time. In the experiments, we used a simple threshold model but other techniques should be investigated.

Lastly, if we want to exercise a control on the number of tasks (e.g. in the case of some Divide-and-Conquer problems), there is the issue of detecting the optimum partition depending on the problem and the characteristics of the physical machine. If this optimum partition is detected, a mechanism is required to stop the creation of tasks once this partition is reached.

9. ACKNOWLEDGMENTS

We would like to thank Murray Cole, Andy King, Geoffrey Burn, Simon Peyton-Jones and the National Transputer Centre for their help and support.

10. REFERENCES

[1] A.V. Aho, J.E. Hopcroft, J.D. Ullmann, *Data structures and algorithms*, Addison-Wesley, (1983).
[2] L. Augustsson, 'Compiling Lazy Functional Languages, Part II', *PhD thesis, Department of Computer Science, Chalmers University of Technology*, Goteborg, (1987).
[3] L. Augustsson, T. Johnsson, 'Parallel Graph Reduction with the $<v,G>$-machine', *Proc. Conference on Functional Programming Languages and Computer Architecture*, London, September 1989, ACM Press.
[4] D.I. Bevan, G.L. Burn, R.J. Karia, J.D. Robson, 'Design Principles of a Distributed Memory Architecture for Parallel Graph Reduction', *The Computer Journal*, 32, no 5, (1989).
[5] G.L. Burn, 'A shared-memory Parallel G-Machine based on the Evaluation Transformer Model of Computation', In *Workshop on the Implementation of Lazy Functional Languages*, Aspenas, Sept. 88.
[6] M. Cole, 'Algorithmic skeletons : a structured approach to the management of parallel computation', *PhD thesis, University of Edinburgh*, October 1988.
[7] B.F. Goldberg, P. Hudak, 'Serial Combinators : Optimum Grain of Parallelism', *Proc. Conference on Functional Programming Languages and Computer Architecture*, Nancy, France, Sept.1985, Jouannaud J-P. (Ed.),Springer Verlag, LNCS 201, (1985).
[8] B.F. Goldberg, 'Multiprocessor execution of functional programs', *PhD thesis, YALEU/DCS/RR-618, Department of Computer Science, Yale University*, April 1988.
[9] H. Kingdon, D.R Lester, G.L. Burn, 'The HDG-machine : A highly Distributed Graph Reducer on a transputer network', *ESPRIT 415 Research Report*, March 1989.
[10] D. McBurney, M.R. Sleep, 'Transputer-based experiments with the ZAPP architecture', *Proc. PARLE Parallel Architectures and Languages Europe*, Eidhoven, Netherlands, June 1987, de Bakker et al. (Eds), Springer Verlag, LNCS 258, (1987).
[11] S.L. Peyton-Jones, *The Implementation of Functional Programming Languages*, Prentice Hall International (1987).
[12] S.L. Peyton-Jones, C. Clack, J. Salkild, 'High-Performance Parallel Graph Reduction', *Proc. PARLE '89 Parallel Architectures and Languages Europe*, June 1989, Odijk E. et al. (Eds.), Springer Verlag, LNCS 365, (1989).
[13] F.A. Rabhi, G.A. Manson, 'Using complexity functions to control parallelism in the parallel evaluation of functional programs', *Report CS-90-1, Department of Computer Science, University of Sheffield*, (1990).
[14] F.A. Rabhi, G.A. Manson, 'Divide-and-Conquer with a parallel graph reduction machine', *Department of Computer Science, University of Sheffield*, (1990).
[15] M.R. Reeve, M. Cripps, 'An introduction to ALICE : a multiprocessor graph reduction machine', in *Functional Programming, Languages, Tools and Architectures*, S. Eisenbach (ed.), Ellis Horwood, (1987).
[16] V. Sarkar, *Partitioning and scheduling parallel programs for multiprocessing*, Research Monographs in Parallel and Distributed Computing, Pitman (1989).

The Solution of Radiation Engineering Problems on a Transputer Based System

S A Khaddaj[1,2], H AL-Bahadili[2], A J H Goddard[1], C R E de Oliveira[1] and J Wood[2]

[1]Nuclear Power Section
Mechnical Engineering Department
Imperial College
Exhibition Road
London SW7 2BX

[2]Nuclear Group
Mechnical Engineering Department
Queen Mary and Westfield College
Mile End Road
London E1 4NS

Abstract. Monte Carlo and finite element methods are numerical techniques used for solving complex problems in reactor physics and radiation shielding. In this paper we are concerned with the implementation of existing research-level codes based on these two methods, written originally for serial computers, on an MIMD transputer based system. Results and performance of the parallelised codes are presented.

1. Introduction

This paper reviews SERC sponsored research aimed at developing highly parallel algorithms for nuclear engineering applications in shielding, criticality and related aspects of safety design. Achievements since the beginning of the project in July 1989 are presented.

The research is concerned with the parallelisation of alternative methods for the solution of radiation transport problems. In general, the Boltzmann transport equation can be solved either by stochastic or by deterministic methods [1]. Of the two methods selected for investigation, the Monte Carlo (the stochastic method) is in wide industrial use for this purpose, while the deterministic finite element method is coming to be adopted by industry as a result of research at the two Colleges over the last decade.

A transputer based Meiko Computing Surface has been used as the parallel machine. The research places emphasis on the development of parallel application programs using the new user friendly advanced parallel programming system, Meiko CStools [2], based on the use of standard FORTRAN and C, which removes the need for the user to work in OCCAM.

For most applications three common broad strategies of parallelism may be considered in modelling physical systems on MIMD arrays [3]. A brief description of these three forms of concurrency is given here; a more general discussion, and the application of these three strategies to different problems, can be found in [3,4]. The three classes of parallelism are :
(a) Event Parallelism, or Processor Farm
This may be considered as the simplest form of parallelism in which each processor is executing the same program independently from all the other processor, each operating on a different part of the total data.
(b) Geometric Parallelism
In this form of parallelism, each processor is executing more or less the same program, but now the data is distributed in a manner which requires extensive communication between the processors, for example, each processor might be used to simulate one part or more of a large system of similar objects interacting with each other.
(c) Algorithmic Parallelism, or Algebraic Parallelism
Here the whole algorithm is split into a number of sections, each of which is assigned to one processor, but data relating the whole system flows through each processor like a production line. Thus, elaborate communication is required in transferring the data from one processor to another.

As the life-history of individual particles is followed independently, the Monte Carlo method, particularly for fixed-source problems, is inherently parallel and well-suited to parallel computer architectures. Use of the process farm strategy requires the ability to generate independent random numbers on each processor: We tackle this problem by using the 'leapfrog method', which is described later.

Application of the finite element method to radiation transport is still a subject of active research. Parallelism can be exploited at two stages. Firstly, parallelism can be exploited in the generation of the global stiffness matrix and, secondly, in the solution of the finite element equations. In the latter stage, a preconditioned conjugate gradient method is used; the method is well parallelised and reduces the amount of storage required compared with direct methods.

First, an overview is given of the parallel architecture that has been used. The particle tracking Monte Carlo code is described and results presented. The particular finite element developments are then presented, finally, some conclusions are drawn.

2 Architecture and Software Tools

This research makes use of a Meiko Computing Surface consisting of a local host (MK014), which can be used as system master or slave, and two MK060 computing element boards. The host consists of a single IMS T414B, 3 Mbytes of DRAM, 128 Kbytes of EPROM, and an IEEE-488 interface. The MK060 Computing element board consists of four IMS T800 with up to 8 Mbytes of DRAM. The transputers communicate with the outside world through a host machine, a SUN SPARK station 330 in our case. Thus, at any one time up to nine processors can be run simultaneously (or ten if we include the SUN processor).

Application programs can be written in OCCAM, FORTRAN and C. Several parallel programming systems for running FORTRAN and C programs on transputers are, in principle, available. The Meiko Computing Surface has hitherto required the use of OCCAM and the OCCAM programming system (OPS). Recently, however, a new advanced parallel programming system, Meiko CStools, based on the use of standard FORTRAN and C (without using OCCAM) has been developed, and the beta-release version has been used in the work reported here.

Meiko CStools is designed to support concurrent applications in which different parts of the program can be executed simultaneously. It allows programmers and designers the use of concurrency in programming and system design. As in OCCAM, processes can operate sequentially using a single transputer, or in parallel using a network of transputers. CStools provides communication services and configurations tools for parallel programming.

In CStools the communication between different processes is provided by system library calls (a set of message-passing library routines) which are included in and called from application programs written in FORTRAN or C. Interprocess communication and synchronisation takes place through system-global message ports.

In order to allocate different processes to different transputers and execute them in parallel, CStools provides a configuration mechanism which is based on what is called the *parafile loader*. This program reads a simple file called the .par file which contains information about the allocation of different processes to different processors and the required configuration of the processors. More information about CStools can be found in [2].

3 Monte Carlo Application

3.1 Description of the Serial Monte Carlo Code

The code which has been chosen to be implemented on the Meiko Computing Surface, is a serial analogue research-level fixed-source particle transport Monte Carlo code, called SMOP [5], for studying the attenuation and leakage of gamma ray photons in an homogeneous shielding material for simple geometries (e.g. sphere, infinite slab and infinite cylinder). It is based on two previous codes, MONTERAY and MOPP [6,7].

In the particular form of the Monte Carlo method used here, there is a close analogy between the physical particles, and the 'mathematical' particles followed by the program. The code simulates the history of a large number of particles from 'birth' to 'death', one particle at a time (i.e., sequentially). The particle is 'killed' if it escapes from the system, or, due to successive scatters, its energy becomes less than a preset minimum; in either event, a new particle is started from the source. The only sophistication employed is the concept of survival weight, by means of which the effect of absorption is accounted for by modifying the particle weight after each collision [6]. In order to accelerate the termination of the unimportant (i.e. low weight) particles, when a particle weight becomes less than a pre-assigned minimum value, a game of Russian Roulette is played to determine whether or not the particle survives; should it survive, its weight is increased appropriately so that the resulting scores are unbiased. Clearly, in our treatment of Monte Carlo the concept of particle weight is important, as it also is in all production-level particle transport codes.

A version of the Monte Carlo code SMOP was implemented on the AMT DAP-610 parallel computer [5], and in order to simplify the implementation of the code on the DAP, two modifications were introduced in modelling two physical events in the program. The same version of the serial code is implemented here so that a comparison can be made between the performance of the DAP (SIMD architecture) and the performance of a transputer based system (MIMD architecture), by running the same programs for equivalent problems.

The modelling of the two important physical events in the program is now described.

(a) Compton Scattering

The basic model simulated is the well-known Klein and Nishina model of Compton scattering. In the parent program [7] the rigorous Kahn procedure is used to sample from the corresponding probability density function. Instead, in SMOP, we use two direct sampling procedures:

(i) for photons with energies greater than 2 MeV, the rigorous Koblinger method [8].
(ii) for photons with energies less than or equal to 2 MeV, the approximate, Carlson method [2].

After a Compton scattering, a particle is allowed to take the energy (wavelength) given by the sampling procedure; the corresponding cross-section values are determined by reference to a set of data tables (based on 5300 energy mesh points) prepared, once for all, at a preliminary stage of the calculation.

(b) Pair Production

In the original serial program, MOPP, when a pair production event occurs, the two annihilation gamma rays released are followed separately. In SMOP, when pair production occurs, only one photon (with double weight) is followed.

The implementation of the code on the DAP, and the effect of these two approximations on the results obtained from SMOP, which is shown to be negligible, are described in detail in [5].

3.2 Parallel Implementation of the Code

Since, in a fixed-source Monte Carlo computation, the life history of the individual particles must be scored independently, the processor farm strategy is well suited to this type of computation. Using CStools, a straightforward implementation of serial fixed-source particle transport Monte Carlo codes can be made subject to two main constraints: (i) Enough memory is available to accommodate the whole program on each processor. (ii) The ability to generate independent random number sequences on each transputer. Of course, these sequences of random numbers must have suitable statistical properties within themselves. In this paper, the problem of random number generation for parallel computation on the transputer array is tackled by using the leapfrog method. As will be discussed later.

In our implementation of particle transport Monte Carlo on the Meiko Computing Surface, in order to minimise the interprocess communications, the relationship between the master (T414 transputer) and the slaves (between 1 to 8 T800 transputers) can be summarised as follows :

(i) The master reads in the basic data for the calculation and passes it down to the slaves.
(ii) The slaves carryout both the preliminary computation and all of the particle tracking computation, and the results are passed back up to the master.
(iii) In the master, results of the calculations from the individual transputers are combined and then printed out.

It is obvious from the above discussion that the master transputer, after sending the data to the slaves, is idle while waiting until they complete their calculations. It is possible, of course, to use the master as an additional processor, but in fact we did not do so, because it does not have a floating point capability equivalent to the slaves.

3.3 Pseudorandom Number Generation

If Monte Carlo calculations are to be performed, a very large supply of uniformally distributed, independent, pseudorandom numbers must be readily available. A widely used algorithm for generating such sequences is the linear congruential method suggested by Lehmer [9], which may be summarised as follows:

$$X_i = (a X_{i-1} + c) \bmod M \qquad (1)$$

where

M, is the modulus;	$M > 0$
a, is the multiplier;	$0 < a < M$
c, is the increment;	$0 < c < M$
X_o, is the starting value or 'seed';	$X_o > 0$

The pseudorandom numbers themselves (lying between 0 and 1) are generating by forming the sequence $\{x_i = X_i / M\}$. When suitable choices are made for the integer parameters a, c, X_o and M, a sequence of integers is produced which has many of the desired statistical properties. The procedures for selecting these parameters is well-illustrated by the work of Fishman and Moore [10].

One method of generating random numbers for use in a parallel processing environment is to generate appropriate portions of sequences such as (1) in each of the parallel processors in an efficient manner. In addition to having suitable statistical properties within themselves, the individual subsequences must be independent of one another. To this end, we use the leapfrog method suggested by Bowman and Robinson [11]. This method, which is easily implemented, produces disjoint subsequences of the original pseudorandom number sequence in each of the parallel processors.

In the leapfrog method, for n parallel processes, the first n values from the sequence (1) are delivered as initial seeds to each of the processors, along with the 'jump' multiplier a_n defined by :

$$a_n = a^n \bmod M \qquad (2)$$

Then each processor generates its own subsequence according to (1) with a_n replacing a, and c taken to be zero. Each subsequence consists of every nth member of the original sequence, starting in each prosess at a different point. Only the starting information need be passed as interprocess communication (and even this could be built into the program running on the parallel processors, if necessary).

The leapfrog algorithm shows great promise, but further detailed study, particularly of the statistical properties of the individual subsequences generated, is needed. In the leapfrog algorithm the optimal choice of multiplier may well be different from what it would be for a single sequence generator. It is perhaps worth pointing out that the leapfrog method does not increase the total number of independent random numbers available, which may be a consideration in large computations in which many random numbers are used in an individual particle case history.

3.4 Description of Problems and Results

Two simple radiation shields, a sphere and infinite slab, are considered, with a monoenergetic gamma ray source of 9 MeV photons in both cases: (i) The sphere: in this problem we consider a homogeneous lead sphere of 3 mfp radius (5.6366 cm) with a uniform, isotropic, volume source confined to an inner region of 1 mfp radius (1.8789 cm). (ii) The infinite slab: in this problem we consider a homogeneous infinite lead slab of 3 mfp thickness (5.6366 cm) with a cosine weighted source (isotropic flux) impinging on the left hand side of the slab. The mfp referred to above is evaluated at the photon source energy.

The shield material is lead, a high Z-material, in which the pair production event is significant for high energy gamma rays. The nuclear cross-sections used are taken from the photon interaction cross-section library, PVC, which has 36 energy groups and allows up to P_5 anisotropy of scattering [12].

All the results shown are normalised to unit source particle, and in Figures 1 and 2 the spectra are divided by the energy interval, ΔE, and normalised to unit area. The estimated standard deviations on the Monte Carlo results are shown adjacent to the parameters-in brackets-in the conventional way. The value of the total particles created, shown in the tables, includes the source particle. For the case of the slab, the leakage spectra shown refer only to leakage at the right hand side. The results, unless otherwise stated, are for 201,600 case histories followed.

In order to validate the random number generator used, and the accuracy of the results obtained from the parallel version of the Monte Carlo code, Table 1 shows a comparison of integral parameters between serial and parallel Monte Carlo, and with an independent deterministic finite element method (FEM) transport code, called TRIPAC [7]. Figures 1 to 4 show a comparison of differential parameters (flux distribution and leakage spectra) for the two problems. The variation of the speedup factor achieved with the number of processors used is shown in Fig. 5. This shows that the speedup factor varies linearly when the number of processors is varied between 1 to 8, and we would expect it to remain so even if the number of processors were considerably increased. This is because the processor farm strategy requires minimal interprocessor communication between master and slaves. Fig.5 demonstrates that the efficiency achieved is over 95%. In Table 2 the performance of the Meiko Computing Surface is compared with other serial and parallel computers for equivalent computations.

Table 1. Comparison of Integral Parameters for the Two Problems (total of 201600 case histories followed)

Parameters	Sphere			Infinite Slab		
	Monte Carlo		FEM	Monte Carlo		FEM
	Serial*	Parallel**	P_{11}/P_5	Serial*	Parallel**	P_{11}/P_5
Particles absorbed	2.31 (0.0041)	2.313 (0.0041)	2.313	2.276 (0.0040)	2.277 (0.0040)	2.281
Particles escaped	0.127 (0.0008)	0.126 (0.0008)	0.126	0.242 (0.0013)	0.243 (0.0013)	0.241
Energy absorbed (MeV)	8.293 (0.0081)	8.291 (0.0081)	8.383	8.659 (0.0091)	8.655 (0.0091)	8.765
Energy escaped (MeV)	0.707 (0.0050)	0.705 (0.0050)	0.703	0.341 (0.0030)	0.341 (0.0030)	0.319
Total particles created	2.440 (0.0018)	2.439 (0.0018)	2.439	2.518 (0.0020)	2.520 (0.0020)	2.522

* Results from running the program on the ICL-3900 using the NAG-Library routine G05CAF as the RNG.
** Results form running the program on 8-T800 tranputers using Leapfrog method as the RNG.

Table 2. CPU Time in Seconds for the Two Problems on Different Computers

Computer	Sphere	Infinite Slab	Wordlength
8 Transputers	133.53 (8.0)**	82.11 (8.0)	Real *8 - Integer *4
DAP-610	54.27 (20.0)	29.50 (22.3)	Real *4 - Integer *4
ICL-3900	707.40 (1.5)	396.56 (1.7)	Real *8 - Integer *4
CRAY XMP*	115.80 (9.2)	69.95 (9.4)	Real *8 - Integer *8
VAX 11/750	2761.28 (0.4)	1432.10 (0.5)	Real *4 - Integer *4
SUN 4	519.00 (2.1)	281.00 (2.3)	Real *8 - Integer *4

* The CRAY XMP in scalar mode.
** Number of transputer required to give the same performance.

4. Finite Element Application

4.1. Finite element development

The finite element method (FEM) is a powerful numerical technique for the solution of many problems in engineering and science. While research into the use of finite element methods in radiation transport problems began in the two colleges more than a decade ago as a complementary tool to the Monte Carlo method, FEM is now seen as a powerful method in its own right and is still under development.

Significant progress has been made in recent years in the application of the finite element method to neutron and gamma-ray radiation transport. The most favoured formulation, which

Fig. 1 Leakage Current Spectra From Lead Sphere

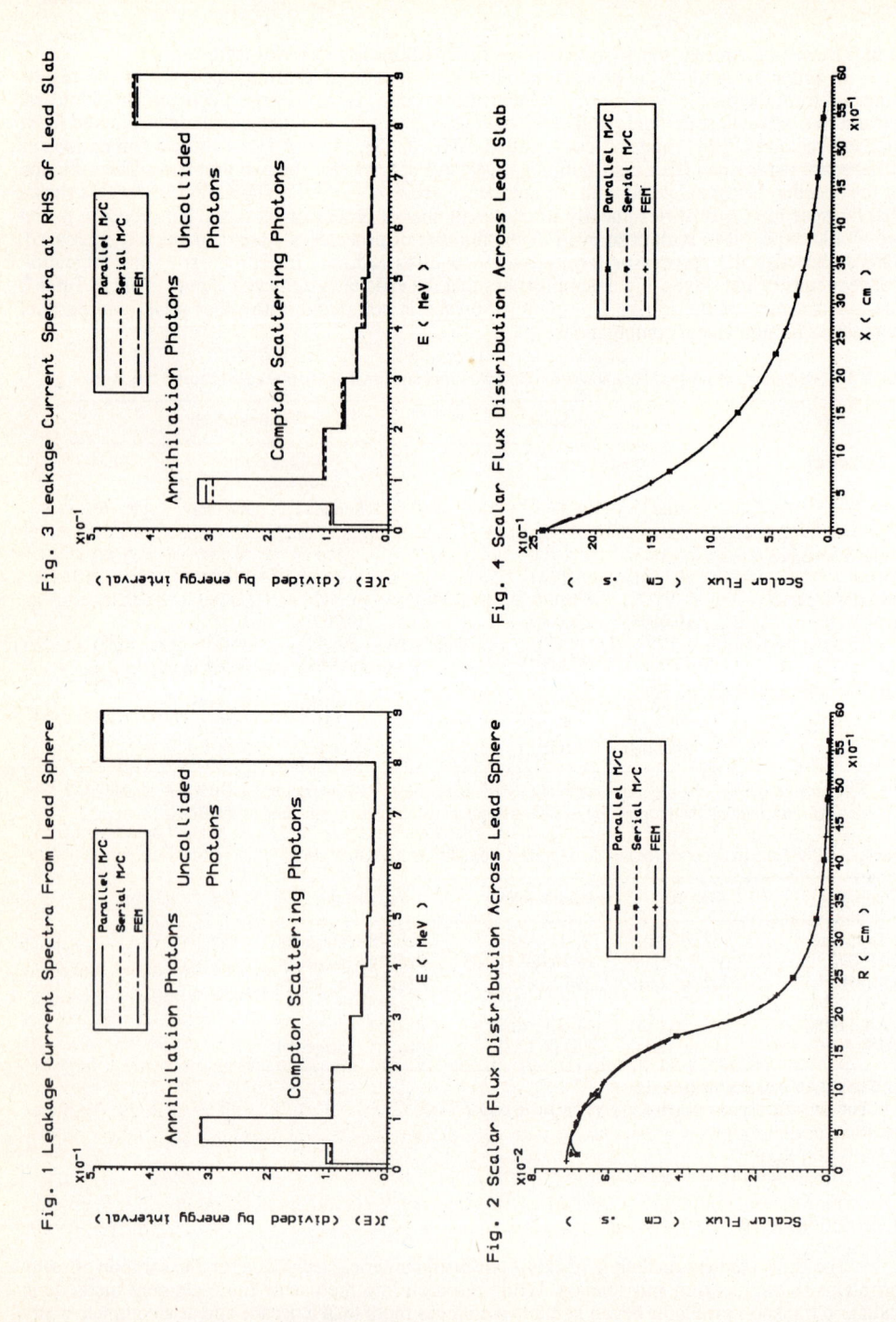

Fig. 2 Scalar Flux Distribution Across Lead Sphere

Fig. 3 Leakage Current Spectra at RHS of Lead Slab

Fig. 4 Scalar Flux Distribution Across Lead Slab

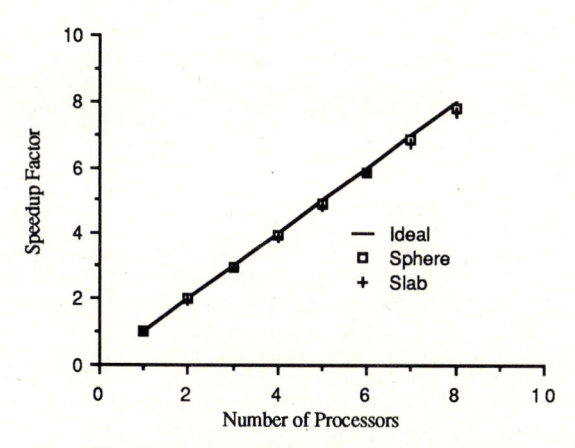

Fig. 5 Speedup Factor against Number of Processors

combines finite elements in space and spherical harmonics in angle, is based on a variational principle for the steady-state, second-order, even-parity transport equation. It has been developed successfully to a stage where it can now be applied to the solution of realistic problems. The demonstrated strengths of the method, i.e. accuracy, geometrical flexibility and ray-effect-free solutions, renders it a highly attractive alternative method to longer established techniques, such as the discrete ordinates and Monte Carlo methods.

However, experience in using the finite element method for radiation transport has also shown that the solution of realistic, complex problems can require very substantial resources on serial machines. Despite the method's near optimum vector performance on the CRAY XMP, computational times and memory requirements for the type of problems for which the method is envisaged are likely to put a restraint on its use for large problems, thus compromising the attractiveness of the method. This has led to the assessment of parallel computer architectures. In the research described here we are concerned with the implementation of radiation transport FEM on a transputer based system.

The problem of achieving parallelism in finite element calculation has been considered widely in the literature [13,14]. In general, parallelism can be exploited in two aspects of the FEM which require extensive computational resources:
- generation of the global stiffness matrix.
- solution of the finite element equations.

The first aspect is straightforward, and is addressed by dividing the mesh into a number of regions which are attached to different processors with the associated data structure to describe the element topology (shape, number of nodes etc..) and the element geometry (geometrical location of the element), and treated in parallel by a sequential algorithm without the need of interprocess communications.

For the second aspect, direct and iterative methods can be used for the parallel solution of the linear system of equations. In the FEM the global stiffness matrix is positive definite symmetric and banded. These properties affect the choice of the linear solver, other factors such the degree of parallelisation of a given solver should also be taken into account. The efficient parallelisation of a solver will require:
(i) Minimisation of the interprocess communications
(ii) Avoiding load balancing problems when some processor are busy doing calculations while other are idle. This means that the amount of work should be equally distributed among processors.

There are various parallel direct solvers available, mainly based on Gaussian elimination, Cholesky factorisation and LU decomposition. However, the development of banded and frontal solvers has been particularly important for the parallel solution of linear equations arising in FE calculations [15].

An alternative to direct methods are the iterative methods. The iterative methods seem to be more attractive to most researchers seeking the solution of FE equations on parallel computer architectures. Iterative methods reduces the amount of storage required by direct methods on each processor since no fill-in zero positions of the coefficient matrix occur during the calculations. Moreover, these methods can be better parallelised and reduces the load balancing problem. In the development of iterative methods for the parallel solution of FE equations most of the work has been concentrated on the conjugate gradient method which requires a preconditioning strategy in order to speed up the convergence rate [16].

4.2 Description of the Serial Finite Element Code

In this section a brief description of the radiation transport finite element program TWODOG is given [17]. The program TWODOG solves the two-dimensional (X-Y geometry), one-speed, even-parity neutron transport equation by a variational finite element approximation. The trial functions are linear triangular elements in space and spherical harmonics in angle. New trial functions can be implemented. The mesh is arbitrary (apart from the use of symmetry boundary conditions). The standard method of assembly is used and a banded, in core, direct-solution Gaussian elimination procedure is used for the solution of the system of linear equations. So, TWODOG in many respects is a standard finite element program and thus shares many features with them.

4.3 Parallel Implementation of the Code

Since the solution of the linear equations is an expensive part of the computations we started the parallel implementation of the program by solving these equation simultaneously. The conjugate gradient method is chosen for the parallel solution of the linear systems, the method is well parallelised and reduces the amount of storage otherwise required by direct methods.

First, we started by the implementation of a preconditioned conjugate gradient (PCG) in TWODOG, rather than the original Gaussian elimination based solver. The conjugate gradient is used for the solution of a symmetric positive definite system of equation, this type of system arising when TOWDOG is used. The PCG was incorporated in TWODOG, then the program was run on a serial machine (the host machine of the Meiko Computing Surface) in order to identify the cost of the different parts of the computation required by the program. The timing information are reported in Table 3 which shows that as the number of linear equations (and the bandwith) in the FE problem increases, the time spent on the solution of the linear equation becomes dominant comparable with the other computationally expensive part the assembly stage.

The PCG for the solution of the system of linear equations in the form $\mathbf{Kx} = \mathbf{b}$ (where $\mathbf{K}$ is the global stiffness matrix, $\mathbf{x}$ is the vector of unknown flux moments and $\mathbf{b}$ is the applied nodal forces) is given below:

$$x_0 = M^{-1} b$$
$$r_0 = b - K x_0$$
$$p_0 = M^{-1} r_0$$

for $k = 0, 1, 2, \ldots$ until convergence

$$\alpha_k = \frac{r_k^T M^{-1} r_k}{p_k^T K p_k}$$

$$x_{k+1} = x_k + \alpha_k p_k$$

$$r_{k+1} = r_k - \alpha_k K p_k$$

$$\beta_k = \frac{r_{k+1}^T M^{-1} r_{k+1}}{r_k^T M^{-1} r_k}$$

$$p_{k+1} = M^{-1} r_{k+1} + \beta_k p_k$$

M is called the preconditioner. In this work we started by a common choice of the preconditioner **M** = diag **K**, this is not a very effective preconditioner but is fast and easy to implement. It is clear from the above algorithm that PCG has three basic kinds of operations: matrix vector product, inner product and vector additions. For the parallel implementation the rows of the matrix **K** are distributed amongst the processors, the vectors **x**, **r** and **p** are also distributed between the processors.

During distributed matrix vector multiplication, processors need the most recently updated values of the direction vector element which are assigned to neighbour processors. During the inner product stage, each processor works on the slice of the vector assigned to it, and sends the resulting value to the master processor where the sum is accumulated, then the value of α and β are calculated and broadcast to the slaves. Finally we mention that the vector addition can performed concurrently without any interprocess communications. The convergence test of the algorithm is:

$$[<r_k, r_k>/<b, b>]^{1/2} < 10^{-8}$$

The implementation of the algorithm was carried out on the Meiko Computing Surface where the program TWODOG was run on the master processor and when the linear solver is called the parallel part started and the PCG linear solver is executed on different processors. Speed up ratio for the initial implementation is reported in Table 4.

Since the work is done on a distributed memory environment, it is inevitable that some form of segmentation is required for the problem. The choice of segmentation strategy, therefore, plays a crucial role in the parallel implementation. Several choices of segmentation strategies will be considered in future work, including that which treats the different material regions of the problem as different segments. This natural segmentation strategy has wider benefits in treating problem features, but has the drawback that if region effort is too dissimilar then load balancing problems might occur.

Table 3. Comparison of the CPU Time in Seconds of the Different Stages of the FE Program

Number of Unknowns	Assembly Stage			The Solution Stage		
	Number of Moments			Number of Moments		
	4	9	16	4	9	16
25	0.15	0.64	1.98	0.06	0.28	0.98
81	0.57	2.39	7.56	0.37	2.13	7.16
121	2.84	15.73	49.01	9.30	56.02	187.38

Table 4. Run-Time in Seconds

Number of unknowns	Number of moments	SUN 4	p = 1	p = 2	p = 3	p = 4	p = 5
9	16	0.83	3.10	2.27	1.89	-	-
25	4	0.34	1.39	1.43	-	-	-
	9	1.98	6.14	-	3.51	-	3.79
	16	6.56	20.98	11.39	-	8.11	7.51
121	4	8.06	23.83	13.70	-	10.42	-

5. Conclusion

We have demonstrated that for fixed-source particle transport Monte Carlo a straightforward implementation of existing serial codes can be made on transputers with the aid of CStools. The comparison of computing times we obtained suggest that a transputer based system can provide cost-effective computing for nuclear radiation engineering problems. As far as the FEM work is concerned, at this early stage of the investigation the results obtained from the implementation of the PCG method show that saving in the solution time of the linear equations can be achieved with the increase of the number of processors, provided the size of the problem also increases.

However, this has been restricted by the early release version of the CStools which only allows interchanging of small arrays between the processors. Further investigation of the PCG on a larger number of processors with different preconditioning strategies, and the parallelisation of first aspect of the FE program, is under consideration.

Acknowledgement

This research has been partially funded under SERC grant GR/F/04667 (investigators A J H Goddard and J Wood). The authors also express their appreciation of the help of Meiko staff during system installation.

References

[1]   A. F. Henry, Nuclear-Reactor Analysis, The MIT Press (1975).
[2]   Meiko Ltd., "Programmer's Introduction to Meiko CStools", (1990).
[3]   C.R. Askew et. al, " Monte Carlo Simulation on Transputer Arrays", Parallel Computing **6**, 247-258 (1988).
[4]   A.J.G. Hey, " Role of MIMD array of transputers in Computational Physics", Comp. Phys. Comm. **56**, 1-24 (1989).
[5]   J. Wood and H. Al-Bahadili, "The Implementing of Particle Transport Monte Carlo on the DAP Parallel Computer", First International Conference on Supercomputing in Nuclear Applications, Japan (1990).
[6]   J. Wood, Computational Methods in Reactor Shielding, Pergamon Press (1982).
[7]   J. Wood and C. R. E. De Oliveira, "A Finite Element of Gamma Ray Transport", Ann. Nucl. Energy **17**, 195-205 (1990).
[8]   L. Koblinger, "Direct Sampling from the Klein-Nishina Distribution for Photon Energies Above 1.4 MeV", Nucl.Sci. Eng. **56**, 218-219 (1975).
[9]   D. E. Knuth, The Art of Computer Programming, Vol. 2 Chap. III, Addison Wesley, Reading, MA (1981).
[10] G. S. Fishman and L. R. Moore, "An Exhaustive Analysis of Multiplicative Congruential Random Number Generators with Modulus 2^{31}-1", SIAM J. Sci. Stat. Comput. **7**, 24-45 (1986).
[11] K. O. Bowman and M. T. Robinson, "Studies of Random Generators fpr Parallel Processing",
[12] R. W. Roussin, "DLC-48/PVC". RSIC Report, ORNL (1977).
[13] R. E. Fulton, "The Finite Element Machine: an Assessment of the Impact of Parallel Computing on Future Finite Element Computations", Finite Elements Anal. Design 2, 83-98 (1986).
[14] D. W. White and J. F. Abel, "Bibliography on Finite Element and Supercomputing", Communications in Applied Numerical Methods 4, 279-294 [1988].
[15] R. G. Miles and S. P. Havard, "Multifronts and Transputer Networks for Solving Fluid Mechanical Finite Element Systems" , Int. J. Numer. Methods in Fluids 9, 731-740 (1989).
[16] C. J. Willis and R. Wait, "Distributed Finite Element Calculations on a transputer array", paper presented at the International Conference on Transputer Application, Liverpool (1989).
[17] B. A. Splawski, "TWODOG : A Finite Element-Spherical Harmonics Program for the Solution of the One-Speed, Even-Parity Neutron Transport Equation", Dept. of Mech. Eng. Report, QMW (1981).

An occam implementation of an asynchronous algorithm for calculating polynomial zeros

T. L. Freeman and M. K. Bane,
Department of Mathematics,
University of Manchester,
Manchester.
M13 9PL

Abstract

Frequent synchronisations have a significant effect on the efficiency of parallel numerical algorithms. In this paper we consider the Durand-Kerner algorithm for the calculation of the zeros of a polynomial and analyse, both theoretically and numerically, the effect of removing the synchronisation restriction from this algorithm. We also discuss the occam implementation of the resulting asynchronous algorithm.

1 Introduction

In this paper we consider the problem of calculating, on a local memory parallel computer, all the zeros of the nth degree polynomial,

$$P_n(x) = x^n + a_1 x^{n-1} + a_2 x^{n-2} + \cdots + a_{n-1} x + a_n, \tag{1.1}$$

where the coefficients $a_i, i = 1, 2, \ldots, n$, are assumed to be real. We also assume, without loss of generality, that $P_n(x)$ is normalised so that the leading coefficient is one, and that the zeros of $P_n(x)$ are $\alpha_j \in \mathcal{C}, j = 1, 2, \ldots, n$, so that

$$P_n(x) = \prod_{j=1}^{n}(x - \alpha_j). \tag{1.2}$$

Throughout the paper, we shall assume, for the sake of brevity, that all summations and products are over the range $1, 2, \ldots, n$, unless explicitly stated otherwise, so that, for example,

$$\prod_{j \neq i} a_j \equiv \prod_{\substack{j=1 \\ j \neq i}}^{n} a_j.$$

Calculating all, rather than a few of, the zeros is the form of the problem usually considered by software library routines (for example, routines C02AEF and C02AGF in the N.A.G. library ([15]), routines ZRPOLY and ZPOLR in the I.M.S.L.([13]) and routine PA07 in the Harwell library ([11]).

However it should be noted that the algorithms used in these library routines determine approximations to the polynomial zeros one or two at a time and eliminate these calculated zeros by deflation. Thus they are thus too fine grained to exploit parallel computers.

2 The Durand-Kerner Algorithm

There exists a class of algorithms which calculate approximations to all the polynomial zeros simultaneously. These algorithms are coarser grained and are therefore suitable for implementation on a local memory MIMD parallel computer (see [9]). An example of such an algorithm is the Durand-Kerner algorithm (see [1], [6] and [14]), the kth iteration of which is given by

$$x_i^{(k+1)} = x_i^{(k)} - \frac{P_n(x_i^{(k)})}{\prod_{j \neq i}(x_i^{(k)} - x_j^{(k)})}, i = 1, 2, \ldots, n, \qquad (2.1)$$

where $x_i^{(k)}$ is the kth approximation to the ith zero of $P_n(x)$.

A local memory parallel version of this algorithm can be implemented by performing the updating of the approximate zeros on separate processors. At the end of each iteration the processors need to communicate their current approximate zeros to each other, but there is no other communication required by the algorithm. As in [9] we assume that there are $p \leq n$ processors and that the lth processor handles j_l approximate zeros and that $i_l = \sum_{m \leq l-1} j_m, l = 1, 2, \ldots, p$; the *parallel Durand-Kerner algorithm* is then given by:

step 1 *(i)* $k = 1$,

   (ii) define initial approximations $x_i^{(1)}, i = 1, 2, \ldots, n$.

step 2 IN PARALLEL, on the lth processor, for $l = 1, 2, \ldots, p$,

   for $i = i_l + 1, i_l + 2, \ldots, i_l + j_l$,
   (i) calculate $p_i^{(k)} = P_n(x_i^{(k)})$,
   (ii) calculate $q_i^{(k)} = \prod_{j \neq i}(x_i^{(k)} - x_j^{(k)})$
   (iii) set $x_i^{(k+1)} = x_i^{(k)} - \frac{p_i^{(k)}}{q_i^{(k)}}$.

step 3 For $i = 1, 2, \ldots, n$, communicate $x_i^{(k+1)}$ to all the other processors.

step 4 *(i)* check for convergence,

   (ii) set $k = k + 1$,

   (iii) return to step 2.

The algorithm can be shown to be locally convergent and to have a quadratic rate of convergence (see [3], [8] and [17]).

Further the algorithm can be implemented in a partial Gauss-Seidel fashion by replacing *step 2 (ii)* by *step 2 (ii) calculate* $q_i^{(k)} = \prod_{j=1}^{i_l}(x_i^{(k)} - x_j^{(k)}) \prod_{j=i_l+1}^{i-1}(x_i^{(k)} - x_j^{(k+1)}) \prod_{j=i+1}^{n}(x_i^{(k)} - x_j^{(k)})$

This modification leads to a minor increase in the R-order of convergence (see [16]) of the algorithm. This result can be proved using an analysis similar to that given in [3] for the Durand-Kerner algorithm implemented in a *conventional* Gauss-Seidel fashion. Extensive numerical testing of an occam implementation of the algorithm described in this section is reported in [9].

3 An Asynchronous Durand-Kerner Algorithm

The algorithm described in Section 2 is highly synchronised, since at *step 3* of every iteration each different processor needs to broadcast its updated zero approximation(s) to all the other processors. If this synchronisation restriction were removed then each processor would continue to update its approximation(s) rather than wait for new approximations to be received from the other processors. Thus the algorithm would not necessarily be using the most up-to-date approximations to the zeros being dealt with by the other processors. The kth iteration of this *asynchronous Durand-Kerner algorithm* is given by

$$x_i^{(k+1)} = x_i^{(k)} - \frac{P_n(x_i^{(k)})}{\prod_{j \neq i}\left(x_i^{(k)} - x_j^{(k_j)}\right)}, i = 1, 2, \ldots, n, \quad (3.1)$$

where $x_j^{(k_j)}$ is the k_j^{th} approximation to the jth zero of $P_n(x)$ and $k_j \leq k$. We note that, for a given i, $\max_{j \neq i}(k - k_j)$, provides a value for the *asynchronism measure* of this partially asynchronous algorithm, as defined in [5].

If we write the error in the ith approximate zero on the kth iteration as

$$\epsilon_i^{(k)} = x_i^{(k)} - \alpha_i, \ i = 1, 2, \ldots, n,$$

then the following local convergence theorem can be established (see [10]).

Theorem 1 *For* $\epsilon_i^{(1)}, i = 1, 2, \ldots, n$, *sufficiently small, the approximations given by the iteration* (3.1) *satisfy*

$$\epsilon_i^{(k+1)} = -\epsilon_i^{(k)}\left[\sum_{j \neq i}\frac{\epsilon_j^{(k_j)}}{(\alpha_i - \alpha_j)} + O(\epsilon^2)\right],$$

for $i = 1, 2, \ldots, n$, *and for* $k = 1, 2, \ldots$, *where* $|\epsilon| = \max\left\{|\epsilon_i^{(k)}| \ ; \ |\epsilon_j^{(k_j)}|, j \neq i\right\}$.

Thus the algorithm is locally convergent under conditions which are similar to those for the synchronised algorithm. However we note that the global convergence properties of the two algorithms may be different; extensive numerical testing indicates that, as expected, the asynchronous algorithm is less robust as the *asynchronism measure* of the algorithm increases (the algorithm becomes less synchronised) and does not have such reliable global convergence properties. This is because the global convergence behaviour of the Durand-Kerner algorithm depends, amongst other things, on the rate at which information is interchanged between the iterations for the different polynomial zeros and the rate of this interchange is reduced as the *asynchronism measure* of (3.1) is increased.

Theorem 1 also shows that the asynchronous algorithm (3.1) converges at a superlinear rate as compared with the quadratic rate of convergence of the Durand-Kerner algorithm (2.1). Further, as the *asynchronism measure* of the algorithm (3.1) decreases (the algorithm becomes more synchronised) the superlinear rate of convergence increases. A detailed, R-order of convergence, analysis of the rate of convergence of the algorithm is given in [4].

4 Numerical Results for a Durand-Kerner Algorithm with a Fixed Communications Delay

To test our theoretical results on the convergence rate of the algorithm we have experimented with the *parallel Durand-Kerner algorithm* but with a more restricted communications algorithm in *step 3* of the algorithm given in Section 2; approximations to the zeros are exchanged between the processes after every m iterations rather than after every iteration so that the *asynchronism measure* of the algorithm can be controlled. In this case the asynchronous algorithm (3.1) can be written as

$$x_i^{(km+l+1)} = x_i^{(km+l)} - \frac{P_n(x_i^{(km+l)})}{\prod_{j\neq i}(x_i^{(km+l)} - x_j^{(km)})}, i = 1,2,\ldots,n, \qquad (4.1)$$
$$l = 0,1,\ldots,m-1; \ k = 0,1,2,\ldots.$$

We note that when $m = 1$ this algorithm is the same as that described in Section 2. We also note that the algorithm (4.1) can be implemented in the partial Gauss-Seidel fashion described at the end of Section 2 and the results quoted in this section are obtained from such an algorithm.

We would expect the algorithm (4.1) to require more iterations to converge to the polynomial zeros as m, the number of iterations between communications, is increased and also as the number of processors p is increased, since each of these changes increases the *asynchronism measure* of the algorithm. However, even though the number of iterations increases, the algorithm suffers less synchronisation delays than the algorithm of Section 2. In Table 1 we quote the number of iterations and the time required to find the zeros of some of the higher degree polynomials in the set of test polynomials suggested in [12] (see also [18]) for different values of p, the number of processors and m, the number of iterations between communications. The results were obtained using the Edinburgh Concurrent Supercomputer (see [19]), with the T800 transputers configured as a doubly linked chain. The termination condition for the algorithm is based on the convergence test suggested in [2] (see also [9]). ** indicates that the algorithm failed because of a floating point overflow in the convergence test, which results from two different approximations tending to converge to the same polynomial zero; a strategy to avoid this difficulty could be incorporated in the algorithm.

The results are as expected; as m, the number of iterations between communications, increases, the number of iterations required for convergence increases. When the number of processors, p, is small, the savings resulting from the more limited communications strategy are outweighed by the cost of the extra iterations. However, for larger p, when

Table 1: The effect of communication delays on the Durand-Kerner algorithm

Table	Problem	Degree	p	m	Iterations	Time
1	29	13	1	1	81	0.461
			7	1	87	0.134
			7	2	112	0.142
			7	3	129	0.152
			13	1	89	0.126
			13	2	114	0.112
			13	3	135	0.113
1	30	15	1	1	28	0.223
			8	1	33	0.0643
			8	2	44	0.0691
			8	3	45	0.0660
			15	1	30	0.0568
			15	2	38	0.0508
			15	3	45	0.0509
1	31	18	1	1	44	0.497
			9	1	47	0.102
			9	2	88	0.152
			9	3	120	0.189
			18	1	47	0.0984
			18	2	60	0.0875
			18	3	72	0.0881
1	32	19	1	1	47	0.587
			10	1	50	0.115
			10	2	**	**
			10	3	**	**
			19	1	52	0.113
			19	2	74	0.110
			19	3	78	0.0994
2	11	15	1	1	62	0.490
			8	1	68	0.123
			8	2	110	0.160
			8	3	102	0.138
			15	1	73	0.120
			15	2	88	0.102
			15	3	102	0.100
2	12	18	1	1	54	0.587
			9	1	72	0.151
			9	2	72	0.126
			9	3	84	0.136
			18	1	58	0.118
			18	2	74	0.105
			18	3	87	0.104
2	13	36	1	1	34	1.414
			18	1	41	0.181
			18	2	**	**
			18	3	**	**
			36	1	37	0.183
			36	2	48	0.164
			36	3	60	0.168

the communications costs are higher, the communications savings of the asynchronous algorithm more than compensate for the extra iterations required by the algorithm and typically lead to a 10–20% reduction in the time taken by the algorithm.

We have also investigated, both theoretically and numerically, the third order simultaneous polynomial root-finding algorithm suggested in [7]. In this case the asynchronous algorithm is more robust; it is also more efficient and it outperforms the synchronised version for smaller numbers of processors (see [10]); this is probably due to the increased granularity of the algorithm.

5 Numerical Results for an Asynchronous Durand-Kerner Algorithm

Further, we have developed, in occam, a *completely* asynchronous Durand-Kerner algorithm; each transputer continues, *without synchronisation*, to perform iterations on its approximate zeros whilst, concurrently, data is being passed between all the processors.

An occam implementation of this algorithm is achieved by running three parallel processes;

Compute process performs the Durand-Kerner iterations using the available data.

Communicate process passes data to and from neighbouring processors.

Buffer process communicates between the compute process and the communicate process on a given processor.

In our current implementation, a compute process passes new approximate zeros to its buffer process after updating its block of zeros. At the same time the compute process reads from the buffer process new values, if they have changed, for the approximate zeros being dealt with by the other processors.

The communicate process performs a continuous sequence of global broadcasts of the latest available data in the buffer processes. Once such a global broadcast has been initiated it continues to completion with the given data, even though the compute processes continue to generate new approximations and continue to send these new approximations to the buffer processes. When any of the data which is being broadcast by the communicate process reaches a processor it is immediately passed to the buffer process on that processor. On each processor a *PRI PAR* is used to give the communicate process the highest priority so that the interprocessor communications can proceed as rapidly as possible. A more sophisticated data-driven global broadcast routine is currently being developed and tested.

The buffer process provides *soft* links between a compute process and its corresponding communicate process. Currently it reads new approximate zeros from either its own compute process or from other compute processes via its communicate process. A *PRI ALT* is used to give preference to reading new approximations from its communicate process.

Note that, in this algorithm, the compute processes are updating their approximate zeros using data about the other approximate zeros (those being dealt with by the other transputers) which may well be an (*undetermined*) number of iterations old; the age (number of iterations since it was calculated) of the data obtained from the other transputers will be proportional to the length of the communications path and thus each compute process will depend on relatively young data from neighbouring transputers but much older data from more distant transputers.

In Table 2 we give some performance figures for this completely asynchronous algorithm for different numbers of processors, p, and for those test polynomials in the collection suggested in [12], which have high degree, n. On this very limited numerical experience we find, as expected, that the time/iteration of the *completely* asynchronous algorithm is considerably better than the corresponding time/iteration for the synchronised algorithm, but that the number of iterations required for convergence is so considerably increased that the overall execution times are worse. By comparison with the performance figures in Table 1 we conclude that this dramatic increase in the number of

Table 2: Performance of the completely asynchronous algorithm

Table	Problem	n	p	SYNCHRONISED			ASYNCHRONOUS		
				Iterations	Time/Iteration	Total Time	Iterations	Time/Iteration	Total Time
1	31	18	1	44	0.0113	0.497	44	0.0130	0.573
			9	47	0.00217	0.102	113	0.00212	0.239
			18	47	0.00209	0.0984	129	0.00143	0.184
1	32	19	1	47	0.0125	0.587	47	0.0144	0.678
			10	50	0.00230	0.115	131	0.00218	0.286
			19	52	0.00205	0.113	148	0.00143	0.212
2	12	18	1	54	0.0109	0.587	54	0.0126	0.678
			9	72	0.00210	0.151	106	0.00210	0.223
			18	58	0.00203	0.118	160	0.00139	0.223
2	13	36	1	34	0.0416	1.414	34	0.0449	1.526
			18	41	0.00441	0.181	91	0.00352	0.320
			36	37	0.00494	0.183	**	**	**

iterations is caused by the slowness of our current communicate process (for the larger problems, each transputer can typically perform four or five iterations in the time taken to complete one global broadcast), which means that the compute processes are using *very old* approximations to some of the polynomial zeros. This difficulty should be alleviated by the data-driven global broadcast process which is currently under development.

6 References

[1]. O. Aberth, *Iteration methods for finding all zeros of a polynomial simultaneously*, Math. Comp. **27** (1973), 339-344.

[2]. D. A. Adams, *A stopping criterion for polynomial root finding*, Comm. A.C.M. **10** (1967), 655-658.

[3]. G. Alefeld and J. Herzberger, *On the convergence speed of some algorithms for the simultaneous approximation of polynomial roots*, SIAM J. Numer. Anal. **2** (1974), 237-243.

[4]. M. K. Bane and T. L. Freeman, *On the rates of convergence of asynchronous polynomial root-finding algorithms*, N.A.Report, Department of Mathematics, University of Manchester, to appear, 1990.

[5]. D. P. Bertsekas and J. N. Tsitsiklis, *Parallel and distributed computation: numerical methods*, Prentice-Hall, Englewood Cliffs, New Jersey, 1989.

[6]. E. Durand, *Solutions Numériques des Équations Algébriques. Tome I*, Masson, Paris, 1960.

[7]. L. W. Ehrlich, *A modified Newton method for polynomials*, Comm. A.C.M. **10** (1967), 107-108.

[8]. M. R. Farmer and G. Loizou, *A class of iteration functions for improving, simultaneously, approximations to the zeros of a polynomial*, B.I.T. **15** (1975), 250-258.

[9]. T. L. Freeman, *Calculating polynomial zeros on a local memory parallel computer*, Parallel Computing, **12**, pp.351-358, 1989.

[10]. T. L. Freeman and M. K. Bane, *Asynchronous algorithms for calculating polynomial zeros*, N.A.Report, Department of Mathematics, University of Manchester, to appear, 1990.

[11]. Harwell, *Harwell Subroutine Library: A catalogue of subroutines*, Harwell Report AERE-R9185, Harwell, 1989.

[12]. P. Henrici and B. O. Watkins, *Finding zeros of a polynomial by the Q-D algorithm*, Comm. A.C.M. **8** (1965), 570-574.

[13]. I.M.S.L., *I.M.S.L. User's Manual*, I.M.S.L., Houston, 1985.

[14]. I. O. Kerner, *Ein Gesamtschrittverfahren zur Berechnung der Nullstellen von Polynomen*, Numer. Math. **8** (1966), 290-294.

[15]. N.A.G., *N.A.G. Fortran Library Manual, Mark 13*, N.A.G. Ltd., Oxford, 1988.

[16]. J. M. Ortega and W. C. Rheinboldt, *Iterative Solution of Nonlinear Equations in Several Variables*, Academic Press, New York, 1970.

[17]. M. D. Prešić, *A convergence theorem for a method for simultaneous determination of all zeros of a polynomial*, Publications de·l'Insititut Mathématique **42** (1980), 159-168.

[18]. R. F. Thomas, *Corrections to numerical data on Q-D algorithm*, Comm. A.C.M. **9** (1966), 322-323.

[19]. D. J. Wallace, *Supercomputing with Transputers*, in *Applications of Transputers 1*, L. Freeman and C. Phillips, eds., IOS Press, Amsterdam, 1990.

Machine Code Implementation of Basic Vector Subroutines for the T800

D.C.B. Watson, R. Wilkinson, C.J. Willis and P.G.N. Howard

Abstract

The implementation and optimisation of basic algebraic routines for the T800 is described.

The Liverpool Single Node Library consists of 162 routines callable from either occam or FORTRAN. The library includes implementations of the Level 1 BLAS (Basic Linear Algebra Subprograms) [1], the Level 2 BLAS [2] and a set of general vector operations (FLO routines [3]) in both single and double precision for complex and real arguments. The techniques used to optimise the performance of these routines form the basis of this paper. The paper is couched in terms of FORTRAN callable routines but the same techniques have been applied to the occam libraries.

The routines are all encoded directly in the Transputer assembly language and are designed to work specifically on the T800 series processors. Since the architecture of the chip has a profound effect upon the style of encoding, some brief remarks about the chip itself are pertinent. The basic instruction set is RISC-like [1] in that complex instructions and large operands are constructed from byte-length instructions in an operand register. This implies that instructions with operands outside the range $(0-15)$ require extra pre-fixing and thus take longer to execute. The CPU and FPU are both implemented as 3 register stacks and are capable of concurrent operation. Limited stack manipulation instructions exist so there is scope for optimisation of stack usage. There is a hardware implementation of time-slicing to facilitate multiprocessing. Time-slicing of a process invalidates the state of its registers, but may only occur at certain instructions in a program. The chip has 4 Kbytes of fast DRAM, access to which is up to 5 times faster than external memory [7]. Since most of the routines are vector or higher order operations the majority of the computation is performed within loops. Thus the most significant performance improvements are obtained by optimising these structures. In order to facilitate the extraction of the effects of the various optimisations the performance of the Level 1 BLAS routines was investigated in terms of the asymptotic performance [2] ($r_{\inf}$) and the half-performance length[3] ($n_{\frac{1}{2}}$)[4]. In order

---
[1] the instruction set does contain some 'high level' instructions which perform complex operations such as channel communication which are perhaps contrary to the RISC philosophy.

[2] the maximal rate obtained when the operation is performed upon a vector of 'infinite' length (10,000 in this case!!)

[3] the vector length required to achieve a performance $\frac{1}{2}r_{\inf}$

Table 1: Performance figures for FORTRAN and assembler codes for the LEVEL 1 BLAS routines. The timings are for calls made to single precision REAL FORTRAN routines and librified assembler BLAS routines using the on-chip RAM manager described in this paper. The total size of such a library is well in excess of the amount of on-chip RAM available so this is thought to be a fair comparison since the equivalent FORTRAN library would not have the fast RAM available to it.

Routine	operation	FORTRAN $r_{\inf}$ (Mflops)	Assembler $r_{\inf}$ (Mflops)	speedup	Assembler $n_{\frac{1}{2}}$
SAXPY	$y \leftarrow y + \alpha x$	0.26	1.06	3.9	~ 15
SCOPY[†]	$y \leftarrow x$	0.21	0.86	4.1	~ 30
SSCAL	$x \leftarrow \alpha x$	0.18	1.16	6.6	~ 40
SSWAP[†]	$x \leftrightarrow y$	0.11	0.60	5.5	~ 25
SDOT	$\leftarrow x^T y$	0.31	1.50	4.8	~ 25
SDSDOT	$\leftarrow \alpha + x^T y$	0.13	0.91	6.8	~ 15
SNRM2	$\leftarrow \|x\|_2$	0.39	1.67	4.2	~ 30
SASUM	$\leftarrow \|x\|_1$	0.23	1.32	5.6	~ 40
ISAMAX[†]	$\leftarrow min(k) : \mid x_k \mid = max\{x_i\}$	0.22	0.63	2.8	~ 20
SROTMG[*]	generate modified plane rotation	0.19	0.26	1.4	N/A
SROTM[§]	apply modified plane rotation	0.35,0.35, 0.47,0.16	1.10,1.11, 1.33,0.72	3.2,3.2 2.8,4.3	<10 , <10 <10 , ~ 30
SROTG[*]	generate plane rotation	0.21	0.29	1.4	N/A
SROT	apply plane rotation	0.52	1.55	3.0	<10

[†] These are not floating point operations. The figures quoted are in M operations/s.

[*] These are not vector operations so $r_{\inf}$ and $n_{\frac{1}{2}}$ are not applicable. The rate quoted is for an average number of operations over many calls.

[§] SROTM performs different operations according to the parameters passed and the sets of figures correspond to these parameters.

to put the performance results into perspective a comparison is made to FORTRAN versions of equivalent codes compiled by the 3L FORTRAN compiler [5]. The assembler routines presented were all generated using the TASM assembler [6].

The first point we consider is whether or not it is worth coding such operations at a low level at all. Is the performance gain obtained worth the man-effort? From the speedups listed in Table 1 it is apparent that significant improvements in performance have been achieved. The higher order LEVEL 2 BLAS show greater speed-ups in general since they perform more computation e.g. SGEMV, the general matrix-vector multiply routine, shows a speed-up over a comparable FORTRAN code of the order of 7. As the routines perform simple operations they are widely applicable and can easily be substituted into existing applications code. Whilst the use of such routines will never give order of magnitude acceleration, their substitution into compute intensive regions of an application will decrease its execution time markedly. Recently, two parallel application codes, from the fields of SAR imaging and Finite Elements, have been trivially modified at Liverpool University to use this implementation of the LEVEL 1 BLAS and both show speedups in excess of 2 for the *whole* application. Thus we conclude that libraries of elemental vector (and higher order) routines are worthwhile tools.

Table 2: Comparison of behaviour of FORTRAN and assembler codes for the routine SAXPY with and without unrolling. The timings are all for codes resident in on-chip RAM. The righthand colmn of performance improvement refers to the improvement in $r_{\inf}$ for the degree of unrolling used.

Unroll Factor	8			1			performance
	$r_{\inf}{}^8$ (Mflops)	$n_{\frac{1}{2}}{}^8$	code size (Bytes)	$r_{\inf}{}^1$ (Mflops)	$n_{\frac{1}{2}}{}^1$	code size (Bytes)	improvement (%)
assembler	1.00	16	589	0.83	8	361	18
FORTRAN	0.37	5	1003	0.33	5	540	12

We now proceed with a discussion of the optimisations applied. This will be done in terms of the routine SAXPY which has been analysed in detail in order to separate the various contributary factors. Other routines will be mentioned where pertinent.

The most significant factor affecting code performance is the efficiency of utilisation of the register stacks. If variables can be duplicated and kept on the register stacks (both CPU and FPU) the number of memory references can be reduced and the execution speed of the code correspondingly increased. In particular, for SAXPY, the floating point (FP) constant α can be kept on the FP stack throughout the calculation and is thus only loaded once. The computed address of the vector elements x_i can similarly remain on the CPU stack removing the need to store and load it for each element. The non-vector routines SROTG and SROTMG do not show any marked performance gain due to hand coding. This is because the arithmetic operations are largely unrelated so that little stack optimisation is possible. For the simplest of operations such as SASUM and SNRM2 it is possible to keep all addresses and accumulated values on the appropriate stacks throughout the computation, hence the high Mflop rates for these routines.

As mentioned earlier, Register-Register operations on the FPU are performed independently from CPU operations. The CPU can thus perform useful work whilst the FPU is busy. This is particularly useful for vector operations since much of the address calculation can be overlapped with the FP calculation. The BLAS 1 routines SDOT and SNRM2 seem to fully saturate the FPU operating at the maximal rates for the FPU - 1.50 and 1.67 Mflops respectively. This is because the address calculation for the operands for the next step is completely hidden by the 2 floating point operations of the current step. The difference in performance between the two can be explained since there is one less FP load operation for the operation SNRM2. As DOUBLE PRECISION operations generally take longer, there is even more scope for hiding CPU operations in the double precision routines. However, it is not always possible to use this extra time. In the test routine SAXPY complete overlap of FPU and CPU is not possible as this routine also requires an address to store the result of each step.

There is a small overhead to pay in order to keep variables on the register stacks as loops must be coded so as not to be 'deschedulable'. This means that the unconditional jump (J) and the microcoded loop end (LEND) instructions must be replaced by a conditional jump (CJ) with the condition forced to false. The penalty for this is typically only 3 processor cycles per loop iteration. Pre-loading of the loop counter and overlap with the FPU sometimes enables the loop overheads to be partially masked with careful loop end coding. The loop counter itself is negated and then successively incremented rather than decremented. This avoids the prefixing instruction associated with loading negative constants.

There is little scope for choice in the instructions used to implement operations. Certain floating point instructions have load and operate forms which can be utilised to compact the code. This can have a knock-on effect in reducing the span of code jumps and thus the need for prefixes. Where possible (small) constants have been used, particularly in addressing. This limits the applicability of the codes to 32-bit processors but this is not regarded as a drawback since the libraries are specifically targeted at the T800.

The (standard) technique of unrolling the loops over vector elements was employed to further optimise the vector routines. Unrolling generally has the effect of reducing the ratio of loop overhead to computation and, thus improves r_{inf} . For hand coded routines there is an additional benefit to unrolling. Generally the end-loop code will require an item from the register stack to be stored and re-loaded at the loop start. The larger the unroll factor the less often this must be done so that for the majority of the the time the code is only operating on values in registers. An extra overhead is introduced in splitting the problem into chunks of size $unroll.factor$ plus odd iterations and the code size is increased by a factor $\sim (unroll.factor + 1)$. This causes a slight degradation in $n_{\frac{1}{2}}$. Table 2 compares both FORTRAN and assembler coded SAXPY routines that have been unrolled. Beyond a factor of 8 the increased code size far outweighs the performance improvement obtained (e.g. for a factor of 16 no improvement in r_{inf} is observed for FORTRAN and the assembler coded version improved by only 1% which does not justify the two-fold increase in code size). The fractional increase in r_{inf} for the assembler coded routine is larger than that for the corresponding FORTRAN implementation, since the the assembler FP code is more efficient, and thus the end loop code is more significant. As Table 3 shows, the degree of unrolling to be applied to a loop is very much a property of the particular code. As a general rule, the largest performance gains are made by unrolling loops for those codes which make effective use of stacks during the loop. SROT with 6 FP operations and a lot of address calculation gains little from massive unrolling whilst the code size increases greatly due to the complexity of the routine. SASUM benefits greatly from unrolling since there is little computation in the routine and at little cost in terms of code size since the loop code is small. SSWAP and ISAMAX are CPU dominated and derive benefit from unrolling to a small degree due to maximal use of the stack. The overhead in loading and storing a variable per loop iteration soon becomes negligible, however.

The routines discussed so far are all general stride versions ; better performances can be obtained for versions specifically coded for constant (e.g. unit) and/or equally strided vectors. In general the performance increase obtained for specialised codes did not warrant the additional effort required, other than in a few specific cases for equal unit strides. For example, a specially coded unit stride dot product routine runs no faster than the generally coded routine listed in Table 1. That this is so is proof that the FPU is completely saturated for this routine. Routines which show increased performance for constant strides are those in which address calculation is not completely hidden by FPU/CPU overlap. Table 4 shows the performance for those routines which in fact test for the unit stride condition and execute an appropriate version of the code in the case of all arguments having unit stride. The SCOPY figure is included for comparison only. In actual fact the unit stride version for this routine utilises block moves and achieves a rate of 2.5 Moperations/s. The other major

Table 3: Performance of Assembler coded routines as a function of the degree to which the loop was unrolled.

routine	unrolling factor					
	32	16	8	4	2	1
SROT	–	1.57	1.55	1.54	1.48	1.39
SASUM	1.37	1.32	1.24	1.11	0.92	0.69
ISAMAX	–	0.63	0.62	0.58	0.53	0.44
SWAP	–	0.60	0.59	0.56	0.52	0.40

factor affecting performance is the physical location of the code in memory. Code will run faster if located in on-chip RAM. Thus codes placed early in the link list will tend to be 'on-chip' and run faster. An idea of the magnitude of this effect can be gained by examining the figures given in Table 5. The speedup over FORTRAN is reduced on-chip since the FORTRAN code is enhanced to a greater degree. This in turn is due to the fact that the code is less efficient and therefore executes more instructions.

In the opening remarks it was noted that there are only 4 Kbytes of on-chip RAM. 3L FORTRAN reserves 2 Kbytes of this for its own use, so it is a precious commodity on the T800. To make efficient use of the remaining RAM, a routine was written to manage the various Library codes and move them into on-chip RAM as required. This obviously requires some care and there is a penalty overhead for using the technique, but this is small and its utility can be seen immediately if we look at the size of the unrolled codes in Table 2 : only one or perhaps two FORTRAN routines can ever reside on-chip, whereas any number of assembler routines can be moved on-chip. The full manager routine checks first to see if a code is already resident in on-chip RAM and allows as many codes as will fit: the codes are effectively cached. The full overhead is thus only incurred once. There is a worst case possibility of a routine being called within a loop with several intervening calls to different routines, the total code length of which exceeds the size of the claimed on-chip RAM, so that the code must be loaded at each iteration. This worst case behaviour is reflected by $n_{\frac{1}{2}}$ which increases to 46 for SAXPY; the 'break-even' vector length with a FORTRAN implementation is only 15, however. We also note that code size is now an important issue since this (largely) governs the overhead in placing code segments into the code cache and the number of codes which will fit into the allocated space at any one time. Thus there is a trade-off between unrolling of loops and code size. This is not too serious for the LEVEL 1 BLAS and FLOS but can be a restriction on the LEVEL 2 BLAS which perform matrix-vector operations and have significantly larger codes. This is overcome to some extent by loading only the critical

Table 4: Comparison of performance on unit and general stride vectors for routines which check for the occurrence of equal unit strided arguments.

routine	SSWAP	ISAMAX	SASUM	SCOPY	SAXPY
r_{inf} - general (Mflops)	0.60	0.63	1.32	0.86	1.06
r_{inf} - unit (Mflops)	0.85	0.68	1.55	1.42	1.21

loops in the codes into fast RAM. Finally, the user may not wish to use the on-chip RAM for Library routines. If the 'code cache' is placed off-chip then the manager detects this and runs the routines without penalty [4]. To gain an impression of the overheads involved in using the fast RAM it is useful to note that the LEVEL 1 BLAS routines operate at 70-90% of the equivalent FORTRAN code for a vector length of 1 and all show speed-up for a vector of length 4. The non-vector routines SROTG and SROTMG are so computationally light that the overhead in placing these in on-chip RAM is larger than any performance gain so these routines run *in situ*.

We conclude that it is worthwhile implementing vector routines in assembler, and that moving code into on-chip RAM proves beneficial to performance with negligible overhead even for small vectors.

---

[4] well, almost ... the penalty is about 10 processor cycles.

Table 5: Comparison of the behaviour of unrolled FORTRAN and assembler codes for the routine SAXPY resident in on- and off- chip memory.

	$r_{\text{inf}}^{\text{on}}$ (Mflops)	$r_{\text{inf}}^{\text{off}}$ (Mflops)	performance improvement
FORTRAN	0.37	0.29	22%
assembler	1.01	0.88	13%
speedup over FORTRAN	2.73	3.03	

References

[1] LAWSON, C.L., HANSON, R.J., KINCAID, D.R., AND KROGH, F.T.
Basic linear algebra subprograms for Fortran usage
ACM Trans. Math. Softw. 5,3 (1979), 308-323

[2] DONGARRA J.J, DU CROZ J., HAMMARLING S., AND HANSON, R.J.
An Extended Set Of FORTRAN Basic linear algebra subprograms
ACM Trans. Math. Softw. 14,1 (1988), 1-18

[3] Liverpool single-transputer machine-code library manual
Extended FLO Fortran Implementation
C.M.S.R, University of Liverpool (1988)

[4] HOCKNEY, R.W. AND JESSHOPE, C.R.
Parallel Computers 2 , IOP Publishing Ltd (1988)

[5] Parallel Fortran User Guide , 3L Ltd.

[6] TASM 2 Reference Manual, Mark Ware Associates

[7] Transputer Instruction Set - A compiler writers guide. INMOS Ltd.
Prentice Hall (1988)

Parallel Algorithms for Finding Optimal Paths on Digital Maps *

A. D. Hislop

Concurrent Computation Group
Department of Electronics and Computer Science
The University
SOUTHAMPTON S09 5NH
United Kingdom

Abstract

Working out the best route to take in a land vehicle from its current position to a certain destination can be done fairly quickly and easily by a human, given a map of the area. If however, the map is large and complex and there are many different constraints on the route taken, then it may be faster to find the route using a computer. This could especially be the case if the process is speeded up by having several computers working on the problem in parallel. The work described in this paper is on the development of a fast and efficient program to run on a transputer array that can find the least cost route to cross a terrain, given a map of the area in a machine readable format. Shortest path algorithms are investigated and the results of distributing the fastest sequential algorithm are described. Reasons for its poor performance are given and the results of developing a fast parallel program are reported. Proposals are made for the development of fast parallel program based on the fast sequential algorithm, building on the experiences gained from the first parallel implementation.

1 Introduction

The work described in this paper is aimed at developing fast and efficient parallel algorithms to run on a transputer array to work out optimal paths on a digital map where the vehicle can travel across land as well as road. Although not specifically designed to be used for an Autonomous Land Vehicle (ALV), the algorithms could be applied in part of the navigation system for an ALV.

The map information was given in the form of a machine-readable file containing the average height and culture information about each area in a 256 x 256 grid of areas covering the map terrain. Culture information included the type of terrain to negotiate, e.g. road, trees, water and buildings. The problem was modelled as a graph network, with a node representing each map point and a directed, weighted arc representing the cost of moving between the neighbouring nodes. The problem was then to find the least cost path between any two nodes in the graph. Originally, for simplicity, only 4 movements were allowed between

---

*The work described in this report was carried out in collaboration with the Royal Signals and Radar Establishment MoD, Great Malvern.

neighbouring nodes (north, south, east and west). Now, north-east, south-east, south-west and north-west movements are allowed.

The cost function was also kept simple so that the relative performances of the different programs for solving the problem could be compared. Times taken to work out optimal paths depended heavily on the choice of start node and the edge costs so these were kept the same when comparing different programs.

If h_i is the height of node i and h_j is the height of node j, then the cost function is simply

$$\text{cost} = |h_j - h_i| \tag{1}$$

i.e. the magnitude of the height difference between the two points.

There are two classes of algorithms for solving optimisation problems — deterministic and non-deterministic algorithms. Deterministic algorithms always find the best, or one of the best solutions to a problem. Non-deterministic algorithms however, seek a "good" solution that is close to the best solution, but found in less time.

Section 2 of this paper describes the shortest path algorithms studied and relevant work carried out by others. The results of comparing the performances of three of the algorithms are given in section 3. Section 4 describes the development of the parallel programs so far, and the design of what will hopefully be a very efficient parallel program.

2 Algorithms Studied

2.1 Dynamic Programming

The foundations of Dynamic Programming were established by Richard E. Bellman [1]. Dynamic Programming is the name given to a broad area of mathematics that is concerned with analysing sequential decision processes. Such processes occur in everyday life, whenever a series of stages exist at each of which a decision about the next stage needs to be made, e.g. walking to a local newsagent may involve going out the front door, turning right, walking along the road etc. A key feature of Dynamic Programming, *The Principle of Optimality*, can be expressed informally by saying that every part of a shortest path between two points is itself a shortest path. It can also be expressed as an iterative process where every node is examined at each iteration to see if a better route to arrive at the node via one of its neighbours, is possible. Initially node costs are infinite but their costs can only decrease so eventually they converge to a solution. It can be shown that the algorithm has worst can complexity of $O(n^2)$, where n is the number of nodes in the map database.

Simple Dynamic Programming is very inefficient when applied to the optimal path problem as much of the work is redundant. Its performance can be improved using methods attributed to Yen [2], which reduce the worst case complexity to $O(n^{3/2})$. The algorithm speeds up convergence to a solution by using values already computed during the current iteration. Low cost paths are traced more quickly and less redundant work is carried out. Yen's algorithm was implemented on the "Warp Machine" at Carnegie Mellon University by Bitz and Kung [3].

2.2 Dijkstra's Algorithm

This algorithm was originally published by E. W. Dijkstra in 1959 [4]. Nodes in the graph are in one of two sets: one whose nodes have reached their final costs, the "permanently labeled" set, and the other whose nodes are still having their costs determined, the "tentatively" labeled set. Initially, only the start node is in the permanently labeled set with a cost of 0, while all

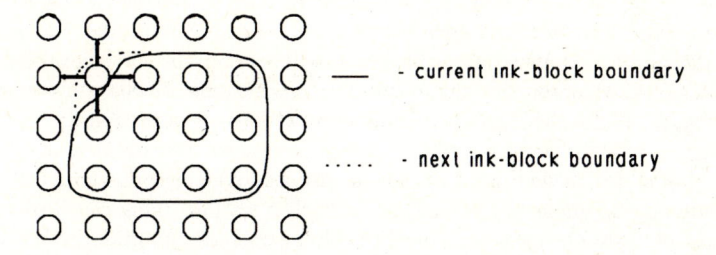

Figure 1: Updating the costs of neighbouring nodes in Dijkstra's algorithm. Also shown is the "expanding ink-block".

others are in the tentatively labeled set with costs equal to that of the moving from the start node to the node directly. This gives an initial cost of ∞ for all the nodes except the start node and those connected directly to it. At each iteration, the node with the lowest cost in the tentative set is removed from the set and put in the permanent set. It can be shown that this node has reached its final value. The costs of the node's neighbours are then adjusted with respect to the cost of the new permanently labeled node. This is shown in figure 1. The process can be thought of as an "expanding ink-block" centred on the start node and expanding outwards, covering the least cost node just outside the boundary at each iteration. When all the nodes, or a particular destination node have been covered, then the algorithm terminates. This is also illustrated in figure 1. In the worst case, the algorithm can have a complexity of $O(n^2)$ but the operation of finding the least cost tentatively labeled node can be made more efficient, e.g. by maintaining a sorted list of tentatively labelled nodes. There are ways of splitting up the work so that the algorithm can run in parallel [5, 6], but these tend to rely on having a very fine grain of parallelism with one process for each node, or having shared or global variables. It would be undesirable to implement either of these methods on transputers, the first method because the transputer is more suited to doing large grain tasks, and the second because it would be necessary to implement a message passing system to handle shared or global memory which would have a large communication overhead.

2.3 Moore's Algorithm

This algorithm was first published by E. F. Moore in 1957 [7]. It is similar to Dijkstra's algorithm in that at each iteration, one node is chosen and its neighbours have their costs adjusted with respect to the cost of the chosen node. The difference is that instead of having permanently labeled and tentatively labeled sets, a queue of nodes is maintained. At each iteration, the head of the queue is removed and the costs of its neighbouring nodes are adjusted. If any have had their costs decreased then they are put to the end of the queue. Initially only the start node is on the queue, and the algorithm terminates when the queue is becomes empty. Nodes can be put on the queue more than once but the algorithm is guaranteed to terminate since node costs can only decrease and all the nodes get put on the queue at least once.

The algorithm can be made more efficient by an adjustment attributed to d'Esopo [8] and developed by Pape [9]. Instead of always putting nodes to the end of the queue, a node is put at the head of the queue if it has been on the queue before and it is not currently on it. This has the effect of giving priority to those nodes that have been processed before such that nodes affected by the change are reprocessed as soon as possible. Assuming that the time taken to insert and remove nodes from the queue is constant, the time complexity will depend on the number of iterations. This varies depending on the edge costs of the graph and the choice of start node. For the graph of a typical map database however, it has been found to be proportional to n, giving a complexity of $O(n)$ (see section 3).

Distributing the algorithm on a parallel machine was studied by M. J. Quinn [10] as part of his PhD. thesis. He showed how Moore's or d'Esopo's algorithm would still work if more than one node on the queue was processed at each iteration. This can lead to a variety of different ways of distributing the algorithm. These include maintaining the queue on one processor and farming out the nodes to be processed by other processors. Another way is to distribute the graph over the processors and have each processor maintain its own queue, exchanging node costs that lie on the boundaries between neighbouring segments of the graph. From running parallel programs on a simulated shared memory multi-processor machine, the Heterogeneous Element Processor (HEP) [11], he found that the best speed-up was obtained when each processor maintained its own queue but that some processors would be idle if the distribution of nodes among processors was uneven.

2.4 The Branch-and-Bound Technique

The Branch-and-bound method [12] performs a restricted search of the decision tree graph of a problem. The root of a tree graph represents the initial state, and each node represents either a state where decisions need to be made, or an end state if it is a leaf node. Instead of simply carrying out an exhaustive search of the tree, branch-and-bound records the lowest cost route found so far to get to a given leaf node, and uses this to exclude subtrees from the search. If the cost of getting to a subtree from the root exceeds this upper bound cost, then the subtree is not searched.

The problem with branch-and-bound is that in the worst case, the time taken to search the graph can grow exponentially with the size of the graph. Normally however, the performance is much better, and can be improved further by incorporating more efficient methods of searching the subtrees, e.g. searching the subtrees in the order of increasing subtree cost.

Much work has been carried out by others on parallel branch-and-bound algorithms, some theoretical [13, 14], some carried out on simulated parallel architectures [15] and some carried out on transputer array and other multi-processor architectures [16, 17]. They are all mainly concerned with solving NP-hard problems. Although the map problem is only $O(n^2)$ complexity at worst, techniques used in parallel branch-and-bound could be combined with one of the other algorithms to restrict the search space.

2.5 Work Carried out at RSRE on the DAP

Contact was maintained with work on the same problem being carried out at the Royal Signals and Radar Establishment (RSRE) Great Malvern [18], using a Distributed Array Processor (DAP) [19].

A parallel version of Dynamic Programming was implemented on the DAP, and its performance was compared with a sequential version of d'Esopo's algorithm written in FORTRAN and running on a VAX 8600. The parallel program was found to take 6.2s to work out the best paths to all points from the top left-hand corner of the map. The sequential program running on the VAX took 19.5s for the same map and starting point. It was concluded that it is not cost effective to solve the problem using a DAP since a sequential program running on a VAX, which is cheaper and easier to program, is not much slower.

2.6 Summary of Expected Algorithm Performance

To summarise, the main algorithms studied were expected to have the performances given in table 1, where n is the number of nodes in the graph.

Table 1: Expected performances of the algorithms studied

Algorithm	Complexity	Type of estimate
Dynamic Programming	$O(n^2)$	worst case
Dijkstra's Algorithm	$O(n^2)$	worst case
Pape d'Esopo Moore Algorithm	$O(n^1)$	average case
Branch-and-Bound	$O(e^n)$	worst case

3 Sequential Algorithm Comparison

Dynamic Programming, Dijkstra's Algorithm and d'Esopo's algorithm were each coded in occam [20] and run on a single T414 transputer [21, 20]. The results are shown in figure 2 and in tabular form in table 2. Both axes are scaled logarithmically and the performance can be understood by considering the relationship:

$$\text{time} \approx c * n^k$$
$$\Leftrightarrow \ln \text{time} \approx \ln c + (k * \ln n)$$

For a set of points plotted for an algorithm's performance therefore, k is the slope of the best fitting line through the points. The results show d'Esopo's algorithm to be the fastest, which agrees with literature read on experimental comparisons between the algorithms [22, 23].

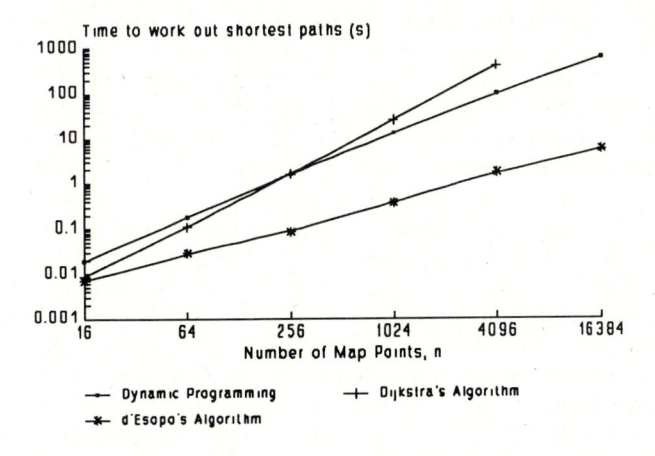

Figure 2: Comparison of Sequential Algorithm Performances

Table 2: Results of sequential algorithm performance comparison.

Algorithm	Complexity:	
	Estimated	Measured
Dynamic Programming	$O(n^2)$	$O(n^{1.2})$
Dijkstra's Algorithm	$O(n^2)$	$O(n^{1.9})$
d'Esopo's Algorithm	$O(n^1)$	$O(n^{1.0})$

4 Parallel Program Development

The parallel programs were developed on a prototype of the Reconfigurable Transputer Array (RTP) "Supernode". The Supernode was developed as a result of ESPRIT project 1085 [24] whose objectives were to produce a modular parallel processing machine that would be powerful but have a low cost, and to provide system support software and a range of demonstration programs. A Reconfigurable Array of Transputers, or RAT-cage for short, is the prototype of the Supernode. It generally has 16 IMS T414 "worker" transputers and a "controller" transputer that is used to program the switch that connects up the links in the array. The switch can be programmed to form a network of any desired topology, subject to the number of transputers in the array and the fact that each has four links. Each of the 16 "worker" transputers in the RAT-cage used had 256 kbytes of external memory.

Although the limitations of occam data structures made writing the programs difficult, it was decided to continue using occam as it would be the easiest language to use for developing a fast and efficient program to run on a transputer array.

As Dijkstra's algorithm seemed unsuited for implementing in parallel on a transputer array, Dynamic Programming and d'Esopo's algorithm were distributed.

4.1 The Parallel d'Esopo Algorithm

In d'Esopo's algorithm, nodes can be taken off the queue and processed in parallel. This will still result in the correct solutions being found but the advantage of giving priority to processing nodes at the head of the queue may be lost. If however, each processor maintains its own queue and is working on its own section of the wavefront, then the priority scheme would still operate successfully. A distributed queue was considered to be superior to having a master processor maintaining a global queue and worker processors doing the processing because there would not be a communications bottleneck between master and worker processors.

The first method of distributing d'Esopo's algorithm that was tried was a simple geometric distribution. The map was evenly distributed over the transputer array and each transputer worked on its own section of the map, communicating with neighbouring processors at regular intervals. This also meant that map data did not need to be moved around after the initial distribution, and the initialisation of variables for each map point could also be distributed.

The program used a geometric "harness" written by Dr. B. Carpenter of the Southampton University Concurrent Computation Group to provide the basic communication routines for the distributed program. The transputers were configured as a 4 x 4 array and the map distributed evenly over the array. Each processor maintained its own queue of nodes to process and exchanged boundary values with each of its neighbours at every iteration. The main program loop is outlined in figure 3. The test for termination is a test for all queues being empty and is carried out every t iterations where t can be set at compile time. Every t

```
{{{ Main ''worker'' process loop
SEQ
  ... initialise variables
  WHILE running
    SEQ
      IF
        NOT Q.empty
          SEQ
            ... remove node at head of Q
            ... adjust neighbouring node costs and put on Q if necessary
        TRUE
          SKIP
      ... exchange boundary node costs with neighbouring processors
      ... update boundary node costs and put on Q if necessary
      ... test for termination
  ... output results
}}}
```

Figure 3: Main loop of the parallel d'Esopo algorithm.

iterations, each processor sends a message to the host indicating the status of its queue. The host then checks if all the queues are empty and sends a message to each processor telling it to either terminate or continue, depending on the result of the termination test.

There is an option to display the costs of the nodes as they are being worked out. It represents the costs by a colour scale that cycles through 256 different colours and was useful for understanding how the program worked. A black and white representation is shown in figure 4. The program ran very slowly however, taking 157s to work out all the paths, which compares with 125s taken by the fast sequential program. This was attributed to the overhead of exchanging boundaries, which took up 45% of the time for each iteration. It was also attributed to the uneven progression of the wavefront. In the sequential program, the wavefront advanced as a regular diamond shape with the start point at the centre. When nodes need to be reprocessed, the wavefront stops advancing and they are reprocessed before advancing further. Also, the wavefront only expands to the next layer of nodes once all those of the previous layer have been processed at least once. With the parallel program however, the wavefront became fragmented crossing segment boundaries, slowing the process down. Another unsatisfactory feature of the program was that processors would only be active while the wavefront passed through them. One way to get around this problem could be to divide the map up into smaller sections and "fold" the sections over the fixed size array such that each processor works on more than one section and is kept busy for most of the time. More communication would be necessary in this method but the optimum balance of useful computation to communication time could be found by experiment.

4.2 Parallel Yen's Algorithm

Although Yen's algorithm (see section 2.1) had already been implemented in parallel on the CMU Warp [3], it was decided to implement it on a transputer array as it was estimated that it would result in a fast parallel program. Let

Figure 4: Display of nodes costs as they are calculated for parallel d'Esopo program. Decreased shading represents increased cost and shades cycle through 256 different values.

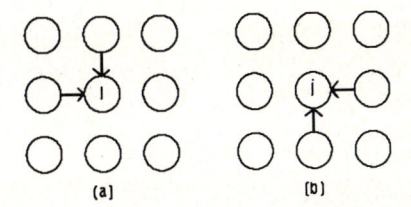

Figure 5: Yen's equation illustrated. (a) Red sweep, (b) blue sweep.

$U_i^{(m)}$ = the cost of the shortest path from the origin to node i such that it contains no more than m arcs.
a_{ij} = the cost of moving from node i to node j.

Assuming that there are only four allowed directions of movement on the map, north, south, east and west, then the algorithm can be expresed as:
Initialise
$$U_j^{(0)} := a_{sj} \text{ for } j = 1, 2, \ldots n.$$

Then repeat

$$\left. \begin{array}{rl} U_j^{(2m-1)} := & \min\left\{U_j^{(2m-2)}, \min_{i<j}\left\{U_i^{(2m-1)} + a_{ij}\right\}\right\} \text{ for } j = 2, \ldots, n. \\ U_1^{(2m-1)} := & U_1^{(2m-2)} \end{array} \right\} \quad (2)$$

$$\left. \begin{array}{rl} U_j^{(2m)} := & \min\left\{U_j^{(2m-1)}, \min_{i>j}\left\{U_i^{(2m)} + a_{ij}\right\}\right\} \text{ for } j = n-1, \ldots, 1. \\ U_n^{(2m)} := & U_n^{(2m-1)} \end{array} \right\} \quad (3)$$

Nodes are scanned at each iteration in one of two orders which are carried out alternately. On a "red sweep", nodes are scanned starting from the top left corner of the map to the bottom right corner, going from left to right along each line from the top line to the bottom. This is given by equation 2 and is illustrated in (a) of figure 5. On a "blue sweep", the same is done except in the reverse direction, as described by equation 3 and illustrated by (b) of figure 5. Red and blue sweeps are carried out alternately until a scan passes in which no changes are made.

Two methods of distributing the algorithm were tried by Bitz and Kung on the CMU Warp [3] but only one of these was considered suitable for implementing on a transputer array. The other would have had a too large communication time compared with the computation time.

The chosen method of distributing the algorithm divided the map up into vertical strips and distributed them geometrically on a linear chain of processors (see figure 6).

In this method, the processing of horizontal lines is pipelined. If P_n is the nth processor, then at the start of a red sweep, P_1 processes the first section of line 1 and passes the cost of the last node of the section to P_2. Processor P_2 then starts working on the second section of the first line while P_1 starts on the first section of line 2. Once P_2 has finished its section of the first line, it passes the cost of the last node of the section to P_3 and receives the cost of the last node of the first section of line 2 from P_1 before processing the second section of line 2. Eventually, all processors are working in parallel on different line sections, and then

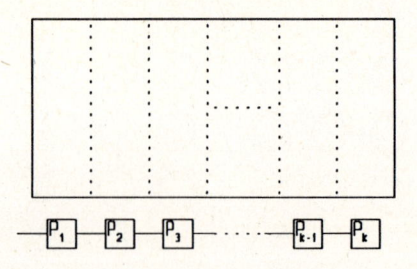

Figure 6: Vertical distribution of Yen's algorithm

when all the lines have been processed, a blue sweep can begin. Again, this is similar to the red sweep except it goes in the opposite direction.

Using all 16 T414 transputers on a RAT-cage, the time to work out the paths was found to be 12s. This was encouraging and it is expected that the performance will scale with the number of transputers applied until the size of the line sections become small making the computation time small in comparison to the communication time. More investigations into this parallel program may be carried out but it is not expected that there is much scope for improvement. Also, the algorithm has already been implemented on other MIMD architectures such as the Warp at CMU and on transputers at Jet Propulsion Laboratory. The parallel Yen algorithm still has to do redundant work which might make its performance deteriorate for larger maps. For these reasons, it was decided to develop further the parallel d'Esopo algorithm.

4.3 Further Developments of the Parallel d'Esopo Algorithm

Other methods of distributing d'Esopo's algorithm were considered. In a "processor farm" distribution of d'Esopo's algorithm, one processor, the "master", would maintain the queue of nodes. At each iteration it would split the queue up into equal sized groups and send them, together with their neighbouring node costs, to be processed by the "worker" processors. The workers would send the results back to the master which would then update the queue and the global copy of the node costs. If the queue was then found to be empty, the master would tell the workers to terminate, otherwise it would start the next iteration. One problem with this method would be that the time to process a group of nodes would be small compared with the time to transfer the group to and from a worker. Another problem would be that each worker would need to have a global copy of the map. This would not be practical as the memory requirement would be too large.

In order to be as efficient as possible at paralellising d'Esopo's algorithm, it would be necessary to concentrate processing power on the wavefront. The wavefront expands very regularly and the order of processing nodes on the queue is such that at any time, the layer of nodes outside the current wavefront are not processed until all the nodes of the current wavefront have been processed. Also, if any nodes need to be reprocessed, the expansion of the current wavefront is suspended while they are reprocessed.

This regular feature of the expanding wavefront could be exploited by a parallel program by having the processors connected in a ring and each working on a different section of the wavefront. The queue nodes, which are effectively the same as the wavefront nodes, would be distributed among the processors in the ring and each processor would be assigned a relevant portion of the map by the master. Synchronisation between the processors would be necessary to prevent processors advancing their wavefronts further that their neighbours but if the program is made more asynchronous then communication would only occur when necessary. Also, the distribution could be made less rigid, allowing the sections of the map to be shared dynamically such that each processor has an equal amount of work to do. One problem with this method however, may be the transfer of sections of the map to the worker processors, as it would be unreasonable for each to have a copy of the entire map. The problem of "paging" sections of the map in and out of each worker transputer's memory would be difficult. To start with, therefore, the system could be tested with a small map such that each transputer could have a copy. By concentrating processing power along the wavefront, it is hoped that this method of distributing d'Esopo's algorithm will run faster than the parallel Yen algorithm, and that its performance will improve as the size of the map increases.

5 Conclusions

Two parallel programs on a transputer array have been developed. The first, ran slowly because of large communication overheads, poor load balancing and because the expanding wavefront of computation became fragmented. It lost the smooth progression that was possible with the sequential program. The second method was much more satisfactory, but it is expected that it will not perform well for larger maps because of the amount of redundant work being carried out. Another method was proposed, based on the first method but improved by reducing the communication overhead and concentrating processor activity along the expanding wavefront of computation. It is expected that this method will not only be fast but will also perform well for larger maps because it will not loose its efficiency as the problem size increases. The use of a reconfigurable array of transputers has allowed the flexibility of trying or considering these and other methods of distributing the work, flexibility which would not be possible with most other parallel architectures and machines.

References

[1] R. E. Bellman. *Dynamic Programming*. Princeton University Press, Princeton, NJ, 1957.

[2] J. Y. Yen. An algorithm for finding shortest routes from all source nodes to a given destination in general networks. *Quarterly of Applied Mathematics*, 27:526–530, 1970.

[3] F. Bitz and H. T. Kung. Path planning on the warp computer: Using a linear systolic array in dynamic programming. *SPIE — Advanced Algorithms and Architectures for Signal Processing II*, 826:215–222, 1987.

[4] E. W. Dijkstra. A note on two problems in connection with graphs. *Numerische Mathematik*, 1:269–271, 1959.

[5] K. M. Chandy and J. Misra. Distributed communication on graphs: Shortest path problems. *Communications of the ACM*, 25(11):833–837, November 1982.

[6] P. Mateti and N. Deo. Parallel algorithms for the single source shortest path problem. *Computing*, (29):31–49, 1982.

[7] E. F. Moore. The shortest path through a maze. In *Proceedings of the International Symposium on Theory of Switching*, pages 285–292, 1957.

[8] M. Pollack and W. Wiebenson. Solution of the shortest-route problem — a review. *Operations Research*, 8:224–230, 1960.

[9] U. Pape. Implementation and efficiency of moore — algorithms for the shortest route problems. *Mathematical Programming*, 7:212–222, 1974.

[10] Michael J. Quinn. *The Design and Analysis of Algorithms and Data Structures for the Efficient Solution of Graph Theoretic Problems on MIMD Computers*. PhD thesis, Computer Science Department, Washington State University, Pullman, USA, 1983.

[11] D. J. Smith. A pipelined, shared resource mimd computer. In *The International Conference on Parallel Processing*, pages 6–8, Aug 1978.

[12] Michael J. Quinn. *Designing Efficient Algorithms for Parallel Computers*. McGraw Hill, 1988.

[13] T. Lai and S. Sahni. Anomalies in parallel branch-and-bound algorithms. *Communications of the ACM*, 27:594–602, Jun 1984.

[14] T. Lai and A. Sprague. Performance of parallel branch-and-bound algorithms. *IEEE Transactions on Computers*, C–34(10):962–964, Oct 1985.

[15] J. M. Troya and M. Ortega. A study of parallel branch-and-bound algorithms with best-bound-first search. *Parallel Computing*, 11:121–126, 1989.

[16] E. W. Feltern. Best-first branch-and-bound on a hypercube. In *3rd. Conference on Hypercube Concurrent Computers and Applications*, volume 2, pages 1500–1504, 1988.

[17] R. P. Pargas and E. D. Wooster. Branch-and-bound algorithms on a hypercube. In *Proceedings of the 3rd. Conference on Hypercube Concurrent Computers and Applications*, volume 2, pages 1514–1519, 1988.

[18] R. Haynes, C. Packer, J. B. G. Roberts, and P. Simpson. Computing optimal routes across terrain using dap. Technical Report 4299, Royal Signals and Radar Establishment, Great Malvern, Worcs., UK., 1989.

[19] R. W. Hockney and C. R. Jesshope. *Parallel Computers*. Adam Hilger Ltd., 1988.

[20] INMOS Ltd. *Occam 2 Reference Manual*. Prentice Hall, 1987.

[21] Inmos Ltd. Ims t414 transputer data sheet, 1987.

[22] E. V. Denardo and B. L. Fox. Shortest-route methods: 1. reaching, pruning, and buckets. *Operations Research*, 27(1):161–186, 1979.

[23] R. B. Dial, F. Glover, D. Karney, and D. Klingman. A computational analysis of alternative algorithms for finding shortest path trees. *Networks*, 9:215–248, 1979.

[24] J. G. Harp. Phase 2 of the reconfigurable transputer project — p1085. In *Proceedings of the 4th. Annual ESPRIT Conference*, volume 1, pages 583–591, 1987.

DACAPO-III: Parallel Multilevel Hardware Simulation on Transputers

Peter Grabienski
University of Dortmund
Department of Computer Science 1
P.O. Box 500 500
D-4600 Dortmund 50
Federal Republic of Germany
Tel.: (+49) 231 755 - 2124
Fax.: (+49) 231 755 2386
e-mail: grabiens@unidocv.uucp

April 24, 1990

Abstract

Digital simulators are widely used in the design of digital integrated circuits. The complexity of these circuits is increasing leading to higher simulation times. One strategy to increase simulation speed is parallel processing. In this paper the implementation of the DACAPO-III simulation system is described in two steps. In the first step this system was implemented on one Transputes and in a second step to multiple Transputers. For synchronization between the processors the Time Warp method was choosen. Problems and results in using parallel processing for distributed simulation are discussed.

1 Introduction

The design of digital integrated circuits is a challenging problem due to the increasing complexity of this problem. Therefore the first design of a circuit is done on a high level of abstraction. In a stepwise manner this design is refined down to the lower abstraction levels until the layout level is reached. However, each of these intermediate designs has to prove whether it still matches the specification, the design on the next higher level and the constraints given by the actual fabrication technology. One tool widely used for this purpose is simulation. The actual design is modeled using a hardware description language and this model is simulated to get information about the behaviour of the circuit to be expected. The simulators can be divided into two subclasses: analog and digital. In an analog simulator times and values are continuous and the circuit is modeled by a system of differential equations (eg. SPICE). A digital simulator, which is the point of interest in the following, handles values and times in a discrete manner. It can be used from the switch level up to the system level of abstraction. Existing simulators are either specialized on one level or can be used on many levels (perhaps all).

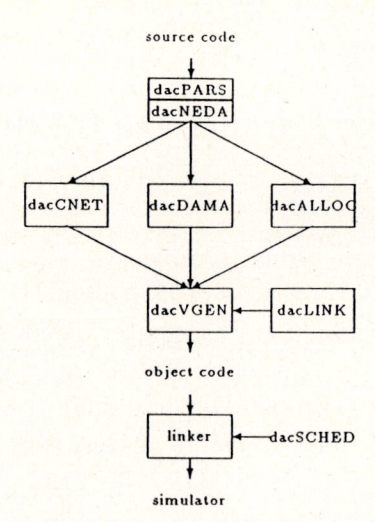

Figure 1: Structure of the DACAPO-III compiler

The DACAPO-III system [1, 2] is an example of a digital multilevel simulator. The main features of this system are: the model can be modularized, mixed mode simulation on all discrete abstraction levels is possible, abstract data types and generic types are available etc. DACAPO-III is a code generating simulation system, so each model is compiled into a specific simulator. This strategy was used to increase performance[1]. But in times of increasing chip complexity models are growing and simulation times are increasing. One way of speeding up simulators is to use parallel processing. On an integrated circuit all transistors are working in parallel, so parallelism is potentially available to increase simulation speed. The goal of parallel simulation is to exploit this potential. In the following the design of a parallel version of DACAPO-III and its implementation on a Transputer system is described.

2 The DACAPO-III system on one Transputer

The DACAPO-III simulation system developed at the University of Dortmund is a multi level and mixed level hardware simulation system which is used for the design and verification of integrated circuit models. The lowest possible abstraction level is the switch level, and all higher levels (gate, register-transfer, algorithmic, system) can be used. To achive this capability each model is mapped to a Petri Net representing the control flow and to a set of data manipulation statements which are related to the transitions of the Petri Net. Each time a transition fires the corresponding data manipulation takes place. However, on the lower levels (gate) no explicit control flow exists. Gate evaluation always takes place and actions are data driven. Therefore data driven actions are transformed into special Petri Net transitions. But from the point of view of the simulator all transitions are handled in a uniform manner so that data driven and control driven constructs can be mixed in the model without problems.

One additional feature is the possibility of modular programming like in MODULA-2. The model is given by a set of definition and implementation modules, one main module and a stimuli module. After transforming one module into a Petri Net this net is of course

---

[1]The ancestor of DACAPO-III, the DACAPO-II system, was an interpreting system and more than 10 times slower.

incomplete. There are "open" places which have only connections to one transition. These places are connected after compiling all the different modules.

The structure of the DACAPO-III compiler is shown in figure 1. The model is given as a set of modules: definition modules (interface and structural definitions) and corresponding implementation modules (circuit description) and a stimuli module describing the model environment. Each module is compiled in the following manner: the components dacPARS and dacNEDA perform the model analysis and construct the Petri Net, the data manipulation code in a high level representation and a symbol table. These parts are now compiled down to the so called LLIR (low level intermediate representation), a machine independent assembler like language. After compling all the modules to this level the component dacLINK generates LLIR code for connecting the different Petri Nets of the modules and to manage global dependencies. The whole LLIR code is then compiled to the assembler code of the given machine using the code generator dacVGEN, which itself is generated by the code generator generator SMAUG [3]. The assembler is compiled to object code and then linked with the precompiled module dacSCHED which contains the model independent code (envent queue, time manager, initialization, protocol functions). The result is an executable program dacSIM.

In a first step the DACAPO-III system was implemented on a single Transputer. Since all the source code of the different dac* parts had been written in C the 3L-C compiler [4] was used to implement the DACAPO compiler. A new code generator dacVGEN was implemented now generating assembler for the TASM 2 Transputer assembler [5]. The whole system is running on a B004 compatible board (T800, main memory 4 MB) running in an IBM-AT host. Since this was only an intermediate step no exact performace comparisons were made at this point. But one problem became visible implementing and using this sequential Transputer-DACAPO: the file I/O throughput. Using the standard B004 interface and the 3L-C routines the maximum output rate to the AT hard disk was below 30K bytes/sec. On the other hand each event in the DACAPO simulator leads to a protocol entry in the result file. Using this configuration mentioned above the simulator was always waiting for file acess. This could be easily verified switching off the protocol functions which leads to an extreme increase of simulation speed. Actually this problem has been solved using a high speed DMA-I/O board [6] which increases the throughput rate to 250K bytes/sec. It must be emphasized that this is only a temporal solution because the faster parallel version of DACAPO in the next section leads to the same bottleneck again.

3 Parallel DACAPO-III on multiple Transputers

Digital simulation is done along a virtual time axis. The most interesting term in this area is the event. The main difference to conventional programming is the difference in time between the reason of an event and its effect concerning this time axis. In a distributed multiprocessor simulation enginge this axis causes problems because the term *at the same time* does not exist. There are different synchronization schemes available which are able to handle this problem. The simplest strategy is to use one global clock for all processors. After receiving the clock signal each processor performs the events at this time and sends messages to other processors if there exists a global dependency in the simulation model. After finishing the tasks for the actual time it sends an acknoledgement to the clock which itself sends the next clock signal after receiving all the acknowledge signals from all processors. Obviously this strategy leads to a heavy communication load and therefore to poor performance. The second strategy is the so called Chandy-Misra synchronization [7, 8, 9] scheme which does not need a central clock. Each processor manages its own time axis, it works only up to the minimal time of all incoming communication channels. The time of a channel is defined as the timestamp of the last message received from this channel. This scheme overcomes the communication load for

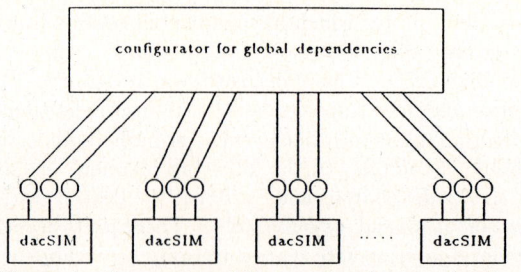

Figure 2: Connecting different circuit part simulators

clock synchronization but involves the danger of deadlocks. To prevent deadlocks additional so called NULL-messages are sent frequently increasing communication at this point.

The third strategy is the Time Warp distributed simulation concept [10] which was used for the DACAPO-III implementation on a set of Transputers. In this concept each processor runs its own simulation without waiting for anything. If a message from another processor arrives the message is checked for its time stamp. If this value is bigger than the local simulation time of the receiving processor the message is stored into the event list and simulation continues. If the time stamp value is smaller then a so called rollback occurs and the processor goes back to the time of this time stamp. All the results produced are *undone* and simulation continues again. To perform such a rollback each processor manages a state saving information pool for the reconstruction of past states and an output queue for storing each message sent so far. The problem of undoing is that messages which are already sent are impossible to undo. In case of a rollback for each message in the output queue an *antimessage* is sent which kills the original message in the receiving processor. This is the global idea of the Time Warp concept, details can be found in [10, 11, 12, 13, 14].

In order to use such a distributed Time Warp simulator the user has to partition his model into a set of submodels which can be simulated in parallel. In a model written in DACAPO these submodels can be easily identified exploiting the module and procedure structuring. Especially the *conbegin* statement which explicitly describes concurrent control flow is well suited for this task. Each submodel is then mapped to one processor[2]. But in normal cases these submodels are not totally independent between each other. For handling these "global" dependencies" messages must be sent to other processors. So the user has to describe the dependencies in a configuration file. This configuration file is an additional input to the parallel DACAPO compiler. The task to generate a parallel simulator is now the following: each submodel is conventionally compiled to the LLIR level. Then the new component dacCONF (see figure 2 is started which generates information for the new dacLINK component, which by itself generates code for sending messages to other processors when necessary. dacCONF performs the "wire routing" between the submodels on different processors. For all this purpose the following modifications of the DACAPO compiler were performed:

- The Time Warp related routines were integrated into the component dacSCHED. They are model independent and were implemented in 3L-C.

- The component dacCONF was implemented (see above). It uses a configuration file written in a new defined small language, checks whether the user tries to use more processors than available and generates also the configuration file for the 3L-C configurator.

- The component dacLINK was modified. Beneath its "normal" tasks it now generates code for sending messages to other processors. Since the LLIR grammar does not contain

---

[2] It is also possible to map more than one submodel to one processor. In general this leads to less performance than the one to one mapping.

rules for this, subroutine calls are generated instead to the component dacSCHED which contains the message handling routines.

- The Transputer is not able to route messages to other processors than its direct neighbours. A set of multiplexor processes were implemented to handle message passing to remote processors. Additionally the multiplexors route the simulation results to the root Transputer (the processor directly connected with the host) and then to the hard disk. On the root Transputer a so called *Master-I/O* process serves the I/O requests.

The parallel version of DACAPO-III was implemented on a four Transputer board (4*T800, 4 MB memory each) in an IBM-AT host. The software configuration is the same as for the sequential version. Up to now the speedup of the parallel version is only measured against the sequential one. Using the parallel simulator only on one Transputer leads of course to decreasing performance against the sequential one because many additional Time Warp related data structures are managed. Therefore the increase in speed using two processors is very poor. But after overcoming this initial threshold the results are quite promising. However, depending of the model, the partitioning quality and the protocol load speedup varies from nearly linear down to less than one. This is not surprising since a poor partitioning leads to a high communication load degrading performance to less than that of one processor. Due to this fact no *speedup diagrams* are published in this paper.

4 Future work

In this paper the structure and the implementation of the DACAPO simulation system on a multi Transputer system was described. Typical problems in parallelizing a digital event driven simulator were discussed. The main result after building the parallel DACAPO version was a promising potential increase in speed against the sequential version and the fact that the partitioning quality is strongly responsible for the speedup. Therefore future research about heuristic and knowledge based partitioning will attack this problem which is, however, not restricted to Transputer based implementations. Additionally the Time Warp mechanism contains a lot of parameters which must be adjusted for optimal performance. Most of the articles in the literature [15, 16] handle this problems from the theoretical point of view. Practical experiments will be made for validating these results. Additionally the problem of the I/O bottleneck will be attacked. One strategy is to integrate filter processes which annihilate the main part of the protocol information so that only the information requested explicitly by the user is stored onto the hard disk. This is the only "real" solution to this problem because the best I/O system becomes saturated using more and more simulation processors.

References

[1] DOSIS GmbH Dortmund. *DACAPO III User Manual*, 1.0 edition, November 1988.

[2] Ch. Ohsendoth and J. Poppensieker. Combined Hardware and Software Development with DACAPO-III. In *IFIP WG 10.2 Workshop*, 1987.

[3] Ch. Ohsendoth. *SMAUG — Code Generator Generator User's Manual*. Forschungsbericht Universität Dortmund Nr. 219, 1986.

[4] 3L Ltd. *3L Parallel C User Guide*. 3L Ltd, 2.0 edition, February 1988.

[5] Mark Ware. *TASM 2 User's Guide*. Mark Ware Associates, June 1988.

[6] J. Sang. The ml-dma file accelerator. Technical report, SANG Computersysteme, 1990.

[7] K. M. Chandy and J. Misra. Distributed Simulation: A Case Study in Design and Verification of Distributed Programs. *IEEE Transactions on Software Engineering*, pages 440–452, September 1979.

[8] K. M. Chandy and J. Misra. Asynchronous Distributed Simulation via a Sequence of Parallel Computations. *Communications of the ACM*, 24(11):198–206, 1981.

[9] K. M. Chandy et al. Distributed Deadlock Detection. *ACM Transactions on Computer Systems*, 1(2):144–156, 1983.

[10] D. R. Jefferson. Virtual Time. *ACM Transactions on Programming Languages and Systems*, 7(3):404–425, 1985.

[11] B. Samadi. *Distributed Simulation: Performance and Analysis*. PhD thesis, Dept. of Computer Science, UCLA Los Angeles, 1985.

[12] A. Gafni. *Space Management and Cancellation Mechanism for Time Warp*. PhD thesis, University of Southern California, 1985.

[13] Y. B. Lin and E. D. Lazowska. The optimal checkpoint interval in time warp parallel simulation. Technical report, University of Washington, Seattle, 1989.

[14] Y. B. Lin and E. D. Lazowska. Optimality considerations for time warp parallel simulation. Technical report, University of Washington, Seattle, 1989.

[15] O. Berry and G. Lomow. The Potential Speedup in the Optimistic Time Warp Mechanism for Distributed Simulation. In *2nd International Conference on Computers and Applications*, pages 694–698. IEEE, 1987.

[16] G. Lomow et al. A Performance Study of Time Warp. In *Proceedings of the Conference on Distributed Simulation*, pages 50–55. SCS, 1988.

Distributing Gate-Level Digital Timing Simulation Over Arrays of Transputers

Kenneth R. Wood
Programming Research Group
Oxford University Computing Laboratory
11 Keble Road
Oxford OX1 3QD

krw@uk.ac.oxford.prg

Abstract. Continuing advances in VLSI fabrication technology are allowing circuit designs to become more and more complex and are thereby fuelling the need for ever faster digital simulators. In this paper, we present a multi-transputer-based method for speeding up gate-level digital timing simulation, the acknowledged "workhorse" of the digital circuit design verification process. In particular, we describe a variant of the basic conservative method for distributed discrete-event simulation and we present PARSIM, a gate-level digital timing simulator which is based on this method and which runs on arrays of transputers. Preliminary results indicate the possibility of simulation speed rising significantly as the number of processors is increased.

1. Introduction

The last decade has seen a phenomenal increase in integrated-circuit densities and a corresponding increase in the complexity of digital circuit designs. It is not uncommon today for a VLSI chip to contain a million or more transistors, and it is expected that by the year 2000 it will be possible to manufacture single chips housing circuits of 100 million transistors [1]. Gate-level timing simulation has established itself as "the 'workhorse' of the [digital circuit] design verification process" [2] and thus the design verification of increasingly complex circuits will require faster and faster gate-level timing simulators. Even today the simulation of large designs can take *days*, so in the not-too-distant future faster simulators will be not just a luxury but an absolute necessity.

Clearly, one approach to speeding up gate-level simulation is to distribute the problem over a number of processors. This is, in fact, already common practice in that many circuit design houses employ specialized hardware accelerators which use SIMD parallelism to increase simulation speed. A good overview and comparison of many commercially available accelerators can be found in [3]. These accelerators usually provide very great speedup, but they are limited to a specific underlying circuit model and to a fixed maximum circuit size.

The theory of distributed discrete-event simulation (DDES) [4, 5, 6, 7] provides a much more general method of distributing simulations over multiple processors. The target platform in this case is typically a loosely-coupled MIMD system such as a transputer array or hypercube and therefore the restrictions on model and size are eliminated: DDES can be used to simulate anything from military combat scenarios [8] to general queuing networks [9] and the problem size is no more restricted than for traditional software-based approaches.

There are two fundamental approaches to DDES: the conservative approach as described in [4, 5, 7] and the optimistic approach typified by the *virtual time* paradigm described in [6]. Some work has been done in applying the optimistic method to transistor-level timing simulation [10], and a distributed gate-level timing simulator based on the conservative method is described very briefly in [11]. In general, however, the application of DDES to digital circuit simulation seems to have been largely neglected. We have begun to redress this neglect by investigating the application of a modified form of conservative DDES to gate-level digital timing simulation.

2. Partially Distributed Simulation

The main idea behind DDES—as described in much greater detail in [4, 5, 7]—is that each *physical process* (PP) of a given physical system is simulated by a corresponding *logical process* (LP). The LPs execute concurrently and operate autonomously except for communicating with other LPs by sending and receiving time-stamped messages along inter-process channels.

In the case of gate-level digital circuits, we could model each gate as a separate PP and thereby require the distributed simulation of a given circuit to consist of as many LPs as there are gates in the circuit. Variations of this one-process-per-gate approach have been attempted in [11, 12, 13] but it is recognized that in general this approach is suited only to the simulation of synchronous circuits and not to the detailed timing simulation of asynchronous circuits [11].

Our approach involves partitioning the circuit into a number of subcircuits each of which is regarded as a single PP. The simulation of the physical system is then only *partially* distributed in the sense that within each LP some sequential simulation technique must be used to simulate that LP's subcircuit. This is, of course, not a startling concept: in any distributed simulation for which the number of gates is greater than the number of processors, at least one subcircuit *must* be sequentially simulated. In the case of the one-process-per-gate approach described above, for example, the "sequential" technique used would simply be the parallel technique serialized via process management within a single processor.

However, by explicitly coding the sequential technique one gains flexibility. We have found that by using slightly modified event-driven simulation within each LP, the standard conservative DDES algorithm can be modified to considerable advantage. We present the details in Section 4 below.

3. Resolving Deadlock

The conservative approach to DDES ensures that an LP proceeds with the simulation of its PP only when it can guarantee to do so correctly. This restriction necessitates some way of resolving deadlock in the network of LPs. The most straightforward method of resolving deadlock is to ensure that it never occurs by transmitting appropriate *null messages* as explained in [4, 7]. We have adopted this method for the time being.

There are also methods for detecting deadlock and subsequently recovering from it rather than avoiding it altogether [5, 14], and there is evidence that these methods may outperform the null-message approach in some cases [5, 9]. In the future we hope to compare the effectiveness of the various methods of deadlock resolution in the context of distributed gate-level circuit simulation.

4. A Modified DDES Algorithm

Our algorithm stems from the standard conservative DDES algorithm as presented in [4, 7]. However, we exploit the additional knowledge of the simulation technique used *within* each LP to implement the LP as a (RECEIVER, SIMULATOR) pair of parallel processes which simultaneously access an event queue managed by a third parallel process. (See Figure 1.)

We consider in turn the three subprocesses which comprise each LP. Note that we describe the algorithm in terms of gate-level circuit simulation so that, for instance, the time-stamped

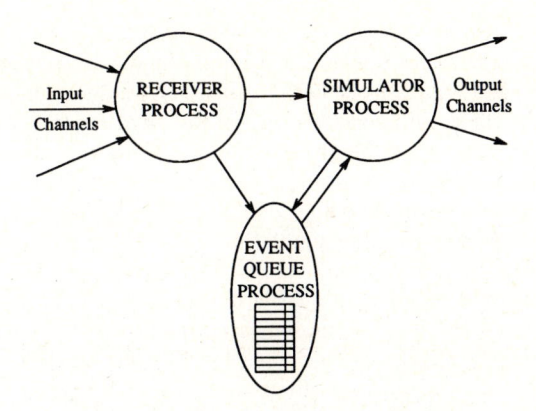

Figure 1: Structure of a single logical process.

messages which travel among the LPs are events of the form "signal S goes to value V at time T". However, the algorithm applies equally well to any physical system for which standard event-driven simulation is suitable. It is intended, of course, for systems amenable to partially distributed simulation—i.e. systems consisting of a number of PPs much greater than the number of processors on which the simulation is to be run.

4.1. The Receiver

The receiver process is very simple:

- it continuously waits on all input channels, receives each incoming message and puts the corresponding event onto the event queue by sending it to the event-queue process.

- as it does so, it keeps track of the channel clock value (CCV) of each of the subcircuit's input signals and of the clock value (CV) of the LP. Whenever the CV changes, the receiver sends the new CV to the simulator process. (Recall from [7] that each signal's CCV is simply the time-stamp of the last message received for that signal and that the CV is the minimum of the CCVs and is therefore the time up to which the subcircuit can be safely simulated.)

- it stops when the CV reaches the predetermined simulation stop time.

Note that there is not necessarily one input *channel* for each input *signal* of an LP's subcircuit. Because the receiver waits continuously on all channels, signals with common source and destination LPs can be mapped onto a single channel.

4.2. The Simulator

The heart of the simulator process is a standard event-driven simulation algorithm as described in general in [7] and in the specific context of gate-level digital simulation in [2]. However, in order to be used in partially distributed simulation, the sequential algorithm has been modified slightly to extend the concept of fanout to include the notions of *internal* and *external* fanout [15].

A signal's internal fanout is simply the standard fanout restricted to one subcircuit: i.e. a list of the gates within the subcircuit which have the signal as an input. A signal's external fanout, on the other hand, is a list of (signal',subcircuit') pairs each of which indicates that the given signal is identified with signal' in subcircuit'. Each external fanout entry includes enough information to send events for the given signal along the appropriate channel to the LP associated with subcircuit'. We will occasionally refer to the fanout (internal or external) of an *event* and by this we mean the fanout of that event's signal.

When an event is processed during simulation, its internal fanout indicates which gates within the subcircuit need reevaluation. Its external fanout determines any corresponding messages which must be sent along the LP's output channels to propagate the event to connected subcircuits. We will use the phrase "broadcast an event" to refer to the transmission of the set of corresponding messages determined by the event's external fanout.

We now turn to the operation of the simulator process. It repeats the following sequence of steps until CV reaches the predetermined simulation stop time:

- it waits for a new CV to arrive from the receiver process.

- it simulates its PP (i.e. its subcircuit) up to time CV using standard sequential event-driven simulation modified as explained above. In performing this simulation, the process removes events from and possibly adds events to the event queue by sending appropriate requests to the event-queue process. The process typically also broadcasts one or more events according to the external fanout of the events processed during the simulation phase.

- it broadcasts synchronization events for each output signal of the subcircuit. (Each synchronization event may be a null message or a real event—see Section 4.4 below.) An output signal is any signal with non-empty external fanout.

4.3. The Event Queue

The event-queue process simply maintains a time-sorted queue of events and performs the operations (adding an event, removing an event, etc.) requested by the receiver and simulator processes. Note that the receiver and simulator will never clash in their requests since the receiver will always be adding events to the queue which are not needed by the simulator for its current simulation.

The event-queue process also provides a facility to flag individual events as "internal only". The simulator uses this facility to reduce null-message traffic as described in Section 4.4 below.

4.4. Reducing Null-Message Traffic

For each output signal X of a given subcircuit, we can determine a value $\delta_X \geq 0$ such that when the subcircuit has been simulated up to time T we can guarantee that signal X will not change value until after time $T + \delta_X$. (For example, if each gate G is modelled as a single-output device with propagation delay P_G, we can set $\delta_X = P_{g(X)}$ where $g(X)$ is the gate for which X is the output.)

Then by one of the fundamental results of [4] (adapted for our modified algorithm) we can conclude that our distributed simulator will not deadlock if the simulator process broadcasts synchronization events as follows:

    For each output signal X •
        - broadcast a null event with time-stamp $CV + \delta_X$

However, we can do better than this. We can (potentially) reduce the number of null message transmissions by having the simulator process broadcast synchronization events as follows:

> For each output signal X •
>> - For each event on the event queue for signal X •
>>> - broadcast the event
>>> - flag the event as "internal only" on the event queue
>> - If the last event broadcast for signal X has time-stamp strictly less than $CV + \delta_X$, then broadcast a null event with time-stamp $CV + \delta_X$

This method is possible because after the subcircuit has been simulated up to time CV any event on the queue for output signal X must have a time-stamp in the interval $(CV, CV + \delta_X]$ and any events created in the future for that signal will have a time-stamp greater than $CV + \delta_X$. Thus, all queued events for X can be safely broadcast (in time-stamp order, of course) to any other LPs for which X is an input signal.

However, the queued events for X cannot be processed *within* the LP because of possible conflict with future internal events. This is the reason that the queued events are not removed from the queue after being broadcast, but instead are flagged "internal only". In order to implement this method the sequential simulation algorithm must be modified such that it ignores the external fanout of any event marked "internal only".

4.5. Benefits

Our algorithm is relatively easy to code and yields the following benefits:

- it ensures that at most *one* channel is required for message transmission from LP_i to LP_j, thereby providing maximum freedom in partitioning a simulation to run on a processor network of given topology.

- it provides a mechanism for reducing the number of null message transmissions required to avoid deadlock. This reduces the likelihood that communication costs will override the benefits of concurrency.

- the event queue also acts as a single centralized buffer for *all* inputs to an LP. Because the event queue is typically allocated most of the available memory within the LP, each input effectively has an infinite buffer. Thus, the determination of optimal buffer sizes is not an issue: each input gets exactly the amount of buffering it needs, thereby reducing the potential for temporarily blocked communication between LPs and increasing the degree of parallelism theoretically realizable for a given simulation.

We should point out, however, that our algorithm does negate the bounded memory requirement provided by the standard algorithm. To guarantee successful completion of an arbitrary simulation, we would require truly infinite buffering and hence event queues of unbounded size. However, we do not believe that this is of practical concern. A distributed simulation whose patterns of interprocess communication necessitate huge event queues is unlikely to run faster than its sequential counterpart. Thus, an intelligent circuit-partitioning scheme which aims to maximize speedup will also obviate the need to worry about unbounded memory requirements. In extreme cases such a partitioning scheme would advocate performing the simulation sequentially, although this is unlikely to be necessary for any reasonable circuit design.

Table 1: Netlist description of a simple circuit

```
/*****************************************/
/* Netlist for a 2-4 Line Decoder split */
/* into 4 subcircuits of 2 gates each.  */
/*****************************************/

CIRCUIT=
0: AND,    OUT0,   T2,    T3,    10;
0: INV,    T3,     IN1,          5;
1: INV,    T2,     IN0,          5;
1: AND,    OUT1,   T0,    IN0,   10;
2: INV,    T0,     IN1,          5;
2: AND,    OUT2,   T1,    IN1,   10;
3: INV,    T1,     IN0,          5;
3: AND,    OUT3,   IN0,   IN1,   10;

STIMULI=
PERIODIC 20 20 FROM 1 TO 1000 SIGNAL IN0;
PERIODIC 40 40 FROM 1 TO 1000 SIGNAL IN1;

MONITOR=
UNTIL 1000
SIGNALS OUT3 OUT2 OUT1 OUT0;
```

5. PARSIM

Based on our modified conservative DDES algorithm, we have developed a gate-level timing simulator (PARSIM) which runs on arrays of transputers. PARSIM reads circuit descriptions written in a simple netlist language and generates Occam2 programs which implement the distributed simulation of the circuit. Table 1 shows the description of a small circuit in our netlist language. The language is formally described in [15].

The circuit model we currently employ consists of a three-valued (0,1,X) logic and seven primitive gate types each with variable propagation delay. The sequential simulation program we use within each LP is straightforward and is formally specified together with the circuit model in [15]. (The formal specification excludes the modification mentioned at the end of Section 4.4 because [15] presents the original version of PARSIM which was based on standard conservative DDES.) We intend to increase the complexity of the model in future versions of PARSIM, incorporating at least one more logic value (for high impedance), several more primitive gate types, additional delay parameters, and perhaps a capability for user-defined behavioural models.

For the moment the circuit partitioning is done manually with a construct of the netlist language. The mapping of processes onto transputers and channels onto physical links is also done manually after PARSIM has generated the network-independent Occam2 code. Future work will investigate techniques for automatic partitioning and mapping.

6. Results

The original version of PARSIM generated distributed simulations which ran on a single processor with parallelism implemented via context switching. We simulated several test circuits with this version and—using specially developed metrics—determined that the potential for significant speedup in a truly distributed environment is high [15].

We are now starting to assess the validity of this projection by simulating circuits on multiple transputers with the current version of PARSIM. In Table 2 we see that a small

Table 2: Some preliminary PARSIM results

Circuit	Number of Gates	Number of Processors	Speedup[1]
2–4 line decoder	8	4	3.41
4-bit ripple counter	52	2	1.42

[1]Speedup is relative to single-processor simulation speed. Thus, for example, the decoder's simulation was 3.41 times faster on four processors than on one.

circuit partitioned into independent subcircuits yields a very significant speedup, while a larger circuit with interdependent subcircuits speeds up less dramatically. Although our preliminary results are encouraging, a thorough analysis of a wide range of PARSIM simulations is required before any meaningful conclusions can be drawn. Such an analysis will be the subject of a subsequent paper.

References

[1] S.M. Sze. Historical developments and future performances of MOSFET. In *Proceedings of the International Conference on VLSI Technology, Systems and Applications*, pages 232–236, 1987.

[2] Gordon Russell and Ian L. Sayers. *Advanced Simulation and Test Methodology for VLSI design*. Van Nostrand Reinhold, 1989.

[3] T. Blank. A survey of hardware accelerators used in computer-aided design. *IEEE Design and Test of Computers*, (1):21–39, 1984.

[4] K.M. Chandy and Jayadev Misra. Distributed simulation: A case study in design and verification of distributed programs. *IEEE Transactions on Software Engineering*, SE-5(5):440–452, 1979.

[5] K.M. Chandy and Jayadev Misra. Asynchronous distributed simulation via a sequence of parallel computations. *Communications of the ACM*, 24(11):198–206, April 1981.

[6] David R. Jefferson. Virtual time. *ACM Transactions on Programming Languages and Systems*, 7(3):404–425, July 1985.

[7] Jayadev Misra. Distributed discrete-event simulation. *ACM Computing Surveys*, 18(1):39–65, March 1986.

[8] Frederick Wieland et al. The performance of a distributed combat simulation with the time warp operating system. *Concurrency: Practice and Experience*, 1(1):35–50, September 1989.

[9] Daniel A. Reed et al. Parallel discrete event simulation using shared memory. *IEEE Transactions on Software Engineering*, 14(4):541–553, April 1988.

[10] J.M. Arnold and C.J. Terman. A multiprocessor implementation of a logic-level timing simulator. In *Proceedings of the International Conference on Computer-Aided Design*, pages 116–118, 1985.

[11] Yves Ansade et al. Highly parallel logic simulation accelerators based upon distributed discrete-event simulation. In Tony Ambler et al., editors, *Hardware Accelerators for Electrical CAD*, pages 69–79. IOP Publishing, 1988.

[12] P.H. Welch. Emulating digital logic using transputer networks. In J.W. de Bakker et al., editors, *Lecture Notes in Computer Science #258, PARLE Proceedings, June 1987, Volume I: Parallel Architectures*, pages 357–373. Springer-Verlag, 1987.

[13] R.D. Dowsing. *Introduction to Concurrency using Occam*. Van Nostrand Reinhold, 1988.

[14] K.M. Chandy, L.M. Haas, and Jayadev Misra. Distributed deadlock detection. *ACM Transactions on Computer Systems*, 1(2):144–156, May 1983.

[15] Kenneth R. Wood. Accelerated simulation of digital circuits using distributed discrete-event techniques. M.Sc. Thesis, Oxford University, 1989.

Transputer Based Neural Bearing Estimator

Sanjay Jha[*]   Gary Kelieff[+]   Tariq Durrani[*]

* Signal Processing Division, Strathclyde University,
Glasgow, U.K.
+ The Scottish Regional Transputer Centre,
Glasgow, U.K.

Abstract. *The bearing estimation problem is concerned with determining the directions of sources radiating an array of sensors, in the presence of additive noise. Traditionally, it has been solved using computationally-complex linear-algebra methods. In this paper, a novel neural networks based solution to this problem is presented. The benefit of this approach is its fast relaxation into the solution, given an adequate implementation. In the absence of technology for practical analogue neural circuits, an array of closely coupled transputers have been used to perform the random asynchronous neural updates in parallel. Comparative results are presented to show the performance of different topologies in performing the neural updates.*

1.0 Introduction

The bearing estimation problem is concerned with determining the directions of sources radiating an array of sensors, in the presence of additive noise. Traditionally, it has been solved using time series modelling methods such as AR/MA, Maximum Likelihood (ME) or Linear Prediction (LP) [1]. ME and LP involve the inversion of the input covariance matrix, which requires $O(n^3)$ operation for an n sensor array. A major limitation of these methods is their inability to resolve closely located sources. High resolution methods such as Pisarenko and MUSIC offer asymptotically unbiased estimates of the direction of the radiating sources, but are computationally more expensive [2]. These methods and their enhancements, such as ROOT-MUSIC and ESPRIT [3], are based on the Eigen-decomposition of the covariance matrix of the input. A number of parallel, regular array architectures have been proposed [4] to find the eigen-decomposition, however, these still do not deliver a real time performance for the subspace based methods.

There is a resurgence of interest in the use of neural networks to solve some of the problems arising in signal processing applications [5]. Hopfield and Tank [6] have applied a single layer network of fully inter-connected neurons to solving optimization problem such as the Travelling Salesperson Problem (TSP). Following [13], we have mapped the cost-function of the bearing estimation problem on to the quadratic energy function of the Hopfield model network. The over-whelming benefit of this method, over the linear-algebra based methods, is the fast relaxation of the network into the solution because of its global connectivity, and the massive parallelism. However the above assumes a suitable implementation of the neural network algorithm onto hardware.

Three approaches to neural implementation have been used: the first is the use of a dedicated analogue implementation in VLSI [7], the second is the mapping of neural algorithm onto a general or dedicated parallel array hardware [8,9], and the third approach has been to use general purpose accelerator boards to increase the speed of simulations. While analogue neural devices have been demonstrated, they remain at an experimental stage, with a limited number of neurons, and a pre-programmed synaptic matrix.

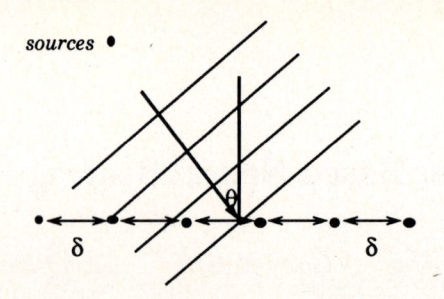

Fig 1 *The Bearing Estimation problem is that of determining the direction of the radiating sources.*

In the absence of analogue networks, dedicated parallel array architectures have been presented [8] , but they do not implement the *random asynchronous* updating procedure required for the Hopfield Model. In this paper, the random asynchronous update procedure of the Hopfield model based bearing estimator has been mapped onto an array of transputers, using the technique of *chaotic relaxation* [10]. This involves the random allocation of variable blocks of neurons to the worker transputers for neural update calculations. Results are presented for different topologies, and their performances are compared. Section 2 presents the neural algorithm, the bearing estimation problem is formally introduced in section 3. The mapping of the bearing estimation problem onto the neural network energy function is also presented here. Section 4 looks at the computation requirements of the neural update procedure and presents the chaotic relaxation algorithm. Simulation results are presented in section 5, and we conclude on the viability of these implementations in section 6.

2.0 The Hopfield Networks Algorithm

2.1 Neural Network Energy Function

The synaptic link between the *i-th* and the *j-th* neurons, in a network of P neurons, form a symmetric matrix [11]:

$$T_{ij} = T_{ji} \text{ and } t_{ii} = 0 \quad \text{for} \quad 1 < i, j < P \quad (2.11)$$

The network changes state using the following dynamic equation:

$$C_i \, du_i / dt = \sum T_{ij} v_j + I_i \quad (2.12)$$

Where, C_i is the input capacitance of the *i-th* neuron, I_i is the input from outside the network and u_i is the internal state of each neuron. The state vector v consists of the neuron outputs v_i

$$v_i = g(u_i) = 0.5 \, (1 + \tanh(u_i / \lambda)) \quad (2.13)$$

where $g(u_i)$ is the sigmoid transfer function of the *i-th* neuron, and $1/\lambda$ is the gain of the neuron. The network dynamic equation (2.12) defines a complex system, but it is possible to find an energy function satisfying the Liapunov's stability criterion [11]:

$$E(v) = -1/2 \sum\sum T_{ij} v_i v_j - \sum I_i v_i \quad (2.14)$$

2.2 Gain Annealing

The decision space of a *P-neuron* network is represented by a *P-dimensional* hypercube $D = [0,1]^P$. Each of the corners of this hypercube represent a possible digital output state of the network; one of these states is the solution states and one or more of the other states correspond to the local-minima of the network energy function. The network starts from some initial state within the hypercube D, and evolves towards one of the corners which corresponds to a minima. If the neuronal transfer function $g(u_i)$ is digital than the network has a smaller degree of freedom and it is constrained to changing states along the edges of the hypercube, thereby increasing the probability

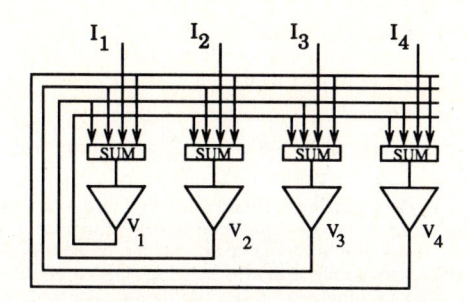

Fig 2 *The Hopfield network has a single layer of fully-interconnected neurons with feed-back.*

of being trapped in a local minima. However, if the network has low gain, it can traverse through the interior of D. This has the effect of smoothing out some of the local-minima, but a digital output is not guaranteed. Following [6], we have adopted an annealing strategy whereby the gain of the network is increased for successive iteration. This has the effect of perturbing the energy function $E(v)$ (eqn. 2.14), such that:

$$\widetilde{E}(v) = E(v) + \sum P(v_i, \lambda) \quad (2.21)$$

where, $\widetilde{E}(v)$ is the perturbed form of the energy function, and $P(v_i, \lambda)$ is selected such that:

$$\lim_{\lambda \to 0} \sum P(v_i, \lambda) = 0 \quad (2.22)$$

If the internal state u_i is defined by a non-linear transformation $u_i = f(v_i, \lambda)$, then the perturbation energy function is defined by:

$$\tau \, d P(v_i, \lambda) / dv_i = f(v_i, \lambda) \quad (2.23)$$

The gradient of $\widetilde{E}(v)$ is now given by:

$$d\widetilde{E}(v)/dv = -\sum T_{ij} v_j - I_i + u_i/\tau \quad (2.24)$$

Using Pontryagin's adjoint equations:

$$du_i/dt = -u_i/\tau + \sum T_{ij} v_j + I_i \quad (2.25)$$

Therefore, the dynamics of the network is now defined by equation 2.25.

3.0 The Bearing Estimation Problem

3.1 The data model

The data vector x_t incident upon the N sensor linear equi-spaced array is described by:

$$x_t = \sum s_{it} d_i \quad \text{for } 1 < i < M \quad (3.11)$$

where, M is the number of sources, s_{it} is the narrow-band signal emitted by the i-th source at time t, and d_i is the direction vector corresponding to each source, given by:

$$d_i = (1, e^{-j\tau_i}, e^{-2j\tau_i}, \ldots, e^{-(N-1)j\tau_i}) \quad (3.12)$$

For source-wavelength λ, and inter-sensor spacing of $\lambda/2$, τ_i is related to the source bearing θ_i by:

$$\tau_i = \pi \sin \theta_i \quad (3.13)$$

3.2 The Mapping of Bearing Estimation onto the Energy function

The mapping is performed by formulating a quadratic *least squares* cost function for the bearing estimation problem and relating it to the Liapunov energy function of the Hopfield model [12]. This can be done either for the wide-band scenario, or the narrow-band scenario. For the wide-band scenario, the amplitude, frequency and the bearing spaces of interest are discretised to *p-levels* and each neuron is used to represent a unique combination of the three parameter. This mapping therefore requires p^3 neurons in the network. The values of the T_{ij} and I_i for the wide-band scenario is given by:

$$T_{ij} = - real\,[\,s_i^*\,s_j\,],\ for\ \ 1 \leq i,j \leq p^3\ ;\ T_{ij} = 0,\ for\ i = j \quad (3.21)$$

$$I_i = 0.5\,real\,[\,y^*\,s_i\,],\ for\ \ 1 \leq i,j \leq p^3 \quad (3.22)$$

where, y is the incident data vector at the array of sensors, and p^3 is the number of neurons in the network. For a narrow-band scenario, only the bearing-space is discretised to p *levels*, and consequently, only p neurons are required in the network. However, this mapping requires the calculation of the *projection matrix* P_i, and the modified T_{ij} and I_i are given by:

$$T_{ij} = -\,real\,[y^*\,P_i^*\,P_j\,y\,],\ for\ \ 1 \leq i,j \leq p\ ;\ T_{ij} = 0\ for\ i = j \quad (3.23)$$

$$I_i = 1/2\,real\,[\,y^*\,P_i\,y\,]\quad 1 \leq i,j \leq p \quad (3.24)$$

where the projection matrix P_i is given by:

$$P_i = s_i(\,s_i^*\,s_i\,)\,s_i^*\quad for\ \ 1 \leq i,j \leq p \quad (3.25)$$

Note that the synaptic matrix in the *p-neuron* model is dependent on the input data y, and therefore, has to be recalculated for each incident input data vector y.

4.0 Transputer Implementation

4.1 Computational Requirements of the Neural Bearing Estimator

The computations involved can be divided into two distinct parts: the pre-processing computations and the random asynchronous neural updates. The pre-processing computations are defined by equation 3.21 and 3.22 for the p^3 *neuron* model, and by equation 3.23 - 3.25 for the *p neuron* model. These involve linear-algebraic operations like vector and matrix multiplications, and can be performed in parallel using a fully connected 2-D array of transputer. The computation involved in the neural update is considered below.

4.1 Random Asynchronous Neural Updates

The dynamics of the Hopfield model neural network is defined by the differential equation in 2.25, and it has been solved using Newton-Raphson method. However, this method is not suitable for parallel implementation, therefore, we have discretised the equation into the following difference equation:

$$u_i\,(t+1) = u_i + T\,v + I_i \quad (4.11)$$

Where, $u_i(t+1)$ is the value of the internal state at time $(t+1)$, and T and v are the matrix and vector form of the synapses and the output state respectively. The output vector $v(t+1)$ is then generated by using the non-linear transfer function of equation (2.13). Kung et al [8] have proposed the use of a systolic array architecture to implement this equation in parallel. However, their scheme does not implement a random asynchronous neural update.

There are two ways of mapping the above equation onto a processor array: the first is the fully parallel, fully inter-connected array of processors which reflects the connectivity of the network exactly. This required one processor per neuron, and because of its high hardware and connectivity costs, it is more suited to the massively parallel VLSI implementation, rather than an array of transputers. A more suitable approach for implementing the neural update onto a transputer array is to map a block of neurons to each transputer in the array.

4.2 Implementation Details

This block-iterative procedure requires the availability of v to all the processors. To overcome this bottleneck, a *Random Asynchronous Update* technique is used. This is based on the *chaotic relaxation* technique of parallel linear algebra [10]. In this scheme, the updates of u are allowed to

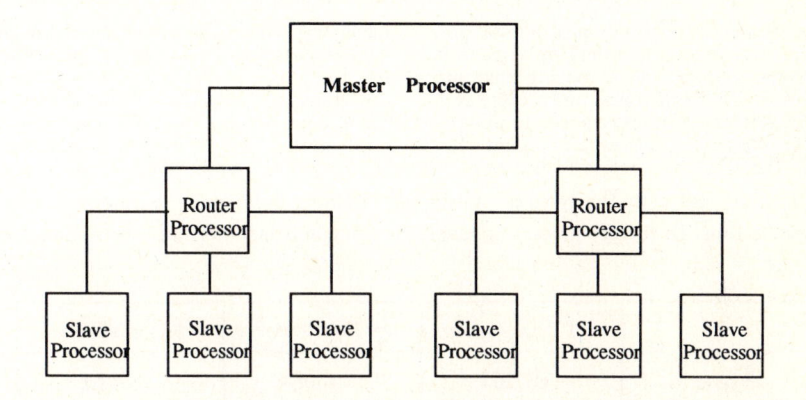

Fig 3 *The processor topology for a one-master, eight-slave transputer array. The router processors also perform the tasks of the slave as well as handling the communication. The master selects the slave processors randomly and updates the output vector.*

become "out of step" with each other, by allowing the current state of v to be used by successive processor, rather than waiting for v to be completely updated by the other processors.

The system had one *master* processor and 4 *slave* processors. In addition, for larger numbers of slave processors, routing/controller processors were used. Fig 3 shows the topology of a one-master, eight-slave transputer implementation. Each slave processor stores a part of the synaptic matrix, and the pre-processed input I, and based on these they update their block of the output vector. The master processor then randomly select the updated output vector blocks and updates the output vector. The output vector is then made available to the other processors. The recursion is stopped when the change in the output vector falls below a threshold level.

5.0 Simulations and Results

The data impinging upon an array of sensor, y_t, was generated by :

$$y_t = x_t + \eta_t \qquad (5.01)$$

where, x_t was generated as in section 3.1. A complex independent Gaussian random process with a mean of zero and a variance of σ^2, was used to generate the noise:

$$\sigma^2 = \frac{\sum |A_i|^2}{20 * 10^{SNR/10}} \qquad 1 \leq i \leq N_s \qquad (5.02)$$

where, A_i are the amplitudes of the N_s sources radiating the array and SNR is the signal-to-noise ratio of the simulation scenario. The Initial internal states of the neurons were set to 0.0 and the external states were set to 0.001. The bearing space from 0.0 to 45.0 degrees was discretised using a network of 88 or, 180 neurons. Three sources at 12.0, 20.0 and 32.0 degrees were used to generate the data at 5dB SNR. The initial value of λ was 10.0, and the annealing schedule used was:

$$\lambda_t = (0.85)^t * \lambda \quad 1 \leq t \leq max\_itern \quad (5.03)$$

where t is number of the iteration. In figure 4, the neuron-bearing values have been plotted against the output states of the neurons at each iteration to show the evolution of the network. As the gain of the sigmoid function increases in the later iterations, the neurons representing the sources assume the value of 1.0. Figure 5 shows that the 28th, the 46th and the 72th neurons represent the bearing of the source. Both figures refer to a simulation for a 25 sensor array.

5.1 The performance of the Transputer Array implementation

Simulations were carried out to evaluate time required to perform the above algorithm on three topologies: one transputer working sequentially, 4 transputer without routing processors, and finally, 8 transputers with 2 routing/slave processors. Table 1 and Table 2 present the timings for a network of 88 neurons, and 180 neurons respectively. It should be noted that the single transputer implementation requires to update of all the neural outputs per iteration. The 4 and 8 transputer implementation require only a quarter or an eighth of the neurons to be updated in each iteration. The time t_{init} refers to the time required to do the pre-processing (that is, create the hypothesis vector, calculate the synaptic matrix and the input data), and the time t_{iter} refers to the neural update time. Of the pre-processing tasks, for a single transputer implementation, 50s out of

	1 Transputer	4 Transputers	8 Transputers
T_{init}	16.551	8.084	6.971
T_{iter}	23.889	2.458	0.458
T_{total}	40.440	10.542	7.429
Iterations	35	35	35

Table 1 *The times (in seconds) for the neural bearing estimator implementation on three different arrays. For these simulations: the number of neurons in the network = 88; number of sensors in the array = 25; number of sources = 3, @5dB SNR.*

	1 Transputer	4 Transputers	8 Transputers
T_{init}	54.707	21.168	16.177
T_{iter}	98.126	10.315	2.165
T_{total}	152.832	31.482	18.342
Iterations	35	35	35

Table 2 *The times (in seconds) for the neural bearing estimator implementation on three different arrays. For these simulations: the number of neurons in the network = 180; number of sensors in the array = 25; number of sources = 3, @5dB*

54s was spent on calculating the synaptic matrix. The wide-band scenario will yield better results because it requires considerably smaller amount of pre-processing.

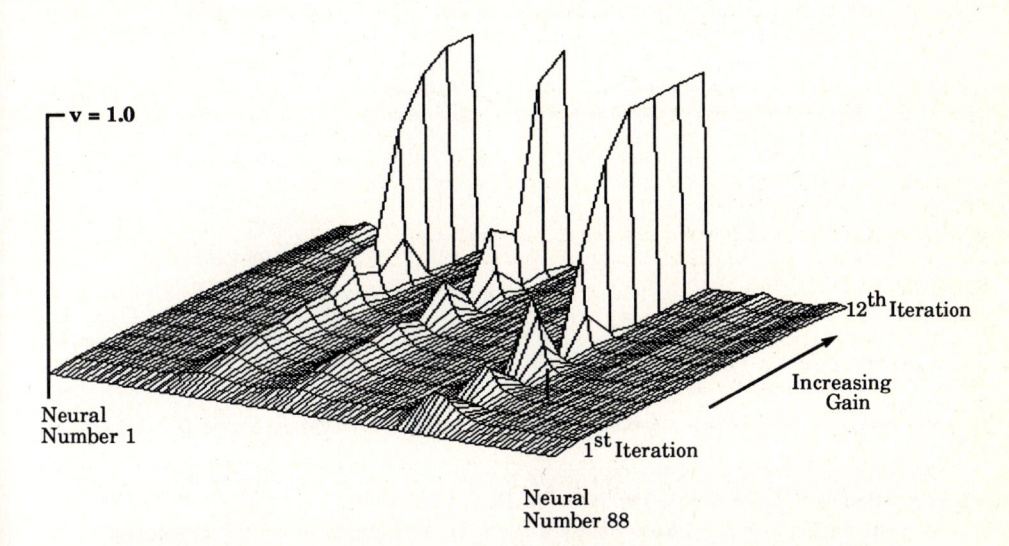

Fig 4: *The diagram shows the evolution of the network. Neurons representing the the bearing of the sources converge to the value of 1.0,*

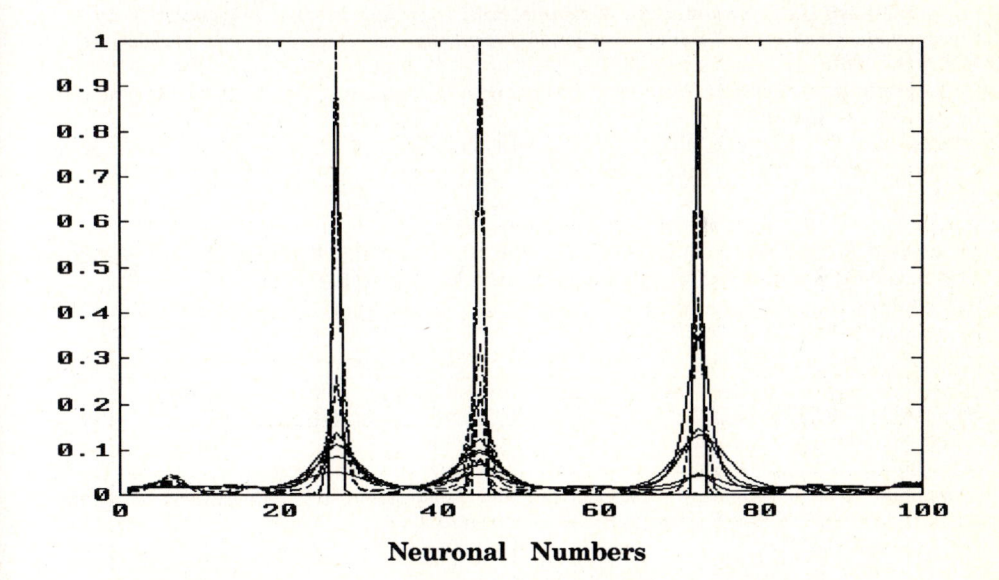

Fig 5: *This figure shows the convergence of the 28th, 46th and the 72nd neuron to the value of 1.0. These neurons indicate the position of the sources at 12.0, 20.0 and 32.0 degrees. The data was generated with 5 dB additive noise.*

6.0 Conclusions

A neural network based scheme for bearing estimation has been presented. The random asynchronous neural update procedure was implemented on an array of transputers, using a technique called chaotic relaxation. Simulation results for different size topologies have been presented. The speed-up gained through using larger number of processors seem to justify their use. It was found that because of the need to store n^2 synapses for an n neuron network, the memory requirement of neural implementation is extremely high, and for large arrays, memory access becomes the limiting factor in the speed-up gain.

7.0 Acknowledgement

This work has been carried out with support from the US Office of Naval Research under contract No. N00014-88-J-1198.

8.0 References

[1] **Kay S.M., Marple S.L. Jr.,** *"Spectrum Analysis - A modern Perspective"*, Proc IEEE vol-69, pp 1380-1419, Nov 1981.

[2] **Johnson D.H., Degraaf S.R.**, *"Improving resolution of bearing in Passive Sonar Arrays by Eigenvalue Analysis"*, IEEE Trans. Vol. ASSP-30 No.4, Aug. 1982.

[3] **Paulraj A., Kailath T.,** *" Eigenstructure methods for direction of Arrival Estimation in the presence of Unknown Noise fields"*, IEEE Trans., ASSP - 34, Feb. 1986.

[4] **Schrieber R.,** *" Systolic Arrays for Eigenvalue Computations"* SPIE, Vol. 341, Real-time Signal Processing V, 1982.

[5] **Rumelhart D.E., Hinton G.E., Williams R.J.,** *"Learning Internal representation by Error Propagation"*, Chapter 8, Parallel Distributed Processing, Ed. Rumelhart and McClleland, The MIT press, 1986.

[6] **Hopfield J. J., Tank D. W.,***"Neural Computation of decisions in optimisation problems"*, Biol. Cybern. 52, 141-152, 1985.

[7] **Murray A., Smith A.V.W.,** *"Asynchronous VLSI Neural Networks using Pulse Stream Arithmetic"* IEEE Journal of Solid State Circuits and Systems, Vol. 23, No. 3, pp. 688-697, 1988.

[8] **Kung S.Y., Hwang J.N.,** *"Parallel Architectures for Artificial Neural Nets"*, 1st IEEE International Conf. on Neural Networks, San Diego, 1987.

[9] **Forrest B., Roweth D., Stroud N., Wallace D., Wilson G.,** *"Implementing Neural Network Models on Parallel Computers*, The Computer Journal, Vol. 30, No. 5, 1987.

[10] **Chazan D., Miranker W.,** *"Chaotic relaxation"*, Linear Algebra and Its Applications, Vol 2 No 2, pp. 199 - 222, April 1969.

[11] **Hopfield J.J.,***"Neural Networks and physical systems with emergent collective computational abilities"* Proc. Natl. Acad. Sci. USA, April 1982.

[12] **Rastogi R., Gupta P.K., Kumerason R.,** *"Array Signal Processing with inter-connected neuron-like elements"*, Proc. ICASSP, pp 54.8.1 - 54.8.4, 1987.

[13] **Jha S., Chapman R., Durrani T.S.,** *"Investigation into Neural Networks for Bearing Estimation"*, Signal Processing - IV: Theories and Applications, Ed. Lacoume J.L., Chehikean A., Martyin N. and Malbos J., Elsevier Science Publishers, 1988.

AN INVESTIGATION INTO THE PARALLELISING OF GENETIC ALGORITHMS

G. D. McClurkin, R. A. Geary and T. S. Durrani
The Scottish Regional Transputer Support Centre
Exchange House,
George Street,
Glasgow G1 1RX
(TEL : 041-552-4400 x2499)

Abstract. *This paper concerns the parallel implementation of a Genetic Algorithm on a number of transputers. Genetic algorithms are a type of function optimisation technique modeled on biological concepts, they are a very powerful method known to perform well with 'difficult' cost criteria. The structure of a genetic algorithm is inherently parallel and is therefore ideally suited for use with a network of transputers. The aim of this paper is to compare various types of topologies and to assess their efficiency for this particular problem.*

1. Introduction

This paper describes the implementation of Genetic Algorithms (GAs) on Transputer networks. A variety of network topologies are considered, including a Flood-filled configuration, a Linear Array and Mesh. Genetic algorithms are a powerful optimisation technique with mechanisms based on naturally occuring processes (e.g. evolution, reproduction). They are known to perform well in problems where the cost function is multi-dimensional and with mulitple local maxima, as dealt with in this paper. Genetic algorithms have a number of advantages over conventional search techniques. For example, gradient based methods tend to become 'stuck' on local maxima, Genetic Algorithms do not; the calculation of a gradient is not required and a Genetic Algorithm can be started with random parameter estimates. Another advantage of a Genetic algorithm is that the underlying mechanisms are such that the algorithm can be easily parallelised, allowing a significant reduction in computation time.

The paper provides results which show the improved performance of GAs when implemented on multi-processor networks. Various topologies will be implemented and the paper will discuss the relative merits of each topology.

2. Genetic Algorithms

Genetic Algorithms are a class of stochastic function optimisation technique first proposed by John Holland in the seventies [1]. The GA method borrows concepts from the biological theory of natural evolution and population genetics. They are one of a family of 'natural' optimisation methods that mimic naturally occuring process (such as simulated annealing which is based on statistical mechanics and thermodynamics). The mechanisms of a GA include (i) chromosomal representation of problem solutions, (ii) reproduction, (iii) 'Survival-of-the-fittest' and (iv) mutation. GAs have been applied in many diverse areas, including Artificial Intelligence [2], Control [3], and Game playing [4]. Regarding function optimisation specifically, genetic algortihms have been studied extensively, for example [5,6]. Interest in this latter application is due to the fact that Genetic Algorithms have been observed to perform well in areas where the function space is multi-modal and/or multi-dimensional. The only assumption that the algorithm makes is that there is a degree of regularity in the search space (which there will be unless the space is totally random - in which case no optimisation technique can perform well). Conventional optimisation methods (such as gradient-based techniques) tend to fail dramatically when confronted by non-linear spaces due the possibility of becoming 'stuck' in local, non-optimal stationary points. However, incorporated into a Genetic Algorithm are mechanisms which allow the algorithm to prevent entrapment in local minima (e.g. the mutation operator).

2.1 The Genetic Algorithm Method

Unlike other techniques that produce parameter estimates (potential problem solutions) on a one-at-a-time basis, Genetic algorithms produce a number of candidate estimates in a single time-step, or *generation* These potential solutions are held together and are termed a *population*. Each succesive iteration of the algorithm results in a whole new population of estimates. The members of the new population are determined from the preceding one by combining attributes of solutions in the old population. Each member in the new population is a combination of two members of the original population (the *parent* solutions) and is termed an For the genetic approach to be applicable the solutions must be represented by finite length strings of attributes or *chromosomes* and there most be a method of assigning a measure of *fitness* to each member of the population in order that the better solutions can be identified (this is simply the result of the optimisation cost function).

The algorithm concentrates its search in areas of the space that have been found to contain many better than average estimates. This is accomplished by choosing as parent strings those whose fitness value is greater than the average fitness of the entire population. If a member of the population is relatively much fitter than the rest it will produce many offspring, hence propagating its attributes more widely than the others. Poorly rated strings (those with low fitness values) tend to produce no offspring and will die-out. (This is essentially the survival-of-the-fittest idea). The two chosen parents are combined using stylised genetic operators termed *Crossover* and *Mutation* to form the offspring. These operators allow attributes from both parents to be passed on to the offspring. The theory behind Genetic algorithms states that, as time proceeds (generations pass) 'good' attributes become widespread throughout the population, and therefore better solutions predominate. It is the reproduction phase incorporating crossover that is at the heart of the algorithm with mutation being merely a (less important) background operator.

In summary, most implementations of a genetic algorithm will have a similar appearance to Fig 1.

```
BEGIN
  Initialise :
  {
      Select Initial Popualtion (randomly)
      Evaluate Fitness of Population
      Gens = 1
  }
  For 1 to MAXGEN :
  {
      Select Parents
      Reproduce
      Evaluate Offspring
      Create New Population
      Replace Old Population with New
      Gens = Gens + 1
  }
END
```

Genetic Algorithm Structure
fig 1.

3. Implementation

It is obvious from examination of a Genetic algorithm that the structure of the algorithm lends itself readily to parallel implementation. In the simplest case, for example, the evaluation of each member of the population could be carried out simultaneously rather than sequentially. There are, of course, other more involved implementations possible which may not appear so obvious, such as the approach featured in [7], where the concept of a Nodal Genetic Algorithm is introduced (NGA). This method basically entails straight-forward, sequential GAs running independently on each Transputer node in the network, each operating on a small population. The major difference between the NGA and the sequential GA is that at certain times (e.g. after each generation) each node will send to its neighbours the best performing string in its own population and at the same time will receive the best individuals from its neighbours. One of the main advantages of parallelising a GA in this manner is that increasing the population size by adding another processor will not greatly slow down the overall execution time whereas increasing the population size in a sequential GA does increase the time taken. (Or, similarly, dividing the population and allowing each processor to operate on a subpopulation will result in a decrease in execution time).

The problem is now to determine which type of architecture or network topology is best suited to implementation of a parallel genetic algorithm. Different topologies will lead to varying evolutionary possibilities. Five implementations were considered : (i) Sequential, (ii) Flood-Filled Network (iii) Linear Array, (iv) Ring, and (v) Mesh (Fig.2 a-d). The Array, Ring and Mesh topologies are nodal GAs but the Flood-filled configuration is a simple master-worker process where the master processor sends out the parents to be processed and collects the offspring from the worker tasks. Only the master process holds any information about the population.

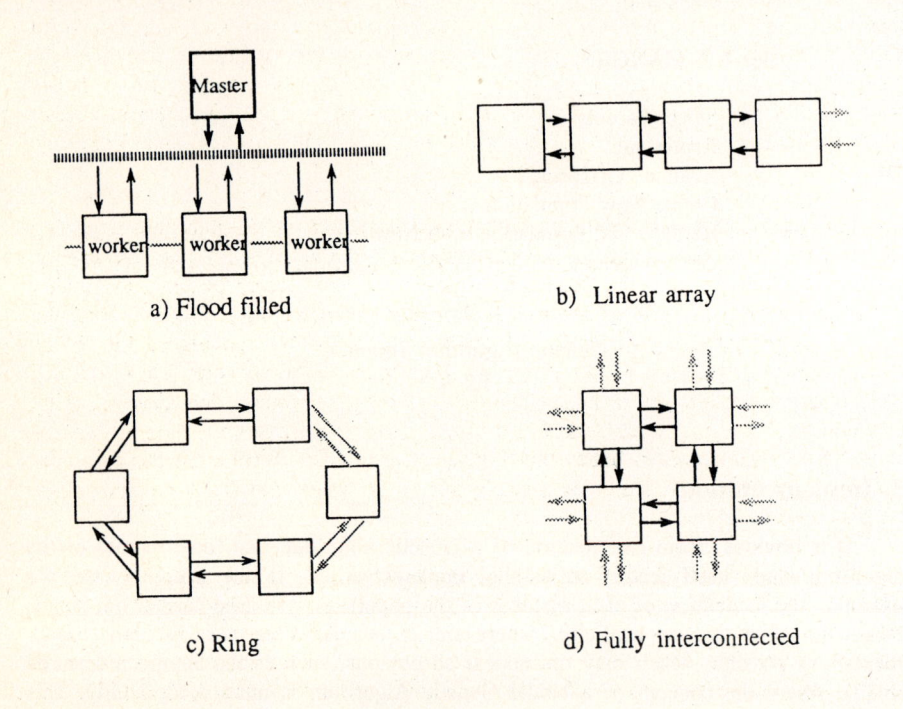

a) Flood filled

b) Linear array

c) Ring

d) Fully interconnected

Network Topologies
fig. 2

4. Results and Conclusions

For the purposes of comparison, a 'difficult' cost function was used. This *Porcupine* function, as described in [8] and shown in Fig. 3 is a multi-modal cost criterion with many 'trap' points where a traditional optimisation method (e.g. gradient-based techniques) would fail or get 'stuck', but the more complex genetic algorithm can cope with easily. Each implementation was tested using the same set of GA parameters and in the case of the Nodal GA an extra parameter is required to determine at which point each node in the network is to communicate with its neighbours. In an 'N' processor Nodal GA, each node has a subpopulation 1/N times the size of the population used in the sequential GA.

Comparing the execution times of the different topologies (Fig. 4), it is not surprising that (excepting the flood-fill) the times for each nodal GA are almost identical. This is because the speed increase is due to the splitting of the population into smaller subpopulations, each being operated on in parallel. In an ideal situation, with no communication overhead, the speed-up for N processors would be N, but it was found that an extra processor gave at best a 30% reduction in execution time. In the flood-filled configuration, the maximum speed-up gained was just 20%, this is a result of the inefficient master/worker process which involves a great deal of (small) message passing.

Figures 5 and 6 are concerned with the performance of the algorithm regarding convergence times and accuracy. It can be seen that the Nodal GAs tend to converge much more quickly than the sequential algorithm. This occurs because in smaller populations a 'good' or fitter string will dominate the population rapidly. Also, the more inter-connected the network, the quicker the algorithm converges, due to the much faster propagation of better strings to other nodes in the network. However, this rapid convergence may have some drawbacks as Figure 6 notes. The mesh topology may converge much *too quickly* and find a point close to but not the optimal. Because of the rapid domination of better (but not necessarily best) individuals, the algorithm unnecessarily restricts it search to a small area of the space and therefore cannot find the true optimal point.

In conclusion, it is obvious that if considering a parallel implementation of a Genetic Algorithm then a trade off between accuracy and convergence times is required, also there are a number of parameters in the algorithm that have to be set at optimal values (e.g. population sizes, swap times etc). One interesting area to be looked into maybe randomly connected networks, which may suit the generally stochastic nature of the Genetic Algorithm itself.

References :

[1] Holland J.H. *Adaptation in Natural and Artificial Systems.*
University of Michigan Press, 1975.

[2] Smith S. "A Learning System Based on Genetic Algorithms",
Ph.d. Thesis, University of Pittsburgh, 1980.

[3] Goldberg D. "Computer-Aided Gas Pipeline Operation Using Genetic Algorithms", Ph.d. Thesis University of Michigan, 1983.

[4] Axelrod, R. "Evolution of Strategies in the Iterated Prisoner's Dilemma", in *Genetic Algorithms and Simulated Annealing*, Pitman, London, 1987.

[5] McClurkin G.D. Sharman K.C. and Durrani T.S. "Genetic Algorithms for Spatial Spectral Estimation", 4th IEEE Workshop on Spectrum Estimation, University of Minnesota, Minneapolis, 1988.

[6] Bethke A.D. "Genetic Algorithms as Function Optimizers",
Ph.d. Thesis, University of Michigan, 1981.

[7] Pettey C.B. et al "A Parallel Genetic Algorithm", in Proc. of the 2nd International Conf. on Genetic Algorithms, 1987.

[8] Ackley D.H. "An Empirical Study of Bit Vector Function Optimization", in *Genetic Algorithms and Simulated Annealing*, Pitman, London, 1987.

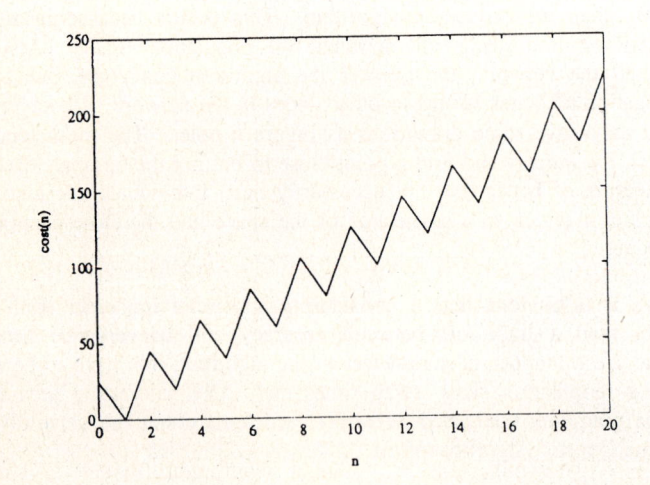

Porcupine Function
fig. 3

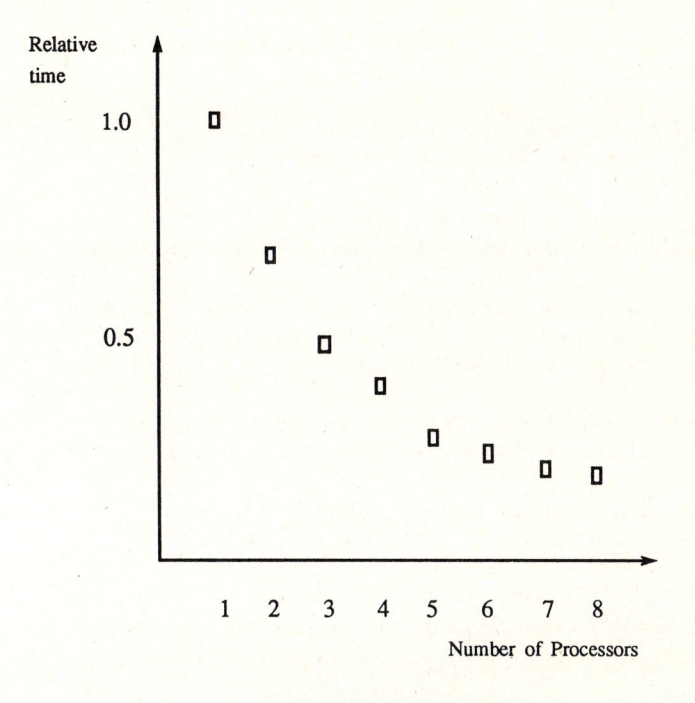

Typical timings for Nodal GA

fig 4

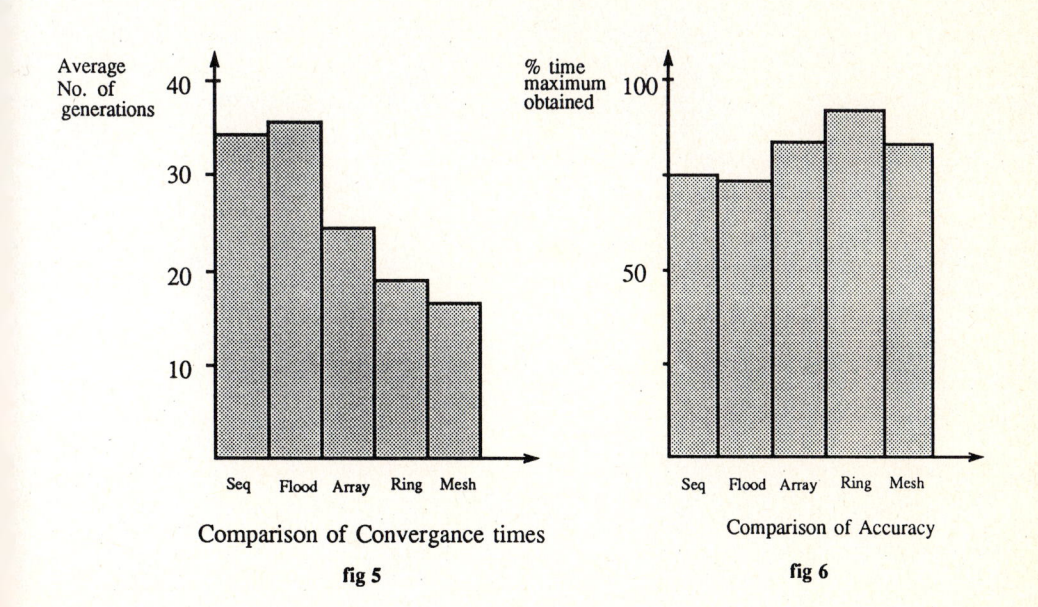

Comparison of Convergance times

fig 5

Comparison of Accuracy

fig 6